Liberating Women's History

# Liberating
# Women's History

## Theoretical and Critical Essays

EDITED BY

## Berenice A. Carroll

*University of Illinois Press*

URBANA CHICAGO LONDON

for
Jacqueline Flenner
and
A Woman's Place
Urbana-Champaign, Illinois

**Library of Congress Cataloging in Publication Data**

Main entry under title:

Liberating women's history.

Includes bibliographical references.
1. Women—Historiography—Addresses, essays,
lectures. 2. Women—History—Addresses, essays,
lectures. I. Carroll, Berenice A.
HQ1121.L56     301.41'2'09     75-45451
ISBN 0-252-00441-8
ISBN 0-252-00569-4 pbk.

# Preface

The essays in this book have been collected with the intention of meeting certain needs not yet satisfactorily filled in the rapidly growing body of works on women's history: first, the need for a critical historiography of the field; second, the need to test a variety of old and new theories or assumptions against the evidence of women's historical experience, on a comparative basis across time and cultures; third, the need to find greater conceptual clarity and define new directions for research in women's history.

Certainly it would be too much to claim that this one volume, collected in an early phase of development of the field, fully satisfies these needs. What is hoped is that it may introduce to a broader public some of the main issues in debate, and reflect the current state of work and thought on these issues.

Most of the essays are published for the first time in this volume. A few are reprinted and others revised from previous publication in journals or books. The essays are highly diverse in character, and no attempt has been made to impose upon them a consistent structure or viewpoint. This reflects a conscious decision to sacrifice easy digestibility in favor of representing the diversity, range, and quality of the current work bearing on theoretical and critical issues in women's history.

The essays in this volume fall broadly into two categories: essays of critical historiography which raise general questions of theory and conceptualization in the field; and case studies or surveys which are primarily empirical in character, but in which the authors suggest, explore, or illustrate some theoretical questions or models. These two categories have been further subdivided according to substantive emphasis.

Thus Parts I and IV are closely related to each other, and overlap to some degree, but in Part I the emphasis is upon the critique of past work in women's history, whereas in Part IV the emphasis is more fully upon current questions of theory and new approaches to research.

The essays in Parts II and III are also similar to each other in general character, but are divided roughly according to whether ideological or class factors are given stronger emphasis. None of these essays is simplistic, and some might well have been classified differently. On the whole, however, those in Part II tend to emphasize the influence of ideology, attitudes, tradition, or consciousness on the position of women, while those in Part III tend to emphasize or give primary attention to economic and class conditions. Some further comment on these points will be found in the introduction to each part.

The editor would like to thank all the contributors for their excellent cooperation and extraordinary patience with the many delays which have been experienced in the gradual evolution of the volume over several years. I would also like to thank the University of Illinois Press for encouraging the publication of this volume, and Carole S. Appel for her painstaking editorial attention to the entire work while it was in press. Though formal acknowledgment can hardly be adequate, my special thanks here go also to some who have provided personal support at one stage or another of the development of the book, or direct assistance in a variety of onerous tasks such as proofreading; in particular, thanks go to my mother, Margaret Jacobs, and to Robert W. Carroll, Helen K. Curley, Clinton F. Fink, Miriam Lowinger, and Hilda Smith. Finally, I wish to express my gratitude to the many women I have come to know in the women's movement in recent years, who have transformed my own conceptions of myself, of women, and of history.

# Contents

# Introduction

*Berenice A. Carroll*

There has been a recurrent demand for theory in the field of women's history, but the reasons for this demand are not entirely self-explanatory. Historians have been inclined, on the whole, to be suspicious of theory or openly hostile to it. In the pages of *History and Theory* one may find learned debates about whether, or to what extent, historians make conscious or unconscious use of explanatory laws and theoretical models in their work, but in the workaday world of most professional historians, theoretical excursions remain relatively rare. Descriptive monographs and narrative texts are still the mainstays of historical writing. Though not averse to "illuminating analysis" of *"man* in *his* social conditions," historians are generally unwilling "to pre-suppose an all-embracing framework for history" or to venture far outside "the specific physiognomy of concrete human situations."[1] Those who do so, are likely to encounter echoes of James Harvey Robinson's rebuff to the philosophers of history for imagining that they could "discover the wherefore of man's past without the trouble of learning much about it."[2]

It is therefore not at all surprising that there has not been much theoretical work in the fledgling field of women's history. The emphasis has been overwhelmingly on the fundamental tasks: resurrecting and reassessing the lost women of history, individually and collectively; recovering source materials and making them accessible through library collections, reprint editions, and anthologies; and working to expand and coordinate efforts to develop women's history as an academic field of teaching and research.

Nevertheless, there has been a marked strain of dissatisfaction with these modes of historical endeavor, which would seem to be quite normal in any other field of history. In one of her contributions to this volume, an essay which was one of the earliest to pose the current questions of theory, Gerda Lerner wrote:

> The literature concerning the role of women in American history is topically narrow, predominantly descriptive, and generally devoid of interpretation. Except for the feminist viewpoint, there seems to be no underlying conceptual framework. . . .
> A new conceptual framework for dealing with the subject of women in American history is needed. The feminist frame of reference has become archaic and fairly useless.

Lerner's essay, "New Approaches to the Study of Women in American History," appeared in 1969. It was soon apparent that others shared her sense of need for conceptual clarification. At the conventions of the American Historical Association in December, 1970 (Boston), and the Organization of American Historians in April, 1971 (New Orleans), women historians presented panel sessions on "Why Women's History?" and "New Perspectives in Women's History," as well as a number of papers in other sessions, offering both critical and constructive historiography. This volume is heavily indebted to the participants in those meetings, not only for a number of the papers which appear here, but also for launching the necessary process of debate and analysis.[3]

Still, it remains somewhat curious that historians in the field of women's history find it so necessary to develop an "underlying conceptual framework" for their field. And indeed it appears that this demand for theory arises from three interrelated sources, quite specific to this field: first, a low evaluation of past work in the field, closely related to skepticism about its legitimacy within the discipline of historical study; second, the unique character of the group which the field seeks to study; third, the existing tradition of theories attempting to explain the historical experience of women.

Whether historical writings about women do tend to be of inferior quality, or did in the past, is an open question. Has there really been a higher proportion of narrow, noninterpretive, hagiographic and nonsensical work in this field than in any other field of historical writing? Considering the vast quantities of such work produced by historians in all fields, one may doubt this; but there can be no doubt that the impression is fairly widespread: past writings in the field tend to be held in low esteem, and the field itself is felt to lack legitimacy.[4]

One may even be told outright that women's history is "not intellectually interesting." This may be stated so explicitly only in a rare fit of candor, but the idea is echoed in manifold ways by both men and women in the profession at large and in the field itself. As Alan Graebner attests, to admit that one teaches courses in the history of women is to risk finding "the same look on the faces of other historians as appears after an off-color joke."[5] There can be little doubt that this particular response reflects underlying attitudes toward women more than it reflects any considered judgment on women's history as an academic field. But the same devaluation of women and their history appears also, more subtly, in the following statement by a prominent male historian, on the rationale for theory in women's history:

> I think it is particularly important to try to introduce some conceptual clarity into the field, which so desperately needs it; it is my firm belief that progress is not going to come simply through the accumulation of monographic work. Still less is it going to come from an insistence that women have been neglected as historical actors, that is, from a historiography of compensation, devoted merely to righting the balance. What we need to know, and I think need particularly to know in a general and theoretical way, is: what are the consequences of this neglect? What do we fail to see by not looking at women's history, or by not

looking at it in the proper light? What do we learn from it that we did not know before? That is: how does a better understanding of the history of women enhance our understanding of other issues as well?[6]

These remarks reflect a common bias against women's history for its own sake, or "merely" for the sake of righting the imbalance and neglect in past historical writing. From this point of view, women's history is justified only insofar as it illuminates what "we" want to know about "other issues."

In fact it seems likely that writing women into history "implies not only a new history of women but also a new history" (Gordon, Buhle, and Dye, "The Problem of Women's History," in this volume). Yet many women might reasonably feel that writing their own history is justified, not merely for the purpose of "righting the balance," but for its own sake alone. We don't normally ask Jews, or Italians, or Blacks, or Chinese, to justify their interest in their own history by demonstrating that it tells us what *we* want to know about "other issues"—then why ask this of women?

The main reason undoubtedly lies in the second source of pressure for theory in the field of women's history: the special character of the group under study, "women"; and the disjunctions between the historical experience of this group and the categories, assumptions, and criteria which shape most scholarly writing on history.

At the most obvious level, the reluctance to accept work in women's history for its own sake is a reflection of the low esteem and stereotypic images in which women themselves are held. On the one hand, most of the events, institutions, movements, and written documents of the past which historians hold to be important have been led or produced or symbolically represented by men, and insofar as women have been active in these endeavors, they are thought to have identified themselves with the leadership and models presented by men. On the other hand, insofar as women have not been active in ways which historians deem significant, they are conceived to have lived out their lives in a limited number of stereotypic roles, essentially changeless over time and therefore irrelevant to the "intellectually interesting" questions of historical change. Within the context of such a system of beliefs and values, it is not surprising that historians should be skeptical about whether women's history can tell us anything "that we did not know before," and that some of the search for theory should be a defensive effort to give assurance that it does.

It is doubtful that any such assurance can be derived from theory alone, in the absence of a far broader base of information about women's past than we have at present. Seeking conceptual clarification in a knowledge vacuum can be as sterile as writing narrowly conceived monographs "devoid of interpretation." Theory cannot wholly precede the detailed monographic, descriptive, and narrative work which, in the field of women's history, has been so badly neglected. Such work need not be devoid of analysis and interpretation, but it must inform us of "the specific physiognomy of concrete human situations." Without that base of information, theory must remain at best hypothetical, at worst unreal and barren. It is with this point in mind that Parts II and III of this volume present case studies and surveys dealing with the experience of selected groups of women in diverse cultures and time periods. In all cases, the authors suggest, explore, or illustrate some theoretical questions or models, but the substance of these essays is more empirical than theoretical. This seems essential as a foundation against which to test both the doubts of the skeptics and the positive analyses of those committed to work in women's history.

The latter have felt the need for theory and conceptual clarification primarily as a guide to work in a field whose subject is full of paradoxes and does not conform to the patterns of social experience with which historians have mainly concerned themselves in the past. Women, as a category of historical study, are at once clearly distinct and hopelessly indistinct from men and their activities. As Hilda Smith argues in "Feminism and the Methodology of Women's History," the customary language of historical writing, which uses categories such as "civilization" and "class," is built on the historical experience of men, and may be largely inapplicable to the distinct historical experience of women. Yet as Gordon, Buhle, and Dye suggest in "The Problem of Women's History," we are only beginning to confront seriously the question: "On what basis do women share an historical existence?" If women's oppression cannot be denied, neither can it be denied that its character varied greatly by time, place, and class; nor that women have also played powerful roles in history. These themes are treated at length in a number of the essays in this volume, and it would not be appropriate to rehearse the arguments here. We may note, however, a few continuities and contrasts among the viewpoints represented in these essays.

One question which recurs in a number of the essays is that of the relationship between feminist perspective and the writing of women's history. Gerda Lerner, as we have seen, argues that the "feminist frame of reference has become archaic and fairly useless." Lerner has in mind here the biases of early feminist historians, particularly "their belief that the history of women is important only as representing the history of an oppressed group and its struggle against its oppressors." This bias led to a distorted image of women's real existence in the past, indiscriminate praise for women's "contributions," and inordinate attention to the women's rights and suffrage movements. Gordon, Buhle, and Dye also take to task the nineteenth-century feminists who conceived of women's past as a history of undifferentiated subjugation, and contemporary liberationists who regard women as a subject caste. They argue that this not only fails to explain women's energy and positive action (as Mary Beard had suggested earlier) but fails also to explain or help overcome "the historic reality of antagonisms and conflicting experiences among women. We must know as much about what kept women apart as we know about what situation they shared. . . . It is precisely the interrelationship between women's oppression and ethnic and class experience that enables us to understand why, for example, industrial experience did not necessarily undermine the strength of patriarchal authority over immigrant women."

On the other hand, Hilda Smith argues that a feminist perspective is essential to the understanding of women's history, and that it provides fruitful approaches to methodology, where the standard methodologies break down. Nor is Smith alone in taking this position, though she presents it more explicitly than others. The authors of "Historical Phallicies: Sexism in American Historical Writing," argue that the works they analyze are distorted precisely by the failure to take seriously the feminism of the women they study, and the tendency to blame women for their own oppression, rather than recognize "the real social conditions which are the source of women's problems and rebellion." Gordon, Buhle, and Dye also seem to suggest that what is needed is a new feminist perspective which allows for a complex analysis of family, class, and individual conditions, yet which "locates the lives of women, all women, at the center of efforts to comprehend and transform social structures."

Another recurrent issue is the relative weight to attribute to ideology and attitudes as opposed to material conditions in determining women's status in any given society or era. While Smith argues explicitly for the primacy of attitudinal factors (e.g., 374–75), Alice Kessler-Harris gives greater weight to economic conditions, especially changing labor needs of employers ("Women, Work and the Social Order"). The case studies in Parts II and III are divided according to the relative emphasis of the authors on these points.

Finally, the impetus to theory in the field of women's history has been fed by the challenges posed by an existing body of explicit or implicit theories, ranging from biblical explanations of women's subjection, through an array of matriarchal and patriarchal theories of social evolution, to the contemporary debate over women's "subjugation" or "force" in history. If women's history has not seemed "intellectually interesting," it has not been for lack of controversy, paradox, and conflicting opinion.

We are now more than a century away from the height of the debate, launched by J. J. Bachofen's *Mother-Right* in 1861. In the intervening time there have been periods in which the flurries of controversy produced a considerable literature, and periods in which the entire subject of women's history was apparently forgotten. It is impossible to review here even the main outlines of this rising and falling interest, nor the main issues and positions in the debate—much less to consider in detail the ideas of the protagonists. But the essays in this volume reflect the fact that the issues have been revived in recent years, the protagonists recalled from obscurity, and the arguments carried forward in new directions.

### NOTES

1. John Higham, *History* (Englewood Cliffs, N.J.: Prentice-Hall, 1965), 369, Felix Gilbert commenting on Marc Bloch; 387, Gilbert, concluding remarks; and 143, Higham, on the contemporary historian.

2. *Ibid.*, 115.

3. This process of debate and analysis is a continuing one, as witness a number of sessions at the Second Berkshire Conference on the History of Women, held at Radcliffe College, Cambridge, Mass., October 25–27, 1974. Particularly noteworthy in this context were the sessions on "Women's History in Transition" and "Effects of Women's

History upon Traditional Conceptions of Historiography," both chaired by Gerda Lerner, and including papers of special interest by Natalie Davis, Joan Kelly-Gadol, Renate Bridenthal, and Carroll Smith-Rosenberg.

4. Thus, for example, Sheila Johansson in her essay in this volume, suggests that "past interest in women's history has had a faddish character," and that scholars may "wonder whether topicality isn't the sole reason for the increasing attention paid to the history of women."

5. This remark was made by Graebner in a paper read at a session on "Women's Experience in History: A Teaching Problem," annual meeting of the American Historical Association, Boston, December 1970, subsequently published in *American Women and American Studies*, ed. Betty Chmaj (Pittsburgh: KNOW Press, 1971).

6. Christopher Lasch, in a letter to Berenice A. Carroll, April 24, 1971.

# PART I

# On the Historiography of Women

The papers in this section are devoted to critical historiography. The first two essays, by Ann J. Lane and Berenice A. Carroll, present critical assessments of two major contributions to the theory of women's history: Frederick Engels's *The Origin of the Family, Private Property, and the State;* and Mary Ritter Beard's *Woman As Force in History.* While Engels and Beard were both persuaded that women in early times held a position higher, relative to men, than they do today in "civilized" societies, their work is otherwise poles apart. As Lane points out: "With [the woman's] fall from equality and independence in primitive periods, Engels ceases to see her as an engaged member of society." In contrast, what Beard is concerned primarily to show is "women active, competent and recognized in their own time in a wide range of occupations and endeavors." Whereas Engels sought to offer an explanation of "the world-historic defeat of the female sex" and the subsequent general oppression of women, Beard was at pains to show that the notion of women as "members of a subject sex" is a myth, distorting and concealing the complex realities of women's status and role in history. But as the critical essays here show, the work of both Engels and Beard was severely marred by problems of conceptual confusion and lapses in logic and continuity.

The last three essays in this section focus on evaluating the body of recent and contemporary historiography of American women. Dolores Barracano Schmidt and Earl Robert Schmidt surveyed the treatment of women in leading textbooks used in college-level American history survey courses in 1970 and concluded that the space devoted to women in these texts was consistently miniscule and badly skewed in terms of selection and presentation. The five coauthors of "Historical Phallacies: Sexism in American Historical Writing" present a more detailed analysis of the work of a number of male historians who have written biographical or general works on the history of women in America. This essay is a strongly stated attack on sexist bias in current historical writing on women, and has already provoked some controversy in the field.

Finally, Gordon, Buhle, and Dye in "The Problem of Women's History" offer a broader survey and analysis of the literature on women in American history. They suggest that these can be classified into four predominant modes or methodological approaches: (1) institutional histories of women in organizations; (2) biographies of important women; (3) histories of ideas about women and their roles; and (4) social histories of women in particular times and places. After surveying and assessing past work in these categories, the authors enter into a discussion of the relationship of feminist theory to historical writings on women.

This discussion, as well as a number of points raised by other authors in this section, opens the exploration of new approaches to the study of women's history, which is carried forward more fully in the essays in Part IV.

# Women in Society:
# A Critique of Frederick Engels

*Ann J. Lane*

## Introduction

The question before us today is: is Frederick Engels alive and well? Until recently he had not fared well in the American academy, but perhaps for the first time in this country his work is soon to be examined seriously. The growing numbers of serious, younger Marxist intellectuals producing important work and holding respectable university posts make neglecting Marxism no longer easy. Nor is academic Marxism viewed as a serious threat, largely because it is no longer associated with a threatening political movement, as it once was. The onus is currently placed on those who act, not talk or write or teach.

Finally, Engels is current because of the kinds of questions to which he directed his attention, particularly the family and women. Many in the woman's movement, both in the university and outside of it, have turned with enthusiasm to Engels's work on the family and the subjugation of women, and have found in his hypotheses and assertions easy ways to reach presumably radical conclusions about a variety of legitimate concerns. One of the ironies of time is that Engels's study, *The Origin of the Family, Private Property, and the State,* which has catapulted him to current prominence, is hardly his central or most important work.[1]

The very reasons for renewed interest in Engels explain the importance of reappraising his work; that is, they focus attention on the overlapping of interests, of those concerned primarily with a further exploration of Marxism and of those concerned primarily with the *subject* of women. While scholars of Marxist humanism who have emerged in recent years seem concerned with rescuing Marx from Engels, by that very concern they have thereby demonstrated the relevance of reexamining the contributions of both men. It is with both of these aspects, then, Engels as theoretician and Engels as analyst of women, that I will deal. To what extent, for example, do Engels's views on women help clarify the kinds of questions with which social critics have yet to grapple: to begin with, the very concept of women's history and women's

An earlier version of this essay was read at the annual meeting of the Organization of American Historians, April 8, 1972, in Washington, D.C.

oppression? Women have been written out of history and should be written in, as a matter of justice. But redressing balances, however desirable, has limited theoretical significance. And on the Marxist end, to what extent do Engels's historical and anthropological investigations deepen our understanding of the historical process? Using the subject matter of women and the family, has Engels enabled us to understand better the workings of the whole social order? By approaching Engels's investigations, in the words of one interpreter, "not as a metaphysical doctrine but as an instrument for the interpretation and explanation of social life,"[2] one can assess Engels's empirical work on women as a giant research project, designed to test the validity of his hypotheses about social organization and change.

Engels's work on the family was inspired in large part by Marx's notes, and although his work came after Marx died, it was a product of many years of joint discussion. Although there are many and important differences between the two, for this discussion I am blurring those distinctions, as well as generational ones, that is, those concerned with the debate over early and late Marx.

I

If anthropologists have been peeved by Marx and Engels, they had some early justification, for the opening line of the *Communist Manifesto* showed their initial disrespect for primitive society. "The history of all hitherto existing society is the history of class struggles" assigns to oblivion those thousands of years of what then became known as "prehistory." In a footnote to the 1888 edition of the *Manifesto*, Engels tried to wriggle out by claiming that what they meant was "written" history, but then he offered a more convincing explanation: when the *Manifesto* was written "the social organization existing previous to recorded history was all but unknown."[3] The neglect was compensated for thirty-six years later with the publication of Frederick Engels's *The Origin of the Family, Private Property, and the State in the Light of the Researches of Lewis H. Morgan;* by 1892 it had undergone its fifth printing. It is the only sustained work on that subject written by either Marx or Engels; indeed it is the only major work in Marxist literature to date on the family.

The empirical work upon which Engels relied for *The Origin of the Family* was that done by Lewis Henry Morgan in his major work *Ancient Society*. "Morgan in his own way," Engels said, "had discovered afresh in America the materialist conception of history discovered by Marx forty years ago."[4] Whether Morgan's contributions warrant such an assertion or whether Engels made more of Morgan than Morgan justified is one of the many questions still unsettled by generations of anthropological debate. What Engels certainly did was to impose a larger order, his conception of society and history, upon Morgan's studies. He used Morgan's extensive work done with American Indians to confirm his already developed hypotheses, particularly as they concerned the evolution of class antagonisms and the emergence of the state. Morgan's work began with the Iroquois Indians in New York State. Initially drawn by the system he found among them of naming kinsmen, he then accumulated data on kinship systems among other American Indians and offered hypotheses concerning the structure of tribal society and the emergence of private property.

Engels was, despite the views of later critics, relatively modest about the claims he made for his study. *"So long as no important additional material makes changes necessary,"* he wrote at the opening of *Origins,* Morgan's "classification will undoubtedly remain in force."[5] Several years later he confidently stated: "Some of Morgan's hypotheses have been shaken or even disproved. But . . . the order which he introduced into primitive history still holds in its main lines today."[6]

## II

Now to the book. To begin at the beginning, " . . . the determining factor in history is, in the final instance, the production and reproduction of immediate essentials of life."[7] Morgan and Engels accepted the widely held notion of the division of human history into successive stages: savagery, barbarism, and civilization, each then subdivided. The means by which humans provide the essentials for life is key: "technology discloses man's mode of dealing with Nature, the process of production by which he sustains life, and by which also his social relations, and the mental conceptions that flow from them are formed," Marx said in *Capital.*[8]

Savagery is divided into three stages. At the lower stage, the "childhood of the human race," human beings lived in forests, partly as tree-dwellers, and gathered food. *"Of all people known to history,"* said Engels, *"none was still at this primitive level"* (emphasis added). Although there is "no direct evidence to prove its existence," such a transitional stage "must necessarily be assumed." During this period articulate speech was developed. The middle period began with the utilization of fish for food, which required the use of fire. Human beings were now more mobile. With the invention of the "first weapons, club and spear, game could sometimes be added." But Engels denied that any society could live exclusively by hunting: "the yield of the hunt was far too precarious." At the upper stage came the invention of the bow and arrow, whereby "game became a regular source of food and hunting the normal form of work" (persumably for men, that is—AJL). "The bow and arrow was for savagery what the iron sword was for barbarism and fire-arms for civilization—the decisive weapon."[9]

Barbarism is characterized by the domestication and breeding of animals and the cultivation of plants. It too is divided by Engels into three stages; the lowest dates from the introduction of pottery. At this point the "natural endowments" of the two hemispheres take societies in different directions. In the Eastern Hemisphere there were animals capable of being domesticated and many cultivable cereals. The Western Hemisphere had only the llama to domesticate and only maise to cultivate. The middle stage of barbarism began in the East with domestication of animals and in the West with the cultivation, by means of irrigation, of plants for food, and the use of adobe brick and stone for building. But then the Spanish conquest cut short further development in the Western Hemisphere. In the Eastern Hemisphere the herding of animals led to a pastoral life. The upper stage of barbarism began with the smelting of iron ore, and "is richer in advances in production than all the preceding stages together." Engels places at this level of development the Greeks of the Heroic Age, the tribes of Italy just before the founding of Rome, the Germans of Tacitus, and the Norsemen of the Vikings. For the first time an iron plowshare is drawn by cattle, thus making large-scale agriculture possible and permitting "a practically unrestricted food supply in comparison with previous conditions."

Briefly then, Engels's distinctions, following Morgan, can be summarized as follows: savagery is a period "in which man's appropriation of products in their natural state predominates"; barbarism is "the period during which man learns to breed domestic animals and to practice agriculture, and acquires methods of increasing the supply of natural products by human activity," now commonly viewed as food-gathering and food-producing periods. Civilization is introduced with the written alphabet and is distinguished by "a more advanced application of work to the products of nature, the period of industry proper and of art."[10]

How does Engels describe the social relationships that existed in these different periods of human history? The development of the family "takes a parallel course," he says somewhat ambiguously, but the distinguishing periods "have not such striking marks of differentiation." Beginning with middle savagery Engels describes, in a significant paragraph, the division of labor as "purely primitive, between the sexes only. The man fights in the wars, hunts and fishes, procures the raw materials of food and the tools necessary for doing so. The woman looks after the house and the preparation of food and clothing, cooks, weaves and sews. They are each master in their own sphere, the man in the forest, the woman in the house. Each is owner of the instruments which he or she makes and uses: the man of the weapons, the hunting and fishing implements, the woman of the household gear."[11]

But with an increase in productivity of labor inevitably came new social relations. The herds provided great wealth. To the man belonged the cattle.

All the surplus which the acquisition of the necessities now yielded fell to the man. The woman shared in its enjoyment, but had no part in its ownership. The "savage" warrior and hunter had been content to take second place in the house, after the woman; the "gentler" shepherd, in the arrogance of his wealth, pushed himself forward into the first place and the woman down into the second. And she could not complain. The division of labor within the family had regulated the division of property between the man and woman. That division of labor had remained the same; and yet it now turned the previous domestic relation upside down, simply because the division of labor outside the family had changed.

The same cause which had ensured to the woman her previous supremacy in the house—that her activity was confined to domestic labor—this same cause now ensured the man's supremacy in the house: the domes-

tic labor of the woman no longer counted beside the acquisition of the
necessities of life by the man.[12]

Engels postulated family relationships to parallel the stages of evolution.
He accepted Morgan's assumption that at a very primitive stage "unrestricted
sexual freedom prevailed within the tribe, every woman belonging equally to
every man and every man to every woman." With great, grim irony, Engels
described the Victorian shock of scientists of his age in dealing with such a
concept of group promiscuity, but he offered a reasoned explanation for its
evolution. Humans, defenseless alone, had to band together for protection.
What was needed, he said, was "mutual toleration among the adult males,
freedom from jealousy," as "the first condition for the formation of those
large, permanent groups in which alone animals could become men." Group
marriage, whole groups of men and whole groups of women mutually possessing one another, "leaves little room for jealousy." Jealousy and incest are
thus late inventions. This is what Engels called the consanguine family. There
are "no verifiable examples" but *it must have existed,* he asserted (emphasis
added). "The whole subsequent development of the family presupposes the
existence of the consanguine family as a necessary preparatory step."[13]

In all forms of group family the paternity is uncertain; only the mother is
known. Descent thus can only be traced on the mother's side and therefore
only the female line is recognized—a state applicable to all people in savagery
and lower stages of barbarism.

Gradually, Engels said, as social organization advanced, parents and children were excluded from intercourse with one another, then sister and
brother. As the history of the family in primitive times led to progressive
narrowing of the circle as to whom one could marry, ultimately group
marriage became practically impossible. The result was what he called the
"pairing family," not yet monogamy, for the bond is very loosely linked and
the marriage is easily dissolved. In general, group marriage is characteristic of
savagery, the pairing family of barbarism, and monogamy of civilization.

The position of women in group marriage and even in pairing marriage
remained free and honorable. "Communistic housekeeping . . . means the
supremacy of women in the house; just as the exclusive recognition of the
female parent, owing to the impossibility of reocgnizing the male parent with
certainty, means that the women—the mothers, are held in high respect." And
again, "The communistic household, in which most or all of the women
belong to one and the same gens [clan—AJL], while the men come from
various gentes, is *the material foundation of that supremacy of women* which
was general in primitive times."[14]

The transition from group marriage to pairing marriage is the transition
whereby the woman "acquires the right to give herself to *one* man
only."[15] (A charming bit of chivalry, a good deal of which sits uneasily but
significantly in Engels's otherwise unsentimental analysis). As wealth increased, the question of inheritance became pertinent. Then mother-right
became a liability. Presumably by now the biology of paternity was discovered and the pairing relationship permitted designation of the father.

"Mother-right had to be overthrown, and overthrown it was. . . . The over-throw of mother-right was the world historical defeat of the female sex. The man took command in the home also; the woman was degraded and reduced to servitude, she became the slave of his lust and a mere instrument for the production of children."[16]

The monagamous family developed out of the pairing family in the transtional period between the middle and upper stages of barbarism. Its ties are stronger than those of the pairing family. Ordinarily only the man can dissolve the monogamous marriage. To insure the wife's fidelity and the paternity of the children, "she is delivered over unconditionally into the power of her husband." Monogamy thus developed in no way connected to love, but as a way to protect property, a marriage of convenience. "It was the first form of the family to be based, not on nature, but on economic conditions—on the victory of private property over primitive, natural, com-munal property." And it is the existence of "slavery side by side with monogamy, the presence of young, beautiful slaves belonging reservedly to the man, that stamps monogamy from the very beginning with its specific character of monogamy for the woman only. . . . And that is the character it still has today."[17]

In summary, in pre-class societies, before surplus wealth was produced and thereupon struggled over, the household functioned communally and the division of labor between the sexes was equitable. Not so under monogamy.

Engels then moves on chronologically in a rather schematic way, first contrasting women's position of honor in primitive society with the deteriora-tion that followed in Greece and Rome. He then runs through feudal Europe and leaps into industrialization. In his far-ranging discussion of class society in *The Origin of the Family,* Engels concentrates largely on the upper-class family and the role of the upper-class woman, who is now projected as victim, oppressed, passive in the historical process. With her fall from equality and independence in primitive periods, Engels ceases to see her as an engaged member of society. The remaining pages in *The Origin of the Family* deal primarily with the emergence of the state after the development of an antagonistic class structure.

### III

Most of the criticism by anthropologists has centered on Morgan's concept of primitive collective society. Even Engels's friends, such as Marxist sociolo-gist Bernhard Stern, have conceded that some of the data "later anthropolo-gists have found to be invalid," although Stern may have conceded too much. Stern described *The Origin of the Family* as a book that "abounds in insights and establishes many fundamental principles of sociological analysis of the family that are of great value." Still he believes that anthropologists "for good reason" do not support the hypothesis that group marriage was the earliest form of family relationship, a view upon which Engels relied heav-ily.[18]

But a careful reading of Engels suggests that his concept of group marriage was misunderstood by many critics, partly as a result of his own ambiguity. He did not claim that a stable group family prevailed.

> Group marriage, which in these instances from Australia is still marriage of sections, mass marriage of an entire section of men, often scattered over the whole continent, with an equally widely distributed section of women—this group marriage, seen close at hand, does not look quite so terrible as the philistine, whose mind cannot get beyond brothels, imagines it to be.

> . . . The Australian aborigine, wandering hundreds of miles from his home among people whose language he does not understand, neverthe-less often finds in every camp and every tribe women who give them-selves to him without resistance and without resentment.[19]

What Engels described is not a stable marriage of whole groups of people but a system of sexual prerogatives.

Although Stern recognized the generalized way in which Engels's group marriage was projected, still he defined this area to be Engels's weakest. Engels assumed that the clan terminology could be explained only by postu-lating an earlier form of group marriage, from which these terms were thought to be survivals. Stern insisted that such an explanation is unnecessary "for they are explicable in terms of their social functions." Those generaliza-tions of Engels that depend upon the premise of an initial group marriage, for example, the assertion that the incest tabu came late in human history, need to be reevaluated in terms of present knowledge, Stern maintained. He insisted, as do many others, that monogamous families frequently are found among simple hunting and food-gathering societies.[20]

Kathleen Gough, another anthropologist whose point of view is sympa-thetic to that of Engels, also insists that there is no evidence that "either matriarchy (rule of mothers) or sexual equality has ever existed. All known societies have been male dominant to some extent, although the extent varies greatly; and it seems to be true that, in general, pre-state societies (bands, tribes, and chiefdoms) offer greater freedom for women than do primitive or archaic state, and matrilineal horticultural tribes the greatest freedom of all."[21]

There are certain observations about the anthropological debate that even an outsider may feel equipped to hazard. Engels built his case on data culled from anthropology (in whatever state it then existed), history, linguistics, and ultimately inference based upon a broadly defined view of society and social change. Anthropologists through the years who have participated in the debate with Engels tend to deal most narrowly with solely his anthropological assertions; they assert and try to demonstrate that no known societies show those familial arrangements Engels described. Primitive societies, those by definition outside the mainstream of the historical process, may hold great clues for understanding early stages of human development, but it is with great delicacy that such evidence must be drawn from these vestigial remnants of an earlier time. In using data that depend so heavily upon the perception of the observer, evidence must be entered with great caution. As Eleanor

Burke Leacock observed, years ago Frank G. Speck's investigations of the Montagnais Indians of the Labrador peninsula became the standard proof that Morgan, and by extension, Engels, was wrong. Speck asserted that private ownership of hunting grounds preceded the penetration by Europeans into the New World. Later work among Speck's very Indians "showed that the hunting ground system had indeed developed as a result of the fur trade with Europeans, and further, that it did not involve true land ownership."[22]

Engels's claim that matrilineality preceded patrilineality, which has also been subjected to great criticism, perhaps suffers from a similar kind of anthropological myopia. How much of what we know about women in primitive societies reflects the vision of the earliest observers? Do we know so much about the sex lives of Eskimos, Leacock asks, because they were first contacted by whalers and not missionaries? In anthropological literature, women are often described as being "isolated" in menstrual huts so that men will not be contaminated. Where men's huts exist they are written about as if reflecting high status. Are these really the attitudes reflected by the natives themselves or are they projected upon them by missionaries and traders?[23]

The entire discussion surrounding Engels has suffered all these years partly because it was locked in the old debate with Marxism. Marvin Harris in *The Rise of Anthropological Theory* states that one of the purposes of that book was "to decontaminate the materialist approach to history."

> The principle of techno-economic and techno-environmental determinism [which is Harris's idiosyncratic variation on Marx—AJL] has never been consistently applied across the range of phenomena with which anthropologists are familiar, despite the fact that anthropologists have played a crucial role in discrediting this option. . . . This failure is all the more remarkable in view of the . . . inability of the science of man to develop a viable alternative to the prematurely discredited strategy, and in view of the passion with which anthropologists have argued that they have remained free of ideological bias.[24]

Discussion of the family has also suffered from a one-discipline approach. If historians have tended to ignore the important materials on prehistoric times, or more accurately, history before written language, if we tend to cut out of our view anthropology and archaeology, the same limitation is true of anthropologists: their view of humankind could use some historical perspective.

## IV

The attention focused on the Morgan material has obscured other aspects of Engels's highly provocative essay. Important questions that he raised are still to be answered. What was the effect of the rise of surplus wealth on relations between men and women? How valid is the assertion that in non-wealth-producing societies, when women's work was as important for survival as men's, that is when, in Engels's terms, both were equally involved in the production process, equality between men and women prevailed? What was the impact of excluding women from the process of production, not as an act of male perversity, but as a result of the shift of production outside of the home, leaving the women in an economically, and therefore presumably socially and sexually, vulnerable position?

Many problems remain. Underlying all of Engels's anthropological assumptions is a unilinear world view. It is one thing to assert that all societies are in constant process of change. It is quite another to insist that they are all moving in and must move in precisely the same direction. Morgan's and Engels's unilinear view has been much exaggerated by critics. They did account for great variations in the evolution of social structures: for example, different resources in the Old and New World taking early societies in varying directions and (see Engels's entire discussion in *The Origin of the Family*) different ways in which the state evolved in class societies. Still, Engels contructs the world's order with a disquieting assurance.

Engels's definition of the role of the family is imprecise. The preface to the first edition of *The Origin of the Family*, later reprinted without change, postulates what appears to be a fundamentally independent role for the family. The determining factor in history, Engels says, the production and reproduction of the essentials of life, has a twofold character. On the one side, "production of the means of existence. . . ; on the other, the production of human beings themselves. . . . The social organization under which the people of a particular historical epoch . . . live is determined by both kinds of production; by the stage of development of labor on the one hand and of the family on the other."[25]

The implication that the family is an independent organism, of comparable significance to the means of producing essentials for survival, is not compatible, the way it is expressed here, with his general theory of society. Later in the book, after outlining stages in history, Engels asserts that "the development of the family takes a parallel course," which again sounds the note of an independent family evolution. It is certainly ambiguously presented; indeed the notion is essentially repudiated by the weight of the entire book. Engels never explains the independence of the family in relation to the general community or tribe in pre-class societies or to antagonistic classes in more advanced ones.

As an extension of that confusion, Engels did not clarify the relationship of the subjugation of women to class exploitation. Exploitation has a precise meaning to Engels: it is the extraction of surplus labor by one class of another. He never integrated the most primitive division of labor, male-female, with class relations, and the fuzziness reappears. In *The Origin of the Family* he quotes Marx as follows: "The modern family contains . . . in miniature all the contradictions which later extend through society." And later, Engels himself: "Monogamous marriage comes on the scene as the subjugation of the one sex by the other; it announces a struggle between the sexes unknown throughout the whole previous prehistoric period. . . . The first class opposition that appears in history coincides with the development of the antagonism between man and woman in monogamous marriage, and the first class oppression coincides with that of the female sex by the male."[26]

What does that mean? In the context of the discussion Engels describes monogamy as the "cellular form of civilized society"—it seems as if Engels means the subjugation of man by woman in monogamy *was* (not *coincides with*) class exploitation. What does it mean to say that "the modern family contained in germ . . . all contradictions?" The knotty problem, how to relate the concept of female oppression, whatever that means historically and theoretically, to class exploitation, when women are distributed throughout the class structure, is not even confronted. Does Engels mean women are a class oppressed, or is he speaking symbolically, rhetorically, analogously?

The cohesion of Engels's entire theory of the origin of the family and the historic role of women in society rests upon his assertion that sex differentiation, the first form of differentiation, is different from sex stratification—sex roles were different but equal. Juliet Mitchell, Kate Millett, and Shulamith Firestone, among others in the woman's movement, deny the possibility that this division of social labor along sexual lines could have been anything but oppressive. To them the first division of labor between man and woman was at the same time the first formation of oppressor and oppressed.

To Engels the oppression of women came with class division: "One of the most absurd notions taken over from 18th century Enlightenment is that in the beginning of society woman was the slave of man. Among all savages and all barbarians of the lower and middle stages, and to a certain extent of the upper stage also, the position of women is not only free, but honorable."[27] If Engels were to pose a pre-class society in which men oppressed women, his whole notion of exploitation as he developed it would have to be reexamined. Could Engels accept the idea of the oppression of women in societies before an exploitative class structure had split humanity into antagonistic relationships? Not very easily. So long as he has created models in which women's oppression is organically tied to class exploitation, his argument requires equality of women in pre-class society. But a careful look at the way his argument reconstructed early society leaves one with an uneasy feeling that his case is weak.

On what basis does Engels assert the equality of women rested? The quotation of page 8 warrants repeating. "Communistic housekeeping . . . means the supremacy of women in the house; just as the exclusive recognition of the female parent, owing to the impossibility of recognizing the male parent with certainty, means that the women—the mothers, are held in high respect": not necessarily. Ignorance of paternity undoubtedly explains the prevalence of early matrilineality—that is, descent on the female side. Such descent patterns do not translate into female equality.

Engels asserts that with the rise of surplus wealth—presumably by then paternity could be known and the pairing family permitted designation of the father—inheritance on the mother's side was abruptly ended. "The overthrow of mother-right was the world historic defeat of the female sex," Engels said. This revolution, "one of the most decisive ever experienced by humanity . . . was by no means so difficult as it looks to us today . . . a simple decree sufficed," transferring inheritance from the mother's line to the father's line.[28] That the revolution could be achieved so easily suggests that women were hardly in the position of equal power Engels projected.

Look again at the important paragraphs quoted on page 7 that describe the way in which, he says, surplus wealth naturally and simply fell into the hands of the male. The division of labor was first between the sexes only. "The man fights in the war, hunts and fishes . . . the woman looks after the house and the preparation of food. . . . They are each master in their own sphere." But eventually "the herds provided great wealth. To the man belonged the cattle."

But where is the evidence for that statement? On the contrary, the weight of evidence suggests that it was the women in whose sphere fell agricultural production and control over domesticated animals. If when the wealth was produced, it was wrested from women, the suggestion is that the power was already in the hands of the men.

"To procure the necessities of life had always been the business of man," said Engels. Not so, for as even Engels admitted, in its early stages society could not survive on the precarious rewards of hunting alone. Women were jointly involved in food production, not just by processing that which the men brought home. If men grabbed the surplus it was more likely a result of their superior strength, the hunting tools that are easily transformed into weapons, the vulnerability of women during pregnancy and nursing—essentially biologically rooted reasons that are hard to fit into Engels's model.

Even Engels's own words question his insistence on the early status and power of women. His references to marriage by force always mean men abducting women. He recognizes female infanticide in early societies. In describing the transition from group marriage to pairing marriage, he alludes to "the man [who] had a chief wife, among his many wives." The Australian aborigine wandering from his home and finding sexual consolation (p. 10) is a male. All these illustrations imply unequal status and power. If Engels's other evidence does indicate that oppression of women was not necessarily unrelieved in all societies throughout all time, his own case is no more convincing: that women occupied positions of power and status in all early societies and until the emergence of private property.

Engels's commitment to group marriage, whatever its validity in general, does not have to be tied to the idea of equality of women, sexual or otherwise. If survival of mankind required cooperative defense efforts—and that meant "mutual toleration among adult males"—then female equality was quite irrelevant. A system in which "every woman belong[ed] to every man" did not at the same time have to include the extension: that "every man belong[ed] to every woman."

Engels's tendency to make easy and tidy generalizations does not end with unconfirmed pronouncements of female equality. To get from group marriage to pairing marriage to monogamy he relied on a few more. In group marriage there were no inhibitions against incest of any kind, Engels proclaims. The "first advance in organization consisted in the exclusion of parents and children from sexual intercourse with one another, the second was the exclusion of sister and brother. On account of the greater nearness in age, this second advance was infinitely more important."[29] Despite the extraordinary importance of such a change in social outlook, Engels has no evidence to offer to substantiate his first assertion, that there were no prohibitions against incest, or to explain why such incest taboos suddenly came about.

How did group marriage break down? Living together communally had a "natural limit." "As soon as the idea arose that sexual intercourse between children of the same mother was wrong," Engels says (again not explaining why and how this idea arose or fell), it affected the way new social units were established. Then when a "social ban on sexual intercourse between brothers and sisters" evolved, a new family unit was established with common possession of husbands and wives but from which brothers of the wives and sisters of the husbands were excluded.[30] A wonderfully imaginative exercise, but how defend it?

Only twice does Engels take note that he has not provided some explanation for the sudden emergence of incest taboos. He refers to "the obscure impulse towards the restriction of inbreeding" and later: "What is significant is how the urge towards the prevention of inbreeding asserts itself again and again, feeling its way, however, quite instinctively, without clear consciousness of its aim."[31]

How extraordinary that Engels can casually rely upon "an obscure impulse" to explain an enormously important change in human history and yet maintain tenaciously and with assurance that group marriage, sexual promiscuity, and female equality were characteristics common to all pre-class societies.

If the move from group marriage to pairing marriage was such a great step forward, as Engels says, because woman "acquires the right to give herself to one man only," her earlier position could not have been so enviable. Either Engels is guilty of the kind of Victorian priggishness that he accused others of, or he is right: group marriage for a woman may have meant she was to be sexually available to many men. In that circumstance one man is undoubtedly an improvement over many, but such a situation hardly bespeaks great power or status.

In summary then, Engels's hypotheses too often straitjacket what might have been provocative insights. A unilinear view of the world leads him to seek identical patterns in all preliterate societies, and one wonders what distortions result. For instance, his belief that class exploitation, which developed late in human history, is somehow identical with or at least connected to oppression of women, leads him to conclude that in pre-class societies women's position had to have been "free and honorable." Yet the evidence is not compelling. While it is certainly possible to postulate the notion of female oppression long preceding class exploitation, Engels's ambiguity somehow has so merged those two separate phenomena as to make them appear inseparable.

## V

The imprecision with which Engels has examined women in pre-class societies carries over to his discussion of women in class society, particularly under capitalism—women as wives, workers, mothers, rulers. Despite some remarkable insights, the earlier unresolved question—the relationship of the subjugation of women to exploitative class relations, and all the ramifications that follow—becomes increasingly significant. While he does not discuss women and the family in later societies as systematically as he did in earlier ones, in *The Condition of the Working-Class in England in 1844* Engels assesses the impact of industrial life on familial relations and institutions. The book was originally published in 1845, but a new edition was issued in 1892 with no major modifications. By that time *The Origin of the Family* had appeared. In *The Condition of the Working-Class* Engels describes the life of the spinner and weaver before the introduction of large-scale machinery and the factory system. Capitalism was dominant, but the factory system had yet to triumph. He describes a life of production centered in the household, with a kind of natural division of work among men, women, and children. Not that life was easy or leisurely, but it was a piece, unfragmented. With the introduction of machinery and the emerging dominance of the factory came the "unfeeling isolation of each in his private interest." And "the employment of women at once breaks up the family; for when the wife spends 12 or 13 hours every day in the mill, and the husband works the same length of time there or elsewhere, what becomes of the children?[32] Grim descriptions follow of the human degradation that followed the factory. Households were turned upside down when the woman earned more than the man, to the great humiliation of the husband. In general there are two prevailing themes, although neither is systematically developed: first, before the onslaught of the factory the family had been unfragmented and based upon a division of labor that seems not to have been internally exploitative; and second, widespread employment of women under the factory system devastated the stability of the household.

Now let us return to *The Origin of the Family* and recapitulate Engels's analysis of the evolution of the family from group marriage to pairing marriage to monogamy. With the rise of the patriarchal family, beside slavery, "household management . . . became a private service; the wife became head servant, excluded from all participation in social production. Not until the coming of large-scale industry was the road to social production opened to her again—and then only to the proletarian wife." And again, "in the great majority of cases today, at least in the possessing classes, the husband is obliged to earn a living and support his family, and that in itself gives him a position of supremacy."[33]

What emerges is a confusion as to when the household was removed from the process of production, and thus at what time in history the role of women did become detached from the larger social community. Engels suggests that the detachment came with both the rise of surplus wealth and the emergence of antagonistic classes, that is with the disintegration of primitive communal society, and then also as late as the eighteenth century with the dominance of the factory system. He suggests that the position of supremacy men have achieved is based upon their wage-earning support of the household, implying first, that the problem would be over if women went to work; and second, that supremacy of males does not serve ruling-class men as a vehicle to protect their property and insure inheritance.

The confusions do not end here. Speaking of marriages of convenience among the rich, Engels finds that the average woman differs from the ordinary courtesan only "in that she does not let out her body on piecework as a wage worker but sells it once and for all into slavery." Love can be real, Engels insists, only among the oppressed class, the proletariat, because here there is no property "for the preservation and inheritance of which monogamy was cleared away; hence there is no basis for any kind of male supremacy left in the proletarian household."[34] There is no basis only if one restricts male supremacy solely to a question of property and chooses to exclude questions of psychology and ideology as relevant to male-female relations. While Engels is capable of such theoretical simplicity, the data he describes add a richness in spite of himself. In *The Condition of the Working Class* Engels poignantly describes brutalities and humiliations perpetrated by workingmen against their wives and children—actions resulting from lives of bitterness, despair, and futility, and quite unrelated to matters of property inheritance.

What of the future? "The first condition for the liberation of the wife is to bring the whole female sex back into public industry and . . . this in turn demands the abolition of the monogamous family as the economic unit of society." He goes on: " . . . to emancipate woman and make her the equal of man is . . . an impossibility so long as the woman is shut out from social production labor and restricted to private domestic labor. The emancipation of woman will only be possible when women can take part in production on a large social scale, and domestic work no longer claims anything but an insignificant part of her time."[35]

Here may be the source of one of the confusions still prevalent in the current woman's movement. When Engels describes proletarian life, it is dreadful, brutal, demeaning, dehumanizing. Why then is the emancipation of women to be found in placing them in social production? Why is equality to men desirable if men are exploited? Having a paying job may give women an important sense of independence but it hardly emancipates them. If Engels is projecting to the future why does he limit himself to capitalist categories at all? The very concept that Marx and Engels used of "social production" leaves the woman at home involved in "non-activity," from which she must escape if she is to become "productive." As capitalism became more complex the limitations of this idea of "socially productive labor" proved more serious as it included increasingly more "nonproductive labor." Thus Engels's difficulty in groping with the problem of "unproductive" domestic labor points to a general rigidity in his analysis.

What we are left with is a thesis that describes monogamy as evolving to protect property—either during Roman slavery or eighteenth-century England—so working-class marriages alone can be based on love. Women's oppression began when new processes of production left them out—either several thousand years ago or a couple of hundred—so to emancipate women put them in a position to be exploited along with men. A partial explanation for this peculiarly confused discussion of women is that it lacks a context that includes men. The very concepts of exploitation, oppression, liberation, make no sense unless they are in a total context.

An explanation for these unusually sloppy formulations must go beyond matters of logic. One of Engels's great strengths was his insistence that *all* forms of social life, including those sacred ones of love, marriage, and family, be subjected to the same standards of analysis as other aspects of culture. His data were not always sufficiently extensive or appropriate but the standards were set. It is disquieting to notice the creeping sentimentalism in his analysis of the evolution of family structure. Monogamy was brought about originally by women, Engels says. As the traditional sexual relations lost the

> naïve primitive character of forest life . . . the more oppressive and humiliating must the woman have felt them to be and the greater the longing for the right of chastity, of temporary or permanent marriage with one man only as a way of release. This advance could not in any case have originated with the men, if only because it has never occurred to them, even to this day, to renounce the pleasures of actual group marriage. Only when the women had brought about the transition to pairing marriage were the men able to introduce strict monogamy— though indeed only for women.[36]

And later:

> sexual love is by its nature exclusive . . . the marriage based on sexual love is by its nature individual marriage. If now the economic considerations . . . disappear . . . the equality of women thereby achieved will tend infinitely more to make men really monogamous than to make women polyandrous.[37]

As much as he tried to break with his conventional sexual attitudes, they clung. Engels, in the following quotation he reproduced from Morgan, concedes that the family "must advance as society advances and change as society changes, even as it has done in the past. . . . Should the monogamian family in the distant future fail to answer the requirements of society . . . it is impossible to predict the nature of its successor."[38]

Engels can encourage the change to public child-rearing but he cannot really conjure up the possibility of an entirely new form of marriage. For all his utterances about the beauties of monogamous marriage for men and women (one conventional view he could not question), he is not even certain that men will be able to achieve it (another conventional view): "The intense emotion of individual sex-love varies much in duration from one individual to another *especially among men* and if affection definitely comes to an end or is supplanted by a new passionate love, separation is a benefit for both partners" (emphasis added).[39] He is not really very far from the nineteenth century after all.

## VI

Slipped between the glaring oversimplifications and confusions are many important ideas. As early as 1845, in *The Condition of the Working Class in England*, while recognizing the life of misery to which the working class was subject, Engels saw as well what is a commonplace today, the importance of the city as a center for community-building and the growth of political consciousness. Unhappily, he did not pursue that insight with women in capitalism, perhaps because for him the overriding concern was the shattering of the family with large-scale factory employment of women. He did not examine its other side: the effect of the factory community upon women, not as mothers or wives only, but as members of the larger community, as workers.

The same book contains an extraordinary and subtle paragraph on the implications for the household when it is sustained by the wife's employment (notice, though, it contradicts specifically his assertion, in the same book, that it is women's wage-earning that establishes the basis for genuine marriages of love among proletarians):

> this condition, which unsexes the man and takes from the woman all womanliness without being able to bestow upon the man true womanliness, or the woman true manliness—this condition which degrades . . . both sexes . . . is the last result of the much-praised civilization. . . . If the reign of the wife over the husband, as inevitably brought about by the factory system, is inhuman, the pristine rule of the husband over the wife must have been inhuman too. . . . If the family of our present society is being thus dissolved, this dissolution merely shows that at bottom, the binding tie of this family was not family affection, but private interest lurking under the cloak of a pretended community of possessions.[40]

Among the most provocative of Engels's ideas is his idea of sex-love, which was, he said, unconnected in its origin to monogamy. Where it existed during antiquity it ordinarily was outside official society: among shepherds and slaves. And "the chivalrous love of the middle ages, was not conjugal. . . . In its classic form . . . it heads straight for adultery." "Marriage," after all, "was openly a political act," and made no other pretense.[41]

The question to which Engels turns is why the victory of capitalism brought with it the triumph of the idea, though not the reality, of marriage for love. Capitalism, by changing "all things into commodities . . . dissolved all inherited and traditional relationships and . . . set up purchase and sale, 'free' contract." The "free" contract is a fraud, as all "free" contracts under capitalism are, by virtue of their veiling of oppressive class relations. At the same time, the eighteenth-century demand for freedom established a genuine commitment to independence that carried with it substantial change.

> Marriage, according to the bourgeois conception, was a contract, a legal transaction, and the most important one of all, because it disposed of two human beings, body and mind for life. . . . [While formally made between two free people] everyone knew only too well how this assent was obtained and who were the real contracting parties in the marriage. But if real freedom of decision was required for all other contracts, then why not for this? Had not the two young people to be coupled also the right to dispose freely of themselves, of their bodies and organs? Had not chivalry brought sex-love into fashion, and was not its proper bourgeois form, in contrast to chivalry's adulterous love, the love of husband and wife. And if it was the duty of married people to

love each other, was it not equally the duty of lovers to marry each other and nobody else? Did not this right of the lovers stand higher than the right of parents, relations and other traditional marriage-brokers and matchmakers. . . . These questions inevitably arose at a time which was loosening all the old ties of society and undermining all traditional conceptions. . . . What did a young man care about the approval of respectability, or honorable gild privileges handed down for generations, when the wealth of India beckoned to him, the gold and silver mines of Mexico?[42]

And again:

Marriage remained class marriage, but within the class the partners were conceded a certain degree of freedom of choice. . . . In short, the love marriage was proclaimed as a human right, and indeed not only as . . . one of the rights of man, but also, for once, in a way, as . . . one of the rights of women.

These are, I think, extraordinary paragraphs, but then he throws it all away, and reverts to sentimentality: "The ruling class remains dominated by . . . economic relations and therefore only in exceptional cases does it provide instance of really freely contracted marriages, while among the oppressed classes . . . these marriages are the rule."[43]

## VII

One can also look at *The Origin of the Family* and other writings not so much from the perspective of women and/or the family, but as an effort to deal with the theoretical weaknesses in the historical and anthropological work of Marx and Engels. Primary among those lapses is an analysis of the transitions from one stage of society to another. Both Marx and Engels postulate the earliest division of labor as that between man and woman in the sexual act. But how this initial division is integrated into the more complicated and varied social division of labor neither of them explained. Their discussions, briefly in *The German Ideology* and expanded in *The Origin of the Family*, refer to the crucial importance of that division, but the discussion never goes beyond the descriptive to the analytic. It is as if having laid out the relationship neither Marx nor Engels knew how to proceed with it. Take for instance Marx and Engels's periodization of historical epochs. As Eric Hobsbawm has noted, what emerges from all their writings is "so very little" on transitions and internal contradiction. And yet it seems clear that the family must have played a vitally important role and a profoundly different one in many of these early societies. In *Precapitalist Economic Formations*, Marx refers to the "germanic system" as a particular "sub-variety of primitive communalism made up of a self-sustaining family unit." Each household, thought Marx, contained an entire economy. But how this system evolved into feudalism, how the family unit was integrally connected to the operating of its system is ignored, even for speculation.[44]

What have recent Marxist scholars been doing on this and other questions related to women and the family? In regard to the transition from one stage to another, there have been recent efforts to fill out and project further Marx and Engels's search for "fundamental laws" of the formation of each stage of society. These efforts have not been especially successful. *The Origin of the Family* constituted a beginning in the attempt to expand the theoretical models to describe the passage from what Engels believed to be a universal primitive communal stage to class society. Little progress has been made since that time with comparable general laws of feudalism and slavery. Little effort has been made in Marxist circles to study the family as a factor in the historical periodization problems currently being debated. How unfortunate that the fundamental social division of male-female has been given such minimal attention beyond the stating of its fundamental importance. Twentieth-century Marxist theorists instead have directed their energies largely to political questions, or to reexamining and reapplying Marxist economic principles to the current scene.[45]

Just as Engels ceased viewing women as active agents of change or as part of a larger cultural community once they were deposed from positions of alleged equality, so Marxists since then have largely continued that tradition. Even E. P. Thompson, who pulled the English working class from a world of silence, left women out. "The inarticulate, by definition, leave few records of their thoughts," said Thompson. Yet brilliantly, painstakingly, imaginatively, he re-created working-class consciousness. But it is male. Thompson reconstructed the impact of the evolution from pre-industrial work habits to the demands of industry, from the rhythm of the spirit, a more flexible way of living, to frugality, industriousness, persistent discipline of the machine. Still we know little of women in that process as workers, wives, mothers, sustainers of the family in the face of those terrible blows. Here and there Thompson whets our appetite. He describes the members of the Female Reform Society who pledged themselves "to use our utmost endeavor to instill into the minds of our children a deep and rooted hatred of our corrupt and tyrannical ruler."[46]

Most references to women deal with women as recipients of some action. "It added to the weaver's shame his dependence upon his wife or children, the enforced and humiliating reversal of traditional roles."[47] What impact did it have on the wife and children, on the functioning of the family, on the relationship between men and women, as marital partners, but also in trade union activity and in their work?

Thompson describes in much detail the passionate struggle between "the old way of life and the new discipline," "the old moral order as against the economy of the free market" in many areas but not in the family. In the family he shows us the impact of that struggle, the disintegration of the home, the result of the battle. Perhaps the traditional view that the family was a key socializing agency to establish discipline and undermine old patterns of behavior is incomplete. Perhaps the family also made a desperate effort to retain that sense of community and affection that was being eroded everywhere else.

We do not even know precisely how women fit into the capitalist world as economic beings, or if indeed women fit at all as a group. Casual comments are common to the effect that women are a constant surplus population to be called upon when needed and sent back to the kitchen when the crisis is over. It is undeniably accurate in many specific situations, but is it valid generally? Marx's famous "reserve army of labor" or "relative surplus population" is crucial to his assertion that wages are constantly kept in check so that they cannot threaten the system. Unemployed workers by their pressure on the labor market exert a continuous downward pressure on wages. But not one of the leading Marxist economists has examined seriously the role of women as part of that surplus labor force. Connected questions concerning demographic shifts, levels of economic development, technological changes, the speed and intensity of occupational shifts suggest a picture far too complicated for generalizations without a great deal of empirical research, which shows no signs of being undertaken.[48] Without it we are still ignorant of the most basic information concerning the role of women and whether or not such a group as a group is "external" or not to the working principles of a capitalist economy.

## Conclusion

Frederick Engels never did account for the nature of the oppression of women. He did not adequately explain why division of labor, or even the extraction of surplus wealth, became oppression. The woman's movement has not advanced the argument. From the 1848 Seneca Falls statement, "The history of mankind is a history of repeated injuries . . . having in direct object the establishment of an absolute tyranny over [women]," to Juliet Mitchell's intelligent book, *Woman's Estate,* which asserts that "oppression of women is intrinsic to the capitalist system as it is not to the socialist,"[49] we are left with invigorating polemic that is yet to be more than asserted. The ultimate key to Marxian analysis is the recognition that society is a series of relationships. By relegating one-half of the participants in those relationships to a world of invisibility we inevitably must destroy our understanding of the past. But how, and in what ways, we still do not understand.

Engels's efforts were worthy; he made some important, tentative first steps and faltered, faltered for two reasons. First, already committed to the idea that exploitation flows from social relations rooted in the productive forces, from the extraction of surplus value, he was unable to connect the notion of exploitation of women, or a derivative idea, the oppression of women, to that source. Second, it seems apparent that Engels, among others, could not subject the whole matter of women, marriage and the family to the same critical analysis as he did other human relations and institutions.

The idea persisted in Engels and Marx, and was later shared by Trotsky and Lenin, that if society removed all the "burdens" placed upon the family—child-rearing and housekeeping—then the parents, the man and woman, would be "free" to establish a genuine monogamous relationship based on "pure" affection. Such a belief presupposes that the responsibilities of home and family, and the economic ties that bind them together, are not an important part of what establishes their cohesion, that society can remove a vital function of an institution in order to perfect it. Socialist society will strip the family of most of its traditional jobs, but the family itself, in its pristine state, untouched by history or reality, shall remain. Emotional needs were not part of the historic reason for the family unit, according to Engels. And yet when the other considerations are removed, they remain alone.

Said Engels: "Full freedom of marriage can . . . only be established when the abolition of capitalist production . . . has removed all the economic considerations . . . then there is no motive left except mutual inclinations." [50] Once again the rigidity of the social analysis in regard to women and marriage points up a more general weakness. Marx, Engels, Lenin, Trotsky—all of them—maintained a simple belief that ending exploitation was a sufficient precondition for creating the new socialist man—and woman. This miraculous transformation, to be achieved automatically by an end to capitalist exploitation, has obviously not occurred.

Not just Marx, Engels, Lenin, Trotsky, et al., but many feminists share the assumption that the liberation of women carries with it freedom from household chores, which, when enumerated, seem always to include child-rearing, as if that were on a comparable level to cooking dinner. Household chores can be altered immensely. But child-rearing is a key to the way a society re-creates itself each generation.

Leon Trotsky, in a typical comment, asserted, "As long as woman is chained to her housework, the care of the family, the cooking and sewing, all her chances of participation in social and political life are cut down." [51] The "care of the family" is, under different circumstances, perhaps, one of the most important political and social activities, depending on how it is organized and for what purpose. The assumption is that intrinsic to the job of child-rearing is oppression. But this is an assumption based on a marketplace society where work is defined by its wage and not by its use. Listen to Lenin on women: "Public dining rooms, creches, kindergartens—these are examples of . . . the simple everyday means which . . . can in fact emancipate women." [52] The first implication of these remarks is that it is eternally woman's job to rear children. Second, whatever woman's oppression is, it is easy to eliminate it by the introduction of some rather significant but feasible reforms, such as we may indeed have in this country soon. Thus the oppression of women remains not only of an entirely different nature from that of exploitation as Marxists traditionally have defined it, but without any seeming connection to the complex of social relations in this and every other society. The liberation of women is reduced to a technical, not social problem.

Such a solution flows from an acceptance of traditional capitalist economic categories. Productive and unproductive labor are defined in terms of a market price. A job that merits a monetary reward is useful; without a market price to define it, labor is unproductive. But this is circular reasoning, judging, as Paul Baran said, "a socioeconomic structure by a yardstick that itself represents an important aspect of that very socioeconomic structure." [53]

Feminists and Marxists frequently lock themselves into highly uncreative visions by assuming that women's emancipation can be achieved by providing allegedly productive labor. Socialists project an end to "wage slavery" not by abolishing work but by redefining and reestablishing its relationships. "Domestic slavery" is to be abolished by eliminating its entire existence, without regard to the significance of the socialized nature of child-rearing on children, who seem regularly to be overlooked, and without a satisfactory understanding of the intricate human relations established by family patterns. But in reality it is not to be taken very seriously, this whole idea of easy, mechanical solutions, which more than any other stands as a profound criticism.

Said Marx, peel away the narrow form of bourgeois wealth and what remains is an elaboration of human creative disposition, "the evolution of all human power as such, unmeasured by any previously established yardstick." In a projected future society, man "does not reproduce himself in any determined form, but produces his totality . . . where he does not seek to remain something formed by the past, but is in the absolute movement of becoming."[54]

That is where we should begin.

## NOTES

1. Frederick Engels, *The Origin of the Family, Private Property, and the State in the Light of the Researches of Lewis H. Morgan* (New York: International Publishers, 1942). All references hereafter are to this edition.

2. T. B. Bottomore, introduction to Karl Marx, *Selected Writings in Sociology and Social Philosophy* (London, 1956), 42.

3. Karl Marx and Frederick Engels, *The Communist Manifesto* (New York: International Publishers, 1948), 46n.

4. Engels, *The Origin of the Family*, preface to the first edition (1884), 5.

5. *Ibid.*, 19.

6. *Ibid.*, preface to the fourth edition (1891), 17.

7. *Ibid.*, 19.

8. Karl Marx, *Capital: A Critical Analysis of Capitalist Production*, vol. 1, facsimile reprint of 1889 edition (New York: Modern Library, 1947), 367n. Also quoted in Marx, *Selected Writings*, 64.

9. Engels, *The Origin of the Family*, 19, 20.

10. *Ibid.*, 21–24.

11. *Ibid.*, 145.

12. *Ibid.*, 147.

13. *Ibid.*, 27, 33.

14. *Ibid.*, 42–43.

15. *Ibid.*, 44.

16. *Ibid.*, 49–50.

17. *Ibid.*, 51, 57, 56.

18. Bernhard J. Stern, "Engels On the Family," *Science and Society* 12 (Winter 1948), 44.

19. Engels, *The Origin of the Family*, 39.

20. Stern, 50.

21. Kathleen Gough, review of Kate Millett, *Sexual Politics*, in *Monthly Review* (February 1971), 52–53.

22. Introduction to a new edition of *The Origin of the Family* (New York: International Publishers, 1972), 19.

23. *Ibid.*, 40.

24. Marvin Harris, *The Rise of Anthropological Theory* (New York: Columbia University Press, 1968), 4–5.

25. Engels, *The Origin of the Family*, 5.

26. *Ibid.*, 51, 58.

27. *Ibid.*, 42.

28. *Ibid.*, 49.

29. *Ibid.*, 33.

30. *Ibid.*, 34–35.

31. *Ibid.*, 38, 39.

32. Frederick Engels, *The Condition of the Working-Class in England in 1844* (London, 1892), 24, 142.

33. Engels, *The Origin of the Family*, 65.

34. *Ibid.*, 63.

35. *Ibid.*, 66, 148.

36. *Ibid.*, 46.

37. *Ibid.*, 72–73.

38. *Ibid.*, 74.

39. *Ibid.*, 73.

40. Engels, *Condition of the Working-Class*, 146.

41. Engels, *The Origin of the Family*, 62, 69.

42. *Ibid.*, 70–71.

43. *Ibid.*, 72.

44. See excellent introduction by Eric J. Hobsbawm to Karl Marx, *Pre-Capitalist Economic Formations* (New York: International Publishers, 1964), esp. 42–44.

45. A few Marxist scholars, such as Herbert Marcuse in *Eros and Civilization* or Marc Bloch in *Feudal Society*, have considered the question, if insufficiently.

46. Edward Palmer Thompson, *The Making of the English Working Class* (New York: Pantheon, 1963), 717–18.

47. *Ibid.*, 308.

48. For a discussion, not related to women, of the problem in general, see Paul A. Baran, *The Political Economy of Growth* (New York: Modern Reader Paperbacks, 1957), 66ff.

49. Juliet Mitchell, *Woman's Estate* (New York: Pantheon, 1971), 95.

50. Engels, *The Origin of the Family*, 72.

51. Leon Trotsky, *Women and the Family* (New York: Pathfinder Press, 1970), 14, from an article in *Pravda*, July 13, 1923.

52. V. I. Lenin, "Women and Society," quoted in *The Woman Question: Selections from the Writings of Karl Marx, Frederick Engels, V. I. Lenin, Joseph Stalin* (New York: International Publishers, 1951), 56.

53. Baran, *The Political Economy of Growth*, 32.

54. Marx, *Pre-Capitalist Economic Formations*, 85.

# Mary Beard's
# *Woman As Force in History:*
# A Critique

## *Berenice A. Carroll*

### I

When *Woman As Force in History* appeared in 1946, it was greeted with mixed reviews, and it has had an equally mixed fate. Reviews written for the lay public appear to have been generally sympathetic, calling the book "scholarly," "bright and learned," "delightful," and "only occasionally tiresome and talky." Sometimes it was felt to be "ponderous in content" or "a trifle oppressive" in argument, but on the whole these reviewers found it persuasive. R. A. Brown, writing for the *Christian Science Monitor* (April 17, 1946), thought its impact would be so significant that it seemed "reasonable to prophesy that no sound historian of the future will neglect the role of women, as was done in the past." When Mary Beard died in 1958, the general press recalled *Woman As Force in History*. The *New York Times* provided a full-column obituary, much of it devoted to Mary Beard's efforts to develop the field of women's history. Even the brief notices in *Time* and *Newsweek* made reference to this book in particular, *Time* with its characteristic tongue-in-cheek,[1] *Newsweek* with a quotation.

But professional historians met the book with attitudes ranging from marked caution[2] to outright hostility,[3] and within a decade they had seemingly consigned it to oblivion. In the few lines which the *American Historical Review* (January 1959) accorded Mary Beard by way of obituary, she was identified first as Charles A. Beard's wife, next by the works she co-authored with him, finally by a few of the books which the *AHR* noted—as though by surprise—came "from her own pen"; the *AHR* had no comment on her work. Two decades after R. A. Brown had prophesied that "no sound historian" would henceforth neglect the role of women in history, the University of Chicago historian William H. McNeill capped the irony of this remark by publishing *A World History*, a college textbook published by Oxford University Press (1967), which features the name of exactly one

This essay is reprinted from the *Massachusetts Review*, © 1972, The Massachusetts Review, Inc.

woman in the index, Catherine the Great of Russia, and no general index entry for "women."[4]

Yet in recent years Mary Beard's book has experienced a curious rebirth. It never achieved a second printing in hardcover, and one wonders a little what moved Macmillan to reissue it in 1962 (rather before the "new feminist" wave) as a Collier paperbound. But in the past two or three years it has won increasing attention, primarily in the women's movement; the paperbound edition is now in its second printing, and it is being used in a number of college courses on women's history or women's liberation. It even begins to seem possible that R. A. Brown's prophecy might yet be fulfilled, if only after two or three decades' delay.

## II

As we read *Woman As Force in History* carefully today, we can hardly deny that it was in many ways a failure—a failure in design, in execution, in conception, and (until recently) in impact. Yet we can as little deny that this is a unique and important book, a work of complexity and subtlety, which raises, even if it fails to answer, a number of significant questions for contemporary historiography. It is these contrasting characteristics, of failure on the one hand, and significance on the other, I wish to explore here.

*Woman As Force in History* may be read as an effort to reconstruct the history of women, from prehistoric to modern times, and to interpret its significance. But this reconstruction of women's history is set in a complex polemic: first, against a "myth" of female subjection in history; second, against feminists who adopted and propagated the myth; third, against historians—mostly male—who have contributed to the myth either directly or by minimization or sheer neglect of women in the writing of history; finally, against the slogan of "equality" as escape from that mythical subjection of women. And this polemical setting is at once responsible for many of the defects of the book and for some of its most provocative and significant features.

The core of the polemic is the argument that contemporary ideas about the relations between men and women are deeply influenced by the notion that women have been "members of a subject sex throughout history," and that this notion is easily shown to be a myth by reference to historical realities. The treatment of this argument is in some respects heavy-handed and ill-designed, giving rise to some of the complaints of reviewers already noted, and to the more ample complaint of J. H. Hexter that some "rather simple points" are proved "well past the hilt, with a copiousness of repetitious quotation that suggests a positive aversion to condensation and conciseness in the author."

Hexter here refers to a portion of the book which presents a subordinate line of argument, namely that the myth of subjection must be attributed largely to Sir William Blackstone and to the easy acceptance of his common-law bias by American lawyers and American feminists in the nineteenth century. Common-law doctrines, as formulated by Blackstone, appeared to extinguish the very person of the married woman before the law, but Mary Beard argues that besides the common law there existed a "vast" body of other law, composed of equity, legislative acts, and customary law and practice, in which such common-law doctrines had no force, and under which the married woman was a fully competent legal person.

To these subordinate aspects of her main theme, Mary Beard devoted five of the twelve chapters of her book—over one-third of its length, not including shorter passages in other chapters. The rest of the material is dealt with in approximately reverse chronological order, beginning with an examination of contemporary attitudes of women and men and concluding with a survey chapter, much of which is devoted to prehistory and the ancient world.

This scheme of organization, dictated in part by the structure of the polemic, was undoubtedly an unfortunate choice, for it is the main source of that repetitiousness or oppressiveness of which the critics complain. On close examination, there is actually very little repetition of content, but the argument doubles back on itself again and again, each time taking up a different aspect, or a different chronological slice of the subject—now focusing on Blackstone's time in England, now on colonial America, now on medieval England, now on classical Rome; now dealing with equity, elsewhere with legislative or customary law, now with the education of women, elsewhere with their economic or social status. With each doubling-back, Mary Beard is obliged to repeat some part of the connective tissue of the polemic. The argument thus repeats itself, but the historical content, the information communicated, is for the most part different in each case.

In fact, had Hexter not let himself become so impatient with the apparent repetitiousness, he might not have been so ready to concede that Mary Beard had proved her points—least of all "well past the hilt." For what those "repetitious quotations" really show is that the legal subjection of women was no myth invented by Blackstone and American feminists, but was a very real and substantial part of the "historical reality" in which women lived, at least from the early medieval period in England to the nineteenth century in America. If we are to credit the quotations from Maitland, the legal position of women in England was at best equivocal in the thirteenth century, and probably became rather worse with the development of the common law in subsequent centuries.

Mary Beard herself is obliged to remark that "had it not been for the growth of equity, the position of women before the law in the eighteenth century would have been lower in many respects than it had been in the thirteenth century" (208).[5] And when we examine the effects of equity, we must recognize that what this statement implies is that the position of many women, perhaps most women, before the law *was* "lower in many respects" in the eighteenth century than it had been before. For no matter how large a body of law relating to property equity became, with respect to married women it protected *only those* whose affluence, knowledge, prudence, or careful relatives led them to make special contractual provisions, before and after marriage, for the protection of their property and legal rights: "Informed men and women of property," Mary Beard tells us, " . . . knew that the disabilities of married women in respect of property under common law could be avoided by a resort to trusts, and that equity, liberally construing the rights of such women, would protect them and their heirs in the enjoyment of the rights so vested" (213).

Thus equity provided only a limited avenue of escape through specified rights vested by contract or trust in particular individuals. It did nothing for women in general, nothing for unpropertied women, ignorant women, imprudent women, or women of ill-disposed families—and of all these one can hardly doubt that there must be large numbers in all times and places. For all these, then, it was the disabilities of the common law which defined their legal status, not the liberal advantages of equity.

### III

Similarly, with respect to the "myth" of subjection in general, we may say that Mary Beard has proved a point—a point of considerable significance—but she has not disposed of the notion that women have been a "subject sex." (To the latter we return below.) The point she has proved is that history will not support "the dogma of women's complete historic subjection to man," nor "the image of woman throughout long ages of the past as a being always and everywhere subject to *male* man or as a ghostly creature too shadowy to be even that real" (155, 87). On the contrary, what *Woman As Force in History* shows most clearly is women active, competent, and recognized in their own time in a wide range of occupations and endeavors. In some places the examples are packed in so tightly that one reviewer remarked: "At moments the listing of individual women and their achievements suggests a catalogue overmuch."[6] In the concluding chapter, which is something like an abridged version of Mary Beard's earlier book, *On Understanding Women* (Longmans, 1931), the compression is so great that it struck Hexter as "one of the great historical grab-bags of all time." Grab-bag, catalogue, or whatever, one thing is certainly clear from this material: women were far from being totally passive, inactive, ignorant, submissive, uncreative, unassertive, subordinate, and invisible through the course of human history.

But can we really call this point significant? Isn't it positively superfluous? Would anyone seriously maintain the contrary? Unfortunately, yes.

The worst offender in recent times, perhaps, is Simone de Beauvoir. In *The Second Sex*, which first appeared in 1949, three years after *Woman As Force in History* and nearly twenty years after *On Understanding Women*, which had already made similar points, Simone de Beauvoir wrote boldly: "Throughout history [women] have always been subordinated to men, and hence their dependency is not the result of a historical event or a social change—it was not something that *occurred*."[7]

The proletarians, she continues (not stopping to ask whether there were any women among them, nor what role they played), have accomplished the revolution in some countries and are battling for it in others, "but the women's effort has never been anything more than a symbolic agitation. They have gained only what men have been willing to grant; they have taken nothing, they have only received. . . . They have no past history . . . of their own . . . woman has always been man's dependent, if not his slave." Worse still: "in the past all history has been made by men."[8]

While one may not find such bald assertions of this notion in the work of professional historians, they are not without responsibility for propagating the idea. Certainly that is the inference one is bound to draw, if only unconsciously, from the numerous textbooks, readers, and even more specialized works which conform closely to the example of McNeill's *A World History*. In a recent study of twenty-seven textbooks currently in use in college courses in American history, Earl and Dolores Schmidt found that the space devoted to women in the textual material of these works ranged from a low of .05 percent to a *high* of 2 percent.[9] Jack Hexter, in his review of *Woman As Force in History*, was at pains to deny that the omission of women from the history books should be attributed to the bias of male historians.[10] But in defending the historians, Hexter resorted to arguing, in effect, that women are not mentioned by historians because they weren't there to mention—not, anyway, in the places worth looking at, the places in which history is made. (We return to this point below.)

We also find this view expressed from time to time among the writings of the women's liberation movement today. Shulamith Firestone, in *The Dialectic of Sex*, adopts not only the subjection theory, but Simone de Beauvoir's biological explanation of it as well: "Women throughout history before the advent of birth control were at the continual mercy of their biology—menstruation, menopause, and 'female ills,' constant painful childbirth, wet-nursing, and care of infants, all of which made them dependent on males (whether brother, father, husband, lover, or clan, government, community-at-large) for physical survival."[11] Thus not only government but even clan and "community-at-large" become *male* in character, and one wonders how women so described ever could or did find the resources to invent agriculture and most of the primitive industrial arts, to do most of the heavy labor in many so-called primitive societies, to acquire learning, property, and independence at least for some of their number throughout the history of literate societies, to engage in military exploits, and to become rulers in their own right, regents, or the "power behind the throne" at various times in the history of almost every nation in the world (the United States being perhaps the preeminent exception).

A similar view of women's subjection is reflected in the "Redstockings Manifesto," which declares: "Male supremacy is the oldest, most basic form of domination. . . . All power structures throughout history have been male-dominated and male-oriented. Men have controlled all political, economic and cultural institutions and backed up this control with physical force. They have used their power to keep women in an inferior position."[12] This kind of rhetoric is cited by Gerda Lerner in concluding of the radical feminists today that "the essence of their concept is that all women are oppressed and have been throughout all history."[13]

In short, the myth of "complete historic subjection of women," which

Mary Beard sought to overthrow, is still very much with us today, and still presents the same problems. In its extreme forms it is not only irreconcilable with the verifiable data of history, but as Gerda Lerner points out, it is "politically counter-productive, since it lends the authority of time and tradition to the practice of treating women as inferiors."[14] And as Mary Beard recognizes (with her usual fidelity to facts even when it is inconvenient to her argument), those very feminists whom she holds largely responsible for the myth of subjection were also quite conscious that women had played an active role in history. Thus she writes that the authors of the *History of Woman Suffrage* (Elizabeth Cady Stanton et al.), "confronted with the question as to how a creature who had been nothing or nearly nothing in all history could suddenly, if ever, become something—something like a man, his equal— . . . used history to show what force women had displayed in history" (168).

On the other hand, the myth of subjection can also be politically useful. Mary Beard concedes this herself, though she seems to view it rather as an accusation:

> Each construct or version of this doctrine fitted into the requirements of some political party of faction as a convenient instrument of agitation for the vindication of traditions or for the reform or overthrow of social and economic institutions. The doctrine in its totality or special phases of it were utilized in all media of literary expression. . . . It haunted the dreams of Freudian disciples and incited women to brave police and prison in passionate struggles for equality with their historic "masters." [115]

This passage, we may note in passing, illustrates nicely one of the virtues of Mary Beard's work—an unwillingness to cling to oversimplification for the sake of consistency. Having attributed primarily to the feminists the formulation and propagation of what she regards as a damaging myth, she does not hesitate ultimately to present a rather different and rather more valid conclusion: namely, that the myth of subjection was one which suited the interests and purposes of a variety of groups, male and female, political and intellectual; that it was developed, modified, and used in a variety of ways accordingly; and that among its many functions it did serve to inspire some of the energy of struggle of the early feminists and the suffrage movement—not surely an entirely negative consequence, even in the eyes of Mary Beard.

## IV

The last two passages quoted from *Woman As Force in History* touch tangentially on another target of Mary Beard's polemical fire: the feminist goal of "equality" with men. This is one of the most obscure and least successful aspects of the book, yet it too raises interesting questions.

The attack on the feminists in the matter of "equality" is unmistakable by its tone (which Hexter calls "waspish" in another context), but it is indirect, and not easy to pinpoint, even though a separate chapter is devoted to "Equality As the Escape from Subjection." As well as I am able to discern,

Mary Beard's main objections to the slogan of "equality" lie in its vagueness, its links with egalitarian socialism or communism, and its inadequacy in application to real circumstances.

In her brief review of the history of the ideal of equality, she shows how variously it was conceived, how little it represented a clearly understood principle, and how easily it could lead to contradictory programs—for example, as between the libertarian ideal of equality, which was "atomistic in its social effects" and which exalted the individual and the competitive urge, and the communistic ideal of equality, quite the contrary in character. She concedes that the feminists did try to define their objectives more narrowly in terms of political and legal rights: "equal protection of the laws; equal opportunity in all 'fields of endeavor'; equal suffrage; and equal privileges and immunities, including the right to hold public offices" (169). But even these she refers to as "formulas" and "phrases," and she adds that " . . . the favorite line of assertion was simplified to the absolute and unconditional demand for 'equal rights' and 'no discrimination on account of sex' anywhere in any relation" (169).

Her chief objection to these formulas and demands, beyond their vagueness, appears to center on what she regards as their inapplicability in practice. Here she considers primarily the difficulties arising from the married women's property acts which were passed in many states in the late nineteenth century. Here too, by implication, she admits the disabilities which had prevailed for most women before the passage of such acts:

> Such an act meant the abolition of numerous common-law rules respecting the right of the husband to control his wife's real estate and take possession of her personal property, in case no pre-nuptial or post-nuptial settlements or arrangements intervened. Rights which prudent parents had long secured for daughters under Equity were now to be extended to all married women as a matter of written law . . . and special precautions in the form of elaborate legal documents, drawn by skilled lawyers, were no longer necessary to assure the possession of property to the married woman as against her husband and his creditors. [170]

There is nothing in this to suggest that Mary Beard opposed the married women's property acts; nevertheless she did emphasize the difficulties they raised in practice. In particular, she devoted a number of pages to raising questions and describing particular cases which came to be adjudicated under the new laws: May the wife require the husband to pay rent to her for the house she owns separately, in which the family lives? Is the wife's property liable for payment of domestic servants engaged in doing the household work of the family? And so forth. The questions are left unanswered and unanalyzed, but one point is clear: Mary Beard is certain that no abstract principle of "equality" can answer such questions. From her point of view, wife and husband are caught up in a network of social, emotional, and economic entanglements to which no legislative act, designed to protect the rights of married women, could hope to do justice.

This is undoubtedly true, particularly where the legislative acts impose only a somewhat artificial and limited equality in property rights upon a system of much more basic inequality, a system which expects and even tends to enforce the dependence of wife upon husband for support. But is there an alternative? The answer is less than explicit, but it does appear that Mary Beard saw an alternative in equity, as principle, and as practice. And what is equity? Mary Beard describes it here mainly in institutional terms, or by contrast with the common law: "a body of precedents and law which was concerned with 'justice' rather than prescriptions of the feudal State" (209). John of Salisbury, centuries before, had offered a more general definition, of which Mary Beard would surely have approved: "Now equity, as the learned jurists define it, is a certain fitness of things which compares all things rationally, and seeks to apply like rules of right and wrong to like cases, being impartially disposed toward all persons, and allotting to each that which belongs to him" (*The Statesman's Book,* 1159).

But is this principle, which in itself presents many difficulties, really a practical alternative? Even John of Salisbury added that "of this equity, the interpreter is the law"; and the Courts of Equity were after all courts of law, though more flexible than the common law. In this context, it seems doubtful that even Mary Beard would deny that the married women's property acts were an improvement in equity over the common law, that women's suffrage was an improvement in equity over manhood suffrage alone, and that "equal privileges and immunities" would be an improvement in equity over the exclusion of women from public offices. And if the slogan of equality helped to secure these improvements, as Mary Beard does not deny, then it may be a valuable slogan to hang onto, despite its vagueness and inadequacy.

V

But we must note one other aspect of Mary Beard's attack on the slogan of equality: one which hits curiously close to the rhetoric of women's liberationists today, and which has important implications with respect to the study of women's history. This is the charge that for many women "equality" means "taking the stature of man as the measure of excellence and endowing woman with his qualities, aims, and chances in the world for personal advantages" (163).

Taken seriously, this challenge to "taking *man* as the measure" has a double thrust. On the one hand it challenges all prevailing standards of excellence, honor, and authority (which today clearly do accord to men the lion's share of both material and intellectual rewards, privileges, and "power" in society). On the other hand it challenges the value premises and principles of selection by which historians have been guided in writing histories devoid of women.

To this extent, Jack Hexter missed the point of *Woman As Force in History* in his argument in defense of the historians. What he argued was that historians are primarily interested in the processes of change in "the framework of society" or in "the pattern of culture" from one period to another, and that accordingly they have looked mainly "where the power to make change" is, namely:

> in the councils of the princes, in the magistracies of the towns, in the membership of the great leagues of traders, in the faculties of the universities—and they found men. On the occasions on which they happened to find women they usually noted the exception;[15] but through no conspiracy of the historians the College of Cardinals, the Consistory of Geneva, the Parliament of England, the Faculty of the Sorbonne, the Directorate of the Bank of England and the expeditions of Columbus, Vasco da Gama and Drake have been pretty much stag affairs.

Now there can be no doubt that the institutions which Hexter mentions have indeed been "pretty much stag affairs"; and there can be almost as little doubt that these types of institutions are those we conventionally regard as authoritative, influential, and "powerful."

Moreover, by virtue of their exclusion (not total, but certainly general) from such institutions, women have certainly been deprived of access—at least direct access—to the opportunities, rewards, privileges, honor, authority, and "power" available to the men who did have entry into these institutions. From this point of view, the idea that women have been a subject sex, through much if not all of "civilized" history, appears to be no myth. Mary Beard has demonstrated that women have been active participants in a much wider range of economic and social pursuits than is usually recognized, that some won acclaim from contemporaries, and some reached even the highest positions of governing authority and material rewards. The demonstration is essential and nontrivial, and insofar as it is incomplete or inadequate, it needs to be expanded and reinforced. But it is doubtful that any amount of expansion and reinforcement will do away with the historical reality of the subjection of women in this sense, that is, the exclusion of most women from the honorific statuses and ruling positions of the societies in which they lived.

## VI

But it may be that "subjection" is a phenomenon as little understood as "power," and Mary Beard, while aiming at the wrong words, may have been striking at the right target in deliberately turning her eyes away from those institutions which do preoccupy historians, and urging them to look elsewhere. For, looking back at Hexter's remarks, we may well feel that they raise more questions than they answer: *Why* were the institutions he mentions "pretty much stag affairs"? *Does* the power to make change in society lie wholly—even mainly—in the hands of the men who predominated in those institutions? What kind of change *is* change "in the framework of society" or in "the pattern of culture"? Or—what kinds? Are all kinds of significant social and cultural change in the same hands? What is "power" anyway?—in particular "power to make change"? Are the kinds of institutions which are ordinarily said to hold "power" generally much disposed toward making fundamental changes in society? If and when they are, from what sources does the initiative for change come? Does it never come from "subject" people? (Some today might ask: does it ever come from anyone but "subject" people?) Are historians anyway so completely preoccupied with change rather than with continuity, inertia, reversions, comparisons across time or across cultures, or simply trying, on occasion, to reconstruct "wie es eigentlich gewesen war"? (J. P. Nettl's biography of Rosa Luxemburg suddenly springs to mind here.) And finally, *should* historians focus their attention so heavily on the kinds of institutions Hexter mentions?

Mary Beard answers the last question explicitly, in the negative. She suggests in her preface that she means to outline in the book "the kind of studying, writing and teaching which I believe to be mandatory if a genuine interest in understanding human life is to be cultivated," and that for such an understanding, "the personalities, interests, ideas and activities of women must receive an attention commensurate with their energy in history." Thus for example in discussing the historians' treatment of medieval education, she argues that they have been too preoccupied with formal education, particularly in the universities, as a consequence of which they have overlooked or ignored the fact of women "receiving an education by some process, pursuing intellectual interests, reading, writing, expounding, and corresponding with one another and with learned men" (257). Finally, she asserts that "being men as a rule, [the historians] tend to confine their search for the truth to their own sex in history. This is in accord no doubt with the caution of their professional training. Yet the caution which eliminates the quest for truth about women in long and universal history may in fact limit the ideas of such scholars about long and universal history or any of its features . . ." (282). And she adds: "While exaggerating the force of men [read "rulers"? or "the powerful"?] in the making of history, they miss the force of women [read "the subject"?] which entered into the making of history and gave it important directions" (282).


## VII

Unfortunately, it must be said that the major failure of *Woman As Force in History* is the failure to develop these points coherently. There are hints, but no more than hints (and sometimes mutually contradictory hints), as to what consequences would follow from the broadening of the historians' perspective which Mary Beard calls for here. And there are hints, but no more than hints (and again sometimes mutually contradictory hints), as to what "important directions" were contributed by women in the making of history. Nor is it at all clear, upon setting down this book, wherein lies the distinctive "force" of women in history.

Sometimes it appears that Mary Beard conceives woman's "force" in history as a civilizing mission. This idea is set in a discussion of various theories of history with which she opens the chapter on "Woman As Force in Long History." She begins with a brief rundown of some generalizations of the "all history proves" variety, such as: "Universal history . . . is at bottom the history of the Great Men who have worked here" (Thomas Carlyle); "The history of the world is none other than the progress of the consciousness of freedom" (Hegel): "The history of all hitherto existing society is the history of class struggles" (Marx and Engels); and so forth. She dismisses each of these with a rapidity which undoubtedly contributed to Hexter's feeling that he is confronted with a "grab-bag." But the selection is neither random nor pointless. Her purpose is to contrast these theories, which she regards as too dogmatic and limited—as well as the less dogmatic but even more narrow forms of specialization pursued by professional historians—with a theory which she attributes to Condorcet and Guizot, and with which she later associates herself more directly.

This is an approach to history rather unfashionable to state today, yet probably still more widely held by historians—even those who count themselves sophisticated—than they might care to admit: namely, the idea of history as progress in "the human struggle for civilization against barbarism in different ages and places, from the beginning of human societies" (281).

In the concluding paragraphs, Mary Beard spells out more fully what is meant by this idea of history as the progress of civilization:

> In its composite formulation it embraces a conception of history as the struggle of human beings for individual and social perfection—for the good, the true, and the beautiful—against ignorance, disease, the harshness of physical nature, the forces of barbarism in individuals and in society. . . . Inherent in the idea is the social principle. That is to say, the civilization of men and women occurs in society, and all the agencies used in the process—language, ideas, knowledge, institutions, property, arts, and inventions, are social products, the work of men and women indissolubly united by the very nature of life, in a struggle for a decent and wholesome existence against the forces of barbarism and pessimism wrestling for the possession of the human spirit. [339]

But she goes beyond the assertion that, as social products, the agencies of civilization are the work of "men and women indissolubly united by the very nature of life," to claim further that women play a special role in the civilizing process: "Despite the barbaric and power-hungry propensities and activities in long history, to which their sex was by no means immune, women were engaged in the main in the promotion of civilian interests. Hence they were in the main on the side of *civil*ization in the struggle with barbarism" (229).

This sounds rather like a bad pun, but that it is meant seriously is suggested not only by the context, but by the fact that the theme had already been set in the chapter on "Women in the Age of Faith—the 'Judge of Equity'," where Mary Beard devotes considerable space to Henry Adams's interest in the influence of women in medieval France—the preeminent influence of the Virgin Mary, and that of her earthly counterparts in politics and literature:

> Thus the Virgin signified to the people moral, human or humane power as against the stern mandates of God's law taught and enforced by the Church. As such, her position made trouble for the Church; but the Papacy, if it had been so minded, could scarcely have suppressed the

urge of the people to Virgin worship, however successful it was in excluding women from the priesthood and the . . . choir. In the popular devotion to Mary was asserted a passionate attachment to the feminine qualities so directive in the long history of the human race. [216]

Yet it still remains somewhat unclear just what these "feminine qualities" were, or in what way they are specifically feminine, or in what ways they exerted their "force." Partly through the words of Henry Adams, partly through her own, Mary Beard here leads us to understand that the qualities she has in mind are qualities of mercy, morality, humanity, and pity—qualities upon which suppliants could rely in hoping for the Virgin's intercession in their behalf before the stern judgment of God the Father and the Son (i.e., the male principle). This then is woman the Mother, comforting, protecting, helping, indulgent (while man plays the conventional role of authority).

On the other hand, it appears that "civilizing" qualities per se were something else. For Mary Beard suggests that the Virgin's power sprang not only from her role as advocate and intercessor for sinning humanity. "An immense, if immeasurable, portion of it sprang from the fact that she was regarded as the most convincing expression of civilized aspirations and ways of life . . . " (223). She represented in this regard: intelligence, calm, strength, emotional stability, inspiration and the standard of refined taste (221).[16]

But still we are not on sure ground, for it is clear in this same chapter, and even from the same source—Henry Adams—that Mary (or woman in general) was not all sweetness and light. Mary is a Queen, imperial and imperious, able to do as she pleases, above earthly judgment. Woman was a power, often an evil power: "The idea that she was weak [wrote Henry Adams] revolted all history; it was a paleontological falsehood that even an Eocene female monkey would have laughed at. . . . One's studies in the twelfth century, like one's studies in the fourth, as in Homeric and archaic time, showed her always busy in the illusions of heaven or of hell—ambition, intrigue, jealousy, magic" (218). And as Mary Beard added: "If on the whole [medieval women] were more Christian in habits, they could be even more perfidious in the arts of crime" (221).

Moreover, she herself questions the designating of some human qualities as "feminine," others as "masculine." She objects to the tendency to ascribe the energies and power of Eleanor of Aquitaine or Blanche of Castile to "their 'masculine' qualities, as the sensibility of men is often ascribed to their 'feminine' qualities" (226).

### VIII

We are thus left entirely at sea with respect to woman's civilizing force in history, and those "feminine qualities so directive in the long history of the human race." And in general it appears that when Mary Beard refers to the force of woman in history, she has in mind simply the active presence and participation of women engaged in all the same kinds of activities as men: "From modern times running back into and through the medieval ages of Western feudalism and Christian contests with barbarism, the force of woman was a powerful factor in all the infamies, tyrannies, liberties, activities, and aspirations that constituted the history of this stage of humanity's self-expression" (282). The bulk of the contents of the book surely leans in this direction, seeking to show women active in buying and selling, contracting, laboring, joining in or forming guilds, patronizing the arts and fine craft industries, founding churches and hospitals, negotiating diplomatic agreements between states, going into battle with men, directing armies, directing governments, drafting political programs, agitating for change, writing and engaging in all intellectual pursuits, competing (via Mary) for dominance in the Church, etc.

Unfortunately, this interpretation of woman's force in history also has its problems. To begin with, it does not suggest any "important directions" contributed specifically by women as distinct from men. And if it is intended to show that women are simply persons, *like men*, it falls into a double trap: first, it is a retreat into "taking man as the measure"; second, in so doing it leads back to the admission that, by that measure, women by and large don't come out very well. If women were simply doing—or trying to do—the same things as men, and failing to achieve equal success, at least in terms of recognition, rewards, status, and authority—then it might seem difficult to escape Hexter's conclusion that it is history itself, not the prejudice of male historians, which warrants looking mainly at men, acting in the predominant, and predominantly male, institutions of their societies.

The dilemma is a hard one, at least to anyone who does not feel comfortable with that conclusion—and that includes not only women interested in women's history, but blacks interested in black history, radicals interested in heretical and revolutionary movements and in the history of the "inarticulate" or in "street history," people anywhere interested in the "losers" or the "subject" of the earth, people interested in the role of mass action in social change—as well as in the nature and sources of mass consent as the foundation of social stability—and a host of others who, in some way, reject the view that in the College of Cardinals, the Consistory of Geneva, the Parliament of England, the Faculty of the Sorbonne, the Directorate of the Bank of England, and all like institutions, lie all the qualities worthy of the attention and admiration of historians.

But however much one may reject this view, however much one may want to look elsewhere, it is not easy to do so. This is manifested even in Mary Beard's work. She raises one of the key questions, in discussing the three queens: Eleanor, Blanche, and Mary of Champagne. "How could the force of the three queens in the private and public affairs of Western Europe be measured or appraised? That it was pronounced and wide in its ramifications was scarcely to be questioned. But measurement was difficult" (225). Mary Beard neither spells out the difficulties nor provides us with an answer to her question. What she does in practice is to take man as the measure: to suggest the power of these women over states or over men. This is generally true in other parts of the book as well: a woman's significance is measured by her influence on men, or by the recognition she won from men. In what seems like one of his nastier moments, Hexter notes that even in *Woman As Force in History*, men outnumber women in the index (by a ratio of 13:10)—but the point is significant after all, though not in the way Hexter intended, for it reflects the continued practice of "taking man as the measure."

In fact, Mary Beard is remarkably uninterested in the influence of women upon each other, or their judgment of each other. She notes the great interest of Queen Isabella of Spain in learning, and how she "watched with eagle eyes and sharp ears the progress of this education among her retinue. She collected texts for the courtiers to read and for students to use in the universities." She adds that "one woman was commissioned to lecture in classics at Salamanca; another on rhetoric at Alcalá," but she does not find it worthwhile to mention their names, and their importance seems defined not by what they did or were, but by their appointment to those male sanctuaries, the universities. She does not mention the pains taken by Isabella for the education of her daughters—of which we know more from Garrett Mattingly's biography of Catherine of Aragon, Isabella's daughter. (Mattingly also names the two distinguished women: Doña Lucia de Medrano in classics at Salamanca, and Doña Francisca de Lebrija in rhetoric at Alcalá.) Hexter may smile in triumph: the male historian outdoes the female proponent of women's history—at least in this instance—in a faithful portrayal of women and their influence upon each other, as a matter of importance in itself!

## IX

In sum, *Woman As Force in History* surely failed in many respects. It failed in design and execution by its involuted, unbalanced organization, which weakens the argument and makes the book seem "repetitious" and "oppressive," sometimes confused or superficial. It failed in appeal and persuasiveness partly also by its method—strangely scholarly and unscholarly at once: relying all-too-heavily on long excerpts from scholarly works, demanding of the reader a level of knowledge and sophistication "not common," yet without the trappings of rigorous historical scholarship, without the footnotes sometimes really needed to identify sources, and without much recourse to "original sources." It failed in conception by its contradictions and aborted beginnings, hints of big ideas left undeveloped, polemics left unfinished. And it failed in impact not only by these defects, and by its appearance on the very edge of the postwar antifeminist wave, but also because it alienated its two main potential sources of support by sharply attacking both: the feminists and the historians.

Yet today it must be said that *Woman As Force in History* is an important book. This is in part because of significant changes in education and outlook in the reading public, which make Mary Beard's ideas and her subject more welcome and more congenial than they were in 1946. It is more particularly because of the growth of the women's movement, and the outlook of that movement, which on the whole today is more likely to cry "Our history has been taken from us!" than to subscribe to the myth of subjection in its extreme forms.

But it is essentially because of the richness and inherent virtues of the book that it has come to life again in this changed climate. Certainly it provides an essential resource, in the information packed into its pages, the references in its long bibliography, and the interpretations—however full of difficulties—of the material. But beyond that, much more can still be said. I do not know of another book in the field of women's history which has the sweep, the depth, the mastery of detail, and the grasp of complexities that this one has. I do not know of many books in any field of history which pose challenges as fundamental to the preconceptions and practices of professional historians. There are few books which attempt as much and emerge as full of life and force, as free of bombast as of sterilized textbook style, and as provocative and readable after twenty-five years, as this one. At the risk of seeming as foolish as R. A. Brown might have seemed, I will prophesy that *Woman As Force in History* will prove as significant and enduring a work of history as any which appeared in that quarter-century.

## NOTES

1. "Mary Beard argued that, between the sexes, women hold the lesser place in history because men write the history books." *Time*, August 25, 1958, 66. *New York Times*, obituary, August 15, 1958, 22; *Newsweek*, August 25, 1958, 61.

2. See the review by Jeannette P. Nichols in the *American Historical Review* 52, no. 2 (January 1947), 292–94. Professor Nichols opened her review by remarking that "more than one male historian has expressed doubt whether [this book] should be reviewed by a woman," thus "warning the reviewer that any comments will meet piercing scrutiny." As a consequence her comments on the book seem strangely involuted, though basically sympathetic. Ultimately she concludes that "this book is not a rash challenge but is couched in constructive rather than denunciatory terms"; and that it "has demonstrated sound historical techniques and its indictment holds against a great many historians." Nevertheless, Nichols is uncomfortable with this indictment of historians, and ends by arguing that Mary Beard had addressed the wrong audience—that instead of addressing herself to historians, in such a "sober treatise," written for a "reading level which is not common," she should have written a popular paperback book designed "to interest many thousands of women" readers. For that time, Nichols may have been right; neither historians nor the female public was ready for the book Mary Beard wrote. Perhaps the recent growth in interest in the book is witness both to the increased numbers of women to whom the reading level of the book is now common, and to significant changes in the ranks of historians.

3. See the review by Jack H. Hexter in the *New York Times Book Review*, March 17, 1946, 5. This review can only be described as condescending and derogatory in tone, yet in its hostility it strikes closer to the real importance of the book than do many more sympathetic reviews. Substantive points raised by Hexter are discussed elsewhere in this essay.

4. McNeill's earlier and larger work, *The Rise of the West: A History of the Human Community*, is a little better; it mentions four women (Jane Austen, Catherine II, Fatima, and Isabella of Castile); three female deities (Athena, Isis, and Mary); and *Alice in Wonderland!* Some authors, of course, do better than McNeill. Gordon Craig's *Europe Since 1815* (1961) has the ratio of women to men up to about 1:40; on the other hand some do worse: Herbert Heaton's *Economic History of Europe* (1948, 769 pp.) has not a single woman's name in the index. See also below, notes 8 and 9.

5. Numbers in parentheses refer to pages in the Collier edition of *Woman As Force in History: A Study in Traditions and Realities* (New York: Collier Books, 1971).

6. Mary S. Benson, *Political Science Quarterly* 61 (June 1946), 299.

7. Simone de Beauvoir, *The Second Sex* (New York: Bantam Books, 1961), xviii.

8. *Ibid.*, xix, xx. The historical section of Simone de Beauvoir's book, however, fails to bear out these generalizations, despite the reiteration in the opening words of that section: "This has always been a man's world. . . ." Though one may argue that there is some sense in which this may be true, Simone de Beauvoir herself shows women active, demanding, independent, even commanding, and certainly in no way bearing out the assertion that "They have no past." It is Simone de Beauvoir, not Mary Beard, who writes of Mme. de Pompadour and Mme. du Barry that they "really controlled the State." This contradiction is one very frequently encountered in dealing with women's history, a part of the extraordinary phenomenon by which, no matter what women actually do in history, they continue to be perceived—even by those who have extensive information to the contrary—as having done nothing.

9. See "The Invisible Woman: The Historian as Professional Magician," in this volume. The high figure of 2 percent was for Charles and Mary Beard's own *Basic History of the United States,* which according to the Schmidts is now out of print.

10. To some extent, Mary Beard agreed that the blame should not be laid only to *male* historians, though she held them primarily responsible, if only because they write most of the history books. In *On Understanding Women*, however, she also had some acerbic comments on women historians, who, once permitted "to study with the high priests in Clio's temple, . . . easily slid into the grooves worn smooth by tradition, assuming with humility and without thought the garb of the disciple." (*On Understanding Women*, 14.)

11. Shulamith Firestone, *The Dialectic of Sex: The Case for Feminist Revolution* (New York: Morrow, 1970), 8–9.

12. "Redstockings Manifesto," in: *Sisterhood is Powerful*, ed. Robin Morgan (New York: Vintage, 1970), 534.

13. Gerda Lerner, "The Feminists: A Second Look," *Columbia Forum* XIII, no. 3 (Fall 1970), 26.

14. *Ibid.*, 27.

15. "Usually" seems dubious here, if not excessive.

16. For amplification, see Henry Adams, *Mont St.-Michel and Chartres.*

# The Invisible Woman:
# The Historian As Professional Magician

## Dolores Barracano Schmidt and Earl Robert Schmidt

According to Garland C. Parker, professor of history and educational records, University of Cincinnati, who collated recent data on 1,089 institutions of higher learning in the U.S., "... it seems safe to assume that 7,750,000 or more students will be counted in the approximately 2500 collegiate institutions in the nation." Of all full-time students, women comprise 40.6 percent; of those majoring in education, women comprise 71 percent. There can be little doubt, therefore, that women are a highly visible element on American campuses, at least at the consumer level: they pay tuition, they buy books. Education today is big business, and the historical profession is an important part of that business.

Most educators would agree with Sidney Hook that "There is a universal need for all individuals to understand the society in which they live" and "that the key to the wise selection out of the illimitable materials of the past is the notion of relevance." There is not a state in the union, for example, that does not require some evidence of formal training in American history before granting teaching certification. Let's go back to our visible women— 3,146,500 of them, among whom are 71 percent of all students working toward a teaching certificate, and watch how quickly they disappear from view.

There is a 100 percent likelihood that an American woman college student majoring in education will take an American history course. The chances that the course will be designed so that she will better understand the society in which she lives and/or that the materials selected are relevant to her experience as a member of the largest minority in American culture are considerably lower. If she attends a women's college, she has a 33 percent chance of having a woman as history professor; at a coeducational liberal arts college the probability falls to 5½ percent. Were she to go to graduate school at one of the top ten departments, the likelihood of her having a woman professor in any area of history would be 1½ percent. (Committee on the Status of Women, American Historical Association, December 1970 report.)

This essay is reprinted by permission of the authors from *Women Out of History: A Herstory Anthology,* ed. Ann Forfreedom (Los Angeles: Forfreedom, 1973); © 1971 by Dolores Barracano Schmidt.

Assuming, even, that a woman college student taking an American history survey course breaks the odds and draws a woman professor, there is no possibility whatever at this writing that the textbook she will use will be written by a woman. (Charles and Mary Beard's *Basic History of the United States* is now out of print. Century Publishers was considering a text written by a woman to be ready for 1972-73.) Education, after all, is big business and business is a man's field.

American history college texts represent four to five million dollars a year in sales. A textbook company invests hundreds of thousands of dollars in the preparation of survey texts, and few businesses will take any unnecessary risks with that kind of money. Though there may seem to be little risk involved in putting a woman's name on the title page of a textbook if the book itself is sound, scholarly, and well written, the facts are that: (1) even the smallest risk is strenuously avoided by the demonstrably uncourageous crew comprising textbook publishers; and (2) the risk might be considerably greater than any rational, educated person is likely to assume. For one thing, Lawrence Simpson's dissertation, "A Study of Employing Agents' Attitudes toward Academic Women in Higher Education," clearly shows that those who practice discrimination against women in academic employment also hold general views concerning female inferiority and that such views are strongest among men who have been in teaching and/or administration for a period of from five to twenty-five years. As the AHA Committee Newsletter observes, "This age group may be assumed to constitute the majority of decision makers in almost any department." The same situation surely prevails in all major publishing companies. Thus, why read beyond the title page when one already knows the work will be inferior? Studies conducted by psychologists Phillip Goldberg and Sandra and Daryl Bem in which subjects were asked to rate a number of professional articles from each of six fields, the articles being collected into two equal sets of booklets with the name of the author changed so that identical articles were attributed to male authors in one set of booklets and to female authors in another set, showed that the identical article received significantly lower ratings when it was attributed to a female author than when it was attributed to a male author. The results proved constant with both male and female subjects and whether the professional fields of the articles were those generally considered the province of men, engineering and medicine, for example, or of women, dietetics and elementary education. The Bems concluded that the subjects, male and female, rated male authors as better at everything, agreeing with Aristotle that "We should regard the female nature as afflicted with a natural defectiveness." Apparently, college administrators and textbook publishers also consider women in this light.

A study of the twenty-seven leading textbooks used in the college-level American history survey course and accounting for almost 99 percent of the total market was recently completed by one of the authors (E. R. Schmidt). The study tabulated all references to women, comparing the total number of pages of each text to the number of pages devoted to women and the total number of illustrations in each text to the number depicting women. In addition, one woman from each century of American life (Anne Hutchinson, Harriet Beecher Stowe, and Eleanor Roosevelt) was deemed of sufficient importance to her time to be mentioned in survey texts, and each text was checked for inclusion and extent of treatment. This study reveals some rather interesting statistics. (See Table 1.)

The hefty tomes of the survey texts, which range from about four hundred to over two thousand pages, devote from a high of 2 percent (Beard) to an infinitesimal .05 percent (Sellers and May) of the textual material to American women. Predictably, in illustrated texts, women are seen far more frequently than they are written about, claiming as much as 6 percent of the total number of illustrations. Thus in Morison's book only 6 of the 1,830 pages discuss women (.33 percent but 4 of 76 pictures (over 5 percent) are of women, those insignificant but decorative creatures, fifteen times more appealing to the eye than to the mind. Morris and Greenleaf, one of the latest texts to appear on this multimillion-dollar market, likewise devotes .5 percent of the printed matter to women, though they permit them 5.5 percent of the pictorial content. *A History of the American People* (Graebner, Fite, and White) carries this theme to its logical extreme, presenting "The Fight for Women's Suffrage" as a pictorial essay, thereby reducing a political and intellectual movement to a quaint visual experience providing comic relief to the overburdened history student.

*The American Pageant* (Bailey), however, is, if anything, consistent: of 1,047 pages only 3 are devoted to women; of 285 illustrations, only 2 depict women: one a derogatory cartoon of Amelia Bloomer, the other a chart of rising divorce rates. The references this author makes are sardonic and offensive. These include such devices as referring to women as "petticoats." He speaks of the "petticoat vote" and tells how "militant petticoats entered the alcoholic arena." When tiring of this offensive epithet, Bailey speaks of "the softer sex." Surely the author's concern with the texture and underwear of his subjects—he mentions neither of these factors in discussing men—interferes with the presentation of any objective view of their social and political contributions. This is sexism in its most blatant form. As is to be expected, Bailey's description of women in history reflects his adolescent condescension:

> The woman's rights movement in America was mothered by some arresting characters. Prominent among them was Mrs. Lucretia Mott, a sprightly Quakeress, whose ire had been aroused when she and her fellow delegates to the London anti-slavery convention of 1840 were not recognized. Mrs. Elizabeth Cady Stanton, a mother of seven who had insisted on leaving "obey" out of her marriage ceremony, shocked her fellow feminists by going so far as to advocate suffrage for women. Miss Susan B. Anthony, a militant lecturer for woman's rights, was the target of both rotten eggs and vulgar epithets. Mrs. Lucy Stone retained her maiden name upon marriage—hence the later-day "Lucy Stoners," who follow her example. Mrs. Amelia Bloomer revolted against the current "street sweeping" female attire by donning a semi-masculine short skirt with Turkish trousers—"bloomers," they were called—amid much bawdy ridicule about "Bloomerism" and "loose habits." A sneer-

Table 1. Space devoted to women in twenty-seven college-level American-history textbooks

| Book | Pages about women/total no. of pages | Pictures of women/total no. of illustrations | Material on Hutchinson | Material on Stowe | Material on E. Roosevelt |
|---|---|---|---|---|---|
| *America: A History*, Oscar Handlin (New York: Holt, Rinehart, 1968) | 10/1098 | 11/337 | 1 par. | 2 sen. | 0 |
| *American Civilization*, 2d ed., Maurice Boyd and Donald E. Worcester (Boston: Allyn and Bacon, 1968) | 2/787 | 0 | mention | 0 | 0 |
| *The American Nation*, John A. Garraty (New York: Harper and Row, 1966) | 2/978 | 1/300 | 1 par. | 1 page | 1 sen. |
| *The American Pageant*, 4th ed., Thomas A. Bailey (Lexington, Mass.: D. C. Heath, 1971) | 3/1047 | 2/285 | 1 par. | 3 sen. | 0 |
| *American Political and Social History*, 7th ed., Harold U. Faulkner (New York: Appleton-Century-Crofts, 1965) | 5/1100 | 0/42 | 1 sen. | 0 | 0 |
| *The American Profile*, Morton Bordon, with Otis L. Graham, Roderick W. Nash, and Richard E. Oglesby (Lexington, Mass.: D. C. Heath, 1970) | ½/372 | 0 | 0 | 2 sen. | mention |
| *The American Republic*, 2d ed., 2 vols., Richard Hofstadter, William Miller, and Daniel Aaron (Englewood Cliffs, N.J.: Prentice-Hall, 1970) | 9/1445 | 3/314 | ½ page | mention | 1 sen. |

*Continued*

Table 1—*Continued*

| Book | Pages about women/total no. of pages | Pictures of women/total no. of illustrations | Material on Hutchinson | Material on Stowe | Material on E. Roosevelt |
|---|---|---|---|---|---|
| *Basic History of the United States*, 2d ed., Charles and Mary Beard (New York: Doubleday, Doran, 1944) | 9/504 | 0 | mention | 1 par. | 0 |
| *The Democratic Experience*, 2d ed., Louis B. Wright, Clarence L. Ver Steeg, Russel B. Nye, Holman Hamilton, David M. Potter, Vincent P. DeSantis, William H. Harbaugh, Arthur S. Link, Thomas C. Cochran, and Carl Degler (Glenview, Ill.: Scott Foresman, 1968) | 2/536 | 0/36 | 0 | 2 sen. | 0 |
| *Empire for Liberty*, 6 vols., pb. ed., Dumas Malone and Basil Rauch (New York: Appleton-Century-Crofts, 1960) | 9/2290 | 0 | ½ page | mention | 2 sen. |
| *A History of American Democracy*, 3d ed., J. D. Hicks, G. E. Mowry, and R. E. Burke (Boston: Houghton Mifflin, 1966) | 3/915 | 2/197 | 1 par. | 1 par. | mention |
| *A History of the American People*, 3d ed., 2 vols., Harry J. Carman, Harold C. Syrett, and Bernard W. Wishy (New York: Knopf, 1967) | 4/1658 | 1/265 | 2 par. | 2 sen. | 0 |
| *A History of the American People*, 2 vols., Norman A. Graebner, Gilbert C. Fite, and Philip L. White (New York: McGraw-Hill, 1970) | 8/1405 | 33/504 | 1 par. | 1 par. | 1 sen. |

| Book | | | | | |
|---|---|---|---|---|---|
| *History of the American People*, 5th ed., Samuel Eliot Morison, Henry Steele Commager, and William E. Leuchtenburg (New York: Oxford University Press, 1966) | 6/1830 | 4/76 | 0 | 0 | 1 sen. |
| *History of the United States*, Russel B. Nye and J. E. Morpurgo (Baltimore: Penguin, 1956) | 4/766 | 0 | 0 | 1 sen. | 0 |
| *A History of the United States*, 3d ed., 2 vols., Harry T. Williams, Richard N. Current, and Frank Freidel (New York: Knopf, 1969) | 9/1688 | 10/414 | 1 par. | 2 par. | 1 sen. |
| *Living America*, Norman C. Lumian (New York: Van Nostrand Reinhold, 1970) | 4/538 | 5/183 | 0 | ½ page | 1 par. |
| *The National Experience*, 3d ed, John M. Blum, Bruce Catton, Edmund S. Morgan, Arthur M. Schlesinger, Jr., Kenneth M. Stampp, and C. Vann Woodward (New York: Harcourt Brace Jovanovich, 1968) | 2/908 | 2/210 | ½ page | 1 par. | ½ picture |
| *New History of the United States*, 3d ed., William Miller (New York: Dell, 1969) | ½/526 | 0 | 2 sen. | 1 sen. | 0 |
| *Out of the Past*, Donald V. Gawronsky (New York: Glencoe Press, 1969) | ¾/430 | 0 | 2 sen. | 0 | 0 |
| *Society and Thought in America*, 9th ed., ed. Harvey Wish (New York: McKay, 1950, 1969) | 19/1256 | 7/112 | ½ page | 1 page | 0 |

*Continued*

Table 1—*Continued*

| Book | Pages about women/total no. of pages | Pictures of women/total no. of illustrations | Material on Hutchinson | Material on Stowe | Material on E. Roosevelt |
|---|---|---|---|---|---|
| *Stream of American History*, 4th ed., 2 vols. in 1, Leland D. Baldwin (New York: Van Nostrand Reinhold, 1969) | 2/897 | 2/162 | 0 | 1 par. | 2 sen. |
| *Survey of American History*, 2d ed., Leland D. Baldwin and Robert Kelley (New York: American Book Co., 1967) | $\frac{1}{2}$/515 | 0 | 0 | mention | 0 |
| *A Synopsis of American History*, Charles Sellers and Henry May (Chicago: Rand McNally) | $\frac{1}{4}$/448 | 0 | 0 | mention | 0 |
| *The United States of America*, Henry Bamford Parkes (New York: Knopf, 1968) | 3/831 | 0/22 | 1 par. | 2 sen. | 0 |
| *The United States of America*, 2d ed., 2 vols., Dexter Perkins and Glyndon G. Van Deusen (New York: Macmillan, 1968) | 6/1711 | 5/215 | 0 | 1 page | 0 |
| *USA: The History of a Nation*, 2 vols., Richard Morris and William Greenleaf (Chicago: Rand McNally, 1969) | 11/1949 | 15/255 b/w 9/159 col. | 1 page | 2 par. | 2 par. |

ing rhyme of the times proclaimed: Gibbery, gibbery gab; The women had a confab; And demanded the rights; To wear the tights; Gibbery, gibbery gab.

Approximately three-fourths of the page or half the space devoted to the nineteenth-century woman's rights movement by Bailey is on Amelia Bloomer, though no mention is made of her motives nor of the very real need for dress reform at that time. The "rotten egg" association seems, to Bailey's mind, a hilarious touch which is mentioned three times in the brief space accorded women in the two-volume work, and Susan B. Anthony's sole contribution to American history appears, in Bailey's version, to have been to serve as a target for rotten eggs. Bailey's text has been a best seller for twelve years now, having gone through four editions and revisions, so his appeal, at least for professors, is undeniable. Textbook publishers need not worry about the sensibilities of their customers, they need only sell the professor, whose students constitute a captive audience. Though Bailey intends, as he says, "Not so much to entertain as to create a sympathetic understanding of the problems confronting our statesmen, and to implant a more lively concern for the lessons of the past," he displays little concern for the feelings of female readers, undergraduate students caught between a democratic educational theory which tells them that each man and each woman has the right to develop to her or his highest intellectual potential, and a conflicting, confining social attitude which dictates, in Vivian Gornick's words, that the prime vocation of their lives is to prepare "for the love of a good man and the responsibilities of homemaking and motherhood. All the rest, the education, the books, the jobs, that's all very nice and, of course, why not? But, Dolly, you'll find out what is really important for a woman." Bailey's ridicule of women who dare to counter the accepted stereotype of female submissiveness merely reinforces the damaging social attitudes which keep women from becoming what they might. Who wants to be the subject of derogatory cartoons, of jeering ballads, the target of rotten eggs?

There is a whole psychological world between Bailey and Faulkner (*American Political and Social History*), between the quotation given above and the one which follows:

The agitation for "women's rights" commenced in America with the visit in 1820 of a young Scotchwoman, Frances Wright, who appeared on the platform in advocacy of many reforms. As the first woman to deliver public lectures, she painfully shocked the conservatives, but her work was an object lesson to women on the possibilities open to them to influence public opinion. Many noble women, who had been actively engaged in various reforms, now sought the lecture platform. Among them were Ernestine Rose, a Polish exile who attained great influence; Lydia Maria Child and Margaret Fuller, representing the finest product of intellectual New England womanhood; Angelina and Sarah Grimke of South Carolina, among the most famous of Southern anti-slavery agitators; Mrs. Lucretia Mott, a Quakeress reformer of Philadelphia; and Mrs. Elizabeth Cady Stanton of New York. . . .

Other women reformers would carry the emancipation of women further. Lucy Stone asserted that married women should keep their maiden names; Amelia Jenks Bloomer advocated a more sensible cloth-ing and designed a costume consisting of loose Turkish trousers gathered at the ankle with an elastic band, a skirt that came below the knees, a short jacket, and a straw hat. Modern students of style are scarcely impressed by this costume, but all will admit that from the point of view of comfort and hygiene it was a step in advance over the tight corsets and hoop skirts of the day. . . . [342] The whole women's rights movement lent itself easily to ridicule, and the smug respect-ability of the time agreed thoroughly with Harper's New Monthly Magazine, which asserted in November, 1853, that the movement had an "intimate connection with all the radical and infidel movements of the day. . . . It is avowedly opposed to the most time-honored proprie-ties of social life; it is opposed to nature; it is opposed to revela-tion. . . . In this respect no kindred movement is so decidedly infidel, so rancorously and avowedly antibiblical." With such language are great movements for reform usually greeted.

Faulkner's text, now in its seventh edition, has been selling well since 1948, and though the author is, as indicated, generally fair and respectful in his discussion of the women's rights movement, mostly he manages to ignore women altogether. One might expect from the words "social history" in the title a more detailed treatment of qualitative changes in American family life, but women do not even appear until page 332, and then only in relation to a discussion of the agitation for women's rights, a subject even a historian cannot discuss without mentioning women.

Leland D. Baldwin and Robert Kelley, *Survey of American History*, do manage, however, to leave women out of the agitation for women's suffrage, making the passage of the nineteenth amendment strictly a political maneuver between men:

> The Democrats had no choice but to steal TR's thunder, as was seen most clearly in agricultural and labor legislation. Too, the historic Democratic "tariff-for-revenue-only" policy was modified by accep-tance of "rational" tariff protection, and a politically independent Tariff Commission was created (1916). The Webb-Pomerene Export Act (1918) relaxed the antitrust laws in order to permit a certain amount of combination among exporters. Two reforms born, as it were, out of time, were the Nineteenth, or Woman Suffrage Amendment (1920), and the Federal Water Power Commission (1920). The FWPC was to be reorganized in 1930 as the Federal Power Commission, and was given considerable authority to regulate interstate utilities. [292]

This is the only mention of woman suffrage in the twentieth century in this text. These writers are the most adept magicians in the profession when it comes to making women disappear. They manage to discuss the reform of insane asylums in the first half of the nineteenth century without mentioning Dorothea Dix, muckraking without mentioning Ida Tarbell, and the Mont-gomery bus-system boycott without mentioning Rosa Parks. They *do* men-tion Peggy Eaton and Harriet Beecher Stowe, as do 89 percent of the texts examined, making these two women the most important females in American history! It is interesting, indeed, when one considers the role of textbooks in reinforcing female stereotypes, that the women most likely to be discussed are those deemed responsible for bringing on the Civil War: Woman as troublemaker—Eve, Helen, and our very own Peggy Eaton, a beauty of questionable reputation whose social ambitions supposedly fired sectional strife, and Harriet Beecher Stowe, one of the "mob of scribbling women," immortalized by Abraham Lincoln as "the little lady who started the big war."

What of those women who *really* changed the quality of life in America, women who could serve as positive role-models for college undergraduates? What of Margaret Sanger, whose efforts to free the American wife from the bondage of annual child-bearing caused her to be reviled and jailed? What of Jeanette Rankin, who first made women visible in the operations of federal government, a female voice for peace heard in this country from the First World War to Vietnam? What of Eleanor Roosevelt, staunch advocate of civil rights, a woman who proved that one could retain a separate identity even though married to a very important man? They are, for the most part, invisible women, Eleanor Roosevelt mentioned, if at all, as an asset to her husband, her humanitarian instincts and activities reduced to political machinations calculated to get her husband votes. And though she continued to be a significant voice in the civil rights movement and in keeping the Democratic party on its toes regarding its obligations to minorities for many years after FDR's death, she disappears from the history texts long before he does.

Malone and Rauch, in their six-volume survey of American history, a series of paperbacks allowing for maximum flexibility in course division, though under-representing women, do at least mention Eleanor Roosevelt, Emma Goldman, Margaret Sanger, Gertrude Stein, and the Women's Peace Party of 1914. On the whole, their work is marred by a strongly moralistic tone: the flapper "confused equality with men with the right to be immoral"; "Flaming youth was first of all composed of eager young women. They ignited young men" (5:154). These quotations, while more sensational than those made by other historians, follow the general sexist party line which maintains that though women have nothing whatever to do with the making of American history, they alone are responsible for the breakdown of American family life, the decline in birth rate, the increase in divorce, the increase in juvenile delinquency. Malone and Rauch, who are to be commended for their efforts to define qualitative changes in American life, seem peculiarly secretive about the important role played by women in making these changes possible. For them the power of woman is sexual and she is a destructive force unless directly engaged in her natural function—supporting men.

Thus, "Eleanor Roosevelt discarded the conventional social role of First Lady and plunged with energy and imagination into the New Deal turmoil, served as another pair of eyes and legs for her husband" (203). (In twenty-seven textbooks, only one mention is made of Martha Washington, describing her shock, after a presidential reception, at finding a greasy mark on the wallpaper [Bailey, 243]—an image of American womanhood surely better suited to TV commercials than to college classrooms.) Women are not credited, however, for bringing about dramatic changes in standards of living.

According to Malone and Rauch, "High school education for the children of workers became common . . . class differentiation in clothing was reduced as mass-produced garments improved in quality, declined in price, and closely imitated the simplified fashions of the wealthy. Foreign observers were deeply impressed by the rarity of 'class-consciousness' . . . among American workers" (138). The writers are speaking of the 1920s, by which time both elementary and secondary school systems had long been staffed almost entirely by educated, dedicated, underpaid women, and it was their less educated, less fortunate sisters who had made the triumph of the American ready-to-wear clothing industry possible. The authors fail to mention these latter facts, a failure shared by the authors of 95 percent of the other texts in this study.

Harvey Wish in his two-volume work, *Society and Thought in Early America* and *Society and Thought in Modern America,* presents the most detailed discussion of social and cultural contributions made by American women, though as a text for the traditional American history survey course, its systematic exclusion of political and economic history presents a serious drawback. Again, its exclusive concern with the cultural and social history eliminates women whose activities were primarily of a political nature— Jeanette Rankin, Emma Goldman, Mary E. Lease, Frances Perkins, Eleanor Roosevelt, to name some—while emphasizing women in their more traditional roles as educators, novelists, poets, actresses, social workers, office and factory personnel, and store clerks. Women's political contributions are restricted to the battle for women's rights, a subject which Wish treats soundly and sympathetically. He also gives relatively detailed accounts of Anne Hutchinson, Mother Anne Lee, and Mary Baker Eddy, three female religious leaders who had the courage of their convictions, the latter two managing to establish institutions attracting many followers.

It would seem these three figures are "relevant" in Hook's sense for a number of reasons: Anne Hutchinson represents early dissent and, rather than choosing conformity and acceptance or becoming one of the silent majority, she suffered the consequences for her beliefs; Mother Anne Lee established a social alternative which functioned for many years without serious conflict with the rest of society, a commune which developed functional design in everyday objects to a high art; Mary Baker Eddy founded a religious sect still powerful today, a sect which publishes one of the great newspapers of our time. The three also happen to be women. As Hook says, "Not everything is relevant to everything; although all subject matters and all experiences have some worth to someone, they do not all have the same quality or the same worth in the educational enterprise, which seeks to make the individual feel at home in a world of change—mastering events by understanding and action instead of being altogether mastered by events, growing in such a way as not to obstruct further growth in insight and maturity." The relevance of citing women in history who acted rather than were acted upon, who did things deliberately rather than caused mischief unintentionally, has undeniable relevance for female students. But beyond that, examples of moral courage, of successful communes, of "late bloomers"—Eddy was fifty-eight when she first gave serious thought to religious philosophy—are relevant to the young of both sexes, and that these three figures are women may have an even more subtle significance for the male students, helping them to see women as individuals rather than stereotypes. Perhaps it is time even historians take their obligations to educate seriously enough to consider the social and psychological implications of their course content and its effect on the attitudes of the young men and women they teach.

"Men make history," states a twenty-two page brochure from Harcourt, Brace and World, Inc., announcing the second edition of *The National Experience* by Blum, Catton, Morgan, Schlesinger, Stampp, and Woodward. The outside cover shows us men making history; inside twelve pages of pictures repeat the theme; and the words themselves are repeated and expounded upon on three pages: "A recurrent theme of the first edition—one that made the study of American History more meaningful for undergraduates— was *men make history.*" And then, so that the innocent will not assume that "men" is a synonym for "people," seven samples of "narrative characterizations of outstanding personalities" intended to implement the theme are given, all of them of men. This is followed by a page which begins with the words, "The 'men make history' theme is just one of the features of *The National Experience* that reflect the authors' concern for the needs of undergraduates." Of which undergraduates? Surely not of half the population, of 40.6 percent of the full-time undergraduates, of 71 percent of the undergraduate education majors. It is unthinkable that any responsible publisher would advertise, "Whites make history"; racism is taboo, but sexism, apparently, is still permissible among gentlemen and scholars.

The statistics are irrefutable; the quotations are unequivocal; the solution remains to be found. Major revision of textbooks, an expensive but not impossible task, would seem to be in order. But who is to do it? The textbook writers have demonstrated a marked insensitivity to the injustice they are doing their students. Supplementary reading offers a more direct solution, one not dependent on profit-making book companies or sexist historians whose financial success is proof to them that they are doing something right. Courses in women's history have been established at a number of colleges and are certainly helpful antidotes to the other history courses in the curriculum. A device used by Mary Beard and successfully revived by Hofstadter, Miller, and Aaron in *The American Republic* is that of quoting women commentators on a wide variety of subjects, not only on women's rights or matters traditionally associated with women's roles. Thus, Martha Gelhorn is quoted on the psychological state of the United States in the time of the Great Depression, Mabel Dodge Luhan is quoted on the relationship between psychology, art, and society, Fanny B. Ames, a factory inspector in Massachusetts at the turn of the century, is quoted on labor conditions. In this way, without "creating" or exaggerating the role of women in American history, textbook authors can present a positive image of women, an indication of respect for their ideas and observations, a sense that women were present and were active citizens throughout American history. Susan R. Resnick of Reed College has suggested ways in which individual undergraduate women studying history may help bring about a history curriculum which has relevance for women: "Petitioning departmental search committees to hire women, encouraging fellow students to do independent study in the history of women, alerting history professors to the validity of and demand for curriculum dealing with the history of women, alerting the student body to the socio-economic oppression of women resulting from the absence of their historical consciousness, initiating student-led seminars on these topics." Thus, consciousness-raising in this area of women's liberation, as in others, is a first order of business.

On the educational scene today, American history textbooks are a prime example of academic sleight-of-hand, of that marvelous trick whereby the hand proves quicker than the eye, in this case the writer's hand and the student's eyes. More mysterious even than the ability to depict a world without women, a world whose existence is clearly denied by the writers' and readers' own experiences, is the fact that until very recently not a single professor protested that historical "truth" should be so unlike reality, not a single paying customer demanded her money back on the basis that she had paid for a history course and had been sold a male fantasy instead.

### Postscript

Since 1971, the changes that have taken place include the publication of one basic text by a woman, the rise of the junior-college text, and the growth of readers on women designed to accompany the basic history text. For a variety of reasons, the one text written by a woman and two texts which have women as working contributors have followed the usual path of devoting less than 1 percent of space to women. This same space allocation holds true for the junior-college texts. The rising number of anthologies on women in American history put out by publishers of major texts is little improvement; few instructors use these works in addition to a major text in a course.

# Historical Phallacies:
# Sexism in American Historical Writing

*Linda Gordon, Persis Hunt, Elizabeth Pleck,*
*Rochelle Goldberg Ruthchild, and Marcia Scott*

Most historians, no matter what their subject, have neglected the history of women's lives.[1] Pick any textbook on American history or Western civilization and look in the index under women, or for the names of specific women.[2] Though women are half of humanity, their lives are usually relegated to special, secondary categories of concern, e.g., "Social Life in Victorian England" or "Women's Rights Movement—*see* Suffrage." In some ways the neglect of women in history is parallel to the racism implicit in much Western history; in other ways, it is more similar to the ignorance of the lives of lower class people of both sexes. In still other ways, it is unique, since women have been at once so close and yet so far from wielding real power.

At the end of the nineteenth century a great feminist movement spread throughout much of the Western world and created significantly more freedom for women than they had experienced before. In the 1960s the feminist movement reemerged and created a widespread interest in the earlier feminism.[3] As a response, many books and articles appeared on that subject, and undoubtedly many more are to be expected.[4] This is a welcome development. But we will argue that many of these books and articles are inferior history because they are sexist. Sexism is basically the belief in the inferiority of women to men. Sexism and good historical writing are incompatible since history deals with change over time while sexist analysts apply immutable and inherent (as well as unproven) character attributes to women, and then proceed to write history with these attributes in mind. Thus the genital difference between men and women assumes cosmic proportions and is used to explain entire sets of social and cultural phenomena as emanating not from external forces—forces in the society operating on women—but from the nature of women themselves.

This essay is reprinted by permission from *Women's Studies* I, no. 1 (1972), ed. Wendy Martin, Queens College, CUNY. Some revisions have been made for publication in this volume. An earlier version was read at the annual meeting of the American Historical Association, December 1970, in Boston, Mass. Cynthia Kneen edited the earlier version.

The books and articles we review here are still among the most prominent about women in America.[5] The authors, all well-known historians, are male; they were chosen not for their biology, but for their ideology. The books and articles are not all alike; their authors have different points of view and the subjects of their writings are different. But the works we will review do have one thing in common: a belief that anatomy is destiny; in short, sexism. In this paper, we will identify and analyze the sexism in each of the historian's works and show how it makes for distorted and misleading historical interpretation.

## I

While both men and women who have advocated social change have been seen as irrational and illogical, this charge has fallen particularly on women, since it coincides with the sex-role stereotype of women. Robert Riegel, author of several books on American women, contributes to the belief that women are emotional creatures and thinks emotionality is a negative trait. Although Riegel, in his *American Feminists*, admits that Mary Wollstone-craft's writings were "far more influential than those of any Americans of that period," he nevertheless believes that "one can well argue that Wollstone-craft's emotionalism and radicalism did more to anger and antagonize than to persuade."[6] Orthodox historical scholarship often shows preference for those thinkers who appear dispassionate, unemotional, and nonpartisan.

An interesting typology of character traits is employed by Riegel to measure the abilities of the women he discusses. He admires some character-istics, those which are usually associated with men: Elizabeth Cady Stanton is thus praised for being realistic and practical. Other characteristics, however, he downgrades. Stanton is denigrated for not being theoretical. So, too, Susan B. Anthony is praised for being "straightforward" and theoretical, but faulted for being anti-male.[7] In these character typings of women, Anthony and Stanton are not treated as people, but as reflections of male values.

Believing that women's lives should be defined by their relations with husband and children, Riegel again reflects these male values, emphasizing as he does the importance of home and marriage for feminist leaders. When discussing "Mrs." Eliza Farnham (he does not similarly preface men's names with "Mister"), writer and lecturer on women's issues, he notes that when she felt an "urge to express herself in numerous books, she wrote nothing about her husbands, which leads to speculation that her marriages were far from satisfying emotional experiences. A further bit of evidence is her embarkment upon a personal career at the very time she was taking care of a husband and small children."[8] If a woman wants a career and does not mention her husband in her books Riegel assumes that she has an unsatisfying marriage.

In an article on "Women's Clothes and Women's Rights," Riegel sees the antebellum dress-reform movement of the feminists as a fad, a diversion which "took attention from more important matters and created unnecessary hostility."[9] The innate frivolity of women is his explanation for dress reform.

But his own evidence indicates how important it was: corsets reducing women's waists to eighteen inches, tight shoes, numerous petticoats, avoidance of "unattractive" rubbers or overshoes in bad weather, infrequent bathing because women were "naturally" clean, all served to confine and debilitate women. Mary Livermore, a nineteenth-century doctor, diagnosed "corset-liver": "These livers were so deeply indented where the ribs had been crowded against them that a wrist could easily be laid inside the groove."[10]

Riegel does not take dress reform seriously. If they worry about their looks, women are condemned for vanity. But woe betide any of them, like "plump Mrs. Stanton" in her baggy pants, who put comfort and practicality before convention. In a more recent book, he asserts that "women who copied male attire were not infrequently sexual perverts or people trying to evade the law."[11] But the dress-reform movement, an attempt by women to define their own humanity and sexuality, was enormously important in changing sexual, educational, medical, and social customs for the whole society. It was an important aspect of feminism and Riegel has completely misunderstood it.

## II

William O'Neill's treatment of the feminist movement is more comprehensive than Riegel's *American Feminists*, but is also a much less sympathetic view of the movement. The argument in *Everyone Was Brave* is that the feminist movement failed because it did not have a fully developed radical critique of American society and of woman's place. Apart from their inadequate analysis of society at large, the feminists' greatest lack was an inability to formulate a radical theory of marriage and the family. What was the reason for their failure? Here the book is not clear, arguing at times that it was the Victorian prudishness of the feminists themselves, at other times, that it was the Woodhull-Claflin doctrine of free love and the attendant scandal which turned women against sexual radicalism. But mostly, he argues that it was the personal inadequacies of the feminists which made them unable to construct a durable ideology. His characterization of "Ten Who Led the Woman Movement" is a good example of his inclination to blame the feminists by focusing on what he considers negative qualities:

> Josephine Shaw Lowell: "Mrs. Lowell was guided by certain principles, but they hardly added up to an intelligible system of ideas."
> M. Carey Thomas: "[She] was the kind of feminist that was easily caricatured. Sharp-tongued, ambitious, a confirmed man-hater, she charged through life, leaving behind her a train of bruised feelings and wounded egos."
> Margaret Dreier Robins: "Mrs. Robins demonstrated that one could be both feminine and a feminist. . . ."
> Jane Addams: "The crowning irony of Jane Addams' life, therefore, was that she compromised her intellect for the sake of human experiences which her nature prevented her from having."

Anna Howard Shaw: "No one else in the woman movement fitted so perfectly the stereotype promoted by anti-suffragists of the sharp-tongued, man-hating feminist."

Carrie Chapman Catt: "Among suffragists she was uniquely rational."

Alice Paul: "[She] was an absolute fanatic."

Charlotte Perkins Gilman: "She was a mother and a heterosexual, unlike some feminists. Thus the degree of her sexual maladjustment was probably less than might have been expected, given her start in life." [12]

The references to hatred, maladjustment, and fanaticism in these character sketches serve to shore up O'Neill's thesis that the feminists were irrational in one way or another. Feminism emerges as incompatible, therefore, with the "serious analysis" which would have led the feminists to what he considers a coherent political philosophy.

In explaining their deficiency in this matter, O'Neill distinguishes two kinds of feminists, the hard-core and the social feminists. He judges both groups unfavorably. The hard-core feminists, "who were chiefly interested in woman's rights," failed because they were too angry. "If the extreme feminists had been more reflective and less emotional—that is to say, if they had not been extremists—they might have reasoned their way to a socialist solution to their dilemma." The social feminists, held somewhat higher in his esteem because they gave priority to other social issues over woman's rights, were also too emotional, but in a different fashion. Some of them had "theoretical perceptions" like Florence Kelley, but in general, like her, they let sentimentality prevail over rationality. Even this social feminist, for whom O'Neill has the highest regard, "had the mind of a socialist, [but] she lacked the requisite temper." [13]

What this means is that Kelley and others of her persuasion were too caught up in the need to alleviate human suffering in the short run to concentrate on a revolutionary program.

> She believed in the long-range program of the Socialist Party, but she could not devote herself to it while misery and want stalked the land. She needed immediate results, and they were to be gotten only through bourgeois reformist organizations like the NCL [National Consumers League]. Her abundant energies, and the impatience they contributed to, made it impossible for her to work for a distant revolution when so much needed doing now. Thus her emotional needs militated against her theoretical perceptions. This response, so typical of American radicals, might well be called the pragmatic fallacy, because by concentrating on reform at the expense of revolution one ended up with neither. Nonetheless, Mrs. Kelley's decision did her credit. It requires a certain hardness of character to put abstract propositions, like The Revolution, ahead of human wants, and to work for a distant event when present evils are so compelling. [14]

O'Neill has created a false opposition between socialist revolution and the satisfaction of human wants, as if it were possible to be a true socialist only by ignoring present misery and want and waiting for these specters to cease stalking the land. What was really needed, O'Neill continues, was the universal adoption of the principles of Debs's Co-operative Commonwealth, since only that could answer the country's needs. "Yet their very virtues prevented generous, impassioned men, and *women even more,* from heeding the call of reason. Their hearts cried out so insistently that the claims of intellect went unmet" (emphasis added). Passion and generosity preclude socialism, especially in women, because they impair the thinking process which O'Neill believes can and should only take place in a social and psychological vacuum. "The example of Florence Kelley is especially dramatic, therefore, not by reason of its uniqueness, but rather because she was one of the few reformers whose mind was sufficiently disciplined and whose experience was sufficiently broad to lead her beyond reformist maxims. That she succumbed to them all the same indicates how desperately high were the odds against socialism in the United States."[15]

It is of course impossible for anyone to live up to the abstract perfection of O'Neill's socialism. Perhaps he senses this, for the somewhat anticlimactic advice which he offers is that the feminists should have joined the Socialist party. But this suggestion takes no account of the fact that even if they had joined it, the Socialist party would almost certainly have subsumed their demands under the rubric of class struggle. Although it is true that the Socialist party went on record in favor of women's rights, in practice the women members often found their concerns not taken seriously and their desire for equality suppressed.[16]

Claiming socialism as the answer, he really finds those who wanted radical change abnormal: ". . .when a position, however false or anti-social, becomes deeply entrenched it is even more irrational to contest it." Or again, that "radicals often more correctly analyze a given situation than their adversaries, but that the very traits responsible for their insight prevent them from exploiting it successfully."[17] Although O'Neill acknowledges the need for social change, he rejects both reformist and radical strategies, leaving no possibilities for action. His fund of ideas ultimately comes down to acquiescence in the status quo.

### III

Both William O'Neill and Christopher Lasch, author of *The New Radicalism in America,* consider the behavior of the radicals a sign of their irrationality and false consciousness. Lasch's argument closely resembles O'Neill's contention that American feminists lacked a class analysis. But the reasons for this failing are different for Lasch than for O'Neill. Lasch argues that the intellectuals were actually in revolt against middle-class values, the patriarchal family, and the cult of gentility, and their failure to recognize this as the true source of their anger was their undoing.

We will discuss two main points in Lasch's book. First, he argues that men and women intellectuals suffer equally a sense of alienation from middle-class values. Second, he polarizes the sex-roles in a way which allows for no human characteristics shared by both sexes. *The New Radicalism in America* attempts to explain twentieth-century American radicalism by examining the emergence of intellectuals as a social type. However, his description of Jane Addams and the feminists springs from his misguided belief that sexual matters can be separated from cultural and political issues. To Lasch the "alienage" which Charlotte Perkins Gilman, Olive Schreiner, and Jane Addams felt was very much the same as what Lincoln Steffens or John Dewey perceived. Lasch acknowledges the fact that Gilman had to leave her husband in order to be free, but he feels that marriage was confining to all intellectuals, male and female.

Women were alienated from middle-class values, but their alienation was two-fold: from these values and from the values which stereotyped women's place. Taking the evidence from Randolph Bourne's life, Lasch argues that the envy of men and women was mutual: "The fact that it was possible for men to envy in women the very things women envied in men makes it clear that the sense of 'alienage' was a highly subjective state of mind, one which cannot be traced to any such simple source as the deprivations of American women. . . ."[18]

What Lasch has done is to take two groups, unequal in power, wealth, legal status, and position in the patriarchal family, and to declare on the basis of their similar feelings toward each other that both groups had similar status. While Lasch contends that middle-class intellectuals of both sexes were alienated from their background, his own evidence contradicts him. His quotations from Inez Haynes Gillmore illustrate clearly her anger at the unequal treatment she received in her family. The poverty of her childhood bore more heavily on her than on her brothers, who enjoyed more freedom. Moreover, Lasch notes complaints like Gillmore's, but ignores their implications, and their frequency among other such intellectual women as Jane Addams, Charlotte Perkins Gilman, and Margaret Sanger.[19]

The feminists failed to realize, according to Lasch, that their sense of alienation was not a woman's problem, but a problem faced by all middle-class intellectuals. How is it, Lasch wonders, that these women could maintain such false consciousness? "Why did they persist in attributing their suffering not to class but to sex, not to their being middle-class intellectuals in rebellion against what had come to seem a sterile and meaningless existence, but to the simple fact of their being women?"[20] Writing on "Woman as Alien," Lasch answers this question.

> Sometimes it amounted to outright antagonism. The feminists talked a great deal about the need for a freer and more spontaneous companionship between men and women, but in practice they often seemed to assume a state of perpetual war. Even when the envy of men did not reach the point of hostility—and it is possible to exaggerate the Lesbian and castrating aspects of the feminists' revolt—the envy nevertheless remained. So did the unconcealed abhorrence of everything connected with the middle-class family and with middle-class life in general, an abhorrence of which the envy of men, in fact, was probably a single facet.[21]

From a position of equality of envy, Lasch suddenly introduces into the feminine sentiments a note of strident "antagonism." Even his language changes, as he sweeps aside their stated desire for "companionship" with men and fastens on their "antagonism," their "hostility," their desire to make war with men.[22] From antagonism, hostility, and perpetual warfare, it is but an easy step to that bogus charge which men raise so often, the alleged female desire to castrate men. By ignoring the real inequality between men and women Lasch is left with no explanation for feminist anger. If one agrees with the feminist analysis that they were enraged by their inferior status, then their anger becomes perfectly understandable and justifiable.

According to Lasch, the feminists failed to see their problems as those of middle-class intellectuals because they were obsessed with the issue of their femininity. Even Jane Addams could not escape the fear "that in pursuing a *masculine* ideal she had betrayed her own *femininity*" (emphasis added).[23] These words make no sense. Perhaps the sentence might have read more correctly if Lasch had written that Addams feared that in pursuing a *career* she had betrayed *marriage* and *motherhood*.

Lasch's tendency to polarize the sex roles leads him to overemphasize the importance of Jane Addams's spinal operation of 1882, on the assumption (incorrect, as it turns out)[24] that it left her unable to bear children and hence condemned her to celibacy. Lasch's acceptance of this myth is shown in the following quotation:

> Cut off . . . from a whole range of feminine experience, she must have begun to wonder whether she was not in danger of losing touch with femininity altogether. A woman bent on a man's career, committed to her father's unyielding masculine example, she now ran the risk of finding herself altogether unsexed. To the invalid, turning over the meaning of her most recent misfortune, lying in bed with her books while the women around her busied themselves, in the immemorial tradition of women, with the details of her care, it must have seemed that she was in danger of losing contact with one whole side of her nature.[25]

If a woman wants a career, she is following a masculine example. Otherwise, she must choose the female role, in "the immemorial tradition of her sex" which is to busy oneself with the details of care. Nowhere is this polarization of sex role more apparent than in Lasch's discussion of a letter Jane Addams wrote as a girl to a friend in a neighboring girls' seminary. The friend criticizes the promiscuous kissing among her schoolmates and pledges to Pythias (Jane Addams) that their friendship and love are sacred. That Addams and her friend chose such names is of great significance to Lasch.

> It is touching and revealing that . . . girls of more serious habits should have found themselves addressing each other as "old fellow," as "Damon" and "Pythias." It is an unimportant detail in itself, this assumption of masculine pseudonyms; but it symbolizes the feminist dilemma. The determination to be a "true woman" forced one in effect to lead a man's life. That was exactly the point made by the most uncomprehending critics of the feminist movement. What was so maddening was that there was finally no answer to this easiest of cliches. The search for woman's nature led always in circles.[26]

The dilemma which Lasch poses for women is false, because, as Charlotte Perkins Gilman says, "The whole area of human life is outside of, and irrelevant to the distinctions of sex."[27] Lasch does notice something very important—that women who dared to take their lives seriously often assumed male identities in their fantasies—but he is blind to the correct interpretation of this practice. The fact is that these young women lived in a world in which only men were permitted to have exciting, challenging lives; thus to many women it was natural that femininity spelled tedium. Their feminine identity crises were produced not by psychological immaturity or inadequate understanding but by objective conditions.

Lasch's analysis is oriented around notions of "feminine experience," "masculine example," "the immemorial tradition of women," "woman's nature." No attempt is made to insist on the social character of these concepts. Lapsing back into a notion of sex roles as eternals, part of nature, fixed since "time immemorial," Lasch carries his analysis outside of history and situates himself amidst the clichés so typical of the sexist analysis of women's role.

## IV

In an opening statement in an article on Anna Howard Shaw, James R. McGovern acknowledges his intellectual debt to the "sophisticated treatment" of the feminists in Lasch's *New Radicalism*. McGovern goes Lasch one better; whereas Lasch indulges in psychologizing, McGovern psychoanalyzes. (He comments that Shaw's writings about her childhood "reveal an invariable pattern of feeling and identifications which serve, in approximation, the same function as a patient's recall to the analyst."[28]) In the age of Masters and Johnson, of persons of all persuasions raising serious doubts about the efficacy of psychoanalysis, psychologists may no longer be so widely disposed to believe in penis envy and feminine hysteria as they used to. But no matter; what psychologists discard, historians recycle.[29] James McGovern in his article on Shaw claims he has discovered a "new approach to feminism"; actually he has revamped the oldest approach of all.

McGovern realizes that the private lives of the feminist leaders did indeed reverberate with their public commitments. But he misses the point: it is true that many outstanding feminists recorded painful memories of their own upbringing as women precisely because they regarded their personal lives as political. Since women were oppressed by being forced into servile sexual and marital roles, many feminists sought liberation by rejecting these roles as well as acting against more public forms of social and economic oppression. It was precisely because so many feminists were attempting to integrate theory with their own lives that they often had to suffer so much pain. McGovern, as well as Lasch, O'Neill, and Riegel, seems to consider unhappiness a sign of inferior emotional adjustment. The truth might be exactly the reverse: the very unconventionality of the feminists' lives was a healthy response to a society which degraded women.

McGovern, through his case study of Anna Howard Shaw, concentrates on the "important contributions of the neurotic personality to historical change." McGovern explains Shaw's life in terms of identification with her father. She was a famous minister, one of the outstanding orators of her day, and president of the National American Women's Suffrage Association. Like several other famous feminist leaders, she did not marry. She was aggressive in her criticism of men and enjoyed some unusually close relationships with women. These feminists, notes McGovern, "were critical of men and lacked sustained, pleasurable sexual contacts with them." The dislike of men and warm feelings toward women committed many women to the feminist movement. But it was more than dislike, McGovern thinks. It was "antagonism toward men by finding fault with them while seeking to *deprive them* of feminine companionship . . . "(emphasis added). McGovern's concern here is not with Shaw's personality at all, but only with the issue of whether men would be deprived. McGovern develops this same theme a little later on, in discussing Shaw's mental "masculinization," which we assume means that she thought like a man instead of a woman. Here McGovern writes: "She adopted and preferred characteristics which, conventionally at least, are more identifiable with men than with women."[30]

Putting aside the question of what "conventionally at least" constitutes masculine and feminine characteristics, we may wonder at the baroque twists of the psychoanalytic mentality that can go to such absurd lengths to find motivation when there is a perfectly good and much simpler explanation right at hand. Shaw's personal experience with a society that debases women is a much more obvious explanation of her motivation. She had a difficult childhood: her father was brutal and oppressive, her mother long-suffering. Despite the objections of her family, she graduated from college and received a degree in theology from Boston University. Shaw also took a degree in medicine, and ministered to both the bodies and souls of immigrant women in the slums of Boston. But she found that "in my association with the women of the streets, I realized the limitations of my work in the ministry and in medicine. As minister to soul and body one could do little for these women. For such as them, one's efforts must begin at the very foundation of the social structure. Laws for them must be made and enforced, and some of those laws could only be made and enforced by women."[31]

McGovern criticizes Shaw because he cannot understand how anyone could become deeply involved, indeed, dedicate one's whole life to a social movement. "Shaw's commitment to feminism," McGovern writes, "was so complete that it becomes irrational and compulsive. Indeed, she had lost her freedom to be anything but a feminist."[32] (How strange, since we think one of the greatest barriers to freedom is the traditional role of women!) McGovern does not argue that the goals of the feminist movement were invalid (although he hints at the problems of unwitting followers getting caught up in the "excesses" to which leaders are easily committed), but he concludes that Shaw's pursuit of feminist goals was overenthusiastic, as if there were something especially creditable about ambivalence and hesitancy. In his final summation of the feminist movement, McGovern writes:

A new dimension is obtained through depth study of a model feminist, especially when it is possible, perhaps even likely, that the same influence, relatively speaking, prevailed among some other feminist leaders of the period. At the very least, this approach permits the historian to view the feminist movement in dynamic terms as a relationship between the drives of leaders and its social achievements. It also demonstrates the real role of fantasy in sustaining what for most followers of a movement are merely its "truths." But it underscores as well the important contributions of the neurotic personality to historical change and conversely illustrates how ideology and organization serve underlying needs and purposes of such personalities.[33]

Further "depth" studies of feminist leaders such as McGovern suggests would only further distort understanding of the feminist movement. Here again, McGovern urges the approach taken by Riegel, O'Neill, and Lasch: a social movement is little more than the sum total of the drives, wishes, and neurotic fantasies of its leaders. Surely, the great movements for human equality cannot be reduced to the neurotic fantasies of a few leaders.

The counterpart of the emphasis on feminist leadership is the disregard for the less articulate members of the feminist movements. History, to Riegel, O'Neill, and McGovern, is made by powerful individuals, urging along a mass of unwitting followers. Thus, from this perspective, historians study the feminist movement by analyzing its leaders. There is no sense of the excitement and power of a mass movement, though that quality was precisely what was most special about the movement. This failure to deal with it as a broad social phenomenon is what permits them to indulge in their incessant psychologizing without seriously considering the social forces which produced nineteenth-century feminism.

## V

For McGovern, Carl Degler, and Page Smith, ideology is an artificial imposition on a social reality which was not so bad after all. Ideology represents a "loss of freedom." For McGovern, this "loss of freedom" is symbolized by the commitment of a handful of neurotic leaders to the feminist movement. For Degler, David Potter, and Page Smith, American women have progressed by working within the system, typing their way to happiness as "supple-fingered secretaries" and happy homebodies. Their lot has improved along with American prosperity, and they have no future outside that prosperity. As Degler says in his article, "Revolution without Ideology: The Changing Place of Women in America," "When women became ideological . . . they faced their greatest opposition and scored their most disappointing triumphs."[34] In his opinion, America has never had any sympathy for ideologies. There is no need for such rhetoric in a country with an innate "feminist bias" and such "high esteem for women." Though Degler tries to make a case for the uniqueness of America, he provides no proof that America has less ideology and more "feminist bias" than any other country.

David Potter is another believer in the American way of life. "As a symbol, the typewriter evokes fewer emotions than the plow," Potter notes, "but like the plow it played a vital part in the fulfillment of the American promise of opportunity and independence." Though he extols the "supple fingers and ready adaptability" of American women as the key to their success,[35] we think it was rather the low wages at their command which led to the mass hiring of female typists, forcing out the higher-paid male secretaries.

Potter's article "American Women and the American Character" attempts to show that the generalizations about the character of American men do not apply to American women. We agree with Potter here. But Potter goes on to argue that these generalizations do not apply to American women because of women's contentment as housewives and their biological suitedness to female occupations. Women's character is different from men's, Potter asserts, since so many women are occupied with a job which Potter characterizes as self-directed, affording a great measure of independence. What is this occupation? Housework. He writes:

> Millions of housewives continue to exercise personal choice and decision not only in arranging their own time-table and routine but also in deciding what food the family shall have and how it shall be prepared, what articles of purchase shall have the highest priority on the family budget, and, in short, how the home shall be operated. Despite strong tendencies toward conformity in American life, it is clear that American women excercise a very wide latitude of decision in these matters, and everyone knows that there are great variations between the regimes in various American homes. Indeed it seems fairly evident that the woman of today, with the wide range of consumer goods available for purchase and the wide variety of mechanical devices to free her from drudgery, has a far broader set of alternatives for her household procedure than the farm wife of two or three generations ago.[36]

To be sure, the farm wife of two or three generations ago was the victim of the drudgery of household work, but today's housewife is the victim of an ideology which makes child-rearing a full-time career. The farm wife of two or three generations ago was never totally confined to household and child-rearing tasks. Potter sees no social or economic reasons for millions of housewives being stuck at home. He believes that woman's condition is what she wants and has always wanted; he does not see the connection between woman's role and the American economy which needs a reserve and scab labor force, an obedient army of consumers, a divided working class, and a group prepared to do the dirty work and raise children well programmed for their proper station in life. In essence, Potter believes that the choices American capitalism offers women—whether to serve frozen beans or frozen peas for dinner—are meaningful.

To Potter, most American women are suburban housewives with ranch wagons, a husband who makes $15,000 a year or more, and two kids. Excluded from mention are the 49 percent of all women between the ages of eighteen and sixty-four who are in the work force, one-third of them employed in seven occupations—secretary, saleswoman, cleaning woman, teacher in elementary school, bookkeeper, waitress, and nurse.[37] Potter thinks housewives are generalists, that is, expert in many domestic roles:

interior decorator, dietician, child psychologist, transportation manager (in the role of driver in the car pool), and economist. But this is a completely false issue. The real problem is not the multiplicity of tasks but their low status and confining nature.

Women are different, Potter explains, since so much of their time is spent in housewifery. Their lives are actually better than men's since they do not face a "traumatic, sudden transition from daily work as the focus of life to enforced idleness" which men encounter upon retirement. But finally, even though women are important as housekeepers, consumers and cultural arbiters, there is still a barrier to women's equality. It is their biology. Since women have been content to be wives and mothers, there will always be some inequality because of this "biological fact."[38] Potter does not appreciate that it is culture, not women's genital equipment, which makes motherhood a barrier to women's equality.

## VI

These age-old biological facts to which Potter refers are further underscored by Page Smith, author of a history of American women from colonial times to the present. The book manifests an antiquarian concern with heroines, easily recognized from the title, *Daughters of the Promised Land: Being an examination of the strange history of the female sex from the beginning to the present, with special attention to the women of America, illustrated by curious anecdotes and quotations by divers authors, ancient and modern.* Smith's knowledge of women comes from autobiographical experience, as he confesses in the book:

> I would thus be less than candid if I did not state frankly that this is basically an autobiographical work. It is based upon my knowledge of those women to whom this book is dedicated [his daughters, Ellen and Anne; the ladies of Cowell College; the women in his life, his mother, Ellen, and his wife, Eloise; and Mary, Barbara, Frances, Sarah, Jacquey, Hattie, Lee, Maxine, Betty, Liz, Claire, Dorothy, Jean, Jane, Janet, Margie, Eve, Ruth, Freya, Alice, Betsy, Hermia, Lois, Helen, Fawn, Rosalind, Ginny, Libby, Linell, Pat, Nancy, Ann, Marcelle, Beatrice, Clarissa, Josephine, Ida, LaVerne, Maria, Emma, Marilyn, Virginia, Kim, Bertie, Tatty, Cleon, Eleanor, Emmy, Carol, Gretchen, Eunice, Laura, Fredericka, Mitzi, Vee, Marion, Susan, Edna, Dixie, Matilda, Cette, Marjorie, Madeline, Sandra, Gay, Peggy, Haddie, Kathy, Allen, Priscilla, Hillary, Genevieve, Maile, Elaine, Lucille, Connie, Rosanna, Florence, Louise, Teddy, Della, Gina, Kitty, Julia, Ella, Janis, Maggie, Judy, Emily, Phoebe, Phyllis, Flora Mae, Amanda, Sandy, Kris, Sheila, Charlene, Candy, Julie Giselle, Sushila, Daphne, and Corda] and above all on twenty-eight years of married life. . . . I cannot imagine that my wife could do so graciously and gracefully the things she does if they were not as much of a delight to her to do as they are to me as the principal though by no means exclusive beneficiary of them.
>
> If she does all these things so marvelously well under the illusion that she enjoys them, tricked by the masculine-dominant culture's

notion of her proper role, then, I can only say, we should be the happier in the shadow of such illusions.[39]

Thus, Smith argues that if it is true that women are socialized into female roles, then we should "all be the happier in the shadow of such illusions." Indeed, much of the history of this book is illusory.

Smith's first illusion is that the history of women in America is the history of Anglo-Saxon, white, middle-class women.[40] Black heroines, such as Harriet Tubman, are not mentioned. Sojourner Truth appears in only one sentence followed by a quotation from her, even though Smith spends several chapters discussing women in the antislavery movements. Two additional black women are mentioned, however: "Mrs. Martin Luther King," in one sentence, and Sally Hemmings, allegedly the mistress of Thomas Jefferson, in a whole paragraph. Smith does write the history of white working girls, quoting as his source the evidence of two Philadelphia society women who remarked on the favorable conditions for working girls in various factories.[41] He concludes, "For the most part they [working girls] did not need enough money to 'make a living,' only enough to bedeck themselves in hope of attracting a husband." In one of the few places where he mentions ethnic immigration to America, Smith remarks that the tide of Irish immigration pushed women out of the industrial jobs they held.[42] While Yankee women were forced out of their jobs by the presence of a surplus labor force willing to work harder for less money, he neglects to mention that it was Irish women and children who were forced into such jobs. In conclusion, on the nature of working women and the American class structure, Smith writes:

> Since women are essentially classless, industrialism provided them with jobs which provided them with money which provided them with clothes which provided them with that middle-class appearance which was the wonder of foreign visitors. Thus the fluidity of American society was in large part the consequence of the fluidity of American women. The wives of workingmen, adopting a middle-class style, dragged their husbands along with them and thereby helped to create that ample and commodious catchall, the American Middle Class, which includes, with a truly splendid lack of discrimination, everyone from judges to plumbers, leaving out only Negroes, Mexicans, Puerto Ricans, and those whites below the so-called poverty line.[43]

Our objection to Smith rests both with his attitudes toward women as well as with his orthodox and narrow social history approach. Since women are half of the inarticulate, one-half of all persons oppressed by class and race, to omit their lives from a history of American women produces a very biased historical account.[44]

At first glance Smith's attitude toward women seems quite flattering. He sees them in many ways as better than men: "They are more open, more responsive, more religious, more 'giving,' more practical than men; more loyal, far more the natural enhancers and celebrators of life; more passive or more capable of passivity, more elemental and more passionate." Smith's manly diffidence extends even to the most delicate of all areas. In a discussion of penis-envy, he admits that the penis is "after all, in purely aesthetic terms, a rather poor object." Indeed, men may have womb-envy: "Certainly anyone who has seen a mother with her infant can hardly doubt that it is the primal act of creation and suspect that all of men's restless creativity is not entirely satisfactory compensation for it."[45]

To Smith, women, then, will be man's salvation. Men have "almost wrecked" the world; women will save it: "I believe that it is to women primarily that we must look for the opening up of those areas of our life which touch the spontaneous, the joyful and the responsive." Thus Smith sees that the qualities he ascribes to women arise from male needs: "The world is so sadly in need of being enhanced, adorned, celebrated, so in need of rituals, pageants, processions, and similar delights, that *women must serve these needs*" (emphasis added). It is hard to take seriously a historian who says, "Perhaps the basic difference between the sexes is that women are made of 'sugar and spice and everything nice,' while men are made of 'snips and snails and puppy dog tails.' "[46]

Though Smith seems to realize the interrelationship between male needs and female roles, he refuses to consider its implications. Instead, like Potter, he resorts to crude biological determinism to fix women in their present position. The nature of women becomes immutable, foreordained by a force outside humanity—not God anymore, but Biology. "A woman's life turns inward. Her 'internality,' her privateness, is symbolized if not directly related to the fact that her sex organs and above all, her womb, are interior."[47]

Since to Smith, women are innately private, internal, and, in essence, passive, he is totally mystified by independent and self-assertive women who break out of their so-called biologically determined roles. These women are denying their natural destiny; they will become part of the male world, which is in a state of chaos, and the effort will not be worth it. "If they simply battle their way into all the dreary and routine tasks performed by men (and this is indeed so far exactly what they have done, taking over the vast portion of the least interesting and most poorly remunerated jobs in our society) they will have won that famous hollow victory."[48] Smith's class bias and his patronizing attitude toward women emerge in this statement. He blames women for taking these jobs—the only jobs open to them—as if they had an alternative. The loaded phrase "battle their way" suggests that it is terribly unfeminine for women to demand paying jobs.

## VII

David Potter and Page Smith argue that women are satisfied as home-makers, but to Andrew Sinclair, author of *The Better Half: The Emancipation of the American Woman*, their very satisfaction is a tragedy. He argues that it is because of laziness and lack of ambition that women have not left the home. They sink willingly into their sex-roles as middle-class house-wives and wallow in their bourgeois domesticity. They are "Victorian," conventional, unimaginative, their brains addled by too much child-rearing, too much fussing about the house. The American woman is and has been parochial, irrational, and worst of all, lacking a compelling class analysis. Basically women do not want total freedom. They have spun the web of their imprisonment, first, because they have not chosen to use their leisure time to better society, and second, because they have chosen to see themselves as "the better half." About the first point, Sinclair says that "the fact is that most American women have done little with the leisure of the home, in terms of developing themselves. . . ."

> They have made too much of the work of mothers and housewives, too little of the quest to become free in mind and spirit. As their opportunity for leisure and self-improvement has increased, they have expanded their care of their children and their homes to take in the slack of the superfluous hours. They have cultivated their progeny more than their own gardens, their rooms more than their own brains. . . . The very move of the American family from the urban apartment to the huge suburban house seems to be more a woman's drive to find more floors to clean than an urge to find more space to live in. For breadth of view can well exist in a narrow room.[49]

Both Potter and Sinclair encompass in their discussion only the concerns of the upper-middle-class woman who does not use her leisure to the best advantage. While Potter exalts the potential of the work of mothers and housewives, Sinclair finds this occupation meaningless. The idea that women have voluntarily expanded their housekeeping to fill the hours ignores the problem of female socialization, and the mystique which Betty Friedan described, in which women were persuaded to become housewives as a way of coping with their superfluity in the labor market. Even the movement for suburban growth is "blamed on women," who want to find bigger houses in order to have more floors to clean.

For Sinclair, women have proved to be a disappointment. Now that they are enfranchised, now that they own washing machines and electric food blenders, why is it that they have not used their freedom? Why is it that they persist in living in suburban homes? It must be because women are either stupid or stubborn. Basically women do not want freedom. If they did, they would take advantage of the traditional high status of women in this country, Degler's supposed innate "feminist bias" of America. If women wanted to be free, they would be. Sinclair writes: "If most women continue to see themselves chiefly as reproductive females, they will work within the limitations of the weaker sex and the better half. If they choose to see themselves chiefly as human beings, they will live and work as human beings for the better whole."[50]

In the same manner as Lasch, Sinclair imagines that women's faulty consciousness has led them astray. Sinclair does not examine women's consistently lower wages and exclusion from the more profitable jobs, the exploitation of women's bodies by the male-controlled corporations, the destruction of women's minds and self-esteem by schools. Instead, Sinclair believes that if women really want to be equal they will be, and that anything less than full equality of the sexes is proof of women's lack of will.

## VIII

The books and articles we have reviewed are quite different in approach, extent of research, and ideology. Some would criticize these books for poor scholarship, since the authors have not done the requisite research. But this is not the issue. No amount of research, given sexist attitudes, will produce a meaningful history of women. Some of the authors are candid about their attitudes toward women, boldly stating that they believe biological differences will always make women unequal. Others hedge the issue, denying biological determinism, but writing in a way which suggests that even if differences do not arise out of biology, they remain immutable.

For many of these historians women are the source of their own oppression. Each historian has a different explanation for how this deficiency has come about, but in the end women have failed to see the proper explanation for their condition. Some say it is biology; others, psychology. Women have chosen domesticity, for the better (Smith, Potter) or for the worse (O'Neill, Sinclair). Whatever the explanation, if women have problems, they have only themselves to blame. Nowhere in these books do we find a sustained investigation of the real social conditions which are the source of women's problems and rebellion. Most American women, except for the few women with independent incomes, are dependent on men. Punished when they violate the unwritten rules which keep them in their place, women are vulnerable to physical and psychological abuse.

The historians we have reviewed include both those who have no basic complaint with American society (Smith, Degler, and Potter) and those who believe real problems exist (Lasch, O'Neill, and Sinclair). Since women have all the emancipation they could reasonably want, there is no need to fuss. They have education, leisure, and money. To be sure, there do exist those few "inadequate providers" in Degler's words, whose wives must work in rather unrewarding jobs, but the opportunities for mobility in our society are so great that even these sources of dissatisfaction are fleeting.

Three of the historians, Lasch, O'Neill and Sinclair, find fault with American institutions, and praise those women whose analysis coincides with theirs. They withdraw their approbation when the women put their own problems first. In so doing, women are manifesting false consciousness. They have refused to recognize their lack of ambition or laziness (Sinclair), their inability to criticize marriage and the family (O'Neill), or their refusal to place class before sex (Lasch and O'Neill) as the source of their problem.

The emotionalism of women clouded their perceptions and misled them, according to these writers. By psychologizing feminist anger, Riegel, O'Neill, Lasch, and McGovern are able to dismiss many feminists as abnormal. If we reconstruct the thought processes of these historians, they seem to begin with feminist militancy, proceed to women's hatred of men, and end with Lesbians, whom they often regard as castrators. To these historians, Lesbianism is unnatural, a maladjustment which can be pardoned at times if there are no men available. These historians believe that if women choose to love other women, it is only because they want to punish men.

The male point of view is masked in these books when the authors write as if they are members of a third sex, uninvolved in the struggle against male dominance and unaffected by the demands of the feminists that men give up their privileges. Consider the following quotation:

> To begin with, I have avoided the question of whether or not women ought to have full parity with men. Such a state of affairs obtains nowhere in the modern world, and so, since we do not know what genuine equality would mean in practice, its desirability cannot fairly be assessed. What I have tried to do is indicate the ways in which feminists struggled for equality and the extent to which their ideas and activities were functionally related to their goals. It is possible, I think, to evaluate the relevance of a given strategy, and its strengths and weaknesses, without committing oneself to the cause it was meant to advance.[51]

Let the reader mentally substitute blacks for women in the above quotation. In so doing one would realize how far we have come that we can be shocked by this as applied to blacks, but how far we have to go that it still appears quite acceptable when applied to women in the preface to William O'Neill's *Everyone Was Brave.* This lack of commitment, concealed as objective history, only serves to perpetuate male dominance. Not to participate in the struggle against male supremacy is to support it.

## NOTES

1. One illustration of this neglect is the paucity of doctoral dissertations on women. "Between 1873 and 1960 only 16 historical doctoral theses were on women, one on 'Recent Popes on Women's Position in Society,' by a man. In the same 87 years there were 30 dissertations on the fur trade. In fact, less than 1 percent of all books in the *Subject Guide for Books in Print* are expressly on women." Arlie Hochschild, "The American Woman: Another Idol of Social Science," *Transaction* 8, no. 12 (November–December 1970), 13.

2. Often the graphics of textbooks give important indications of sexist bias. One famous American history text, *The National Experience,* includes only one picture of a black—Booker T. Washington—and only two pictures of women, both in group portraits—Eleanor Roosevelt with Adlai Stevenson, and Jacqueline Kennedy at the funeral of her first husband. John M. Blum, Bruce Catton, Edmund S. Morgan, Arthur M. Schlesinger, Jr., Kenneth M. Stampp, C. Vann Woodward, *The National Experience,* 2d ed. (New York: Harcourt Brace and World, 1968).

3. As a result of this contemporary interest, a great deal of research has been undertaken. The Women's History Research Center published on microfilm its library of all women's serials, 1968–74, and its files on Health, Mental Health, and Law (distributed by Research Publications, New Haven, Conn.). The Coordinating Committee on Women in the Historical Profession publishes a bulletin of work in progress as well as recent publications on women's history. Many other historical and bibliographical works are now also available from other sources, such as KNOW Press, Feminist Press, and the Barnard College Women's Center.

4. Similar reviews on the historiography of women's history appeared in 1971 in other scholarly journals. Ruth Rosen commends the history of women in *Century of Struggle* by Eleanor Flexner, *The Better Half* by Andrew Sinclair, and *Ideas*

*of the Women's Suffrage Movement* by Aileen Kraditor. She is critical of Page Smith's *Daughters of the Promised Land,* William O'Neill's *Everyone Was Brave,* Mary Elizabeth Massey's *Bonnet Brigades,* and Mildred Adams's *The Right to Be People.* Ruth Rosen, "Sexism in History or, Writing Women's History Is a Tricky Business," *Journal of Marriage and the Family* 33, no. 3 (August 1971), 541–44.

The following books are reviewed by Lois W. Banner in her article, "On Writing Women's History": Kate Millett, *Sexual Politics;* Alice S. Rossi, ed., *Essays on Sex Equality* by John Stuart Mill and Harriet Taylor Mill; Emily James Putnam, *The Lady: Studies of Certain Significant Phases of Her History;* Anne Firor Scott, *The Southern Lady: From Pedestal to Politics, 1830–1930;* David M. Kennedy, *Birth Control in America, The Career of Margaret Sanger,* and Page Smith, *Daughters of the Promised Land.* Banner has a particularly useful refutation of the arguments in Smith's *Daughters of the Promised Land.* Lois W. Banner, "On Writing Women's History," *The Journal of Inter-disciplinary History* II, no. 2 (Autumn 1971), 347–58.

Ray and Victoria Ginger reviewed two books by William O'Neill and a collection of essays, *Up from the Pedestal,* by Aileen S. Kraditor. They hold a generally unfavorable opinion of *Everyone Was Brave* and *Divorce in the Progressive Era* by O'Neill. Ray and Victoria Ginger, "Feminist and Family History: Some Pitfalls," *Labor History* 12, no. 4 (Fall 1971), 614–18.

James P. Louis thinks that O'Neill's *Everyone Was Brave* will become the "Bible" for the contemporary woman's movement. Louis argues that the suffrage movement should be judged on its own terms, irrespective of "presentist" values. How can one look at the past without some system of values, whether acknowledged or unconsciously assumed? Along with O'Neill's book, Louis reviews Scott's *The Southern Lady* and Louise R. Noun's *Strong-Minded Women: The Emergence of the Woman-Suffrage Movement in Iowa.* James P. Louis, "The Roots of Feminism: A Review Essay," *Civil War History* 17, no. 2 (June 1971), 162–70.

5. The works reviewed in this paper are: Robert Riegel, *American Feminists* (Lawrence: University of Kansas Press, 1963), and "Women's Clothes and Women's Rights," *American Quarterly* XV, no. 3 (Fall, 1963), 390–401; William L. O'Neill, *Everyone Was Brave: The Rise and Fall of Feminism in America* (Chicago, 1969; University of Chicago Press reprint, 1971), and "Feminism as a Radical Ideology," in Alfred F. Young, ed., *Dissent: Explorations in the History of American Radicalism* (DeKalb: Northern Illinois University Press, 1968); Christopher Lasch, *The New Radicalism in America, 1889–1963: The Intellectual as a Social Type* (New York: Knopf, 1965); James R. McGovern, "Anna Howard Shaw: New Approaches to Feminism," *Journal of Social History* III, no. 2 (Winter 1969–70), 135–53; Carl N. Degler, "Revolution without Ideology: The Changing Place of Women in America," in "The Woman in America," *Daedalus* 93, no. 2 (Spring 1964), 653–70; David Potter, "American Women and the American Character," in Edward N. Saveth, ed. *American History and the Social Sciences* (New York: Free Press, 1964), 427–45; Page Smith, *Daughters of the Promised Land: Women in American History* (Boston: Little, Brown 1970); Andrew Sinclair, *The Better Half: The Emancipation of the American Woman* (London: Jonathan Cape, 1966).

6. Riegel, *American Feminists,* 9.

7. *Ibid.,* 77–78.

8. *Ibid.,* 138.

9. Riegel, "Women's Clothes and Women's Rights," 400.

10. Mary Livermore, as quoted in Sinclair, *The Better Half,* 104.

11. Robert Riegel, *American Women: A Story of Social Change* (Rutherford, N.J.: Fairleigh Dickinson University Press, 1970), 46.

12. O'Neill, *Everyone Was Brave,* 109, 110, 117, 120, 121, 126, 127, 132.

13. *Ibid.*, x, 143, 136.

14. *Ibid.*, 136–37.

15. *Ibid.*, 137.

16. Mari Jo Buhle, "Women and the Socialist Party, 1910–1914," *Radical America*, IV, no. 2 (February 1970), 36–55.

17. O'Neill, *Everyone Was Brave*, 290–91.

18. Lasch, *The New Radicalism*, 101.

19. *Ibid.*, 58, 60–62.

20. *Ibid.*, 64.

21. *Ibid.*, 57.

22. To become conscious of the oppression of women is to become conscious of the way in which our language is not our own. One often feels, reading books by male authors, that they are writing only for men. They seem to generalize male experience into human experience. Reading their books, one comes across phrases, constructed consciously or unconsciously, that reflect a stag-dinner mentality. For example, O'Neill writes: "Judge Lindsey wanted to institutionalize the new pattern of youthful sexual experimentation by introducing a period of trial marriage, safeguarded by contraception, during which time either party could *withdraw* without penalty" (emphasis added). O'Neill, *Everyone Was Brave*, 302. Likewise, Page Smith titles a chapter "The Great Withdrawal." Smith, *Daughters of the Promised Land*, 345.

23. Lasch, *The New Radicalism*, 65.

24. Private communication from reader for *Journal of Social History* (April 16, 1971).

25. Lasch, *The New Radicalism*, 17–18.

26. *Ibid.*, 68.

27. Charlotte Perkins Gilman, *The Home*, as quoted in *ibid.*, 59.

28. McGovern, "Anna Howard Shaw," 138.

29. Psychological interpretations of social movements have come and gone. In the fifties it was fashionable to see the abolitionists as cranks, neurotics, and fanatics who were stirring up a lot of trouble over a problem which otherwise would have been settled amicably. In the sixties the abolitionists returned as admirable, farsighted moral reformers, disturbed by the presence of a social evil. Like the abolitionists, the feminists may again find a more approving audience.

30. McGovern, "Anna Howard Shaw," 146, 144.

31. Eleanor Flexner, *Century of Struggle* (New York: Atheneum, 1968), 237.

32. McGovern, "Anna Howard Shaw," 151–52.

33. *Ibid.*, 153.

34. Degler, "Revolution without Ideology," 665.

35. Potter, "American Women and the American Character," 432.

36. *Ibid.*, 433.

37. Marijean Suelzle, "Women in Labor," *Transaction*, 8, no. 12 (November–December 1970), 51.

38. Potter, "American Women and the American Character," 435, 444.

39. Smith, *Daughters of the Promised Land*, 349–50.

40. Writing the history of women in America, Smith states that the "story properly begins with settlement of the first English men and women in America." There were of course women and men living in America before the first English women and men arrived, but these persons are not mentioned. So, too, Smith notes in error that Virginia Dare was the first feminine historical figure in the American colonies. The significance of Dare's birth is purely a racial one: she was the first white woman born in America. *Ibid.*, 3, 40.

41. Discussing one group of poor white women, Smith paraphrases the Populist leader Mary Ellen Lease, who will go down in history (or at least history texts) as having said the farmers should raise less wheat and more hell. Actually Lease urged farmers to raise less corn and more hell. *Ibid.*, 170. This mistake of Smith's goes against the grain.

42. *Ibid.*, 284, 276.

43. *Ibid.*, 286–87.

44. In his discussion of the woman's suffrage movement, Smith uses the term "suffragette" instead of the term "suffragist." Suffragette was used as a term of opprobrium by misogynists. See *ibid.*, 170, 239.

45. *Ibid.*, 331, 309.

46. *Ibid.*, 332, 329.

47. *Ibid.*, 317–18.

48. *Ibid.*, 332. Smith was a member of an ad hoc Committee on the Status of Women appointed by the Executive Council of the American Historical Association in February, 1970.

49. Sinclair, *The Better Half*, 357.

50. *Ibid.*, 367.

51. *Ibid.*, viii. It is often in the insignificant parts of a book that one finds important clues to the author's point of view. One such place is the acknowledgments. Often the spouse of an author is acknowledged, many times for the labor (generally unpaid) performed in typing, editing, researching, or even in some cases, writing and rewriting the book. Ther than this typical acknowledgment, O'Neill writes: "My wife Carol did not help me write this book. Instead she gave *me* love, happiness and two beautiful daughters, for all of which I am grateful beyond words" (emphasis added). *Ibid.*, xi.

# The Problem of Women's History

## Ann D. Gordon, Mari Jo Buhle, and Nancy Schrom Dye

The difficult task of reconstructing the past, locating women, recording their "force" and points of resistance, has resumed after a half-century of virtual silence. At such a juncture it is essential to define our research carefully. We have organized our discussion along two lines: first, historians' methodology for writing about women; second, feminist theory about women's collectivity. The problems of each intersect in theory and in practice, but more explicitly than historians, feminists employ categories to define "woman" as an historical being and explanations to describe her status as the second sex; these in turn inform their programs for social change. Historians may implicitly hold similar concepts, but their work is based on notions of historical significance that tend to deny history to women or equate women's experience with that of men.

### I

Historians' neglect of women has been a function of their ideas about historical significance. Their categories and periodization have been masculine by definition, for they have defined significance primarily by power, influence, and visible activity in the world of political and economic affairs. Traditionally, wars and politics have always been a part of "history" while those institutions which have affected individuals most immediately—social relationships, marriage, the family—have been outside the scope of historical inquiry.

Because most women have lived without access to the means of social definition and have worked outside the spheres of reward and recognition, they have not had a history as historians have defined the term. Men, given the traditional definition of historical significance, have been active; women, passive. As long as historical inquiry equates initiative and mastery with life, the lives of women are historical anomalies.

Then too, historians are accustomed to measuring change by tangible and discrete events: wars are declared, presidential administrations begin and end.

This essay is a substantially revised version of Part I of "Women in American Society: An Historical Contribution," which first appeared in *Radical America,* 5, no. 4 (July-August 1971).

By comparison, women's lives throughout Western history are characterized by an apparent timelessness: their lives have focused on bearing and raising children and have been isolated within the confines of the family. The processes affecting women's lives frequently have been slow and without immediate impact. To assume that as a result, however, their lives were without time and without change is to ignore very real developments and changes over history and to neglect the role the subjection of women has played in world development.

Because the processes affecting women's lives have not been accorded importance, because women have rarely been in positions of power and autonomy, because, in other words, women frequently have been the objects of history rather than historical subjects in their own right, historians have long assumed that "woman" was a trans-historical creature who could be isolated from the dynamics of social development.

These assumptions have been crucial in shaping the forms historical writings on women have taken. Women who look to the current body of historiography in order to gain a better understanding of the social forces which have shaped their lives will find that writing on women falls into four categories: (1) institutional histories of women in organizations, (2) biographies of important women, (3) histories of ideas about women and their roles, and (4) social histories of women in particular times and places. The most exciting changes in recent years have occurred in the last category as attitudes and methods new to historical inquiry have met with questions new to feminist inquiry. The other modes persist, however, and their assumptions continue to influence our conceptions of women's past. Each mode of historical writing manifests assumptions about historical significance, about the nature of women and femininity, and about social change.

## 1. Histories of Women in Organizations

Histories of women in organizations make up the largest number of works on women. These institutional studies are more precisely labeled as histories of feminism rather than histories of women, for the history of women's rights movements dominates their content. The scope of organizational studies has been limited further by the virtually exclusive concentration on the suffrage campaign within the larger woman movement. One is led to assume through such studies as Eleanor Flexner's *Century of Struggle* and Mildred Adams's *The Right to Be People* that American feminism—or even women's history generally—is virtually synonymous with the fight for the vote.[1] In these studies, women's history begins in 1848, with the Seneca Falls Convention, and ends abruptly in 1920, with the ratification of the woman suffrage amendment. The subjects of institutional histories are women who were articulate, conscious, organization members.

Although the abundance of source material on the women's rights movement helps explain why historians have devoted so much attention to it, this fact alone does not fully explain why scholars have paid so little attention to women who were not involved in organized feminism. More important by way of explanation is the fact that institutional studies reflect historians' assumption that it is only when women are behaving in ways usually regarded as masculine—that is, politically and collectively—that they merit historical discussion. In all other matters, many writers seem to assume that women's experience can be dismissed as "women's work"—an inappropriate or irrelevant subject for historians who have always dealt with power relations and institutions. Thus, writers of institutional studies assume that women have had a history, properly speaking, only when they have managed to step out of their proscribed sphere and enter the world of men.

The implicit belief that organizations initiate social change in and of themselves is a second major assumption which many institutional studies share. Although some historians have made superficial mention of the importance of industrialization, urbanization, and other socioeconomic changes on women's lives and social relationships, often these are not meaningfully integrated into institutional narratives or seriously analyzed. The early studies of the suffrage movement, such as the mammoth compendium by Susan Anthony, Elizabeth Cady Stanton, and Mathilda Gage, *The History of the Woman Suffrage Movement*, and Carrie Chapman Catt's *Woman Suffrage and Politics*, as well as many of their more recent counterparts seem unaware of the changes that the nineteenth century brought to women's lives.[2]

Finally, the writers who have dealt extensively with women's rights and suffrage movements often have shared a view of American society and the nature of historical change that make organizational history an appropriate focus for their work. All share a faith in American political democracy and social institutions and a belief in the linear progression of American history. For most of them, women's history is set in an evolutionary framework depicting the development of Western civilization as the unfolding progress of humanity toward democracy. In this conception, the woman's movement can be interpreted as "another chapter in the struggle for liberty."[3] Although most recent studies have been more sophisticated in writing and research than the studies of suffrage workers themselves, they have often shared the optimistic Progressive notion of historical development. Mildred Adams, for example, writes in *The Right to Be People:*

> It was a remarkably selfless campaign. The women who spent their lives in it were working not for themselves, but for the common good. They were working for the better status of women in a democracy and for the better conduct of that democracy. They honestly believed that women . . . should have the vote because they were citizens and as a tool with which to improve not only their own legal status, but also the laws and government of the nation.[4]

This Progressive viewpoint, largely unconscious in the early writers who chronicled the progress of their own movement with optimism and sincerity, obscures many important facets of the women's rights movement, not to mention the general condition of women throughout history. Women enlisted in the suffrage movement for a variety of reasons. A women's club member, for example, had different reasons for working for suffrage than did a young industrial worker. Progressive interpretations have usually neglected the racist aspect of the early suffrage movement, its limited, middle-class concerns, and its lack of feminist ideology.

Aileen Kraditor's *The Ideas of the Woman Suffrage Movement,* William O'Neill's *Everyone Was Brave: The Rise and Fall of Feminism in America,* and William Chafe's *The American Woman: Her Changing Social, Economic, and Political Roles, 1920-1970* serve in some ways as correctives to older studies.[5] Kraditor traces the development of the suffragists' ideology from nineteenth-century arguments based on natural rights to the arguments based on the necessity of women's participation in social and political reform in the early twentieth century. Her work illuminates the suffragists' abandonment of far-reaching feminist reform in favor of an expedient rationale for voting rights based on traditional notions of femininity. In addition, her study sheds light on the suffragists' class base. She emphasizes the middle-class nature of the movement and its basic failure, despite assertions of "sisterhood," to overcome the limits of class interests and outlook.

William O'Neill, in *Everyone Was Brave* and in his article, "Feminism as a Radical Ideology,"[6] also emphasizes the suffrage movement's middle-class base and the suffragists' failure to formulate a radical critique of the existing social structure. He documents the process by which American feminists discarded potentially radical ideas about marriage and the family and replaced them with the goals of "social feminism" geared toward general social reform.

William Chafe's study, *The American Woman,* departs from traditional institutional studies by analyzing women's historical experience in the years *after* the suffrage amendment became a reality rather than dealing with the women's rights movement itself. In discussing the failure of the early twentieth-century woman's movement to bring the goal of women's equality to fruition Chafe applies sociological role theory and the anthropological concept of the division of labor by sex to his analysis. He argues that the suffrage amendment failed to alter woman's role in any fundamental way in the period after it was enacted because it offered a political solution to a social problem. The vote, and the ideological arguments feminists advanced in its favor, could not affect American society's division of labor by sex. Changing employment patterns and a greater acceptance of women in the work force, rather than feminist arguments, Chafe maintains, were responsible for altering woman's role. In addition, Chafe provides a detailed chronicle of legal, political, and economic developments which have affected women in recent American history.

All three historians, however, despite their greater sophistication in analyzing the women's movement and its ideological limitations, are still confined by the traditional emphasis on organizations. The writers define the history of women through an organizational perspective and are concerned primarily with the thought and activities of women in public life. The content of women's everyday experiences is lost. Even the best of the strictly institutional studies, then, are inherently limited in the scope of their inquiry.

Histories of the women's rights movement and women's organizations are important, and, despite the numerous studies already published on the early movement, many questions remain unanswered. New questions need to be asked, drawn from our experience in the present movement. Why did the first feminist movement ultimately lose sight of feminist goals? What can we learn from tactics of the early women's rights movement? Then too, the history of organized feminism could tell us a great deal about the nature and development of feminist consciousness. The overwhelming historiographical emphasis on the suffrage movement has precluded study of women in other types of organizations. The women's club movement, the temperance crusade, women's participation in labor unions, and the special role women played in early twentieth-century social reform organizations and the settlement movement are just being written or have yet to be explored.

## 2. Biographies of Women

Biography, the second major form of historical writing on women, has often served as the only way to reconstruct the lives women led. Sources which exist for writing about the world of men do not exist for the majority of women during most periods of history. Biographies are inherently limited, however, in that they can tell us very little about the life-style of the overwhelming majority of women who were not members of a small social elite or who did not pioneer in one of the professions. The work of reconstructing the history of the inarticulate has just begun, and women make up the largest and probably the most silent of society's inarticulate groups. Anyone who has attempted genealogical and demographic research knows that even basic facts about the birth, death, and parenthood of a woman in most historical periods are difficult to find.

Relatively few women have left diaries, letters, and other written sources with which to assess their role and their experience. The very existence of written materials on a woman tells us that she was exceptional: she had the leisure and ability to write, she had the opportunity to experience something other than basic production for her household, and she lived in a family conscious enough of its heritage to preserve family records. Sometimes the existence of written sources on a woman indicates only that she was married to a famous man. Alice Desmond's biography, *Alexander Hamilton's Wife,* is a good case in point.[7] Even when written sources exist, they often prove sadly inadequate to the task of reconstructing a meaningful narrative of a woman's life. The lack of feminist consciousness characteristic of a pre-industrial society made it highly unusual for a woman to write of herself in letters or diaries in a self-conscious way, distinguishing her experience from the experiences of her husband and children. Thus, biography can be a useful tool for understanding the exceptional woman who stands out in history, such as Anne Hutchinson, the Grimké sisters, Margaret Sanger, or Emma Goldman. Uncovering the experiences of "typical" women, or even defining what "typical" means, however, is far more difficult.

Most biographies are limited also because they are narrative and anecdotal: characteristics singled out as unique or eccentric are often emphasized at the expense of analyzing how the subject fit into her social environment. A woman's uniqueness is exaggerated because biographers do not know the options and expectations their subject had, nor do they have perspective on the time, place, and conditions in which she lived and worked. In essence, then, the woman is removed from history.

The psychological assumptions with which biographers have approached their subjects have also affected their work. Writers have worked, often unconsciously, within the confines of psychological theories of woman's nature. Freudian constructs have been the basis for most of their conceptualizations. American historians, in the tradition of psychoanalytic theory, have generally assumed that woman is a naturally passive creature. Although recent debate over the validity of psychoanalytic constructs has made historians more reluctant to make broad generalizations, comprehension and use of Freud's ideas continue at a popular level, providing norms for judging deviance. The recurring statement that Mary Wollstonecraft, or any other feminist, refused her passive social role because of an extreme case of penis envy is the most obvious example of a loose application of a Freudian model to women's history. Explanations of women's motivations for rejecting proscribed roles which center on unresolved Oedipal conflicts or fixations at immature developmental stages are additional examples.[8]

Some historians have rejected the psychoanalytic model in favor of more unsystematized personality theory. They have employed trait theories to explain individual women's personality and motivation. The end result is the same: the historian asks what unique factors forced outstanding women to reject their "natural" role. Robert Riegel, for example, in his book *American Feminists,* criticized historians for underestimating the complexity of feminists' personalities. Too often, he asserted, these women were portrayed as stereotypic spinsters or as simple humanitarians devoted to a maternal concept of social reform. By contrast, he proposed to assess the personalities of feminists and concluded in his collective biography that most American feminists have shared the characteristics of good health, good education, and physical vigor. His biographical vignettes centered on the personal lives of his subjects and downplayed their accomplishments. Again, the historian attempted to explain his subjects in purely individualistic terms and almost completely ignored the social conditions in which they lived.[9]

Recent psychological theories have stressed the cognitive component of motivation and the ability of individuals to formulate and adhere to ideologies as the result of rational observation of their environment's need for change rather than as an attempt to work out unconscious conflicts. Margaret George's biography of Mary Wollstonecraft, *One Woman's Situation,* is an excellent example of a study which does not confound the subject's personal psychological make-up with her feminist politics.[10] For the most part, however, biographers have employed psychological theories in an unsophisticated, piecemeal, and reductionistic manner, failing to realize that psychological theories cannot, and are not intended to, explain the totality of historical experience.

### 3. Histories of Social Ideas

The third form of women's history—the history of social ideas—poses a question common to all historical writing: what is the relationship between ideas and social practice? Histories of social ideas are often based on prescriptive literature such as etiquette books, child-rearing and marriage manuals, and home economics texts; literature, in other words, written to inform contemporaries how they ought to conduct their lives.

These prescriptive studies ask important questions about the nature of social institutions. They attempt to chart changes and developments in child-rearing practices, marriage and divorce customs, and sexual mores, and to relate those developments to a larger ideological framework. Edmund Morgan in *The Puritan Family,* for example, used sermons and Puritan writings to relate seventeenth-century Puritan theology to New England family life. Bernard Wishy, in *The Child and the Republic,* placed changes in attitudes toward children within a context of changing conceptions of environment as a determinant of a child's character.[11]

Although such studies ask important questions, they are often weak in the evidence they employ to answer them. After reading such works, we are left with vague and sometimes inaccurate notions about the nature of actual cultural behavior. We cannot assume that the models of behavior and attitudes found in sermons, books, or magazines accurately reflected how people really acted. Was a Puritan minister describing how his congregation behaved when he wrote about child-rearing or woman's role, or was he describing ideals for his congregation to emulate? Did articles in *Godey's Lady's Book* and other women's magazines describe how middle-class and upper-class parents treated their children, or were the articles largely unrelated to daily life? Prescriptive studies assume a relationship between ideology and social practice which may not always exist.

Histories of social ideas also fail to distinguish between women of different classes. Even if we take the largest estimate of *Godey's* circulation, an estimate which assumes that women handed one issue around among themselves, the majority of American families never saw a copy. Their own practices in any of the areas for which the magazine set standards were not influenced by this source. To say "the child" or "the mother" on the basis of such literary and class-oriented work greatly oversimplifies the complexity of behavior and the class differences in social practice. Finally, too little attention is given to social and economic factors in the histories of social ideas by concentrating on the words of a few taste setters.

### 4. Social Histories

The fourth category of studies in women's history, which we have given the general label of social history, holds the greatest possibilities for future work. New advances in historical methodology coupled with feminist questions promise to expand our knowledge of women's lives throughout American history.

Social histories of women are not new. In the early years of the twentieth century, when a feminist movement was strong, a number of women wrote of their past with historical skill and feminist consciousness. Although their books appear oversimplified when judged by today's standards of social history, works such as Julia Spruill's *Women's Life and Work in the Southern Colonies,* Elisabeth Dexter's *Colonial Women of Affairs,* and Edith Abbott's *Women in Industry*[12] still stand out as exemplary efforts to describe the tasks that women performed, the resources they had, the values they held, and the self-assertion they exhibited. Each book required painstaking surveys of sources which had only peripheral bearing on family life to discover hints of women's activities. The best of these authors recognized that women do not constitute a monolithic and undifferentiated historical category, and they distinguish between women in cities and in rural areas, between planters' wives and female slaves, between European immigrants and established American families. Their generalizations help reconstruct the outline of woman's sphere in different times and places.

Most of these earlier studies presented static vignettes of women's activities at various times. The best of them, however, took account of changes in women's sphere over time. Elisabeth Dexter's study of women in the colonial period is a good case in point. Dexter was familiar with nineteenth-century feminist histories which stressed proscriptions on women's participation in public and economic life. She was aware of the need to account for the contraction of woman's sphere in the late eighteenth and early nineteenth centuries. She looked outside the history of women to such phenomena as the codification of the law, increasing emphasis on wealth and consumption, expanded educational opportunities for men, and the professionalization of occupations such as medicine and law, and she linked the limits on women's lives to those changing conditions.

Recent social histories of women in America have also stressed the ways woman's role and sphere have changed over time. There has been a growing recognition of the fact that the world women have inhabited has its own history, intimately related on one hand to changes in women's lives and, on the other, to developments in world history which have affected the lives of men and women. The organization of society around age differentiations, the privatization of the family, the emergence of a class society, and the development of a cult of motherhood around a biological function, are instances of change, subject to analysis, in women's lives. As Phillippe Ariès asserted in *Centuries of Childhood,* the history of the intimate world of the family and of social relations among family members reflects changes in all modern social and class relations. Thus, some historians are beginning to adopt new ideas about historical significance. They are beginning to integrate women into history, rather than assuming that women's lives and roles have been part of an unchanging, passive, and silent past.[13]

In concrete terms, historians have begun to look at the relationship of women's movements to major social changes in American society, rather than as isolated groups of atypical and eccentric women. Social changes in mid-nineteenth-century America affected women's role in the family, the work that women performed, and ideas about femininity. Although we still do not have precise notions about how burgeoning industrialization affected women, we are beginning to look for connections between social change and the emergence of the nineteenth-century women's rights movement.[14]

In similar fashion, a number of biographers recently have examined the interaction of their subjects with their social environment rather than removing the women they are studying from history and elevating them into heroines. Without denying that women such as Sarah and Angelina Grimké, Mary Wollstonecraft, and Margaret Sanger were exceptional individuals, recent biographies of these women have placed them squarely within the historical context of their lives. Gerda Lerner in her biography *The Grimké Sisters from South Carolina* deals with Angelina and Sarah Grimké as women who grew up in the American antebellum south, and analyzes the content and development of their feminism and abolitionism in this frame of reference. Margaret George discusses Mary Wollstonecraft in *One Woman's Situation* as an archetypal example of the eighteenth-century bourgeois woman, delineates the options open to a woman of her class, and analyzes Wollstonecraft's feminism as a product both of her personal life and her historical situation. David Kennedy, in *Birth Control in America: The Career of Margaret Sanger*, traces Sanger's career within the context of attitudes toward sexuality and medical developments in contraception. All three studies serve as examples of sympathetic analyses which attempt to integrate personal motivational factors and the external social environment.[15]

Social historians are also beginning to probe the connections between women's role in the home and the work she has performed in the labor force. We are becoming aware that we cannot separate women's role in the workplace from her role in the family. Because different class and ethnic groups within American society have had varying family structures and cultural mores regarding woman's role, industrialization did not affect all women in the same ways. Virginia McLaughlin's study of Italian immigrant family patterns in Buffalo, New York, is an excellent example of new ways of examining the impact of social change on women. Her study illustrates the strength and adaptability of traditional pre-industrial family patterns in an industrial society. In addition, her study is important for pointing out the necessity for separate analyses of women's experiences in different classes and ethnic groups.[16]

New social histories, then, are attempting to connect women's experience with historical developments in American society. At the same time, historians of women are beginning to delve more deeply into women's responses to the social changes which affected their lives. Historians are attempting to document women's awareness of social change and their ways of dealing with it. In addition, we are trying to understand how women resisted or tried to circumvent the restrictions placed upon them and how they came to terms with their societal role. In other words, feminist historians are asking what it was like to be a woman at various times in history and are exploring women's subjective responses to their environment. We are trying to learn more about how women interacted with their children, husbands, and parents, and how they began to develop a consciousness of their distinct role in society.

At present most of the new feminist histories are biographical essays of nineteenth-century women writers who revealed their feelings about womanhood through the medium of fiction. Tillie Olsen's biographical essay on Rebecca Harding Davis in the Feminist Press's edition of *Life in the Iron Mills* combines literary analysis of Harding's writings with an insightful discussion of how Harding's fictional characters expressed her own sense of frustration at being confined to a life of " 'unused powers, thwarted energies, starved hopes.' "[17] Other essays such as Ann Wood's "The 'Scribbling Women' and Fanny Fern: Why Women Wrote" attempt to analyze why women felt the need to express themselves through writing.[18]

Women's literary works, of course, make up the most fruitful source for an analysis of women's inner experience. Writing was one of the few options available to women in the years before the twentieth century. Other avenues for self-expression when professional careers of all sorts were closed to women included religious, charitable, and social-reform organizations. Some of the new studies of women in organizations have not focused entirely on the organizational activities themselves, but have tried to explore what needs women were fulfilling by participating in moral reform societies, religious movements, and settlement houses.[19] The history of organized feminism, if undertaken from this viewpoint, would have much to tell us about the process by which women began to think of themselves as women, with a distinct status and distinct problems. Finally, we need to know much more about the subjective responses of working-class women to industrialization and unionization, and how a woman worker's responses to life in the workplace were affected by her perceptions of her role as a woman.

In short, new approaches to women's history are attempting to integrate women into the mainstream of American historical development rather than isolating women as a separate category. Although most new social histories could still be classified in institutional, biographical, or prescriptive categories, more historians are placing their work in a larger historical and social context.

## II

Feminism today challenges society's organization of personal relations at the most intimate level of human experience. It locates the lives of women, all women, at the center of efforts to comprehend and transform social structures. How we identify the essence of history shared by women directly affects efforts to transcend the imposition of contemporary institutions and values on our lives. Without knowledge of historical roots, our view of daily life remains at the level of individual reaction to what strikes us as intolerable. Our analyses tend to document our feelings of subjection rather than the underlying conditions of the subjection of all women. Through *historical* studies of women, as changing diversified participants in social development, we can begin to answer the question, on what basis do women share an historical existence?

The current interest of women in their history is analogous to black Americans' interest in uncovering their past. During the last decade, blacks have shown the role of history in defining a social movement. The search to understand collective conditions and the relation of race to the dominant society has enabled blacks to locate their strengths, their social importance, and the sources of their oppression. Furthermore, this process has provided an analytical framework for recognizing their unity through historical experiences, rather than simply through their racial difference from the ruling caste.[20]

The discovery of women in history begins with a very simple concept: women shared a sexual identity and whatever they did adds substance to their history. To stop at that categorization leaves women outside the dynamics of world development and prevents historians *and* feminists from probing the fullest meaning of history. Once "discovered," women's history has been used to show where things were once better or how women fought in the past or when individual women proved their ability to share fully in society; in short, history somewhat apologetically legitimizes the current struggle.[21] But repeatedly the realization hits us that the past does not contain our vision; we haven't any model of liberation. As feminists we demand something new, a total reconstitution of social relations in order to overcome the alienation we feel.

We barely know the outlines of what has occurred in women's lives and know much less of what within their sphere mediated changes from one period to the next. But if we start from an assumption that women are isolated, timeless, then we impose such a monolith on women's history that we cannot begin to analyze changes women have undergone, especially changes in their consciousness of being a collectivity, and neither can we begin to differentiate the experience of women in different social situations. It is precisely the *interactions* between women's sphere(s) and the "rest" of history that enable us to discover women's contributions to world history and the meaning of their subjection.

The historical analyses of nineteenth-century feminists are readily available for the new movement but with our advantage of hindsight and our perspective on developments in American capitalism, we need to examine them critically. Woman's rights advocates analyzed women's bond as oppression by men and offered definitions of changes necessary to alter that relationship. They found their evidence, as Mary Beard pointed out in 1946, in Blackstone's commentaries on the common law, and, as Elisabeth Dexter wrote in 1931, in the constrained circumstances of their nineteenth-century lives.[22] Their history basically described limits on their lives without a sense of the changes which had occurred in their lifetime. Suffrage proposed access to political power; property-law reform opened avenues to economic power; education broadened access to work; each program chopped away at the roots they identified. Their own emergence as the first fighting force of women in history seemed to them a natural consequence of time passing. In the spirit of democratic optimism, they believed their turn had come in the struggle for freedom. They internalized the "myth" of their secondary status and placed their hopes for change outside of their lives in the industrial revolution or in inevitable progress. Their analysis of women's oppression tended to blur distinctions in women's lives through world history and to blunt their own initiative in nineteenth-century change.

The particular formulations offered by the woman's rights movement as keys to change appealed to very limited sectors of the population. White, middle-class, Protestant women formed the base and, not surprisingly for their time, manifested racist and nativist attitudes toward the other Americans.[23] Their particular historical situation was obscured. They failed to realize that their own consciousness had been made possible by their class position based on the new roles of woman as producer and reproducer introduced by recent industrialization. Abstractly, they sought freedom for all women but without ever defining the condition which all women shared.

This summary is, of course, an oversimplification and an affront to a few really outstanding theorists of woman's rights who pointed out unheard-of directions for social change. But the problems inherent in their analysis recur and the weakness of ahistorical concepts is compounded by repetition. We cannot afford to locate the logic of our movement in apparently anonymous forces, such as "civilization" or "technology," which lie outside women's lives, for by doing so we accept the dominant ideology that the inner dynamics of "woman's sphere" are too slight to examine and too insignificant to have an impact on the course of history.[24]

The nineteenth-century notion that women are bound together by common oppression freezes and levels their enormously diverse experience. That women have suffered oppression is not to be denied. Sexual exploitation, ego damage, the double standard, stereotyping, and discrimination are past as well as present realities. But oppression, even as women consciously employed the concept, meant different things at different times to different groups and classes of women. A historical perspective on women's realization of sexual exploitation as the core of oppression clarifies some of the weakness in leveling historical differences. Today women view sexual exploitation partially in terms of the repressive nature of monogamy that binds a woman to one man. Many complaints center on the denial of equal pleasure to women. For nineteenth-century feminists, sexual exploitation also focused on the unnatural marriage relationship which gave a husband command over his wife's body. But they accepted much of the Victorian double standard and denied feminine sexuality, expressing their grievance at the necessity of vile sex to satisfy their vulgar, sensual husbands. Liberation in practice meant chastity rather than free love.

The conceptual confusion created by unvarying and undifferentiated use of "oppression" to analyze women in the same period of time can be illustrated by the situation of women on an antebellum plantation. For the slave woman, oppression meant physical cruelty and sexual exploitation. For the leisured, financially comfortable plantation mistress, oppression, realized or not, was not physical hardship but social and legal constriction and repressive sexuality. Focusing entirely on the bond women share by virtue of sex, the concept of oppression does little to explain the dynamics of either woman's life or of the historical conditions underlying it. It does violence to the lives of black women and men under slavery and sidesteps white women's role in that enslavement.

In fact, women have been kept apart in their oppression, yet the generalization of their condition, as in the notion of undifferentiated subjugation, implies that women constituted a caste throughout human history. "Caste," in this usage, is an idea imposed on women, a definition derived from their subordinate position in male-dominated culture and applicable to all forms of social organization. It defines the *negativity* of women's relationships with the larger society and, consequently, divorces women's history from its content. To explain the upsurge of collective actions in reform societies, cultural organizations, and woman's rights politics in the nineteenth century, for instance, it is necessary to step outside of women's simple sexual identification and to look at the interactions between their "sphere" and the larger society. That women's activities were proscribed in a given society cannot alone explain their energy; Anne Hutchinson and Anne Bradstreet, for example, could not see common cause in their relationship to the social structure of Massachusetts Bay Colony and yet each resisted her limits individually. [25]

Simone de Beauvoir, who made a decisive contribution in defining the usefulness of what women have shared, specifically rejected the idea that women constitute a caste, because they have not reached the required consciousness of self. [26] Our history must record the movement of women toward consciousness over time and not assume that caste relationships necessarily define its inevitability. Changes in the family structure, the relationship of the family to production, the valuation placed on children, all suggest more useful explanations for women's self-realization between 1630 and the early nineteenth century than do labels of static conditions.

Within time, "caste" subordinates all other class, race, and historical conditions to its primary, sexual contradiction; the dichotomy or antagonism between the sexes is transformed into the theoretical principle underlying history. To assert centuries of sisterhood will not explain, nor help overcome, the historic reality of antagonisms and conflicting experiences among women. We must know as much about what kept women apart as we know about what situation they shared. Working-class women in the last century felt their oppression in class terms and organized around their work; women in ethnic communities recognized the alienation and subjection they shared with men of the same nationalities more than they identified common bondage with Anglo-Saxon women.

The rejection of class in the modern liberation movement is often based on the observation that a woman received her class (or race or nationality) through a man and not through her own productive relations. [27] The historical relevance of that assertion in a period when women increasingly enter the work force is immediately suspect. But more important, the insight explicit in the rejection negates differences in class experience in America. Economic well-being, social relations, life expectancy, and ranges of personal choice are all dependent on the changing relations of classes, and those conditions of daily life are as real for women as for men. It is precisely the interrelationship between women's oppression and ethnic and class experience that enables us to understand why, for example, industrial experience did not necessarily undermine the strength of patriarchal authority over immigrant women.[28]

Calling themselves a caste enabled nineteenth-century women to mobilize around their common feelings of alienation and to begin finding their history. Paradoxically, they transformed their very isolation from male culture into a positive metaphor of shared consciousness. On the one hand, women were said to have been denied the feeling of strength and possession of real power which defined men's control over the world. On the other hand, by virtue of powerlessness women retained a kind of moral superiority over aggressive warlike men. Thus distance from decision-making in society was translated from a description of oppression into a source of strength. A major argument for women's suffrage was the public necessity for an expression of moral values that had been saved in the isolation of woman's sphere. Today the argument surfaces in new dress: women will make the revolution because their hands are clean from the blood, profit, and power with which men have ruled the world.[29]

This argument not only accepts a view of the past in which women were outside of history, but also asserts that now and in the future, the condition which has separated them from men will be the basis for their entrance into history. The very real powerlessness felt and frequently expressed by women of the last two centuries becomes, ironically, a source of misunderstanding about the complexity of women's role. Generalization from specific forms of subjugation may serve only to mystify the real sources of women's strength in their historical evaluation and the specific form of their dependency on the predominantly male world.

Examples of women who gained power within their own sphere by capitalizing on their superiority in moral and cultural realms illustrate the difficulties to come from expecting historical change through the liabilities of women's subjection. Sentimental novelists, motherly reformers, and feminine businesskeepers obviously exerted greater power than their immediate predecessors enjoyed under the constraints of "true womanhood." They may in fact have opened new avenues to social power through the back door of acting very "female." But the experience of twentieth-century women, suffering under a resurgence of femininity, belies the assertion that women thereby transformed the dimensions of sexual differentiation or the repressive demands of monopoly capital.[30]

In essence, analyses of women based on static concepts such as caste or oppressed group render history an external process, a force which presses against women's lives without a reciprocal interaction. Women become in the truest sense the *objects of history,* bound by their peculiar situation as victims of oppression. Without denying what we share as women we must develop categories to fit women into history. The dynamics of women's history occur along two interwoven threads: changes in the multiplicity of women's roles over time and across class, race, and ethnic lines, and movement of women as a group toward consciousness of their common condition.[31] If our histories recognize this dual nature of change we can begin to define the basis of women's experience to include *all women* and to lay the foundation for women to initiate history. Our alienation can then appear in terms of historical development rather than as expressions of personal failure or unique insight. Our situation will begin to appear as a moment in history rather than as a condition of history.

Social and historical definitions of women popular until recently have been essentially characterizations of *womanhood* as a biological fact in the civilization. Only slowly and unevenly have these definitions broken down to allow more complex, closer perspectives on the specific conditions of family, class, and individual role. To the extent that feminism has been active in the process of redefinition, women's "sisterhood" has been affirmed with the ambivalent effect of raising new interest in the study of women *and* providing new forms of potential confusion about women's caste-like position. Historians similarly have often made half-steps toward understanding. Women were assessed at closer range, but too often only through institutions or the narrow range of their own individual biographies (often enough hinging on a psychological interpretation of the woman's inability to achieve happiness by the "normal" routes), further clouding central issues even while providing worthwhile information for a later accounting. Perhaps, as recent work suggests, we are now at a turning point in the nature of the researches. At last, some categories have been established for a social history which seeks the story of women not only as such, but also within the general historical developments that have shaped human action and understanding. We are learning that the writing of women into history necessarily involves redefining and enlarging traditional notions of historical significance, to encompass personal, subjective experience as well as public and political activities. It is not too much to suggest that, however hesitant the actual beginnings, such a methodology implies not only a new history of women but also a new history.

## NOTES

1. Eleanor Flexner, *Century of Struggle: The Woman's Rights Movement in the United States* (New York: Atheneum, 1968); Mildred Adams, *The Right to Be People* (Philadelphia: Lippincott, 1967). Other studies which concentrate chiefly on the suffrage movement are Abbie Graham, *Ladies in Revolt* (New York: Woman's Press, 1934); Olivia E. Coolidge, *Women's Rights: The Suffrage Movement in America, 1848–1920* (New York: Dutton, 1966); and Emily Taft Douglas, *Remember the Ladies* (New York: Putnam, 1966). Over one-half of Eleanor Flexner's *Century of Struggle*, probably the best-known and most widely read general study of American women, is devoted to the suffrage campaign, and the last quarter of the book is devoted to the twelve years before the vote was won. Flexner's work is a detailed and valuable narrative study of the women's rights movement from its beginnings in the abolitionist movement through the ratification of the Nineteenth Amendment. Flexner recognizes the importance of events and developments outside the scope of the movement, but, generally speaking, these aspects of women's history gain significance in her book only through their relation to

the suffrage movement. The chapter on working women, for example, deals with working women's participation in the movement. Adams's *The Right to Be People* is also a narrative account of the women's rights movement, but with an even heavier emphasis on the suffrage campaign. Like Flexner, Adams gives a detailed account of factional struggles within the suffrage movement and a year-by-year account of the fight for the vote.

2. Elizabeth Cady Stanton, Mathilda J. Gage, and Susan B. Anthony, eds., *The History of Woman Suffrage* (New York: Arno Press, 1969), 6 vols.; Carrie Chapman Catt, *Woman Suffrage and Politics: The Inner Story of the Suffrage Movement* (New York: Scribner's, 1926).

3. Belle Squire, *The Woman Movement in America* (Chicago: McClurg, 1911), 285.

4. Adams, *The Right to Be People*, 3.

5. Aileen Kraditor, *The Ideas of the Woman Suffrage Movement* (New York: Columbia University Press, 1965); William O'Neill, *Everyone Was Brave: The Rise and Fall of Feminism in America* (Chicago: Quadrangle, 1969); William H. Chafe, *The American Woman: Her Changing Social, Economic, and Political Roles, 1920–1970* (New York: Oxford University Press, 1972).

6. William O'Neill, "Feminism as a Radical Ideology," in Alfred Young, ed., *Dissent* (DeKalb: Northern Illinois University Press, 1968).

7. Alice Desmond, *Alexander Hamilton's Wife* (New York: Dodd, Mead, 1952).

8. See, for example, Ferdinand Lundberg and Maryna Farnham, *Modern Woman: The Lost Sex* (New York: Harper, 1947). Christopher Lasch, *The New Radicalism in America* (New York: Vintage, 1965) also employs psychoanalytic theory.

9. Robert Riegel, *American Feminists* (Lawrence: University of Kansas Press, 1963).

10. Margaret George, *One Woman's Situation* (Urbana: University of Illinois Press, 1970).

11. Edmund S. Morgan, *The Puritan Family: Religion and Domestic Relations in Seventeenth-Century New England* (New Haven: Yale University Press, 1948); Bernard Wishy, *The Child and the Republic* (Philadelphia: University of Pennsylvania Press, 1967); Margaret Benson, *Women in Eighteenth Century America: A Study of Opinion and Social Usage* (New York: Columbia University Press, 1935) is another good example of prescriptive history.

12. Julia Spruill, *Women's Life and Work in the Southern Colonies* (Chapel Hill: University of North Carolina Press, 1928); Elisabeth Anthony Dexter, *Colonial Women of Affairs: Women in Business and the Professions in America before 1776* (Boston: Houghton Mifflin, 1931, rev. ed.); Edith Abbott, *Women in Industry* (New York: D. Appleton, 1910).

13. Philippe Ariès, *Centuries of Childhood: A Social History of Family Life* (New York: Vintage, 1962). For a good example of one of the first efforts to integrate the history of American women into American social and economic development, see Carl Degler, "Revolution without Ideology: The Changing Place of Woman in America," in Robert Jay Lifton, ed., *The Woman in America* (Boston: Beacon, 1964).

14. See for example Gerda Lerner, "The Lady and the Mill Girl: Changes in the Status of Women in the Age of Jackson," *Midcontinent American Studies Journal* X (1969). Also see Carl Degler, "Revolution without Ideology," and Nancy Cott, ed., *Root of Bitterness* (New York: Dutton, 1972).

15. Gerda Lerner, *The Grimké Sisters from South Carolina* (Boston: Houghton Mifflin, 1967); George, *One Woman's Situation*; David Kennedy, *Birth Control in America: The Career of Margaret Sanger* (New Haven: Yale University Press, 1970).

16. Virginia McLaughlin, "Patterns of Work and Family Organization: Buffalo's Italians," *Journal of Interdisciplinary History* II (Autumn 1971).

17. Tillie Olsen, "A Biographical Interpretation," in intro. to Rebecca Harding Davis, *Life in the Iron Mills* (Old Westbury, N.Y.: Feminist Press, 1972), 79.

18. Ann Wood, "The 'Scribbling Women' and Fanny Fern: Why Women Wrote," *American Quarterly* XXIII (Spring 1971), and Ann Wood, "Mrs. Sigourney and the Sensibility of Inner Space," *New England Quarterly* XLV (June 1972), 163–81.

19. See for example J. P. Rousmaniere, "Cultural Hybrid in the Slums: The College Woman and the Settlement House, 1889–1894," *American Quarterly* XXII (1970); Carroll Smith-Rosenberg, *Religion and the Rise of the American City: The New York City Mission Movement, 1812–1870* (Ithaca: Cornell University Press, 1971); Gail Parker, "Mary Baker Eddy and Sentimental Womanhood," *New England Quarterly* XLIII (March 1970); Barbara Welter, "The Feminization of American Religion, 1800–1860," in William L. O'Neill, *Problems and Issues in Social History* (Minneapolis: Burgess, 1973).

20. An example which might serve as a model for work in women's history is Harold M. Baron, *The Demand for Black Labor: Historical Notes on the Political Economy of Racism,* pamphlet (Cambridge, Mass.: Radical America, 1971).

21. See for example the selection made in Leslie B. Tanner, ed., *Voices from Women's Liberation* (New York: New American Library, 1970); Miriam Schneir, ed., *Feminism: The Essential Historical Writings* (New York: Random House, 1972).

22. Mary Beard, *Woman As Force in History* (New York: Macmillan, 1946); Dexter, *Colonial Women of Affairs.* For a discussion of Beard's uses of history and critique of feminists see Berenice A. Carroll, "Mary Beard's *Woman As Force in History:* A Critique," in this volume.

23. For critical appraisals of nineteenth-century woman's rights, see Kraditor, *The Ideas of the Woman Suffrage Movement*; O'Neill, *Everyone Was Brave* and "Feminism as a Radical Ideology."

24. Shulamith Firestone, *The Dialectic of Sex: The Case for Feminist Revolution* (New York: Morrow, 1970) argues that technology will liberate women. Mary Beard relies to some extent on "civilization" and "progress" to accomplish the same ends.

25. Roxanne Dunbar, "Female Liberation as the Basis for Social Revolution," in Robin Morgan, ed., *Sisterhood Is Powerful* (New York: Random House, 1970), 477–92 presents the most cogent argument for caste as the descriptive category for women's position. See also Ti-Grace Atkinson, "Radical Feminism," in *Notes from the Second Year: Women's Liberation* (New York, 1970) and "Redstockings Manifesto," in the same publication. Both of these use the word "class" but to the same effect as others use the word "caste." Elizabeth Wade White, *Anne Bradstreet, The Tenth Muse* (New York: Oxford University Press, 1971) discusses the historical coincidence of the two Annes along with other rebellious women of the Bay Colony.

26. Simone de Beauvoir, *The Second Sex* (New York: Modern Library, 1969), 129.

27. The "Redstockings Manifesto," for example, says "We repudiate all economic, racial, educational or status privileges that divide us from other women." Kate Millett, *Sexual Politics* (Garden City, N.Y.: Doubleday, 1970), also argues on the basis of a repudiation of historical conditions.

28. McLaughlin, "Patterns of Work and Family Organization."

29. See Branka Magas, "Sex Politics: Class Politics," *New Left Review,* no. 66 (March–April 1971), for a lengthy discussion of this point.

30. Glenda Gates Riley, "The Subtle Subversion: Changes in the Traditionalist Image of the American Woman," *Historian* XXXII (1970), 210–27. A good critique of the "sentimental subversion" is in Jill Conway's "Women Reformers and American Culture, 1870–1930," *Journal of Social History* V (1971), 164–77.

31. In two edited works, Mary Beard attempted such history by collecting women's

descriptions of their own work, humor, and sense of history; both books are still valuable source collections as well: *America through Women's Eyes* (New York: Macmillan Co., 1933) and, with Martha Bensley Bruere, *Laughing Their Way: Women's Humor in America* (New York: Macmillan Co., 1934). More recently, Juliet Mitchell, in *Woman's Estate* (New York: Pantheon Books, 1971) offers a theoretical framework for differentiating women's historical experience through the changing relationship of their roles; she also applies her model to recent (post-World War II) history. Sheila Rowbotham, *Women, Resistance and Revolution* (New York: Pantheon Books, 1972) examines the relationship between feminism and socialism; her analyses are sensitive to the uniqueness of feminists among all women and the need to understand women's position in terms of a comprehensive history.

# PART II

# On Ideology, Sex, and History

The papers in this section, as well as those in Part III, offer case studies and surveys relevant to testing various theories, assumptions, or models. In this section, the papers tend to emphasize the influence of ideology and tradition on the position of women, or seek to assess these influences as compared with the effects of class differences or other material conditions. The premise is stated most explicitly by Hilda Smith in the first paper, on "Gynecology and Ideology in Seventeenth-Century England": "It will be the purpose of this paper to explore the extent to which ideological preconceptions and values relating to woman's 'nature' influenced both the medical treatment accorded to women in seventeenth-century England, and also helped justify the exclusion of women from the practice of medicine." In the second essay, Adele Simmons traces the influence of attitudes toward women upon the educational goals and practices of American educational institutions in the nineteenth century.

Amy Hackett's essay, "Feminism and Liberalism in Wilhelmine Germany," examines the dilemma of German feminists whose goals and values for women came into conflict with their loyalty to liberalism as it was known in the political milieu of their time, even though they believed that ideally the women's movement and liberalism were one. In an ideological climate in which national welfare was high on the scale of liberal values while equal rights for women were not, and in which feminists generally identified themselves with the liberal parties, there seemed little choice but to compromise feminist goals.

But the same problem confronted working-class women, as Robin Jacoby shows in "Feminism and Class Consciousness in the British and American Trade Union Leagues, 1890–1925." The indifference or hostility of working-class men toward feminist issues, and the primacy of goals and values based on class consciousness among the trade-union women, caused feminist goals to be compromised or abandoned in the trade-union league movement the same way they were among German liberals. As Jacoby notes, in 1922 Gertrud Hanna, speaking for German working women, opposed the International Federation of Working Women on the basis that ". . . women do not and cannot unite independently of existing parties for the furtherance of their own interests, but that their resolutions are influenced by their political outlook, and that men and women both vote for the party to which they belong, without regard to sex." To what extent this phenomenon, reproduced in parallel fashion across class lines, should be attributed to class differences in themselves, or on the other hand to an ideology of class loyalty and subordinacy of women's interests as such, remains to be determined.

The two papers which follow offer more broad-ranging surveys of the history of women in Latin American and Afro-American cultures. Ann M. Pescatello traces the changing conditions of women in Ibero-American societies from their background of Iberian, African, and native American cultures to the present status of women in Argentina, Mexico, Cuba, Peru, and Brazil. She observes the strong influence of traditional patterns and attitudes toward women throughout, but also shows significant variations by class. In general, Pescatello concludes, working-class women "seem to share circumstances and values in common, across cultures," while the constraints and opportunities of women in upper and middle strata may vary more widely in response to traditional cultural influences and ideological change.

Joyce Ladner, in the excerpt reprinted here from her book, *Tomorrow's Tomorrow*, considers the contemporary debate concerning the character of the black family and the position of women in black American society, focusing upon the relative influence of precolonial West African cultures on the one hand, and slavery and other forms of structural oppression on the other hand. Ladner does not offer a clear-cut conclusion on this issue, but introduces the views of some of the main participants in the debate, and some of the supporting evidence.

In the last paper in this section, Kay Boals attempts to apply to the study of women in Algeria a model she suggests for studying "the dialectic between culturally dominant and culturally oppressed groups." Boals distinguishes six types of consciousness as significant in the process of self-liberation of oppressed groups, and suggests that such groups (as groups, though not necessarily their individual members) will tend to pass through these types or stages of consciousness in a certain sequence. Though some readers will be inclined to challenge details of the proposed model, or the central emphasis it places on consciousness, Boals's essay contributes an unusual and provocative development and application of theory in women's history.

# Gynecology and Ideology
# in Seventeenth-Century England

## Hilda Smith

It will be the purpose of this paper to explore the extent to which ideological preconceptions and values relating to woman's "nature" influenced the medical treatment accorded to women in seventeenth-century England, and also helped justify the exclusion of women from the practice of medicine. I will consider first the influence of such preconceptions and values on the content of some gynecological texts of the period; second, the presence of these ideas in the works of more prominent physicians; and third, the role of these concepts in preventing women from entering the medical profession.

Understanding the gynecological texts of seventeenth-century England is not a simple task. Perhaps the greatest difficulty in reaching such an understanding is that of placing these works in historical perspective. This difficulty stems from two sources: first, the inadequacy of the available histories of gynecology, and second, the fact that we know nothing about most of the authors who were writing about obstetrics and gynecology during the 1600s. As is the case with most histories of medicine, the authors tend to be physicians rather than historians, and often fail to pose proper historical questions. There is little, if any, attempt at generalization, and when an author does attempt a judgment it is often so vague or wide-sweeping as to be meaningless.

For instance, both Richard A. Leonardo and Theodore Cianfrani in their histories state that scientific gynecology did not exist until the eighteenth century.[1] What is meant by such a statement is never clarified, and no real distinction is made between the gynecological improvements before and after 1700. The works jump from unsupported broad-scale generalizations to a series of individual exploits of contemporary physicians. Perhaps two quotations from the introductory material to Cianfrani's chapter on the seventeenth century will help suggest the nature of these histories: "The 17th century was an era of great names such as Thomas Hobbes, Sir Isaac Newton, Francis Bacon, Pepys, Burton, Dryden, John Locke, Sir Thomas Browne, the Chamberlens and greatest of all, William Harvey," and "The seventeenth century has often been called the 'age of physiology' because of the discovery of the circulation of the blood by Harvey in 1616 in England, an event that has been considered the greatest physiological discovery of all time."[2] Cianfrani then follows this discussion with a listing of the accomplishments of seventeenth-century physicians. Although some of what he says is interesting, it is useless in helping one form a theoretical framework for understanding seventeenth-century gynecology either in its contemporary setting or in its relationship to earlier or later writings in the area.

Further, as noted earlier, the men who wrote gynecological texts were often obscure individuals. It is difficult to find information about their medical philosophies or particular role, if any, in seventeenth-century medicine. Normally one can find only a short entry in the *Dictionary of National Biography* limited to a brief biographical sketch. The more important physicians gave little, if any, interest to the study or practice of obstetrics and gynecology, and one can find only brief passages concerning women's diseases in the works of Thomas Willis or Thomas Sydenham. Even William Harvey's *De Generatione Animalium* deals only briefly with the topic of human reproduction; the bulk of his work is devoted to reproduction in chickens and deer. There was little original work done in gynecological research and most of the gynecological texts were either translations, plagiarisms of earlier works, or works whose authors readily admitted their only source of authority was the ancient texts. The one exception to this mediocrity may be Nicholas Culpeper, but his originality is confined more to the area of proper treatment rather than medical research. The difficulty, then, is the inability to discover any underlying theoretical framework in these works on which their description of various drugs or treatments are based.

Although histories of medicine in general are often of an inferior quality, those dealing with gynecology have special difficulties. First, since they are not dealing with the great discoveries of medicine, the authors often include material less for its significance than for its curiosity. Second, and most significant for the scope of this paper, the authors have managed to write the history of gynecology and ignore the fact that they are writing about women. The one unifying factor among gynecological texts is an accepted view of women's social and physical character and its relationship to the state of their health. Yet, historians of gynecology totally ignore this sexual framework. By so doing they have omitted a fundamental element in the physician's diagnosis, in his treatment, and even in his most basic understanding of what is a "healthy" or a "sick" woman. Further, not only was a general attitude of women's peculiarity the basis for special medical treatment, it influenced who could read these texts and who could practice the medicine contained within them, as well. The seventeenth century was a crucial period in removing women from their traditional role as caretakers of the family's and village's health. Alice Clark in *The Working Life of Women in the Seventeenth Century* outlines the tactics used by newly formed medical guilds to exclude women from their number and from their particular practice.[3] The question of what medical treatment women should receive and who should treat them was inextricably connected with the view of women's special nature.

I

The gynecological and obstetrical literature of the seventeenth century presents a picture of women as beings whose health was determined, most basically, by the fact that they were female. To be a woman meant that one was subject to fevers and ill vapors arising from a malfunctioning menstrual cycle, to hysteria resulting from a diseased womb, and to general bad health developing from a life of ease. Women as dictated by their anatomy were less healthful creatures than men. This assumption, with its myriad corollaries, was a basic tenet of seventeenth-century gynecology.

This is not to dispute the fact that medical care in general during this period was based on ignorance and often did as much harm as good. However, the writers on women's diseases provided sexual stereotypes of women's physical inferiority as explanation for an internal sexual structure they did not understand. Since medical research was backward in the field of gynecology and their theories agreed with the general social attitudes toward women, they held sway until quite recently. It was quite late when medicine discovered the most basic facts of women's reproductive functions. It was not until 1827 that the existence of the ovum was discovered and only with the twentieth century that ovulation was finally understood. Only well into the nineteenth century was there any significant reduction in maternal deaths.[4] Seventeenth-century gynecology was a combination of ignorance about internal medicine, bias against women, and an almost total reliance on the ancients.

In 1651 Nicholas Culpeper wrote *A Directory for Midwives; or, A Guide for Women, In their Conception, Bearing and Suckling their Children.* Culpeper's work was followed during the decade by four other books, texts on women's diseases and guides for midwives written by others partly to cash in on the financial success of his work and partially as an attack on Culpeper's lack of practical knowledge. On his title page Culpeper described himself as a "Gentleman Student in Physick and Astrologie." Although he had had some practical experience as a physician, Culpeper's aim was to establish principles of self-help for women and midwives, not to write a medical textbook.[5] Although I will discuss Culpeper's advanced views concerning the role of midwives in a later section, at the moment I am concerned with his work merely as an example, and one of the earliest, of medical guides for women. His work was organized similarly to other texts of the period—the first section being devoted to a description of the genital organs of first men, then women; the second to the formulation of the child in the womb; the third to hinrances to conception and remedies for barrenness; the fourth to furtherance of conception; the fifth to a guide for women during conception; the sixth to miscarriage; the seventh to a guide to women in labor with live children; the eighth to a guide for women in their lying-in; and the last to nursing children.[6] However, the chapter headings here are deceptive, as they are in other medical guides for women written during the 1650s, because they give an illusion of having a straightforward informational approach which the chapters themselves did not have. All sections of these texts included moral and religious admonitions along with warnings against sexual taboos. For example, Culpeper in his section on women in labor with live children included a paragraph in which he advised women to: "Learn, to know your first Evil, which was Pride. To be humbled for it. To look after a Spiritual Being, seeing your natural is so defective."[7]

In attempting to analyze or evaluate Culpeper's work and those of his successors it is necessary to remember the primitive level of internal medicine and the dependence of the authors on ancient sources as respected authorities. Galen and Hippocrates were continually quoted or referred to in the various texts. Although many writers included independent judgments and individual criticisms of the ancients, they had no independent criteria for medical expertise and their criticisms are normally based on personal, practical experience or hearsay evidence. This lends a tone of defensiveness to the texts in general. The works, in general, closely resemble one another; and there is little impressive about them.

The section of each text which most reveals medical attitudes toward women is the introductory material which establishes the physiological and anatomical structure for the diseases and medicines which appear later in the work. This section is of particular significance because the material it contains is referred to regularly in the subsequent sections; the physiological structure of women in contrast with men was thought to be the most important factor in diagnosing and treating their ailments. The meshing of cultural values and physiological description is well revealed in the first chapter of *The Womans Doctour: or, an exact and distinct Explanation of all such Diseases as are peculiar to that Sex.* The first sentence of that 1652 work sets the tone:

> Women were made to stay at home, and to looke after Household employments, and because such business is accomplished with much ease, without any vehement stirings of the body, therefore hath provident Nature assigned them their monthly courses, that by the benefit of those evacuations, the feculent and corrupt bloud might be purified, which otherwise, as being the purest part of the bloud, would turne to ranke poyson; like the seed ejaculated out of its proper vessells.[8]

That menstruation is necessary because women supposedly live sedentary lives is a typical example of the manner in which physicians integrated their daily observations of women into their views on women's physical make-up. In this way they filled in the gap created by the general ignorance among doctors and laymen. It is difficult to stress too greatly the constant interweaving of woman's social and sexual functions in the determination of her proper diagnosis and treatment.

First, the structure of women's sexual organs formed the basis for any disease which they might contract. In continuing with the physiological analysis in *The Womans Doctour,* the author stated that Hippocrates "had a perfect understanding of these things" when he stated "that the Matrix [meaning the womb, or often the entire female sexual structure] is the cause of all those diseases which happen to women." It is interesting to read at length a section which reveals the practical application of this viewpoint:

> the Matrix hath a Sympathy with all the parts of the body; as with the Braine by the Nerves and Membranes of the parts about the spine, from whence sometimes ariseth the paines, in the fore part, and the hinder part of the head, with Heart also, both by the Spermatick, and the Epigastrick arteries, or those that lie about the abdomen at the bottome of the bellie, from hence cometh the paine of the heart, fainting and

swounding fits, the passion of the Heart, anxietie of minde, dissolution of the spirits, insomuch as you cannot discerne, whether a woman breaths or not, or that she hath any pulse; it hath likewise a consent with the breasts; and from hence proceed those swellings, that hardness, and those terrible cancers that afflict those tender parts, that a humour doth flow upwards, from the Matrix to the Breasts, and downwards again, from the Breasts to the Matrix. . . .[9]

As is obvious from the above quotation, women's sexual make-up was not only related to sexual diseases but to more general illnesses ranging from headaches to consumption.

The author points out that the above is agreed upon by Galen, Hippocrates, Laurentius, and Duretus. That sexual functions and relationships were the controlling factors in a treatise on women's health problems is revealed even more clearly by the four classes of women's diseases. This list, following the discussion on the womb, included: diseases common to all women, those peculiar to widows and virgins, those relating to both barren and fruitful women, and those of pregnant women and women nursing babies. A woman's sexual status played an integral role in the condition of her health. Sexual intercourse was considered a proper cure for many diseases and married women were believed to be the most healthy of the above classes: "Married women overcome menstral difficulties by lying with their husbands, so loosen the passages of the seed and so the courses come down more easily thorow them. . . . Wives are more healthfull then Widowes, or Virgins, because they are refreshed with the mans seed, and ejaculate their own, which being excluded, the cause of the evill is taken away."[10]

The most important link between a woman's sexual structure and the status of her health, together with the sympathy between the womb and the other parts of the body, was the universal importance of menstrual periods. Diseases which affect all women "proceed from the retention, or stoppage of their courses, as the most universall, and most usual cause."[11] Almost all of the remedies devised for women's illnesses were designed to either increase or decrease the flow of menstrual blood, depending on whether the physician believed the problem to be one of stoppage or too heavy a flow. These remedies incorporated most of the commonly used medications of the period. Patients were either bled, given herbs in either oral dosage or suppositories, or had suction cups applied, particularly to the breasts, to draw out the evil vapors. Also women's thighs were either tightly bound to stop too heavy a flow or holes were cut in them to remove the evil humors or bile which coagulated and putrified the blood. Scarification was one of the purposes of the cupping glasses applied to the breasts, although there was no explanation as to how scarring the tissue around the breasts would affect a cure for retention of menstrual blood. All of these remedies were directed toward reaching a proper menstrual flow. If a physician wanted the blood to flow upward toward the womb (to decrease its flow) he would bleed the woman in her arms, but if he wanted the blood to flow downward (during a period of retention) then he would bleed her around her knees and ankles and the blood would flow toward the direction of the incision. One of the most bizarre medications for retention of menstrual blood was a solution of ground steel taken orally for the purpose of cutting the thickness of the retained blood.[12] Each of these medications reflects not only the primitive level of medical treatment, but the real dangers involved in the assumption that women's sexual make-up controlled many of their other bodily functions. If it were thought necessary to treat women's diseases by indirectly administering to an internal sexual system which was little understood, many opportunities existed for either useless or even harmful treatments to be employed.

It was not only in the area of proper medication that women's biological structure was deemed crucial, but in the general status of her health as well. The accepted views of women's inferior structure provided the key factor in determining what was the truly "healthy" state of the female. It is in this context of the actual physical make-up of men and women as determined from birth that their proper temperaments, life-styles, and state of health must be judged. Although it was believed that there existed many variations in the sperm (seed) which produced a male or a female, most of these sexual differences were thought to center around the degree of temperature and amount of moisture in the seed. As the author of *The Compleat Midwifes Practice Enlarged* stated: "... that heat extendeth and enlargeth all things, and cold retaineth and closeth them up ... and therefore if the seed be cold and moist, a woman is begotten, not a man; and if the same be hot and dry, a man is begotten, not a woman; whence it is to be inferred that there is no man to be termed cold in respect of a woman, nor woman hot in respect of a man." Men are by nature more hot and dry, while women are cold and moist. There are three degrees or intensities of temperature and moisture, and women of the first degree of moist and cold are most like men. And, as the author continued, women of this first degree are best determined, "First, by the quick apprehension and acuteness of wit in women, for if they be very witty and acute, they are to be judged cold and moist in the first degree onely, if very shallow and simple, in the third degree, but if they partake of a middle nature between these two extreams, it signifieth that they are in the second degree."[13]

In accordance with the ancients' praise of a golden mean the second-degree woman was the one to be most admired. The author continued his list of characteristics for each of the three degrees (from the first, which tended to be slender and possess a voice of masculine volume, to the third, which tended toward obesity and a faint voice), and he found those women of the second degree to be close to perfection. He conceived their qualities as follows: "... a handsome form and proportion of body is the result of the middlemost degree, deformity arising from either extream." He then stated what was the most important attribute of the second-degree woman: "Now from all these signes it may be concluded that those women, who are cold and moist in the second degree are of the perfect temper, and the best capacity as to their own proper nature, of bringing forth children." Further, the woman of the middle range may more easily and successfully mate with men of any of the three degrees of masculine heat and dryness "because she comes nearest in proportion to men of each several temperatures." The woman of the second degree also possessed a good nature, didn't lack hair nor have an overabundance of it, and was of a "fresh and lively colour."[14] Women should imitate (as much as their physical make-up would allow) this feminine epitome of the golden mean. It is interesting to note, as well, how the temperament and mental ability of the woman formed an essential element in her classification into the three physical types.

Of course not all women could be of the median degree of warmth and moisture and it was, therefore, necessary for them to marry a man who would compensate for their failing in being either too hot or too cold. The following explanation of successful mating between a "masculine" woman and a "feminine" man reveals just how varied and established were those categories which divided both men and women on the basis of their emotional, mental, and physical composition: ". . . it is to be concluded that a woman who is wity, ill conditioned, shrill vocy't, lean, swarthy coloured, and deformed, (which are the signs of cold, and moist in the first degree) may conceive by a man, who is ignorant, good-natured, sweet-voyc't, corpulent, having little hair, a well-colured face, and a handsome body, which are the signs of hot and dry in the first degree. . . ."[15]

The broad scope of these sexual categories is made even more clear in the next section of *The Compleat Midwifes Practice Enlarged,* entitled "What course is to be taken that male children be brought into the world, not a female." The author introduced this segment with this reasoning behind the advisability of producing male children: "Those who seek the comfort of having wise children, must indeavor that they be born male; for the Female, through the cold and moist of their Sex, cannot be indowed with so profound a judgement; we find indeed that they take with appearance of knowledge in sleight and easie matters, but seldom reach any farther than to a sleight superficial smattering in any deep Science." The medical opinion that men were naturally more intelligent than women was attributed to their physical construction. As the author noted: "[moisture] stifleth the operations of the rational soul, and also occasioneth sicknesse and short life. . . . so that it appears that a good wit, and a sound body arise from one and the same quality, namely, drynesse. . . ." Supporting this belief are the remedies for dullness, such as the recommendation that children should be washed with salt water at birth to dry up the moisture in the brain and thereby strengthen their wit. This section on the relationship between intelligence and temperature is followed by the typical distinction between the formation of the seed which produces a girl or a boy. Men are produced by seed from the right testicle, which is hot and dry, while women come from the left, which produces cold and moist seed. To prevent the conception of a girl he suggested several remedies, including eating hot and dry meats, eating moderately, not having intercourse until the seed is well developed, and finally, to "procure that both the seeds of the husband and wife fall into the right side of the womb."[16] It was believed that women possessed sperm (seed) comparable to the male's, and that the ovaries were merely internal testes.

It is difficult to adequately portray the sexual stereotypes conveyed in these medical tracts by a standard explication of their contents. The conscious and unconscious interweaving of value judgments on the proper life-styles of both sexes with the accepted medical and physiological analyses of the day created intellectual and respectable bases for viewing woman as both a distinctly inferior and medically unique creature. It is not so much what was argued forthrightly in these texts, but rather those views which were taken for granted that set a tone of unquestioning orthodoxy to their opinions about women. The distinctive roles of men and women, women's major function in child-bearing, and the physiological incapacities which kept women properly at home and away from either responsible positions or intellectual endeavors, were continually recurring themes.

In attempting to catch the spirit of these tracts, apart from their formulation of medical advice, one is struck by the emphasis placed on the relationship between women's illnesses and their immoral and sensual natures. This too, however, evolved from their physical make-up. The right testicle (from which came the seed which produced males) is hotter "because it receives more hot and pure bloud," while the left testicle (which produced females) "are most full of seed, and most prone to venery."[17] Although the term, "venery" was used in various contexts, it basically meant a high degree of sensuality and an excessive interest in sex. This led these authors into the normal dilemma of those who accepted the view of women's greater sensuality while advocating a chaste and modest womanhood. Thus women, who were created with a venerous nature, were required to be as pure as men—indeed, they were required to be purer. There is at least some evidence that seventeenth-century medical writers faced this dilemma more squarely than Victorian authors. This is evident in the advice presented in *The Compleat Midwifes Practice* for widows who had to exist without their normal sexual relationships and who had difficulty doing so:

> We must conclude that if they be young, of a black complexion, and hairie, and are likewise somewhat discoloured in their cheeks, that they have a spirit of falacity, and feele within themselves of frequent titillation, their seed being hot and prurient, doth irritate and inflame them to venery; neither is this concupiscence allaid and qualified, but by provoking the ejaculation of the seed, as Galen propounds the advice in the example of a widow, who was affected with intolerable symptoms, till the abundance of the spermatick humour was diminished by the hand of a skillful midwife, and a convenient oyntment, which passage will also furnish us with this argument, that the use of venery is exceedingly wholesome, if the woman will confine herselfe to the laws of moderation, so that she feele no wearisomnesse, nor weaknesse in her body, after pleasing conflicts.[18]

It was therefore acceptable for a woman to resort to masturbation if she was in sufficient discomfort from lack of sexual activity, and it was even considered sufficiently a medical problem that a midwife could be called in if the woman were unable to find relief. This does not mean, of course, that promiscuity was encouraged either on social or medical grounds; rather, on the contrary, it was believed that too much sexual activity could alter women's internal physiology. It was noted that excessive sexual activity could alter the neck of the womb, and that "in women with often copulation, they are oftentimes worn out, sometimes they are wholly worn out, and the inner side of the neck appears smooth, as it happens to whores."[19] It was contended by physicians writing on the diseases of women that their health was affected by their physical weaknesses, their sensual natures, their life of ease, the primacy of their sexual function, and their cold and moist constitutions which made them more susceptible to illness than men.

## II

Before discussing the general topic of women's declining role in the medical profession during the 1600s, I would like to deal briefly with the views of more renowned physicians toward women's particular medical difficulties. Neither William Harvey, Thomas Willis, nor Thomas Sydenham wrote much about the analysis or treatment of women's diseases, but what they did reveals that they were not greatly advanced over their less-learned colleagues. Ilza Veith, however, in *Hysteria: The History of a Disease,* does view Willis as an enlightened voice in the medical controversy over the cause of hysteria.[20] She points out that he was one of the earliest physicians to argue that hysteria had a cerebral origin and did not develop from a diseased womb, as the accepted medical opinion held. Although William Harvey wrote the first original text on gynecology since the ancients, he had little to say about human reproduction. Thomas Sydenham devoted even less attention to women than Harvey and Willis, and his views differ little from the gynecological writers previously discussed.

In searching William Harvey's *De Generatione Animalium* for references to human reproduction one finds only scattered, unsystematic comments. Although Harvey's work is considered the only original gynecological text of the seventeenth century, it is devoted primarily to reproduction in deer and the development of the chick within the egg. His only significant comments on human reproduction deal with spontaneous generation (the possibility of which he apparently accepted), and the ability of a baby to propel itself from the womb, if the normal muscle contractions were impaired. He presents two examples of children expelled by their own force from the mother when the uterine tract was blocked. One involved a woman who died and whose baby was found between her legs the following morning; the other instance was a child who had sufficient force to push its way out of a diseased and blocked uterus. Harvey attests to the authenticity of both cases.[21] Harvey's gynecological writing was, therefore, both severely limited and highly questionable.

Thomas Willis wrote no specific work on human reproduction or the diseases of women, but he did have occasion to speak of hysteria and puerperal fever in his general work on fevers. Although he held an advanced view on the causes and nature of hysteria, he expressed many of the accepted medical opinions toward women in his writings. In a collection of his writings entitled, *The London Practice of Physick: or the whole Practical Part of Physick contained in the works of Dr. Willis,* published in 1685, Thomas Willis relates difficulties in childbirth to the social station of the woman giving birth. It is useful to present his analysis in its entirety, since he reveals his assumptions on the relevance of woman's morality and social position to her health so clearly here. His comments refer to the likelihood of a woman contracting puerperal fever following her lying-in:

> for poor Women, Hirelings, Rusticks, and others us'd to hard Labours, also Viragoes, and Whores, who are clandestinely delivered, bring forth without great difficulty, and in a short time after, rising from their Bed, return to their wonted Labours; but Women that are rich, tender and beautiful, and many living a sedentary Life, as tho they partak'd of the Divine Curse after a more severe manner, *bring forth in pain,* and presently after their delivery lye in an uneasie and dangerous condition: the reason of which seems to lye in this, that those that use much exercise, continually exagitate, and eventilate the Blood, and therefore after the Menses are stopt, heap together fewer Miasms for the matter of the Disease; Moreover, labouring and active Women, having the nervous Parts more firm, are less subject to convulsive motions, and the affects vulgarly called hysterical: on the contrary, in nice women, and such as live idly, during the time of their being with child the mass of Blood becomes impure and fermentative: moreover, because they have the Brain and the System of nerves tender and weak, upon any light occasion they undergoe Distractions of the animal Spirits, and disorderly motions of the Nervous Parts: and here it is to be noted by the by, that Women before Men, and some of that Sex before others, are troubled with the Affects called hysterical, not so much by reason of the fault of the Womb it self, but by reason of the Weaker Constitutions of the Brain and *Genus Nervosum:* for in Persons so affected, Passions of Anger, Fear, Sadness; also all vehement or strong Objects easily pervert the Crases or Functions of those parts, which when they have once been injur'd, they afterward in a manner always accustom themselves to the same Irregularities.[22]

Although we cannot expect Willis to realize that pain in childbirth is dictated more by the pelvic structure than by personal idleness, or that puerperal fever originated from unsterile delivery conditions, it is significant that he employs the social and sexual stereotypes of women to explain phenomena for which he has no adequate medical explanation. Or perhaps more accurately, phenomena for which he conceives no need for further explanation.

As noted earlier, Willis did differ with general medical opinion on the causes of hysteria. And here his views are relevant to the whole question of women's medical peculiarities. By removing the source for symptoms of hysteria from the womb to the brain, he contends that its origin is mental and not sexual disturbance. Further, males can be susceptible to the disease as well. It is interesting to compare his skeptical, critical views on the origin of hysteria with his previous opinions on childbirth:

> If at any time an unusual sort of sickness, of a very Secret Origine occurs in the Body of a Woman, so that its cause lies hid, and the Therapeutick Indication be wholly uncertain, presently we accuse the evil influence of the Womb (which for the most part is guiltless) and in any unusual Symptom, we cry out that there is somewhat Hysterical in

it; and consequently the Physical intentions and the uses of Remedies are directed for this end, which often is only a starting hole for Ignorance.[23]

Next, Willis notes that he has witnessed hysteria in all types of women—rich and poor, virgin, wife or widow—and, he continues, ". . . nay and men are sometimes troubled with such kind of Passions, instances of which are not wanting."[24] He therefore not only criticizes medical opinion for wrongly accusing the womb as being the seat for hysteria and dismisses the view that it was purely a female ailment, but he does so by laying the blame at the physician's proclivity to designate the womb as culprit for any woman's disease he cannot diagnose.

Thomas Sydenham did not hold Willis's advanced views on hysteria and viewed it not only as a disease exclusively female, but one connected with the patient's social habits, as well. He held that "Such women as are of a crude and lax Habit of Body are chiefly afflicted with this Disease. . . ."[25] He compared hysteria in women to the "Bilious Cholick" in men. Further, he argued that hysteria was often brought on by overzealous and arrogant midwives who, wishing to show off their skill, encouraged weak women to rise too quickly from their bed. Other than these few comments, Sydenham had little to say about the treatment of women.

One comes away from the study of seventeenth-century gynecological writing with an overview of woman as a unique sexual, social, moral, and medical creature. Women's illnesses were viewed in the context of their sexually and socially defined roles. This underlying assumption of their distinctiveness often caused physicians not to investigate behavior or maladies which they believed to be characteristic of women, particularly nervous instability. Further, it encouraged them to focus their analysis of women's illnesses on their sexual make-up. Although there were, without doubt, other bases for irrational judgments about human disease, sexuality was unique to women, and was used to explain their health and behavior in a way never applied to men. It is obvious that by having babies women perform a particular sexual function, but it does not follow, as it did in the mind of seventeenth-century physicians, that this function must dictate the general status of their health. Nor does it follow that there is some natural connection among woman's sexual function, general morality or social status, and health. But it is precisely in these areas that the seventeenth-century physician filled in the gaps of his medical knowledge with the accepted views (both ancient and contemporary) of women's special weaknesses. For this reason, it is not possible to view accurately seventeenth-century gynecological writings as mere guides to women's diseases, without seeing them as well as repositories for the general bias of the population against women.

### III

In areas relevant to the relationship between women and medicine in the seventeenth century, this bias was revealed not only in the treatment given, but also in discussions of who was to administer treatment. Medical care had been a traditional role reserved to women. Only at the highest levels of society, and then often only for serious ailments were physicians called in. It was the duty of the wife to be sufficiently skilled to handle the routine medical needs of her family. On a broader scale a particular woman, either a member of the gentry or simply a "wise" woman of the village, was especially trained to care for the health of her neighbors. Normally her training was limited to medical advice passed down from generation to generation or from the general medical guides which were published at the time. She certainly had no formal scientific or medical training. However, the level of medical practice in general was quite low. Only a few of the people who practiced medicine were university educated and generally their services were limited to the wealthy of London or scattered members of the aristocracy who could afford the services of a private physician. But, for the mass population, women without formal training administered whatever medical aid was given. There were associations of barber-surgeons and local doctors, but their level of training was hardly higher than that of the women, their preparation being primarily a period of apprenticeship.[26]

Alice Clark describes the general level of medical treatment as follows: "The general standard of efficiency among the men who professed medicine and surgery was very low, the chief work of the ordinary country practitioner being the letting of blood, and the wise woman of the village may easily have been his superior in other forms of treatment. . . . "[27] Whatever the relative competence of women and the local surgeon or physician, there was a gradual erosion of women's position within the profession throughout the seventeenth century, and this erosion was based on their supposed lack of competence. Two factors led to the decline of women's medical role. The first was the overt effort by medical guilds to limit all practice to their members, while at the same time excluding women from their ranks. The second was the increasing importance of formal training in the profession, training from which women were excluded. This latter development particularly threatened the traditional hold of women on the profession of midwifery and left them to attend only routine deliveries. Women were the victims of attempts to professionalize medical occupations, and of the increasing demand for theoretical knowledge as well as practical experience. An instance of overt exclusion is presented in the charter granted to the Company of Barber-Surgeons at Salisbury in 1614:

> No surgeon or barber is to practice any surgery or barbery, unless first made a free citizen, and then a free brother of the company. Whereas, also there are divers women and others within this city, altogether unskilled in the art of chirurgery, who do oftentimes take cures on them, to the great danger of the patient, it is therefore ordered, that no such woman, or any other, shall take or meddle with any cure of chirurgery. . . . "[28]

Such an attempt to prevent women from practicing medicine was not without precedent. In an effort to curb the practice of witchcraft among medical practitioners, Parliament, in Statute 3, Henry VIII, established an elaborate system of examinations for physicians residing in London. Those who wished to become physicians had to be first examined by either the Bishop of London or the Dean of St. Paul's on questions of religious orthodoxy and then by a committee of four physicians or surgeons, depending upon the applicant's area of specialty. This was believed to be necessary because ". . . common Artificers, as Smiths, Weavers, and Women, boldly and accustomably took upon them great Cures, and Things of great Difficulty, in the which they partly used Sorceries and Witchcraft, and partly applied such Medicines unto the Diseased, as were very noyous, and nothing meet therefore."[29]

Alice Clark, in her analysis of women's declining position in medicine, sees this decline as a part of the general downgrading of women's traditional hold on service occupations. It had been the wife's duty to administer to the needs of her family, whether educational or medical. Through village records, Clark documents the general practice of paying certain women for medical advice and treatment. She even notes that Sir Ralph Verney and Thomas Hobbes relied on women for medical treatment rather than men who were physicians. However, with the increasing scientific sophistication of trained physicians it was inevitable that a woman whose only claim on the profession was traditional, would lose out to her more skilled colleague. It is therefore not surprising that women were pushed out, but the question that arises is how and when their position was undermined during the seventeenth-century beginnings of the professionalization of medicine. Although it is difficult to be exact in this area, there is evidence to support the conclusion that physicians and surgeons were attempting to squash competition from women by applying monopolistic privileges granted by charter while they yet lacked the professional skills to justify exclusive privileges.[30]

The controversy over women's role in midwifery is probably the most interesting of the conflicts. Women had long held a monopoly in this area, and the fight to redefine their position as midwives often took on sexual overtones. Further, women fought the entrance of men into this field, and we have a better picture of their side in this battle than we do in any of the other areas. The issues in the debate centered on the advisability of employing either male midwives or physicians rather than the traditional female midwife for a difficult delivery. Related topics were the competence of the respective groups and the proper level of training and education for each. In the battle, men made some headway during the seventeenth century in becoming accepted as midwives, while the traditional midwives, who were primarily female, were prevented by physicians from securing adequate education or organization.

The most important family to enter the field of midwifery was that of the Chamberlens. William Chamberlen came to England in 1569 and practiced midwifery following his emigration. He had two sons who were members of the Barber-Surgeon's Company and, who, in addition, practiced obstetrics. This family was of such importance because of their use of an effective forceps. They were able to maintain a reputation of success and expertise because they kept their discovery a secret throughout the century. It was their reputation, above all, that helped support the view that men were more skilled than women as midwives. Quite early the Chamberlens sought to establish a dominant position within the profession. William Chamberlen's sons, Peter Chamberlen the Elder and the Younger, came into conflict with the College of Physicians for supporting a plan to incorporate midwives. The plan was presented in 1616 in the Humble Petition of the Midwives in and about the city of London "that the said midwives be incorporated and made a Societye." The Chamberlens were criticized by the College because they "impudently advocated the cause of these women."[31]

The role of the Chamberlens in seventeenth-century efforts to organize midwives is not totally clear. In the 1616 attempt they appear to be disinterested supporters of the proposal, but by 1634 Peter Chamberlen the Elder wanted to organize midwives with himself as their head. The College of Physicians, acting as arbiter at the request of the House of Lords, opposed both efforts to unify and professionalize midwives. Of the first attempt they stated the following: ". . . the Colledg of Physitions doe hold yt very convenient that a Reformation were had of such abuses as are menconed in the peticon. And allso some meanes used for the bettringe of the skill of the Midwives (who for the most part are very ygnorant). Nevertheless they think yt neither necessary nor convenient that they should be made a Corporacon to govern within themselves, a thinge not exampled in any Commonwealth." Rather, the college suggested that the midwives should be judged by the president of the college and two or three "of the gravest of that Society" before they were examined by the bishop in his routine investigation. Further, they offered to act as a consulting body for any midwives who were troubled. The college opposed Chamberlen's attempt to control the profession in 1634 and appeared to support the midwives against Chamberlen's move. In the account given by the college they reported that Chamberlen had had "them to meet at his house once every month without authority and with intention to bring about a project of his to have the sole licensing of them or approving of all such as shall hereafter be licensed. . . . " It should be kept in mind that the College of Physicians opposed any efforts to organize midwives and it is uncertain whether its members merely felt threatened when Dr. Peter Chamberlen attempted to usurp their licensing prerogative or whether they honestly believed his proposal was detrimental to other midwives. There is little doubt that the college was correct in stating that his actions came "out of an opinion of himself and his own ability in the Art of Midwifery." He refused to attend upon any difficult case for midwives who would not conform to his standards, and he would not come if his consultation fee was not sufficiently great. This does not mean, of course, that his actions might not have led to an advancement of midwives as well as to an aggrandizement of his own position.[32]

Not only were midwives prevented from organizing themselves into a corporation which could set general standards and provide the means for educating prospective members, but writers of gynecological texts purposely omitted material which would have made them more competent in their work. Dr. Hugh Chamberlen in his translation of Maurice's work on midwifery omits the anatomical drawings because "there being already severall in English; as also here and there a passage that might offend a chast English eye. . . . " James McNath carries the justification for this censorship even further in his *The Expert Midwife* when he states that he has

> of purpose omitted a Description of the parts in a woman destined to Generation, not being absolutely necessary to this purpose, and lest it might seem execrable to the more chast and shamfaced through Baudiness and Impurity of words; and have endeavoured to keep all Modesty, and a due Reverence to Nature: nor am I of the mind with some, as to think there is no Debauchery in the thing, except it may be in the abuse.[33]

This last sentence is particularly amazing. It gives the impression that midwives may be immodest by gazing upon the nude female body, whether lust is involved or not. Obviously it reveals McNath's failings as a physician as greatly as it does his low opinion of midwives. This was not the only reason, however, that he wanted to omit anatomical drawings from his work. It was unnecessary for midwives to be learned in anatomy for the limited role he envisioned for them. As he continued: "Natural Labour, where all goes right and naturally, is the proper work of the Midwife, and which she alone most easily performs aright, being only to sit and attend Nature's pace and progress . . . and perform some other things of smaller moment, which Physicians gave midwives to do, as unnecessary and indicent for them. . . . "[34] It was, therefore, almost impossible for a midwife to obtain an adequate preparation in medicine to aid her in her profession. She was forced to follow other midwives and observe their techniques in delivery, and even though her model might be a skilled practitioner from whom she could gain an acceptable practical knowledge, her theoretical learning was greatly limited.

These circumstances did not go uncriticized, however. Among physicians, Nicholas Culpeper, author of *A Directory for Midwives,* was the most outspoken critic against the entrance of men into the field of midwifery and the general exclusiveness and elitism of physicians. He contended that physicians maintained exclusive control over recipes for medication that should be dispensed to the population generally. People lost their lives merely to keep doctors in their privileged position. The primary purpose of his medical writings, including the guide for midwives, was to instruct those who actually needed the information, in this case midwives and women themselves. In criticism of his fellow physicians he says: "For we [physicians] must borrow terms of other nations that we may make the common people believe wonders, that so ourselves may grow rich and proud, and keep folk in ignorance though to their own undoing, and the loss of many a dear life." [35] Culpeper wanted to upgrade the level of midwives, and wrote his guide for them so they could educate themselves and become competent in their profession. Basically, Culpeper wanted to get medical information to those to whom he felt physicians were preventing its distribution, and midwives were among them. He advised them to read his work so that ". . . you need not call for the help of a man-midwife, which is a disparagement not only to yourselves, but also to your profession. . . . "[36]

Culpeper was not alone in wanting to upgrade the profession of midwifery or in hoping to discourage men from dominating the field. Two of the best educated and articulate midwives, Elizabeth Cellier and Jane Sharp, worked to organize midwives and argued for women's rightful place in the profession. Sharp, in *The Midwives Book, or the Whole Art of Midwifery*, sets forth the issues in the controversy and supports women's traditional dominance in the area:

> she that wants the knowledge of Speculation, is like one that is blind or wants her sight: she that wants the Practice, is like one that is lame and wants her legs. . . . Some perhaps may think, that then it is not proper for women to be of this profession, because they cannot attain so rarely to the knowledge of things as men may, who are bred up in Universities, Schools of Learning or serve their Apprenticeship for that end and purpose, where Anatomy Lectures being frequently read the situation of the parts both of men and women . . . are often made plain to them. But that objection is easily answered, by the former example of the Midwives amongst the Israelites, for, though we women cannot deny that men in some things may come to a greater perfection of knowledge than women ordinarily can, by reason of the former helps that women want; yet the Holy Scriptures hath recorded Midwives to the perpetual honour of the female sex. . . . It is not hard words that perform the work, as if none understood the Art that cannot understand Greek. Words are but the shell, that we oftimes break our Teeth with them to come at the kernel, I mean our brains to know what is the meaning of them; but to have the same in our mother tongue would save us a great deal of needless labour. It is commendable for men to employ their spare time in some things of deeper Speculation than is required of the female sex; but the art of Midwifery chiefly concerns us.[37]

Sharp notes a conflict that often existed between the midwife with considerable practical experience and the physician whose knowlege was primarily theoretical and who seldom, if ever, witnessed a childbirth. Her views agree with Culpeper's and she has little admiration for the Latin-spouting physician who wished to displace her in all except routine deliveries.

Elizabeth Cellier organized one of the many efforts to unify midwives during the 1600s. At the time of her proposal she noted the listing of deaths of six thousand women and more than thirteen thousand infants in the bills of mortality for the London area over the last twenty years. She believed that they "have in all probability perished, for want of due skill and care, in those women who practice the art of midwifery." She asked that the government establish a self-governing corporation for midwives through which standards could be enforced. She also asked the government to establish requirements for their instruction. The government set up the corporation, but went no further, and the project was dropped.[38] There were, then, conscious efforts, primarily by midwives themselves, to advance the level of care given by midwives, but these efforts did not succeed. Their most steadfast opponent was the College of Physicians, and this opposition reflected the divergent views of physicians and midwives over what properly constituted their duties.

## IV

It is difficult to believe that a link did not exist among the sexual and social stereotypes of the gynecology texts, the general view of women's limited position, and the desire to restrict the role of midwives and to keep them ill-educated and unprofessional. Although there is not a direct connection established between the sexual attitudes present in the gynecological tracts and the downgrading of women's role as midwives, those attitudes aided the physician in his contest with the midwife. The accepted view of women's general incompetence supported the contention of the College of Physicians that the midwives not be allowed to govern themselves. Further, essential anatomical information could be kept from midwives for fear that it "might offend a chast English eye." For his efforts to establish a society of midwives, Peter Chamberlen was criticized for "impudently advocating the cause of these women."

Midwives were inadequate because of their lack of professional training; but this lack was directly related to their sex. First, because a general assumption of female incompetency prevented them from following skilled occupations; and second, because their sex excluded them from such training. Also, on questions of competence, it should be remembered that the choices open to women who needed gynecological care were the trained physician who had little if any gynecological experience, the local surgeon, and the experienced midwife. It is not at all clear which of the three was actually the most skilled in child delivery or treating sexual disorders. Even so, the College of Physicians worked from the assumption that the midwife was incompetent.

If, as was stated by all groups, the goal was improved obstetrical care, why not educate the midwives who bore by far the greatest burden of this care? How can one justify the notion that it is immodest for the midwife to view women's reproductive structure if it is her job to deliver babies? It is difficult to see how anyone could conceive that such drawings could prove shocking to an experienced midwife. One can only understand these arguments by placing them in the context of the early formation of a medical profession. It was necessary for the physician not to be associated with the uneducated midwife; no one must ever think he was on her level or he would lose his status as a professional. Unfortunately, women, both as patients and as medical practitioners and midwives, often were the victims of the physicians' quest for respectability.

## NOTES

1. Theodore Cianfrani, *A Short History of Obstetrics and Gynecology* (Springfield, Ill.: C. C. Thomas, 1960), 170; Richard A. Leonardo, *History of Gynecology* (New York: C. C. Thomas, 1944), 209.

2. *Ibid.*, 155–56.

3. Alice Clark, *Working Life of Women in the Seventeenth Century* (London, 1919), 259–63.

4. Leonardo, *History of Gynecology*, 255.

5. Nicholas Culpeper, *A Directory for Midwives: Or, A Guide for Women, In their Conception, Bearing, and Suckling their Children* (London, 1651), title page.

6. *Ibid.*, pp. 3–191.

7. *Ibid.*, 166.

8. Nicholas Fontanus, *The Womans Doctour: or, an exact and distinct Explanation of all such Diseases as are peculiar to that Sex with Choise and Experimentall Remedies against the same* (London, 1652), 1.

9. *Ibid.*, 2–3.

10. *Ibid.*, 3, 4.

11. *Ibid.*

12. *Ibid.*, 17–20.

13. *The Compleat Midwifes Practice Enlarged* (London, 1659), 285, 284a.

14. *Ibid.*, 284–85a.

15. *Ibid.*, 289.

16. *Ibid.*, 288a, 295, 290–91.

17. *The Compleat Midwifes Practice in the most weighty and High Concernments of the Birth of Man* (London, 1656), 3–9.

18. Fontanus, *The Womans Doctour*, 6.

19. *The Compleat Midwifes Practice* (1656), 28.

20. Ilza Veith, *Hysteria: The History of a Disease* (Chicago: University of Chicago Press, 1965), 132–34.

21. Arthur W. Meyer, *An Analysis of the De generatione animalium of William Harvey* (Stanford, Calif.: Stanford University Press, 1963), 45–55; 130–31.

22. Thomas Willis, *The London Practice of Physick: or the whole Practical Part of Physick contained in the works of Dr. Willis* (London, 1685), 631–32.

23. *Ibid.*, 297.

24. *Ibid.*

25. Thomas Sydenham, *The whole works of that excellent practical physician Dr. Thomas Sydenham* (London, 1722), 147.

26. Clark, *Working Life of Women in the Seventeenth Century*, 257–58.

27. *Ibid.*, 258.

28. *Ibid.*, 259–60.

29. *Ibid.*, 259.

30. *Ibid.*, 257–61.

31. Herbert R. Spencer, *The History of British Midwifery from 1650 to 1800* (London, 1927), iii.

32. *Ibid.*, iii, v.

33. Clark, *Working Life of Women in the Seventeenth Century*, 281.

34. *Ibid.*, 282.

35. Culpeper, *A Directory for Midwives*, 7.

36. *Ibid.*, "Dedicatorie" (pagination confused).

37. Clark, *Working Life of Women in the Seventeenth Century*, 271.

38. *Ibid.*, 274–75.

# Education and Ideology in Nineteenth-Century America: The Response of Educational Institutions to the Changing Role of Women

## *Adele Simmons*

Only recently has attending college been a realistic and generally acceptable goal for young women in the United States. However, the nature of the institutions that today provide educational opportunities for young women was defined in the nineteenth century. During this time, teacher training colleges were established, the eastern women's colleges and coordinate colleges were founded, and coeducational institutions opened in the Middle West. Since that time, the number and diversity of educational opportunities for women has increased. But within this trend toward increasing opportunities, there have been fluctuations. The goals of the institutions and the nature of the curricula have changed from decade to decade to reflect the prevailing social attitudes about the role of women. Universities incorporated and then legitimized new views about women's place. Part I of this essay outlines the different kinds of institutions that were established for the purpose of educating women, and examines the close relationship between societal attitudes toward women and the nature and availability of educational opportunities for them.

As Part II of the essay shows, institutions dedicated to providing educational opportunities for women shared the society's ambivalence about what women should do with their education. In the nineteenth century as well as today, these institutions failed to reconcile increased accessibility to higher education with the lack of opportunities available to educated women.

## I

### Early Justification: Women As Teachers

Colonial America believed that women were intellectually inferior to men, and that women's place was in the home. Whatever skills women needed, they

This essay was originally prepared for the Eastern Sociological Association Conference, April 1971, in Boston, Mass. The author is indebted to Elinor Yalen for research assistance.

learned by working in apprenticeship to their mothers. There was no room for institutional female education.

It is not surprising, then, that at the end of the eighteenth century only a few men and women conceived of an education for women that would extend beyond the home. And even advocates of female education, including Benjamin Rush, professor of chemistry at the University of Pennsylvania and an outspoken advocate for women's education, felt that school should teach women to be better assistants to their husbands and better educators of their children.[1] In a speech at a female academy in Philadelphia in 1787, Rush outlined an elaborate "feminine curriculum" to educate women about the "duties of social and domestic life."[2]

Emma Willard, long viewed as a pioneer of female education in this country, agreed with Rush. Education should focus on preparing women for the home. In her proposal to Governor Clinton for a female seminary, Willard explained, "It is believed that housewifery might be greatly improved by being taught, not only in practice, but in theory."[3] In addition, Willard argued that it was especially important for mothers in America to be educated, for in the new democracy women would bear the responsibility for the early education of men who would later govern. If these women continued to have little understanding of the world beyond the home, and even less of child development,[4] they would fail the country. Still, when Willard's seminary opened in 1821, there was nothing in the curriculum to help women better understand children, in part because the field of child development as we know it did not exist. Rather the curriculum focused first on natural philosophy and domestic science.

The curriculum of Willard's school, as well as of other seminaries in the early nineteenth century, changed considerably as a new role for women was defined. By the 1820s, common schools for all male children were established throughout the country. The new schools urgently needed teachers and the taxpayers wanted cheap teachers. Women had already been teaching their own children at home; thus the step from being a teacher at home to being a teacher outside the home was relatively easy, and in keeping with one traditional female role. Moreover, since the profession was itself new, women would not compete with men for existing places in the labor force. Even so, the image of women working as professionals outside the home in pre-industrial America was unusual. A certain sense of desperation pervaded the comments of those who justified the importance of women becoming teachers. Thomas Dallaudet, writing in the *Connecticut Common School Journal,* argued, "We must look more to the other sex for aid in this emergency and do all in our power to bring forward young women of the necessary qualifications to be engaged in the business of instruction."[5]

Catharine Beecher, another leader in the field of women's education, agreed: ". . . it is woman who is to come to this emergency and meet the demand . . .woman whom experience and testimony have shown to be the best, as well as the cheapest guardian and teacher of childhood in a school as well as the nursery."[6]

But unlike most contemporary advocates, Beecher saw also the greater implication of the growth of teaching as a profession for women. Even though among teachers, women were paid between one-fourth to one-half of what men were paid, Beecher emphasized that at last a woman could have a profession "as honourable and as lucrative for her as legal, medical and theological professions are for men."[7] The opportunities were enormous. By 1850, two million school-age children engaged the services of two hundred thousand teachers.[8]

Catharine Beecher devoted a great part of her life to recruiting and training women teachers for ill-equipped schools in the western and southern parts of the country. By 1872, 101 "normal" schools, particularly in the East and Midwest, were training women specifically to be teachers. At the same time, the nation's elementary and secondary schools adapted so readily to women teachers that the job became rapidly identified as female. As early as 1850, the state of Pennsylvania had 81 male teachers and 646 female teachers in its common schools.[9]

The entry of women into the teaching professions established a pattern that has become familiar. Whenever new jobs emerge which require some of the qualities associated with homemaker and mother, and where men are not available to fill these positions, women are employed,[10] and the job becomes low-status, low-paying and only for women. So it was in the nineteenth century and so it is today.

## Imitative Colleges

By the 1850s in America, the Beecher view of the professional possibilities offered by female higher education was challenging the Willard view that education for women should be primarily training for homemaking and child rearing. If women were to grow intellectually, they would need new institutions which would offer a collegiate education similar to that offered at men's colleges. Beecher understood this and realized as well that these institutions must be endowed to be permanent.

The shift in emphasis to a liberal education which Beecher advocated did not begin until the 1850s. In some circles, "Teaching the mind how to take up a subject, investigate it and draw conclusions" became a goal of women's education.[11] For the first time, some educators advised girls to acquire discipline and reasoning abilities, and the broad outlook which young men learned in college. It is important to remember that these views about education for women were consistent with reforms taking place in men's colleges, for at this time the curriculum of Harvard was expanding to include what is now the basis of the liberal arts curriculum.[12] However, while the women's schools talked of a curriculum similar to that at men's schools, there was always a special focus on subjects believed to be of interest to women. Thus the new schools were to ". . . furnish young women with that general yet appropriate discipline of all their powers and faculties which will qualify them, in a fully developed womanhood, with a sound mind and a pure heart in a healthy body, to do work of life for which God has made them, in any place to which in His providence they may be called."[13]

Vassar, Wellesley, and Smith were all founded with this goal in mind. These schools were not the first to admit women. (Oberlin graduated four women from its regular college course in 1841, and Vassar was not incorporated until 1861.) But the eastern colleges for women were significant because they were permanent institutions with high academic standards and considerable prestige, and were generously endowed by their founders, Matthew Vassar, Henry F. Durant, and Sophia Smith.

It is important not to lose sight of the purposes of the founders. Each of the three benefactors had a deep religious and social commitment. Each looked at other projects before deciding to found a woman's college. In the end they followed the contemporary view that women were a particularly powerful moral force in the society and according to Durant, "the uplift of women meant the uplift of humanity." Similarly, Smith hoped that "by the higher and more thoroughly Christian education of women . . . their weight of influence in removing the evils of society will be greatly increased." Specifically, she hoped that the "educated women will sweep the filth out of literature."[14]

The founders of the eastern women's colleges all commented on the existing injustices in a system of higher education that excluded women, but they failed to appreciate the practical effects of widening opportunities for women and proving that women could perform intellectually as well as men. In spite of, rather than because of, the views of the founders, their institutions served as a testing ground for students and faculty who were dedicated to proving to themselves, as well as to men, that higher education with rigid standards was appropriate for women.

This view was not popularly held in the 1870s. A former professor at the Harvard Medical School, Edward H. Clarke, published *Sex in Education* in 1872, elaborating on his views of the physical dangers of higher education to women. Drawing upon clinical evidence from six patients, Clarke hypothesized that the active use of the brain required excessive blood and that in the case of women this blood would be drawn from the nervous system and the reproductive organs. Women who went to college, Clarke concluded, were likely to suffer mental and physical breakdowns and possibly sterility.[15]

It is difficult for us to appreciate the significance of Clarke's book to educators of the time. Distinguished editors refuted Clarke.[16] But the number of female college graduates was tiny, and the number of women who had become scholars or professionals was even smaller. Thus most of Clarke's readers had little experience with women who could contradict Clarke's evidence. As late at 1895, the faculty of the University of Virginia announced its considered opinion that "women were often physically unsexed by the strains of study."[17] M. Carey Thomas, president of Bryn Mawr, had met only one female graduate when as a young woman she packed her bags and left home for Cornell. Even someone as determined as she was haunted by fears that women were physically and intellectually inferior to men. Speaking to a group of Bryn Mawr graduates, she described her doubts about women: "I remember often praying about it, and begging God that if it were true that because I was a girl, I could not successfully master Greek and go to college and understand things, to kill me for it."[18]

Only when large numbers of women had successfully completed the rigid curriculum of the men's institutions would Thomas's fears, as well as Clarke's, be put to rest. Until then, some people at the women's colleges self-consciously tried to provide a curriculum similar to that of more established schools. Maria Mitchell, a Vassar astronomer, found this particularly frustrating and wrote, "Our faculty meetings try me in this respect: we do things that other colleges have done before. We wait and ask for precedent."[19]

On one hand, some people at the colleges stressed the ability of women; on the other, official publications of the eastern women's colleges reflected an ambivalence about the purpose of the schools as well as uncertainties about the abilities of women. Women's colleges were concerned about the need to provide a climate that would develop "healthy women" as well as the need to avoid placing undue strain on frail females. Thus at Smith, "stairs were reduced to a minimum because they were thought to be harmful to female health."[20] At Vassar, the president's reports always included lengthy sections on student health, and elaborate programs in hygiene and physical exercise were part of the curriculum.

While some professors struggled to maintain the imitative aspects of the curriculum, Catharine Beecher, who had supported the idea of such colleges, deplored their failure to prepare women for their "distinctive profession as mother, nurse, and chief educator." She continued to believe that women should develop professional skills only in those areas which were related to a woman's role as wife and mother. In this she was supported by *Godey's Lady's Book*, which condemned the Vassar curriculum, calling the system "a false one," not based on the real needs of its students.[21] At the same time, it is interesting that Beecher argued that the colleges were not meeting the needs of women, in part because the boards of trustees were composed primarily of men, and because the colleges often had male presidents and few women faculty members.[22]

In fact, the imitative colleges did pay more attention to the needs and interests of women than Beecher suggested. Preparing women for marriage and homemaking was still one of the goals. A survey of women's colleges in 1868 showed that in comparison to men's schools they offered in general more modern languages and less Greek, and more science, especially biological sciences. Women's colleges emphasized "aesthetic culture" and were likely to offer courses in music and art, though not always as part of the regular curriculum.[23] In the sciences, adjustments were often made to satisfy parents or students who valued studies which had practical applications. Vassar's "practical application" of chemistry, for example, included "general culinary chemistry, toxicology and its antidotes . . . , curing, tanning and dressing of leather."[24] At Wellesley, all the students helped perform the necessary domestic tasks as a required part of their college preparation.

The eastern women's colleges did succeed in proving that women could perform as well as men intellectually, but still the idea gained little acceptance. The colleges were providing an institutional framework and an academic degree more or less equal to that of men's colleges, but it was clear to everyone that the results were not identical; nor were the opportunities offered upon the completion of degree requirements. While teacher-training colleges had clearly prepared women for a profession, albeit a temporary one, the graduates of the eastern women's colleges whose education was more diverse than that of teacher-training graduates had no other professional opportunities. The problem of what to do with a college education, as we shall see later, was born in these times.

### Coeducation

While "separate but equal" education was struggling for acceptance in New England, the question of coeducation was being settled in the western parts of the country. Oberlin had been coeducational in its secondary department since its opening in 1833. In 1837, when four women who had requested admission to the college course were found to be sufficiently prepared, Oberlin became the first college in the United States to admit women and to grant them the regular arts degree. However, it was largely the state institutions of the Middle West, particularly those in Iowa, Wisconsin, and Michigan, which were responsible for the growing acceptance of coeducation.

Questions of propriety and principles of democracy were frequently cited in the controversy over full coeducation; but the most influential argument in favor of coeducation was the economic one. Once admitted, women paid tuition to the established universities. In addition there was simply not enough new capital to create adequate institutions of higher learning especially for women. In 1876, Charles Van Hise, president of the University of Wisconsin, pointed out that "The western states in those early days were too poor to support two high-grade educational institutions. Yet the justice was recognized of the women's demand that they have equal opportunity with men. There was no way to afford such opportunity but to adopt co-education."[25] President Eliot of Harvard was more explicit: "For the education of the two sexes together, there is but one respectable argument, poverty."[26]

While the economic reasons for coeducation were forceful, the different role of women in the Middle West provided another reason for coeducation in that part of the country. While women in the East had a more clearly defined secondary role, women in the Middle West had to assume considerable responsibility for the daily operations of the farms. Their responsibilities increased with the Civil War—just after many of the state schools were established and at a time when the number of men who had the time for higher education was at a low. Indeed, at Wisconsin women exceeded men in numbers all through the war, owing both to the scarcity of male students and the demand for women trained as teachers.

In 1866 the University of Wisconsin was explicitly reorganized to open all departments equally to men and women. The new president, Paul Chadbourne, objected to this policy and planned a special "female college" with separate courses of instruction. He did not, however, prevent women from enrolling in the regular course if they were prepared. Since no women enrolled in the women's college, Chadbourne was forced to discontinue it. [27]

In spite of the Wisconsin experience and in spite of the fact that coeducation was working successfully at several universities, its merits continued to be debated. Some educators argued that "Woman is no more capable of enduring the same severe and protracted study with the other sex by day and by night through all the months and years of her early life than she is able to perform the same labors on the farm or in the shop."[28] Others felt that coeducation would cause loss of femininity. Clarke himself suggested that "coeducation would make girls half boys and boys half girls."[29] The strongest resistance to coeducation was in the eastern states, where arrogance and a disdain of anything western led to the conclusion that the eastern solution, "separate but equal," was best.

But in spite of eastern opposition, coeducation was sufficiently entrenched in American education to be able to withstand the considerable opposition that arose in the next decades.

### Coordinate Colleges

By the turn of the century, the success of Smith, Vassar, and Wellesley had long since proved that a woman's institution could approach a standard equal to that of a man's. There was no doubt that women had the ability to learn. But old questions about whether women ought to go to college and for what reason were raised with new forcefulness. Attitudes toward women were changing, in part as a result of the arrival of large numbers of immigrants, and statistics about the influence of college on women's life styles were at last available. As a result, a major reaction against both imitative and coeducational schools took place.

By the 1890s, it had become an accepted principle that women of the elite should have as many children as possible. At a time when the establishment was facing the influx of immigrants from Italy and Ireland, statistics showed that 45 percent of female college graduates over fifty years of age were not married. Only 10 percent of non-college women did not marry. Those college graduates who did marry, usually remained single for eight years following graduation. Furthermore, they tended to have small families.[30] It was logical, then, that at the turn of the century, many well-to-do eastern women were discouraged from continuing their education.

The educational institutions were not unhappy with a move away from both coeducation and higher education for women. Women had excelled in their college work, and in particular were concentrating in the humanities. Male students began to leave these fields for others, and educators as well as students began to oppose coeducation openly. Revised views of coeducation found expression in revised educational structures. Coordinate colleges in particular became popular. Some coordinate colleges, such as Radcliffe, offered new opportunities for women.[31] Other coordinate colleges were an attempt to isolate women who were already on campus. Believing that Tufts had declined in popularity since its becoming coeducational in 1892, President Hamilton went so far as to state that "The future of the academic department of Tufts College as a man's college depends upon the immediate segregation of the women into a separate department or college. . . . I regard this as the most pressing education problem we have before us. . . . I have no fear that a failure to solve it would involve imminent disaster to the College of Liberal Arts."[32] In 1910 Jackson College was then founded, not out of concern for providing higher education for women, but because it was the most expedient way of removing women from the College of Liberal Arts at Tufts. For similar reasons, Western Reserve began a separate College for Women, and Barnard, Pembroke, and Sophie Newcomb were founded. Wesleyan College, in Middletown, Connecticut, solved the problem in a more final way. In 1912 Wesleyan closed its doors to women, and did not reopen them until 1970.

The coordinate colleges offered women a third institutional choice, a compromise between a single sex college and a coeducational college. But like the other alternatives, these coordinate colleges were founded in response to prevailing ideology about women, their role, and the kind of educational experience which could best prepare them for that role. The coordinate colleges were an effort to postpone the complete integration of women into the country's educational system at a time when there were serious concerns about the appropriateness of higher education for women. While the shift in ideology in the late 1960s led to the full integration of some coordinate colleges with the nearby male colleges, others have retained their names but little else. Barnard, which was one of the few coordinate colleges with its own faculty, has decided to maintain its separate status in the belief that, given Barnard's particular strengths and its unusual relationship to Columbia, it can best serve the interests of women by remaining separate.

## II

### Education for What?

The belief that women should have the right to intellectual pursuits prompted the opening of colleges for women in the nineteenth century. The reaction against higher education for women at the turn of the century was in part a reflection of the difficulty college women had in putting their education to practical use. As early as 1875 many female college graduates, although grateful to have been part of a major educational experiment, were left wondering what to do with their skills. As William O'Neill explained, "Suddenly they found themselves not merely alone, but alone in a society that had no use for them. Their liberal education did not prepare them to do anything in particular, except teach, and the stylized, carefully edited view of life it gave them bore little relation to the actual world."[33] The plight of four Vassar graduates led one person to write, "A $3,000 education prepared them to do work in a house which a moderately paid servant could do as well."[34]

These women were acutely aware of their dilemma. As Inez Gillmore wrote: "A professional career . . . puts me beyond reach of the average woman's duties and pleasures. The conventional limitations of the female lot put me beyond the reach of the average man's duties and pleasures."[35] A college graduate of three years complained to Alice Freeman Palmer, a former president of Wellesley: "I have not done what is expected of me. . . . I am so tired of going to teas and ball games and assemblies! I don't care the least in the world for foreign missions and I am not going slumming among the Italians. I have too much respect for the Italians. And what shall I do with the rest of my life?"[36]

While colleges planned to turn out efficient housewives, some graduates became frustrated by a sense that they should use their education in some way that society had not yet defined. They sensed that they would not be welcome in the professions which were male-dominated, but they lacked realistic goals and their college performance sometimes suffered for it.[37] They were concerned, but most were not adventurous.[38] Most were not ready to challenge the view that women's first goal in life was to marry and have children and that such a role excluded all other possibilities. There were a few women like Maria Mitchell, who believed that "We must not only be ready to help women into new occupations, but we must make women willing to enter them."[39]

Although the first women graduate students to enter M.I.T., Yale and Johns Hopkins were Vassar graduates, the challenge to women's traditional place did not come from universities or university graduates. Rather it was the feminists who led the way. Few of the 1,235 women preachers, 208 women lawyers and 4,000 women doctors had been to college, since college was not required for professional training.[40] Similarly, few of the suffragists were college graduates. Political action was inconsistent with the behavior expected of a college girl. Other women provided the precedent; college women followed, establishing professional schools for women or insisting that existing male schools become coeducational. College women took a lead in institutionalizing the opportunities defined by the feminists.

What, then, did college women do? Teaching was the main outlet for college women for decades. A survey of eight thousand college graduates in the 1880s showed that five thousand married and did not work outside the home, and of the remaining three thousand, two-thirds taught.[41] Seventy percent of the women who graduated from Mt. Holyoke during the first forty years of the school's existence taught at the elementary or secondary level.[42] While colleges showed little concern for placing their alumnae in jobs or helping them after they graduated, Catharine Beecher started a placement service for teachers. She found jobs for a limited number of college women in the western states, but her placement effort collapsed as unfavorable reports of western life filtered east.

It was not until the 1890s that women had a second respectable profession: social work. Jane Addams helped to define a new field where women could again work without competing with men, and which emphasized feminine virtues. However, social work and teaching were not permanent careers for most women.[43] Rather, these occupations provided an interlude between school and marriage. In spite of the availability of quality higher education, and in spite of all the discussions about woman's place and rights, the message was the same: a woman's primary duty was to marry and raise a family. The small group of women who dedicated themselves to a career rarely married. Having no families of their own, they were expected to use their feminine skills caring for a portion of society, often assuming a position of moral leadership in the community.[44] Thus women in the nineteenth century had to choose between using their education in one of the few accessible professions and not marrying, or retaining their accepted feminine role and never fully using their education. For decades, most women made the choice, rather than question the society which forced the choice upon them.[45]

After 1920, it became increasingly possible to combine a career and a family. However, society viewed the wife-mother-professional of the twentieth century very differently from the professional single woman. The latter, without family obligations, was contributing to society. The wife-mother-professional was seen rather as a self-serving person who chose to pursue personal interests at the expense of her immediate community, her family. She had home obligations which were sufficient to keep her occupied, and the choice to work was a selfish one, to stimulate her own intellect or to fulfill a personal psychological need. Those women who found a career and a family more than they could manage, gave up their careers. As in the nineteenth century, they did not question the social institutions which created their dilemma nor did they recognize the lack of institutions to help them deal with it.[46]

The conflict which women have felt between pressures to make full and direct use of their education and those to focus on family life is not new. In the nineteenth century, much as today, women were painfully aware of the discrepancy between the nature of the education they received and the role they were expected to fulfill upon graduation. As the number of women attending universities has grown, awareness of this conflict has increased. Yet very few people have thought about the implications of providing women with higher education without simultaneously providing occupational opportunities. For many years women were convinced that if properly educated they could succeed as professionals. Equal education would lead to equal opportunity. Barriers were to be overcome but not removed. And education was the principal means of overcoming the barriers. These women did not recognize the social and economic pressures that placed them at a clear disadvantage no matter what their training. Only recently have women begun to equate the limitations of opportunity with sex discrimination.

This review of the history of women's education in the United States has emphasized the ambivalence both men and women have felt about the place of educated women in society. I have described the shifts back and forth between curricula and structures which focused on the special role of women and those which focused on identical education for men and women. While these shifts have been dramatic, they reveal a consistent trend over the century toward preparing women for more opportunities and choices. Yet only rarely were colleges or other social institutions directly concerned with helping women use their abilities. This is the concern of women today. They are asking that they be welcomed in jobs for which they have been and can be trained. They are also asking for changes within universities to better prepare them to participate in a broader spectrum of careers. Past experience suggests that the institutions of higher education themselves will again not take the lead in bringing about change, but as before, will only slowly respond to pressures to reassess women's education. As the university redefines equal education to include equal opportunity, it will, in turn, legitimize it.

## NOTES

1. Frederick Rudolph, *The American College and University* (New York: Knopf, 1962), 309.

2. Thomas Woody, *A History of Women's Education in the United States* (New York: Octagon, 1966 [1929]), I, 303.

3. *Ibid.*, 310.

4. Rudolph, *The American College and University*, 309.

5. Quoted in Woody, *History of Women's Education*, I, 462.

6. Catharine Beecher, *The True Remedy for the Wrongs of Woman* (Boston: Phillips, Sampson, 1851).

7. *Ibid.*, 23.

8. Woody, *History of Women's Education*, I, 236.

9. *Ibid.*, I, 432.

10. See Valerie Kincade Oppenheimer, "The Female Labor Force in the United States," Ph.D. thesis, University of California, Berkeley, 1966.

11. Woody, *History of Women's Education*, I, 194.

12. Rudolph, *The American College and University, passim.*

13. Quoted by M. A. Robson, "The Development of Higher Education of Women in the Eastern United States" (M.A. thesis, Oxford University, 1968), 60, from Smith Archives, *Smith College Official Circular* (September 10, 1872), 6–7.

14. Quoted in *ibid.*, 22, 24.

15. Edward H. Clarke, *Sex in Education; or, A Fair Chance for the Girls* (Boston: J. R. Osgood, 1873), 157.

16. Julia Ward Howe, ed., *Sex and Education: A Reply to Dr. E. H. Clarke's "Sex in Education"* (Boston: Roberts Brothers, 1874); Eliza Bisbee Duffey, *No Sex in Education; or, An Equal Chance for Both Boys and Girls: Being a Review of Dr. E. H. Clarke's "Sex in Education"* (Philadelphia: J. M. Stoddart, 1874).

17. Rudolph, *The American College and University*, 326.

18. M. Carey Thomas, "Present Tendencies in Women's College and University Education," *Education Review* XXV (1908), 64–85, quoted in Barbara M. Cross, *The Educated Woman in America* (New York: Teachers College Press, 1965), 159.

19. Maria Mitchell, *Maria Mitchell, Life, Letters and Journal* comp. by Phoebe Mitchell Kendall (Boston: Lee and Shepard, 1896), 174.

20. Quoted by Robson, "Development of Higher Education of Women," 50, from Smith Archives, *Smith College Official Circular* (October 1, 1874), 6–7.

21. Woody, *History of Women's Education*, II, 216, 217.

22. Catharine Beecher, *Educational Reminiscences and Suggestions* (New York: J. B. Ford, 1874), 184.

23. Louise Schutz Boas, *Woman's Education Begins: The Rise of the Women's Colleges* (Norton, Mass.: Wheaton College Press, 1935), 256.

24. Woody, *History of Women's Education*, 112; Boas, *Woman's Education Begins*, 253.

25. Woody, *History of Women's Education*, II, 256.

26. Charles W. Eliot, Commencement Address at Smith College, 1879. See also Ely Van de Warker, *Woman's Unfitness for Higher Coeducation* (New York: Grafton Press, 1903), 7.

27. Helen Maria (Remington) Olin, *The Women of a State University, an Illustration of the Working of Coeducation in the Middle West* (New York and London: G. P. Putnam's Sons, 1909), 47.

28. W. S. Tyler, "The Higher Education of Women," *Scribner's Monthly*, February 1874, 158, quoted in Robson, "Development of Higher Education of Women," 86. See also Van de Warker, *Woman's Unfitness*.

29. Clarke, *Sex in Education*, 180.

30. Willystine Goodsell, *The Education of Women: Its Social Background and Its Problems* (New York: Macmillan Co., 1923), 34–61. A decline in marriage rate among college-educated men in the 1900s suggests that marriage as an institution was being questioned by other than college women. Among 509 married women who graduated from Vassar between 1867 and 1892 there was an average of 1.91 offspring. *Ibid.*, 52, 35.

31. Although Radcliffe was officially established in 1893, women had been taking courses from Harvard professors since 1879 through the Society for Collegiate Instruction for Women.

32. Woody, *History of Women's Education*, II, 319.

33. William L. O'Neill, *Everyone Was Brave: The Rise and Fall of Feminism in America* (Chicago: Quadrangle, 1969), 79.

34. Woody, *History of Women's Education*, II, 218.

35. Christopher Lasch, *The New Radicalism in America (1889–1963): The Intellectual as Social Type* (New York: Knopf, 1965), 58.

36. Alice Elvira Freeman Palmer, *Why Go to College?* (Boston: T. Y. Crowell, 1897), 18.

37. Marion Talbot, *The Education of Women* (Chicago: University of Chicago Press, 1910), 238.

38. Robson, "Development of Higher Education of Women," 107.

39. Mitchell, *Maria Mitchell*, 187.

40. Woody, *History of Women's Education*, II, 322.

41. *Ibid.*, 323.

42. Mabel Newcomer, *A Century of Higher Education for American Women* (New York: Harper, 1959), 77.

43. Jill Conway, "Jane Addams, an American Heroine," in Robert Lifton, ed., *The Woman in America* (Boston: Houghton Mifflin, 1965), 247. See also Christopher Lasch, *New Radicalism*, chap. 1, "Jane Addams: The College Woman and the Family Claim."

44. Conway, "Jane Addams," 265.

45. It is interesting to note that when Alice Freeman, president of Wellesley, married George Palmer, a Harvard astronomer, the trustees of Wellesley offered Palmer several choices, "including the presidency of Wellesley alone or with his wife." Palmer stayed at Harvard. Freeman moved to Cambridge. Dorothy Gies McGuigan, *A Dangerous Experiment* (Benton Harbor, Mich.: R. W. Patterson, 1970), 79.

46. For a more general discussion of the career expectations of women, see Lotte Bailyn, "Notes on the Role of Choice in the Psychology of Professional Women," in Lifton, ed., *The Woman in America*.

# Feminism and Liberalism
## in Wilhelmine Germany, 1890-1918

*Amy Hackett*

I shall discuss the women's movement in Wilhelmine Germany as a "liberal" movement, for so virtually all German feminists understood it. Examination of the interrelationships between German liberalism and feminism will, I hope, be provocative for those interested in integrating women into history.

One expects feminists to be motivated as women, that is, to be reacting against a role which society, or men, foists upon them. German feminists refused the traditional and legal restriction of women to a few "feminine" activities; they insisted that women themselves decide what they might or must do. But, far more than American feminists, they wished to maintain, even to cultivate and exalt, traditional "feminine" qualities—especially women's maternal, nurturing "instincts"—as unique and valuable additions to culture.

"Feminist" is at least an incomplete appellation for women torn by several often conflicting identities. Feminists are never solely women. Differentiating among the sources of a feminist's behavior is no easy task, because they combine organically as a single personality.

The German women's movement proclaimed itself an outgrowth of liberalism, integral to which was a lively concern for what was felt to be the national well-being. I shall emphasize this asexual, liberal influence on German feminism. Only a handful of women were fairly single-minded about improving the situation of their sex. Many liberal men, moreover, did not sympathize with feminism as ideological reason seemed to warrant. Liberal women often had to establish priority between liberalism and feminism.

I shall deal primarily with the "bourgeois" women's movement. Non-socialist women themselves used this term. Though feminists thought the class conflict dividing Germany to be regrettable, their class origin was a matter of fact. (For Social Democrats, of course, "bourgeois" implied a critique.) Germany had two women's movements—bourgeois and Social Democratic—if by "women's movement" one means an organized effort, supported by ideology, to improve women's lot. In fact, Protestant and

This essay was first presented at the convention of the American Historical Association, December 1971, in New York City.

Catholic women claimed more or less independent status as branches of a "religious women's movement." The German Protestant Women's Association joined the central federation of women's organizations, the *Bund deutscher Frauenverein*, or BDF, in 1908. (They left in 1918 over the BDF's suffrage demands and its cooperation with socialist women.) The Catholic group remained separate. Thus feminism had to contend with and accommodate itself to the considerable fissures in German society.

Liberal women did not suffer their identity conflicts alone. But Catholic women, subservient to the church and abhorring radicalism, experienced relatively slight distress. The Social Democratic party was so far ahead of the liberal parties in acceptance of feminist goals that comparison of socialist and liberal women's relationship to their respective parties is hard.

Although socialist women confronted their version of the conflict, liberal women were in a quandary. I shall first discuss the philosophical connections these women drew between their cause and liberalism; then the historical ties between the two movements; and finally, the choice between their allegiances which faced liberal women.

Feminist leaders were overwhelmingly liberals, tending toward the more left or "progressive" wing of liberalism. Feminist ideology insisted that consequent liberalism must include women in its concern for the unfettered development of human potential. Liberal women assumed that the force of ideas must someday triumph in the form of outspoken liberal party programs. Meanwhile, in the metaphor of a Bavarian feminist, they waited for their likely parliamentary beaux to show interest.[1] Alice Salomon cited the community of ideology in Theodor Barth's left-liberal journal *Nation* in 1903. Few feminists had then entered politics. Salomon discounted the need for sacrifice once they did. "After all," she noted,

> the women's movement is the product of an individualistic, liberal historical current; a movement with thoroughly progressive tendencies, which can only grow out of a modern world view. It is the belief in the right of self-determination, in the blessings of individual freedom, which . . . has let women strive to free themselves from intellectual, economic and legal bonds. The women's movement *has sprouted on the same ground from which political liberalism too once drew its nourishment;* . . . the similarity of world-view will naturally lead most supporters of the women's movement to the liberal parties. Not, because above all they can there hope for support for women's cause, rather because the world-view which they have gained in fighting for women's rights in regard to politics can only push them into progressive paths. . . .[2]

Feminism would thus convert women to liberalism. More likely, feminists, at least the vocal ones, grew up with a liberal world-view—however imprecisely formulated. Liberalism flourished in their social milieu; their brothers were probably liberals. Why did most women growing up in "liberal" surroundings *not* become feminists? What differentiated those who *did*? How formative were their personal experiences; how important was ideology? Unfortunately there is biographical information on only a few leaders.

Feminist language abounded in liberal turns of phrase. Feminist and liberal rhetoric alike teemed with unfolding and developing personalities. Liberal idiom was so compelling that the Conservative Paula Mueller, the Protestant women's leader, occasionally verged on it. The Christian women's movement, for example, aimed to create "independent personalities, responsible for themselves."[3] Linguistic nonpartisanship seemed unattainable. In 1901 and 1902 nearly all feminist leaders decried the government's high tariff policy. Only Marianne Weber criticized frequent feminist treatment of low tariffs as a "woman's cause." ("Woman as consumer" was the usual line.) She did not want the bourgeois feminist movement tied to a party or interest group. "The goals of the women's movement as such," Weber explained, could only be "those demands which are raised from woman's standpoint as such and for woman as such." She had only uncovered the problem. Noumenal "woman as such" may well be indifferent to tariff schedules. Grain at three and a half marks per ton was probably not a "feminine" tariff. Weber was right on the impediments to feminine unanimity on material issues. But her own ideal woman was not value-free. Weber thought feminism was motivated by ethical ideals, for example, woman's right to "self-determination and independence without regard to her peculiarity as a sexual being." This required the "elimination of all external barriers which oppose her development to full humanity." Weber's vintage liberal rhetoric is far from "neutral." Yet just these ideals, she thought, gave feminism its "stamp of universal validity."[4]

Even less-democratic liberals recognized feminism's link with liberal ideology. The National Liberal Heinrich von Sybel in 1870 wrote a booklet *On the Emancipation of Women* in which he suggested that law and civil society should not discriminate against women. The democratic *Zeitgeist* demanded equal rights. Sybel identified this spirit with the "correct and noble basic principle" of equality before the law for "every reasonable being" regardless of physical or economic strength. Though he credited women with reason, Sybel did not infer total equality. For one thing, Nature made maternity an overwhelming occupation, even as it rendered men's "rougher hands" unfit for infant care. Sybel was torn between his liberal premises and his prejudices about women. His concept of marriage was conservative-organic: man and wife being one, the marital unit should have one electoral will, expressed of course by the man. Sybel hastily added that few unattached women would want to vote. But, he admitted, if political suffrage were a human right, women could not fairly be deprived. Certainly it was unbearable to deny the most educated lady what the most stupid shoemaker's helper was granted.[5]

The Conservative Paula Mueller also deemed woman suffrage "the final consequence of liberal-democratic thought," although she realized that those of other persuasions might support it. Mueller personally opposed suffrage beyond the local level—effectively allowing a limited, property-based franchise, such as was typical of municipalities. Principle did not move her so much as the practical fear that the female masses would vote for the Social Democratic or Catholic Center parties. She also voiced a fastidious distaste for women's being pulled into ugly election campaigns. For liberals, however, woman suffrage was *"the* consequence," as was a high regard for the individual voter.[6] Socialists agreed that rights were essentially a demand of the liberal bourgeoisie. Socialists believed rights meant little without basic socioeconomic revolution, but remained the most avid parliamentary defenders of women's rights. (It was in fact a Social Democratic commonplace that the party must take up those historic tasks which pitiful German liberals were not up to.)

Liberal and feminist history ran parallel.[7] Women shared in the political and national enthusiasm of 1848. An incipient feminism arose, then fell to censorship and repression. Feminist and liberal timidity had similar roots. The movement only revived in the mid-sixties, when feminists began to organize. The year 1848 was, incidentally, that of the Seneca Falls convention in the United States; but the subsequent developments were shaped by vastly different conditions in the two countries.

German unification was crucial to liberalism, but as the accomplishment of Bismarckian diplomacy and Prussian might it provided no rationale to expand women's political rights. German men furnished no useful precedent for a suffrage campaign. Bismarck granted universal male suffrage by fiat. Attempts by some men to popularize suffrage by making it a reward for those who bravely fought for unification hardly helped women. (Women did sometimes recall that they bore the nation's defenders.)

The antisocialist law cast a pall on political life in the eighties. Stagnation hit the women's movement too; new issues were not forthcoming and diffidence increased with the dissolution of several organizations for aiding working-class women. Feminist resurgence in the 1890s coincided with a general intensification of political and cultural life following the death of Wilhelm I, Bismarck's dismissal, and Wilhelm II's lifting of the antisocialist law. Even so, women suffered from old laws of association and assembly in some German states, including Prussia and Bavaria. These laws barred women from political organizations and meetings. The laws were most zealously applied against socialist women, but they reinforced the circumspection of bourgeois feminists, against whom they were at times used. Imperial law removed the state barriers in 1908.

Virtually all nonsocialist men sympathetic to feminism were liberals, mostly on the left or progressive wing of liberalism. Liberal men were instrumental in some of the first women's organizations. Karl Schrader and Rudolf Breitscheid's wives, Harriet Schrader-Breymann and Tony Breitscheid, were prominent feminists. Hellmut von Gerlach spoke at feminist rallies and Barth's *Nation* began publishing feminist articles in the eighties. But Julie Bassermann, wife of the National Liberal leader Ernst Basserman, was a feminist, as was Rudolf von Bennigsen's daughter Adelheid, who was a leader in the Protestant women's movement.

Still, liberals were slow to recognize feminist issues. (Women are, of course, not alone in being ignored by those out to win rights for themselves in the name of humanity.) Liberal Reichstag deputies greeted the socialists' first woman suffrage proposal in 1895 with silence. Education and employment opportunities for women won liberal favor long before woman suffrage. Liberal reluctance about the vote was compounded of general male prejudices and specific fears that women would not vote liberal. The Free Conservative Wilhelm von Kardorff, speaking only for himself, was in 1902 the first bourgeois parliamentarian to support woman suffrage in the Reichstag.[8] (He thought that women would vote conservative.) Liberal deputies left the subject to the socialists.

If the Reichstag seemed indifferent to suffrage, German feminists hesitated to ask for it. When the socialists made their 1895 proposal, radical feminists had just begun to petition for free association and assembly; in December 1894 Lily von Gizycki (later the socialist Lily Braun) made the first feminist public speech demanding the vote outright. Anita Augspurg founded the first suffrage organization in 1902. Seeking German participation in the incipient International Woman Suffrage Alliance, she realized that suffragists might organize in Hamburg, which had no laws against political women. Radical women soon pushed moderate feminists to discuss woman suffrage for Germany. Moderates feared radical competition, but also wanted their own "responsible" approach to prevail. Moderates were always solicitous that things be said properly, that they be inoffensive to the authorities and to more timid women, inside and outside the movement. Harmony within the organizations and movements was a fetish. Feminists long circumlocuted suffrage as a "contribution to culture," a "far goal," the "crown" which would top all else, or the "reward" for women's prior achievements. Hardly anyone bothered with the vote's potential usefulness. These attitudes no doubt reflected in part the Reichstag's weakness.

The feminist consensus said that community activities were most likely to merit suffrage: service on poor-law boards and school boards, public guardianships, and the like. These purportedly "feminine" activities would elicit women's greater compassion, their innate maternal feelings. Community work, an extension of women's role at home, was a gradual next step from traditional charitable involvements. These ideas parallel the tendency in most governments to mark off preserves for women, excluding them from such "masculine" monopolies as finance and military committees,[9] though these might have some effect on the realization of plans for health and education where women are presumed competent.

German feminists were notably uneasy about "rights." American feminists easily slipped into natural rights language, the Declaration of Independence serving as a ready model at Seneca Falls. Historical theories of right superseded natural law in Germany, with consequences for both its liberalism and feminism. Rights were contingent, not inalienable. Suffrage was a civil right. Enfranchisement should be decided, in the words of one feminist, "merely *according to considerations of political expediency."* It was "contrary to duty" to give the vote to persons who might "endanger the state or general well-being." Property or educational requirements might then be desirable, or wisdom might delay suffrage until women could handle the responsibility. Perhaps they should first fight for a role in municipal administration, which had been men's "best school of political education."[10] To demand rights carried a stigma of unladylike behavior. German feminists skirted rights with anxiety or coupled their requests with duties or responsibilities. They did not want women voting to Germany's detriment. Here one may often substitute: to the advantage of the Center and socialists. Feminists often seemed to hope that "maturity" would bring to women a "reasonable" liberalism.

For all their regard for ethics and despite the principles binding feminism to liberalism, German feminists were pragmatic about suffrage. They occasionally referred to the injustice or impossibility of men's representing women, particularly on "women's issues." But their most usual argument approximated that of the socialists—without their imputation of inevitable class hatred. Women in the Progressive People's party summarized the position in a 1912 party resolution: "Economic and social developments have extraordinarily increased the number of women employed. This development, which will undoubtedly continue, and the increasing participation of women of all classes in public life leads necessarily . . . to women's *political equality.*"[11]

Consistent with the notion of rights as an outgrowth of women's role in the economy, needed above all to protect their economic interests, feminists emphasized representation on such bodies as trade and industrial councils. Friedrich Naumann saw women's role in the economy as central to the determination of their status, just as his liberalism centered on economic productivity. Not only socialists viewed politics as a struggle of economic forces.

Whatever theory and history might suggest, most liberal men opposed woman suffrage. Roughly, the further "left" the liberal, the more favorable he was to feminism. National Liberals were least sympathetic. Though National Liberal women organized in 1912, and some worked in elections, various local party groups excluded them. At national party congresses they were only visible when the ladies were toasted.

Naumann's tiny National Social party admitted women from the outset where the laws allowed. Given feminists' predilection for the "social," as well as their economic orientation, this cultural-political movement attracted many women. Naumann himself rejected the equation of liberalism with woman suffrage. He especially feared the threat to Prussian suffrage reform from women's radical demand. At the 1908 congress of the Radical Union, with which his movement had merged in 1903, Naumann held up the model of male liberals, who had begun in local administration. The need for woman suffrage could not, he asserted, be self-evident, since liberals were still discussing it. History proved that liberal demands for equality did not implicitly include women. The liberals in the *Paulskirche* in 1848 had bypassed woman suffrage. In fact, Naumann argued, rights *became* "self-evident" when the group wanting them was too evident to overlook. Only recently had organized women prevented liberal men from ignoring woman suffrage. Still, it was not yet realistic for Germany. It might become such if the government could not cope with the present parties or if feminists stirred up continual unrest on the suffragette model.[12]

Naumann softened a Radical Union demand for women's political equality, including suffrage, with a phrase about "recognition in principle."[13] (Incidentally, party women had fashioned a yet weaker formulation that spoke of "admission to" political bodies, but not suffrage.[14] A more explicit wording came from two men, one the trade unionist Anton Erkelenz.) The party also urged the recruitment of women members and officers. The radical suffragist Else Lüders was elected to the national executive committee. Thus this tiny liberal group, almost without Reichstag representation, surged ahead of the other liberal parties.

Yet at this 1908 congress the Union lost three of women's most eloquent allies: Rudolf Breitscheid, Hellmut von Gerlach and Theodor Barth. Precipitating their exit was, ironically, the party's backing of the law on associations which lifted the barriers to women's political work. For that law also included a "language paragraph," requiring that political meetings be held in German. This amounted to exceptional legislation against national minorities. Nor did the law satisfactorily protect working-class organizations. More generally, the secessionists were dissatisfied with the party's compromises with the government and in the so-called "Bülow Bloc" of liberal and conservative parties. They re-formed as the miniscule and short-lived Democratic Union, decidedly feminist, but electorally insignificant.

The most outspokenly prosuffrage element of German feminism agreed with those who opposed the new law, no matter that it freed women. Minna Cauer, a radical feminist who had long urged the women's movement into political paths, argued against trading women's oppression for that of Poles. Increasingly "political," Cauer moved ever further from the women's movement. She introduced the term "feminism" to Germany, but pejoratively, as "Nur-Feminismus," an interest *only* in *women's* rights. Cauer's attacks on "feminism" coincided with dissension in the suffrage movement over the desired kind of woman suffrage. "Feminist" suffragists wanted the same suffrage granted men. Theory aside, this meant application of Prussia's reactionary three-class suffrage to women. Socialists and radical feminists argued that this "lady's suffrage" would not enfranchise women as such, but would confirm the reign of property. National Liberal women were especially fond of the "feminist" position. They claimed that support for universal female suffrage breached the suffrage organization's nonpartisanship. That group nonetheless proposed the basic Reichstag suffrage—universal, direct, equal, and secret—for women at all levels of government. Men were at first included in the demand, which was narrowed to apply only to women in 1911. The demand for an expressly democratic suffrage remained, in the absence of an agreeable substitute formula. But by the time of the war, broader political issues had split the suffrage movement.

Cauer clung to the fiction of her "neutrality." She wanted only the Reichstag suffrage, on which principle the German empire was based. This was perhaps disingenuous, certainly naïve, since the German empire was created through concessions to undemocratic state institutions. More cogently, Cauer noted that any suffrage based on property or education would in fact discriminate against women. Wives would be subsumed under their tax-paying husbands; women alone did not, because of their sex, earn much to be taxed. Cauer finally admitted that she was really a democrat—and that a single suffrage organization was doomed in a politically divided Germany.

Cauer urgently hoped for a union of progressive elements in a single, "decisively" liberal party that would even cooperate with socialists. This party would naturally support women down the line. In 1910 the three main left-liberal parties united in the Progressive People's party. Women's gain was not apparent. The South German People's party strongly opposed woman suffrage. Some members of the largest constituent group, the Radical People's party, sympathized, but the majority hardly desired it. The tiny Radical Union, friendliest of the three, had lost its most vocal proponents of women's vote. Not to endanger unity for the sake of women's outlandish wishes, the new party's program contained an innocuous paragraph, coming before a final tribute to universal peace, on desired changes in education and employment for women—most of them already won by feminists. After some outraged murmurs, progressive women put liberal unity first and looked to the 1912 congress.

They were again disappointed. A women's committee proposed for the party program: "Full equality of citizenship rights for women."[15] The party executive committee's spokesman, however, pointed out that "many outstanding friends of the party"—indeed "true and genuine liberal men"—could not reconcile a woman-suffrage plank with their principles. The party could not rebuke them in a matter of no practical importance. Liberal unity, it was emphasized, rested on the lowest common denominator of principle. Liberals could be for or against suffrage. But all should be wary of imperiling Prussian suffrage reform for men. One progressive's earlier plea to impatient women was invoked: "Let us first become men, before we solve the woman question." The executive committee opposed any program change, but graciously allowed individual members freedom to go beyond it in work for women's rights.[16]

Women members did not hide their annoyance. Yet, as concerned for liberalism as for women, they would not secede. Liberal women were not, Gertrud Bäumer explained, suffragettes looking for a new battlefield, indifferent to the havoc they might wreak. They came "as members of our liberal party, not in the first instance as feminists." "We stand here," she asserted, "because liberalism with its principles of the individual's independence . . . , of responsibility for oneself, has given us all the weapons with which women too have tried, in a spirit of freedom, to overcome the difficult crisis in which they were placed through economic development." Bäumer, no doubt echoing Naumann's demand for a clamor, disputed liberalism's ambiguity as to woman suffrage. The women's movement was a liberal issue because *"a broad stratum of our people demands equal rights in the state."* Bäumer, chairwoman of the nonpartisan feminist federation, admitted that the BDF was hurt by its leaders' identification with the party. But, she claimed, "We have brought this sacrifice in full consciousness. Out of the wish, as liberal citizens, to confess our liberalism, even if we thereby forfeit successes which liberalism today cannot bring us, rather which we could only expect from other parties."[17]

The women finally agreed to a nonbinding resolution on suffrage (see p. 132). Conrad Haussmann noted with relief: ". . . the whole question shifts onto the academic level of expression of sympathy for the movement." Haussmann "welcomed the women's movement" but thought it wrong "to give it the direction of politicizing women."[18]

Despite feminists' own efforts to prevent it, the German women's movement was long since politicized. Most feminists identified with the liberal parties. Their unwillingness to accept liberal defeat hamstrung their ability to bargain with other parties for the feminist cause.

To women outraged by a fellow progressive's patronizing remarks about women, the progressive Reichstag deputy Ernst Müller-Meiningen once replied: "According to its whole position on culture, the *bourgeois* women's movement can find protection of its legitimate interests only by progressive liberalism" (emphasis added).[19] Middle-class feminists had no other resort, short of eschewing parties altogether. Feminist consistency might have led them toward socialism, but this path was inconsistent with the rest of their lives. Conservative and Center parties offered less to feminists than the liberals, and were repugnant to feminists in any case.

German women were finally enfranchised by the revolutionary socialist government in the postwar upheaval of November 1918. To the end, few feminists expected more than municipal suffrage as the reward for women's wartime service to the Fatherland. The last document of the old Reichstag was a proposal by the parliamentary interparty committee that state governments reform their undemocratic franchises, including the granting of woman suffrage. Progressives, National Liberals, and Centrists more or less willingly approved what was essentially a socialist demand. Wartime cooperation among these parties had lessened fears that women's votes would strengthen a rival whose victory was unthinkable. Yet the parliamentarians' action had no effect; it simply confirmed what the spontaneity of revolution had already brought to pass.

Today's feminists may wince at the concessions made by German feminists to liberals for whom one could adapt Harriet Taylor Mill's description of men who were Chartists because they were not lords; they were "levellers who would level only down to themselves."[20] But if German feminists were truer to liberalism than the "liberals," all the less could they acquiesce in the triumph of political elements which they found disastrous. They subordinated women's rights to their version of the national welfare, all the while maintaining that Germany could not prosper if its women did not. Given the illiberality of German liberals regarding women, liberal women had to compromise either their liberal or their feminist principles—though for them the two were inseparable. When it came to that, they sacrificed the feminist goals. This was in keeping with traditional feminine "virtue," which German feminism never entirely disavowed, though it extended the objects for self-sacrifice well beyond husband and children. Their self-sacrifice also involved an assignment of top priority to what they deemed Germany's national interest. And this had little to do with feminine "virtue" or feminism.

## NOTES

1. Ika Freudenberg, "Die Forderungen der Frauen an den bayrischen Liberalismus," *Centralblatt der Bund Deutscher Frauenvereine* VII (December 1, 1905), 129–30. (Hereafter *CB.*)

2. Alice Salomon, "Politik und Frauenbewegung," *Nation* XX (May 16, 1903), 516.

3. Paula Mueller, "Ziele und Aufgaben des Deutsch-Evangelischen Frauenbundes," in Paula Mueller, ed., *Handbuch zur Frauenfrage* (Gross Lichterfelde, 1908), 60.

4. Marianne Weber, "Politik und Frauenbewegung," *CB* III (December 1, 1901), 129–30.

5. Heinrich von Sybel, *Ueber die Emancipation der Frauen,* (Bonn, 1870), esp. 17.

6. Paula Mueller, "Wie steht der Deutsch-Evangelischen Frauenbund zum Frauenstimmrecht?" *Die Frau* XX (October 1912), 98.

7. The best discussion of early feminism is found in Margrit Twellmann-Schepp, *Die deutsche Frauenbewegung im Spiegel repräsentativer Frauenzeitschriften, ihre Anfänge und erste Entwicklung (1843–1889)* (Meisenheim/Glan, 1972).

8. *Verhandlungen des Reichstages,* X Leg. Per., 2d sess., 1900/03, 3586–87.

9. See Maurice Duverger, *The Political Role of Women* (Paris, 1955), 95–101. The "feminine" fields are health, family, welfare, children, women, social questions—generally low priority concerns. Finance, defense, and foreign affaris are virtually "off limits" to women deputies.

10. Elisabeth Altmann-Gottheiner, "Grundsätze und Forderungen der Frauenbewegung auf dem Gebiet des öffentlichen Lebens," in *Grundsätze und Forderungen der Frauenbewegung* (Leipzig and Berlin, 1912), 30 ("Flugschriften des BDF," no. 1).

11. *Der zweite Parteitag der Fortschrittlichen Volkspartei zu Mannheim, 5–7. Oktober 1912* (Berlin, 1912), 96.

12. *Dritter Delegiertertag des Wahlvereins der Liberalen zu Frankfurt a.M. am 21. und 22. April 1908* (Berlin [1908]), 102–10.

13. *Ibid.,* 111–12.

14. *Ibid.,* 92.

15. *Mannheim Parteitag,* 82.

16. *Ibid.,* 83–87.

17. *Ibid.,* 87–91.

18. *Ibid.,* 92–93.

19. Ernst Müller-Meiningen, "Offener Brief an die Herausgeberin," *Die Frauenbewegung* XIII (May 1, 1906), 65.

20. Harriet Taylor Mill, "Enfranchisement of Women," in John S. Mill and Harriet T. Mill, *Essays on Sex Equality,* ed. Alice S. Rossi (Chicago, 1970), 96–97.

# Feminism and Class Consciousness in the British and American Women's Trade Union Leagues, 1890-1925

*Robin Miller Jacoby*

A comparative history of the British and American women's trade union leagues between 1890 and 1925 provides an illuminating test case of the response of certain women in this period to the issues of feminism and class consciousness. This study developed out of an interest in feminism and a desire to explore its intersection with the ideology and actuality of class differences.[1] Existing during a period of an active male-dominated labor movement, and a middle-class-dominated feminist movement, the British and American women's trade union leagues were autonomous but related reform organizations of leisured and working-class women concerned about the problems of women workers. This article will examine two aspects of this intersection of feminism and class consciousness through a discussion of the relationship between the British and American women's trade union leagues and the women's suffrage movement in each country and an analysis of the short-lived (1919-24) International Federation of Working Women, an organization that came into existence under the sponsorship of the British and American women's trade union leagues.[2]

Feminism and class consciousness are obviously complex notions in themselves, and little serious theoretical attention has been paid to the relationship between them.[3] Feminism simultaneously complements and conflicts with the ideology of the primacy of class consciousness. It is complementary in that it implies equal rights and opportunities for women within sexually mixed, class-based settings; it is conflicting in that it also implies that the sexual identification creates a solidarity among women that transcends class divisions. Another aspect of the complexity of these issues is that feminism and class consciousness are both ideologies that have ideal or utopian as well as historical dimensions. That is, the ultimate vision of a sexually equal and classless society is expressed and struggled for in different ways in different periods, and all people involved in struggles related to the lives and rights of women and workers do not necessarily share the same ultimate vision.

In the context of the period under discussion, feminism was an ideology that centered on two somewhat contradictory premises: one was that women should have the same political, legal, educational, and economic rights as men; the other was that due to women's reproductive and maternal roles, women were intellectually, psychologically, and physically different from men in certain fundamental ways. Feminist thought held that the combination of these two situations—women as oppressed members of a society and women as potential or actual mothers—created a bond of sisterhood between all women that theoretically transcended class, racial, and national differences.[4]

Within the British and American women's trade union leagues, class differences were clearly defined. This was true even though it was during this period of the late nineteenth and early twentieth centuries that the lines between working- and middle-class women were beginning to blur due to the expansion of the service sector of the economy and the significant growth in the number of white collar workers.[5] The trade union leagues, however, were primarily concerned with the problems of women in the industrial labor force, so that the distinction between working-class and middle-class members, who were called allies in the American league, was obvious to all concerned. Thus, in the historical context of the women's trade union leagues, class definitions were quite clear; what was less clear to league members was what feminism meant in the concerns and activities of the leagues.

The women's trade union leagues must be seen in the broader context of the impact of industrialization on women. Industrialization basically involved the separation of work from the home, and some of the earliest processes to be industrialized were those related to the production of food and clothing, processes that had traditionally fallen within the sphere of work done by women. The result of this was that working-class women simply moved their work from the home to the factory; the result for middle- and upper-class women was the loss of an economically productive role.

The problem faced by women in the industrial labor force in the late nineteenth and early twentieth centuries was that they were characteristically unskilled, clustered in the lowest paying jobs, and unorganized.[6] These factors, plus prevailing attitudes regarding the role of women, were all interrelated, and they combined to produce a significantly different industrial experience for women than for men.

Organizing women workers into trade unions was a difficult and discouraging process because of several factors: the age of women workers, the length of their employment, the types of jobs they did, their wage scale, the structure of the labor movement, and the prevailing concepts of femininity. The archetypal woman worker in this period was a young (sixteen to twenty-six), single woman who expected to work for a few years prior to her marriage. Thus, women considered themselves and were regarded by male workers as only temporary members of the labor force. This fact was a major reason why women were used as the labor pool to fill the needs of an expanding industrial economy for unskilled workers.

Within most factories the different processes were rigidly defined as men's jobs or women's jobs; the men's jobs were consistently those calling for the most skill and commanding the highest wages. For example, in the garment industry, cutting the cloth was invariably done by men, while the finishing work, such as sewing on buttons, was always done by women. The general rule regarding wages was that full-time male workers[7] earned on the average twice as much as full-time female workers. In New York and Chicago the average wage for women factory workers was around six dollars a week;[8] in Britain women's wages averaged seven shillings sixpence a week (about $1.80).[9] An example of the difference organization and the chance to work at a skilled job could make is revealed in the fact that in the one place where women were not denied access to skilled jobs and to union membership—in Lancashire—it was not exceptional for women textile workers to earn 24 shillings a week.[10] Women's wages were low partly because of the unskilled nature of their jobs, but also because it was assumed that their income was a supplementary, rather than a primary, income for a family.

Since the labor movement in both countries was more interested in skilled workers, locals covering women's jobs simply did not exist. Women were therefore forced to create organizations to encompass their job categories and then to convince an existing union to extend its definition of the craft to include unskilled and semiskilled workers. This process involved going to meetings, often at night, and pushing forcefully for recognition from male workers and employers. Since such behavior was contrary to notions internalized by both men and women about the proper behavior for women, it was difficult for women to initiate and sustain such activity.[11] A serious obstacle to the organization of women workers was the lack of places in which they could meet; union meetings were often held in pubs or social halls where women neither felt comfortable nor welcome. A major activity of both the American and British women's trade union leagues was finding and renting places where women could comfortably meet with other women workers or with male co-workers or employers.

An additional obstacle to the organization of American women workers was the ethnic heterogeneity of the American labor force. Language barriers and ethnic differences impeded the development of feelings of solidarity among workers, and employers often exploited these differences to keep their work force divided. It was not uncommon for an employer to arrange his workers so that people of dissimilar backgrounds were clustered together in a factory; for example, a group of workers could include a Russian Jew, an Italian, a Scandinavian, and a Slav. During the major strikes in the garment industry in this period, there were sometimes as many as nineteen groups of workers meeting simultaneously to discuss strike issues and tactics in their own language with their own people.

Intrinsically related to the economic changes involved in industrialization[12] was the codification of what has become known as the Cult of Domesticity—the ideology that women belonged demurely and submissively in the home and that their primary function was to be the moral guardians of society through their maternal and wifely roles.[13] Some version of this ideology permeated all classes of British and American society, even though all classes could obviously not afford to live out its implications. The women's movement that developed primarily among middle-class women in Britain and America in the mid-nineteenth century reflected both an attack on the restricted definition of what was considered to be women's sphere and an internalization of prevailing notions on the nature of women. The former led to the women's rights movement—the demand for legal, political, and educational equality; the latter was expressed through what has been termed social feminism.[14]  Social feminists were women who expanded the scope of their role as moral guardians to include society at large as well as their individual families, and who then focused their reform energies on problems that particularly affected women they viewed as "their less fortunate sisters."

The process of industrialization served to define more sharply class differences between women;[15]  it created an oppressive work life for most women in the industrial labor force, and it created an oppressive leisure life for many middle-class women. The juxtaposition of industrialization and the Cult of Domesticity explains the existence and development of organizations like the British and American women's trade union leagues.

The women's trade union leagues of Britain and the United States were autonomous organizations connected by some personal contact between the leadership of each organization and by a common focus on the problems of women workers.[16]  The publication of each organization carried news of the activities of the other, and on occasion there was an exchange of delegates to each other's conventions, but there was no formal structure binding the two organizations.

Somewhat ironically, the British organization was established first, as the result of a visit to the United States in 1873 by Emma Paterson. Paterson had served an apprenticeship as a bookbinder and had followed that with a stint as a governess, before moving into social work and becoming the assistant secretary of the London Working Men's Club and Institute. A few years later she married Thomas Paterson, a cabinet maker and the secretary of the Institute. Thomas Paterson possessed some private means, and they used this money for their honeymoon trip to America.

While in New York, Emma Paterson was intrigued by what she later described as "some successful unions consisting of and managed by working women."[17]  Not much is known about any of these unions; they were apparently part of the group of short-lived, independent, benefit-society oriented[18]  unions that characterized the history of most artisan guilds and trade unions in nineteenth-century America.[19]

Emma Paterson had been peripherally involved with similar groups in England in the 1860s, and her contact with these New York unions revived her commitment to the possibilities of organizing women into trade unions. On her return to England she published a series of articles discussing the sweated conditions and low pay of most women workers and the need for the organization of working women. She followed her articles with a call to a meeting of "sympathetic ladies and gentlemen," most of whom were middle-class social reformers.[20]  However, the group did include a few influential men trade unionists, such as the secretary of the London Society of Journeymen Bookbinders and the secretary of the London Trades Council. In the course of this 1874 meeting, it was decided to form the Women's Protective and Provident League. The words "trade union" were consciously not used in the title of the new organization, in an attempt to placate men trade unionists, who on the whole were hostile to the idea of women joining trade unions. They believed it was bad enough that women were becoming competitors with them in the industrial labor force; they were certainly not about to let them into their unions. Since one of the goals of the league was to create awareness and gain support for the problems of women workers among the middle and upper classes as well as the working class, the title chosen also reflected a desire not to offend these elements of the population, which at this time were still relatively hostile to the idea of trade unions, for men or for women.[21] The league organized some women's unions, but the focus of the groups that were formed was very much on benefit-society activities rather than any kind of genuine trade union struggles.

By 1890, due to changes in the climate of public opinion and to changing leadership in the league (Emma Paterson had died in 1886), the name of the organization was changed to the Women's Trade Union League (WTUL), and the focus shifted much more solidly to organizing women into existing men's unions where possible, or into newly created unions composed solely of women in a particular trade. Initially the WTUL served as the umbrella organization uniting these women's unions; later (1906) the league created the National Federation of Women Workers to serve this purpose. Because of its mixed-class membership, the league had never been able to become an affiliated member of the Trades Union Congress, the British equivalent of the American Federation of Labor. The National Federation of Women Workers, however, was totally composed of women workers; it was recognized as a bona fide trade union and was allowed to affiliate with the Trades Union Congress. The Women's Trade Union League, whose membership consisted of affiliated unions with women members and individuals sympathetic to the goals of the league, remained in existence until 1921, when it dissolved and became the women's section of the Trades Union Congress.[22]

The American Women's Trade Union League was established in 1903 as the result of a visit to England by an American, William English Walling, a wealthy progressive who eventually became a Socialist. Influenced by Jane Addams, Walling had become a settlement worker in the New York University Settlement House, and through his life in the settlement house, he had become interested in the problems of women workers. He came back from this trip to England impressed with the philosophy and work of the British WTUL and began talking with various people about the possibility of creating such an organization in the United States. These discussions led to a meeting of interested persons in Boston in conjunction with the 1903 American Federation of Labor convention. As with the establishment of the British league, the people attending this meeting were men and women who represented primarily the settlement house and labor movements. The result of the meeting was the creation of the American Women's Trade Union League. The first slate of officers included Mary Morton Kehew, who was a socially prominent Bostonian active in the women's movement and who was also known as a friend of labor; Jane Addams, the well-known founder and head of Hull House in Chicago; and Mary Kenney O'Sullivan, a bookbinder who had been briefly employed as an organizer by the AFL in the 1890s, and who, along with Walling, had been the key figure in calling the meeting to form the Women's Trade Union League.

The American league was headquartered in Chicago, and it developed branches in various cities, mainly in the East and Midwest, with Boston, New York, and Chicago becoming the first local branches and remaining the most important ones over the years. Its main purpose was the organization of women into trade unions. Like the British, their idea was to organize locals of women in a particular trade and then try to get the appropriate AFL affiliate to accept the local; failing that, the local WTUL would serve as the parent organization. However, since the league was endorsed by but not affiliated with the AFL (and the American WTUL never developed an organization comparable to the British National Federation of Women Workers), it meant that these women's unions did not have the full force of the labor movement behind them.

In addition to its organizing activities, the American league often put as much or sometimes even more energy into lobbying for protective legislation for women workers. The issue of protective legislation for women workers is extremely complex, for it raises ideological as well as economic and physiological questions. The basic justification for such legislation has been that women are physically weaker than men and that since all women are potential or actual mothers, it is in the public interest to regulate the hours and working conditions of women (preservation of the species was the kind of phrase used in discussions of this issue in the late nineteenth and early twentieth centuries).

The women's labor movement in both Britain and the United States consistently supported and lobbied for protective legislation for women. Groups such as the women's trade union leagues agreed with the above justification, and they regarded protective legislation as a way of significantly improving conditions for women workers, who were not sufficiently organized or politically powerful enough to gain such improvements on their own.

Male workers and the labor movement in each country usually supported such legislation for women. Their support was sometimes based on the assumption that they too would benefit from the proposed changes. Often, however, their support reflected an attempt to keep women out of the labor force; they hoped the restrictions would make it more difficult to hire women, and, therefore, they would not have to contend with women as potential competitors for their jobs.

Feminists in both countries tended to oppose protective legislation on the basis that it was discriminatory toward women. It never became quite as controversial in Britain as it did in the United States, although there were various instances when feminists and women labor leaders clashed over the issue. After suffrage was won in the United States, the National Women's Party proposed the Equal Rights Amendment and focused all its activity on lobbying for the amendment. The American WTUL spent an enormous amount of time, energy, and money in the 1920s fighting the Women's Party and its proposed amendment. The WTUL argued that women still needed protection, that the existing legislation helped more women workers than it hindered, and that the Equal Rights Amendment would wipe out all gains that had been achieved for women in the industrial labor force.[23]

The American WTUL also stressed educational activities for middle- and working-class women. The intention was to awaken middle-class women to the problems faced by working women and to gain their financial and moral support for the efforts of women workers to better their conditions. This educational effort was a significant attempt to develop a sense of sisterhood across class lines. The educational activities aimed at working-class women consisted of English classes for immigrants and programs involving academic study and fieldwork training for women organizers to develop women labor leaders. The best known women labor leaders identified with the WTUL were Agnes Nestor, Rose Schneiderman, and Mary Anderson. Nestor, a glove worker, became one of the few women officers of an international union (the International Glove Workers Union), and she was also president of the Chicago league for many years. Schneiderman, a Russian Jewish immigrant, was a cap maker by trade. She worked at different times as an organizer for the National Women's Trade Union League and for the International Ladies Garment Workers Union. She eventually became president of the New York league and was the only woman on the Labor Advisory Board of the National Recovery Administration (NRA) in the 1930s, an honor of which she was enormously proud. Mary Anderson was a Swedish immigrant who was an active member of the Boot and Shoe Workers Union before she became a full-time organizer for the Chicago Women's Trade Union League. She was selected as the first director of the Women's Bureau in the Department of Labor when the bureau was established shortly after World War I, and remained in that post until her retirement in 1944.[24]

Thus, organization, education, and legislation were the major concerns of both the British and American women's trade union leagues. Over the years however, the British league emphasized organization to a much greater extent than the American league, which divided its energies and priorities more evenly among all three areas. Involvement in the leagues also provided social fellowship for the members; relationships between various members were strained at times due to personal and political differences, but the friendships that existed were important sources of support and pleasure in the lives of many league members. Involvement in the leagues gave a sense of purpose to the lives of many of the leisure-class members. The leagues, especially the American one, have been criticized for being middle-class dominated organizations, genuinely concerned about improving the conditions of working women, but nevertheless, benevolently intent on keeping women workers in their lower-status position in society and within the leagues.[25] There is, however, evidence that many of the working-class members valued the broadened intellectual, political, economic, and cultural horizons that involvement in the leagues brought to them.[26]

With the preceding sections as background, it is now possible to return to a discussion of the issues of feminism and class consciousness through an examination of the relationship of the British and American women's trade union leagues to the women's suffrage movements and an analysis of the conflict that developed between the American and British leagues concerning the International Federation of Working Women.

The struggle for suffrage was merely one thrust of the nineteenth-century movement for women's rights, but by 1890 it had become the dominant focus of the women's movement in both countries.[27] However, the British and American leagues responded quite differently to the suffrage movement in their respective countries, partly because of the attitudes of the leadership within each country, but mainly because the suffrage situation was so different.

The most basic difference was that Britain did not have universal suffrage for men until 1918. Until then suffrage was based on property qualifications. These qualifications had been lowered at various times in the course of the nineteenth century,[28] but in 1910 only 58 percent of the adult male population was enfranchised.[29] The 1918 bill gave universal suffrage to all men over the age of twenty-one but only to women over the age of thirty; it was not until 1928 that women from twenty-one to thirty were granted the right to vote.[30] The women's suffrage movement began seriously in 1866, so that it took fifty-six years of almost constant agitation for British women to win the right to vote. One reason the suffrage struggle was so protracted was that the Conservatives, who stood to gain politically from a limited enfranchisement of women, i.e., the extension to women of the same property qualifications applying to men, were philosophically opposed to the idea; the Liberals, on the other hand, were more sympathetic philosophically but opposed women's suffrage on pragmatic political grounds.[31]

Thus, the demand of the women's suffrage movement in Britain was not for votes for all women, but for suffrage for women on "the same grounds as it is or may be granted to men." The suffragists' demand reflected both a somewhat sophisticated political strategy (the women feeling it was not politic to ask for broader rights for women than those granted to men) and the undemocratic attitudes of a certain percentage of those in the movement who were not interested in extending the franchise beyond themselves and others in their social position. An example of this attitude is found in a manifesto of the Conservative and Unionist Women's Franchise Association which stated that one of the objects of the association was the opposition to "manhood suffrage in any form."[32]

The British WTUL was not opposed in principle to the idea of women's suffrage. However, the league largely ignored the suffrage movement because of its class-based nature and demands, in order to retain its credibility with the labor movement. The British league never participated in suffrage demonstrations, and, in contrast to the American experience, no effort was made on the part of the league leadership to educate women in the suffrage movement to make them more understanding of and sympathetic to the needs of women workers, one need clearly being the power of the vote.[33] The league, however, did give a certain amount of straightforward publicity to the activities of women's suffrage groups in its publication *The Woman Worker*. When the Labour party began its campaign for adult suffrage in 1905, the league was solidly but not very actively behind this position.[34] However, a series of political events caused the Labour party to change its position in 1912. Realizing that the issue of adult suffrage was being used by the government as a delaying tactic in its response to the women's suffrage movement and feeling that some extension of the franchise was long overdue, the Labour party announced after its 1912 convention that it would henceforth support a bill for the limited enfranchisement of women. Up to this point the Labour party had only supported bills that would lead to universal adult suffrage; it changed its position on the assumption that if the limited enfranchisement of women could be instituted, it would serve as an opening wedge for further extensions to follow. Mary Macarthur, head of the WTUL and active in the Labour party from its inception, was a key figure in urging this change of policy. She reminded those at the 1912 Labour party conference how many times she had opposed a limited women's suffrage bill based on property qualifications, but she went on to explain why she thought it was now important and necessary for the Labour party to support the women's suffrage movement.[35] Despite her role at the convention and the WTUL's support for the changed position of the Labour party, league members and leaders continued to eschew participation in suffrage activities to concentrate on their organizing and legislative lobbying work.

When the 1918 bill was passed extending the franchise to men at age twenty-one and to women at thirty, the rationale was that it was a reward for service rendered by men and women during World War I. *The Woman Worker* pointed out that this still left most women workers disenfranchised since they were predominantly under thirty years of age; it also noted the irony of finally giving women the vote as a reward for their work during the war and then excluding the largest group of war workers.[36]

Just because the WTUL was not particularly involved in the suffrage movement did not mean there were no working-class women involved. However, looking for indications of working-class involvement in the women's suffrage movement outside the membership of the WTUL reveals only a limited number of examples of active individuals or groups. The earliest involvement came from women textile workers in the Manchester Women's Trades and Labour Council who supported a petition campaign sponsored by the National Union of Women Suffrage Societies in the late 1890s. Although working-class women did spend time collecting signatures and speaking to trade unions and Labour clubs, the initiative for this activity came from the influence of two middle-class women, Esther Roper and Eva Gore-Booth, who were interested in bringing working-class women into the suffrage movement.

The Women's Cooperative Guild, an organization of married working-class women, also supported the women's suffrage movement rather than aligning with the Labour party movement for adult suffrage. Probably the best-known group of working-class women actively working for women's suffrage was the

East London Federation of Suffragettes, led by Sylvia Pankhurst. There were also some working-class women involved as individual members of the militant Women's Social and Political Union (the organization headed by Emmeline and Christabel Pankhurst) and in groups comprising the more moderate National Union of Women's Suffrage Societies, headed by Millicent Garrett Fawcett. The Women's Social and Political Union quickly moved away from its 1903 origins in the Independent Labour party; it made no further efforts to relate to working-class women as workers or as wives, and it gave no support or recognition to Sylvia Pankhurst's efforts in East London.[37]

The papers of the National Union of Women's Suffrage Societies were largely destroyed during World War II, but there is some evidence in the extant papers of certain efforts on the part of suffrage groups to reach out to working-class women.[38] How much of this was due to genuine interest in the problems of women workers and how much a way of simply increasing support for the cause of suffrage is difficult to assess, but it seems to be primarily the latter. One indication of the attitudes of women in the National Union comes from an incident involving its leader, Millicent Garrett Fawcett, in 1898. Fawcett was a shareholder in the Bryant and May Match Company, which had been the scene of one of the first uprisings of women workers in 1888. In 1898 a campaign was in progress by concerned liberals urging the government to pass legislation prohibiting women from working with phosphorus because of the dangers of necrosis (phosphorus poisoning). Fawcett wrote to one of the leaders of this campaign saying that she had gone to an East End club to talk with some of the matchgirls, as the women workers in this industry were called. She reported that she found them unanimous in being quite content with their employment at Bryant and May and not at all fearful of contracting necrosis (known to the workers as "phossy-jaw.") She went on to say that the workers expressed great indignation when she told them that some people wanted to forbid women and girls working where phosphorus was used. The letter gives no indication of Fawcett's sensitivity to what was undoubtedly the real situation—that the workers had many complaints about the hardships and danger of their work, but they were terrified of losing their jobs and responded to Fawcett in the way they did because they assumed she was a spy sent by the firm to uncover potential troublemakers.[39]

The American situation differed considerably from the British since universal suffrage for men already existed in the United States; thus, women's suffrage would bring the enfranchisement of all women. From its beginning in 1903, the American WTUL incorporated the demand for suffrage into its statement of goals, and in addition, some of the league's leading members were quite active in the suffrage movement.

The American suffrage movement began in the 1850s by claiming that women should have the vote on grounds of basic justice and equality. By 1890, owing to changes in the leadership of the movement and the general social climate in the United States (particularly in urban areas), the rhetoric of the movement had shifted to focus on what Aileen Kraditor calls arguments of expediency.[40] Sharing and capitalizing on prevailing racist and nativist prejudices, suffragist speeches and publications began to claim that being excluded from a political right that was extended to immigrant, black, and working-class men was an insult to native-born, white, middle-class women. Speaking to the 1889 convention of the National American Woman Suffrage Association (NAWSA), Olympia Brown, a Universalist minister, noted that "the foreign influence" was threatening "our free school, our free church, and our republican government," and since there were "three times as many American-born women as the whole foreign population, men and women together," giving women the vote was "the only means of overcoming this foreign influence and maintaining our free institutions." She went on to add, "Women are well-educated; . . . they are reading and thinking and writing; and yet they are the political inferiors of all the riff-raff of Europe that is poured upon our shores. It is unbearable. There is no language that can express the enormous injustice done to women. . . . "[41]

The delegates to the 1893 NAWSA convention expressed their continuing agreement with Brown's position when they passed the following resolution, adopted unanimously: ". . . we call attention to the significant facts that in every State there are more women who can read and write than the whole number of illiterate male voters; more white women who can read and write than all negro voters; more American women who can read and write than all foreign voters; so that the enfranchisement of such women would settle the vexed question of rule by illiteracy, whether of the home-grown or foreign-born production."[42]

Belle Kearney, a Southern suffragist, added a note of explicit racism in her address to the 1903 NAWSA convention. Reiterating the statistical argument on the proportion of white, native-born women to the rest of the population, she told the convention delegates, "The enfranchisement of women would insure immediate and durable white supremacy. . . . The South is slow to grasp the great fact that the enfranchisement of women would settle the race question in politics."[43]

While these attitudes never totally disappeared from the suffrage movement, by about 1910 they became much more muted toward immigrants and working-class people. (The same was not true regarding blacks; in order not to antagonize southern congressmen and suffrage supporters, black women were consistently discouraged from participating in the suffrage movement.)[44] This change in attitude was due partly to the realization on the part of suffragists that whether they liked it or not, such groups of men did have the vote, and it made more sense to have them as allies than as enemies toward the women's cause. Another factor in the shift was the influence of women like Jane Addams and Margaret Dreier Robins, the middle-class president of the American WTUL. They acted as liaisons between the women's movement and immigrant and working-class women, and their speeches and writings attuned many suffragists to the needs and problems of women workers.

Some of this change was sincere, but there is evidence that it also stemmed from pragmatic considerations of self-interest on the part of NAWSA leaders.

A letter in the NAWSA papers reveals the offer of a first vice-presidency of NAWSA to Margaret Dreier Robins was "a bait for the labor vote."[45] Robins declined the offer, claiming her time was fully occupied with WTUL work, and there is no indication that she questioned the motivations behind the NAWSA offer. Carrie Chapman Catt, the president of NAWSA in this period, indicated some of her feelings about workers and immigrants in another letter which stated: ". . . I am a *good* democrat in theory but my faith weakens when it meets bad air, dirt . . . and horrid smells. I rather enjoy onions for instance when the odor pervades a clean home and is diluted with good air. To my nostrils it becomes a real aristocratic perfume, but when it is a democratic odor diluted with perfumes of beer and uncleanliness, the blood of my royal ancestors boils in protest. Of course I do not know positively that I had any royal ancestors but if I had not why this shrinking from my fellow beings because of smells?"[46]

However, the WTUL gave its whole-hearted support to the issue of suffrage in its conventions and publications, and Margaret Dreier Robins was a frequent speaker at suffrage meetings. There was also a regular exchange of delegates between the conventions of the WTUL and NAWSA. Delegations from the WTUL participated in suffrage parades, and, especially in urban areas, there was an increasing tendency to include factory women as speakers in large suffrage rallies and meetings. Rose Schneiderman and Leonora O'Reilly, the latter one of the early working-class members of the WTUL who later established the New York Wage Earners Suffrage League, spoke often at mass suffrage meetings in cities throughout New York State on topics such as "The Right to Organize" and "The Importance of the Vote to Working Women." As one working-class member of the WTUL wrote to Rose Schneiderman: "I knew that you would make good on the road. For the 'cultured' ladies may be very sincere in their desire for the balot, I don't doubt their sincerety, but because their views are narrow, and their knowledge of social conditions limited, they cannot do as well as some of us can. And as I come in contact with these women day after day, they are beginning to see the necessity of having a working girl tour a State rather than some professor."[47] Agnes Nestor participated in the Illinois Suffrage Special, a caravan that traveled throughout that state in 1910 seeking support for a state referendum on women's suffrage, and she was often featured as the principal speaker in industrial areas. Three women from the New York WTUL headed the Industrial Section of the New York State Suffrage party, which focused its activities on winning support for women's suffrage from trade-union men; women from the Boston league engaged in similar activities in Massachusetts.[48]

However, interaction between working-class and middle-class women in the suffrage movement was not always harmonious. A delegate from San Francisco to the 1909 WTUL convention reported that the mixed-class suffrage organization in that city had fallen apart because the middle-class women had refused to support a strike of streetcar conductors. The suffragists regarded the strike as an inconvenience to themselves and displayed no sense of sympathy or identity with the labor cause. On the basis of this incident, the working-class women decided they could no longer work in the same group with the other women, and they withdrew to form their own independent suffrage organization, which they called the Wage Earners Suffrage League.[49]

Another example of tension is found in the letter of a young worker and member of the WTUL who had been active in the Industrial Section of the New York State Suffrage Association. While attending a suffrage conference in New York, she wrote to Leonora O'Reilly:

> . . . I feel as if I have butted in wher I was not wanted. Miss Hay gave me a badge was very nice to me but you know they had a school teacher represent the Industrial workers if you ever herd her it was like trying to fill a barrell with water that had no bottom not a word of labor spoken at this convention so far . . . after the hole thing was over some people came to me and said I had a right to speak for labor but they kept away until it was over.
>
> . . . I am not goying to wait for sunday meeting I am goying home satturday.[50]

The American league was much more oriented toward public relations work than the British. This activity took the form of letters and speeches to a variety of women's organizations, not necessarily connected with the suffrage movement. The point of this work was always to gain support and sympathy for general or specific struggles of women workers. Agnes Nestor was sent by the Chicago WTUL to a 1906 General Federation of Women's Clubs convention in Illinois to give a speech on women in industry. She writes in her autobiography that "it was a bold step" for the clubwomen to consent to having a worker speak to them on trade unionism and that she was anxious to present her case effectively. Wanting to look her best in the company of these society women, she had a lovely silk blouse made for the occasion and described herself as looking as "gay as a butterfly." After the event, she was pleased to have her speech described as "stirring and informative," but she was terribly disappointed by a newspaper reference to her "dark and shabby appearance." So much for her beautiful new blouse and her attempts to appear stylish and well-dressed before a middle-class audience![51]

A typical attempt on the part of the Women's Trade Union League to gain the support of middle-class women was the league's response to a 1912 strike of women workers at the Kalamazoo Corset Company. In addition to sending organizers to help the strikers form a union and carry out negotiations with the employers, the league sent letters to a variety of women's organizations explaining the causes of the strike and the demands of the workers and asking the recipients of the letters not to buy corsets made by this company until the strike was over. It is of course virtually impossible to assess the extent to which middle-class women supported the strike in this way; the significant point is that the league leadership thought such a tactic was potentially effective and was willing to devote a portion of the league's limited financial resources to efforts along this line.

Probably the best known instance of the league's generating a response from leisured women was the supportive activities of what Rose Schneiderman called "The Mink Brigade" during the 1909–10 strike of women garment workers in New York.[52] Prominent women, such as Alva Vanderbilt Belmont and Josephine Sykes Morgenthau, staged fund-raising benefits and served as observers of police treatment of the strikers' picket lines. Their involvement generated extensive publicity for the strike. However, as Theresa Malkiel, one of the strikers, pointed out, the financial contributions of these women, while significantly helpful, were not as great as they could have been. In reference to the well-known Hippodrome rally sponsored by Alva Belmont, Malkiel wrote in her diary: "The most of our girls had to walk both ways in order to save their car fare. Many came without dinner, but the collection baskets had more pennies than anything else in them—it was our girls themselves who helped to make it up, and yet there were so many rich women present. And I'm sure the speakers made it plain to them how badly the money was needed, then how comes it that out of the $300 collected there should be $70 in pennies?"[53] Other than the continuing activities of the allied members of the WTUL, this instance of strike support was virtually the only one in this period when nonworking women actively joined workers in their struggles.

To summarize the relationship of the women's trade union leagues to the women's suffrage movement in each country: the class-based nature of the British suffrage movement meant that there was little effort made on the part of working-class or middle-class women to join together as sisters fighting for a right that was denied to all women. The American movement reveals more of an attempt to transcend class divisions, but the evidence indicates that despite some genuine instances of leisured- and working-class women joining together in a common cause, on balance class differences were not significantly overcome. Thus, despite the dominant rhetoric of the American suffrage movement about the bonds holding all women together, a pervasive sense of sisterhood clearly did not develop among American women in this period.

An analysis of the International Federation of Working Women (IFWW) provides another revealing instance of the intersection, and in this case, more explicit conflict, between feminist and class attitudes. The leadership of the American WTUL was interested in establishing an international forum for working women, and they discussed the idea with the leaders of the British WTUL, who agreed there was a need for such an organization. Part of the impetus for forming an international women's labor organization came from the concern of women in both leagues that the interests of women workers were not going to be fully or properly represented in the new International Labor Office that had been created as part of the League of Nations. On the basis of these discussions, the American WTUL called a meeting in Washington, D.C., in the fall of 1919 to coincide with the first meeting of the International Labor Organization. Representatives of seventeen nations (mainly European) attended this first conference, which issued a series of resolutions giving "the women's point of view" on topics that were to come up at the ILO conference. The participants also decided to form a permanent organization and elected Margaret Dreier Robins, president of the American WTUL, the first president.[54]

Subsequent conventions were held in ·Geneva in 1921 and in Vienna in 1923. The purpose of the meetings was to give women involved in the labor movements of their respective countries an opportunity to come together to discuss common problems and possible solutions. The stated goals of the federation were: the promotion of "trade union organization among women"; the development of "an international policy giving special consideration to the needs of women and children"; the examination of "all projects for legislation proposed by the International Labor Conference of the League of Nations"; and the promotion of "the appointment of working women on organizations affecting the welfare of the workers."[55] The positions adopted by the IFWW conventions were not legally binding; however, it was expected they would be taken seriously as guidelines for action by women's labor groups in each country. The members hoped the new organization would gain publicity for their cause, and they expected their status as an international body would strengthen the legitimacy of their demands on the governments and labor movements of their respective countries for legislative and organizational changes.

However, the IFWW lasted only five years (1919–24) because a split developed between the Americans and the Europeans, led by the British, over the future direction of the organization. The debate related directly to the issues of feminism and class consciousness. Specifically, it focused on whether the federation should continue as an autonomous women's organization, seeking support from and interaction with other international women's organizations such as the Women's International League for Peace and Freedom and the International Women's Suffrage Alliance, or whether the federation should dissolve itself to become the Women's Division of the International Federal of Trade Unions (IFTU).

The IFTU had been formed in 1901, but it had fallen apart during World War I, when, despite the hopes of many socialists, national sentiments had overcome a sense of international working-class solidarity. As part of the effort toward reconstruction after the war, the federation was revived in 1919. The British rejoined—in fact, an Englishman was elected president—but, and this is significant in terms of the split that later developed among the women, the Americans did not. Samuel Gompers, president of the American Federation of Labor, had never been comfortable with the socialist and political (as opposed to strictly trade-unionist) orientation of the prewar federation, which the AFL had not joined until 1910. Gompers was upset about the nature of the revived federation, for both political and personal reasons. He was strongly opposed to a trade-union movement concerning itself with issues of political power or socialist ideology, and such concerns were clearly part of the IFTU. Furthermore, there is some evidence that Gompers had envisioned himself as the leader of the postwar international labor movement. However, given the political orientation of the revived federation, he realized that was clearly out of the question. For these reasons Gompers was decidedly not interested in having the AFL associated with the international labor movement, at least the aspect of it represented by the International Federation of Trade Unions.[56]

By the 1923 convention of the IFWW, the British women had decided their primary interest was in identifying the organization with the international labor movement and that the most effective way of demonstrating their solidarity and having their concerns taken seriously was to become an integral part of that labor movement. The British delegation came to the 1923 convention with a proposal to this effect, and the main issue of the convention was the question of affiliation with the International Federation of Trade Unions, "the middle ground of the great trade union movement of the world."[57]

German women had never joined the IFWW, claiming there was no need for a separate women's labor organization. They had been suspicious of an organization that included bourgeois women, such as Margaret Dreier Robins, and they felt the feminist orientation of the new organization was too strong and potentially too divisive. The Germans agreed that women workers faced different problems, but they argued that such problems were best solved by men and women discussing them together in the context of class-based organizations. Speaking for German women workers, Gertrud Hanna told a 1922 IFTU convention that she opposed the IFWW because:

> The first idea was to form an organisation solely to champion the rights of women. This is evident from the resolutions adopted at Washington. From the opening address of the President . . . and from numerous documents I have received since the Congress, it is obvious that the intention of the officers of the IFWW was to induce women to organise as a separate movement, with the object of taking action solely from the woman's standpoint. This view is extremely naive. . . . Our experience of the countries where women have the vote is that the women do not and cannot unite independently of existing parties for the furtherance their own interests, but that their resolutions are influenced by their political outlook, and that men and women both vote for the party to which they belong, without regard to sex.[58]

Hanna's perception of the separatist tendencies of the IFWW was somewhat exaggerated, but it was clear at the 1923 IFWW convention that most of the delegates had come to share her feeling that there was no longer a need for the IFWW to continue as a separate women's organization. British women had indicated in 1921 that their aim was to establish an international organization "which will link up working women . . . and which will in its turn be linked up with the international movement of working men and women."[59] Contact with the IFTU had been established shortly after the 1921 IFWW convention, which had reelected Margaret Dreier Robins president but had decided the headquarters should be moved from Washington, D.C., to London, since the secretary and treasurer were British (there was a vice-president for each member country) and the organization itself was primarily European in its orientation.

The idea of formal affiliation with the IFTU was discussed by letter prior to the 1923 convention; it was clear the British felt strongly that such a step should be taken, but the proposal created a considerable amount of controversy within the American WTUL. Robins, an extremely warm but also forceful and somewhat domineering woman who was accustomed to having things go her way, was staunchly opposed to the proposal. However Maud Swartz, a member of the Typographical Union, the current president of the American WTUL (Robins had retired from sixteen years in office in 1922), and the American vice-president of the IFWW, was strongly in favor of the merger idea and conducted a vigorous campaign to gain support for the idea among members of the American WTUL.[60]

The 1923 Vienna meeting was a turbulent one, at least for the Americans, and it resulted in the decision to affiliate with the IFTU; the only negative vote came from the American delegation. There were three reasons for the opposition of the Americans. One was that the decision to affiliate with the IFTU would put the American WTUL in an awkward position vis-à-vis the AFL, whose genuine support the WTUL was constantly trying to cultivate. There was no question in the minds of the Americans that if the IFWW merged into the IFTU, the Americans would have to withdraw, given the attitude of the AFL toward the IFTU. Another reason was that American women sincerely felt it was in the best interests of the IFWW to maintain itself as an autonomous women's labor organization. They reasoned that belonging to the IFTU would mean that women could not take independent stands on various issues; that the proposed structural relationship, which did not provide for a representative of the Women's Division to be on the IFTU Executive Board, would mean that women's issues would be put in a subordinate position; that women's labor groups would get involved in general IFTU activities and would have less time to focus on specifically women's issues; and that the proposed plan would provide fewer opportunities for the development of women labor leaders.

Margaret Dreier Robins was extremely upset by the convention's decision; she took it as a rejection of her leadership (which to some extent it was), and as a crushing blow to her hopes that women could achieve sisterly solidarity despite class differences. She recognized that "European delegates could not quite understand the American point of view. They were unaccustomed to women who were not industrial workers being interested in them and trying to help them better their industrial conditions and establish fellowship among women generally." However, she could not understand why, "When there were differences of opinion as there inevitably were, they wrote it down to the 'middle class' point of view and to the women who simply could not comprehend the workers' viewpoint."[61]

The American Women's Trade Union League's assessment of the reasons for the dissolution of the IFWW was summarized in the following statement:

Underlying the different points of view of the American and the European working women on this proposal, are their different conceptions of economics and social structure. American women have recognized the necessity for a woman movement within the labor movement; hence, the existence of the National Women's Trade Union League of

America, an autonomous body working in co-operation with the American Federation of Labor, but specializing upon the problems of working women, which are admittedly different in many vital aspects from the problems of working men, and need to be emphasized by women in Women's own way. The European labor movements, on the other hand, emphasize class-consciousness and deprecate a woman movement within their class. European working women agree with European working men in this.[62]

It is impossible to estimate how much strength or effectiveness the IFWW would have had had it remained an autonomous women's organization. British women were aware that women "must fight all the time to get attention focused on women's affairs within a general organization of workers";[63] they realized such struggles were necessary, were committed to putting energy into them, and were hopeful of success. However, it is clear in retrospect that the American women were in fact correct in their perceptions of what would happen to women within the IFTU. An advisory women's committee was established, but its function did not include any independent activities, and it rarely met with the IFTU leadership, although its advice was "always available to the IFTU by correspondence."[64] The committee held infrequent conferences, which were presided over by a male officer of the IFTU, where discussions were held and resolutions were passed, but that was as far as things went. Despite protests from the women members of the IFTU, virtually no money was allocated to support work leading toward the implementation of any of the women's resolutions, and the IFTU never made the problems of women workers a priority or even a significant aspect of its work.

There is no clear solution to this structural problem of how women should operate—whether they have the best chance of making progress through autonomous structures or through pushing from within. What a study of the International Federation of Working Women reveals is that, while the decision to affiliate with the International Federation of Trade Unions was in many ways a logical one, being part of the IFTU did not significantly further the cause of women workers.

When white, middle-class women in the United States and Britain (then and now) become aware of their inferior status in their respective societies, it is very clear that their oppression is directly related to their sex. For working-class (and black, Chicano, or Indian) women, the issue is less clear, for it is much more difficult for them to sort out in what ways they are oppressed because of their sex and in what ways their oppression is due to their class or race.

An examination of the relationship between the British and American women's trade union leagues and the women's suffrage movement in each country indicates that despite feminist ideology and rhetoric about sisterhood, it was extremely difficult for barriers of class not to come between women. On the other hand, an analysis of the International Federation of Women Workers shows that when women choose to focus their activities within sexually mixed groups of their own class, they must have feminist consciousness to struggle for their rights within that group.

There were many differences between the British and American women's trade union leagues, but the most significant one was the different priority they gave to the issues of feminism and class consciousness. The British league consistently chose to work for women's rights within sexually mixed, class-based contexts, while the American league tended to focus its efforts on interaction with women across class lines. However, the more fundamental point is that despite the differences between the two organizations, which in their own ways responded to conditions in their own countries, the women of the British and American women's trade union leagues were essentially participating in the same struggle.

## NOTES

1. This article grows out of work in progress on a comparative history of the British and American women's trade union leagues. The broader study is comparative on three different levels: it involves a national comparison of Britain and the United States; a comparison by sex of the different but interrelated experiences of men and women in the labor force; and a comparison of the ideologies and activities of two different social movements—the women's movement and the labor movement. The conceptual analysis focuses on questions of feminism and class consciousness.

I would like to thank Berenice Carroll, Phyllis Erenberg, and Alice Kenney for their helpful suggestions regarding the revision of this paper from an earlier version which had been presented to the Comparative History Colloquium at the University of Michigan.

2. The main sources of information on the British and American women's trade union leagues are the papers and publications of each organization, including the *Women's Trade Union Review* and the *Woman Worker* for the British and *Life and Labor* for the American. The British league's papers are in the Trades Union Congress Library in London; the American league's papers are in the Library of Congress and the Schlesinger Library of Radcliffe College.

Virtually all the secondary literature on the leagues discusses them from a labor history point of view. There is no study that explores in any depth the mixed-class character of the leagues or the complexity of their status as mixed-class, women's labor organizations influenced to varying degrees by the ideologies of feminism and class consciousness.

The main secondary works that discuss the British league are Gladys Boone, *The Women's Trade Union Leagues in Great Britain and the United States of America* (New York: Columbia University Press, 1942); Barbara Drake, *Women in Trade Unions* (London: George Allen and Unwin, 1920); and B. L. Hutchins, *Women in Modern Industry* (London: G. Bell and Sons, 1915).

Discussion of the American league is found in the following secondary sources: Mary Anderson, *Woman at Work* (Minneapolis: University of Minnesota Press, 1951); Boone; William H. Chafe, *The American Woman: Her Changing Social, Economic, and Political Roles, 1920–1970* (New York: Oxford University Press, 1972), chap. 3; Allen F. Davis, "The Women's Trade Union League: Origins and Organization," *Labor History* V (Winter 1964), 3–17; Mary E. Dreier, *Margaret Dreier Robins: Her Life, Letters, and Work* (New York: Island Press Cooperative, 1950); Alice Henry, *The Trade Union Woman* (New York: D. Appleton, 1915), chap. 4; Alice Henry, *Women and the Labor Movement* (New York: George H. Doran, 1923), chap. 6; Agnes Nestor, *Woman's Labor*

*Leader* (Rockford, Ill.: Bellevue, 1954); William O'Neill, *Everyone Was Brave: The Rise and Fall of Feminism in America* (Chicago: Quadrangle, 1969), 98–102; and Rose Schneiderman, *All for One* (New York: Paul S. Eriksson, 1967).

Comparative approaches to an analysis of the women's trade union leagues are found in Boone, which has only one chapter on the British league, and in William O'Neill, ed., *The Woman Movement: Feminism in the United States and England* (Chicago: Quadrangle, 1971), 63–69.

3. The classic nineteenth-century works on this subject are August Bebel, *Woman under Socialism*, trans. Daniel DeLeon, (New York: Schocken, 1971) and Frederick Engels, *The Origin of the Family, Private Property and the State* (London: Lawrence and Wishart, 1940). The most important contemporary analyses are Juliet Mitchell, *Woman's Estate* (London: Penguin, 1971) and Sheila Rowbotham, *Women, Resistance and Revolution: A History of Women and Revolution in the Modern World* (New York: Pantheon, 1972).

4. See Aileen Kraditor, *The Ideas of the Woman Suffrage Movement, 1890–1920* (New York: Anchor, 1971); Kraditor, *Up from the Pedestal: Selected Writings in the History of American Feminism* (Chicago: Quadrangle, 1968); O'Neill, *Everyone Was Brave;* and O'Neill, *The Woman Movement* for discussions of feminist ideology.

5. The number of women office workers increased from 1.1 percent of all women workers in 1890 to 12.0 percent in 1920. Janet M. Hooks, *Women's Occupations through Seven Decades*, U.S. Department of Labor, Women's Bureau, Bulletin 218 (Washington: Government Printing Office, 1947), 75.

6. There were approximately seven and one-half million women over the age of sixteen in the American labor force in 1910, accounting for 20.6 percent of the total labor force. It is very difficult to get accurate statistics on union membership, but a 1910 assessment of the major trades in which women were employed (e.g., bookbinders, boot and shoe workers, garment workers, textile workers, laundry workers) showed that only 3.3 percent of the women workers in the fifteen trades considered were members of trade unions. Joseph A. Hill, *Women in Gainful Occupations 1870–1920*, Department of Commerce Census Monographs (Washington: Government Printing Office, 1929), IX, 52. See also John B. Andrews and W. D. P. Bliss, *History of Women in Trade Unions*, Senate Report on the Condition of Woman and Child Wage-Earners in the United States (Washington: Government Printing Office, 1911), X, 138.

In Britain there were approximately 5,500,000 women in the labor force in 1911; 335,000, or approximately 6 percent, of the employed women were members of trade unions. B. R. Mitchell and Phyllis Deane, *Abstract of British Historical Statistics* (Cambridge, Eng.: Cambridge University Press, 1962), 60, 68.

7. See Mabel H. Willett, *The Employment of Women in the Clothing Trade*, Columbia University Studies in History, Economics, and Public Law, vol. XVI, no. 2 (New York: Columbia University Press, 1902), chap. 3.

8. National Women's Trade Union League of America, *Some Facts Regarding Unorganized Working Women in the Sweated Industries* (Chicago: NWTUL, 1914), 5–6. A typical weekly budget of a single woman living away from her family was:

| | |
|---|---:|
| One half of furnished room | $1.50 |
| 7 breakfasts, rolls and coffee, at 10¢ | .70 |
| 7 luncheons, coffee and sandwich, at 10¢ | .70 |
| 7 dinners, at 20¢ | 1.40 |
| Carfare | .60 |
| Clothes at $52 a year—weekly | 1.00 |
| Total | $5.90 |

The remaining 10 cents had to cover laundry, doctor bills, newspaper, recreation, and savings. *Ibid.,* 4.

9. Mary R. Macarthur, "Trade Unionism," in *Woman in Industry*, ed. Gertrude Tuckwell (London: Duckworth, 1908), 66.

10. *Ibid.*, 67.

11. Illustrating this problem, Rose Schneiderman, who became a well-known labor activist, mentioned her mother's opposition to her involvment in union organizing in 1903. She wrote, "It was such an exciting time. A new life opened up for me. . . . The only cloud in the picture was Mother's attitude toward my becoming a trade unionist. She kept saying I'd never get married . . . a prophecy which came true." Her mother was also concerned about her daughter, "being out of the house almost every evening." Schneiderman, *All for One,* 50. Another woman wrote of her father's and boyfriend's opposition to her participation in union and strike activities. Both men were trade unionists, but her father spoke for both of them when he said, ". . . I don't think it's a woman's place to be hangin' around street corners. . . . Union is all good and well by itself, but it was never meant for the women." Theresa Malkiel, *The Diary of a Shirtwaist Striker* (New York: Co-operative Press, 1910), 12.

12. For further discussion of the impact of industrialization on women, see the following: Edith Abbott, *Women in Industry: A Study in American Economic History* (New York: D. Appleton, 1918); Henry, *Women and the Labor Movement;* Hutchins, *Women in Modern History;* Ivy Pinchbeck, *Women Workers and the Industrial Revolution 1750–1850* (London: G. Routledge and Sons, 1930); Helen L. Sumner, *History of Women in Industry in the United States, Senate Report on the Condition of Woman and Child Wage-Earners in the United States,* vol. IX (Washington: Government Printing Office, 1911); and Tuckwell, ed., *Woman in Industry.*

13. See Barbara Welter, "The Cult of True Womanhood: 1820–1860," *American Quarterly* XVIII (Summer 1966), 151–74.

14. See O'Neill, *Everyone Was Brave* and *The Woman Movement.*

15. For further discussion on this point, see Gerda Lerner, "The Lady and the Mill Girl," *Midcontinent American Studies Journal* X (Spring 1969), 5–15.

16. The following summary of the history of the British and American women's trade union leagues is based on the papers and publications of both organizations and the secondary works cited in note 2.

17. Drake, *Women in Trade Unions,* 10.

18. "Benefit-society oriented" meant that the emphasis was on creating savings and insurance funds, mainly to cover illness and unemployment, rather than on aggressive action vis-à-vis employers regarding wages, hours, and working conditions.

19. The most comprehensive study of the early history of women in trade unions in the United States is the work done by Andrews and Bliss.

20. Those present included Canon Kingsley, Arnold Toynbee, the Reverend Stewart Headlam, Harriet Martineau, Anna Swanwick, and Mr. and Mrs. Hodgson Pratt.

21. Legislation in 1871 legally recognized trade unions and protected their funds, but it left trade unionists open to criminal prosecution for all forms of picketing, and laws against conspiracy could still be applied to strikers. The legal situation was improved by new legislation in 1875, but British trade unionists were concerned about the security of their legal rights through the end of the nineteenth century and into the early years of the twentieth. The position of trade unions was not legally secure until 1906, when a Liberal government with a large number of Labour MP's came to power. See Henry Pelling, *A History of British Trade Unionism* (London: Macmillan and Co., 1963), chaps. 5–7.

22. The National Federation of Women Workers had become part of the National Union of General Workers in 1919.

23. Further analysis of the issue of protective legislation is part of the work in progress for the larger study referred to in note 1.

24. For further information on these women, see their autobiographies (cited in note 2) and their personal papers. Anderson's are in the Schlesinger Library of Radcliffe College, Nestor's are in the Chicago Historical Society collection, and Schneiderman's are in the Tamiment Library of New York University.

25. See for example, Gladys Meyerand, "Women's Organizations," *Encyclopedia of the Social Sciences*, vol. XV (New York: Macmillan Co., 1935), 465.

26. The statements in this paragraph are based on a cumulative impression of personal letters in the papers of the women's trade union leagues and of Margaret MacDonald, Leonora O'Reilly, Rose Schneiderman, and Margaret Dreier Robins. They are further supported by the biography of Robins, the autobiographies of Anderson, Nestor, and Schneiderman, the unpublished autobiography of Gertrude Tuckwell in the papers of the British WTUL, and by interviews with Elizabeth Christman and Nora Jones, surviving members of the two organizations.

27. This situation was partly the result of gains having been achieved in other areas, notably education and legal rights, but it was even more a reflection of the growing attitude that winning the right to vote would give women greater power in working for other aspects of women's rights and general social reform.

28. The first major extension of the franchise was the result of the Reform Bill of 1832. Further extensions came with the Reform Bills of 1867 and 1884. For a summary of the property qualifications determining the eligibility of male voters at the beginning of the twentieth century, see Constance Rover, *Women's Suffrage and Party Politics in Britain, 1866–1914* (London: Routledge and Kegan Paul, 1967), 27.

29. David Butler and Jennie Freeman, *British Political Facts 1900–1967*, 2d ed. (London: Macmillan and Co., 1968), 155.

30. Suffragists were willing to accept this age discrepancy in the interest of establishing the principle of women's suffrage, although they did fight to lower the proposed age from thirty-five to thirty. One reason the higher voting age for women was an issue was that due to British losses in World War I, there were more women than men in the British population, and politicians were very hesitant to create an electorate with a majority of women voters.

31. See Rover, *Women's Suffrage and Party Politics*, chap. 8, for a detailed discussion of the way each British political party dealt with the issue of women's suffrage.

32. *Ibid.*, 23–24.

33. The minutes of WTUL meetings are very frustrating in this regard. They merely indicate that discussions on this issue took place which resulted in the consistent decision to avoid participation in the suffrage movement. Unfortunately the minutes do not give the gist of these discussions, nor do they indicate the points of view expressed by the members present.

34. Margaret Bondfield, who later became the first woman cabinet member when she was made minister of labor in the Labour government of 1924, was the most active WTUL member in the adult suffrage movement. Her position is clearly stated in the account of a well-attended debate between Bondfield and Teresa Billington-Grieg, a prominent women's suffragist. See *Verbatim Report of Debate on December 3, 1907: Sex Equality (Teresa Billington-Grieg) Versus Adult Suffrage (Margaret G. Bondfield)* (Manchester: Women's Freedom League, 1908).

35. See Marian Ramelson, *The Petticoat Rebellion: A Century of Struggle for Women's Rights* (London: Lawrence and Wishart, 1967), chap. 14, and Rover, *Women's Suffrage and Party Politics*, 146–67, for a more complete discussion of the Labour party and the women's suffrage movement.

36. See *The Woman Worker* for 1918.

37. See R. S. Neale, "Working-Class Women and Women's Suffrage," *Class and Ideology*

*in the Nineteenth Century* (London: Routledge and Kegan Paul, 1972), 143–68; E. Sylvia Pankhurst, *The Suffragette Movement: An Intimate Account of Persons and Ideals* (London: Longmans, Green, 1931), books 4, 5, 8, and 9; and Ramelson, *The Petticoat Rebellion*, chaps. 9, 12, and 13 for further information on the relation of working-class women to the women's suffrage movement.

38. These papers are found in the Fawcett Library in London.

39. See Ramelson, *The Petticoat Rebellion*, 106–8 for a fuller account of this incident.

40. See Kraditor, *Up from the Pedestal*, for documents pertaining to the suffrage movement; see Kraditor, *The Ideas of the Woman Suffrage Movement* and O'Neill, *Everyone Was Brave* for analytic accounts of the American suffrage movement.

41. "Olympia Brown on the Foreign Menace," in Kraditor, *Up from the Pedestal*, 258–59.

42. "Resolutions Adopted at a Convention," *ibid.*, 260.

43. "Belle Kearney, The South and Woman Suffrage," in *ibid.*, 264.

44. See Kraditor, *The Ideas of the Woman Suffrage Movement*, chap. 7, for a discussion of this issue.

45. Clara Hyde to Mary Gray Peck, Sept. 26, 1917, NAWSA papers, Library of Congress.

46. Carrie Chapman Catt to "Francis and Pan," October 15, 1910, Carrie Chapman Catt papers, Library of Congress.

47. Pauline Newman to Rose Schneiderman, July 26, 1912, Rose Schneiderman papers, Tamiment Library, New York University.

48. It is interesting to note the different rhetoric used in both countries in suffrage propaganda aimed at working-class and middle-class audiences. The working-class-oriented material stressed the need for women to have the political power of the vote to better specific working and domestic conditions; the middle-class-oriented propaganda stressed issues such as women's basic rights, their interests as mothers, and the social impact of giving the special moral qualities of women a political voice. See for example, *Why Women Should Have the Vote* (Kirkby Lonsdale, Westmoreland: Women's Cooperative Guild, n.d.) and the series of open letters published by the Industrial Section of the New York State Suffrage party in the Rose Schneiderman papers, Tamiment Library.

49. "Proceedings of the 1909 Convention," 26–27, WTUL papers, Library of Congress.

50. M[argaret] Hinchey to Leonora O'Reilly [1913?], Leonora O'Reilly papers, Schlesinger Library.

51. See Nestor, *Woman's Labor Leader*, 66–68, for a more complete account of this incident.

52. Schneiderman, *All for One*, 8.

53. Malkiel, *Diary of a Shirtwaist Striker*, 40–41.

54. Information on the IFWW, which was initially called the International Congress of Working Women, is found in the WTUL papers in the Library of Congress and in the IFWW papers in the Schlesinger Library.

55. International Congress of Working Women, "Second International Congress of Working Women: Summary of Proceedings, October 17–25, 1921," 1, WTUL papers, Library of Congress.

56. See Lewis L. Lorwin, *Labor and Internationalism* (New York, Macmillan Co., 1929) and Louis S. Reed, *The Labor Philosophy of Samuel Gompers* (New York: Columbia University Press, 1930) for a fuller discussion of the international trade union movement and Gompers's relationship to it.

57. International Congress of Working Women, "Second International Congress . . . ," 1.

58. International Federation of Trade Unions, *Report of the IFTU Congress* (Amsterdam: IFTU, 1922), 45–46.

59. "Working Women at Geneva," *The Labour Woman* (November 1921), 176.

60. See Anderson, *Women at Work*, chap. 15, for a discussion of the IFWW and the American WTUL.

61. Dreier, *Margaret Dreier Robins*, 165.

62. "International Federation of Working Women," *Life and Labor Bulletin* II (November 1923), 2.

63. Edith W. Donald (IFWW secretary) to Maud Swartz, April 29, 1924, WTUL papers, Library of Congress.

64. John Price, *The International Labour Movement* (London: Oxford University Press, 1945), 67.

# Latina Liberation:
# Tradition, Ideology, and Social Change
# in Iberian and Latin American Cultures

## Ann M. Pescatello

In recent years scholars have developed interpretations of Iberian and Ibero-American civilization in terms of racial and ethnic relations, land and labor systems, immigration and urbanization, or industrialization and modernization. These are fruitful and obvious topics for analyses of our neighboring cultures, so it is surprising that few have focused on the largest single subgroup, the female. Since there is not yet available on the female in Iberian cultural milieux a basic general essay, for purposes of comparison and contrast with other cultures, I hope that this essay will begin to redress that neglect.

On the surface it would appear that social changes have occurred in western European societies, specifically Scandinavia, England, Germany (and the United States) on a wider scale than they have in southwestern European societies, particularly Spain, Portugal (and Latin America). Our heritage and our interpretation of traditions have been shaped by the allegedly "progressive" Anglo-Saxon *Weltanschauung*, and consequently we tend to analyze other cultures according to our values. But is this approach applicable to Iberian cultures? In Iberian cultural traditions, what of the woman?

## I

There are two paradoxical attitudes toward females in Iberian cultural tradition, one of which contends that "women . . . have been and are the repositories of the essential virtues of the race and the transmitters of its moral vitality across all the infinite accidents of our history. . . ."[1] The other attitude is reflected in Iberian laws which identify woman as an *imbecilitas sexus*, one classed with children, invalids, and delinquents in all the codes of Castile.[2]

As to why such conservative attitudes toward females developed and prevailed in Iberian traditions, two theories have currency. One emphasizes the impact of Moorish civilization, and, if true, is thus so primarily for Spain, and there only for the southern and central sections of Castile and Andalusia, home of most of Latin America's earliest immigrants and most enduring bastions of Moorish influence in the peninsula. In those areas, particularly the cities, it is likely that Spanish urban upper classes adopted the Moorish custom of keeping women secluded; at home women were restricted from appearing at windows, squatted on cushions instead of chairs, and were semi-veiled in all areas of Spain except the North and Northwest.[3]

The other view contends that rather than Moorish influence in particular it was the turbulent and uncertain conditions in medieval Iberia in general which caused elaboration of a protective system which ultimately segregated women from involvement in changing society.[4] This latter view would seem to me more likely, since Moorish influence can only exhibit analogies to but not explain much of Portuguese and northern Spanish attitudes. In societies in turmoil it is possible to see development of behavior patterns in which lines of inequality between the sexes were drawn to the disadvantage of women, and yet in which males were publicly protective of the other sex.

These two paradoxical attitudes toward women seem much more applicable to the upper classes than to the lower classes. Spanish proverbs are rife with directives on the division of male-female responsibilities in society, with specific rules for behavior between males and females of the upper classes.[5] Our classic conception of the depressed and deprived Latin female derives from the fact that these attitudes and rules, born of turmoil, hardened into tradition in more tranquil times for some visible groups within the bounds of Iberian culture.[6]

Women of the lower classes, less restricted by the growing codes of proper behavior, were able to continue their involvement in occupations outside the home and often engaged in activities considered "improper" for ladies. Due to the perpetuation of medieval family patterns among the lower classes, these women remained dominant in their own households and wielded considerable influence in the economic and social affairs of their kin groups.[7] Many women, especially in Seville and Lisbon, were domestic servants or slaves who took charge of household activities for wealthy families, nursed children, and produced and sold wares in the urban markets. Plays and novels of the sixteenth through the eighteenth centuries emphasize the intimacy of female servants or slaves with their mistresses; they often served as confidantes and love-brokers for their secluded and idle Iberian ladies.[8]

Lower-class women belonged to farming or pastoral families in the countryside or to artisan, laboring, shopkeeping, and service families in the cities. Legally, their rights were as circumscribed as they were for all classes of women, but in practice they had more freedom than other women since their jobs and their husbands' occupations often took them out of their homes to help supplement meager incomes. The mode of sexual behavior among the lower classes was different from that of the upper classes. Due to their life's circumstances, working-class women were far removed from upper-class ideals of female chastity and marital fidelity. These women worked in fields, shops, or factories in which they were in constant contact with men and in situations which provided a relatively free atmosphere for sexual relations.

Thus we have two paradoxical attitudes regarding women, two theories regarding the development of those attitudes, and two separate feminine traditions based on socioeconomic status emanating from the Iberian peninsula at the end of the Middle Ages.

## II

The medieval or "pre-modern" family was communal, often polygamous, served basically as a transmitter of family property and names, and was frequently characterized by common-law marriage.[9] This seemed to be the case both in its chronological contexts and geographical contexts, be it fourteenth-century France or parts of nineteenth-century Latin America.[10] Females were at once a casual, expendable item, often wasted early through the rigors of childbirth, and yet a necessary, often powerful influence, since they ran households and contributed equally to work in fields and decision-making in societies dominated by massive kin networks.

Europe after the late Middle Ages witnessed profound changes in the image of the child from one in which a child had little importance and was considered a young adult ready before puberty to support his or her family, to one in which the first obligation of a family was to educate the child and to raise him or her according to new precepts of child-rearing.[11] Concurrently with the changing image of the child there evolved a new conjugal, "modern," patriarchal family. The establishment of this nuclear family induced new concepts of sociability based on privacy, isolation, and narrow and confining codes of morality.

Within this new family milieu the position of the female seems to have changed; her role as a wife and mother became idealized in the sense that her world, her society had become prescribed and her duties were solely of the family rather than of the larger society. On the one hand she became the paragon of chivalric virtue while on the other she was isolated from decision-making and public activities except those which concerned rites of passage, in a world-view epitomized by the Victorian age.[12]

Reformation and Enlightenment ideologies spread ideas of liberty and equality and demands for economic, social, and political reform, as well as for education for all (including women). Nevertheless, the nuclear family was never more restrictive and oppressive to women in western Europe and North America than in the nineteenth century.

These changes in family social order occurred in the West in tandem with the Industrial Revolution, although it is not possible to claim that one was cause or effect of the other. Rather, industrialization seems to have been aided by the new type of family while the conjugal family appears to have achieved dominance because, of all family structures, it could best respond to the particular needs of industrialization.[13] We have now to determine what influences the Reformation, the Industrial Revolution, and the Enlightenment had on Iberian female traditions.

## III

Reformation ideas filtered into Iberia and for a time generated some following among certain groups and classes, primarily those budding bourgeoisie of the capitalistic-oriented coastal towns. But the permanency of Reformation ideology was not to be in Iberia; after the death of the Erasmian Emperor Charles (I of Spain, V of the Hapsburg Empire) the kings of the

Iberian peninsula opted to bolster their authority against the incipient powers of the bourgeoisie and influential urban aristocrats by strengthening their ties with the Church and rural oligarchy in the era known as the Counter-Reformation.[14] Spain was the epitome of the Counter-Reformation state, and the pillars of tradition—the Church, the landed aristocracy, and the nobility—successfully countered the implantation of such ideals as individualism, education, and equality.

Similarly, there failed to take root in Iberia those changes which were taking place elsewhere in Europe, changes in the image of the child and a shift from a kin to a conjugal family.[15] They failed because Iberia had already undergone severe social changes which by the time of the Reformation had hardened into tradition. The role of the female had already changed, not as a result of Reformation ideology but much earlier than the Reformation, as a result of conditions peculiar to medieval Iberia itself. Change had occurred from sources outside of the realm of Reformation ideology and acquired a permanency of its own within the Iberian context. These differences in causes and timing of change in Anglo and Iberian traditions aid our analysis of the present position of the female. In both traditions the result of change—reduction of the public role and influence of women—suggests why it is possible to make cross-cultural generalizations according to class, while the causes and timing of change indicate why female traditions are different in Latin America than in Anglo-America.

As the Reformation ideology failed to impress Iberian society, so did the Industrial Revolution find an inhospitable environment in southwestern Europe. Iberia's rulers had opted for state absolutism; monies which could have been utilized for investment in manufactures, industrial development, and other capitalist ventures were used instead to support a massive, cumbersome bureaucracy. The bureaucratic system of the Spanish Hapsburg state may have encouraged state capitalism but discouraged free enterprise; this transpired at a time when the state was concerned about generating income by extractive means (from mines and plantations) rather than by supporting scientific experimentation and economic-industrial development.[16] A large-scale Industrial Revolution did not prevail in Iberia, nor was there a conjugal family to aid its development; at the same time, the nuclear family had no industrialization process to which it could respond.

As the ideologies of the Reformation and the Industrial Revolution had failed to obtain a general hearing in Iberian cultures so, too, did those of the Enlightenment. To be sure, the French Bourbons brought to their new throne in eighteenth-century Spain some of the ideals and zeal of the Enlightenment, and Charles III did apply some technological and rational ideas to the development and ordering of his empire. Yet, the success of the Enlightenment depended on certain prerequisites, none of which existed in Iberia: lessening of influence of the Roman Catholic Church, a few "enlightened despots" to champion the cause of a free and independent nation-state. Furthermore, Iberia's incipient and small middle classes had atrophied and those elites who possessed the power and the money to make cities grow had turned them instead into stagnant centers of absentee-landlordism. Consequently the Enlightenment in Iberia had neither soil in which to take root nor a flourishing plant to which it could give light and life.[17]

Modernizing processes did enter the Iberian peninsula primarily as a result of the nineteenth-century development of transportation and communication facilities. During the past century-and-a-half Iberia has been influenced gradually by trends and conveniences of industrialization, urbanization, and modernization made possible by the intrusion of European ideologies. Iberia has seen a new flush of urban growth, expansion of the middle class, and increased industrial development, and with them inevitable changes.

Yet, rooted in the Iberian medieval past the female legacy has persisted throughout the twentieth century in the peninsula and in Latin America. Today in the Spanish countryside the ideal is that woman should be submissive, secluded, frugal, and industrious, but in practice she perpetuates the myth of male supremacy for her own purposes and remains the household's center by exerting influence through her children and the routines of family life.[18]

In Spain's cities, women of all classes are becoming more independent, although their societal role is supposedly still determined by their official occupation as housewife, *sus labores*. Among the unmarried, chaperonage is continued for a girl until she is eighteen; thereafter she is allowed to appear in public accompanied by girls of similar age and status, whose families are approved by her parents. Freedom of action for young women varies according to their families' position but generally greater freedom is allowed those of upper classes due to the opening of professions and other occupations previously restricted to males. Women attend the universities, they travel, and many study abroad. About one in every seven women in Madrid is employed, and in the last thirty years or so women's wages have risen much faster than men's.[19] Although prostitution was officially outlawed in 1956, professionals and brothels abound in the cities catering to customary prerogatives of extramarital sexuality. The double standard is prevalent still; marriage is the ideal for most Spanish, the "honest" female is accorded chivalrous attention while the prostitute or mistress is treated as a woman of impropriety.

In Portugal much the same pattern persists. The lower-class woman is a housewife in addition to her other tasks as a field worker, factory laborer, food preparer, domestic servant (usually prior to marriage), or public service worker (especially in the post office and primary schools). The life of the lower-class woman is basically hard, her diet meager, and her monetary resources inadequate to purchase decent food and clothing, to light or heat her small home, or to supply sanitary facilties. The upper-class woman, on the other hand, enjoys the material advantages that money allows and if her family is "enlightened" she uses her leisure for clubs, shopping, and travel.

For the working woman, not only of the agricultural north but also in the pastoral south, work pays poorly (only one-third a man's salary) and offers few possibilities for advancement, even in jobs created by the state, in which, incidentally, women are quite prominent. Since World War II there has been a noticeable growth in the percentage of women workers in the labor and public works sectors, which used to be male preserves. As in Spain, the social and economic position of urban and upper-class woman is changing gradually, yet at a much faster pace than that of her rural and lower-class sisters, who are still bound by a tradition underwritten by centuries of national poverty and decline.[20]

IV

Until the wars for independence (1808–26) Latin America's nations were considered by Spain and Portugal to be "kingdoms" in their respective empires; consequently the same laws were applied and attitudes toward and opportunities for women in economic, social, and other activities were as circumscribed as in the peninsula. Iberia was the culture-mold into which South America's countries were cast; Iberia's traditions, values, attitudes, language, religion, and laws provided the pinions for cultural development of the twenty or so nation-states comprising Ibero-America. The development of plantation societies in Latin America helped perpetuate the "pre-modern" family in new lands long after it had disintegrated in many Western nations. In these plantation societies the late-medieval life-style was characterized by intimacy among family, servants, and slaves, a behavior pattern which seems to hold true for North as well as South America.[21] As some plantation families and societies prospered, the life experience of females became defined more sharply than it had been in the amorphous atmosphere of medieval society. Lower-class women continued to be influential in the economic and social affairs of their families, but while upper-class women enjoyed more leisure, they were more segregated than in the past, a feature common to both Anglicized and Iberianized societies.[22]

Yet the Ibero-American nations were influenced also by the two racial groups which Iberians encountered: the resident Amerindian cultures and the enslaved African groups. Did these elements modify or in places give distinctive character to Latin America's female traditions?

In Amerindian societies, those of the so-called high cultures and the less technologically developed cultures, the position of the female has analogies to that of Iberian women.[23] Probably a more accurate comparison could be made between Iberian classes and Amerindian tribal levels rather than between cultures. In the less technologically developed Indian groups, females often dominated the economic activities and all household affairs. As mothers, food producers, traders, and the like they exerted considerable influence within their kin groups. Yet, in government, religion, and inheritance they seldom enjoyed influence.

In the more highly technologically developed civilizations of the Inca, Aztec, and Maya, women were workers within and without the home, yet did not seem to enjoy the measure of powers derived from economic activities that their tribal counterparts did. Women became surplus to a society and economy which had limited means to support them; they were seen as expendable and were often used for sacrifice or kept as a leisure class of concubines.

Women of the aristocracy enjoyed some legal prerogatives, especially in Aztec society, and in a few instances held high administrative, religious, and social positions.

In most areas of Latin America where the less technologically advanced Indian tribes lived, the tribes have disappeared. Of those resident in Argentina, Chile, Brazil, Paraguay, Uruguay, and the Caribbean, only in Paraguay do these Amerindians (the Guaraní) play an influential role in shaping a society which lost its Iberian males to wars and which is dominated by Amerindian women. In the areas inhabited by the "high cultures" and which are part of the colonial *hacienda* socioeconomic tradition—Mexico, Peru, Bolivia, Ecuador, and Guatemala—some of the Amerindian heritage continues but represents the lesser strain in societies dominated by Iberian elite traditions. The heritage of the Amerindian female was too similar to the Iberian to exert profound changes in that tradition.

In African cultures it seems as if sexual roles were more equal, or at least that the female enjoyed substantial prerogatives. In those areas of central Africa and the western or lower Congo with which the Portuguese came into contact, not only was descent and succession matrilineal, with females the heads of families in many villages, but also property, houses, and lands were inherited through females. In West African societies, which provided the bulk of labor for the slave societies of America, for example in Dahomey, females were involved in services vital to the functioning of the polity at both state and local levels, and they controlled production and distribution of the market economy. Similar, albeit modified, situations existed among the Yoruba, Ibo, Fon, and Akan-speaking peoples of West Africa. Although females did not escape repression or attitudes which regarded them as inferior, it seems that throughout the western and Sudanic areas of Africa women enjoyed substantial social, economic, and political rights and responsibilities.[24]

These positions of influence the African woman carried to the New World; in areas where the density of blacks was not substantial, including much of continental Spanish America, African values exerted little influence on the position of women. But in sections of the Americas where Africans were numerous—Haiti, Cuba, Colombia, Venezuela, Brazil, and parts of the Caribbean, the powers and prerogatives of the female contributed to formulation of those distinctive cultures we call Afro-American. In these Afro-American cultures black and *mulata* women controlled the distribution of produce in the markets and dominated socio-religious life through their roles as *Maes-dos-santos* in Afro-Brazilian, Afro-Cubano, and Haitian cults.[25] In fact, the black and *mulata* woman who comprised much of the lower class was much more active within the larger society than her white middle- and upper-class counterparts. But the extent of the Afro-American female's influence on Iberian feminine tradition was mitigated by her class position.

Thus, despite substantial encounter with Amerindian and African traditions the Iberian heritage prevailed. Amerindian cultures failed to produce change because their tradition was akin to the Iberian, and the African influence, albeit strong at the lower-class levels, failed to create change precisely because it reflected a lower-class tradition in an elitist, authoritarian, patriarchal culture.

The twentieth-century Ibero-American female lives in societies strongly reflective of their colonial past and bound by attitudes nurtured in the precepts of *Las Siete Partidas* and the Laws of Toro.[26] Laws stated that no married woman could accept or repudiate inheritance except by permission of her husband.[27] For the woman of the Spanish Indies, "In Spanish Law . . . only in exceptional situations, does the woman enjoy full civil rights. . . . The single woman is always submissive to paternal authority . . . the married . . . inside the orbit of a new power as *acusado* as the first. Only the state of widowhood permits the woman to earn her full civil rights."[28]

The American kingdoms of Spain and Portugal strikingly resembled their mother countries, especially in the behavior of the ruling white classes. Brazilian and Spanish American women were, according to tradition, the property of male members of their families, a situation which, in theory, afforded protection to the female but, in practice, isolated her from external social and cultural contacts. In economic matters it appears that some Latin American women of the colonial era had enjoyed a measure of financial power or property privileges; Lockhart has substantiated the participation of women in the early economic development of Peruvian society and both Schwartz and Dutra have noted similar activities for Brazil.[29] Nonetheless, the colonial era encouraged the growth of numerous American societies in which women remained the majority of an almost totally illiterate population which enjoyed no political perquisites, and were an anomaly if involved in economic transactions or public ventures.

The nineteenth century was well under way before changes occurred. During the first half of the century, travel accounts, more abundant for Portuguese than Spanish America, chronicled the humdrum, isolated, and inhumane existence of upper-class women as well as the somewhat permissive life-style of the lower classes. Perhaps the most striking aphorism concerning this situation, and applicable throughout South America, is the statement of an observer that "A woman in Brazil is still the image of what she used to be; she still bears on her wrists the marks of chains; she has not yet taken the place which is rightfully hers. . . ."[30]

Thus, prior to nineteenth-century independence movements, the social position of women had derived from the customary organic fabric of Iberian colonial culture. But after the first quarter of the nineteenth-century, national independence meant national judiciaries and national ideologies which Creole elites had extracted from European and North American models and applied to preexisting traditional social orders. These varied, and often irreconcilable, mixes of customs and codes of "progress" guided Latin American social systems into the twentieth century.

## V

Social change, as it affected women, did come to Latin America, but its impetus, tempo, and style are peculiar to each twentieth-century Latin

American nation. Each has interpreted its past and each has adapted the ideological and technological innovations of western Europe and the United States to its own present needs. In general, the twentieth century brought increasing pressures on the customary pattern of male-female relationships, on family traditions, and on the general social fabric, especially in light of the subtle shifts in the status of females within the family and society. Some of these changes resulted from internal pressures, from gradual reforms, and from implementation of codes of "progress"; others resulted from influences external to Latin America. Not only did more Latins visit North America and western Europe but more "western" ideas and women traveled to Latin America.

A major impetus to change was the growth of cities, making available transportation for increased mobility, and communications which carried the new ideas that threatened traditional family structures. With twentieth-century urbanization came an increase in the tempo of life, from unhurried to rushed, and some alterations in living style; for example, people moved out of patriarchal mansions and into small homes and apartments. These innovations whittled down such notions of privacy and family relaxation as are architecturally represented by the enclosed backyard patios much utilized by Latin families, replacing them with spatial imitations such as are represented (in their openness) by American front yards, which few families use.

In addition to the new ideas represented by urbanization, another major impetus to change was industrialization, which induced changes in the economy and thus in occupational opportunities for women. Urban women traditionally had filled roles in teaching and clerical professions; now they enter business, government, sales, and nursing. Women from the provinces who previously had become domestic servants in suburban households now leave their villages to work in city factories. With their responsibilities and the freedom afforded by wage-earning, women gradually changed their notions about matrimony and maternity; nations made constitutional changes regarding divorce; and civil rights guarantees for women became commonplace. Latin American women slowly but surely moved toward both the benefits and the hazards of behavior norms accepted by twentieth-century Western society.

At the turn of the twentieth century, few women participated in public activities; females of the elite classes attended their public festivities under strict surveillance while the relatively open life of lower-class women was frowned upon as "indecent" and "perverted." In marital relations an entrenched patriarchal pattern determined the legal and social subordination of wife to husband, although this was often done under the guise of protection for females. Nonetheless, husbands owned family estates, including all that their wives brought in dowries and all that they later received as gifts, earning, or inheritance. A wife could not inherit property from her husband and only if she were left penurious by his death could a widow petition to receive a quarter of his estate. In her role as a mother the woman had limited legal rights in relation to her children, her only prerogative being to give permission to any offspring over twenty-five years of age who wished to marry, but that only in the absence of their father.[31]

On the other hand, the female continued to be the core of Ibero-American society by virtue of her idealized role in the family and she was rewarded with supervision of all housekeeping and household crafts. In upper-class families she usually guided the work force of servants, but in lower-class families she usually enjoyed more autonomy, since her husband spent little time at home, or in many families was a migrant worker or a vagrant, and absent from the household for long periods. In fact, one can argue that relative lack of wealth and household accoutrements have probably guaranteed more social fluidity for lower-class women since enforced responsibilities tend to be the foundry for personal freedoms.

The bastion of traditional mores remains the growing middle class but even here women have increased their extramarital activities and occasional disruptions in the sexual double standard which fixes no guilt on the male for discrepancies in social behavior but which imposes a loss of dignity and "face" on females involved in illicit liaisons. Women who know the rules of sexual relationships in their respective classes and who play by the rules usually fit into the idealized scheme of being a "modern" Latin woman. Those who are apt to get caught between custom and fancy are young rural girls who exchange the monotony of village life for the tedium of urban anonymity and often find themselves in illegitimate relationships and maternity clothes. For these legally and socially defenseless women the "modern" world is cruel; rarely do they wish to return home; generally they get rid of their babies one way or another; and due to lack of facilities for social "rehabilitation" they often turn to prostitution. Yet, part of the value-system of the rural tradition from which they escape is such that should a wayward daughter wish to return home she probably could count on the aid of her mother and family in caring for her child.

In addition to differences in class strata, there exists a dichotomy in social attitudes between women in the rural and urban sectors. The basis of rural economy is agriculture, supplemented by household industries, and women represent more than 50 percent of the work force in these activities.[32] The structure of family and society in the countryside is different from urban social organization. Life in the economically underdeveloped rural areas for the lower classes remains essentially pre-modern in terms of social and economic relationships, but among the middle- and upper-class families in the countryside there remains a strong semipatriarchal family organization with all of its implied legal and social subordination of women.

In the cities there are more opportunities to change the social system. In urban areas industries provide more opportunities for labor and more types of occupations in which women could be employed; they also provide a freer atmosphere for contact between sexes which has gradually weakened traditional sexual attitudes and relationships. Separation of the sexes has broken down in schools; more young girls now move into their own or share apartments away from parental tutelage; and unchaperoned dating has become a more acceptable form of social behavior.

In general, Latin America is still a less nuclear and more kin-oriented family society. Many of the community-based public activities and political involvements which are so much a feature of United States society are still under family control in Latin America. According to analysts Almond and Verba, while United States women tend to be actively involved in their communities more than most other women in the world, Latin American women are less so. Latin American women are neither as participatory nor as knowledgeable as their international sisters in social interaction and political affairs. But this may be the result of a peculiarity of Iberian and Latin American cultures: their societies do not have the volunteer, community-action idea of the once-frontier society of the United States. Latin women marry, raise families, "socialize" children, and affect the family as a unit and the way the family is "socialized" in the political system, all within the Iberian tradition.[33]

## VI

As I have noted, social change came to Latin America but the impetus, tempo, and style of change was peculiar to each of the twenty or so Latin cultures. In nations where there has been little industry, slow processes of urbanization and modernization, i.e., Bolivia, Ecuador, Paraguay, and most Caribbean republics, tradition is stronger than in countries which have encouraged these processes, i.e., Argentina, Chile, Cuba, Uruguay, Brazil, and to a lesser extent, Colombia, Venezuela, and Peru. Also, the type of change has been influenced by the nature and number of Indian or African descent-groups in each nation, by the country's status in relation to its mother country during the colonial era, by the rural-urban balance of population and power in the nation, by the influence of traditional elites and modernizing agents.

No one nation is a replica of the others but some can serve as models of different styles of social change in Latin America: Argentina, Mexico, Cuba, Peru, and Brazil.[34] Argentina had been a backwater of Spain's American empire. Originally the home of nomadic and less technologically advanced Indian tribes, it was sparsely settled by Spaniards since it offered little of the glamour or wealth that the conquistadors coveted. Consequently, in the nineteenth century when Argentina was exposed to ideas of "progress" she had few entrenched traditional institutions or groups to prevent receptivity. A nation dominated by the cosmopolitan metropolis of Buenos Aires, Argentina has welcomed industry and immigrants and has been in the forefront of social advances along with Chile, Uruguay, and Costa Rica.

Argentina has one of Latin America's highest literacy rates. The country's educational system was modeled after that of the United States, and since the Roman Catholic Church had enjoyed slight influence in Argentina, Argentines were able to establish a free public educational system staffed only by lay teachers. A free, compulsory public education system has resulted in the high literacy rate, which in the end has benefited women. In the professions, women comprise 20 percent of the nation's doctors and lawyers, 50 to 55 percent of its pharmacists, chemists and dentists, and about 20 percent of its architects, agronomists, and civil engineers. All in all, a much better showing than for female counterparts in the United States.

Argentina has been the Latin American nation most insistent on civil rights legislation. It has also had an active feminist organization. Working-class women, who comprise about 25 percent of the nation's labor force, are beneficiaries of some of the world's most advanced protective labor legislation, designed for both women and men.

If Argentina represents "enlightened" attitudes, Peru is representative of a nation heavily influenced by traditional institutions and elites and, with Mexico, a former pillar of Spain's overseas empire. Despite her prominence in colonial days as a center of learning, Peru has been laggard in upgrading educational opportunities for girls and women, in generating civil rights legislation and feminist movements, or in providing substantial opportunities for women in the labor force, either as professionals or as workers. Peru, along with Ecuador, Bolivia, most of the Central American and Caribbean republics, and to a lesser extent Venezuela and Colombia, represents the classic tradition-bound Latin society.

Mexico is a median case between Argentina and Peru. With Peru, one of Spain's two centers of overseas empire, Mexico was an Indian-populated and hacienda-oriented economy and society, dominated by traditional institutions and elites, her cities bureaucratic or military bastions rather than industrial or commercial cores. In the latter half of the nineteenth century some attempts to make Mexico receptive to modernizing influences culminated in the events of 1910 and the start of the revolution. Industry, modernizing processes, and the adoption of extensive and radical social measures served to erode the influence of traditional organizations and to send some groups underground, including the clergy.

Since the revolution, Mexican women have made great strides in education, in range of occupations open to them, in professional activities, and in the area of civil and political rights. Leaders of the revolution after 1910 have supported strong labor legislation, have encouraged women away from traditional influences of the Church, and made room for them in management capacities in business, labor, and the professions. Even in the area of social mores the Mexican female, like her Colombian, Peruvian, Central American, and Caribbean counterparts faithful to codes of honor and virtue, is gradually moving away from the influence of her family and her church.

One final example of social change in Spanish America is that of revolutionary Cuba under Castro. An island backwater whose only importance was Havana's position as a chief port of the galleon trade, Cuba at the end of the eighteenth century became a full-blown plantation society, heavily populated with blacks, and integral to Spain's economy. As a part of Spain until 1898, and later heavily influenced by the United States, Cuba enjoyed some of the benefits of imperial rule which in that compact, relatively urban and growing middle-class society helped lay the groundwork for revolution.

By the time Castro came to power Cuba already ranked as the third most literate nation in Latin America; the 1953 census showing 78.8 percent, with

79 percent women and 74 percent men. Furthermore, the Church had never been as influential in Cuba as elsewhere in Latin America and there was a patina of more social equality for women than in other Latin American countries. Cuban women were among the first Latins to acquire the franchise (1934) and Cubans regularly elected women to the House and Senate while women also served as justices, ministers, and in other ranking government positions.

With this background Castro had ample bases on which to build. In a revolution whose goals were to establish a classless, egalitarian society, inequality between the sexes was not tolerated. Since 1959, even greater strides than earlier have been made; even more women go to school, partake in the political process, make economic decisions, and direct social measures for change. Extremely important has been the effort of the revolution to mobilize and to resocialize women, with the result that women now are active in positions and roles traditionally thought of as male. That is not to say that traditional attitudes do not still stand but they are being eroded. Cuba represents a semitraditional society receptive to an ideology which radically interpreted the ideas of the Reformation, Enlightenment, and Industrial Revolution and represents a model of widespread social change in Latin America.

One other country in Latin America which seems to be undergoing massive social change with a different style and tempo is Latin America's only Portuguese country, the giant of Brazil. Here the complexities of family relationships reflect the changes inherent in the transference of life-styles from the rural "Big House" to the urban mansions and shanties.[35] There remains in twentieth-century Brazil a dichotomy between the patriarchal, poverty-ridden rural areas and the more permissive, "bourgeois" suburbs and cities, with their own species of poverty. Yet, even considering changes from one area to another, Brazil is more rural than it is urban, not only in percentage of the population but also in attitudes and values, which also vary from area to area. For example, in many states, particularly Minas Gerais and those of the Northeast, the patriarchal family, dominated by the Portuguese *pai* (father) is still the dominant social force in a subsistence economy subculture in which there is a preoccupation with marrying daughters at as early an age as possible—thirteen, fourteen, or fifteen years.[36] In other rural areas of Brazil, especially in the predominantly immigrant-colony southern states of Paraná, Santa Catarina, and Rio Grande do Sul, the situation is somewhat different—not so much directly with regard to changed attitudes of and toward women, as indirectly, in the styles of patriarchy which were transferred to Brazil from various European cultures.

The dichotomy is not merely geographical or ethnic but is also reflected in the different social strata; among the working classes more responsibility seems to be in the hands of women and consequently they assume to themselves more prerogatives within the family. The "family" in these classes is most likely a loose and transitory relationship between a woman and her man of the moment; this is especially true of *favela* (slum) dwellers in the cities, who have a more informalized attitude toward children and mates.

It has been said that the Brazilian middle classes, especially those in the cities, reflect the character of nineteenth-century European bourgeois culture in which females were divided into two groups: respectable and nonrespectable.[37] The "respectable" women are protected by their fathers, husbands, or brothers, who tend to infuse the possessive pronoun—*my* mother, *my* wife, *my* daughters—with heavy personal proprietory meaning. As in Spanish America, the middle class remains a bastion of petit bourgeois morality, but these virtues are being subjected to the stresses and strains of a turbulent and changing society.

The Brazilian upper classes reflect yet another dichotomy, since within this group are found not only the most traditional of attitudes toward and by women, but also the most liberal in the sense that money, power, and position of a family affords some women the opportunity to move within the mores of the international jet set. Some of these young women become society leaders, a few actively enter the spheres of business and high finance, while others turn to the professions, particularly university teaching; it is in this category that Brazilian women have achieved fame for their country's image as a flexible society.

## VII

In both western and southwestern European cultures, then, women are regarded as peripheral to centers of power and are treated as secondary to males in almost all capacities. But they are victims of this attitude as a result of different cultural traditions. For the western European woman, the ideologies of Reformation, industrialization, and Enlightenment influenced the directions of change in family and society and hence of female life.

Ideological and industrial processes in western Europe induced social changes which afforded the general society access to a life-style theretofore reserved for the elites and at the same time were responsible for shifting the position of the female from one of prominence in a kinship-dominant society and economy to that of the far more restrictive purview of a nuclear family. At the time modern Europe was defining its parameters and also building its empires, the Anglo-American woman was ensconced in a subordinate role in a new nuclear, patriarchal family, with far less influence in public affairs than she had previously enjoyed. The Ibero-European woman already had been subordinated to her kinship family, her powers in society abdicated to males in a culture riddled with turmoil and in which military chieftains and feudal lords were absolute. For the Iberian woman, the shift had preceded the advent of ideologically induced change and had been a product of forces integral to the peninsula itself.

In the New World, colonial societies had settled into patterns similar to those of their mother countries, with some modifications resulting from geographic and ethnic influences. The same processes of ideological and industrial revolutionary development peculiar to western Europe were continued in Anglo-America. Similarly, in Ibero-America, just as their mother countries had rejected and later slowly accepted ideological and industrial precepts so, too, the South American countries responded gradually to change.

By the twentieth century in Western societies, proponents of ideologies of liberty, equality, individualism, and reform had encouraged the process of breaking down a status system based on sex and seniority, helped to shift the position of women within the society, and called for changes in economic and social areas commensurate with those already available in political and civic affairs. Once victims of the transformation to modern society, females in the West have begun to utilize to their own advantage the concepts of freedom and equality.

Yet, despite the fact that North Americans consider Latin America to be an underdeveloped area, and its countries to be less technologically advanced than theirs (hence to make the generalization that its women require more liberating than North Americans do), Latin American women seem sometimes to exhibit more influence in their societies than do northern women. Middle- and upper-class Latin women in general appear to demonstrate greater partici- pation at every professional and public level (save politics, the last male preserve in any society) than do their Anglo-American counterparts. It is true that in terms of morality and sexual behavior, Latin women are also still subject to a harsh double standard; however, that constitutes a psycho-social problem which I cannot deal with here. The main question to be asked here is: why are middle- and upper-class Latin American women in positions of influence, more so than in the United States, and why do lower-class women reflect similarities across cultures in terms of their position?

The answer is complex. Regarding the reasons for middle- and upper-class women's positions of influence, I believe the major one is that change has come gradually, that medieval and modern traditions have been in con- fluence. Latin America has been modernizing but doing so in the imposing shadow of medieval tradition. The primary family institution has changed to a nuclear one but retained many of the values and attitudes of the medieval family. Upper- and middle-class women still can rely on an extensive network of kin and servants to handle household and family tasks, thereby being freed for full-time participation in professional and other public activities. Thus, for these women and their families, the Anglo-American liberating ideal for upper-class women seems in the process of being achieved more rapidly than in the United States. The child of these upper classes is pampered and cared for by kin and servants, with the child's mother and father sharing equally in his or her upbringing. These upper- and middle-class families seem to have adopted the features of both nuclear and kin families most useful to them- selves, and within them some women have found the support necessary to conduct their own lives independently. But they have done so at the expense of a servant class of female domestic help and of unliberated members of the kin group, such as grandmothers and aunts.

In general, lower-class women seem to share circumstances and values in common, across cultures. The general exclusion of the lower classes from the centers of economic and political power has encouraged and at the same time made necessary the retention of patterns of behavior and kin relationships common to the medieval tradition. Looser moral codes, fewer restrictions on male-female behavior, and the outright need of women to control or significantly influence their households and the external arenas which their households and families dominate, for example, the local markets, have made lower-class women more visible and more powerful than lower-class males. Yet, because the lower classes in the larger society are almost inarticulate in power terms, the women of these classes across cultures share the misfortunes of all peoples on the peripheries of power. The only relief, and, at the same time, a major difference between lower-class women in Latin America as compared with Anglo-America is that many Latin nations, earlier than the United States, passed and continue to adhere to extensive, radical social legislation which has benefited the working woman.

Thus, the upper- and middle-strata women of Latin America appear to be bypassing or eliminating the entrenched, Victorian antifeminine traditions of a post-Reformation, industrialized Anglo-American world, with its frustrating revolution of rising expectations. The lower strata of women, however, who comprise the majority female voice in *all* American societies, are still victims of their class position, exploited by the more privileged members of their respective societies. For these women, across all cultures, liberation will not come until there is class liberation.

## NOTES

1. A commentary by Marañon on the ancestors of Gaspar de Guzmán, Conde de Olivares, as cited in Alicia Moreau de Justo, *La mujer en la democracia* (Buenos Aires, 1945), 30.

2. The legal position of the Iberian female is discussed in Mercedes Formica de Careaga, "Spain," in *Women in the Modern World,* ed. Rafael Patai (New York: Free Press, 1967), 179.

3. J. H. Elliott, *Imperial Spain* (New York: New American Library, Mentor, 1966), 305.

4. Conversations with Iberian research scholars Thomas Glick, Carlos Diaz-Ortiz, Carla Rahn Phillips, and Francis Dutra.

5. Gonzalo de Correas, *Vocabularia de refranes y frases* (Madrid, 1924), *passim.*

6. Elliott, *Imperial Spain,* 305ff.

7. See A. H. de Oliviera Marques, *Daily Life in Portugal in the Late Middle Ages* (Madison: University of Wisconsin Press, 1971).

8. See Miguel Cervantes, *Novelas Ejemplares* (Madrid: Aguilar, 1960); Lope de Vega, *Cuatro Obras Teatrales* (Madrid: Aguilar, 1960); *The Celestina,* trans. Lesley Byrd Simpson (Berkeley: University of California Press, 1966); and Ruth Pike, "Sevillian Society in the Sixteenth Century: Slaves and Freedmen," *Hispanic American Historical Review* 47, no. 3 (1967), 344–59.

9. See Philippe Ariès, *Centuries of Childhood* (New York: Knopf, 1962) for a classic, pioneering study, based on demographic data and iconographic materials, which overturns previously held notions of the family.

10. Ariès, *Centuries of Childhood, passim;* Edmund Morgan, *Virginians at Home: Family Life in the Eighteenth Century* (Williamsburg: Colonial Williamsburg, 1952);

Gilberto Freyre, *The Masters and the Slaves* (New York: Knopf, 1963) and *The Mansions and the Shanties* (New York: Knopf, 1963).

11. Ariès, *Centuries of Childhood, passim.* According to this study, the child became not one of many to be apprenticed but one of fewer of his or her group in a society in which he or she became a more privileged member. Also see David Hunt, *Parents and Children in History* (New York: Basic Books, 1970).

12. See William O'Neill, *Divorce in the Progressive Era* (New Haven: Yale University Press, 1967).

13. *Ibid.*, 17; William Goode, *World Revolution and Family Patterns* (Glencoe, Ill.: Free Press, 1963).

14. Elliott, *Imperial Spain, passim;* John Lynch, *Spain under the Hapsburgs,* 2 vols. (New York: Oxford University Press, 1965, 1969). Both studies give a lucid and comprehensive exposition of the Counter-Reformation Spanish state.

15. A classic delineation of the medieval "child" in Iberian society is found in the anonymous picaresque novel *Lazarillo de Tormes* (Madrid: Coleccion Austral, 1958).

16. See H. R. Trevor-Roper, *Religion, the Reformation and Social Change* (London: Macmillan and Co., 1967) for a theoretical discussion on the alternate "bureaucratic" and "mercantile" systems.

17. See Richard Herr, *The Eighteenth Century Revolution in Spain* (Princeton, N.J.: Princeton University Press, 1958), Arthur Whitaker, ed., *Latin America and the Enlightenment* (Ithaca, N.Y.: Cornell University Press, 1963), and A. Owen Aldridge, ed., *The Ibero-American Enlightenment* (Urbana: University of Illinois Press, 1971), for comprehensive analyses of the extent and influence of the Enlightenment in Iberian societies.

18. For a comprehensive interpretation of the women of modern Spain, see Michael Kenny, *Spanish Tapestry: Town and Country in Castile* (New York: Harper and Row, 1966). For a more traditional compilatory study see Maria Lafitte Campo Alange, *La mujer en España: Cien años de su historia, 1860–1960* (Madrid, 1964).

19. Kenny, *Spanish Tapestry,* 197, 161.

20. Information on contemporary Portuguese women was made available to me by Professor Raymond Sayers, who kindly lent me the original manuscript of João Baptista Nunes Pereira Neto on Portuguese society since 1945, which subsequently appeared sans materials on women in Raymond Sayers, ed., *Portugal and Brazil in Transition* (Minneapolis: University of Minnesota Press, 1968), under the title "Social Evolution in Portugal Since 1945." References here are from pages 20–21, 44, 55, 63, and 67 of the manuscript. The views of both Kenny for Spain and Nunes for Portugal are confirmed by my own field experiences in 1960, 1967, and 1968.

21. See Ariès, *Centuries of Childhood;* Morgan, *Virginians at Home;* and Freyre, *The Masters and the Slaves;* see also Carl Bridenbaugh, *Myths and Realities: Societies of the Colonial South* (New York: Atheneum, 1963), esp. chap. 3.

22. See *ibid., passim.*

23. For general discussion of the female in Amerindian societies see Julian Steward's six-volume *Handbook of South American Indians* (Washington, D.C.: Smithsonian Institution, 1946–50), and Robert Wauchope's ten-volume *Handbook of Middle American Indians* (Austin: University of Texas Press, 1965-continuing).

24. See Jan Vansina, *Kingdom of the Savannas* (Madison: University of Wisconsin Press, 1968); Karl Polanyi, *Dahomey and the Slave Trade* (Seattle: University of Washington Press, 1966); James Duffy, *Portuguese Africa* (Cambridge, Mass.: Harvard University Press, 1959); Daryll Forde and P. M. Kaberry, *West African Kingdoms in the Nineteenth Century* (London: Oxford University Press, 1969); Michael Crowder, *A Short History of Nigeria* (New York: Praeger, 1966); Philip Curtin, *The Atlantic Slave*

*Trade: A Census* (Madison: University of Wisconsin Press, 1969); and the monographs of the International African Institute Series of the Oxford University Press.

25. Oral-history interviews from my own field research in Spanish and Portuguese America in the 1960s and in 1970 and 1971.

26. These are the legal codification of the thirteenth century and the recompilation of principal civil codes of the sixteenth century.

27. Law of Toro Code, Article 54.

28. A statement from the noted Hispanic-American jurist José Maria Ots Capdequi, as cited in Vera Pichel, *Mi pais y sus mujeres* (Buenos Aires, 1968), 42.

29. James Lockhart, *Spanish Peru, 1532–1560* (Madison: University of Wisconsin Press, 1968); Stuart Schwartz, "Free Farmers in a Slave Economy: The *Lavradores de Cana* of Bahia, 1550–1750," in Dauril Alden, ed., *The Colonial Roots of Modern Brazil* (Berkeley: University of California Press, 1973), and Francis Dutra, "Pernambuco vs. Bahia: Donatorial Privilege, Centralization, and the Struggle for Hegemony in Seventeenth Century Brazil," *ibid.* See also Asunción Lavrin's essay in this volume, "Women in Convents: Their Economic and Social Role in Colonial Mexico," in which Lavrin documents the importance of upper-class women in nunneries to the development of the colonial economy of Mexico.

30. The words of a school teacher in Vassouras *municipio* in Brazil's Paraíba Valley, 1873, as cited in Stanley Stein, *Vassouras. A Brazilian Coffee Country, 1850–1900* (Cambridge, Mass.: Harvard University Press, 1957), 152.

31. Rosa Signorelli de Marti, "Spanish America," in *Women in the Modern World*, ed. Raphael Patai (New York: Free Press, 1967), 192–93.

32. See the *United Nations Demographic Yearbook*.

33. Gabriel Almond and Sidney Verba, *The Civic Culture* (Princeton: Princeton University Press, 1963), 426–28.

34. See Ann Pescatello, *Power and Pawn: The Female in Iberian Families, Cultures, and Socities* (Westport, Conn.: Greenwood Press, 1976), for detailed analyses of these countries.

35. See Gilberto Freyre, *Masters and Slaves* and *Mansions and Shanties, passim*, for description of post-independence rural and urban Brazilian life.

36. Rose Marie Muraro, *A mulher na construção do mundo futuro* (Petropolis, 1967) 122.

37. *Ibid.*, 123.

# Racism and Tradition:
# Black Womanhood in Historical Perspective

*Joyce A. Ladner*

Black womanhood has become a popular topic of discussion during the past decade, when social analysts, policy makers, community leaders, and others became concerned about the so-called plight of the black family and sought to intervene in this institution in an effort to "uplift" it from its alleged decay and disorganization. This focus on the black family and its women began decades ago when E. Franklin Frazier asserted in *The Negro Family in the United States* that the family is matriarchal and disorganized as a result of having inherited the legacy of slavery, and as a result of the mass migration to the cities which causes further disruption. In 1939 Frazier wrote the following:

> when one undertakes to envisage the probable course of development of the Negro family in the future, it appears that the travail of civilization is not yet ended. First it appears that the family which evolved within the isolated world of the Negro folks will become increasingly disorganized. Modern means of communication will break down the isolation of the world of black folk, and, as long as the bankrupt system of southern agriculture exists, Negro families will continue to seek a living in the towns and cities of the country. They will crowd the slum areas of southern cities or make their way to northern cities where their family life will become disrupted and their poverty will force them to depend upon charity. . . . the ordeal of civilization will be less severe if there is a general improvement in the standard of living and racial barriers to employment are broken down. Moreover, the chances for normal family life will be increased if large-scale modern housing facilities are made available for the masses of the Negro population in the cities. Nevertheless, those families which possess some heritage of family life and traditions and education will resist the destructive forces of urban life more successfully than the illiterate Negro folk and in either case their family life will adapt itself to the secular and rational organization of urban life.[1]

During subsequent periods, analyses of various aspects of the black family life were conducted, including the works of Charles S. Johnson (*Growing Up*

This essay is reprinted from *Tomorrow's Tomorrow*, © 1971 by Joyce A. Ladner. Reprinted by permission of Doubleday and Company, Inc.

*in the Black Belt)*, Allison Davis and John Dollard (*Children of Bondage*), St. Clair Drake and Horace R. Cayton (*Black Metropolis*), Hylan Lewis (*Blackways of Kent*) and others. All of these works generally followed the Frazierian thesis by tacitly comparing the black family to that of the white middle class, and thereby emphasizing its weaknesses, instead of attempting to understand the nature of its strengths—strengths which emerged and withstood formidable odds against oppression.

All of the classic studies which have investigated black life and culture have focused on the attitudes and behavior of blacks. None have dealt with the structural effects of oppression, or with specific ways to change the social system so that it no longer produces its devastating effects on black people. Because of this faulty conceptualization of the nature of the real problem—oppression as the source—the attitudes and behavior of blacks became the object of considerable stigmatization because they did not conform to the American status quo. The strong resilience and modes of adaptation which black people developed to combat the forces of poverty and racism, produced by neocolonialism, were *never* recognized as important areas of intellectual inquiry. Indeed, many students of black life and culture so emphasized the "pathological" that the positive features were virtually unknown. Thus, the dominant trend of thought came to be that which purports that blacks do not value family life. Martin Luther King once voiced strong sentiments to the contrary when he said: " . . . for no other group in American life is the matter of family life more important than to the Negro. Our very survival is bound up in it. . . . no one in all history had to fight against so many physical and psychological horrors to have a family life."[2]

The work of black sociologist Andrew Billingsley is the first comprehensive study of the black family that attempts to assess its strengths instead of concentrating on its weaknesses. His volume, *Black Families in White America,* also places the family in a historical perspective as it relates to the African background, slavery in the Americas, etc.[3]

The black woman is again emerging as an important figure within the family and community, to be investigated and reinterpreted in light of the foregoing discussion.

Because there has been much controversy and concern over the black woman, and since there are a great number of misconceptions and myths about who she is, what her functions are, and what her relationship to the black man in fact is, it is necessary that one understand some of the historical background that has shaped her into the entity she has become. It is important to realize that most of the analyses concerned with black women (largely the poor) are ahistorical and do not attempt to place them in the context of the African background, through slavery and into the modern era. Indeed, scholars generally assume that blacks were stripped of their heritage during slavery. (This will be discussed more fully below.)

It would seem impossible to understand what the black woman is today without having a perspective on what her forebears were, especially as this relates to the roles, functions and responsibilities she has traditionally held within the family unit. This, of course, will involve her relationship to her husband, children, and the extended family. Only by understanding these broader sociohistorical factors can we properly interpret her role today.

There are basically three periods relating to the black woman included in this analysis: (1) the African background; (2) slavery; and (3) the modern era. In discussing the black woman from a historical perspective, it is important to know that there is no monolithic concept of *the* black woman, but that there are many models of black womanhood. However, there is a common denominator, a common strand of history, that characterizes all black women: *oppression.*[4] Even though many black women today consider themselves middle class and often are socialized in a tradition similar to that of middle-class white women, the common ancestry and oppressive conditions under which all black people have had to live to varying degrees provide the strong similarities and commonalities. Therefore, this chapter will broadly focus on the black woman, taking into consideration the differences and similarities that have been mentioned.

## The African Background

Before Africans were brought to American shores, they had developed highly complex civilizations along the West Coast, the area where a considerable amount of slave trading occurred. Tribal customs and laws for marriage and the family, property rights, wealth, political institutions and religion revolved around distinct patterns of culture which had evolved out of the history of the African people. Family patterns were viable entities unto themselves and were not influenced by, nor modeled after, the Western tradition of the monogamous unit; and strong protective attitudes toward kinsmen, including the extended family, likewise had their legitimate origin within African societies and were highly functional for African people. John Hope Franklin states that, "At the basis even of economic and political life in Africa was the family, with its inestimable influence over its individual members."[5] The family was extended in form, and acted as a political, economic, and religious unit. All of these institutional functions and arrangements took place within the broader extended family presided over by the patriarch. Another writer has noted that, "Although there were various types of states, the fundamental unit politically . . . was the family. . . . It was a kinship group numbering in the hundreds, but called a family because it was made up of the living descendants of a common ancestor. The dominant figure in this extended community was the patriarch, who exercised a variety of functions. . . . "[6]

A striking feature of precolonial African society was the importance that was attached to the family unit. The extended family was highly structured, with clearly designated roles for its male and female members. Marriage was always considered a ritual that occurred not between two individuals alone, but between all the members of the two extended families. It was a highly sacred ritual that involved bride price and other exchanges of property. Often marriages were arranged by parents of the bride and groom but sometimes by the two consenting partners. The emphasis was placed upon the binding together of two individuals who represented different families, and upon the mutual duties and obligations they were to carry out for each other. The elderly were highly regarded in African society. The patriarch of the extended family, who was sometimes considered a chief, was usually an elderly man.

Since the families lived in tribes, most of the functions now considered extrafamilial were also carried out within the broader extended unit. These included providing for the family's food, clothing, shelter, recreation, religious instruction, and education. The family, through the tribe, also engaged in warfare against other hostile tribes. As a social system, the extended family was complete and autonomous. This independence perhaps encouraged the development of close ties between family members and a high regard for the sanctity of the family.

Notably, the roles of women in precolonial Africa were very important ones and quite different from the understood duties and obligations of women in Western society. Two of the important roles of the African woman perpetuated during slavery and continued until today are: (1) her economic function; and (2) the close bond she had with her children. Politically, women were very important to the administration of tribal affairs. Since lineage was often matrilineal (descent traced through the female), "Queen Mothers" and "Queen Sisters" assumed highly significant duties in the tribe. For example: "Each major official had a female counterpart known as his 'mother', who took precedence over him at court and supervised his work. When officials reported to the King, groups of women were present, whose duty was to remember what had happened."[7]

In attempting to explain the origin of the important roles played by women in precolonial African society, one historian has noted:

> There is a recurring theme in many African legends and mythology of a woman who is the founder or the mother of the tribe who is either a queen or the daughter of a king. She is an aristocratic lady who is involved in politics. For example, the creation myths of the Hausa people in Northern Nigeria or of Niger or Chad begin with a woman who goes out and founds a kingdom. She is the Black Moses who is leading her people into the promised land which is an area near the water where communication is relatively free. She settles down and establishes the traditions of the people.[8]

It is clear that the roles of women in precolonial West African societies were very different from those of women in Western society. Their positions of economic and political power could also be observed in the family.

One of the ways in which the role of women can be observed is in their relationship to children. The Queen Mother or Queen Sister among the Ashanti, who traced descent matrilineally, placed the woman in the highest order because of her role as procreator: "Like a mother's control of her children, a queen mother's authority depends on moral rather than legal sanctions and her position is a symbol of the decisive function of motherhood in the social system."[9] Furthermore, "As Ashanti often point out, a person's status, rank and fundamental rights stem from his mother, and that is why she is the most important person in his life."[10]

The relationship between mother and child was important in all of West

Africa. Although there were clearly defined roles for adult men and women, with the male taking a strong role as the patriarch, there were still vital functions that the mother fulfilled for the children and which were reserved only for her. Thus, "the Ashanti regard the bond between mother and child as the keystone of all social relations."[11] Even in the societies where descent was patrilineal or double, there was a high regard for the mother's function as child bearer and perpetuator of the ancestral heritage. This emanates from the value that is attached to the childbearing powers of women. Barren women are pitied, if not outcasts, even today in much of Africa. Barrenness is often considered a legitimate reason for a man to seek a divorce from his wife. Similarly, women who bear great numbers of children are accorded high status.[12] This emphasis upon the woman's role does not underestimate the importance of the male as provider, disciplinarian, and teacher. The strong patriarchal figure was of utmost importance to the child's rearing, but the day-to-day contact was primarily with the mother.

Another area of importance with regard to women's roles in African society was their economic function as traders in the villages. Meier and Rudwick note that "Women played an important role in the administration of political and economic affairs. . . . They were the chief traders in the village."[13] Even in contemporary West African society, women still fulfill the important economic function as traders. Marie Perinbaum states: "The West African market woman is an institution in West Africa. She is the small capitalist, or the entrepreneur, and is sometimes one of the major cash winners of the family. She is also the one who brings in the consumer goods."[14] Melville Herskovits also describes the prominent role that women played as traders in the market, and indicates that some of them became independently wealthy as a result of their endeavors.[15]

These are the traditions and life-styles to which Africans were accustomed. As products of highly complex civilizations, with a high regard for the family—both living and dead—they must have been totally unprepared for the barbaric conditions to which they would be subjected in the New World. From the early seventeenth century to the mid-nineteenth century when slavery ended, approximately forty million Africans were brought to the United States. Historians note that slavery in the United States assumed the most cruel and harsh form, and was designed systematically to dehumanize its captives. All the highly developed institutions which were an integral part of African society were crushed (from their original form) and slaves had to fight to preserve whatever remnants of their civilization they could.

In this cursory view of the black woman's relationship to the African past one can observe that she was part of a cultural tradition that was very different from that which she was to enter in the New World. Thus, "The Negro who came to the New World varied widely in physical type and ways of life, but there were many common patterns of culture. Whatever the type of state, the varied groups all operated under orderly governments, with established legal codes, and under well-organized social systems. The individual might find it necessary to submerge his will into the collective will, but he shared a deep sense of group identity, a feeling of belonging."[16] The degradation a woman suffered in slavery had total effects on all aspects of her life—her identity as a woman and as an African, her relationship and roles with regard to her husband and family.

## Slavery

When Africans were sold into slavery they were introduced to an alien culture and an attempt was made to force them to adopt the way of life of Western society. The highly organized social order from which they emerged was considered "barbarous" and "uncivilized" because of the inability of Europeans to understand and appreciate the cultural differences which set them apart from the Africans. Because of the fact that slavery was engaged in for economic reasons, Africans became property and were thus denied the rights of human beings. They were not publicly allowed to practice their native religions, speak their native languages, nor engage in the numerous other cultural traditions which were characteristic of African society. Obviously the effects were devastating on the family, which, in fact, could not be recognized as the one they had been part of in Africa, notably in its structure. Legal marriage was denied, allowing for the emergence of the ephemeral quality of male-female liaisons. Men were denied the right to fulfill the long-standing tradition of patriarch over the extended family, and women, in effect, became the backbone of the family. Parents were denied the right to exercise authority over their children, an important aspect of African culture. Especially absent was the function of the economic provider, disciplinarian, and teacher, strong characteristics of the African male.

Of considerable importance is the emphasis slaveholders placed upon the legal contract between slave and master as well as the various informal sanctions of slavery. Quarles notes, "All slaves were inculcated with the idea that the whites ruled from God and that to question this divine right-white theory was to incur the wrath of heaven, if not to call for a more immediate sign of displeasure here below."[17] Numerous legal restrictions were enacted to prohibit the slave from exercising his rights as a free person. In spite of these restrictions, there were many outward signs of rebellion against the mores of the slave masters. The structure and processes of slave family life have not been adequately documented because of the scarcity of information recorded by slaves. Yet there are some data concerning the family and, particularly important for the purposes of this analysis, the role of women in slave society.

Most of the accounts of the relationships between slaves and their regard for each other are to be taken from slave narratives and autobiographies of ex-slaves such as Frederick Douglass, Nat Turner, and Sojourner Truth. These provide information about the role women in particular played within the family and society. It must be noted that these frequently differ from the analyses and portraits some historians have given. One of the positions that has been advanced by social scientists is that slaves rarely developed strong familial bonds with each other because of the disruptive nature of their family and community life. This position runs counter to the firsthand accounts given by slaves. For it will be observed that the family during slavery, with all its modifications, was a strong unit in that parents were able oftentimes to impart certain values and cultural ethos to their offspring. It appears that whenever it was economically feasible for this family pattern to emerge, parents sought to exert this responsibility. The family was also extended in form whenever it was economically feasible.

Nat Turner, the revolutionary, provides information about his relationship with his parents and grandmother. In his own *Confessions*, he speaks of the religious instruction he received from his grandmother, to whom he was closely attached, and of the encouragement he received from his mother and father to become a prophet. He states: "My father and mother strengthened me in this my first impression, saying in my presence, I was intended for some great purpose, which they had always thought from certain marks on my head and breast."[18]

Frederick Douglass, the noted abolitionist, in the *Life and Times of Frederick Douglass* describes the close relationship he had with his grandmother, who cared for him in the absence of his mother. Douglass states: "If my poor, dear old grandmother now lives, she lives to remember and mourn over the loss of children, the loss of grandchildren and the loss of great-grandchildren. . . . My poor old grandmother, the devoted mother of 12 children is left all alone. . . ."[19] On one occasion he remembers his own mother, who had been sold to another plantation, slipping into their home in the night to see him: "I was grander upon my mother's knee than a king upon his throne. . . . I dropped off to sleep, and waked in the morning to find my mother gone. . . . My mother had walked twelve miles to see me, and had the same distance to travel again before the morning sunrise."[20]

Sojourner Truth, the prophet and leader, who referred to slaves as Africans, provides a vivid account of the trauma her mother suffered when she was separated from her children. She recounts: "I can remember when I was a little, young girl, how my old mammy would sit out of doors in the evenings and look up at the stars and groan, and I would say, 'Mammy, who makes you groan so?' And she would say, 'I am groaning to think of my poor children; they do not know where I be and I don't know where they be. I look up at the stars and they look up at the stars!' "[21] When Sojourner's five-year-old son was taken and she was told that he was to be sold into the Deep South (although she was a slave in New York State), she made the statement that she felt as "tall as the world and mighty as the nation," indicating that she had the faith that she and her son would some day be reunited.

Numerous slave narratives provide dramatic accounts of the events surrounding the forced separation between parents and children. The following is one such example.

My brothers and sisters were bid off first, and one by one, while my mother, paralyzed with grief held me by the hand. Her turn came and she was bought by Issac Riley of Montgomery County. Then I was offered. . . . My mother, half distracted with the thought of parting forever from all her children, pushed through the crowd while the bidding for me was going on, to the spot where Riley was standing. She fell at his feet, and clung to his knees, entreating him in tones that a mother could only command, to buy her baby as well as herself, and spare to her one, at least, of her little ones. . . . This man disengaged himself from her with . . . violent blows and kicks. . . . I must have been between five and six years old.[22]

Even when separation was apparent, and fathers and mothers found themselves unable to prevent it, there was evident a profound feeling that the family would one day be reunited. Slaves also tried to instill within their children who were being separated from them a sense of morality: "I was about twelve or fourteen years old when I was sold. . . . On the day I left home, everything was sad among the slaves. My mother and father sung and prayed over me and told me how to get along in the world."[23] This strong bond also transcended actual separation, for when families were not reunited, memories and grief about kinsmen remained strong.

Solomon Northup, who spent twelve years as a slave, recalls one such experience.

On my arrival at Bayou Boeuf, I had the pleasure of meeting Eliza, whom I had not seen for several months. . . . She had grown feeble and emaciated, and was still mourning for her children. She asked me if I had forgotten them, and a great many times inquired if I still remembered how handsome little Emily was—how much Randall loved her—and wondered if they were living still, and where the darlings could then be. She had sunk beneath the weight of an excessive grief. Her drooping form and hollow cheeks too plainly indicated that she had well nigh reached the end of her weary road.[24]

Northup's accounts of Eliza's grief demonstrate the mortal psychological wounds she suffered as a result of being separated from her children. It appears that she would almost rather have been dead than to have given them up.

Indeed, some accounts show that mothers chose death for themselves and their children rather than experience the humiliation and torture of slavery, separation, and the total denial of their humanity. There is much in the oral history of slavery that speaks about the vast number of captives who jumped overboard en route to the Western Hemisphere, preferring to die rather than become slaves. It is said that others threw their newborn infants overboard for the same reason. After arriving on the mainland, women sometimes killed their children rather than allow them to grow up in slavery. This highest form of rebellion can be observed in the following oral historical account, taken from a slave narrative.

My mother told me that he [slave master] owned a woman who was the mother of seven children, and when her babies would get about a year or two of age he'd sell them and it would break her heart. She never got to keep them. When her fourth baby was born and was about two months old, she just studied all the time about how she would have to give it up, and one day she said, "I just decided I'm not going to let ol' master sell this baby; he just ain't going to do it." She got up and give it something out of a bottle and pretty soon it was dead.[25]

This example shows the total commitment this mother had to fighting a system which violated what must have been her most sacred principles.

All of these are some of the symbols of the strong bonds that existed between parents and children (notably between mother and child) during slavery and the strong attachment all the family had for each other. Contrary to popular myth, black parents had a tremendous capacity to express grief when separated from their children. One must also recognize the fact that, because of the inability of slaves to marry legally and have sustained unions, mothers were more often left with the ongoing care of the children, for whatever period they were able to do so. This also meant that they served the vital economic function of providers for their families in the absence of a sustained husband-father figure. Staples notes that "only the mother-child bond continually resisted the disruptive effect of economic interests that dictated the sale of fathers away from their families."[26] The institution of slavery only acted to reinforce the close bond that had already existed between mother and child in African society. It could be argued that this strong attachment, although very positive, in many respects probably would not have developed if Africans had been allowed the basic freedoms and liberties of the Europeans who had settled on this continent. This was a necessary adaptation to the system, and without doubt acted to reinforce the subjugation of men to women. It is clear that within the cultural context of the dominant society, slave women were forced to assume the basic duties and responsibilities toward their families men assumed in the white world. The impact this had on black men is immeasurable, and remnants of this effect can be found today, especially since many of the fundamental conditions are unchanged.

Historians have adequately documented the numerous rebellions/revolts staged by slaves against the social system. The most widely known form of rebellion was the slave revolt but there were a variety of other ways that slaves expressed their indignation, such as the day-to-day feigning of illness or acting "stupid" (recalcitrance). There is little evidence that slaves were a docile, happy lot who without hesitation gave up their African heritage and contented themselves to adapting to whatever life-styles their masters dictated.

The question is often raised as to what the black man's role was in defending his family against all the ravages and mass assaults of the slave system. It seems to be generally assumed that the men did very little, and most often nothing, to defend their mothers, wives, and children. But there are numerous historical accounts of black men lashing out against slavery because of its inhuman effects upon their families. One notable example is David Walker's *Appeal*, given in 1829:

Now, I ask you, had you not rather be killed than be a slave to a tyrant, who takes the life of your *mother, wife, and dear little children?* Look upon your *mother, wife, and children,* and answer God Almighty; and believe this, that it is no more harm for you to kill a man, who is trying to kill you, than it is for you to take a drink of water when thirsty; in fact, the man who will stand still and let another murder him, is worse than an infidel, and, if he has common sense, ought not to be pitied.[27] [Emphasis added.]

One could imagine that Walker voiced the sentiments of the hundreds of thousands of black men who found themselves unable to protect their mothers, wives, and children from the barbarous slave system. Some accounts can be found of black men who attempted to uphold the system of marriage by defending their wives against the attacks of white men. The following is one such account of a man who described the harsh experiences of his father, who had attempted to defend his mother:

His right ear had been cut off close to his head, and he had received a hundred lashes on his back. He had beaten the overseer for a brutal assault on my mother, and this was his punishment. Furious at such treatment, my father became a different man, and was so morose, disobedient, and intractable, that Mr. N. decided to sell him. He accordingly parted with him, not long after, to his son who lived in Alabama; and neither mother nor I ever heard from him again.[28]

This severe punishment is a reflection of the problems black men encountered when trying to exercise their rights and obligations to their families. They were harshly dealt with, sometimes unto death, when doing so. Almost any compassion expressed by slaves toward each other was dealt with severely. The following account was taken from a slave narrative: "They whipped my father 'cause he looked at a slave they killed and cried."[29]

Slave masters, through their demands for absolute obedience, and reinforced by harsh slave laws, attempted to crush every symbol of humanity, affection, and compassion within slaves. There were, of course, exceptions among some slaveholders who attempted to develop a more humane system.

If slaves revolted against the Western political and cultural system in the ways indicated, there is strong reason to believe that in the process of revolting they attempted to preserve some of their African traditions. One could argue that slave revolts (minor and major) were evidence of a two-pronged attack: (1) against the cruelty of slavery; and (2) against the denial to blacks of the right to practice their past cultural traditions, etc. Indeed, both are closely related. This is not to underestimate the effects slavery had in the attempts to crush every single remembrance of Africa, because the impact was obviously devastating. But one could argue that the oppression forced some of the native traditions underground. It is also clear that individual slaves had a strong reaction to slavery and the denial of Africans in this country the ability to relate to the native customs. Sojourner Truth's reference to blacks as Africans is a notable example. It is most clear, however, that slavery forged many distinct adaptations and acted to create a unique set of behavior patterns, attitudes, and values—a black culture—that are more American than African. Yet it would be in error to say that all of the African heritage was destroyed during slavery, because we have observed certain conditions that encouraged the perpetuation of African traditions related to the family. Immediately we can recognize the effects oppression had and subsequent adaptations it caused in the sharp change in status of black men, who were strong patriarchs in African society and mere subhumans in America, with none of the rights and privileges of American household heads. There are numerous other changes that affected the roles of men and women, such as the inability to marry legally and have children within the Western societal framework, and the undue hardships women experienced in being forced very often to accept total responsibility for their families.

A multiplicity of factors—notably slavery—acted to mold the black family. It is too simple an explanation to attribute all of the behavior characteristics of the family during slavery to either Africanisms or to the series of adaptations that blacks were forced to make to the social system. On this point, Herskovits states:

> Slavery did not cause the "maternal" family; but it tended to continue certain elements in the cultural endowment brought to the New World by the Negroes. The feeling between mother and child was reinforced when the father was sold away from the rest of the family; where he was not, he continued life in a way that tended to consolidate the obligations assumed by him in the integrated societies of Africa as these obligations were shaped to fit the monogamic, paternalistic pattern of the white masters.

The economic, political, and social institutions to which Africans had to relate during slavery provided the opportunity for the survival of many of the African traditions. The woman continued to play important functions within the family with regard to the welfare of children, as well as in the economic sphere. This allowed for the strengthening of her role as an independent figure within the family; in the New World her role as an economic provider only assumed a different form. However, the demands in slave society were more acute than those she had experienced in Africa because of the mandatory status that was applied: "That the plantation system did not differentiate between the sexes in exploiting slave labor, tended, again, to reinforce the tradition of the part played by women in the tribal economics."[30] As already stated, had there not been a continuing need for black women to continue to fulfill these functions their roles would probably have been little different from those of most white women, whose statuses were economically secure.

Today a popular debate revolves around whether or not American blacks possess a distinct cultural heritage that is a hybrid of the culture developed during slavery and certain remnants of African culture that were preserved. E. Franklin Frazier argues in *The Negro Family in the United States* that slavery and the Middle Passage destroyed all remnants of African culture:

> Probably never before in history has a people been so nearly completely stripped of its social heritage as the Negroes who were brought to America. Other conquered races have continued to worship their household gods within the intimate circle of their kinsmen. But American slavery destroyed household gods and dissolved the bonds of sympathy

and affection between men of the same blood and household. Old men and women might have brooded over memories of their African homeland, but they could not change the world about them. Through force of circumstances, they had to acquire a new language, adopt new habits of labor, and take over, however imperfectly, the folkways of the American environment. Their children, who knew only the American environment, soon forgot the few memories that had been passed on to them and developed motivations and modes of behavior in harmony with the New World. Their children's children have often recalled with skepticism the fragments of stories concerning Africa which have been preserved in their families. But, of the habits and customs, as well as the hopes and fears that characterized the life of their forebearers in Africa, nothing remains.[31]

In his perceptive analysis, Melville Herskovits disputes Frazier in *The Myth of the Negro Past* and argues that many "Africanisms" survived slavery and are to be observed in contemporary black life-styles, including the family, religion, music, dance, and the arts. The debate continues today among scholars such as Nathan Glazer and Daniel P. Moynihan, who assert that, "It is not possible for Negroes to view themselves as other ethnic groups viewed themselves because . . . the Negro is only an American and nothing else. He has no values and culture to guard and protect."[32] Some black intellectuals have argued that blacks in American society are an African people, and that few of the continuities between Africa and America have been broken.[33] Others propose that black culture is authentic. Charles Keil, whose study of black blues singers demonstrates the distinctiveness of the "soul ideology" and its peculiarity to the black experience, is one of the chief proponents of this thesis: "Like it or not, . . . a Negro culture exists, and its existence ought to be recognized by all concerned, no matter what their policy or proposed solutions to the American dilemmas."[34] Robert Blauner asserts that the peculiar historical experiences of blacks allowed for the development of a distinctive Negro lower-class life-style, although compared to the cultures of other ethnic minorities it is relatively weak.[35] It is very easy to concentrate on the thesis that blacks were denied their heritage, because that idea allows for the perpetuation of various myths regarding the inferiority of black people. Herskovits states: "The myth of the Negro past is one of the principal supports of race prejudice in this country. Unrecognized in its efficacy, it rationalizes discrimination in everyday contact between Negroes and whites, influences the shaping of policy where Negroes are concerned, and affects the trends of research by scholars whose theoretical approach, methods, and systems of thought presented to students are in harmony with it."[36]

It seems more difficult to recognize the unique heritage of blacks because most of the current historical documentations present a stereotyped portrait of the servile slave personality, as well as the "disorganized" family structure. One is forced to perceive black people today in a more positive manner if recognition is given to the rich cultural tradition from which blacks emerged. Such an analysis would put black people close to the same context in which the European immigrants to this country have been placed—immigrants who have been allowed to be assimilated into the mainstream of the society, and whose cultural heritages are highly respected.

Much of the heritage of slavery was passed on to blacks in the modern era. The basic economic inequities and racial discrimination in all walks of life prevented the majority of the black population from entering the mainstream and competing in an open society. Therefore, some of the problems black women faced during slavery, notably those of providing the economic sustenance for the family in the absence of a strong male provider, the maintenance of the extended family and the close ties between mother and children, are also characteristics today.

So black people had no choice but to develop their own distinctive culture with some elements from the old and some from the new and many innovative adaptations. It was necessary to develop this black culture in order to survive, to communicate, and to give meaning to life. For culture is the very way of life of a people.

The debate over the retention of Africanisms and the controversy over whether either a total black social system or a black subculture exists has only relative importance. There are both sharp discontinuities and strong uniformities between Africa and the New World (the United States and the Caribbean), and the principal factor among these should be an understanding of the political context of the black family all over the world. The black families in Africa, the Caribbean, and the United States have all been strongly influenced by the effects of neocolonialism, and thus have suffered similar problems emanating from racism and poverty.

Numerous studies have been conducted on the black family in the Caribbean and all of them provide a considerable amount of information about the way in which the continuities between Africa and this part of the New World have been maintained, although these assumptions are only implicit in most of these investigations.[37] One can recognize the similarities that exist between the Caribbean society and the broader black community in the United States, although the interpretations that researchers have provided vary widely. Blake argues, for example, that lower-class family relations are merely deviations from the traditional Western social system instead of being representative of a distinct culture. This position was challenged by Braithwaite, Rodman, and others who assert that this seemingly disorganized culture is a normal and legitimate one for its adherents.

It is generally recognized that the institution of slavery was less severe in this part of the New World than in the United States, a fact which accounted for, among other things, a higher retention of African culture. Melville Herskovits's pioneering efforts in studying the continuities are perhaps still considered the foremost work in this field, although other scholars have challenged many of Herskovits's assumptions. Hannerz says:

> Noting the strong bond between mother and children in black American households, and the weak and marginal relationship of the husband and father to this household nucleus, Herskovits related this to West African polygyny where he held that the male naturally was somewhat

peripheral to each group of mother and children. West African women are also traditionally rather independent economically, a fact which could contribute to keeping the husband-wife relationship rather weak. West Africans had an idea of the conjugal relationship as relatively weak, and when taken into slavery in the Americas they brought this idea along.[38]

A position that is somewhat different from both Herskovits's and from E. Franklin Frazier's "culturally stripped" thesis is held by M. G. Smith, who maintains that in the West Indies many of the cultural adaptations to the slave system which developed are still transmitted because of their functional value, and other family forms that are closer to the dominant society have developed out of the contemporary social context because certain conditions have been conducive to their emergence.[39]

An understanding of the Caribbean family structure provides the broader perspective that is needed to interpret the common sociohistorical experiences of blacks in the Americas. Such an analysis also generates a proper political context in which to analyze and propose solutions to the problems of the black family in all of the New World.

## NOTES

1. E. Franklin Frazier, *The Negro Family in the United States* (Chicago: University of Chicago Press, 1966), 367–68.

2. Address delivered at Abbott House, Westchester County, N.Y., October 29, 1965.

3. Andrew Billingsley, *Black Families in White America* (Englewood Cliffs, N.J.: Prentice-Hall, 1968).

4. African women were not shaped by oppression and it was only after they came to the New World that they had these experiences.

5. John Hope Franklin, *From Slavery to Freedom* (New York: Knopf, 1956), 28.

6. Benjamin Quarles, *The Negro in the Making of America* (London: Collier-MacMillan, 1964), 16–17.

7. August Meier and Elliott Rudwick, *From Plantation to Ghetto* (New York: Hill and Wang, 1966), 14.

8. Marie Perinbaum, lecture delivered at Spelman College, Atlanta, Ga., 1969.

9. Meyer Fortes, "Kinship and Marriage among the Ashanti," in *African Systems of Kinship and Marriage*, ed. A. R. Radcliffe-Brown and Daryll Ford (New York: Oxford University Press, 1950).

10. R. S. Rattray, *Ashanti* (London: Oxford University Press, 1923).

11. Fortes, "Kinship and Marriage among the Ashanti," 262.

12. Clark D. Moore and Ann Dunbar, *Africa Yesterday and Today* (New York: Bantam, 1968), 33.

13. Meier and Rudwick, *From Plantation to Ghetto*, 14.

14. Perinbaum, Spelman College lecture.

15. Melville Herskovits, *The Myth of the Negro Past* (Boston: Beacon Press, 1958), 62.

16. Quarles, *The Negro in the Making of America*, 18–19.

17. *Ibid.*, 71.

18. "The Text of the *Confessions of Nat Turner*, as reported by Thomas R. Gray, 1831," reprinted in John Henrik Clarke, ed., *The Confessions of Nat Turner: Ten Black Writers Respond* (Boston: Beacon Press, 1968), 93–118.

19. Benjamin Quarles, ed., *Narrative of the Life of Frederick Douglass, an American Slave, Written by Himself* (Cambridge, Mass.: Harvard University Press, 1960), 35–36.

20. *Ibid.*

21. Taken from W. E. B. Du Bois, "The Damnation of Women," *Darkwater* (New York: Schocken, 1969), 179.

22. Josiah Henson, *Father Henson's Story of His Own Life* (New York: Corinth, 1962), 12–13.

23. *God Struck Me Dead: Religious Conversion Experiences and Autobiographies of Negro Ex-Slaves* (Nashville, Tenn.: Fisk University Social Sciences Institute, 1945), 161–63.

24. Solomon Northup, *Twelve Years a Slave* (Baton Rouge: Louisiana State University Press, 1968), 77.

25. Lou Smith and B. A. Botkin, eds., *Lay My Burden Down: A Folk History of Slavery* (Chicago: University of Chicago Press, 1945), 40.

26. Robert Staples, "The Myth of the Black Matriarchy," *Black Scholar* (January–February 1970), 10.

27. Reprinted in Floyd Barbour, *The Black Power Revolt* (Boston: Porter Sargent, 1968), 25.

28. Frazier, *The Negro Family in the United States*, 53.

29. Roberta Manson, quoted in Julius Lester, *To Be a Slave* (New York: Dial Press, 1968), 33.

30. Herskovits, *The Myth of the Negro Past*, 181.

31. Frazier, *The Negro Family in the United States*, 15.

32. Nathan Glazer and Daniel Moynihan, *Beyond the Melting Pot* (Cambridge, Mass.: M.I.T. Press, 1963), 53.

33. abd-L Hakimu Ibn Alkalimat, "The Ideology of Black Social Science," *Black Scholar* (December 1969), 28–35.

34. Charles Keil, *Urban Blues* (Chicago: University of Chicago Press, 1966), 191–92.

35. Robert Blauner, "Negro Culture: Myth or Reality," *Black Experience: The Transformation of Activism* (New Brunswick, N.J.: Trans-action, 1970).

36. Herskovits, *The Myth of the Negro Past*, 1.

37. All of the following scholars have provided penetrating insights into the family structure of West Indians: Edith Clarke, *My Mother Who Fathered Me* (London: George Allen and Unwin, 1957); R. T. Smith, *The Negro Family in British Guiana* (New York: Grove Press, 1956); M. G. Smith, *The Plural Society in the British West Indies* (Berkeley: University of California Press, 1965); Judith Blake, *Family Structure in Jamaica* (New York: Free Press, 1961); William Goode, "Illegitimacy in the Caribbean Social Structure," *American Sociological Review* XXV (February 1960), 21–30; Hyman Rodman, "Marital Relationships in a Trinidad Village," *Marriage and Family Living* XXIII (May 1969), 170; Rodman, "Lower-class Attitudes toward 'Deviant' Family Patterns, a Cross Cultural Study," *Journal of Marriage and the Family* (May 1969), 315–21; Rodman, "The Lower Class Value Stretch," *Social Forces* XLII (December 1963), 205–15; Lloyd Braithwaite, "Sociology and Demographic Research in the Caribbean," *Social and Economic Studies* VI (Jamaica: University College of the West Indies); and F. M. Henriquez, *Family and Colour in Jamaica* (London: Eyre and Spottiswoode, 1953).

38. Ulf Hannerz, *Soulside: Inquiries into Ghetto Culture and Community* (New York: Columbia University Press, 1969), 72.

39. See *ibid.*, 71–76, for a full discussion of the various schools of thought on the black family in the New World.

# The Politics of Cultural Liberation: Male-Female Relations in Algeria

*Kay Boals*

Comparisons among culturally oppressed groups are not new. The term "nigger," for example, has been applied to women and to students to suggest the character of their position vis-à-vis males and professors, respectively.[1] Comparison is also made in common parlance when people speak of the black movement being "ahead" of the women's movement, or of gay liberation as beginning to "catch up with" the feminist and black movements. So far, however, such comparisons have been unsystematic and largely intuitive, and the bases on which they rest have remained implicit and perhaps unconscious. In this paper, an attempt is made to provide a framework for systematic comparative analysis of the process of cultural liberation. The framework suggested is a model for examining the dialectic between culturally dominant and culturally oppressed groups. The case selected for study involves a twofold dialectic: that of male-female relations and that between colonizer and colonized in contemporary Algeria.[2]

By culturally oppressed groups is meant, for example, women in male-dominated and masculine-value-oriented societies; blacks in white America; homosexuals in "straight" society, and colonized peoples in colonial and post-colonial societies. The major similarity among these otherwise diverse cases is that all involve a relationship of dominance which is both "external" and "internal." That is, the dominance is not merely technological or economic or military; it is also emotional, cultural, and psychological, producing in the dominated a pervasive sense of inferiority and insecurity.[3] As one feminist has noted, "It is hard to fight an enemy who has outposts in your head."[4]

The process of self-liberation involves simultaneously both individuals and groups. Although it takes place within the psyches of individuals, it is absolutely central to political analysis because it is the crucible out of which all revolutionary and transforming movements arise. Moreover, though it is necessarily an individual process, it is one which cannot be successfully

This essay is a revised version of a paper read at the 1972 annual meeting of the American Political Science Association, Washington, D.C., September 5-9; © 1972, American Political Science Association.

completed by individuals in isolation since it is their identity as members of a (usually ascriptive) group which is under attack.

In the model proposed here, cultural liberation is seen as composed of six process-oriented types of consciousness: traditional, traditionalist, assimilationist, reformist, revolutionary, and transforming consciousness.[5] We examine first each of the six types of consciousness, and subsequently consider the question of relationships among the various types.[6]

### I

The first of the six types of consciousness which comprise our model is *traditional* consciousness; its most important characteristic is an unquestioning acceptance of the way of life of one's own group. In some cases, as in Islamic traditional culture, it is characterized by a calm conviction of superiority over others and a sense of being at the center of the cosmos.[7] Traditional consciousness is also often linked to a religious belief about the proper "station in life" of various individuals and groups—an attitude which has so nearly disappeared in contemporary America that we too easily forget how pervasive it has been in most societies.

One example of what is meant by traditional consciousness is given by Wilfred C. Smith in his discussion in *Islam and Modern History* of al-Khidr Husayn, the first editor of the journal of al Azhar, Egypt's religious university.[8] According to Smith, what distinguishes this editor from his successor is his clear distinction between the Muslim community as it actually exists and the ideal Islam to which that community must continue to aspire. Neither romantic nor nostalgic, he is not hesitant to point out existing defects, and he focuses on what needs to be done to make the community a better embodiment of the Koranic ideal. Two things are crucial: his firm conviction that the Islamic ideal is the direction in which to move and his commitment to judging the community in terms of standards and criteria derived from that ideal, rather than by criteria external to it. Although writing in the 1930s, he apparently remained essentially unaffected by the British occupation.[9]

In this respect he differed profoundly from many who came under colonial domination in various regions of the world. To the extent that colonialism went hand in hand with a cultural domination that challenged the previously accepted way of life of the indigenous society, it was instrumental in generating new kinds of consciousness in response. One of these was what might be called *traditionalist* consciousness.

The essential characteristic that differentiates traditionalist from traditional consciousness (although not, as we shall see, from other forms to be discussed below) is that the sense of unquestioning acceptance of the traditional way of life is irrevocably gone and in its place is a will to believe without the capacity to do so. In the case of the Islamic community, for example, to use Clifford Geertz's terms, religiousness is replaced by religiousmindedness.[10] Put somewhat differently, faith becomes ideology.[11] In the process there develops an increasingly strident defensiveness. Moreover, the ideology is of a very particular kind, reflecting the situation from which it arose: namely, that of being threatened by a culturally potent other. The traditionalist continues to reaffirm the criteria of judgment of his or her own traditional culture or religion but is unable to do so with internal conviction. There is thus a strong internal incoherence between emotions and thinking, between what one would like to believe and what one "knows in one's bones."

One telling instance of the difference between traditional and traditionalist consciousness is cited by Rama Mehta in *The Western Educated Hindu Woman,* a study of fifty Indian women who were in their twenties at the time of Indian independence.[12] The fathers of these women were in the Indian civil service and the women themselves were educated in missionary secondary schools and had gone on at least to the B.A. in Indian colleges and universities. Their mothers, however, were almost entirely uneducated, spoke only the language of their own province and knew almost no English, remained devout Hindus, and continued both to practice the daily religious rituals and to try to bring up their children, especially their daughters, according to traditional Hindu ideas of modesty, reticence, submissiveness to male domination, and sacrifice of individual personal growth and development in the interests of family harmony and filial respect.

Their mothers, the respondents reported, were not at all embarrassed at their poor English or their unfamiliarity with British manners and ideas, nor did they take the British and Anglicized Indian way of life as a threat or challenge to themselves. Rather, they were so firmly convinced of the unquestionable rightness and morality of their own way of doing things that the British way was not even seen as a possible alternative.

On the other hand, while many of the respondents themselves asserted their belief in the desirability of the extended family, or of sub-caste affiliations, or of teaching their daughters to be women in the traditional style, their own education and life-styles made it both psychologically and practically difficult for them to do so in any consistent or convincing way, and they definitely saw the Western life-style as a threat and challenge to their own.[13]

Thus traditionalist consciousness appears clearly in the respondents, although their mothers were traditional. A parallel in this country would be those women who assert with increasing defensiveness the superiority of the wife-and-mother-only role against the felt threat of feminist challenges. A woman with traditional consciousness would not be similarly defensive, because she would not see the feminist point of view as a threat in the first place.

It is in general fairly easy to discriminate between traditional and traditionalist consciousness by focusing on the tone of assertions. It can also be seen in the content, however, since traditionalists are already in the position of arguing primarily against something (i.e., the external cultural threat), whereas traditional individuals do not take a predominantly comparative stance at all. This may be seen, for example, in comparing al-Khidr Husayn, the editor of the al Azhar journal discussed by Smith, with his traditionalist successor. Whereas al-Khidr Husayn focused on serving God and saw Islam as a transcendent ideal toward which the Muslim needed to strive, the second editor's emphasis was on serving Islam—and Islam conceived not as ideal, but in terms of the actual historical community. This emphasis reflects the fact that he is writing with an eye to refuting attacks and judgments based on standards external to Islam; in so doing he himself takes over some of those standards—and indeed often quotes Western scholars to make his points. As Smith points out:

> In a strict sense, even, such apologetic is more appropriate for non-Muslim consumption.
>
> In fact, a fanciful case could be made out that these writings are really functioning for readers who in the most profound, most religious sense are not Muslim; rather are men who, religiously ex-Muslim, are (or want to be) proud of their heritage, and desperately need reassurance in a hostile world. They believe (or want to believe) ardently in Islam and delight to see it defended. A true Muslim, however, is not a man who believes in Islam—especially Islam in history; but one who believes in God and is committed to the revelation through His Prophet. The latter is here sufficiently admired. But commitment is missing.[14]

Traditionalism is by no means the only possible response when traditional consciousness is undermined by having to come to terms with a culturally potent other, although it is presumably the most widespread initially. An alternative adopted by some is what might be called *assimilationist* consciousness.[15]

The essence of assimilationist consciousness is the attempt to close the gap opened by the destruction of traditional consciousness by identifying oneself wholly and completely with the dominant culture. It is primarily, although not necessarily, an attempt to find an individual solution to the problem by dissociating oneself from the culturally subordinate group to which one originally belonged. Examples would be (1) what one author calls "loophole women," that is, those who feel they have "made it" as individuals, in gaining status and acceptance in the male world;[16] (2) colonized *évolués* who immerse themselves in the colonizer's culture; (3) homosexuals who try to "pass" in the straight world; and (4) blacks who believe that their individual talents and achievements will be sufficient to overcome race prejudice. Inevitably, attempts at individual assimilation are accompanied not only by rejection of identification with one's own culturally oppressed group, but also by contempt for that group as a whole and for individuals within who do not assimilate successfully. There is, of course, an implicit self-denigration in this contempt; particularly where ascriptive groups based on race or sex or culture are concerned, but this may well not receive conscious recognition.

Nor is the assimilationist stance sufficient to overcome internal incoherence within the individual. It may well please an assimilationist-minded woman to be told that she thinks "like a man," for example, but such compliments provide only temporary reassurance that one has "made it" into the dominant group and any trace of what may be interpreted by others as "typically female" behavior may be sufficient to destroy the always precarious acceptance. Moreover—and more important—it is doubtful whether one's ascriptive status as female or black or colonized will be so entirely forgotten as to permit full acceptance in the first place.

Partly for this reason, perhaps, some individuals develop a second version of assimilationist consciousness which focuses on assimilating the culturally dominated group itself to the dominant culture rather than on individuals' disengagement from their initial group. This type of assimilationist consciousness can be seen, for example, among those feminists who hold that achievement of desirable forms of male-female relations requires elimination of all differences that are group differences. It assumes that the pattern of behavior of the culturally dominant group ought to characterize everyone and therefore the culturally dominated group need only take on that already existing way of life. It may well be the case that some of these behavior patterns would be useful and desirable, but the important point here is that they are advocated more because they are part of the culturally dominant life-style than on their own merits.[17]

In group-oriented, as in individually focused assimilationism, one's own culture is rejected in toto in favor of that of the culturally dominant group. There is no attempt to harmonize the two; rather there is a dichotomy whereby whatever belongs to the dominant culture is modern or civilized or otherwise desirable, while whatever belongs to the dominated culture is backward or uncivilized or otherwise undesirable. It is thus easy to distinguish assimilationist consciousness from both traditional and traditionalist consciousness. It is also quite easy to distinguish it from what might be called *reformist* consciousness.

Reformist consciousness is characterized by the attempt to take over valuable aspects of the dominant culture and to ground them in one's own tradition or culture. This process involves a reinterpretation of that tradition to read back into its past the genesis of ideas which in fact have been absorbed from the dominant culture. In the Islamic case, for example, the choosing of the caliph by community leaders is reinterpreted to demonstrate the democratic nature of Islam; Koranic verses about the position of women are given a new reading to demonstrate Islam's superiority in the realm of male-female relations; the religious tax is advocated as a socialist system offering the golden mean between communism and capitalism, etc., and it is conveniently (or genuinely) forgotten that nobody ever saw them that way before.

The situation that reformists are in is rather more difficult than that faced by traditional individuals. Given the commitment of traditional individuals to the transcendent ideal of their own culture, they can easily afford to reinterpret that tradition openly in the light of changing circumstances (although it is also the case that traditions tend to ossify to some degree). The reformists, however, must show that what they advocate has long been part of their own culture and is firmly rooted there, when in fact that is usually not the case. It is not hard to see that in such a dilemma one's desire to succeed would promote easy distortion of the tradition, distortion which is probably both conscious and unconscious.

There are sufficient similarities between traditionalist and reformist consciousness to make the application of the concepts difficult in certain cases. What the two have in common is that individuals having both kinds of consciousness are led by their interaction with the dominant culture to distort their own tradition, to judge it by standards external to itself, and to attempt to demonstrate its superiority to the dominant culture. In both cases, moreover, a similar kind of defensiveness is likely to be found, as is a similar unwillingness to abandon tradition in the face of new problems. The differences between the two are nonetheless profound. Thus in the case of al-Khidr Husayn's successor as editor of the Azhar journal, it appears that the traditionalist is out to defend and affirm his own tradition or culture at any price, using any arguments that come to hand, however subversive to that tradition they may in fact turn out to be. What he is not interested in doing is changing that tradition or reforming it. Reformists, by contrast, are not so much concerned to defend the tradition as they are to change and reform it by a process of incorporation. In the interaction between their own tradition and the dominant culture traditionalists stand squarely in the camp of their own tradition, firing broadsides in the direction of the other, whereas reformists may want to place themselves within their own tradition but in fact keep a foot in both camps. This being the case, the reformists' tone is often rather less strident than that of the traditionalists. Their attitude toward aspects of the dominant culture is "yes, that is good, but we already have it ourselves when our tradition is properly interpreted," whereas that of the traditionalists is "no, that is not good, and what we already have ourselves is far better."

Another alternative which has similarities to both traditionalist and reformist consciousness (and especially to the latter) is what might be called *revolutionary* consciousness. Those with revolutionary consciousness polarize against the colonizer and have a much more cynical or skeptical view of the dominant culture than reformists have. At the same time they carry the remythologizing of traditional culture even further than reformists and develop a much more explicit ideology about the need for self-liberation from cultural oppression. The essence of revolutionary consciousness, then, might be seen as a dual process of demystification of the dominant other and a simultaneous remythologizing of one's own tradition.

In particular, that tradition is remythologized in terms of finding within it episodes and periods of heroic resistance to the dominant culture, episodes which are then interpreted in terms of their own ideology of struggle against the oppressor. Among colonized peoples, revolutionary consciousness often takes the form of making the idea of the nation and of specifically nationalist (rather than merely xenophobic or traditional) resistance to the colonizer retroactive to pre-colonial times, and the entire colonial period is searched for evidence of revolutionary activity. A similar process can be seen in the emphasis among American blacks on slave revolts and uprisings, and among feminists on reinterpretations of female behavior patterns such as indirectness or (seeming) submissiveness as strategies of power, rather than signs of subordination.

The revolutionary attitude holds that while the dominant culture purports to be superior, it is in fact full of hypocrisy, lies, and exploitation. Thus there is nothing to be taken over because there is nothing worth taking. Whatever is needed can be found in the revolutionary's own culture, once that culture is rediscovered. Rediscovery is vitally necessary, however, since the dominant culture has tended to suppress and distort its most positive aspects and to hide them from view.

What the revolutionary seeks in the past, then, is quite different from what either the traditionalist or the reformist looks for. This process of demystification of the other and retroactive mythologizing about the self is central to the creation of a new community, a new consciousness, and a new society. It is thus a crucial stage in the process of self-liberation and a fascinating one to explore. Its predominant tone tends to be a mixture of rage and exaltation, of fury at the way one's consciousness has been distorted by internalized self-images of inferiority and backwardness, and joy, relief, and enthusiasm as self and other are reinterpreted in ways that give the self a new sense of potential and worth.

But if this is the case, why then do we designate six rather than only five types of consciousness in the process of self-liberation? Why is revolutionary consciousness not sufficient to complete the process? There are several answers to be given. First of all, the revolutionary is still caught in a polarized dialectic with the still-dominant other. This can be seen, *inter alia,* from the strength of the need to debunk and demystify. Revolutionary consciousness is thus still engaged in a process of dethroning; it is not yet free to go its own way. Moreover, there is still a large element of defensiveness and touchiness present, often accompanied by a "chip on the shoulder" attitude to the world. In addition, a rigidly held ideology operates to explain the world in terms of rather simplistic and emotionally charged categories. One example among many is the attitude developed by some American feminists in the 1970s, which in slogans like "Women are messed over, not messed up," expresses the view that there is nothing wrong with any woman except that she is being oppressed. All women are innocent and all men guilty. This kind of ideology may well be an emotional necessity at a particular stage in the process of self-liberation, but it hardly reflects completion of that process. What Simone de Beauvoir says about women in *The Second Sex* applies equally well to revolutionaries in other oppressed groups:

> By aspiring to clear-sightedness women writers are doing the cause of women a great service; but—usually without realizing it—they are still too concerned with serving this cause to assume the disinterested attitude toward the universe that opens the widest horizons. When they have removed the veils of illusion and deception, they think they have done enough; but this negative audacity leaves us still faced by an enigma, for the truth itself is ambiguity, abyss, mystery: once stated, it

must be thoughtfully reconsidered, re-created. It is all very well not to be duped, but at that point all else begins.[18]

What begins at that point is what I would call transforming consciousness, a kind of consciousness which would feel genuinely free to forge new combinations of personality traits, life-styles, and ways of being without the need either to imitate the model of the European or white or male other, nor to refrain from seeming to do so; without the need either deliberately to perpetuate previous forms of one's blackness or femaleness or Arabness nor to reject anything having a resemblance to those forms; and without the need for approval nor fear of being judged by the male or white or European other. The quotation from de Beauvoir expresses beautifully the gap that exists between this kind of consciousness and the best that any culturally oppressed group *qua* group has been able to achieve so far.                    .

What makes it seem like a non-utopian possibility for groups in the future, however, is that one can find examples of individual blacks or women or homosexuals or formerly colonized people who seem to have achieved it. But even if that were not the case, it would still be necessary to discuss transforming consciousness in considering the process of self-liberation from cultural domination since genuine liberation is possible only on that basis. None of the other kinds of consciousness heals the wound caused by the destruction of traditional consciousness. Only transforming consciousness allows the individual to have that "disinterested attitude toward the universe that opens the widest horizons" and does not place ideological obstacles in the way of perception. Only transforming consciousness allows the individual to affirm her or his ascriptive group identity without shame or defensiveness while at the same time leaving her or him free to develop new ways of being that are relevant to contemporary problems.

Each of the six types of consciousness presented above is qualitatively different from the others in relationship to the problem of cultural liberation. The first, traditional consciousness, is in a sense prior to the whole process; it is a stage in which liberation from cultural domination has not yet become problematic for the dominated group, either because the relationship of cultural domination has not yet been established or because it is so accepted "as the way things are" that it is perceived as subject to change. The sixth type, that of transforming consciousness, represents successful liberation. The other four types—traditionalist, reformist, assimilationist, and revolutionary— are all partial and inadequate attempts to come to grips with the problem of perceived and internalized cultural domination. Their common characteristic is a kind of strident defensiveness and anxious touchiness foreign to the self-assurance and sense of self of both traditional and transforming individuals. To say that the middle four stages are partial, inadequate, and emotively defensive, however, is not to suggest that all of them can be dispensed with along the way or that it is possible to step straight from traditional to transforming consciousness. I know of no case in which that has occurred; moreover, it is highly improbable that it could. It is as though both individuals and cultures are obliged to pass through a period of crisis, anguish, and psychic incoherence, once traditional consciousness has been destroyed, before coming once again to a sense of wholeness within and without. As one Muslim theologian wrote concerning the shattering of the glass of traditional faith: "That is a breaking that cannot be mended, and a separating that cannot be united by any sewing or putting together, except it be melted in the fire and given another new form."[19]

Yet while there is probably no way of skipping directly from traditional to transforming consciousness, it does not follow that every individual passes through all six stages in relation to every aspect of cultural oppression. First of all, the starting point of an individual who grows up in a group already subject to cultural domination by another group may well not be traditional; that is, one may grow up without ever having experienced the sense of security and unquestioning acceptance of the ways of one's own group that is the hallmark of traditional consciousness. Moreover, to date not many individuals or groups have achieved transforming consciousness; most of us remain stuck in one not very productive dialectic or another between self and other. Some remain traditional while others become traditionalists and still others opt for an assimilationist stance. Thus, at various times the group in question will display a range of responses, conceivably extending from traditional individuals at one end of the spectrum to those with transforming consciousness at the other.

It does seem to be the case, however, that the culturally dominated group *qua* group will indeed pass through all six types and will tend to do so successively in the order in which they have been set forth above. What is meant by this is not that each and every individual in the group will do so, but rather that the politically crucial segments of the group will be successively traditional, traditionalist, reformist, and so forth. This is a statement of probability rather than logical necessity; nonetheless, as evidenced in the case of French colonialism in Algeria, there is a certain inherent dialectic such that one stage in the sequence will tend to generate the next. However, by the time we come to the contemporary period, the full range of orientations is already present.

## II

In contrast to other areas of life, traditional patterns of male-female relations in Algeria were not particularly disrupted by French colonialism, and continued to function without much change. The family became a bastion and a refuge. It was also the one area in which the colonized male could freely dominate others without being himself dominated in turn by the colonizer. During the colonial period, the family continued to be the major institution of socialization into Muslim culture, expecially since much of this socialization was done by women who themselves led very restricted lives that did not bring them into contact with the dominant culture.

Nonetheless, traditional consciousness in this realm was undermined by the interaction with the dominant other for two major reasons: first, it was clear that the traditional Muslim patterns or male-female relations (including polygamy, very early marriage, easy divorce for the man, and wearing of the veil) elicited contempt and derision from the colonizer, making it increasingly necessary to justify those patterns to the self; and, second, it was those patterns, especially polygamy, which were cited by the French as the major reason why Algerians could not be granted French citizenship and political participation. There is also a third reason whose weight is more difficult to assess: namely, the effects of Algerian exposure to French patterns of male-female relations. There is no doubt that Algerians were shocked by and strongly disapproved of some of the freedoms available to French women; however, it seems clear that at least in some circles there was an attraction as well.

Whatever the relative weight of the various factors, they operated jointly to undermine the major aspect of traditional consciousness:[20] namely, its unquestioning acceptance of traditional patterns as the only possible way to do things. Traditional consciousness was probably replaced by traditionalist consciousness for most of the population in the first instance, but other patterns emerged as well. Among males, assimilationist consciousness was least evident; indeed, it is not at all clear that unmixed assimilationist consciouness developed at all even among those *évolués* who so eagerly embraced other aspects of French civilization. There was some intermarriage between *évolués* and European women, but the education and social level of the women was often below that of their husbands, a fact which would tend to make easier the perpetuation of male dominance within the household. Reformist consciousness was rather more prevalent, although perhaps not as much in this as in other realms of life. It was typically a position advocated by men, leading Germaine Tillion to remark that in Muslim countries feminism is a male affair.[21] While reformist consciousness is certainly not feminist in any very far-reaching sense and her remark is thus misleading, she is nonetheless right in saying that in many Muslim countries the theoretical arguments in favor of reforming Muslim practice in the realm of male-female relations were advanced by men: Emir Khalid in Algeria,[22] Qasim Amin in Egypt, and Tahar al-Haddad in Tunisia, for example. This is not surprising, since reformist consciousness is by its very nature most likely to be found among those who have been thoroughly educated in Islamic law and culture and at the same time exposed to Western influence. Such education was normally open only to men. Second, reformist consciousness, by wanting to purify the tradition, takes that tradition very seriously as something of value to be reinterpreted for modern life. It is thus concerned with male-female relations, not directly and in themselves, but rather as they reflect the Koranic prescriptions (rightly interpreted and purified) for relationships between the sexes. Women, by contrast, have tended to be more directly concerned with male-female relations in and of themselves in terms of the possibilities of freedom and self-expression they permit to women.

Algerian male revolutionary consciousness emphasized not the content of the tradition, but rather its function as a symbol of identity and pride vis-à-vis the dominant culture. What this meant with regard to male-female relations was that the revolutionaries lauded women and the family for having preserved and passed on the Algerian cultural heritage, accused the French of having tried to corrupt and undermine that heritage, and stressed the need to build a modern society "on Islamic bases" or "along Arabo-Islamic lines" as part of the revolutionary desire to break the deeply ingrained equation of European with modern, and Algerian or Muslim with backward. This pull in two opposed directions—toward reassertion of the remythologized tradition on the one hand and toward the creation of a modern, developed society on the other—is at the heart of the revolutionary's dilemma, a dilemma that has proved to be particularly painful in the realm of male-female relations.

The differences among Algerian males in kinds of consciousness can be illustrated in brief compass by discussing the changing meaning of a single symbol, namely, the veil. For the traditional Muslim the veil symbolizes feminine modesty, and at the same time, woman as a sexual threat and temptation, weak and amoral, and impure and dangerous to man. It functions as part of the internal nexus of symbols, customs, and patterns of behavior that characterize the traditional Islamic system. For the traditionalist these meanings remain, but added to them is the defensive assertion of the traditional way of life against colonialist inroads. Thus the veil comes to function as part of the dialectic between self and other. For those of assimilationist consciousness it is equally part of that dialectic, but is seen as a symbol of backwardness and degradation of women and as something to be eliminated in favor of European styles of dress. For the reformist the emphasis is once again on the meaning and function of the veil within the Muslim community, and the tendency is to retain it while fundamentally reinterpreting its meaning. Instead of stressing women's untrustworthiness and dangerous sexuality (and therewith the veil's function as a protection for men), the reformist stresses respect for women and the freedom it gives them from unwelcome advances (and therewith its function as a protection for women). Since this reinterpretation takes place in the context of reformist discussions of Islam's provision for appropriate equality between the sexes, it seems clear that it reflects an attempt to incorporate into Islam a modified version of Western ideology on male-female relations. For the revolutionary, however, the traditional meaning of the veil tends to be forgotten or submerged, and only its function as a symbol of cultural separateness and integrity is stressed. Thus, the veil as a symbol becomes politicized as part of the dialectic of cultural domination.

But so far we have spoken primarily of Algerian males. What of the women? How did they respond to the undermining of traditional consciousness? Here two things are crucial for understanding the different responses of women. First, it must be recognized that women experience more repression, restriction, and denial of opportunity, and less freedom, dominance, and status under the traditional Muslim system of male-female relations than do men; they have less reason for commitment to the tradition and more reason to want to change it. Second, whereas male-female relations are only one aspect of the Algerian man's life, they both shape the totality of the woman's life and constitute a far larger proportion of it. Thus, male-female relations are in a sense more directly and immediately relevant to women, and whatever dissatisfactions they entail are likely to be more deeply experienced by women.

The differences to be found between male and female responses are not surprising when viewed from this perspective. With regard to male-female relations, the overall consciousness of Algerian males is traditionalist, and very few show any signs of being willing to give up the privileged position associated with traditional male dominance. Where consciousness is not traditionalist, it tends to be reformist. There is a sense of nostalgia and of affection for the traditional patterns. Nonetheless, on some issues (education of girls, for example), nontraditionalist policies may be adopted even by traditionalist individuals or groups, including the government. First, considerations relevant to concerns other than male-female relations may take primacy (the desire for *cadres* for economic development, for example). Second, the incompatibility between the specific action (educating a daughter, marrying an educated woman) and the perpetuation of traditionalist patterns of male-female relations may not be clearly recognized. There is some desire to have one's cake and eat it too: to take advantage of benefits offered by changing traditional patterns, but to resist giving up the advantages to males inherent in those patterns.

By contrast, the primary concern of a growing number of Algerian females is probably to escape from particular aspects of the traditional patterns that restrict their lives and curb their freedom. They want to be allowed to continue their education instead of being withdrawn from school when they reach puberty; they want to have a say in choosing their husbands rather than being married off by their parents; they want to have some freedom to come and go; and some, in addition, want the opportunity to work at a career or job that will provide a measure of independence and contact with the modern world.[23] What they aspire to corresponds more closely to patterns of male-female relations in European than in traditional Muslim culture. But their outlook is not primarily oriented to the dialectic between Muslim and European culture or to adopting European models. Rather it is oriented to the internal dialectic between themselves and Algerian males.

What complicates the situation, however, is that the dialectic between Algeria and Europe continues to operate and creates an ambivalence or uncertainty with respect to action for change. The woman committed to building a modern society on Arabo-Islamic bases as part of the revolutionary dialectic with the European other may feel vulnerable to charges that she is betraying the Algerian heritage or aping Frenchwomen if she tries to change the patterns of male-female relations that operate in her life. Whereas most Algerian males would like to maintain traditional patterns of male-female relations but are forced to move reluctantly and in part unconsciously toward modifying those patterns, a growing number of Algerian women are eager to change the traditional patterns but are somewhat inhibited in doing so by the internal psychic ambivalence created by the desire to affirm the Algerian heritage and culture.

The general schema presented here can be applied to a series of specific problems in the realm of male-female relations. In the area of political rights, at the time of independence Algerian women were granted full legal and formal equality with men in voting, party membership, and candidacy for office. They thus attained on the formal plane rights which it took European and American women decades of bitter struggle to attain. In actual practice, however, a variety of obstacles continue to exist. Given the novelty of such political participation for women, a good deal of active propaganda and encouragement by the government and party would have been necessary to foster female involvement. While some efforts have been made in this direction, they have been rather limited in scope.[24] At the same time some males, particularly those in the lower echelons of the party, have refused to let women join local party cells, telling them to go instead to the women's organization, the *Union Nationale des Femmes Algériennes* (referred to hereafter as UNFA).[25] Another indication of women's difficulty in achieving actual equality in political participation, is their gross underrepresentation in the government, the parliament, and the higher party *cadres,* as well as the generally subservient and acquiescent role played by UNFA vis-à-vis the government. Nonetheless, the formal commitment to equality is of great symbolic importance and should not be underrated. It appears to stem from two major sources, neither of which is directly oriented to male-female relations: first, the crucial role played by women during the struggle for independence and, second (and probably more important) the fact that the granting of equal political rights to citizens of both sexes had by 1962 become part of the fundamental concept of a modern polity.

In terms of economic rights and opportunities women have been affected by a combination of traditionalist views about women's place being in the home and, perhaps more important, by the staggering rate of unemployment in post-independence Algeria. The position of most men, including that of President Haouri Boumedienne in his speech on International Women's Day in 1966, has been that men should receive first priority in jobs. However, many of the women active in UNFA and the party have sharply disagreed, as they demonstrated by walking out during Boumedienne's speech.[26] Since the war of independence left many women widowed and needing to support themselves and their children, the suggestion that priority in jobs be given to men clearly reflects male prejudice rather than a rational priority derived from objective conditions.[27] Traditionalist prejudice is even more strongly rooted outside governmental circles. Men typically do not want their wives to work and try to restrict their daughters to jobs that do not bring them into contact with men.[28]

In the area of education the government has taken the most progressive position, devoting a great deal of the national budget to education and bringing large numbers of girls into the schools.[29] Government and party leaders have also sharply attacked those who have objected to girls' participation in gymnastics and other athletic activities.[30] The main ground for this attitude to education appears to be that the regime recognizes the necessity and desirability of educating the next generation in order to create a modern society. On the other hand, at the level of primary school (where the major push has been undertaken) girls have not yet reached the age where difficult issues arise concerning puberty, marriage, and the like.

Education is thus a prime case in which the government acts indirectly to change male-female relations because of its dedication to social change in other respects. In general, the areas of political rights, economic opportunities, and access to education are perceived as only indirectly affecting male-female relations. Here the goals of modernity and development dictate that women be accorded greater (if not yet equal) rights. These rights affect women's possibilities for autonomy and self-development profoundly, but at a certain remove.

The case is quite different, however, when we come to matters that touch more directly on the intimate substance of interpersonal relations between the sexes, both inside and outside the context of the family. These matters may be called "women's issues," since they are particularly important to women, though they are relevant to the society as a whole; they include the issues of dress, marriage and divorce law, and birth control.

The matter of dress has been of great symbolic importance in post-independence Algeria. Many letters to newspapers have argued for or against clothing associated with European fashions, in particular the miniskirt.[31] Here, in contrast to the Tunisian government, which has encouraged women to unveil and to adopt modern dress, the Algerian government, particularly since the overthrow of Ben Bella in 1965, has taken a conservative position. Thus in his speech to the first National Congress of UNFA, President Boumedienne referred to the "false problem of the suppression of the veil" only in order to urge his listeners to transcend this merely formal problem. Algerian women, he assured them, already had all of their rights, and the veil was irrelevant.[32] His regime failed to show an equal neutrality on the other side, however, and in 1967 the police rounded up girls whose skirts were considered too short and painted their legs with Mercurochrome from the knee to the skirt hem.[33] What is at stake here clearly goes very deep, as controversies in our own society over hair length and the like indicate. Dress is a very important expression of attitude and life-style, and it is thus not surprising that it has received attention from would-be revolutionary leadership not only in Algeria but in other countries, such as Turkey and China. In the case of the Algerian leadership, the attitudes betrayed by their policies on dress suggest a combination of "revolutionary puritanism," conservative morality, and an underlying suspicion of female emancipation.

In the area of birth control and family planning, the pattern is somewhat different. Very little has been done to develop family planning services in Algeria; there was not even any discussion of the subject during the first few years after independence. Since 1965 there have been cautious discussions and a few model clinics have been set up, but no large-scale program has been undertaken. This inaction occurred in face of a rate of population increase that is one of the highest in the world, in a country in which unemployment and lack of educational facilities are such that even the existing population is forced into massive emigration to France.[34]

However, the reason for inaction is not to be found in Muslim traditionalism, but in the anti-Malthusian orientation currently typical of many Marxists. According to this view, the problem is not to limit population, but rather to develop the productive resources of the country. The effect of this view on official Algerian attitudes toward family planning can be seen reflected in a speech by Dr. Nefissa Laliam, president of UNFA and herself a physician.[35] The first part of her speech offers a compelling presentation of all the reasons why family planning would seem to be highly necessary and desirable in the Algerian context. Nevertheless, Laliam concludes that no decision on the necessity of family planning can be made until investigations into the potential productive resources of the country have been completed. Thus in this area it is modern ideology rather than traditionalist prejudice which is the major obstacle to providing women with control over their own reproductivity—a *sine qua non* of genuine liberation.

This example demonstrates the necessity of investigating the particular factors operating in each case rather than assuming that they can be deduced from a general framework of analysis. On the other hand, in the case of marriage and divorce law, it is again traditionalism which is the obstacle to women's emancipation. The project for a new law that was circulated in 1967 has been extensively analyzed by Fadéla M'Rabet, and there is no need to repeat that analysis here.[36] Suffice it to say that the project, while making certain modifications in traditional Islamic marriage and divorce law, remains squarely within the traditional Islamic code in its overall orientation and major provisions. Polygamy is not prohibited but merely made more difficult; a woman must still have a matrimonial tutor who consents to her marriage for her; divorce is still much easier for the man than for the woman, though its traditional arbitrariness is sharply curbed; and the man is explicitly recognized as the head of the family. In that capacity his wife is legally bound to show him both deference and obedience. While the obstacles to women's emancipation in the political, economic, and educational realms are private and social rather than public and legal, in the realm of marriage and divorce the law itself perpetuates a situation of grave inequality and disadvantage for the woman.

## Conclusion

I have attempted to clarify the nature of what is at stake in particular problem areas by showing their connections to the more general ideological context in which they take place. In the areas of formal political rights, employment opportunity, and equal primary education, traditionalist attitudes toward male-female relations in Algeria have been bypassed in public policy under the pressure of commitment to development goals. In the more private or personal realms of "women's issues," traditionalist consciousness has combined with Marxist ideology to stifle liberating changes in male-female relations.

The model of six types of consciousness presented above is certainly in need of further refinement and development; it may even turn out to be unworkable as a general model when tested against a wider universe of cases.

Nevertheless, the framework will have served a useful purpose if it stimulates further work towards systematic analysis of the politics of cultural liberation.

## NOTES

1. For example, Naomi Weisstein, "Woman As Nigger," *Psychology Today,* October 1969.

2. See my article, "Algeria: A Case Study of the Requirements of Revolutionary Transformation," *Proceedings of the 1967 Princeton University Conference on North Africa* (forthcoming), and "The Liberation of Women in Tunisia, Algeria, and Egypt," a paper presented at the 1971 annual meeting of the Middle East Studies Association. A preliminary sketch of the framework presented in the present essay was set forth in my paper, "The Politics of Cultural Liberation: A Comparative Study of Algerian Nationalism and American Feminism," presented at the HEW-sponsored institute, "Women: Crisis in Higher Education," June 1971 in Pittsburgh, Pa.

3. The lengths to which this sense of inferiority can go were brought to my attention in a conversation with Badi Foster, a Ph.D. candidate at Princeton, whose work on Morocco will add much to our knowledge of the problem of cultural identity. In Morocco, he pointed out, whatever is European in dress, in life-style, and the like is considered "civilized," whereas whatever is Moroccan is thought of as "savage" or "uncivilized."

4. Sally Kempton, "Cutting Loose," *Esquire,* July 1970, 57.

5. As I have discovered since initially developing the framework presented in this article, others have used terms similar to those I thought I was coining. For example, David Gordon speaks in *The Passing of French Algeria* (London: Oxford University Press, 1966), 21, of assimilationists and traditionalists. What others have not done, to my knowledge, however, is to suggest a comparative, process-oriented study of the development of political consciousness which would include women, blacks, and homosexuals, as well as colonized peoples.

6. It might be well at this point to discuss briefly the uses and limitations of the conceptual approach adopted here. It may be objected that this approach neglects the empirical complexity and real differences among the various groups to which I suggest it applies. The "mix" of psychic and economic oppression is rather different from case to case. Moreover, we do not yet have for any of these groups the kind of detailed monographic work which some scholars hold must precede all attempts to generalize and compare at a high level of abstraction. Indeed, black-white relations and male-female relations have become subjects for scholarly study in the United States only very recently.

In contrast to those who say that theorizing must await the collection of masses of detailed, noncomparative studies, I believe that it is precisely at the present initial stage that conceptual frameworks are of particular importance. They provide a preliminary mapping of the area to be explored. They do not provide exhaustive analyses of every inch of terrain, but they do give a sense of the whole, while at the same time providing a context within which more limited and detailed studies can be placed. Moreover, there is some doubt as to whether general theory ever emerges from masses of monographs in the way that those who urge the postponement of generalizing apparently assume. It seems at least as likely that trees will obscure the forest as that tree-by-tree perusal will eventually constellate it. Research in Gestalt psychology lends support to the view that the perception of meaningful wholes is a primary rather than secondary perceptual process.

7. For further discussion of this point see Joseph Campbell, *The Masks of God: Occidental Mythology* (New York: Viking Press, 1964).

8. Wilfred C. Smith, *Islam and Modern History* (New York: Mentor, 1957), 127–37.

9. For additional examples see Elizabeth Fernea, *Guests of the Sheik: An Ethnography of an Iraqi Village* (New York: Doubleday Anchor Books, 1969).

10. Clifford Geertz, *Islam Observed: Religious Development In Morocco And Indonesia* (New Haven: Yale University Press, 1968), 17–19.

11. This terminology comes from Manfred Halpern, a colleague from whose work on modernization I have learned much of relevance to the present theme. Indeed, those who know Halpern's work will have no trouble seeing the types of consciousness proposed in this paper as relevant to Halpern's discussion of emanation, incoherence, and transformation in his forthcoming book, *The Dialectics of Transformation in Politics, Personality, and History.*

12. Rama Mehta, *The Western Educated Hindu Woman* (New York: Asia Publishing House, 1970), 16–32.

13. *Ibid.*, 137–61.

14. Smith, *Islam and Modern History*, 151.

15. Perhaps this is as good a place as any to mention briefly the enormous problems raised by our language for discussions of this kind. People do not "adopt" a particular kind of consciousness—least of all by surveying the range of choices and picking the one they want. It would be more accurate to speak of "finding oneself with" rather than "adopting" a kind of consciousness. "Consciousness" is itself a term that is difficult to use sensibly and consistently, and there is the danger that it will come to be used (or at least sound as though it is being used) as a pseudo-explanatory label rather than as a concept that illuminates the relationship between the individual and his world.

16. See Carolyn Bird, *Born Female: The High Cost of Keeping Women Down* (New York: McKay, 1970).

17. This is particularly true in matters of dress and personal appearance, and can be seen, for example, in the adoption by American blacks of this persuasion of white standards of beauty (straightening hair, bleaching skin, etc.), as well as in the adoption among formerly colonized peoples of the miniskirt. The important point, of course, is not *what* is done, but in what spirit and for what motives it is done.

18. Simone de Beauvoir, *The Second Sex* (New York: Knopf, 1968), 709–10.

19. Al Ghazzali, *Al Munqidh min al-dalal* (Preservation from Error), cited by Manfred Halpern in *The Politics of Social Change in the Middle East and North Africa* (Princeton, N.J.: Princeton University Press, 1963), 31.

20. I know of no material which would shed light on at what stage or under what circumstances traditional consciousness about male-female relations began to give way. It is certainly clear in the post-independence period, however, that traditional consciousness has been thoroughly undermined.

21. Germaine Tillion, *Le Harem et les cousins* (Paris: Editions du Seuil, 1966), 211n. She makes this remark in the context of discussing the support for traditional patterns given by older Algerian women who have finally achieved a position of some power, status, and dominance within the traditional system.

22. J. P. Charnay, *La Vie musulmane en Algérie d'après ta jurisprudence de la première moitié du XX$^e$ siècle* (Paris: Presses Universitaires de France, 1965), 64n.

23. Abundant evidence for this assertion is provided by Fadéla M'Rabet in her accounts of girls' desire for education, their attempts to avoid arranged marriages, and their longing for greater freedom and contact with the world. *Les Algériennes* (Paris: Librairie François Maspero, 1967), 81–112.

24. See the article by Nefissa Bensaadi, "La femme doit remplir son devoir de citoyenne," *El Moudjahid* (May 24, 1969).

25. For illuminating examples of this obstructionism see M'Rabet, *Les Algériennes,* 235–37.

26. David Gordon, *Women of Algeria: An Essay on Change* (Cambridge, Mass.: Harvard University Press, 1968), 77.

27. For a discussion of women in the labor force see M'Rabet, *Le Algériennes,* 144–64.

28. See Flora Lewis, "No Revolution for the Woman of Algiers," *New York Times Magazine,* October 29, 1967.

29. For statistics see M'Rabet, *Les Algériennes,* 168–93.

30. Gordon, *The Passing of French Algeria,* 76–77.

31. For examples see M'Rabet, *Les Algériennes,* 27–29.

32. UNFA, *Bulletin Intérieur,* 4, report on the first UNFA National Congress, November 19–23, 1966.

33. Lewis, "No Revolution for the Woman of Algiers," 28.

34. For figures see M'Rabet, *Les Algériennes,* 208–19.

35. Nefissa Laliam, "Le Planning familial," a speech given to UNFA in Algiers on April 14, 1968, and printed by UNFA.

36. See M'Rabet, *Les Algériennes,* 241–80.

# PART III

# On Class, Sex, and Social Change

Like the papers in Part II, those in this section are surveys and case studies which deal with the specific historical experience of women in particular times and places, while raising at the same time questions of theoretical relevance. In this section, the focus of attention is mainly on class differences and economic conditions.

In the opening essay, Sarah B. Pomeroy offers a cautious assessment of the classical evidence concerning the existence of matriarchy in the late Bronze Age. Pomeroy notes that historians have unjustifiably minimized or ignored the importance of Bronze Age queens, but that the high position of royal women in aristocratic societies does not necessarily imply a high status for women in general. On the whole, Pomeroy concludes that the evidence available from classical scholarship is insufficient to determine the historical existence of matriarchy in the Bronze Age.

Kathleen Casey next offers a wide-ranging analytical survey of the historical experience of medieval women. Writing in a concise style, Casey touches on many provocative questions concerning women's work and women's consciousness, and the relationship of each to stability or change in women's roles and status. After preliminary sections emphasizing the great variations of individual circumstances, regional differences, and personality types in the elusive category of "medieval women," Casey considers more closely the roles and status of women by class: working and peasant women, gildswomen, women of the feudal classes, and the urban middle-class "housewife." Finally, she considers a number of marginal or transitional categories including the nun, the witch, the learned woman, and certain individual examples of deviant or conformist roles. Casey argues that the chances for breaking out of traditional molds were better for medieval women "than in later periods usually associated with the rise of feminism" but that the opportunity was lost. Whether this was more through economic forces or more through a chosen affirmation of traditional values is less clear, but Casey suggests that "those who collectively went down to defeat were, at least in part, collectively responsible."

In the next study, Asunción Lavrin considers the economic and social role of women in convents in colonial Mexico. While the nunneries were indeed centers of spirituality, offering secluded refuge for devout women—even to the exclusion of such service functions as education and hospital work—their social and economic functions went far beyond the religious. Lavrin finds that the nunneries were intimately tied to the racial and economic ruling minorities, both by the exclusiveness of their membership and the use of their extensive endowments: "they were not only expressions of the social order but they reinforced it from an economic point of view." Thus the value system which dictated that women should hold a special responsibility for the preservation of religious values, and that unmarried women of the upper classes should live in a protected spiritual environment, was at the same time a system which guaranteed to the wealthy or elite classes a ready source of fluid capital for loans and investments.

In "Sex and Class in Colonial and Nineteenth-Century America," Ann D. Gordon and Mari Jo Buhle survey the changing interactions of class and consciousness over a period of more than three centuries, during which women's self-awareness "was reflected through the prisms of a colonial community, a transitional Victorian industrializing society, and a commodity-rich but labor-alienated modern capitalist order." Through these changes in economic organization, they argue, self-conscious feminism "has been provoked, transformed or suppressed, and provoked again."

Whereas Casey, in her essay on medieval women, is inclined to emphasize the responsibility of women in all classes for opting "to affirm rather than deny traditional values," Renate Bridenthal and Claudia Koonz in their essay on Weimar women are concerned with exposing the structural realities which made that same option the choice of large numbers of women in Weimar Germany. Contrary to widespread belief, the attraction of many German women to Hitler's call for return to hearth and home was not a rejection of progress in women's emancipation under the Weimar regime. For despite the rhetoric of emancipation, women's political and economic condition actually declined in important respects during the Weimar Republic. While the early promises of political equality rapidly showed themselves fraudulent, the process of industrial modernization proved retrogressive: "women as a group increasingly were pressed into unskilled work with lessened responsibility or out of the economy altogether." Under such conditions, it is hardly surprising that German women turned to the conservative and Nazi parties in hopes of regaining territory which seemed lost or threatened. From this viewpoint, women's conservatism must be seen, not as mere devotion to tradition, but as a response to structural conditions affecting their real interests.

Whether these structural conditions are to be attributed more to an overarching patriarchal ideology, or whether they are specific to particular economic and class circumstances (such as those of modernizing societies) is left an open question by Bridenthal and Koonz, as it is also by Alice Kessler-Harris in "Women, Work and the Social Order." Kessler-Harris tends to emphasize the varying needs of the economy as determinative of changes in family structure and women's roles. On the other hand, these changes create tensions in the social order which have their own momentum. Thus the ideology of the family is an important component of maintaining the social order, while the challenge which women's liberation poses to the ideology of the family "may have the potential for long-term change."

# A Classical Scholar's Perspective on Matriarchy

*Sarah B. Pomeroy*

Did matriarchal societies ever exist? No question in the history of ancient women has generated more controversy. No topic has been approached by both traditional scholars and feminists with less objectivity. How gratifying it would be for a feminist scholar to discover that in pre-history, a period far longer than recorded history, women were not the second sex at all. Then we could rebut all the scholars since Aristotle who have complacently been stating that women are by nature inferior.

I am both a classical scholar and a feminist. I earned my doctorate in classics at a conservative university where I was instructed by an all-male faculty. In more recent years events in my personal life have developed in me a consciousness of myself as a woman, and inspired me to reevaluate the lessons learned at my pedagogues' knees.

No definite answer to the question of whether matriarchal societies have had a historical existence in ancient times can be offered in this paper. The problems of definition and evaluation of evidence, including mythological and archaeological evidence outside the period of the Bronze Age, are too complex to be dealt with briefly. A full-scale analysis of the matriarchal theories of Bachofen and others would itself require another paper[1] (or volume), while adequate evaluation of the evidence calls for the cooperation of archaeologists and anthropologists.

There is, however, certain evidence classical scholarship can offer which is relevant to a discussion of matriarchy and the related topic of matriliny. In this paper I shall outline the sort of evidence available, and offer some notes first on its historical validity, and second on how it has been dealt with at the hands of traditional classical scholarship. I will focus on the late Bronze Age, also known as the Heroic period, or late Helladic III (approximately 1400–1200 B.C.). Reference will also be made to classical authors, especially those who describe the non-Greek world, as well as those who consider the history of earlier times.

This paper was first read at the Berkshire Conference of Women Historians meeting on Historical Perspectives on Women, March 3, 1973, at Douglass College, New Brunswick, N.J. The author is grateful to the American Council of Learned Societies for a grant which facilitated the writing of the essay.

The late Bronze Age is the period renowned for the exploits of the traditional heroines of classical mythology, including Helen, Clytemnestra, Electra, Hecuba, Andromache, Medea, Jocasta, Antigone, Atalanta, Hippodameia, Phaedra, and the Amazons Penthesileia and Hippolyte. Examination of classical legends influenced J. J. Bachofen over a century ago to formulate his theory of the priority of matriarchy and matrilineal descent. The descriptions of non-Greek societies, particularly in the writings of the Greek historian Herodotus, who lived in the fifth century B.C., were a second decisive influence on Bachofen. To simplify the present exposition, it may be said that some of the barbarian customs reported by Herodotus were to Bachofen a corroboration of the customs he discerned in the Greek legends of the late Bronze Age. Bachofen reasoned that while the Greeks of the classical period had progressed into a patriarchal and patrilineal society, the non-Greek world still preserved some of the older customs. Actually, Thucydides (I, 6) had first stated the principle that the primitive universality of a custom could be deduced by observing that a custom was still practiced by some of the less progressive Greek states and by most of the non-Greek world.

A brief résumé of the chronology of Greece is necessary here. As previously stated, the Bronze Age terminated approximately 1200 B.C. The precise date and catastrophic cause has been the subject of extensive debate in recent years, but there is universal agreement that Bronze Age civilizations terminated exceedingly abruptly. The Dark Age, which ensued, lasted for the next four hundred years. This period derives its name from the strikingly inferior quality of the material remains and the total illiteracy of the time, particularly in comparison with the technology and literacy of the preceding civilizations. In the eighth century B.C., tradition tells us, a poet named Homer composed the *Iliad* and *Odyssey,* relating some events which were purported to have transpired in the latter Bronze Age. Also in that century writing was reintroduced to the Greek world, although the works of Homer apparently were not written down until the sixth century B.C.

The evolutionary scheme enunciated by Thucydides, and developed by Bachofen and others, is not generally accepted nowadays by professional classical scholars and anthropologists. Nevertheless, although Bachofen's construct has been discredited, the evidence from which he started has not been invalidated. The tremendous wealth of ancient material indicating the high status of Bronze Age queens, the success of Amazon societies, and the freedom enjoyed by some barbarian women in antiquity cannot fail to impress a modern feminist.

Yet as a serious historian I must remind myself to suppress my burning desire to prove that women long ago enjoyed a position far superior to that of women nowadays, and instead merely identify the existing evidence, evaluate the evidence, and determine what deductions and conclusions, if any, may be drawn from the evidence.

How much can a historian learn about Bronze Age society from the earliest Greek literature, the Homeric epics? The *Iliad* and *Odyssey* stand at the climax of a long tradition of oral poetry going back to the heroic Mycenaean age. There were many such epics. For example, the *Thebaid,* although now lost, was the source of the legends used by tragic poets of the fifth century B.C. for their stories of Jocasta, Oedipus, and Antigone. Through the techniques of oral poetry, illiterate bards transmitted the legends of heroic society. How reliable a picture of the past could the bards have preserved over a period of more than four hundred years? Indeed, poets have never been concerned with journalistic reporting of facts. It is relevant here to notice the Aristotelian distinction between poetry and history: the poet describes the things that might happen, the historian the events that actually did happen (Aristotle, *Poetics*, IX). In addition, we must consider the material evidence for the discontinuity between the Mycenaeans of the late Bronze Age and the Greeks who came after them. With justification, the consensus of modern historians is that whatever the Greeks remembered about the Bronze Age did not correspond to the reality of the past, and that the Homeric poems present the traditions of the Dark Ages rather than of Mycenaean times.[2]

On the other hand, that the break between late Bronze Age civilizations and the oral poetry of the Dark Ages was not total is proven by the reality of the archaeological evidence excavated in such places as Mycenae and Troy. Although the ruins of Mycenae, for example, were obscured in the days of Homer, nevertheless, the epic poems accurately describe some of the material objects found in the excavations in modern times. Let us assume, for the moment, that the *Iliad* and *Odyssey* give a historically valid report of Bronze Age society. Or let us follow the ancient historians, who felt justified in using the legends of epic as history simply because there was no other record of earlier times. Is there sufficient evidence in the epics to support a theory that matriarchy existed at that time? First, it is necessary to point out that the Homeric epic has an aristocratic bias. An intermediate class of poor free women is never mentioned; instead the mortal women in the poems are either members of a ruling family, or slaves in royal households or in the army camp. Actually, the existence of stratified social classes and the holding of private property (including slaves), rather than being compatible with a notion of a golden age of matriarchy, are features which are some of the most conventional characteristics of patriarchy.

On the other hand, Hecuba, Andromache, Helen, and Arete as royalty exert a substantial influence. Yet only in the cases of Arete and the mother of Andromache can an argument be made that the queen actually wielded more power than the king in a given realm. But there is absolutely no evidence, even in realms where queens were powerful, that women were the dominant class throughout the society. Would a historian be tempted to label the British Isles a matriarchy in the sixteenth century because of the activities of Mary Stuart, Mary Tudor, and Elizabeth I? Nevertheless, the power of queens, Bronze Age or Renaissance, should not be minimized.

Yet, the conventional history books describe Bronze Age government exclusively in terms of male-dominated institutions: the monarchy, the council of elders, and the general assembly of warriors. The Homeric descriptions of these political organs can be trusted, historians reason, because these institutions continued to exist in classical times. By the same reasoning, the importance of Bronze Age queens is minimized because in later periods of Greek history women of all social classes played a subordinate role.

The tendency of most historians to minimize the political influence of Bronze Age queens, or to magnify their role into an all-encompassing theory of matriarchy, in my opinion, can be ascribed to the same cause. The political and legal status of women in patriarchal Athens was so low that a "scientific" historian like Thucydides could not imagine that the situation was ever any different. Thus Thucydides (I, 9) states that Agamemnon organized the expedition of Greeks against Troy because of his political and military dominance, rather than, as legend has it, because Helen's suitors had sworn to bring her back if she were ever carried off. Bachofen, in contrast, faced with the discrepancy between the position of women in classical times and their apparent prestige in the Bronze Age, exaggerated the contrast to produce his theory of matriarchy evolving into patriarchy.

The careful historian can irreproachably state that the status of some royal women in the Bronze Age as described in the Homeric epics was remarkably high. The feminist scholar will also point out the efforts of male historians and scholars to diminish the importance of these women. These efforts began in antiquity. Although there are many fantastical elements in the Homeric epics, Thucydides chose to single out and criticize the theory that Helen could have caused the Trojan War. The well-known farewell scene between Andromache and her husband Hector (*Iliad*, VI, 409-96) provides an example of the tendency to minimize Homeric women. Most of Andromache's lines express the dependence of her son and herself on Hector. However, she offers seven lines (433-39) of military advice to her husband. Beginning with Aristarchus, an Alexandrian textual critic of the third to second centuries B.C., these seven lines were said to be inauthentic, because the scholar judged military advice to be inappropriate coming from the mouth of a woman. Another example of irresponsible scholarship concerns the translation of a Greek verb *basileuō*.[3] In all the cases where the verb is applied to males the translation is "to rule"; in the sole case (*Iliad*, VI, 425) where it is applied to a queen, the mother of Andromache, the translation has been "to be the wife of a king."

Relevant to our discussion of whether a theory of matriarchy can responsibly be postulated for the late Bronze Age are the numerous questions concerning the Amazons. These female warriors were said to have lived on the edges of the barbarian worlds known to the Greeks. They were adept at horseback riding, and while they may not have exceeded men in physical strength, their prowess with bow and arrow was probably responsible for their military superiority. As historians we are dealing with a major epistemological problem. Was there ever a totally female society, or at least a society in which women were so dominant that men seemed nonexistent? Were the Amazons ever a historical reality, or are we dealing here with a mythical fantasy? The Greeks themselves did not always separate historical fact from legend. Plutarch, for example, apologizes for resorting to the use of legends as history, and then relates the story of the Amazons' attack on Athens in the days of the Bronze Age hero Theseus (Plutarch, *Life of Theseus*, 27). Plutarch does comment that the sequel about the Amazon queen disrupting Theseus' wedding was false. Presumably, then, for Plutarch the story of the Amazon attack on Athens was a historical fact. Yet, the modern historian notes that Plutarch (*ibid.*, 30) also reports, without comment, the struggle of Theseus against the Centaurs, a race of creatures with men's heads and torsos attached to horses' bodies. Evidently, to Plutarch the story of the Centaurs was as true as the story of the Amazons. In Greek literature and the visual arts as well there are many depictions of the battles between Amazons and various Greek heroes. The metopes of the Parthenon depict the battle of the Lapith people against the Centaurs, a battle of Giants, the capture of Troy, and a battle against the Amazons. The modern historian will determine the first two themes to be definitely mythical; the burning of Troy is probably a fact. In what category is the battle of the Amazons to be placed? Since there is nothing inherently monstrous or impossible about an Amazonian society, it is possible, though of course, not provable, that such a society did exist.

Without making any determination as to the historical veracity of the Amazons, we are on safer ground when we deal with the importance of the Amazons to the Greeks as well as to the modern world as a concept. The Amazons have always been a fascinating mythical theme. Most of the major Greek heroes, including Theseus, Heracles, Bellerophon, and Achilles, fought and defeated them. Once again, among the many legends surrounding these heroes some tales, notably their battles against monsters, are patently false, while some probably have a background of historical reality. Whether the Amazons were real, or are to be relegated to the category of monsters is unclear. Forced to leave the question in abeyance, we can possibly take refuge in one of two psychoanalytic explanations. The idea of Amazons can be interpreted as a mythical fantasy, possibly expressing the repressed male notion of female ferocity, and providing a rationalization for the male's urge to subdue women. A second psychoanalytic explanation can be adopted from a recent study of matriliny in Herodotus.[4] According to this interpretation, the Greeks tended to view the non-Greek world as topsy-turvy and opposite from the Greek world. In most of the Greek world women were in a subordinate position. Hence evolved the symmetrical view that male/female relationships would be the opposite among the barbarians. Herodotus (e.g., IV, 26), indeed, reported that among some barbarians women actually held equal power with the men. The notion of an Amazon society then would be the *reductio ad absurdum* of the distorted Greek view of the non-Greek world.

Another major source of information about the Bronze Age is the archaeological evidence of the period. Specifically, the historian of women would look here for pictorial representations of women. Women are visible in the Bronze Age frescoes of Crete and Thera, as well as on the mainland at Mycenae, Tiryns, and Pylos. The best-known examples are the women depicted in the frescoes at the great palaces of Cnossos and Phaestos. These women are shown playing prestigious sacerdotal roles with male figures in subordinate positions. Another event in which female figures as well as male figures are involved is the dancing and vaulting over a bull. The modern historian would also be startled by the women's décolletage, which dipped under the breasts. Other artifacts include a large number of female statues which have been interpreted as fertility goddesses, plus an assortment of jewelry and other possessions of women of sufficient prestige to have been buried in a durable tomb. The majority of these artifacts, incidentally, would have been unknown to Bachofen, since he lived before the days of modern archaeology.

Still, what can a responsible historian deduce about the sociology of the late Bronze Age from the material remains? Very little. The major deities are mother goddesses, and mortal women played a more significant role than men in religious matters. Actually, in later Greek and Roman religion this pattern is, with some exceptions, retained, in that males are the priests for male deities and females tend to serve female deities. Yet in the classical period the fact that women played a significant religious role did not improve their low political, legal, and social status. Accordingly, although the prestige of Bronze Age women in religious affairs was certainly high, no historian should therefore deduce that their prestige was likewise high in other realms.

When the Minoan linear B script was deciphered, it was hoped that there would be some literature which would give some indication of the social structure of the period. However, most of the tablets seem to be inventories and accounts of the palaces. Some of the tablets from Pylos have been interpreted as telling of the tasks to which women were assigned when they sought refuge in the palace before the great destruction.[5] These tasks were of a humble nature, including fetching water and furnishing baths. The tablets also concern the religious functions of women, and hence confirm what had been deduced from the depictions of women in the fresco paintings.

The material remains of Bronze Age Greek societies do not, thus far, provide sufficient evidence concerning the relative status of males and females. We feel we have contributed to feminist scholarship merely by criticizing the traditional assumption that men enjoy the higher status unless proven otherwise. On the basis of the current archaeological evidence available, it is prudent to withhold judgment.

It remains to turn briefly to the topic of matriliny in Greek society. Greek myths and the Homeric epics preserve sufficient evidence from which we can deduce that in certain cases descent was reckoned through the mother.[6] Moreover, male succession to political power through females is seen in many myths of the Bronze Age. For example, Oedipus, a penniless exile, became king in Thebes by marrying the widowed queen Jocasta. Likewise, Menelaus became king of Sparta, by marriage to Helen. Also, the *Odyssey* suggests that the successful suitor of Penelope will rule over Ithaca. In the fifth century B.C. Herodotus (I, 173) similarly reported that among the Lycians descent was reckoned through the mother. Since Bachofen mistakenly believed that matrilineality was a symptom of matriarchy, Herodotus's report was a potent cornerstone for his theory. Recent studies of the slightly more than one hundred fifty sepulchral inscriptions of Lycia from the fifth and fourth centuries B.C. have demonstrated that in the majority of the inscriptions descent is actually patrilineal.[7] However, Herodotus's statement is not totally disproven, for some of the reckoning is matrilineal. Moreover, the social class of people who were wealthy enough to erect tombstones which have survived twenty-five hundred years may have had different customs from the common population. In short, there is some agreement among classical scholars that some cases of matrilineal descent can be observed, although very few nowadays would say that matriliny has significant implications for the male-female power relationship in classical antiquity.

In summary, as far as the late Bronze Age is concerned, classical scholarship can offer two types of evidence: archaeological findings and myths or legends preserved in the literature of later times. The archaeological evidence is inconclusive with regard to social systems and women's roles, although it does permit us to say that women were dominant in the religious sphere. The literary evidence for the period is highly unreliable; and I feel it does not further the cause of feminism to serve up myths camouflaged as verifiable history. Myth has little independent value for the serious historian, although it can often be used in conjunction with what is known from other sources. Unfortunately for the period under discussion there is little information from other sources. Nevertheless, the literary evidence, though it must be used with extreme caution, does indicate that matrilineal reckoning was sometimes practiced; that some Bronze Age queens wielded a significant amount of political power; and that Amazonian societies, though they may have been purely imaginary, also may have actually existed. I think there is little evidence available to a classical scholar indicating the historical existence of matriarchy in the Bronze Age. An examination of earlier periods of prehistory, perhaps neolithic times or earlier, may prove more fruitful, but this task I must leave to the anthropologists.

## NOTES

1. See "Matriarchy versus Patriarchy: Nineteenth Century Debates over the Status of Women in Prehistory," by Sheila Johansson, revised manuscript of a paper read at the Berkshire Conference of Women Historians meeting on "Historical Perspectives on Women," March 3, 1973, at Douglass College, New Brunswick, N.J.

2. See, for example, M. I. Finley, *Early Greece: The Bronze and Archaic Ages* (New York: Norton, 1970), 83, and Emily Vermeule, *Greece in the Bronze Age* (Chicago: University of Chicago Press, 1964), 312.

3. Some of the ideas in the latter part of this paragraph are set forth in greater detail in my forthcoming article "Andromache and the Question of Matriarchy," *Revue des Etudes Grecques.*

4. Simon Pembroke, "Women in Charge: The Function of Alternatives in Early Greek Tradition and the Ancient Idea of Matriarchy," *Journal of the Warburg and Courtauld Institute* XXX (1967), 1–35.

5. F. J. Tritsch, "The Women of Pylos," *Minoica* ("Festschrift Sundwall," Dt. Akad. der Wiss. zu Berlin, Schr. der Sekt. Für Altertumswiss., XII; Berlin: Akad.-Verl., 1958), 406–45.

6. The Homeric evidence has been collected by Kaarle Hirvonen, *Matriarchal Survivals and Certain Trends in Homer's Female Characters,* Annales Academiae Scientiarum Fennicae, Ser. B, CLII (Helsinki: Suomalainen Tiedeakatemia, 1968), *passim.*

7. Simon Pembroke, "Last of the Matriarchs: A Study in the Inscriptions of Lycia," *Journal of the Economic and Social History of the Orient* VIII (1965), 217–47.

# The Cheshire Cat:
# Reconstructing the Experience of
# Medieval Women

*Kathleen Casey*

## Introduction

The last three medieval centuries in Western Europe, subsuming the ferment of Renaissance and Reformation, witnessed an equal ferment among women. At issue is not *whether* but *how* these experiences are connected. Sex-related activity may have been the principal variable in a complex situation. It may simply have been one of several variables. Perhaps, in this case, as in others, sexual phenomena ought to be regarded simply as the locus, not the origin of conflict.

As the women's movement leaves behind the simpler issues of awareness, rights, and purely personal change to focus upon the reordering of social power and priorities, it becomes increasingly necessary to develop a historical perspective on the function of personal change within major social transformations. Status, and the power conflicts that arise from it, can be explained in both economic and sexual terms. Sometimes the source of all stratification, and hence of all conflict, is perceived as purely economic power; sometimes as the elementary physical and mental coercion believed present in all sexual situations, including the individual encounters of men and women.[1] But historical interpretations need not vacillate between idealist and evolutionary concepts of human and sexual nature, as if these concepts were mutually exclusive. Historians need only be sure when or under what conditions gender and the specifically sexual forms of sensual behavior should be regarded as elementary and fixed, and when they may be purely situational.

Unfortunately, as far as the medieval period is concerned, the key to a full understanding of these questions may be the least well explored area of women's studies: that of women's productive labor as it then related to political power. Women's work in that period is further related to the area least well understood, if far better documented and more extensively discussed: that of women's consciousness. In either case, only the systematic collection and statistical analysis of far more data about far more people than have been used to produce the following preliminary hypotheses can begin to show to what degree, and in what combinations, competing structural models may be complementary. But in substituting measurement for an impression, historians, among others turning to the digital computer for assistance, have found it impossible to dodge or postpone hypothesis building. It is because hypotheses are needed, if only to begin the work of systematically correcting them, that I offer a theoretical framework which at this point can be little more than intuitional.

The basic concern of current quantitative social research happens to be identical with that of women's studies: to reduce to a merely statistical uncertainty the vagueness of terms that describe crucial variables, for example, "woman," or the even more indefinite categories "middle-aged" and "middle-class" woman. Like "family" and "state," the category "woman" and all its subgroups seem to behave so differently in different epochs that sometimes it is hard to compare them at all. Sometimes it is our own terminology, sometimes that of the past that is out of step. Combing the record of medieval women, a historian finds, like Alice, that if "something to which we had been applying the word 'cat' with complete assurance should suddenly begin to speak, or should grow to the height of twelve feet, or should vanish into thin air and then reappear and vanish again from time to time . . ." then "in such cases we should not know whether to apply the term. . . . The number of wild situations we could envisage in which we would not know whether today what was before us was a cat is limited only by the extent of our ingenuity."[2] History, not ingenuity, can supply enough "wild situations" in the case of medieval women to make them as elusive as the Cheshire cat.

The effort of reordering our terminology through quantitative studies is not meant to elaborate the obvious or to make women vanish again from the scene. We already know that in different societies, women have been differently perceived. What might now be considered is that people designated as "women" actually were different, under different circumstances in some, if not in all respects. Not women themselves, but only the effects of sex and gender may vanish, at close range, from some periods of history. Where this seems true, the special difficulties of women may have some other source. A review of the circumstantial evidence about medieval women as producers, consumers, and role transformers points to specific areas in which self-conscious gender (rather than sex itself) remained definitive, while material conditions shaped other areas. Many women found ways to refuse, ignore, or circumvent the burden of irrelevancy with which a literary and religious superstructure depressed their public and private image. But as the experience of subsequent generations fully attests, such efforts proved inadequate in the long run.

## 1. Settings: Economic Growth and Regional Patterns

If access to the control of benefits and resources is an essential precondition of role change and even of personality change, all the evidence suggests that by the fourteenth century, for a growing proportion of the female population, that condition was met. A small but steady population growth, clearly observable if not yet fully measured, from the tenth or eleventh centuries on, created the impetus for an accelerating surge in the direction of sustained economic growth. Though fascination with the conspicuous signs of prosperity and mobility makes it easy to overlook the persistence of almost unimaginable poverty for great numbers of people, medievalists agree that in the later Middle Ages an undetermined but significant proportion of European producers and consumers, both male and female, had attained living standards of relative abundance and variety.

However minuscule that proportion, the activities and attitudes of the whole category of persons called women seem to have made a deep impression on the literary elites whose evidence we normally depend upon. From them, posterity gathers that late medieval women of all ranks were highly visible, restless, and troublesome. But we are left wondering whether the literary accounts really meant to imply rebellion, or whether what was actually seen amounted to that. The chances, certainly, of breaking a mold set during the earlier centuries of Christianity were better then than in later periods usually associated with the rise of feminism. Control of resources has flowed to groups of women at various times before and since without significantly altering their position, but late medieval women were exceptionally favored. They had room to maneuver within a mixed or ambivalent kin set; within a set of religious values that were androgynous or even asexual as often as they were mysogynist and antisexual; and within an unsystematic mosaic of customary law. Private stipulations permitted not only informal equality under formal inequality but also the dubious benefits of limited answerability before the law.[3]

Earlier investigators of the history of women have seen the High Renaissance as the apogee of their "influence" in more recent times, attributing improvement in female status to the very period in which the overall position actually was deteriorating. This is because so much attention has been paid to a tiny, if influential, segment of society. A different approach forces conclusions quite the reverse. Activity that might be called "feminist," whether conscious or simply spontaneous, reached a crescendo in areas temporally, socially, and intellectually removed from what we call the Renaissance. By the sixteenth century it had inspired a backlash affecting women of all ranks and in all regions for several centuries to come. It was in Italy, however, that the expansion of female economic power into political decision-making was earliest and most successfully blocked. It was there that "the first sex war," as I am tempted to call it, first was verbalized. As the Renaissance mode encompassed the rest of Europe, the Italian pattern was repeated.

All this suggests a complex regional-cultural variable likely to have affected power, consciousness, and role change among medieval women. While distinctions cannot be drawn along the lines of national units recognized between the sixteenth century and the middle of the twentieth century, a fourfold organic pattern is visible. It roughly corresponds to regional agglomerations only now reemerging in forms like the European Economic Community, its subgroups and satellites: "Romania," comprising southern France and Provence, parts of the Alps, the Italian peninsula and northeastern Spain; the old

Carolingian heartland, to which "Romania" was axially attached, including not only the present Benelux group but also the Rhineland and France north of the Loire; Ottonian Germany, looking eastward and, last of all, the Atlantic-facing peripheries from Scandinavia and the outer isles to Albion's core and the rest of the Iberian peninsula.

"Romania" inherited from the ancient Mediterranean empires an emphasis on different and unequal life roles for the sexes, roles which fortunately also included a separation of goods. Women of both the "heartland" and of Germany enjoyed a climate hospitable to religious experimentation and freedom to bargain within the law. Their relative independence harked back, perhaps, to the "barbarian" tradition of female self-reliance and a shared, if different and still unequal, life role. Their elite culture descended less than directly from mysogynist classical antiquity, but "heartland" influence mediated even more tenuous connections between the classical superstructure and the "Atlantic" peripheries. If Bede, the historian, almost alone of his kind, spoke constantly and positively of women, and could describe an action as taken "with feminine boldness" (*Life and Miracles of St. Cuthbert,* 24), his evident respect was no doubt induced by the example of active queens, abbesses, and commoners in the Anglo-Saxon setting of that scholar's Latin Christianity.

Yet similarities of outlook and objective conditions in all regions are more striking in perspective than these gross differences, especially in the higher social ranks that shared a unitary lay and clerical tradition. The broad and composite nature of the regional variable makes it a likely culprit in the case of spurious correlations. It should not too easily be assumed responsible either for the backlash itself, or for any self-imposed limitations on role change that helped to make the backlash effective. A discussion of the productive role of women can legitimately begin by ignoring regional patterns.

## 2. Women As Producers and Consumers

While no consensus has yet been reached about the course, the causes, even the existence of a Europe-wide economic "crisis" in the later Middle Ages, women seem to have taken a large and apparently unexpected part in the shifts that are visible. At least some historians have tried to explain events in Keynesian terms and insofar as these may apply, the perspective on history that includes sexual economics suggests a specific role for women in the formation of new patterns of demand. Interpretations of the crisis that stress the side of production need also to take women into account. Whether the major changes that took place are ascribed to structural or to climatic, technological, or demographic forces, one should not underestimate the contribution of women's work at this period or fail to notice the pressure of such forces upon (as well as through) women, both as producers and as consumers. An objective account would presumably try to apply econometric or other data processing techniques to the widest possible range of information in the effort to estimate how many women matched increased expenditure by increased productive work, as compared with the number who only redistributed wealth and did so, as the very existence of a crisis implies, in an unhealthy way. Unhappily, such inquiries cannot be pursued without interval scales of measurement that the medieval data simply will not supply. The making of global estimates of women's contribution, over the period, to gross social product is not presently feasible.

It is a pity that the allegations of literary elites that women did not make constructive use of their resources has to go unchallenged for want of the means to test such charges. That, however, may be less immediately germane to the issue of power and consciousness than assessing the degree of autonomy women managed to inject into their lives at this period, whatever they did. We should at least also ask how many women, or what kind of women took self-assertion beyond acquiring equal weapons in the struggle for sexual mastery—a Pyrrhic victory—and how many instead, while seeking power of a more material nature, also sought self-definition. Such questions are not easy to answer even for the data-rich centuries that follow. What does seem clear is that, unlike the situation in those centuries, the economic structure of the Middle Ages gave women a few advantages.

The traditional work role of women did not at any time before the seventeenth century have anything like the economically marginal character it has since acquired. Before 1600, in an economy geared more to production for use than for the market, the traditional skills of spinning, embroidery, accounting, and supervision were not yet merely peripheral to "gross national product." Most women, in any case, were rural cultivators who shared almost all seasonal labors with men.[4] Only toward the end of the Middle Ages did wage differentials become pronounced, reserving to men the areas of greatest gain, such as the harvesting of wheat. This took place as wool, cereals, and wine became cash products responsive to a rising market. In the thirteenth century there seems to have been little material difference between the day rates for a planter of beans, a woodcutter, or a reaper, despite the traditional segregation of some of these jobs according to sex. Yet in the fourteenth century, a reaper made two or three times as much as the others, whose wages remained the same. (See Table 1.) Meanwhile, changes in relative product and factor prices conferred a new importance on traditionally male work like that of the smith. The prices fetched by his ironware were soaring.[5] By the time that butter, milk, and cheese, the daily products of the farm wife, had found a wide enough market, in the seventeenth century, to become equally important income items, it was too late for her to start asking to be paid what she was worth. The preceding generation or two had by then recreated a "patriarchal" style of law, religion, and state power that effectively delayed any adjustment of sex-based relations of production.

Fine weaving and embroidery, by contrast, began their medieval career not as a pastime but as a valuable economic operation producing a surplus for the community, and ended as symbols of leisured status. Both the convents and the Carolingian workrooms (*gynaeciae*), where female slaves labored in teams under female supervision, produced the exquisite fabrics that either served and enriched the Church or went for export to fastidious Byzantium in return for badly needed gold. In a struggling economy, women's work produced one of the very few income items. If it is true that the compensation (*wergild*) laws rated the lay embroiderers with the highest valued males of their class, the goldsmiths, they were measuring not the intrinsic status of these women but their objective social value.[6] By the onset of the "commercial revolution" of the eleventh and twelfth centuries, the exploitive *gynaeciae* had disappeared, but countless nuns still maintained their traditional and still marketable skills as a labor of love—to use the euphemism by which later periods have described the traditional but unmarketable skills of the married woman. Incidentally, much of the exquisite art work we associate with the early and late Middle Ages was likewise executed by nameless and now unnameable nuns. The credit duly given to one or two artists who did not remain anonymous scarcely measures the total contribution of women to the community in a field of endeavor with a clearly economic as well as cultural and aesthetic value.[7]

In the ever-widening market for more humdrum products during the later Middle Ages, women in a great variety of crafts actively expanded their control and increased their gains, whether employed at day or piece rates as independent traders and manufacturers, or working for a husband with the prospect of inheriting his gild privileges. A process could be very thoroughly learned in a lifetime of collaboration with a man whose workshop was adjacent to the home. Most often, those who attained master's rank in the gilds did so in this way, but (from information relating mainly to the "heartland"), mastery could be acquired independently in a surprising range of trades. Though many bear some relation to what traditionally has been called "women's work"—the preparation of food and clothing—some of the very lucrative occupations in which women predominated or which they actually monopolized (brewing, tavern-keeping) do not. The master's widow operated in nearly the entire range of crafts, including sword-making and smelting.[8] We do not know in what strength, or how it may have fluctuated. That she may not literally have been hammering at the forge or wielding the bellows is economically, if not existentially, irrelevant. It was she who collected the profits.

This promising structure had serious flaws. Certain key gilds would not admit women under any circumstances: the scholars, the lawyers, the notaries, the goldsmiths, and those fast-rising entrepreneurs, the portrait painters. In a process visible in France between the thirteenth and the eighteenth centuries the several branches of medicine slowly edged women out of the corporations and out of lawful practice. In the second place, gild regulations as well as market forces set lower rates for day laborers in specifically female trades than in male occupations. And in the one branch of manufacture that already deserved to be called an industry, wool-making, women never did progress to the more highly paid operations. Yet that industry was of overwhelming importance in the period. In many European cities the preparation, weaving, and finishing of wool products, as well as their sale, were the very foundation of both private and civic prosperity, but since the sheer number of processes involved meant that specialization of labor was un-

Table 1. English male/female wage rates in selected occupations, for fifty-two years between 1268 and 1394

| | PRIMARILY MALE[a] | | | | PRIMARILY FEMALE | |
|---|---|---|---|---|---|---|
| | Hedging, ditching, digging, hoeing, gardening d. per day | Reaping (incl. mowing) d. per day | Spaying and gelding (d. per approx. 10 animals) | Planting peas, beans[c] d. per day | Gathering straw, stubble, chaff; weeding d. per day | Unspecified "women's work"[,e] d. per day |
| 1268 | 2½ | | | | | |
| 1270 | | | 1½–¼ (sows) | | | |
| 1271 | | | 3½ | | | |
| 1279 | | 1 (food) | | | | |
| 1280 | | | ⅛ | | | |
| 1295 | | 1½–2 | 4 | | | |
| 1296 | | 1½–2 | ¾ | | | |
| 1300 | | | | 1 | | |
| 1301 | | | | 1 | | |
| 1302 | | | | 1 | | |
| 1303 | | | | 1 | | |
| 1304 | | | | 1 | | |
| 1306 | | | | | | 1 |
| 1307 | | 3 | | 1 | | |
| 1308 | | 2 | | | | ¾ |
| 1310 | | 3½–4 | | | | |
| 1313 | | | 4 (pigs) | | 1½ | |
| 1314 | 2 | 3 | | | | |
| 1315 | 1 | 2½–3 | | 1 | | |
| 1316 | | | | 1 | | |
| 1317 | 1½ | 3–4 | | | | |
| 1318 | | | | 1 | | |
| 1321 | 2 | | | | | |
| 1322 | | | | 1 | | |
| 1323 | | 1½–2½ | | | | |
| 1324 | | | | | 1 | |
| 1326 | | | | | 1 | |
| 1327 | | | | 1 | | |
| 1328 | | | | | 1 (men) | |

| Year | | | | |
|------|------|------|------|------|
| 1330 | | | | |
| 1336 | 3 | | 2 (sows) | |
| 1340 | | | 6½ (sows) | |
| 1341 | 2½–3½ | | 2½–3 (pigs) | |
| 1344 | | | | |
| 1345 | 2 | | | |
| 1347 | | | | ¾ |
| 1349 | 5[b] | | | |
| 1351 | 3 | | | |
| 1354 | 2 | | | |
| 1356 | 2 | | | |
| 1357 | | | | 2 |
| 1358 | | 4 (pigs) | | |
| 1359 | 3–4 | | | |
| 1360 | 5[b] | | | 2[d] |
| 1361 | 5[b] | | | |
| 1362 | | 5 (pigs) | | |
| 1364 | 3–6[b] | | | |
| 1365 | 3–4 | | | |
| 1369 | | | 2 | |
| 1388 | 8[b] | | | 1½ |
| 1391 | | | | 1–2 |
| 1394 | 3 | | | |

*Source:* Compiled from James Edwin Thorold Rogers, *A History of Agriculture and Prices in England* (Oxford: Clarendon Press, 1866, 1902), II, 576–83. Only those data for which an approximate standardization is possible, and where a daily rate is either specified or implicit, have been used. Information comes from a variety of English regions. Short of a thorough reexploration of all published and manuscript sources, Rogers's compilation is at present the only available substitute for a truly random sample. As a rough gauge of purchasing power, it is worth noting that in 1366, 100 herrings cost 6d.

[a] The economically crucial ploughing operation has had to be omitted because quoted rates are almost always for unstandardized and varying quantities, not for a day's work.

[b] Mowing. This was a task sometimes given to women, according to the calendars. The higher of the two rates cited for 1364 is for mowing.

[c] For setting apple plants (no sex specified) the rate was invariably between 1½d. and 2d.

[d] For cutting stubble the rate was 5d. a day in 1360.

[e] Rogers's phrase.

usually far advanced, by no means every participant shared equally in that prosperity. If the Italian experience is at all typical—and there is reason to believe that it was—all women and large numbers of men in the wool business formed an unskilled proletariat. In the actual growing of wool the situation is not quite so clear. That, in itself, deserves investigation, for in pastoral communities, as we shall presently see, women played an unusual role. But the manufacturing process, increasingly dominated by merchandizing specialists, sharply defined the contrast between a female wool operator and a female ironworker. Work opportunities were restricted less by concern for conventional sexual decorum than by the accidents of control over production.

### 3. Gildswomen and Politics

Not the wool merchant, however, but the alewife was the epitome of exploitive malevolence, according to medieval and Renaissance literature and folk media. Her shrewish prepotence may perhaps be written off as a satirical cliché, but the reference to unfair trade practices, rightly or wrongly charged to women, certainly reflects contemporary, not classical concerns. On the one hand, it may have been pure economic jealousy that motivated gilds to deny women access to the fat profits of wool, painting, and the law. Men may have feared a repetition of the process which earlier had allowed wives and widows to gain a monopoly over certain key occupations. There may even have been an inkling that such control could open the long-barred access route to women's public exercise of civic power. On the other hand, it is questionable how far literary themes could have been mirroring the concerns of businessmen. It is more likely that they were reflecting the anxieties of an entire society grappling with its own guilty failure to live and conduct commerce along Christian principles. Unlike antiquity, that society may have feared the private exploitation of power over resources by either sex or by both, more than it feared any extension of such power by just one of them into the public sphere. Methodical research has yet to find ways of showing whether men were displacing self-contempt upon another object or whether, and in what proportion, women entrepreneurs were indeed exploitive. It is still uncertain whether or not the archetypal alewife had some counterpart in daily experience. Should this prove to be the case, such evidence would have to be considered along with indications from some quarters that women's entry into public life was actively forestalled and from others, that women themselves made no move at all to cross the threshold of the public forum.

Perhaps the most interesting insights are obtained where the facts are ambiguous. No mixed gilds in any region of Europe, even those in which women were a majority, seem ever to have elected women to the highest office in their organization. But in the French experience, at any rate, gilds which did not discriminate and even those in which most of the workers were women, demanded no sex-related advantages either. In such gilds women followed the same hours, submitted to the same judgments, and paid the same fines as men.[9] Constructive in itself, this unwillingness to press for special benefits implies at the same time an inability on the part of gilds-women to recognize that it lay in their power to do so. Even less, apparently, did it occur to them to press for political control where they already had an economic advantage. No doubt the fear of losing that advantage influenced the one kind of reluctance as much as the other, but in the long run such strategies were myopic. A crackdown on apprenticeship rules and tighter consolidation of power in the upper gild echelons during the late sixteenth century was more likely the result of crisis conditions and the ensuing wave of labor unrest than a direct tactic of sex warfare. But the closing off of economic opportunity affected men less than women because a failure to gain access to the decision-making ranks had left women without recourse.

Sometimes, in pastoral as distinct from purely agrarian communities, or in the tightly knit and highly cooperative rural hill settlements of southern Europe, the participation of women in local affairs on an equal basis with men was a tradition. But the experience of sheepherders and of a few urban centers was as exceptional as it was remarkable;[10] it was related perhaps to the peculiar economic structure of such communities. In urban Italy, dominated by the wool industry, women workers do not appear to have had any choice at all about entering the public arena, whether by the back door or the front. The Italian gilds, particularly the *Arte di Lana,* were the fundamental cells of government, cementing it more directly and obviously than its modern counterpart into the economic base of society. But A. Briganti has pointed out that female gild masters did not even appear on the matriculation lists conferring eligibility for civic office. To follow his lead into a more thorough and detailed comparison than yet exists of Italian gild statutes and practices would almost certainly confirm the observation that Italian women outside the wool industry made a massive contribution to the economy at managerial as well as laboring levels, yet still failed to gain direct access to power. Briganti's suggestion that this loss of rights found compensation in the prestige of the Virgin Mary[11] is unintentionally ironic. Unlike women in the flesh, Mary was certainly welcome to preside over gild and city alike. But if Italian business interests made a conscious effort to curtail even further the potential of a female labor force already seriously eroded by conditions in the wool trade, it is unfortunate that support of the cult of Mary by women themselves served only to distract them from what was happening.

### 4. The Feudal Lady

The general pattern, as distinct from the varieties, of female response to political opportunity can be inferred by digressing from the larger to a far smaller segment of the population: the feudal class. The values of this class are far from irrelevant because its standards still tended to dominate society as a whole. The military duties of the feudal lady grew out of an economic role. She was accustomed to running a castle or two in the frequent and lengthy punitive, aggrandizing, or crusading absences of her husband. Household management, however, happened to include collecting taxes, sitting in judgment upon dependents and raising armies—often leading troops in person and in armor, like Jeanne de Montfort displaying her two-year-old son and blasting a defiant promise of future vengeance, or Perrette de la Rivière who held Roche-Guyon against the invading Henry V of England. Marozia degli Ubaldi held out in 1357 at Cesena against the papal legate Albornoz, and the Pisan Cinzia di' Sismondi is said to have organized a night attack against the Saracens. The examples are far too numerous to list,[12] and may even be found in many standard histories, especially those of France where the tradition of military leadership by women seems to have been particularly strong. There is really nothing odd about the emergence of Joan of Arc save her disputed peasant origins and her personal indifference to worldly power.

All over Europe, early and late, feudal ladies were involved in dynastic warfare more often than in government. It is ironic, but not really surprising, that their very bellicosity should seem to diminish them as politicians. As the medieval period drew to a close, politics came once more to mean organized decision-making, at the expense of charismatic power. For Pierre Brantôme, writing in the sixteenth century to celebrate the new "cult of women," the outstanding quality of the combatants was their "great-heartedness" in life and death, and his Seventh Essay manages to convey an irresistible image of them only as superlative cheerleaders. Unspectacular and self-effacing devotion to peace and good government were either rare or uninteresting to those who wrote history.

We hear that the countess of Hainault, sister of Philip VI of France and mother-in-law of Edward III of England, but also abbess of Fontenalles, came out of seclusion to negotiate the truce of Esplechins in 1340 and we are told that the widow Ippolita, who ruled Viterbo, was "much loved," but not exactly why. Ermengarde of Brittany, under whose direction in 1127 the exploitation of shipwrecks was abolished, amended feudal customs favoring male heirs; and Blanche of Champagne not only improved roads and created new towns but also was responsible in 1212 for a ruling restricting the rights of an eldest heir. Jeanne of Flanders may have been the first ruler to use the French vernacular as an official language.

These are among the few known exceptions to the general pattern of female rule. If feudal society often derogated from its own rules where family interest was at stake, so that some women of feudal rank exercised in fact powers that were denied them in law, it was because most of them, like their male relatives, could be trusted not to alter conventional political objectives. Some did make good, creative use of their position. But innovative change, the molding of provisional and temporary powers into an autonomous role or the altering of objectives, can barely be glimpsed at all, although some of the activities of Ermengarde of Brittany or Blanche of Champagne began to move in that direction.

For the most part, all those in control of resources, whatever their sex, thought principally in terms of family. Even a queen was regarded as a special kind of wife. This preoccupation with kin or dynasty was a substitute for the formal political life that had barely existed since the demise of the Roman forum. By the sixteenth century the separation of personal and individual behavior from public and collective responsibility was only just beginning to be recognized. But as this started to happen, the derogations from feudal principle that allowed a woman to be active in what once had passed for politics, rarely brought her into the kind of political life that did develop during the later Middle Ages and the Renaissance: affairs of "state" and of "state" diplomacy. Only in France, predictably, were there a few attempts to include women in formal political discourse: Blanche of Champagne personally attended the royal *parlement* called in 1213 and Mahaut of Artois in 1315 was a member of the court of the Peers of France. The reactionary policy which in 1328 reversed ancient custom and formally barred women from the French throne ended the experimental period.[13]

Much the same pattern is apparent here as that which seems to have emerged in the sphere of paid labor. Most women in a strategic position did not think about molding or extending the position's decision-making aspects to their own advantage. When the uses they did make of their power were outmoded by a more aggressive and impersonal style in government and economic structure, it was too late for formal resistance to formal reaction. Their attitude is understandable, especially among the ruling elites. Satisfied, for the most part, with privilege accruing naturally by marriage as well as by birth, women of feudal rank or in the urban patriciates had little incentive to interfere with the nature of the prince's role. They refrained even when so personal a status involved sticking to some less comfortably personal rules of conduct.

From the last generation that can be called "medieval" comes the example of Catherine of Aragon, who never aspired to independent power despite the profound impact of her decisions upon the course of history. Notwithstanding the imperious style of her mother, Isabella of Castille, and her own humanist training, fit for a Renaissance prince, Catherine disappointed some of those supporters in the divorce dispute who looked to her to raise a rebellion against Henry VIII. She claimed only her rights as a wife. "I shall not ask his Holiness for war," she said; "that is a thing I would rather die than provoke."[14] Yet hers was not quite the impersonal stand on conscience of a Joan of Arc or a Thomas More, people for whom any kind of power seemed a false goal. Deeply involved in her own kin, despite shabby treatment from her father in the course of the marriage game, the queen of England stood stubbornly on her own and her family honor. Catherine and Henry both were, in their separate ways, old-fashioned. Elizabeth, who was not, had shortcomings of a quite different nature and of another age.

Despite the unthreatening example set by women of feudal rank to other women, the last century of this period produced an outburst of vocal hostility to the accession of female rulers. Its occurrence among several great dynasties at once in the late fifteenth and sixteenth centuries, when the personal beliefs of a ruler could be disastrous in a realm already torn by religious warfare, at first seems enough to explain a spate of tracts against women in general and against ruling queens in particular. But this must be placed in the full context of a hardening position on women in legal theory and in the courts,[15] and a revival of "patriarchal" family theory. It was not in the north of Europe, however, that changes in law and speculations on family authority first appeared, but in the Italian peninsula, which was relatively immune from religious turmoil. Patriarchal models for family life were only later used by religious reformers north of the Alps, and the paper barrage that was mounted in sixteenth century England and France surely was but part of a far more encompassing, and unprecedented, literary battle whose opening skirmishes took place as early as the fifteenth century in the humanist circles of southern Europe.[16] Hostility to women in politics was due not only to a fear of their interference in religion; it was but one expression of a more diffuse unease.

Clearly dictated by chronology, a focus upon Italy and Renaissance intellectual concerns as the single source of such unease begs all the usual questions about the interaction of ideas with experience. It seems unlikely that renewed theorizing about the family consortium as a keystone of state power can be explained solely or even mainly in terms of a narrow humanist fondness for classical models.[17] Even the re-formation of conceptual hierarchies that preoccupied all of Christendom's intellectual elite cannot be held responsible for decisions made in every mundane encounter over a dowry or a will. Rationalizations of resentment against women's holding power may just as well have had a basis in everyday living.

Demographic probabilities certainly were at work, bringing a few women to princely authority, as well as many more to the control of wealth at humbler social levels. It is hardly likely, however, that a perception could have existed of the way in which the aggregation and proportion of females in society could effect great changes in its character. Explanation of the belated backlash of the sixteenth century requires a return to the concerns and aspirations of the individual, but statistically "average," woman during the two preceding centuries. Her activities seem to have been the source of an amorphous and diffuse resentment.

### 5. The Townswoman

The role of the urban middle-class "housewife" was in effect a modified extension of the role of feudal lady. Both, after all, lived in an agrarian-based society where "housewife" was the counterpart of the "housebondman" or farmer-householder. If the noblewoman remained "just" a housewife while carrying a heavy load of responsibility, the average married woman was not "just" what the average woman has since become, including the woman who works both inside and outside the home. Many a medieval woman did that, too. Household management in those days carried a burden of sustained effort and organizational talent. Households were supplied in bulk; purchases were made for a season or a year at a time. The manager also used and personally cultivated a great variety, now lost, of grains, herbs, and vegetables, along with the roses and other flowers it was her job to use in decoration. Her life was further complicated by real estate dealings and supervision. In the growing class of substantial townspeople and farmers, women set a sophisticated table, according to the extant recipe books, but high energy consumption and frequent religious fasting may have preserved the fine, willowy frame that was the cultural ideal. In all probability, those women who managed to fulfil as well as create that ideal were neither delicate nor fragile; just wiry. In all ranks they burned up calories in an avalanche of tasks and diversions.

If, however, we are to believe the diatribes of literature and of sermons, first heard in the late thirteenth century and rising to a crescendo by the fifteenth, or the sumptuary legislation endlessly reenacted in city after city throughout Europe during those centuries, the "average" woman was "Noah's wife," a stock character of street drama, or that Alice of a fifteenth century song, drinking with her female friends in a tavern and boasting: "I dread no man!"[18] Middle-class townswomen at dice served to illustrate Barclay's English version of the German *Ship of Fools* (1497), even though both sexes had been seized by the passion for gambling. When the typical woman was not called shiftless or immoral, she was accused of having devouring ambition. Dread of a polymorphous evil found a specific target: women who allegedly put money on their backs instead of on the table, driving their overworked men forward to material success or backward into debt.[19] It was as if a vague awareness already was abroad of the pressures attending a growth economy, projecting anxiety upon a more traditional enemy and on an economic collaborator defined mythologically, if not experientially, as the inactive partner.

Active or inactive, striving or parasitical, the ancient enemy also was taken to task for greedy extravagance of a rather different kind. This time it is the disciplinary vehicle itself which clearly betrays a generalized social disquiet. The sumptuary laws of Greece and Rome, directed against wasteful expenditure in general (but most easily against women with money of their own) were disinterred and refurbished with an up-to-date concern for keeping the proper distinctions of rank expressed in clothing. Women with more money than respect for the rules, apparently, were the principal violators, and by implication, a major threat to the old order. These laws were one more device of social maintenance used unsuccessfully in this period to mend breaches in a time-worn and patently inadequate threefold stratification: fighters, prayers, and workers. People of indeterminate status and both sexes were crossing from one level to another or cracking the old conceptual scheme by the sheer weight of their intrusive and expanding presence. Newer paradigms of social structure did admit the existence of a whole range of non-feudal occupations. They did not, however, include among them an active, independent wife or female worker.[20] All the same, the independent woman's appearance as a social force was implied in the way women were singled out as targets both of the sumptuary laws and of moralists' attacks upon the clothing revolution.

The unprecedented involvement of both sexes in high fashion at this period seems at first sight to carry no special implications for social structure as distinct from social mores. Its most obvious effect was simply to negate the sexually neutral message conveyed by all clothing styles up to the turn of the fourteenth century. True, both men and women went far beyond a mere rejection of long, shapeless robes which hid sexual features, choosing instead clothing which flaunted and even accentuated them, nipping in waists, padding shoulders and genitals, and exposing breasts. Moreover, strong assertion of sex differences, as males sheathed their legs in multicolored hose and females affected languid dependence in sleeves and trains of exaggerated length, was something rather new in Christian society. But if this clothing revolution at least offered each sex an equal opportunity to make of the other a sexual object, it can hardly have been introducing the subject of sex to a society which, despite all efforts by the clerical culture (if not by the clerics themselves) had been neither particularly innocent, nor particularly repressed, nor particularly delicate in its language. This major shift in style implied something more than a shift in sensual awareness, as contemporary critics were not slow to notice, either. Fevered competition in dress and the very notion of "fashion" was an outward expression of unwillingness to be bound by any of the social forms and symbols of the past. But once more it was women who were singled out as major offenders in this process of rejection. The expense and presumption of their bizarre headgear, evolving through a swift and bewildering succession of fantasies, and their use of cosmetics drew the most sustained harangues.

## 6. Researching the Challengers

It is not enough, however, to ask whether more women than men helped to stretch the fabric of society out of shape. A study of women's consciousness as well as power needs also to distinguish between the positive and negative qualities of a force whose very existence is witnessed mainly by hostile sources. When these qualities are identified it will be easier to say how the very agents of change became its victims. Unfortunately, none of the textual records gives direct answers. These have to be sought indirectly by the systematic application of several alternative kinds of research, all of a rather laborious nature.

First, the literary evidence is by no means useless. The Boccaccian-Chaucerian tradition, for example, is too fresh in both style and content to be simply an Ovidean revival, a renewed expression of the classic myth of feminine evil or an elaboration of standard Christian paradigms of vice and virtue. When rhetorical patterns are identified, the crucial inconsistencies that betray what has been conditioned by experience can be located. Certain kinds of computer-assisted textual analysis that already have been tried could throw new light on the topic of women in medieval literature.[21]

Another likely procedure would be to compare self-reliance and simple ambition by measuring each according to indices devised from civil, and especially criminal records. Legal thinking is and always was more used to defining nuances of action and responsibility, avoiding absolute categories and polar oppositions, than the rhetorical, philosophical or aesthetic modes of expression. Henry de Bracton saw no inconsistency in noting three circuit cases where a woman appeared in court as her husband's attorney (*Notebook*, 342, 1361, 1507), while upholding in his systematic treatise the principle of marital "coverture." And the second statute of Westminster in 1285 gave a wife the right to intervene in a plea where her husband defaulted and she was in danger of losing her inheritance.

Formal rules about women are usually set down because their rationale has at some time been challenged, and it should be possible to assess the frequency of these challenges. "Ambitious" behavior, on the other hand, could be defined as abnormally frequent resort to litigation, where an average can be statistically established. Still more specifically, it might be asked what proportion of women in all ranks, but especially within the catalytic burgess class, won a rise in status through their own efforts rather than through an advantageous marriage alone. The example of developing non-European economies suggests that a rise in urban incomes usually has reduced the proportion of women active outside the marital-maternal role.[22] The medieval record hints that this was not the case in Europe until much later on.

Yet another approach is possible. The behavior of a great variety of women, recorded sporadically in legal and financial documents, in chronicles, memoirs, and even in the problematical saints' lives, might well be measured against standards constructed initially from well-documented situations or individual cases. Such standards of "typical" behavior would eventually be modified or refined by the accumulation of evidence. The case studies that now follow are less like such strictly statistical "profiles" than they are intuitional "ideal types" of role transformer and role sustainer.

### 7. The Nun and the Witch

The types that will be considered range across a continuum of behavior, moving from that which is truly "on the edge" of society toward the statistical average. Somewhere along that continuum emerges the role I would define as "sequential" and the true "emergent" type that permanently redirects conventional patterns without completely changing them.

Applied to a role, the terms "marginal" and "transitional" share a sense that they are enacted on the frontier of social experience, between ordinary and extraordinary behavior; between the explicable and the inexplicable. The common heritage of both nun and witch (as defined by the period) was the routinized charismatic role of the sybil of antiquity. Neither witch nor nun made any permanent redefinition of female behavior, although both tried. Both lost status. Some were swept to the margins of society in a literal sense.

The conventional *ordines*—the concept of warrior, monk, and peasant ranks in feudal society—made no allowance for a specialized sex role, only for specifically female behavior within each stratum. Surprisingly, perhaps, the slightly less common twofold division of society into the married and the unmarried—essentially, the laity and the clergy—did imply, at least, that the biological division of labor could be modified. The nun who thus found a place in the religious hierarchy, if not the economic, occupied as a single woman by vocation a well-defined and nearly autonomous role that has since been lost. Rightly or wrongly, seclusion in imitation of martyrdom carried awesome prestige in medieval society, but what is more to the point, the nun's life-style was more self-determining than any other available alternative to the wife-mother complex. At its most subtle, Christianity did offer new possibilities for the female being. Some of the early Patristic writings, notably those of St. Gregory of Nyssa, used neo-Platonic themes out of a Hellenistic milieu long hospitable to women to propose an endlessly transcendent view of human nature and of society. St. Gregory's formulation, unlike many others in such vein, was incorporated into orthodoxy. His exposition of the inner meaning of virginity laid the earliest foundations for the later veneration of Mary, contributing some of the more positive layers of meaning to an image overloaded with negative qualities.

In practical terms, and for all the misuse of medieval convents as dumping grounds for women who were useless in the marriage game, nuns enjoyed a community life, in the company of other women, that was no harsher than in most homes. Their life expectancy was not usually lowered, as it was for other women, by maternity, and they could relish intellectual and other forms of intercourse with men not always as tyrannous as husbands or their own abbess. Those with a taste for administration could indulge it. Some of the early Anglo-Saxons did this impressively. While Church councils issued academic canons elaborating in Christian terms the myth of feminine evil, women were ruling sizable monastic communities, including some with both men and women as members. Toward the end of the Middle Ages, older strictures upon female monasticism gave way before the creative energies of women like St. Catherine and St. Theresa. Whether as mystics or as reformers and innovators, religious women made a notable contribution to resolving tension between the active and the contemplative life that agitated Latin Christendom. Its official representatives always made concessions to those whose piety could be relied upon. Unfortunately for the superstructure under stress, it was sometimes the very zeal of the religious that hastened the process of dissolving what many an early Christian princess or nun, fully internalizing Patristic values, had helped to create.

Convent life itself was not accessible, however, to the vast majority of low-status women without an endowment. There were two substitutes: orthodox lay piety, heavily involved with veneration of the Virgin, and a heterogeneous counter-culture that ran the gamut from recognition of a female creation principle and holistic rather than dualistic perceptions, to a view of matter, sex, marriage, and property which ranged from austere hostility to indifference. Genuine "feminism" should not be sought in the former, a cult of married virginity with useful appeal to rural "pagans" responding late to the Christianity of an elite. Women among those beginning to have more control over their situation could not develop by enshrining a passive, self-sacrificing role that fantasized peace and harmony in a society fatally transformed by demographic and economic pressures. Long an enriched symbol of the Great Mother or the mystery at Eleusis, Mary now became Queen not only of the chivalric courts of Heaven but also the quality of mercy itself; pacifier of city strife and agent of repentance. She stood for women who were expected to soothe all tensions, save their own. Her popularity attests to the overwhelming need of the insecure for an attributed identity. It was ironic that just when conditions were ripe for some women to begin searching for a new life, sensitive but misguided males appended to the Marian image of "woman" their own concept of the *vita nuova*. Dante's exceedingly complex figures symbolized a multilevel perfection of soul. They have little to do with some of the strange forms taken by the "new life" of living women.

Unlike the nun, the ordinary rural witch had traditionally played neither a sublime role nor one that was necessarily marginal in the literal and economic sense: she had not always been old, poor, and impotent; for not all rural women automatically were that. By the fifteenth century, however, her usually harmless prophylactic and therapeutic functions had been formally identified with diabolism and heresy in a movement that cannot all be attributed to Dominican psycho-sexual paranoia, on the one hand, or to the final triumph of a male-dominated university tradition, on the other.[23] The Inquisition's educational and punitive crusade was waged against any attempt, by any person, to acquire full mastery of mind and environment, and it was already two centuries old when it began—almost irrelevantly, it seems—to ensnare thousands of obscure, unexceptional, and powerless women.

If its motives have baffled posterity, its effects are clear enough. They reduced to a position of semi-criminal deviance the routinized activities of many women, who were defined now as subversive. Coincidentally, a large number of them were poor. The polarization of wealth that accompanied an economic and demographic revival dating from the late fifteenth century swelled the ranks of those most vulnerable to inquisitorial pressure. With vagrancy sharply on the rise in the sixteenth century, the formerly respectable "poor of Christ" had turned into the disreputable and "dangerous" classes in whose ragged ranks disrespectful and ungrateful women were prominent—almost indistinguishable, moreover, from that other disturbing newcomer to Europe, the gypsy.

There was nothing new in the fear that a literal construction might be put upon the Gospel's use of the poor, the powerless, and the prostitute as symbols of a quest for perfection that ignored the inequities of the status quo. New, on the other hand, was an apparent extension of the political uses of sorcery, long common in the upper ranges of society.[24] Consciously or not, the most banal kinds of self-assertion were interpreted by persecutors and persecuted alike as social defiance. It was probably quite correct to do so. Women who too readily confessed to special powers were indulging a desire for them: a perverse, but still demonic gesture.

## 8. Deviant and Conformist Models

Contemporaries took as seriously as posterity doubts the claim that witches were interfering with the natural fertility crucial to an agrarian society. It is as if they all clearly saw how dangerous it would be for women to take control over reproduction.

To understand this in terms of quite everyday experience we have to turn back from the hysterical climax of witch-hunting to the year 1320, and the laconic testimony of Beatrice de Planissoles of Montaillou, in Languedoc.[25]

This unpretentious woman expressed her disdain for the role of minor feudal wife in sexual rebellion that was as quiet as it was unselfconscious. Unfortunately for her personal safety, she listened, without undue enthusiasm, to the heretical beliefs of a series of priestly lovers, all secretly of the Cathar faith. Never fully freed from conventional acquiescence in the primacy of male needs, she was at first able to raise only mild protests against Christmas-night copulation behind the locked doors of a church, but eventually she found audacity enough to abandon not only role and family but in the long run, lovers too. Her candor before the inquisitorial court and before the facts of her own life reveal the makings of a liberated spirit, and she did make the important discovery, albeit through Cathar teachings, that marriage was not, after all, divinely ordained. She was lucky that the commonplace charms and mementoes found in her purse were not in those days thought conclusive proof that she was a witch. It is ironic, though, that her private self-assertion should still have been found a threat to society when she simply failed to be overawed by its institutions. She did not go so far as to connect sexual and social rebellion.

The much more radical upheaval foreshadowed in some of the religious heresies never did occur. If the centuries-old struggle over celibacy was in the forefront of Reformation concerns, so were considerations of economic and social reform. But their sometimes haphazard conjunction in diverse attacks on marriage and property were, in the long run, violently rejected.

Though the nun and the witch may have been losers, Margery Kempe of Norfolk won a few moves in her "sequential" version of the marital life-style. Neither as unobtrusively radical as that of Beatrice, nor yet thoroughly satisfactory, her enterprise did move marriage in a positive direction, and in a way that did not endanger her life. Wishing neither to be a cloistered nun, nor altogether to abandon the prosperity, independence, and prominence afforded by her position in trade, she found the key to revolt in her financial surplus. She paid off her husband's debts in return for freedom from the debt of the marriage bed. If many people found her difficult to take seriously, she enjoyed her own pretensions to mysticism, traveled extensively, tried out and cast off the role of Beguine, or wandering holy woman, and still managed to maintain good relations with her son. It is unfortunate that the remarkable record of her own words leaves us uncertain as to what, eventually, she did become.[26] But neither the fully autonomous celibate role nor informal mass rebellion was destined to compete with her prophetic compromise.

In her own time, however, the type she represented can hardly have been numerous. Among women who no doubt more fairly represent the "typical" role than does the Noah's wife caricature, three generations of wool-rich Paston women infused into their voluminous correspondence the high energy and self-organization that amounts to fulfillment of a sort, even where such concentrated activity lacks a personal goal and is not altogether self-directed. True, the Pastons (of East Anglia, like Margery Kempe) marshaled their impressive powers in the lifetime service of a husband, a family, and an estate. But if the first of these women was tough and tyrannical, the second seemed actually to enjoy, not just endure, her role as adjutant. An engulfing enthusiasm for acquiring property and her verve in protecting it betoken a more than economic motivation. The tone she took with her husband was one of unfailingly respectful, yet easy, familiarity, but her handling of tenants and officials was belligerent. In politics, a subject her mother-in-law had never mentioned, she took a genuine interest. Only once did Margaret Paston use a self-deprecating phrase, apologizing for a "simpleness" (March 3, 1451) in which she obviously did not believe.

But if Agnes, Margaret, and Margery moved in three generations from *materfamilias* to marital companion, this change in no way affected fundamental aspects of the maternal role and the raising of male children. Margaret, the career wife, was also the perplexed mother of John Paston II, a tournament fancier and a collector not of wool, but of books and women. Old William's grandson was willing to shrug off responsibility but his disappointed mother seemed neither ready nor willing, despite her acumen and independence, to make changes in the maternal image of dominance and its corollary, the need to be dominated. Indulgent, and careful to hide from her young children the tougher aspects of her personality, she turned dominant-submissive in widowhood, banishing one daughter foolish enough to marry beneath her and exhorting the return of her sons, since enemies "set not by a woman as they should by a man" (1467). Many women must similarly have remained, by their own choice, carriers of a culture that made it hard for them to imagine themselves in a father's place, or present themselves to their children as a fully adequate alternative to the paternal model.

## 9. Learned Women

Among the accumulation of uncoordinated personal decisions to go on creating the apparently fixed qualities of male and female, those of learned and influential women deserve special attention in an account of women's consciousness. A minority, to be sure, they were still much more like the "average" in effect, if not exactly in behavior, than any "atypical" group. They were not "feminists," and contemporaries were right to find for them a quite specific term. In the language of courtly love, they were "ladies." Whereas the term "nun" does not fully convey all its medieval meanings to the modern ear, and though medieval people used the word "witch" for new connotations without troubling to dissolve the old, it is we who have blunted the precision of "lady." Its proper context is the cult of love and romance, an aesthetic mode but also the special style of "Romania."

The culture of courtly romance made it difficult to see sex roles in an honest light. Behind the submergence of self in service, justifying the Christian knight's often pedestrian goals, lurked the mutual humiliation of the sexes and the old contest for mastery that had more recently been expressing itself in mundane economic form. Originally useful in buttressing the eroded identity of the feudal male, it also helped women disguise the brutal truth about their relationship with men and about themselves. Exposed to a harsh environment they were, by and large, neither all that secluded nor all that passive. I believe the question of female passivity is still open. The range of behavior in women was wider, even for unremarkable persons, than is commonly believed. Pilgrimages, on which women were encouraged to go, often were lengthy and far-ranging. Chronicles convey an impression that ships and overland trails were clogged with passengers of both sexes, and they supply attractive anecdotes about the physical and moral agility of women. Marriage, even for those of humble rank, often took them relatively far from their place of birth. Fights between them were frequent and not all their crimes were "women's crimes," committed with male help.[27] To privileged women whose rank always had afforded concrete defenses against the blows of men and fate, the code of courtly love promised only an opportunity to add or commission their own sexual fantasies to the array supplied by men, while to the majority, both less sheltered and more vulnerable, it offered a mere illusion.

Christine de Pisan's bold challenge, in 1399, to the University of Paris and the royal court over alleged slights to the female sex in *The Romance of the Rose*, ignored passages proposing a free and natural relationship between men and women (41, 47). Jean de Meun's late-thirteenth-century version of the *Rose* is neither a frankly pornographic fantasy nor a typical product of courtly romance. It is a popularized distillation of a culture not yet tired of pressing, like Dante, for the principle of complementarity or (to use the terminology of certain Eastern philosophies) "reciprocal exclusion." From this kaleidoscope of ideas the celebrated feminist pulled one or two "dirty" words, dealing with them out of context and *ad nauseam*. Rightly cutting through scholastic disputes over "universals" she denied also that words must be judged by the intention with which they are used, disapproving the poem's suggestion that neither love nor sex are in themselves at fault. As a Christian humanist, she went straight to the point: if a thing is evil, so is the word, "for the first understanding of the thing has already made the name evil." The thing in question: a testicle. It took one of her male adversaries to point out that it was in themselves that Adam and Eve sinned, not in the parts of their bodies.[28]

In many other respects, the work and life-style of Christine de Pisan broke new ground. Nor should it be forgotten that she was also a rhetorician. The controversy over the *Rose* may reflect her personal views less, perhaps, than the work of 1405, *Trésor de la cité des dames*. But too little attention has been paid to the dissimilarities between these writings and, say, her treatise on warfare, a standard piece that incorporates classical authors and fully internalizes the male view of war. It is unexpectedly remote from the themes of *La Cité des dames*. Yet paradoxically, none of these works may be very far from the assumptions and mood of one less frequently read or cited: *The Book of the Duke of True Lovers*. Appearing some time after 1400, this romance may account for the element of conformity in de Pisan's rebellion. It is at one and the same time both a reflection of courtly convention and the personal contribution to its literature of a female victim of "curteysie." In her version of sexual fantasy, a submissive suitor, granted kisses alone, night after night and "more than a hundred times," declares himself highly content, and is banished notwithstanding. His lady's belated concern for her reputation pushes the emphasis on neurotic uncertainty in sex beyond its conventional limits. Whether in earnest or in jest, Christine de Pisan's excursion into the romantic mode could but remove still further that hope for "passive reciprocity," in which Jean de Meun had anticipated some of the themes of Gestalt psychology. The enigmatic Christine de Pisan brings irresistibly to mind the syndrome of the Cheshire cat.

Humanistic education did little to free the well-bred and tastefully literate woman from the sadomasochistic patterns of courtly love. As the ultimate refinements of chivalry in the "sweet new style" ceded to the Platonic cult of beauty, the sex tourney continued in palaces, instead of castles, between adversaries of intelligence and wit. But while a distinction did start to be drawn between "the perfect wife" and "the perfect lady,"[29] the sublimest virtue of that low-keyed paragon was "a splendid silence."[30] A woman who actually, in true Renaissance mode, exerted an audacious will to challenge fate without scruple was dubbed a *virago*, literally, a surrogate male, as if an alternative were unthinkable.

Whether of classical or Christian inspiration, the style of the new education, aiming to develop the whole being of a "well-rounded, universal man," was capable of forming a critical, self-assertive personality. But its content, offering to the well-rounded woman a curriculum perpetuating philosophical prejudice and erroneous biology, formed anything but a whole female being. Formerly, just the reverse had been the case. In the rigor of its vocational training, devoid of much parental closeness and its lack of stress on intellectual attainment, the medieval upbringing had been almost identical for both sexes, irrespective of rank.[31] If a girl's training had also concentrated on inculcating the current morality along with a certain shrewdness, the warmer humanistic style managed only to turn that defensive shrewdness into witty strategies. Learned women passed on its content unmodified by an independent point of view, just as the less erudite but energetic women of no particular distinction had not modified motherhood.

## Conclusion

It appears that the majority of women, irrespective of age, status, milieu, and even the use to which they put their resources, opted in certain crucial respects to affirm rather than deny traditional values, the strategic areas of role recruitment and role replacement. While the débâcle of the sixteenth century was hastened by economic forces largely indifferent to sex, those who collectively went down to defeat were, at least in part, collectively responsible. Unable in some cases but in others unwilling to grasp public power, large numbers of women lost control over institutional adjustment to new relations of production. And in the training of each rising generation they slowed down transformations they had materially helped to initiate. The Pauline injunction against women as teachers (1 Tim. 2:12), which recognizes a real threat to self-maintaining social mechanisms, seems to have been either too well heeded or redundant.

Despite their many burdens, medieval women present a distinctly positive and cheerful aspect. Looming as large, bold and confident, at times, as the Cheshire cat, they could also, like that creature, fade into nothing but a grin. It happened noticeably in the last century of the period and in those regions early associated with the humanistic core of a rising new European culture that cultivated self-conscious gender, if only in the rhetorical sense. But in the end, before the eyes of a puzzled modern Alice, even the grin fades away.

## NOTES

1. Randall Collins, "A Conflict Theory of Sexual Stratification," *Social Problems* **19** (Summer 1971), 3–21. See also, in the present context, E. Kohler, "Les troubadours et la jalousie," in *Mélanges de langue et de littérature du Moyen Age et de la Renaissance offerts à Jean Frappier* (Geneva, 1970). This study of the twelfth-century *paradoxe amoureux* sees it as the psychological expression of class struggle within the feudal ranks.

2. William P. Alston, *Philosophy of Language* (Englewood Cliffs, N.J.: Prentice-Hall, 1964), 94.

3. The marriage and property of the vast majority of women in all countries were regulated not by feudal rules favoring the male warrior, but by custom and customary law. On the Continent and even in England a married woman could acquire the status "feme sole merchant." Inheritance was frequently partible, if not equal. The widow everywhere enjoyed the ancient right of maintenance ("freebench") and dower: one-third (in some places, one-half) of community property. (This was the outgrowth of Germanic "bride-price" and *morgengabe,* or the Lombardic *meta:* a contribution from the male side to marriage always more substantial than that from the female side. It was paralleled in Roman law by the slow evolution of the "donation" from the bridegroom, comparable in value with the *dos* or dowry proper.) In the lower ranks, marriage rites (officially under the jurisdiction of the Church, but still in an unfixed state) often were dispensed with, permitting an ambiguous freedom that the daughters of the propertied could not enjoy. It was not until medieval customary law began to be systematized by Romanizing lawyers in the later Middle Ages that the dower of the non-feudal classes had to be "proved" in court, as noted by Coke's *Institutes.* For a general introduction to this subject, see R. Faith, "Peasant Families and Inheritance Customs in Medieval England," *Agricultural History Review* 14, no. 2 (1966); J. A. Raftis, *Tenure and Mobility: Studies in the Social History of the Mediaeval Village* (Toronto: Pontifical Institute of Mediaeval Studies, 1964), chap. 2; G. C. Homans, *English Villagers of the Thirteenth Century* (New York: Russell and Russell, 1960 [1941]), part 3; F. J. Pollock and F. W. Maitland, *History of English Law before the Time of Edward I,* 2d ed. (Cambridge, Eng.: University Press, 1898–99 [1923]); Paul Gide, *Étude sur la condition privée de la femme,* 2d ed., A. Esmein (Paris, 1885); A. Eyquem, *Le Régime dotale* (Paris, 1903); *La Femme: Recueils de la Société Jean Bodin,* vol. 12 (Brussels, 1962). The brighter side of being "under the rod of her husband" for a woman under English matrimonial law is illustrated by case number 1847 in the *Notebook* of Henry de Bracton, ed. F. W. Maitland (Cambridge, 1887). In a case of forged evidence, in property litigation to which both a husband and his wife were party, he was hanged while she went free.

4. The evidence is mainly pictorial. For an introduction, see J. C. Webster, *The Labors of the Months* (Evanston, Ill.: Northwestern University, 1938).

5. James Edwin Thorold Rogers, *A History of Agriculture and Prices in England* (Oxford: Clarendon Press, 1866, 1902), II, 576–83. It has been suggested that the development of powered flour milling released labor time which women devoted to the

cultivation of vegetables and flax. Sylvia Thrupp, "Medieval Industry 1000–1500," in C. Cipolla, ed., *The Fontana Economic History of Europe* (London, 1972), 234.

6. Thrupp, "Medieval Industry," 229–30, and Andree Léhmann, *Le Role de la femme dans l'histoire de France au moyen âge* (Paris: Berger-Levrault, 1952). For a *wergild* equivalence between embroiderers and smiths, Léhmann cites P. Boissonade, *Life and Work in Medieval Europe*, book 1, chap. 10, who does not quote his source. Since none of the printed Germanic codes seems to contain such a rule, I assume that these authors were aware of some other source which it would be useful to locate.

7. Etienne Boileau's *Livre des Métiers* (1270) refers to gilds of female illuminators and binders in Paris, and in England a copyist received in 1366 as much as 8s. 9d. for one book, a binder 6s. 8d. for a single manuscript, according to the examples of "Sundry Services" quoted in Rogers' *Prices.*

8. See Léhmann, *Role de la femme*, 436–37, citing Boileau and the tax lists of 1292 and 1300. These show 108 occupations (out of 321) open to women, including surgery, butchering, glassblowing, bit- and bridle-making, chain-mail forging. In at least one case, the barber-surgeons admitted a woman before widowhood (1313), and in 1374 the parlement ruled in favor of a female surgeon (*ibid.*, 471–73). Of Boileau's list of 110 gilds, only 5 were restricted to women only.

9. In Paris, as many as half the directors of mixed gilds, numerically dominated by women, were male, according to the *Livre des Métiers.* English gilds, whether commercial or confraternal, did not elect women wardens at all. See Joshua Toulmin Smith, *English Gilds, The Original Ordinances, etc.*, Early English Text Society, vol. 40 (London, 1870); S. Thrupp, *The Merchant Class of Medieval London, 1300–1500* (Chicago: University of Chicago Press, 1948), 169–74 and chap. 5. For Italy, see A. Briganti, *La donna e il diritto statutario in Perugia, secoli XIII e XIV* (Perugia, 1911), 41–43, 49, 53, 61–62. This study draws on material from other parts of Italy as well as Umbria.

10. Léhmann, *Role de la femme*, 242–43; A. Pertile, *Storia del diritto italiano*, 2d ed. (Turin, 1892–1902), II, 43, note 15. In Spain, both early transhumant associations and the national sheepherders' *Mesta* that succeeded them in the thirteenth century granted an equal voice to women.

11. Briganti, *La donna*, 41–42, 57.

12. For many other battle heroes, see also E. Rodocanachi, *La Femme italienne avant, pendant et après la Renaissance* (Paris, 1922). See also Doris M. Stenton, *The English Woman in History* (New York: Macmillan Co., 1957), *passim.*

13. Marion F. Facinger, "A Study of Medieval Queenships: Capetian France 987–1237," *Studies in Medieval and Renaissance History* 5 (1968), 1–48, points out that a special administrative role for the female consort had ceased to develop after royal centralization began in the thirteenth century.

14. Garrett Mattingly, *Catherine of Aragon* (New York: Vintage, 1941), 344.

15. In Italy, systematizing glossators and practitioners stressed the harshest aspects of property law under both Roman and Germanic systems. By the sixteenth century new rules restricted the personal disposition by a woman of her dowry and her right to make a will, beyond the point to which Rome had gone. The exclusion of women from intestate succession was written into the majority of urban statutes at this time. See the statutes listed by Rodocanachi in *La Femme italienne*, 292, 344–66. In Perugia, dowry had to be fixed not simply by the bride's father but by a council of relatives, according to Briganti, *La donna*, 23, 75. The new principles also became authoritative in Germany, where lawyers tended to follow the Italian schools. In England, Tudor-Stuart legal practice hardened against women. Both this case law and the rich but widely scattered collections of manuscript *consilia* (opinions) in Germany, Rome, Florence, and many lesser Italian towns deserve systematic treatment, though most are still unindexed.

My own survey of 350 fourteenth- and fifteenth-century *consilia* in Perugia alone showed that roughly one-fourth of these dealt with disputed dowry and intestate succession.

16. Summaries in translation of many rare treatises may be found in Ruth Kelso, *Doctrine for the Lady of the Renaissance* (Urbana: University of Illinois Press, 1956).

17. For example, Leon Battista Alberti, *I libri della famiglia*, in *Opere volgari*, ed. Cecil Grayson, scrittori d'Italia, vol. 218 (Bari, 1960). Alberti's treatise was written between 1432 and 1434, with additions in the early 1440s.

18. T. Wright, *A History of Domestic Manners and Sentiments during the Middle Ages* (London, 1862), 438.

19. E. Zeydel, trans., *Sebastian Brant: The Ship of Fools* (New York: Dover, 1944). The satire pounces on the tradesman's wife, "Who wears more gauds of various kinds Skirts, rings, cloaks, broid'ries scant and rare It's ruined many a good man's life, He must go begging with his wife," 270. In the fourteenth century, Queen Jeanne of France was shocked to find hundreds of rich burghers' wives in Bruges dressed and bearing themselves as splendidly as she. M. Mollat and P. Wolff, *Ongles Bleus, Jacques et Ciompi: Les révolutions populaires aux XIVe et XVe siècles* (Paris: Calmann-Levy, 1970), 23. Wives of artisans and other men of mean birth who "emulated with their jewels and dress the ladies of noble birth" were much hated by the latter, according to the Perugian chronicler Francesco Maturanzi. E. S. Morgan, trans., *Chronicles of the City of Perugia 1492–1503 written by Francesco Matarazzo [sic]* (New York: Dutton, 1905), 67.

20. Jacobus de Cessoli's *Liber de moribus hominum et officiis mobilium* was many times copied and translated after it first appeared in the fourteenth century, and in 1483 William Caxton printed and illustrated an English version of this analogy between society and the game of chess. Its queen was still the powerless creature of the twelfth-century game, however, moving diagonally and in one direction only.

21. W. Sedelow, Jr., "History as Language; Part 1," *Computer Studies in the Humanities and Verbal Behavior* 1, no. 4 (December 1968).

22. Ester Boserup, *Woman's Role in Economic Development* (London: Allen and Unwin, 1965), 224.

23. For a general introduction to this complex subject, see F. Heer, *The Medieval World: Europe 1100–1350*, trans. J. Sondheimer (Cleveland, Ohio: World, 1962).

24. See, for example, William R. Jones, "Political Uses of Sorcery in Medieval Europe," *The Historian* 34, no. 4 (August 1972), 670–87, esp. 678–87. Though Joan of Arc was considered by political powers to be a threat to them, she herself was not a part of collective female revolt. She seems to have been a true role transformer in being one of those rare individuals who find neither sex nor authority relevant to conduct and thus was both sufficiently behind and ahead of her time to display an interest in the transformation of current social roles. England, it should be remarked, was spared the worst excesses of the witch hunt.

25. Jean Duvernoy, *Inquisition à Pamiers, Intérrogatoires de Jacques Fournier évêque de Pamiers (1318–1325)* (Toulouse: Editions Privat, 1966), 46–71.

26. Her memoirs, available in several editions, were dictated between 1436 and 1438. Margery Kempe was born in 1373, but the date of her death is unknown.

27. For many examples, see Wright, *Domestic Manners, passim;* Rafti's *Tenure and Mobility*, 178–82. In 1309, three unattached Italian women, summoned to appear in the Perugian court for housebreaking and theft, ignored the summons. They were probably never brought to justice. *Archivio di Stato,* Perugia: *Giudizuario,* Podesta, no. 50.

28. These citations from her letters are my translations from documents in Charles F. Ward, "Epistles on the Romance of the Rose and other Documents in the Debate," Ph.D. thesis, University of Chicago, 1911. For the reputation of Christine de Pisan as "the first

feminist," see Rose Rigaud, *Les Idées féministes de Christine de Pisan* (Neuchatel, 1911). A more recent evaluation is Marguerite Favier's *Christine de Pisan* (Paris, 1967).

29. Kelso, *Doctrine for the Lady of the Renaissance*, 134.

30. F. Watson, ed., *Vives and the Renaissance Education of Women* (New York, 1912), 101. Alberti's perfect housewife controlled staff and family without raising her voice (Grayson, ed., *Della famiglia*, 241). An unpublished analysis by Leslie Getz (University of California at Berkeley, 1970) of the vast bibliographical literature on learned women of the Renaissance and after concluded that remarkably few studied any subject outside the humanities; Getz's study confirmed my own impression of their intellectual passivity.

31. Among rural cultivators there was little hard work that women did not share, and in the tiny feudal class, girls as well as boys learned to play chess, to hawk, and to hunt. Women were known to ride astride, not sidesaddle as on formal occasions (Wright, *Domestic Manners*, 312). Coeducation existed in secular or ecclesiastical schools; see esp. Trevisa's Higden, *Chronicles and Memorials of Great Britain* (London, 1865–86), VII, 183; and G. G. Coulton, *Social Life in Britain from the Conquest to the Reformation* (Cambridge, Eng.: University Press, 1918), 434. In 1300 the Norman lawyer Pierre Dubois proposed a task force of specially coeducated young men and women to compose differences between Islam and the West, using a practical instead of a scholastic training that included medicine. *De Recuperatione terrae sanctae*, trans. W. I. Brandt (New York: Columbia University Press, 1956).

# Women in Convents:
# Their Economic and Social Role in
# Colonial Mexico

*Asunción Lavrin*

Recent Latin American colonial historiography appears to be moving away from the study of institutions considered as autonomous structures toward interest in the functional interrelationship of those institutions with the society in which they were rooted and in the changes undergone by both these elements throughout time. There is now a greater interest in studying such socioeconomic subjects as the people who formed the backbone of colonial institutions; their reactions or adjustments to royal policies; the changes in the composition of the personnel of well-known administrative units of the government (which have explained formerly misunderstood political attitudes); and the financial framework of specific groups and corporations, and how they reflected and affected the trends of the regional and the general economy.

With regard to the Church, since the major roles of its secular and regular branches have been already well defined and, in general, successfully studied, new questions are now posed, which demand a closer look at the finer details of this institution. Certain topics have received a large share of historical attention: the great personalities of the missionary period; the expulsion of the Jesuits. Yet, we know very little about the members of the Church, as people; the differences in behavior and roles of the several component bodies of the Church; and have very little reliable information about the much debated economic power of the orders and the secular Church.

In particular, one of these parts of the Church, the feminine orders, has been largely neglected as a subject of serious historical research. Apart from brief references or general statements as to their character, there are still few objective studies about these institutions which are not tinted by paternalis-tic—or maternalistic—condescension. Perhaps the fact that they were popu-lated by cloistered women, coupled with the notion that these women could not have had much influence on society, contributed to the lack of interest in nunneries. We are now discovering that much of the flavor and meaningful nuances of colonial society lies not only in the lives and activities of the eminent, important as they are, but can also be found among its previously assumed dull or unimportant people.[1]

I will then, in this new spirit of curiosity about the relatively unexplored aspects of ecclesiastic history, present a survey of the socioeconomic role of the feminine orders in eighteenth-century New Spain. This is neither 100 percent ecclesiastic history nor 100 percent feminine history, since only a sector of colonial women and a part of the Church are here represented. It is, in part, a survey of the economic importance of the feminine orders, and, in part, a study of a group of women as members of a social institution: the Church. It deals with two main questions: in what way can a group of secluded women reflect their society; and how can such presumably pious and detached establishments influence the economy of the capital of the wealthiest Spanish possession in America?

Although not claiming to have a definitive answer to these questions, I will start with the premise that nunneries, as institutions, went beyond the merely religious and were more than refuges for devoted women who wished to pursue a religious life. From a social point of view they mirrored the society in which they flourished, and they played the role which they were expected to perform. From an economic point of view, they participated quite actively in New Spain's economic development and contributed to its shaping to a degree which has perhaps been suspected, but which has not been properly gauged.

I

Spanish tradition in the sixteenth century assigned a rather restricted social role to women.[2] However, women had a well-defined and powerful role within the family, as mothers and preservers of the moral order.[3] This role they continued to perform in Spanish America. One of the most important tasks of women within the family was to transmit the principles of religion to the progeny. Women, as mothers, aided the Church in this task, and were closely associated to religious activities, which constituted an important part of their social activities.

The close association of women and the Church during the colonial period, and even after independence, had some interesting implications which have not received the scholarly attention which they deserve. From their earliest years, women attended church, daily or weekly, heard sermons which set moral guidelines for their lives, were confessed and advised quite frequently, and consulted their parish priests for all the important decisions in their lives. For those able to read, the most likely readings were devotional books. Altogether, the Church had a great impact on women and must have contributed to a very large extent in the molding of their attitudes, self-concepts, and behavior.

It is not surprising that many women chose to live their lives in convents, where they expected to be protected from wordly imperfections and to be free to pursue the ideals set up by their Catholic faith. There were, however, other aspects to life in a convent, in addition to those purely religious. Not only were convents centers of spirituality, but they also had material concerns as institutions which needed income to survive. In order to insure this income, they established a net of properties and investments which gave them a stake in the development of the economy. Social values set rules as to which kinds of women might profess, and social pressures persuaded many to do so.

As with their male counterparts, the place of Spanish women in colonial society was directly related to their political role as conquerors, and their ethnic origins, as a tiny group of white people in a world of conquered Indians. White women, whether the original Spaniards from the peninsula, or later the creoles (born in America of Spanish descent), enjoyed a high position in the social complex, as wives, mothers, or relatives of the conquistadors and their children. The fact that these women were legally dependent on their husbands or fathers did not diminish their status in society.

The scarcity of Spanish women during the initial period of conquest and settlement led most male Spaniards to mix freely with Indian women. Out of this contact, a new racial group was created: the *mestizo,* already an important social element at the end of the sixteenth century. The addition of black slaves added to the process of miscegenation and contributed to the formation of a truly heterogeneous society. Since usually the first and second generations of *mestizos* were born out of wedlock, the concept of illegitimacy was added to that of racial mixture.[4]

In order to maintain its social supremacy, the group of descendants of the conquistadors, which always remained numerically inferior, preserved a legal concept of racial superiority expressed as *limpieza de sangre,* or lack of blemish by mixture with other races. To this it added the concept of religious purity, which made of old Christians (*cristianos viejos*) a privileged group, in contrast with new Christians, those recently converted to the Catholic faith.[5]

The preservation of that privileged social status depended upon marriage between persons considered equals. Any union with elements of doubtful racial or even religious origin could endanger the social status of the family. For this reason, the marriage of women of Spanish descent received a great deal of consideration and thought from the Spanish political and spiritual leaders. From the sixteenth century marriages were regulated by royal orders and social pressure. Young people were subject to paternal authority until age twenty-five, and religious influence buttressed paternal and royal influence.[6] The persuasive character of royal legislation throughout the seventeenth and early eighteenth centuries hardened into the royal *Pragmática* of 1776, which legislated policies concerning marriages.[7] The *Pragmática* aimed at preventing marriages among unequal parties by punishing with legal deprivation of family and personal rights (such as the right to inheritance) persons who contravened parental dissent in a marriage arrangement, even after age twenty-five. On the other hand, marriage partners were entitled to challenge in court any unreasonable parental dissent, as long as they were of equal or similar social status. This provision tried to prevent unfair coercion from parents.

These rules regulating marriages were intended to protect women, rather than men, since women were thought to be weaker and more endangered by the temptations of the world. The wish to preserve the purity of women, and thus that of the family and the race, moved religious and lay leaders to promote social devices aimed at ensuring the status of women. These devices benefited mostly those of the upper social and ethnic ladder. The two most effective schemes to protect women were: the dowry, which ensured marriage *inter pares;* and the foundation of institutions, such as *beaterios* and nunneries, where honest women could take refuge and resist the temptations, real or presumed, of a pioneer and still unstable society.[8]

Dowries were required from any woman of social distinction whenever she "took state" (*tomar estado*), and all women were expected to take state; that is, to marry or to profess, since spinsterhood was ill-regarded.[9] If a woman did not take the state of matrimony, her alternative was to retire from the world, living as a dependent or protegée in the extended family of a relative, or by becoming a *beata* or a nun. Very few women, especially in the higher classes, had the option of being single and independent, since the traditional roles of women in society were enforced more firmly among the upper classes.

It would be misleading, however, to believe that the Spanish tradition of married home life for women was rigidly enforced in all cases, and that most upper-class women were confined to the menial occupations of housekeeping, or the leisured life of a well-staffed household. There was a special class of women, the property-owners, urban or rural, often mature women, who wielded a great deal of power within their circles, especially if they were widowed. Widowhood conferred on women a great deal of independence, legal and social, since a widowed woman was unlikely to return to the paternal house, and instead became the head of her own household. There were numerous widowed farm-owners (*labradoras*) who, although using over-seers to run their properties, held ultimate control over their often valuable ranches and *haciendas.* Women also owned sugar mills and urban businesses, such as wine stores, wax and cigar factories, and printing houses.[10] Thus, although the prevalent concept of femininity pointed to marriage, mother-hood, and housekeeping as the destiny of women, there was a certain margin for other activities under special circumstances. Those women who found themselves in a position to make use of this margin did not fit the more common stereotype of wife or nun. Women of the lower classes had, per force, a more independent life than their wealthier counterparts. Economic neces-sity pushed them to do some work out of their homes: in the fields, if they were peasants; or domestic work, the sale of clothes and food, if they lived in the cities. However, these menial tasks were performed almost exclusively by Indians and mixed-bloods. Many of the poor white women seem to have found occupations (such as that of seamstress or teacher of girls) which they could perform in their own homes and still maintain a certain amount of "dignity."[11]

Whether or not women could gain a certain degree of freedom in their social class, it was still generally agreed that they should "take state." When women were ready to take state, whether in religion or marriage, arrange-ments for a dowry were required from those in good social standing. Marriage dowries could consist of cash or goods, and the amount was determined by the family's status and financial circumstances. A dowry of three hundred pesos for an orphan, and presumably poor, girl was regarded as acceptable. Women in higher social strata usually brought much larger sums as dowries. Several thousand pesos was a common sum for daughters of governmental employees or aspiring professionals. The daughters of rich merchants or members of the nobility had dowries which were not unusually above ten thousand pesos. In the seventeenth century, it was also common enough for the family of the bride to buy a governmental post for the future son-in-law. Such posts could cost as much as seventy thousand pesos.[12] In cities other than the capital, dowries could be of more modest proportions and could consist, partly, in property or goods. For example, in the isolated northern province of New León, in the middle of the seventeenth century, a woman might bring a dowry in cash and goods such as clothes, metal bars, slaves, and furniture, which were just as useful as money in a pioneering society. In this area cash dowries were rarely larger than three thousand pesos.[13]

Toward the end of the sixteenth century, numerous rich patrons had already created special dowry foundations to provide orphan women who were descendants of Spanish conquistadors with adequate sums of money for their marriages. These dowries, of a minimum of three hundred pesos, purported to insure acceptable husbands for these women. The essential prerequisite for the allocation and receipt of these dowries were legitimacy of birth and *limpieza de sangre*. The candidates had to be Spaniards (a term which came to mean white, and not a person born in Spain), and poor. In this manner, the obstacle of poverty was to be eliminated while the sense of racial and social elitism was preserved.[14]

The notion that the best place for women was home also supported the creation of *beaterios* and nunneries. If the social enclosure of marriage was lacking, it could be substituted by religious enclosure, in which the woman contracted a spiritual marriage with Jesus Christ.[15] *Beaterios* were voluntary religious associations of women (*beatas*) who did not profess in convents, but who took simple vows of enclosure, virginity, and poverty. *Beaterios* did not require dowries and their members were often, although not necessarily, poor, and lived on alms and the making of sweets and clothes. These institutions required the approval of civil and religious authorities. The latter provided them with spiritual directors to confess the *beatas* and perform mass for them. *Beaterios* offered an alternative to profession to those devout women who could not afford to profess in a convent, for lack of a dowry or lack of a nearby convent. *Beaterios* also offered shelter to unmarried women or widows who did not wish to remarry. It is significant, for example, that already in 1599, in a distant and still largely unorganized pioneering community such as New León, there was interest in the foundation of a *beaterio* where women could live until they married, or remain, if they so preferred.[16] There were numerous *beaterios* throughout Mexico during the colonial period. Many were founded by women themselves; others by priests, bishops, or concerned lay patrons. Many of these *beaterios* evolved into nunneries when they found wealthy patrons who underwrote the costs of a building and sustenance for the community.[17]

Nunneries were regarded as socially and spiritually superior to *beaterios*.

Their members took formal religious vows, which made them affidavit members of the Church and gave them a different status before the law and a distinctive and rather privileged social status. The first nunnery of New Spain was founded about 1540, with nuns of the Conceptionist order brought from Spain for the purpose of teaching Indian women.[18] However, throughout its history of over three hundred years, La Concepción, like most of the nunneries founded in colonial Mexico, did not have the education of Indians, or education *per se,* as its primary purpose. Moreover, the contemplative character of Mexican nunneries precluded any hospital or socially oriented work by the nuns. Nunneries became centers of spirituality which, from a religious point of view, emphasized seclusion and the salvation of the soul.

From a social point of view they also fulfilled that role which was deemed so necessary at the time of their foundation: shelter for unprotected women. Many of the founders of convents throughout the colonial period mention the social purpose of the foundation more frequently than the purely religious. Although society was not new any longer in the seventeenth and eighteenth centuries, the rigidity of the class structure remained largely unchanged, and contributed to the preservation of social attitudes about the undesirability of unequal marriages and the positive benefits of institutions where women could profess and be secure.

Sister Mary Gallagher, in a recent doctoral dissertation, examined the major motivating forces behind the foundation of feminine orders in colonial Mexico. She indicated that great emphasis was put on the social problem of unmarriageable women who would be living in the world under conditions thought to be potentially dangerous to their honor.[19] Although not all the convents established in Mexico had the specific purpose of offering shelter to unmarried, often undowered, women, most of those founded in the sixteenth century did, and this purpose is frequently repeated in the seventeenth and eighteenth centuries.[20] There were at least seventeen convents founded from the end of the sixteenth century to the end of the eighteenth century, for which the patrons or founders stated their purposes as being to offer a safe place for retreat to orphans and the unmarried, or to aid poor white girls who could not afford a dowry to profess. Another significant fact is that sixteen convents were founded or directly promoted by widows or single women who wished to help other women withdraw from the world or find fulfillment in religion. Two other convents were founded by young and very rich orphans who themselves professed.[21]

Colonial society acknowledged the validity of such motivations. Many pious individuals acted as patrons of convents with the sincere belief that they were performing a socially and religiously desirable deed. The concept that society had a distinct responsibility for the establishment of nunneries is also reflected in the legal procedure required for the foundations in the eighteenth century. The personal desire of the prospective founders was not considered sufficient to warrant the creation of a new convent. Other religious orders, the *Cabildo* (town government), the leading citizens, and even the Viceregal opinion, were required. The financial resources of the founder and the supporting town people had to be disclosed, and to be judged competent, in order to insure the economic well-being of the convent and to prevent it from becoming a social burden.[22]

The usual dowry for a professing nun was two thousand pesos in the late sixteenth century; three thousand pesos during most of the seventeenth century, and four thousand pesos from the 1730s onward. These sums were not as high as those provided by the very rich to their daughters, but they were still above the reach of most of the poorer members of society. Whether a religious dowry was "cheaper" than a marriage dowry depended on the number of girls in the family, its financial situation, and its social status. An aspiring but ill-paid government official might have trouble providing attractive marriage dowries for all his daughters and might have thought of a convent as a desirable alternative. On the other hand, easy generalizations on this topic should not be made, since a religious profession was not cheap either. In addition to the required dowry, a novice had to provide for her living expenses prior to profession, and for the expenses of profession itself, which in some convents ran into the thousands of pesos. The parents of wealthy nuns also provided an additional sum of money called *reserva*, which, lent out at 5 percent by the convent, provided the nun with an extra income for additional comforts in the convent. It was also common for nuns to own their own cell, which could cost from several hundred to several thousand pesos. Thus, it cannot be said that to have a daughter professing in a convent was a means of avoiding the arrangement of a possibly large marriage dowry.

In the late seventeenth century and throughout the eighteenth century, many nuns came from wealthy families; others from families of bureaucrats and merchants who could afford the dowry and expenses involved. The examination of available records seems to suggest that in the late sixteenth century and throughout the middle of the seventeenth century, there were more nuns who came from less than well-to-do families, and who required the help of patrons in order to provide their dowries. In the late seventeenth century, and in the eighteenth century, there are fewer cases, especially in Mexico City, of outright necessity being mentioned as a motivating factor for profession. In her study of two convents in the eighteenth century, a rich one in the provincial city of Querétaro, and an Indian one in Mexico City, Sister Gallagher has concluded that only 10 percent of the nuns could be classified as coming from poor families. This conclusion suggests that although convents continued to be regarded as places of shelter for women in the eighteenth century, there were fewer economic motivations for profession than in previous centuries. The fact that more nuns were from wealthy families, stresses economic in addition to social elitism.[23]

Thus, profession could be a socially acceptable and personally desirable option for a woman, but it could also pose a formidable economic obstacle for those of limited means. As a result, pious patronage of religious foundations for women and endowments for nuns remained a popular and desirable aim throughout the colonial period.[24] Capuchine and Discalced orders were assumed to take young women without dowries, but they had only a limited number of vacancies available for undowered novices. They did not turn down those novices who brought dowries. The expenses of undowered novices in these, and convents of other orders had to be insured before they professed. Although patrons were not lacking, aspirants always outnumbered the available places.[25]

In addition to providing dowries, women desiring to profess had to meet other requirements which restricted the number of those who would be acceptable for religious life. In order to profess, a novice had to be of perfect Spanish ancestry and born within wedlock. Her certificate of birth, where her race was stated, and the notarized statement of several witnesses were required as supporting evidence. These requirements eliminated the chances of professing for women of some remote Jewish ancestry and for all Indians and mixed bloods.[26] In a society which was mostly composed of Indians and mixed bloods, these requirements turned the convents into elitist institutions, accessible only to a very thin layer of colonial society.

The question of legitimacy could be and was ignored in the case of many aspirants who were backed by families of good social standing. Girls of irregular birth were usually foundlings who had been raised by well-to-do families. Sometimes it was known that their father had been a captain or other high official who had been involved in a not too uncommon youthful relationship prior to marriage. These girls had their "defect of birth" absolved by the religious authorities and were permitted to profess.[27] However, the racial exclusivism of the feminine convents was never or rarely relaxed. Although some of the earliest convents had presumably been founded for teaching Indian girls, Indians were excluded from most convents, including some founded by Indians themselves. Indians, male and female, were regarded as neophytes, too recently converted to take holy orders. Undoubtedly, there was also a considerable amount of racial prejudice among white people. The policy of exclusion set in the sixteenth century persisted throughout the seventeenth century. It was not until 1724 that a convent designed exclusively for Indian women was founded in Mexico City. Although it had its bad times and it was never wealthy, it survived and spread to the provinces.[28] Even in this convent the handful of white nuns who were brought in to organize it attempted to take over the government of the community under allegations that the Indians were not capable of ruling themselves or carrying a proper religious life. The protests of the Indian nuns and several of their protectors prompted an investigation which resulted in the transfer of the white nuns to several other convents. No further white novices were ever admitted in this convent.[29]

It must be remarked that Indians practiced racial and social exclusivism in their convents, as much as the whites did in theirs. They did not admit any aspirants who were not full-blooded Indians of the *cacique* or principal class. *Caciques* were the nobility among the Indians, who were excluded from the payment of personal taxes which other Indians and mixed-bloods had to pay. Principal families were those wealthy and highly regarded among Indians themselves. Indians of the lower classes, employed in manual occupations or domestic services, had very slim chances of placing their daughters in the convents for Indians. The reason given by the convent of Corpus Christi for this policy was similar to that of the white convents; that only the best candidates were fit to become the brides of Jesus Christ.[30]

*Castas,* as mixed-bloods were known, had absolutely no chance of professing as nuns during colonial times, or even after independence. There was an intense feeling of prejudice against these members of society, despite, or perhaps because of the fact that they composed a significant stratum of the inhabitants of the urban centers. Socially, they were regarded as too low to follow religious life in any convent. The most they could hope for was to become servants in the convent. Blacks were barred from profession also. Free black women were sometimes employed as servants. The convents also owned black slaves for the service of the community and nuns were allowed to own slaves for their service.[31]

The previous statements about the social character of many foundations of convents, and the social values involved in accepting candidates for profession, do not rule out the consideration of religious vocation as a very important motivation for profession. During the seventeenth and eighteenth centuries many girls were placed in convents by their parents or guardians and raised by a nun, frequently a relative, who acted as instructor and moral guide. Many pious mothers placed their daughters in convents with the clear hope that they would become "inclined to the religious state."[32] It was quite natural for many women raised in convents to regard the cloisters as their home and wish to profess in order to remain in a world which offered them security and distinctive spiritual rewards.

Girls who were raised at home and wished to profess had received very strong religious upbringing. They frequently had aunts or cousins professed as nuns, or male relatives as members of the orders or the secular Church, and felt a natural familiarity with religious life. In many instances, women made a decision to profess after the death of their mother or father, when the emotional vacuum left by the personal loss could only be filled by religion. There were also a considerable number of widows who professed after their husband's death. Religiosity, thus, was a very strong factor in profession, but in view of other important evidence pointing to social circumstances, as well, it would be misleading to think that religiosity alone motivated all professions. Social, personal, and religious factors were intimately bound into the process of choosing a religious life. Nonetheless, it should be stressed that the peculiar socioeconomic setting of colonial Mexico made the call of vocation accessible to only a few chosen ones.

## II

In addition to being places where some women fulfilled their religious vocation and where others found an acceptable way of life, nunneries have often been cited as the centers of feminine education throughout colonial times. Convents received girls of good families for their education. Since girls allowed to stay in the convents for this purpose were of similar ethnic and social background as the nuns, it can be stated that only a small minority of women received the benefits of convent education. For example, in a description of the Bishopric of Michoacán at the end of the eighteenth century it is stated that the nunneries of the city received many "noble girls" for their education. The adjective "noble," in the context of colonial society, implied girls of socially acceptable families.[33]

The education obtained by the girls who were interned in convents was imparted by the nuns themselves and, ultimately, its quality depended on the knowledge of the nuns, and on the accepted standards of feminine education of the times. These standards were rather low. Women were not supposed to need much learning, and this precluded the teaching of any subject which went beyond their assumed lower intellectual capacity and social requirements. Girls placed at the nunneries learned how to read and write and were also trained in such "womanly arts" as sewing, embroidering, and cooking. [34]

Despite the limited horizons of feminine education, it is surprising to find that many nuns, and some other women, were well educated for their times, although they received little credit for it. Many nuns knew Latin for the services, although it is possible that many knew just enough for this purpose, since it is known that they could be exempted from learning it. Many of them were trained in music, either to sing or to play instruments, and performed in convent celebrations. In fact, many poor girls learned a musical instrument in the hope of earning their entrance into a convent as musicians, with a lowered dowry or none at all. Some other nuns developed a remarkable ability with numbers and accounting, since all convents needed the services of accountants for keeping the records of internal expenses. At times, a group of nuns took over the revision of the finances of their convents and did much better than their majordomos.[35]

Although the majority of women who received any recognition for their intellectual achievements during the colonial period were professed nuns, not many of them had their works printed. The situation is similar for the several distinguished lay women who wrote poetry and devotional works.[36] There are numerous unpublished manuscripts written by nuns, mostly of pious character: biographies, spiritual confessions of their inner life, books of prayer and religious exercises, and sometimes short theatrical pieces of a religious character. Among these can be cited, as an example, the collection of letters of Sister Sebastiana Josepha de la S.S. Trinidad, a nun of the San Juan de la Penitencia convent in Mexico City, whose life was praised as an example of religiosity by two preachers.[37] Her letters and poems reflect an anguished world where her own religiosity seems to offer little happiness or consolation. Her style reveals that she had read Saint Teresa, the Spanish mystic, and it might be that the literary orientation of the times stressed the struggle within the soul rather than the contentment of achievement.

Another unpublished biography is that of Sister María Marcela, a Capuchine nun in Querétaro, who professed in 1778. The serenity and elegance of this biography contrasts strongly with the writings of Sister Sebastiana Josepha, and speaks of an intelligent and well-educated woman. Another manuscript represents yet a different expression of the literary abilities of some nuns. It is a short theatrical piece, a *Coloquio* or dialogue among several virtues and symbolic figures, composed by a nun of Santa Teresa la Antigua for the profession of her protegée. However, the largest number of works written by nuns remain almost unknown, and we only hear of their existence through references in erudite bibliographies.[38] It seems that most nuns were encouraged to write by their confessors and their works are concerned with their spiritual experiences, the history of their institutions, and accounts of religious events of their times. Thus, most of the manuscripts deal with the lives of other nuns, the life of Christ, the Virgin and the saints, novenas, etc. Although the literary merits of these works might not be great, they are evidence that some learning and a basic education were accessible to women who professed.

Several nuns saw their work published. Sister María de Santa Clara, a Franciscan nun, published *Subida al Monte de Mhirra* in 1747.[39] This is a book of spiritual exercises and meditations upon the sufferings of Christ; it purported to help the nuns achieve religious excellence. Sister Maria Anna A. de San Ignacio wrote several books which eventually were gathered into one volume entitled *Devociones* (1758), published by the Bishop of Puebla.[40] Devotional in character, it is nevertheless well written, and shows the influence of the Spanish mystic writers of the sixteenth century.

The best-known writer nun of the colonial period was Sister Juana Inés de la Cruz, poet, playwright, author of essays on religious and worldly topics. Her literary achievements were not surpassed by any male writer throughout the colonial period. She is still regarded as one of the most outstanding women writers produced in Spanish America and in her time she was called the Ninth Muse. Sister Juana (1648–95) was born in a modest family and was mostly self-educated. After a debut in the Viceregal court, which she earned for her intellectual brilliance and not her social position, she lived for a few years in the midst of comfort and public approval. Then, rather suddenly, she "abandoned the world" and decided to profess. It has been suggested that only in a convent could she achieve an independent life as a writer, and she herself made this assertion, adding that she felt a disinclination for the state of marriage. However, since it has been discovered that she was born out of wedlock, it is possible that this fact contributed to her decision, since her "defect of birth" and her lack of family relations made her life in court potentially difficult.

Her literary career was not interrupted by her profession. In fact, she enjoyed the highest regard among her intellectual contemporaries. Only toward the end of her life, and under the influence of her confessors and several religious authorities, did she give up writing and turn to an ascetic practice of religion. Her *Complete Works* were published in 1714, and include courtly and love poems, lyrics for lay and religious songs, sonnets, lay and religious plays, and some devotional exercises. One of her best prose works is an autobiographical letter, *Respuesta a Sor Filotea de la Cruz*, in which she made a case for her right to write and study and for the right of all women to be educated.[41]

This brief survey of the known writings of several nuns suggests that many of them were better educated than has been thought, especially since none of the nunneries of Mexico possessed a library and none can be cited as a center of learning where members were encouraged to pursue any kind of scholarly studies. A large degree of self-motivation must explain the existence of these educated nuns.[42] Much of this personal knowledge could have been passed on to the girls who inhabited the convents. It may reasonably be conjectured that such intelligent nuns would attempt to instruct the girls under their tutelage. However, the education of these girls depended greatly on a very personal relationship with the nuns, a situation of a certain haphazard nature which can scarcely be construed as a formal system of education on the part of the convents. Available records give evidence that there were very few organized schools within the nunneries.

Many of the non-professing girls entered the convents as pupils of the nuns for several years; others stayed for shorter periods, left there by widowed parents or legal guardians until they made a decision about their future. The number of girls in convents was never very large, judging by the sparse figures available, especially if we think in terms of how many girls of school age there must have been in the capital city at any given time.[43] The presence of girls was systematically opposed by many religious authorities. There are several records of the invectives of the Franciscan prelates against the acceptance of girls in convents.[44] Ecclesiastic authorities also complained about the worldly character of many convents (especially those of the Conceptionist order), which they attributed to the presence of servants and girls. The situation went unheeded for most of the colonial period until, as part of a general movement of reform of convent life, girls were banned from the convents in 1774.[45]

As this ruling was carried out, it became apparent that many of the so-called *niñas* (girls) were not as tender in age as this name might have suggested. Many of them were well over twenty years old, an age in those days which was almost too late for marriage. The archbishop of Mexico reported that out of 474 girls living in the nunneries under his jurisdiction, it had been possible to return to their parents, or to intern in other suitable educational institutions, some 265 of them. However, for a large number of the rest, it was found necessary to permit them to remain in the convents, due to their lack of resources or advanced age. The Franciscan prelates also reported that some very old *niñas* had to be allowed to remain in their convents.[46] These women had probably entered the convents in their youth and had neither professed nor married, but remained there as protegées of the nuns.

The banning of girls from the convents was ill-regarded by many parents who preferred a convent to a school for their daughters. However, in the 1770s many lay schools were being founded all over New Spain, opening their doors to girls of all social classes. In addition, a teaching order had been brought to the viceroyalty. These schools were already carrying out the task of educating women in a more thorough manner than the feminine orders. Although the ban on the reception of girls in the convents was lifted in 1796, the importance of convents as educational centers did not increase.[47] In general, it can be stated that the influence of nunneries on feminine education was rather limited since they only reached a very select minority of colonial women.

The only feminine order which fulfilled an important educational role was the Order of Mary, better known as La Enseñanza. This was the only teaching order established in New Spain and the only order which formally trained nuns as teachers. It was introduced in Mexico by the heiress of a very rich family, Sister María Ignacia Azlor y Echevers, of the family of the Counts of Aguayo. After the death of her parents, María Ignacia professed in Spain in 1745. For years she negotiated the approval of the transfer of this educational order to Mexico. Eventually she succeeded in obtaining royal approval and established the Order of Mary in Mexico City, opening the school in 1753.[48] There was a private school attended by girls who paid for their education, but La Enseñanza also opened a public school for girls of all social classes, and the demand was so great that the teaching nuns were almost unable to cope with the number of applicants. The teaching included reading, writing, arithmetic, elements of natural science, and some European history.[49] The Order of Mary was extended to the provinces at the end of the century. Two other convent-schools were founded in Irapuato and Aguascalientes in 1800 and 1804 respectively.[50]    .

### III

It is evident that since their inception, feminine orders in colonial Mexico had a very specific role to play in their society, and were tied by reason of their social connections to the ruling minority of the viceroyalty. In the first half of the seventeenth century many nunneries in Mexico City and in the provinces passed through economic crises due to their poor administration. However, many found wealthy patrons who endowed them handsomely and provided them with the necessary capital to heal their losses. By the middle of that century, there was a well-established situation in which the majority of the nunneries were under the wing of what we might call the PPPs, the pious powerful patrons, who had not only contributed to the founding of many convents, or to the endowment of ones already in existence, but who had also entrusted to them many of their own relatives. Although these ties with the wealthy still did not guarantee the administrative efficiency of nunneries, it did guarantee them a continuous replenishment of their funds, and the moral support of the "establishment" from which most of their professed members were drawn.

The feminine orders were, essentially, urban institutions, but they established very strong economic connections with property-owners, not only in the capital itself, but in the agricultural areas adjacent to Mexico City. A similar process took place in the provinces. This relationship was set through the economic device of the lien (*censo*) and later through loans (*depositos*).[51] Basically, these were mortgages and loans which the convents extended to property-owners, since the latter suffered from a chronic shortage of capital funds. These loans and mortgages paid a 5 percent interest to the convent, and provided a significant percentage of their income. Nunneries also received numerous gifts from patrons, and a constant supply of capital in the form of dowries of the professing nuns.

On examining the lists of liens and loans of several of the leading convents of Mexico City from 1680 through 1800, the most striking fact one notices is that they were in the hands of a rather small segment of society: landowners, merchants, a few wealthy priests, widows, and several masculine orders (largely the Jesuits and the Dominicans). In the case of liens, the relationship with property-owners who had mortgaged their houses and land is understandable. It is in the list of loans where the association of the feminine orders with the socioeconomic elite becomes more evident. Large loans of ten or twenty thousand pesos or more were requested and obtained, indicating that some nunneries were already quite rich at the end of the seventeenth century, and had established a well-recognized position as a source of capital, which was eagerly sought by property-owners and merchants.[52]

Those in the lists of borrowers formed a closely knit group of entrepreneurs who supported each other as bondsmen and requested loans when their friends returned money. A large number of them were captains, lieutenants, knighted gentlemen, members of the governmental bureaucracy, merchants, silver dealers, and a rather small number of qualified women. Widows of rich men, women with houses or land, and a few members of rich families were the women to whom the convents lent money. It was to the members of these socioeconomic groups that the nunneries primarily channelled their financial resources, although not exclusively. Since these people were the usual patrons of the feminine orders and the parents of the nuns in them, this relationship constituted a circle of mutual benefit.

There was little change in the social aspect of this relationship throughout the eighteenth century. However, the character of the investment of the nunneries changed significantly in this century. Liens decreased in volume while loans increased, and both were replaced by urban real estate as the major source of income for the majority of the convents in the capital. The process of cancellation of liens started quite early in the eighteenth century and continued uninterruptedly throughout it. Not only did lay owners cancel liens on their properties whenever possible, but the convents themselves made a point of doing so with the liens on their properties.[53] An excellent example is provided by the powerful convent of La Concepción, which had a list of 110 liens in 1683. At the end of the eighteenth century it had only six perpetual and thirteen redeemable liens.[54] In the case of the convent of La Encarnación, which still appears to have had a large investment in liens at the end of the eighteenth century (129,000 pesos), this situation is explained by the existence of one large lien of 100,000 pesos held on the entailed property of the powerful Villanueva family, which, no doubt, could not afford to cancel it.[55] Not all the convents of Mexico reduced the number of their liens as drastically as La Concepción. In fact, some continued to depend heavily on the income of liens and loans. However, those convents are the exception rather than the rule.

The notion that clerical liens were a heavy burden on rural properties in colonial Mexico (as in the rest of Spanish America), is based on solid documentary evidence. Undoubtedly, at the end of the eighteenth century a large number of properties were encumbered by clerical liens. However, it must be borne in mind that the term lien is broadly applied to any kind of clerical encumbrance: be it a chantry, a pious donation for masses, a dowry, etc. The information provided by the accounts and reports of the feminine convents seems to support the affirmation that, for the nunneries by the end of the colonial period, the lien was an economic remnant of the past, a form of investment rapidly falling into disuse. The lack of direct control over the fate of the lien once granted, despite legal guarantees on behalf of the convents, might have discouraged nunneries from further investments. As liens passed from one property-owner to another, and other liens were added to the same property, the investment became more risky and the chances of default in the payment of interest greater. When this happened, convents became involved in long litigations which could last for years and which did not always guarantee the return of the capital. The loss of the capital of many liens in the seventeenth century and throughout the eighteenth century was quite frequent and enough money was lost by the convents to warrant a change of investment policy.[56]

The gradual cancellation of liens provided the convents with fresh capital to invest in loans or the purchase of houses, although it should not be forgotten that dowries continued to provide a sizable share of the convents' incoming capital. Loans remained secondary to house-ownership as a form of investment, but they were important indicators of the relationship of the nunneries with the elite of colonial society. The capital invested in loans was not fixed at any time. It fluctuated from year to year, as loans were returned and reinvested, or used for another purpose. However, it can be stated that they provided between 10 percent and 30 percent of the income of the majority of the convents of Mexico City.

As loans grew more important, there was an increasing tendency, especially among the wealthiest convents, to grant larger loans to fewer people. In other words, there was a trend toward the concentration of loans in the hands of the powerful social elite mentioned earlier. The examples of the convents of Jesús María and La Encarnación will illustrate this point. In 1724 Jesús María had 43 names in its list of loans, having lent 178,020 pesos. Fourteen borrowers (32.5 percent) received loans amounting to 84,700 pesos (47 percent of the total). The accounts of 1756 record 24 loans for 146,500 pesos. Seven borrowers (29 percent) held 89,000 pesos (60 percent). In 1763 the convent lent 106,000 pesos to one merchant, a truly Gargantuan loan for any institution in those days. By 1795, the convent had only 34 borrowers, having lent 309,500 pesos. Of these, 53 percent held 89 percent of the total sum lent. Three of these loans amounted to more than 100,000 pesos and were granted to a large landowner and two members of the nobility.[57]

Throughout the eighteenth century, La Encarnación lent between 54 and 71 percent of its money to between about 22 percent of its borrowers, in loans which not infrequently ranged between 40,000 and 98,000 pesos. The recipients, as in the case of Jesús María, were rich mine-owners and landowners, and wholesale merchants.[58] This convent was one of the richest and best administered in the viceroyalty. Since the 1750s the sister-accountants had left written guides for the better management of convent funds. One of the shrewdest of these accountants, Sister María Micaela de la Encarnación, advised extreme caution on loans. She preferred loans with houses as collateral, rather than *haciendas,* whose owners tended to exaggerate the value of their property; the houses should be in the good neighborhoods of the city, and not in the poor boroughs. However, the safest loans in her opinion were those placed with merchants of well-known fortune and in good standing.[59] Doubtless, Sister Micaela's advice reflects the policy not only of her convent, but of similarly rich and powerful institutions.

The economic association of the merchants and the nuns was a loyal and long-lasting one, stretching from the last decade of the seventeenth century to the first decade of the nineteenth century. Punctuality in repayment and business reliability on the part of the merchants inclined the feminine convents to grant their numerous requests for loans.[60] Since after the enactment of the decree of free trade in 1778 many merchants rechannelled their capital to agriculture, much of the wealth of the feminine orders went to benefit a social and economic class which defies classification: merchant-landowners, miner-hacendados and noble-latifundistas.[61] But it all amounted to an association of the rich and the privileged, which perpetuated the power of the top social classes of this highly stratified society.

Despite the social and economic importance of the loans, few convents relied entirely on this kind of investment. In fact, urban real estate became the favorite form of investment of the feminine orders of the capital in the eighteenth century. In the seventeenth century, convents did not own many houses. There seems to have been a general lack of interest in the acquisition of urban real estate. Though many convents owned houses, the sales of these properties equaled their purchases, and the number of their houses did not increase. The costs implied in the maintenance of houses might have discouraged such investments at a time when most nunneries in the capital were ill-administered and involved in a constant struggle to straighten their accounts. In 1670, La Encarnación listed 1,982 pesos as the income from its houses. Since the normal rent charged was 5 percent of the value of the house, this figure would indicate property worth 39,640 pesos. But in the same year, the convent had 171,200 pesos in liens.[62]

Toward the end of the seventeenth century, convents started to purchase houses or retain others acquired through litigation. It is difficult to determine any fixed date for this change of policy of investments, but there is no doubt about the change. By 1714, La Concepción had acquired or was building urban holdings worth 157,140 pesos.[63] As for La Encarnación, the convent claimed an income of 11,043 pesos from its property in 1708.[64] The value of such property must have been over 200,000 pesos in order to yield that income. By 1744 the majority of the convents of Mexico City derived the largest share of their income from urban real estate. (See Table 1.) Twelve out of seventeen convents obtained between 52 and 89 percent of their income from their houses, and among them were the leading convents of La Encarnación (67 percent), Jesús María (65 percent) and La Concepción (59.5 percent).

Table 1. Assets of the feminine orders of Mexico City in 1744

| | Houses (Pesos) | Percent | Liens (Pesos) | Percent | Loans (Pesos) | Percent | Total (Pesos) |
|---|---|---|---|---|---|---|---|
| Santa Catalina de Sena | 356,640 | 87.6 | 44,040 | 10.9 | 6,300 | 1.5 | 406,980 |
| Santa Inés | 148,400 | 89.2 | 17,800 | 10.8 | | | 166,200 |
| Santa Isabel | 223,410 | 61.7 | 36,400 | 10.0 | 102,750 | 28.3 | 362,560 |
| San Gerónimo | 442,540 | 85.4 | 56,760 | 11.1 | 18,400 | 3.3 | 517,700 |
| San Juan de la Penitencia | 32,300 | 10.8 | 60,656 | 20.2 | 206,636 | 69.0 | 299,593 |
| San Lorenzo | 204,740 | 52.3 | 77,505 | 19.9 | 108,600 | 27.8 | 390,845 |
| Corpus Christi | No information | | | | | | |
| San José de Gracia | 187,200 | 52.2 | 45,140 | 15.0 | 69,900 | 23.0 | 302,240 |
| La Concepción | 511,480 | 59.7 | 146,620 | 17.0 | 199,620 | 23.3 | 857,720 |
| Santa Clara | 240,000 | 38.9 | 11,213 | 18.1 | 264,450 | 43.0 | 615,663 |
| Capuchines of San Felipe de Jesús | | | | | | | 9,000 |
| Regina Celi | 181,060 | 51.0 | 76,635 | 21.6 | 68,820 | 19.4 | 326,515 |

| | | | | | | | |
|---|---|---|---|---|---|---|---|
| Santa Teresa la Nueva | 12,960 | 9.9 | | | (118,460)[a] | 90.1 | 131,420 |
| Santa Teresa la Antigua | 215,440 | 82.7 | 45,100 | 17.3 | | | 260,540 |
| La Encarnación | 567,380 | 65.1 | 203,670 | 23.4 | 101,000 | 11.5 | 872,050 |
| San Bernardo | 77,200 | 21.7 | 68,356 | 19.2 | 210,591 | 59.1 | 356,147 |
| | | | | | | | 31,915[b] |
| Balvanera | 307,820 | 76.9 | 42,200 | 10.5 | 50,560 | 12.6 | 400,580 |
| Jesús María | 493,760 | 67.0 | 118,680 | 16.1 | 124,100 | 16.9 | 736,540 |
| TOTAL[c] | 4,202,330 | 60.0 | 1,150,775 | 16.4 | 1,531,727 | 21.8 | 7,044,208 |

*Source:* Archivo General de la Nación, Mexico, Bienes Nacionales, Leg. 1151; Leg. 356, exp. 13 (La Concepción); Templos y Conventos, vol. 77 (Santa Clara).

[a]The liens and loans of Santa Teresa la Nueva are not included in the total for either of these columns since it is not possible to determine them separately. The figure 118,460 represents the combined liens and loans sum.

[b]Pious deeds.

[c]Percentages do not add up to 100 since the liens and loans of Santa Teresa la Nueva are not included in the total.

Houses had been acquired as a result of litigation for lack of payment of liens, by cessions of pious patrons, by outright purchase or by building.[65]

Urban real estate ownership offered the convents considerable advantages over the uncertainties and risks involved in the collection of the interest and capital of liens and loans. Houses were usually close to the convents and their rents could be collected by an administrator who kept in frequent touch with the nuns. Houses could be refurbished when necessary or sold at the convent's convenience. The growing urbanization of the capital and the demographic development of Mexico in the eighteenth century suggest that investment in houses was not only logical, but preferable to any other form, especially since houses yielded 5 percent of their value, the same as liens and loans.

The administration of houses had its negative aspects. The most frequent was the irregular payment of rents, which in many instances obliged the administrators to work very hard to collect the rents, and deprived the nunneries of expected income. The expenses caused by the repair of properties and, in the second half of the eighteenth century, property taxes, were other liabilities to house-ownership. But, apparently, convents did not mind these handicaps. Purchase of real estate continued apace throughout the eighteenth century and by its end nunneries owned a considerable number of houses in Mexico City. The richest convents, such as La Concepción and La Encarnación, owned some of the choicest houses in the capital. On the other hand, rural property did not seem to interest the convents of the capital. It was difficult for the nunneries to administer property beyond the boundaries of the city. Even provincial convents found that the administration of their rural estates posed too many problems for cloistered nuns. By 1744, the convent of Santa Clara in Puebla, which owned several rural estates, had sold some of them and was willing to sell the rest.[66] The convent of Santa Clara in Querétaro, which had owned some twenty ranches and farms in the seventeenth century, had put them all for sale in 1695.[67] These sales were "lien sales" whereby the convent continued to receive 5 percent of the income of the properties. However, later in the eighteenth century the sales were made final. Other provincial convents retained their rural properties, such as those convents in Oaxaca, but even in their case, several of them trimmed the number of their estates to that which they could comfortably and profitably administer.[68]

The convent of La Concepción owned the largest number of houses among all the nunneries of the capital. In 1785 it had 55 units of real estate which contained 86 large houses; 48 smaller houses and mezzanines; 86 small houses attached to larger houses; 134 rooms in multiple-tenant houses; 17 stores; 9 large trading stalls and 2 smaller ones. The value of this property was estimated at over one million pesos.[69] La Encarnación was another large landlord. In 1776 it owned 33 units which involved 54 large houses; 24 small and medium size; 77 attached houses; 32 mezzanines; 12 multiple-tenant houses; 2 stores and one barracks leased to the government. This property was worth over 790,000 pesos.[70] With the possible exception of a few large confraternities and the City Council, it is unlikely that any other corporation, lay or religious, owned such extensive and valuable housing as the feminine orders.[71]

The extent and variety of convent property was such that it housed all the existing social classes of colonial Mexico, from the richest to the poorest. La Encarnación rented houses to several nobles, very rich merchants, and members of the bureaucracy. The rent of the large houses varied between five hundred and one thousand pesos yearly. La Concepción and Jesús María also housed similar members of society. With very few exceptions, these tenants paid their rents punctually and even in advance. Their desirability was above mere assumption; their reliability was beyond reproach.

In contrast, there were the far more numerous smaller and cheaper houses inhabited by the lower classes of the viceregal capital. The less affluent convents had more multiple-tenant houses and, consequently, housed more of the poor of the city. The rents yielded by the smaller houses varied between six and twenty pesos, according to their size and location; rooms rented for one to two pesos monthly. There were a few stables and huts, presumably fitted for human habitation, which yielded four to six reales a month. The undesirability of many of these rooms was admitted even by the administrators themselves, and many remained vacant for many months of the year.[72]

There was a large turnover of tenants in the cheaper houses and rooms of all convents, which accumulated large debts from the many delinquent tenants. The administrators tried to obtain a small sum of money as token of payment when they first rented the houses, but such precaution was often meaningless; the rate of delinquency seems to have varied in direct relationship to the efficiency of the administrator and the general economic situation of the viceroyalty. In times of famine or poor crops, many administrators commented on the impossibility of forcing the poor to pay.[73] When a tenant did not pay the rent, his or her property was impounded. The description of such items tells of the meager means of the owners: used clothing, old pieces of furniture, old pictures. This confiscated property was stored for a time and then sold, if the tenants did not repay the debt. In these instances, most of the impounded property hardly ever covered more than a fraction of the debt. In order to prevent impoundment, many tenants who could not pay for their rents escaped at night, taking the keys with them or breaking the locks.[74]

The inhabitants of the low-income houses of the convents were the unknown of the city, the artisans, the unskilled workers, the Indians, and a remarkable number of women listed as main tenants. For example, in the properties of Regina Celi, in 1756, of the more than 255 tenants recorded, at least 75 (33 percent) were women.[75] Were these women married, widowed, or simply the heads of families where men were absent due to the low number of legal unions among the poor? Although a categorical answer to this question is not possible, the results of a census of the four major boroughs of Mexico City in 1753 point to a significant number of households headed by women, widowed or unmarried.[76]

Since the lists of tenants sometimes state the occupation of the tenants, it is possible to gain an insight into the kind of people who populated the cheaper houses of the convents: bakers; washerwomen; cobblers; some priests (presumably not very affluent); small shopkeepers, such as wine merchants or leather tanners; fruit vendors; scriveners; coach drivers and coach builders; tailors; carpenters; blacksmiths; and even a woman porter. No doubt there was a great social distance between this woman porter and the select examples of womanhood who professed in the convents. Yet, they were both contained in the world of the feminine orders: one as the preferred inhabitant of the religious centers; the other as a tenant in the property which the religious centers needed to sustain themselves. Apparently, they had little in common, but in historical perspective they come together as samples of their society at large, and the values which that society lived by.

The dichotomy of values which has been suggested for women of different social classes in Spanish America is quite clear in the setting of nunneries in colonial Mexico.[77] While a greater freedom of life was not only permitted, but often mandatory for the women of the lower classes, a maximum of protection and sheltering was required for the upper classes. Nunneries were created to protect and fulfill that part of the female elite which was not to become married, and they performed this social role quite successfully.

As financial units, the nunneries reflected the trends of the economy in general. Throughout the seventeenth century they experienced the same administrative difficulties as other clerical, lay corporations and economic units, such as *haciendas*. Nunneries adjusted to the character of the times by changing the nature of their investments and blossomed in the eighteenth century, as the Bourbon administrative reforms reorganized the trade and fiscal systems. But the feminine orders did more than simply reflect the economy: they influenced it by offering credit to the entrepreneurial classes of society. Thus, they were not only expressions of the social order but they reinforced it from an economic point of view. In addition, the bulk and value of their property made them as important as some of the most powerful of the masculine orders, and an element of great economic significance in the life of the colonial city.

## NOTES

1. James Lockhart, "Spaniards among Indians: Toluca in the Late Sixteenth Century," paper presented at the Schouler Lecture Symposium, Johns Hopkins University, 1973.

2. José María Ots Capdequí, *El derecho de familia y el derecho de sucesión en nuestra legislación de Indias*, Madrid, Instituto Iberoamericano de Derecho Comparado, 1921; "Bosquejo Histórico de los derechos de la mujer casada en la legislación de Indias," *Revista General de Legislación y Jurisprudencia*, XXIII (Madrid, Ed. Reus, 1920).

3. Guillermo Céspedes del Castillo, "La Sociedad Colonial Americana en los Siglos XVI y XVII," in Jaime Vicens Vives, ed., *Historia Social y Económica de España y América*, 4 vols. (Barcelona, 1968), III, 388–578.

4. Magnus Mörner, *Race Mixture in the History of Latin America* (Boston: Little, Brown, 1967); *Race and Class in Latin America* (New York: Columbia University Press, 1970).

5. Spain discovered the New World immediately after recovering the peninsula from

the Moslems, after eight hundred years of the latter's domination, and also in the same year the Jews were expelled from its territory. Although, theoretically, Jews were not allowed in any of the Spanish possessions, they settled in America as converts. During the sixteenth and seventeenth centuries there was a strong feeling of prejudice against new Christians; thus, the concept of *limpieza de sangre* had both a racial and a religious implication. See Seymour B. Liebman, *The Jews in New Spain* (Coral Gables, Fla.: University of Miami Press, 1970); C. H. Haring, *The Spanish Empire in America* (New York: Oxford University Press, 1947), 13, 203–4; Martin A. Cohen, ed., *The Jewish Experience in America*, 2 vols. (Waltham, Mass.: American Jewish Historical Society, 1971).

6. Ots Capdequí, "Bosquejo Histórico" and *El derecho de familia, passim.*

7. Richard Konetzke, *Colección de Documentos para la Historia de la Formación Social de Hispanoamérica, 1493–1810,* 3 vols. (Madrid, 1953–62), III, 406, 420, 362, 305. Men as well as women were included in all marriage laws, which aimed at preserving the social status of the best families. However, women were more likely to be coerced than men. Although the law included all social classes, marriage was freer and not subjected to much social pressure among lower classes. Members of the military, as a special corps, were subjected to rather strict marriage regulations which demanded they have licenses from their superiors prior to marriage. It was impossible to enforce thoroughly all the laws and regulations, however, and the repeated royal statements about the necessity of enforcing them indicate that they were not universally obeyed. Nonetheless, their existence is a good evidence of the prevailing social pressures with regard to marriage.

8. Dowries, *beaterios,* and nunneries had their root in Spanish tradition. See Antonio Domínguez Ortíz, *La Sociedad Española en el Siglo XVII* (Madrid, 1970).

9. Fr. Fidel Lejarza, "Expansión de las Clarisas en America," *Archivo Ibero-Americano,* no. 54: 131–90; no. 55: 265–310; no. 56: 393–455. See also no. 54: 188; Céspedes del Castillo, "La Sociedad Colonial Americana. . . . "

10. Archivo Histórico de Hacienda (hereafter cited as AHH), Mexico, Anatas, Leg. 267–16; 267–33; 269–82; Archivo General de la Nación, Mexico, Tierras (hereafter cited as AGN); vol. 440, exp. 3; vol. 2488, exp. 9; vol. 2712, exp. 7; vol. 2718, exp. 17. Isabel González Sánchez, *Haciendas y Ranchos de Tlaxcala en 1712* (Mexico: Instituto Nacional de Antropología e Historia, 1969), *passim;* "Licencias para imprimir libros, 1748–1770," *Boletín del Archivo General de la Nación* (hereafter cited as *BAGN*), vol. 15, 1ᵃ época (1944), 67–102. In this article the activities of printer María de Rivera are recorded; she was one of the leading printers of her times but not the only woman who had entered that business. Other well-known female printers were the widows Viuda de Hogal and Viuda de Ontiveros. For a comparison see James Lockhart, *Spanish Peru, 1532–1560* (Madison: University of Wisconsin Press, 1968), chap. IX.

11. Eduardo Báez Macías, "Planos y Censos de la Ciudad de Mexico," *BAGN,* vol. 8, 2d series (1968), no. 3–4.

12. Guillermo S. Fernández de Recas, *Mayorazgos de la Nueva España* (Mexico, 1965), 229–34; Gregorio Martín de Guijo, *Diario, 1648–1664,* 2 vols. (Mexico, 1952), I, 92–93, 112; II, 113; Juan F. Gemelli Carreri, *Viaje a la Nueva España* (Mexico, 1927), 184; Josefina Muriel, ed., *Fundaciones Neoclásicas; La Marquesa de Selvanevada: sus Conventos y sus Arquitectos* (Mexico, 1969), 14; Archivo de Notarías de Mexico, Protocolos de José A. de Anaya, vol. A-23, fol. 21v: AGN, Bienes Nacionales, leg. 213, paquete I, exp. 24.

13. Israel Cavazas Garza, *Catálogo y Síntesis de los Protocolos del Archivo Municipal de Monterrey, 1599–1700* (Monterrey, 1966), 30, 58, 68, 94–95, 100, 248–49. Women of the lower classes were mostly undowered. For further examples see Archives of the

Church of the Latter Day Saints, film 31489, pt. 6, fol. 22v, 78v; pt. 23, fol. 252; pt. 30, fol. 259v.

14. Numerous dowry funds were established throughout the colonial period. They were usually administered by confraternities and bore the name of the donor. The husbands of the recipients had to be acceptable to the dowry administrators. See, for example, AGN, Templos y Conventos, vol. 44, exp. 2–8; vol. 45, exp. 31, 33, 34; Gemelli Carreri, *Viaje a la Nueva España*, 184.

15. Juan José Moreno, *Sermón . . . por el cumplimiento de dos siglos de su fundación del convento de . . . Santa María de Gracia, Guadalajara* (Mexico, 1789); Francisco Fabián y Fuero, *Colección de Providencias Diocesanas* (Puebla, 1770), 34; Fr. Joseph Vega y Santa Barbara, *Oración Panegírica* (Mexico, 1753).

16. Garza, *Catálogo y Síntesis . . .* , 3; Lockhart, *Spanish Peru*, 163.

17. Luis de Velasco y Mendoza, *Historia de la Ciudad de Celaya*, 3 vols. (Mexico, 1947), I, 220–21; José I. Dávila Garibi, "Diligencias generalmente observadas en la Nueva Galicia para la fundación de conventos de monjas de vida contemplativa," *Memorias de la Academia Mexicana de la Historia* XVII, no. 4 (1958), 358–67. There were also other institutions called *recogimientos* which also offered shelter, and sometimes instruction to women of all ages. See José María Zelaa e Hidalgo, *Glorias de Querétaro* (Mexico, 1803), 66; Julián Gutierrez Dávila, *Vida y Virtudes del Siervo de Dios, el Venerable Domingo Perez de Barcia, fundador de la Casa y Voluntario Recogimiento de San Miguel de Belen* (Madrid, 1720). This *recogimiento* became a school in the eighteenth century; AGN, Historia, vol. 92, Beaterio de Santa Rosa, Erección en Convento, vol. 109; Reales Cédulas, 45: 484; 71: 16.

18. Mariano Cuevas, ed., *Documentos Inéditos del S. XVI para la Historia de Mexico* (Mexico, 1914), 56, 61; Joaquín García Icazbalceta, *Fr. Juan de Zumárraga* (Mexico, 1881), Appendix, 94, 102, 107; Luis García Pimentel, ed., *Descripción del Arzobispado de Mexico hecha en 1570* (Mexico, 1897), 290; Library of the University of Texas, Relación del Monasterio de La Concepción.

19. Miriam Ann Gallagher, R.S.M., "The Family Background of the Nuns of Two Monasterios in Colonial Mexico: Santa Clara, Querétaro, and Corpus Christi, Mexico City, 1724–1822," doctoral dissertation for the Catholic University of America (Washington, D.C., 1972), 35–52.

20. Libro Historial del Convento de la Purísima Concepción, Guadalajara. Manuscript lent by the nunnery to the writer; AGN, Historia, vol. 77, Fundación del Convento de Ntra, Sra. del Carmen, Querétaro, fol. 105. In her petition for a royal license to found this convent, the ex-marchioness of Selvanevada stated among several other reasons, that a family with four to six marriageable girls could place two of them in a convent and give the rest of them the possibility of a better marriage.

21. Gallagher, "The Family Background . . . ," 35–52.

22. AGN, Historia, vol. 98, exp. 3; Reales Cedulas 65: 122; 72: 27, 47; 113: 113.

23. The daughter of the marquis of Pánuco, Francisco Javier Viscarra, professed in the convent of Sta. María de Gracia, in Guadalajara, in 1785. She donated ten thousand pesos to the convent, provided eight thousand pesos for the dowries of two other nuns, and endowed a religious feast with two thousand pesos. See Archivo de Instrumentos Públicos, Guadalajara (hereafter cited as AIPG), Protocolos de Blas de Silva, 26: 126 (1785), and see pp. 132, 151, and 177 for other examples of professions; Muriel, ed., *Fundaciones Neoclasicas*, 15. Each of the two professing daughters of the Marchioness of Selvanevada had ten thousand pesos as *reserva*. The peso was the basic coin of the Spanish monetary system in colonial Mexico. It varied in value in the sixteenth century, as there were silver and gold pesos. In the seventeenth century the standard peso was silver and divided into eight *reales*. At the end of this century an unskilled laborer earned

two to three pesos weekly; thus, three thousand pesos was a relatively large amount of money. For further examples of professions of girls of distinguished families, see Fr. Joaquín Gallardo, *Sermón* ... *en la profesión religiosa de Sor María Guadalupe del Sacramento* (Mexico, 1788); Nicolás de Jesús María, *El Cristus ABC de la Virtud* ... *Sermón* (Mexico, 1726).

24. Sister Miriam Ann Gallagher, "The Family Background ...," 36, has concluded that "some problems relative to the secular and religious dowry were solved by the foundation of *monasterios*. For most of them the religious factor was secondary or even incidental; the main concern was that *monasterios* would help relieve society of certain economic and social burdens—undowered women."

25. Muriel, ed., *Fundaciones Neoclásicas*, 33, 35. The convent of Santa Teresa la Nueva, in Mexico City, had fourteen places endowed by patrons. There was a waiting list of thirty-nine girls in 1798. In that decade only one place had been available. Some convents did not accept undowered nuns until they had accumulated three thousand pesos in interest from the original pious donation, which they lent to merchants or landowners at 5 percent interest. As a result, only every twenty or thirty years was there a place available. For example, the convent of Santa Clara, in Mexico, had a pious endowment from Ana de Alemán. It paid one hundred pesos yearly of interest. Only every thirty years did the convent have the three thousand pesos to endow a professing nun. See AGN, Templos y Conventos, vol. 84.

26. In the late sixteenth century and throughout the seventeenth century there were Portuguese settlers in Mexico. The crowns of Spain and Portugal were joined from 1580 through 1640. Many of these Portuguese were Jews recently converted and under the surveillance of the religious authorities for possible heretic practices. In the seventeenth century many of them were condemned by the Inquisition. See Liebman, *The Jews in New Spain*, 210, 214, 225; José Toribio Medina, *Historia del Tribunal del Santo Oficio de la Inquisición en Mexico* (Santiago de Chile, 1905).

27. AGN, Bienes Nacionales, leg. 85, several expedientes; leg. 156, exp. 5; leg. 100, exp. 17; leg. 213, paquete I, exp. 6, 32; paquete II, exp. 30, 31, 33; AHH, Annatas, leg. 100–101. In leg. 85, Bienes Nacionales, is recorded the case of Juana de Sandoval, novice in the convent of San Lorenzo in 1728. She was registered in the baptismal records as daughter of unknown parents. However, a witness in the process for her profession declared that she was the daughter of Andrés Muñoz de Sandoval, a relative of Viceroy Duque de Linares. Leg. 156, exp. 5 and 18, tell of the profession of Juana Josefa de Leyza in the convent of San Bernardo. She was the acknowledged natural daughter of Captain Joseph A. de Leiza, and professed in that year with her half sister, who was a legitimate daughter of the captain and sixteen years younger.

28. Josefina Muriel, *Los Conventos de Monjas en Nueva España* (Mexico, 1946), 225–39; *Las Indias Cacicas de Mexico* (Mexico, 1963); Biblioteca Nacional de Mexico, Archivo Franciscano, Monjas, Informe del Comisario General Fr. Pedro de Navarrete ... sobre la fundación del monasterio de Corpus Christi, 1743, hereafter cited as BNAF; AGN, Historia, vol. 109, exp. 2. The convent of Valladolid was founded in 1734 and the one in Oaxaca in 1782. See AGN, Historia, vol. 109, exp. 4; José Gómez, *Diario Curioso de Mexico* (Mexico, 1854), 130–32.

29. BNAF, Monjas, Carta de Sor María del Sacramento, August 1728; Carta de Fr. Juan de Alcaraz, September 1728; Carta del clérigo Diego Torres, 1743; Carta de Fr. Bernardo de Arratia, October 1745; AGN, Reales Cédulas 52: 20; 63: 263; 72: 369.

30. Joseph de Castro, *Primera Regla de la Fecunda Madre Santa Clara de Asis* (Mexico, 1756); Gallagher, "The Family Background ...," 154–56.

31. AGN, Bienes Nacionales, leg. 101, exp. 2; leg. 186, exp. 2; leg. 1113, exp. 15; leg. 195, exp. 5; Archivo del Instituto Nacional de Antropología e Historia, Fondo Fran-

ciscano (hereafter cited as AINAHFF), vol. 92, fol. 212–13; AIPG, Protocolos de Manuel de Mesa, vol. IV, fol. 42; Protocolos de García de Argomanes, vol. XXV, fol. 115; Gonzalo Aguirre Beltrán, *La Poblacion Negra de Mexico* (Mexico, 1972). There is an interesting case recorded, in which the owner of an eight-year-old slave decided to "dedicate her to religion." She gave the slave to a nun in the convent of Santa Inés, with the proviso that the slave should never leave the convent. See, AGN, Bienes Nacionales, leg. 195, exp. 5; *BAGN,* vol. VI, 1a serie, no. 4 (1935), 541–56, "Un matrimonio de esclavos," relates the story of the troubles faced by a slave in a convent when she decided to get married; Carlos Sigüenza y Góngora, *Paraíso Occidental* (Mexico, 1684), 171–74; Antonio Paredes, *Carta Edificante. Vida ejemplar de la hermana Salvadora de los Santos, India Otomí* (Mexico, 1784). This is the biography of a *principal* Indian from Querétaro who lived a pious life as a maid in the Carmelite *beaterio* of that city.

32. Joseph Bellido, *Vida de la M.R.M. María Anna Agueda de San Ignacio* (Mexico, 1758); Juan Benito Díaz de Gamarra y Dávila, *Vida de la R.M. Sor María Josefa Lino de la Sma. Trinidad* (Mexico, 1831); Juan A. de Mora, *Admirable Vida y Virtudes de la Venerable Madre Sor María Inés de los Dolores* (Mexico, 1729); José A. Ponce de León, *La Azucena entre Espinas; Vida y Virtudes de la V. Madre Luisa de Santa Catarina* (Mexico, 1750). These biographies of nuns are useful for determining the motivations for profession.

33. "Breve Descripción del Obispado de Michoacán," *BAGN,* vol. XI, 1a. época, no. 1 (1940), 125–45; Josefina Muriel, "Notas para la Historia de la Educación de la Mujer durante el Virreynato," *Estudios de Historia Novohispana* (Mexico, 1968), 25–33. The writer states that nuns never taught in any of the schools annexed to convents in Oaxaca. This implies that those schools, wherever they existed, were quite independent of the nunneries. The principal schools for girls in Mexico City were Colegio de Niñas or La Caridad; Las Vizcaínas; San Miguel de Belén; and Ntra. Sra. de Guadalupe, for Indian girls. For information regarding these lay schools, see "La Cofradía del Santísimo Sacramento y Caridad," *The Americas* II, no. 3 (1946), 369–75; Gonzalo Obregón, *El Real Colegio de San Ignacio de Mexico* (Mexico, 1949); AGN, Reales Cédulas 45: 484; Temporalidades, vol. 22, exp. 2; Francisco Sosa, *El Episcopado Mexicano* (Mexico, 1877–79), 170; Gerard Decorme, *La Obra de los Jesuitas Mexicanos durante la Epoca Colonial, 1572–1767,* 2 vols. (Mexico, 1951), I: 333. According to Alexander von Humboldt, who visited Mexico in 1803, there were 165 girls in twenty convents in Mexico City. There were 574 girls in the schools of Las Vizcaínas, Ntra. Sra. de Belén and Ntra. Sra. de Guadalupe. In the convents of La Enseñanza and Jesús María, there were 185 girls. The convent of Jesús María had originally been founded to educate girls, but there are few standing records as to how this teaching was performed. Humboldt states that there were no girls within the cloisters of the convent. See Alexander von Humboldt, *Ensayo Político sobre el Reino de la Nueva España* (Mexico, Ed. Porruá, 1966), 574, 576.

34. J. Muriel, "Notas para la Historia de la Educación, etc."; "Breve Descripción del Obispado de Michoacán," *BAGN* XI, no. 1 (1940). Standards for feminine education were probably lower than those for boys. For the latter, see "La Enseñanza Primaria en la Nueva España," *BAGN* XI, no. 2 (1940), 245–302.

35. AINAHFF, vol. 92, fol. 77–119; AGN, Bienes Nacionales, leg. 146, exp. 57; leg. 140, exp. 15; leg. 213, paquete III.

36. Fr. José Joaquín Granados y Gálvez, *Tardes Americanas* (Mexico, 1778), 396–97; Guillermo Furlong, S.J., *La Cultura Femenina en la Epoca Colonial* (Buenos Aires, 1951). See pp. 42ff. for Mexican women; José Mariano Beristain de Souza, *Biblioteca Hispano-Americana Septentrional,* 2a. ed., 4 vols. (Amecameca, 1883), I: 428; II: 59, 262; III: 325; IV: 60.

37. José E. Valdes, *Vida Admirable . . . de la V. M. Sor Sebastiana Josepha de la S.S. Trinidad* (Mexico, 1765); Ignacio Saldana, *Sermón Funebre en las exequias de Sor Sebastiana Josepha de la Santisima Trinidad,* etc. (Mexico, 1758); BNAF, Manuscript Collection, Sor Sebastiana Josefa de la S.S. Trinidad, "Cartas en las cuales manifiesta a su confesor las cosas interiores y exteriores de su vida" (n.d.).

38. Coloquio que Compuso la R.M. María Vicenta de la Encarnación, 1804; manuscript at the Garcia Collection, University of Texas Library; José Mariano Beristain de Souza, *Biblioteca . . . ,* I: 303, 355, 359, 386, 403, 428; II: 262; III: 59, 104, 122–23; IV: 69, 176, 297; José F. Ramírez, *Biblioteca Hispano-Americana Septentrional. Adiciones y Correcciones* (Mexico, 1899), 387, 443.

39. Sor María de Santa Clara, *Subida al Monte de Mhirra* (Mexico, 1747).

40. María Anna Agueda de San Ignacio, *Devociones; Impresas por orden y a expensas del Illmo, Sr. D. Domingo Pantaleón Alvarez de Abreu* (Puebla, 1758).

41. Sor Juana Inés de la Cruz, *Obras Completas* (Mexico: Ed. Porrua, 1969); Gerard C. Flynn, *Sor Juana Inés de la Cruz* (New York: Twayne, 1971).

42. In the appraisal of the belongings of a deceased nun of the convent of La Encarnación, there is a catalog of her books, which suggests what kind of readings some nuns made. Apart from several books of prayer, there was a *Life of Christ,* a *Life of Saint Teresa de Jesús* and a *Life of Bishop Juan de Palafox* (a seventeenth-century Bishop of Puebla). Altogether, this nun owned twenty-four books described as "of diverse legends and devotions," and valued at nine pesos. See AGN, Bienes Nacionales, leg. 213, paquete I, exp. 41.

43. According to Humboldt, who based his estimates on the first census carried out in New Spain, in 1790, there were 165 *niñas* in convents and 185 in the two convent-schools of Jesús María and La Enseñanza. This makes a total of 350 girls. The number of girls under sixteen years, in the city of Mexico, is calculated as 18,922. Therefore, those girls in convents (not counting those in lay schools) constituted only 1.8 percent of the female population of school age at the end of the eighteenth century. See Humboldt, *Ensayo Político. . . ,* 574.

44. BNAF, Monjas, Caja 75, Real Provisión de 27 de Junio de 1667; Caja 76, no. 1275, Carta del Provincial Fr. Manuel de Nájera.

45. Francisco Fabián y Fuero, "Colección de Providencias Dadas a fin de Establecer la Santa Vida Común," in *Colección de Providencias Diocesanas* (Puebla, 1770), 84–90; AGN, Reales Cedulas, 104: 214; Asunción Lavrin, "Ecclesiastical Reform of Nunneries in New Spain in the Eighteenth Century," *The Americas* XXII, no. 2 (1965), 182–203.

46. AGN, Correspondencia de los Virreyes, 10: 166, 305; 11: 118, 121.

47. Manuel A. Valdés, ed., *Gazetas de Mexico,* vol. 8, no. 19 (Mexico, 1782–1821), 150.

48. *Relación Histórica de la Fundación de . . . Ntra. Sra. del Pilar* (Mexico, 1793); AGN, Reales Cédulas, 65: 122; 72: 27, 47.

49. Obregón, *El Real Colegio de San Ignacio de Mexico,* 92; Bernardo Pazuengos, *Sermón en la creación de . . . Ntra. Sra. del Pilar* (Mexico, 1755).

50. AGN, Reales Cédulas, 122: 39; Colegios, vol. 8, exp. 21; Historia, vol. 109.

51. The lien was a financial operation which had its roots in medieval Spain. It could be the theoretical donation of money to an institution without using cash in the transaction, whereby the owner paid 5 percent interest to the institution which he chose to benefit from then on. It could also be the granting of a sum of money by the institution to a borrower, which mortgaged his property as a collateral, and paid a 5 percent interest yearly. The property remained mortgaged through ensuing owners until the original sum was repaid. Loans were of temporary character, and they also required either bondsmen as security of repayment, or the mortgaging of a property as collateral. Loans paid 5 percent interest. While loans were usually repaid in five or ten years, liens

encumbered the property for several decades. See AGN, Bienes Nacionales, leg. 1221, fol. 50–60; Archivo de la Secretaría de Salubridad y Asistencia, Papeles del Convento de Jesús María, 18–1–17; 18–2–21; 16–7–3. Hereafter cited as ASSACJM. See also José María Ots Capdequí, *El Régimen de la Tierra en Hispanoamérica* (Ciudad Trujillo, 1946), 83–87.

52. See, for example, AGN, Bienes Nacionales, leg. 213, paquete I; AHH, vol. 2168.

53. AGN, Bienes Nacionales, leg. 213, paquete I, exp. 7: leg. 1221, exp. 5. This *expediente* contains the case of the Jesuit College of San Pedro y San Pablo, which in 1683 had a lien of 50,000 pesos lent by La Concepción. This lien does not appear in any of the records of the eighteenth century. The convent of Santo Domingo had a lien for 97,500 pesos in 1656, paying interest to La Concepción. It was cancelled in 1724. See, AHH, vol. 2168, no. 64. For cancellations of the Jesuits in Jesús María, see ASSACJM, 18–1–17, fol. 1–6. See also fol. 40v, 55, 58, 67.

54. AHH, vol. 2168; AGN, Bienes Nacionales, leg. 1029, exp. 9.

55. AGN, Bienes Nacionales, leg. 667, exp. 5; leg. 281, exp. 3.

56. In 1724, San Bernardo had 40,000 pesos in liens and loans in litigation. See, AGN, Bienes Nacionales, leg. 1221, exp. 10. In 1744, San Lorenzo had 43,600 pesos also in litigation; Santa Isabel had 11,400 pesos and Santa Catalina de Seña 32,850 pesos. See AGN, Bienes Nacionales, leg. 1151, Relaciones Juradas, 1744.

57. ASSACJM, 18–2–21; 18–5–30; 18–9–54; AGN, Bienes Nacionales, leg. 82; leg. 1151.

58. AGN, Bienes Nacionales, leg. 667, exp. 5, 10.

59. AGN, *ibid.*, Cuaderno de Apuntes de la Contaduría del Convento de La Encarnación.

60. The merchant's gild (*Consulado*) borrowed 14,000 pesos from La Concepción in 1724. The previous year it borrowed 27,000 pesos from La Encarnación and 36,000 pesos from a confraternity adjunct to this convent. The convent of San Bernardo had provided 16,500 pesos in that same year. In 1744 the Consulado took a loan of 40,000 pesos from Santa Isabel; in 1746 it returned 24,000 pesos to Santa Clara. At the end of the century, the merchants borrowed 12,000 pesos from San Lorenzo and 80,000 pesos from La Concepción. See, AGN, Bienes Nacionales, leg. 1073, no. 24; leg. 111, exp. 19; leg. 1151; Templos y Conventos, vol. 84, fol. 28; AHH, vol. 2168; Consulados, leg. 640–19.

61. For the role of miners and merchants in the economic complex of the late eighteenth century, see David Brading, *Miners and Merchants in Bourbon Mexico, 1763–1810* (Cambridge, Eng.: Cambridge University Press, 1971); Enrique Florescano, *Estructuras y Problemas Agrarios de Mexico, 1500–1821* (Mexico, 1971).

62. AGN, Bienes Nacionales, leg. 667, exp. 10.

63. AHH, vol. 2168, fol. 320–39, fol. 1.

64. AGN, Bienes Nacionales, leg. 356, exp. 10, fol. 113.

65. ASSACJM, 18–1–14; AGN, Bienes Nacionales, leg. 18, exp. 7; leg. 175, exp. 11; leg. 1108, exp. 24, 38. At the end of the seventeenth century, the convent of Jesús María already owned a relatively large number of houses. The convent of Discalced Carmelites of San José was building a new convent and purchasing and building new houses worth 196,723 pesos. Part of this money came from the donation of a rich patron, Captain Juan Mosquera Molina. See ASSACJM, Relacion de las Fincas . . . de Jesús María, 1684–1690; AGN, Templos y Conventos, vols. 36, 37, 43, 86.

66. AINAHFF, vol. 92; BNAF, Monjas, Caja 75, no. 1260, 1280.

67. AGN, Tierras, vol. 417; vol. 2696, exp. 13; vol. 2738, exp. 10.

68. William B. Taylor, *Landlord and Peasant in Colonial Oaxaca* (Stanford, Calif.: Stanford University Press, 1972); see Taylor's chapter on church estates.

69. AGN, Bienes Nacionales, leg. 1029, exp. 9.

70. *Ibid.*, leg. 667, exp. 5.

71. As a matter of interest it is worthwhile to compare the income of the City Council of Mexico City (*Ayuntamiento*) ca. 1740. Its several houses and trading stalls yielded 33,250 pesos of income, suggesting a value of 665,000 pesos, since houses were rented for 5 percent of their value. See José Antonio de Villa-Señor y Sánchez, *Theatro Americano* (Mexico, 1746); AINAH, Colección Lira, vol. 86.

72. AGN, Bienes Nacionales, leg. 281, no. 54.

73. ASSACJM, 18–7–75; 18–2–21; AINAHFF, vol. 73.

74. AGN, Bienes Nacionales, leg. 462, Cuentas del Mayordomo de La Encarnación.

75. AINAHFF, vol. 73.

76. Macías, "Planos y Censos de la Ciudad de Mexico," *BAGN*, vol. 8, 2a serie (1968), no. 3–4.

77. Ann Pescatello, "The Female in Ibero-America: An Essay of Research Bibliography and Research Directions," *Latin American Research Review* VII, no. 2 (1972), 125–41.

# Sex and Class in Colonial and Nineteenth-Century America

*Ann D. Gordon and Mari Jo Buhle*

## I

The changes which took place in the lives of American women during the colonial period—a span of almost two centuries—provide a valuable framework for understanding the relationship between greater economic and social complexity and the emergence of a distinct, and limiting, notion of femininity. At one end of the period there was the Virginia House of Burgesses describing why it granted land to wives as well as to husbands in 1619: ". . . in a new plantation it is not knowen [sic] whether man or woman be the most necessary."[1] At the other there was Mercy Otis Warren, a writer and historian, telling a young woman that learning was useless to a lady (as useless as virtue to a gentleman, she added).[2]

In this discussion we can point out some general outlines of colonial growth and some signs that transformations were occurring in daily life. At a minimum, the suggestions here should provide background for the more familiar tale of the nineteenth century when proscriptions on women and definitions of their limited sphere were fully developed.

Colonial history was in part a beginning again. Each new coastal settlement and each move westward entailed a return to the simplest social organization: a family or a single man produced enough for survival and used virtually all available time for essential work. Farming areas rapidly entered a market economy, exporting surplus foodstuffs and wood and importing manufactured goods. A few towns reached the size of European cities and supported specialized labor forces and artisans. Sequences of development repeated themselves in different locations at different times, so while one city grew to resemble London or Edinburgh, farms on the frontier were more similar to the earliest wilderness settlements. Still no one moved for long beyond the influence of colonial governments, and in most areas churches were established as rapidly as settlers moved in.

Colonial forms of increasing complexity, models for institutions and for

This essay is a revised version of portions of Part II of "Women in American Society: An Historical Contribution," which first appeared in *Radical America* 5, no. 4 (July–August, 1971).

social relations came out of the European (primarily English) experience of the settlers. The majority of colonists, for example, accepted the logic of monogamous marriage, built single-family houses, and assumed their right to own property.[3] They joined churches with British or European counterparts, adopted elements of English common law, and organized their production and marketing along familiar lines. By the middle of the eighteenth century, when commerce, or reliance on commerce, created not only greater involvement with the mother country but greater similarities with it as well, colonists increasingly sought to duplicate the forms of English social life.[4]

Women throughout the period were tied to the fate of the family. Town governments in New England assumed and legislated a family basis for social life, and urged single men and women to live within a family household.[5] In some southern colonies where settlement was conducted initially as an adventure by English investors, men were sent alone to begin productive work. The leaders found that little incentive for producing a surplus existed without families, so they imported women and sold them to men for the cost of their passages.[6] That brief period before women arrived may express as much about the importance of women in colonial development as any time when they were more conspicuous by their presence. Throughout the colonies there were more men than women—a development unique at that time to American society. A woman enjoyed good chances of maintaining herself and of getting married, and her age at marriage was considerably lower than it was for women in Europe. It may have been true as well that the scarcity of women resulted in greater social mobility as they could be more selective about their husbands.[7]

The simplicity of economic and social organization concentrated a variety of essential activities in the family. In family production, each member contributed work of equal importance to the group's survival. Two aspects of this assured women of useful roles: the independence of each family's work and the immediate necessity of it. Most families farmed, produced their own food and manufactured their own clothing, soap, candles, and fuel. The division of work was along sex lines, but within that basic division there were different patterns depending on the family's relative wealth, its degree of participation in the cash economy, the organization of the father's work, and the size of the household—relatives, servants, slaves, children, etc. Under such conditions of work a large family was an asset and thus the woman's reproductive work, as well as her productive work, was valued.[8]

Education for the majority of colonists took place in the family and consisted of learning skills and morals. Boys and girls learned those from the work and daily life of their families. Where families were concentrated and homogeneous, as in New England towns or religious settlements, children occasionally attended schools or lived in another household to learn.[9] Anna Grant, resident in New York before the Revolution, recorded in her *Memoirs* that among the Dutch in Albany, mothers took primary responsibility for educating children, especially about religion. Janet Schaw, an eighteenth-century traveler in North Carolina, remarked that the sharp contrast in civility between men and women resulted from daughters being raised in the cultured environment of their homes while sons learned the rough ways of the woods from their fathers. Whatever its particular form, this responsibility to society, resting with the family, defined a major part of the work of both parents. Where mothers and fathers were unable to provide, as in the case of orphans or bastards, the state stepped in to replace the family.[10]

Not until education was more clearly defined as something that changed the relationship between parent and child by introducing new values into a society, and not until the family unit no longer concentrated the work of both men and women, did learning require new structures and distinct duties of each parent.[11]

The rhetoric of the times described marriage as a partnership between men and women. The institution existed to produce offspring and, at least in Puritan thought, to control natural sexual appetites by providing an outlet for their monogamous expression. In New England, grounds for divorce applied equally to each sex: adultery, impotency, refusal of sexual favors, and desertion. However, the Puritans, so often chided for their repressive attitudes toward sex, delimited only two major forms of deviation: sexuality must never interfere with the ultimate relationship, that between human and God, and it must never take place outside of marriage. In practice, even those limited restrictions may have loosened during the eighteenth century, as records of children born to couples after less than nine months of marriage indicate.[12] Other colonies appear to have accepted a double standard of sexual behavior somewhat earlier, at least in application of the law. The legal and theological partnership had economic reality when the family worked land or in a craft and so long as the wealth provided for children derived from that common work.

Throughout most of the seventeenth century, colonial society was relatively unfragmented, either by sex or age.[13] Individual women occasionally stepped outside the limits set for them (Anne Hutchinson putting doctrinal challenges to Massachusetts leaders, Quaker missionaries demanding religious tolerance, a southern woman refusing to utter the word "obey" in her marriage vow); but in general, neither men nor women seemed concerned with defining what women were or what their unique contribution to society should be.[14] Similarly, studies of children's toys, books, and nurture reveal very little special attention to children as unique creatures in society.[15] Cultural expressions of the time indicate lack of consciousness about the possible differences which later characterized all discussion of women and children. Such silence about sex- and age-roles is a feature of most pre-industrial societies.

Emphasis on the social necessity for women in a wilderness environment and on consequent respect given to their labor must not be mistaken for a society without discriminations against women. Distinctions were made in law, in education, in theology and church affairs, and in political and property rights. No one asserted equality. But the lines around men's work and women's work were flexible. Abstract theories about the proper role of women did not stand in the way of meeting familial and social needs. There is considerable evidence that women engaged in numerous business and professional activities in the colonial period. They worked not simply in those jobs extending their traditional domestic work out into more complex organization, such as producing food or clothing, but they also published and printed newspapers, managed tanneries, kept taverns, and engaged in just about every occupation existing in the colonies. Many of these women learned skills while sharing their husbands' work and continued the businesses as widows to support their families.[16]

This "unique" participation of women in the economy is frequently taken as a sign of the frontier's liberating effect on traditional roles, but comparison with the more carefully documented English events suggests that American women duplicated the work experience of English women.[17] In England, women had belonged to craft guilds, as widows worked in their late husbands' jobs, had professional standing as midwives, and acted with power of attorney in lieu of their husbands. But by the end of the seventeenth century women lost these positions. Nothing in English culture militated against utilizing the talents of men and women in a variety of occupations as long as the economy needed their strength and numbers. The colonies reverted to a form of work disappearing from England; but as the American economy capitalized its productivity, and as individual wage earners replaced families as the basic production units, women found themselves excluded from their earlier work experience. Two activities in the colonies which underwent this limiting process were midwifery and informal exercise of the power of attorney.

Not only was midwifery open to women; their monopoly in the profession was protected. In 1675 officials of York County, Maine, presented "Captain Francis Raine for presuming to act the part of a midwife," and fined him fifty shillings.[18] But less than a century later formal learning started to replace practical experience as preparation for the job. Dr. William Shippen, Jr., a leader in medical education in Philadelphia, announced a series of lectures on midwifery in 1765. He did not exclude women from training, but offered his expertise to women with "virtue enough to own their ignorance." According to Shippen, "unskilled old women" aggravated the serious problem of mortality in childbirth. Women enrolled in separate classes from men.[19] A similar process in granting powers of attorney is documented in Maryland. When law became a career with prerequisites denied to women, gradually the practical flexibility which had allowed a woman to appear in court on her own behalf if single and on behalf of her husband in his absence disappeared.[20]

By the middle of the eighteenth century, urban middle-class women styled themselves after the ladies of England and participated in the development of a distinct, class-linked femininity. Prior to that time, theology served as the primary source of ideas to "define" woman objectively; there her subordinate status was clearly established but not without granting her equal access to the final and more important rewards in the afterlife. The religious ideas were not adequate to the needs of class differentiation in commercial society nor to the demands of rationalizing the existence of male and female spheres of work. New ideas came first through imported and reprinted English essays, novels, and prescriptive books. Later, educated colonial men (and, even later, colonial women) presented their own views on fashions, on whether and how women thought, on the manners of courting these odd creatures and the doom of marrying one. Writing to define social roles developed earlier among English men as the idea grew that gentility, or whatever other qualities men valued, was not inherited but acquired. Supplementing their own self-consciousness, men delighted in describing their ideal woman, an ideal which women would then, of course, emulate. Although it is unlikely that women lived up to this ideal, their concerted attention to an earthly, domestic ideal was assumed. The life of Nancy Shippen, an upper-class Philadelphia belle, unhappily married by her father's wishes, reveals some of the practical pain of living through the literary images of female life.[21]

Education reflected a similar transition from an egalitarian religious justi-fication to an invidious training for the separate spheres of work and leisure. Schools no longer taught primarily God's message but engaged in role defini-tion, by class and by sex. Special schools for young ladies flourished in the major coastal cities, Boston, Newport, New York, Philadelphia, and Charles-ton. After the Revolution, female seminaries extended further inland.[22] Some academic subjects such as appeared in the boys' schools were selected as suitable; these provided what Abigail Adams called the "groundwork . . . of more durable colors." Women learned to respect the serious literature of philosophy and morality, to read history, and thus to talk intelligently with men and to train their children. The rest of learning concerned needlework and table manners, dancing and carriage.

Benjamin Rush, considered the first major American theorist of women's education for an essay he wrote in 1787, defined what social conditions required this limited training.[23] He identified three major responsibilities for which women needed training: all of them centered in the home. The first transformed the old economic partnership by training women in accounts to help their husbands and to "be stewards and guardians of their husbands' property." The second adapted women to the exigencies of raising children without their husbands' assistance; women's education trained them to "in-struct their sons in the principles of liberty and government." And finally women studied to manage their servants who, in America, did not know their place.

Only in the most minimal ways did women react to these changes in terms which showed consciousness of their condition as a social caste. In all the new nation's newspapers men and women argued about women's true nature and American printers republished Mary Wollstonecraft's *Vindication of the Rights of Women* within a year of its appearance in London. Educated men and women discussed her ideas in their correspondence. Some women took up writing as a career, writing for other women and apologizing profusely for their presumption. No framework integrated these responses; none challenged the new restrictions of women's lives.[24]

British "sentimental" novels were read more widely than vindications and feminist dialogues. Such books told tales of seduction and of battles for female virtue against lustful male temptors; sensibility and domestic love triumphed over the temptations of flesh and passion. Samuel Richardson's

*Pamela* won readers' hearts by her heroic struggles against an employer intent on seducing her. In an American counterpart, *The Coquette*, the heroine tried to rebel against decorum but died ignominiously as a result.[25] The morality of sentimentalism defined a series of almost religious tests faced only by women and met by successfully avoiding participation in a masculine world of physical and degrading passion. Not only was the charted course highly repressive of both men and women, but it also set the central conflict of life to be between the sexes. The first victim of that transformation from a common conflict with evil was healthy sex.

## II

By the end of the eighteenth century, the development of a market economy had begun to disrupt and transform the social relations of the family. Pre-industrial labor, as Marx noted, was based upon a spontaneous or natural division of work within the family, depending on tradition and differences in age and sex to determine productive roles. The labor power of each individual member was only a "definite portion of the labor-power of the family" expressed in products—whether crops, livestock, or clothing. By the first decades of the nineteenth century, the growth of manufacturing in home industries had already challenged the basis of these relations by widening the division of labor within the family, and by widening class divisions between families. The development of a true factory system was slow during this period—as late as 1810 two-thirds of the clothing and household textiles of persons living outside the cities was produced by family manufacture—yet, for women, this shift was significant. As products previously produced at home came to be accessible on the common market, whether textiles, various food products, or household supplies like soap and wax, the prestige of women's labor inevitably declined. Moreover, the increasing expression of products as commodities, defined not primarily by their use-value but rather by their exchange-value upon the market, dichotomized those produced under market conditions by socially organized labor (i.e., almost entirely by men) and those produced privately for direct use (i.e., substantially by women and children in the home). The consequent mystification of the exchange process within society was called by Marx commodity fetishism, for it apparently replaced the pre-industrial, direct relationship between producers into "material relationships between persons and social relationships between things."[26] In a society of commodities, the subordinate and secondary value of woman's work and woman herself was necessarily degraded. To replace the spontaneous and relatively egalitarian division of labor in pre-industrial society had come a mode of organization which far more than before thrust women into the role of caring for the home, while men engaged in activities to reshape the world. Furthermore, women's participation in the market economy was mediated through their husbands, thus relegating their own class, status, or privilege to a social function of only their husbands' work.

Similarly, the development of industrial capitalism transformed the roles of the family. While previously the family structure had encompassed a variety of forms and functions, the nineteenth-century family tended to contract into an increasingly private set of relations. The compartmentalization of work and home activities was accompanied by a reevaluation of women (and especially leisured women) as the guardians of traditional moral values. Within rapid industrialization, men were necessarily an increasing part of social changes while women were ironically sacrificed for the preservation of a home which had lost its functional role in the economy. The home became "woman's sphere," fixed in terms of an ideal rather than a realistic evaluation of women's potential roles. The older traditions of feminine usefulness, strength, and duty were cast aside for moral and decorative functions, and subjugation to domesticity became the most revered feminine virtue. Men, on the other hand, commonly were expected to show the inevitable effects of materialistic and base associations of a business life: aggression, vulgarity, hardness, and rationality.[27]

From these new definitions of men and women flowed the reappraisal of the Lady. Earlier, certain colonial imitations of British writings on manners and morals prescribed the gentility, style, limited education, and tolerance that could be expected from women of fashion; and in the South, this imperial practice was greatly emulated. But not until the late eighteenth century did the lady become the paragon for all American women. Colonial women generally, by contrast, had been respected because of the strength and sensuality of their characters, attributes which complemented their participation in the rugged family arrangement of an agricultural and frontier economy. As late as 1890, nearly half of all American women lived and worked in this immediate social environment of a farm family, providing many necessities for the home through daily hard work. Yet the farm wife lost her cultural standing to a new sector of women: the wives and daughters of the rising entrepreneurs and merchant capitalists of the urban Northeast. This new sector remained a numerical minority, while its ethos became central to American Woman's self-definition. Because of their class position, these women gained an hegemony over female cultural patterns never attained by the eighteenth-century elites. Taste, customs, religious and political principles, and above all, morality were reshaped in the nineteenth century through the cultural equivalent of the economic power that capitalists themselves wielded. Thus for all women in the society, this new ideal of femininity became the model, however unrealizable in their own lives.[28]

### III

The nineteenth-century replacement for woman's earlier role in the family was in fact idleness, expressed positively as gentility. The cultural manifestation of this ideal has been aptly called "The Cult of True Womanhood," for the rigid standards held by society amounted to religion-like rites. The True Woman symbolized and actualized stability, expressed in her own cardinal virtues of piety, purity, submissiveness, and domesticity. Religious literature and feminine novels continued and broadened a chaste idealization begun in the eighteenth century, and the newer women's journals emphasized the superficial and fashionable glamour of woman's new image. The functional character of household life was in effect replaced with an *ornamental* attraction of the Fair Lady. Since industrial ethics defined work as masculine, labor of almost any kind was deemed unsuitable for this Lady. Even gardening, a family necessity and appropriate pastime for colonial women, was perceived as a violation of the dainty image. While some contemporary journalists approved of flower cultivation (itself an apparent reflection of Victorian femininity), the usual editorial position unqualifiedly condemned the sight of a virtuous woman tending an onion patch. Thus woman was in a sense transformed from a human being into a living object of art, existing for the pleasure and pride of her husband. She was a creature of solely decorative worth, possessing a beauty which rested upon her frailty, purity, delicacy, and even asexuality. Woman's aesthetic contribution was herself, with her sensuality sublimated in the same sense Freud suggested that all art was sublimated sexuality. Feminine culture was a highly romanticized shell, containing an apparently barren interior.[29]

The new demands on woman were expressed in a subtle but significant *language of repression,* reflecting and reshaping the very conceptions of its users. During this period, for instance, the substitution of "limb" for leg first appeared, to the point of ruthless false consciousness where a breast of chicken was renamed the "light meat." Correct table manners forbade offering a lady the chicken's leg; rather, she always received the "bosum," a common euphemism for this part. In polite company women were referred to as "ladies" or "females," in deference to the risqué connotations of the womb in the more familiar generic label. In the areas of children and family, linguistic repression demanded a sheer absence of some vital discussions. Woman's newer interest in child rearing and infant care was paralleled by an accompanying secrecy involving pregnancy. Despite the rich detail in women's magazines on children's clothing, stories, and habits, talk of pregnancy was proscribed even in the intimate relations of mother and daughter. Gestation was hidden as long as possible and then obscured by the retiring of the prospective mother into confinement. At last, even the term "pregnant" was replaced with the more delicate indirect suggestions as "with child" or "woman's condition." Such conditions viewed as mysterious and wonderful beyond contemplation involved a new level of Victorian myth-making; the stork explanation of childbirth was popular.[30]

New cultural restrictions in Victorian fashion dictated the spread of sexual repressiveness to all aspects of social life. Feminine passivity was ensured by clothing which, through the sheer weight and number of garments, literally enclosed women from the outside world and severely limited their physical mobility. The home was transformed from functionalism to the atmosphere of the showplace, an apt surrounding for the Victorian woman. Similarly, standards of cleanliness for domestic life matched the purity associated with such a feminine setting. More subtle circumscriptions were easily noticed by European travelers such as Harriet Martineau, who, in her accounts of American society, frequently remarked upon the relative severity of woman's domestic subjugation. Martineau implied that the discrepancy between the self-proclaimed democratic ideals of the Republic and the actual condition of American life was best exemplified in the treatment of women. Her books, which pointed to romantic chivalry as sheer substitution for real freedom, were not considered proper reading materials for American ladies. With Mary Wollstonecraft and other rebels, she was vilified as a half-woman or mental hermaphrodite.[31]

Nineteenth-century repression of sexuality was in fact only one manifestation of the total work ethic that required suppression of all social values previously associated with leisure and enjoyment. While new wealth nominally provided new free time, the ascending capitalist norms demanded an individual sacrifice to work, especially among male members of the rising entrepreneurial classes. The accompanying social relationships altered the fundamental conditions of life for man and woman, based substantially upon a sexual polarity established through the industrial revolution. This polarity took various forms of expression. While sex came to be considered dirty, base, and vile, gratification became part of masculine culture, based upon the materialistic functions of male social life. Woman's superior nature depended upon the absence of painful and humiliating sexual participation, save for the satisfaction of her husband and the propagation of the race. Since the relationship between husband and wife was considered based upon property, the male could easily acquire added property without seriously affecting his current holdings. Consequently, promiscuity was allowed only for men, who thereby participated in the rise of prostitution.[32]

Evidence of the effectiveness of female repression may be ascertained in the decline of the birth rate from 1820 to the end of the century. For a society lacking in knowledge of contraceptive measures, such decline could only signify the moderation of sexual relations for the prescribed bearers of society's children. Simultaneously the increasing urbanization and privacy of life enhanced the importance of individual family members. The new status within the family tended to derive from individual worth rather than from group function. Thus while the existence of many children imposed a financial hardship upon the father's income, the single child became more precious and idealized. Childhood was extended to nearly marriageable age, since the presence of few children lowered the burden of dependency. Repression thereby was provided a new outlet, if not a resolution, through the intensified relationship of mother and child.[33]

The double standard ironically intensified the sexual connotations of all social roles. Critics of Victorian society complained of an "over-sexed" concern for life, referring not to the presence of uncontrollable urges but rather to the overly obsessive consciousness of the individual's gender. European travelers often noted the inhibiting effects of the separation of men and women in all public affairs and attributed the low level of American intellectual culture to the stifling effect of women's segregation. Yet, isolation both allowed and forced an advanced sector to search out a special identity, to comprehend and finally act on it. The very nature of Victorian society encouraged women to regard themselves as a special group, as *womanhood*.[34]

The assertion of Woman's moral superiority had important implications. For the first time, women as a group had been attributed an independent power of moral guardianship which, however intellectually degrading, contained the potential of a hidden challenge to woman's traditional political and social passivity. In community reforms, such as schools for the poor and charity and religious organizations, and in social clubs, such as sewing and literary circles, middle-class women recognized the advantages in their forced isolation. Through closer contact with each other, these women gained a new sense of sorority for their common plight and their common aspirations.[35]

These early organizational forms provided models for the later women's rights movement. Political consciousness was added through women's participation in the major reform movements of the times, most of all temperance and abolitionism. Women gained organizational skills and a recognition that leadership was not an exclusively male capacity. By the end of the 1840s, many activists realized that they would not be satisfied with shaping the world indirectly through their moral influence, and they demanded the right to personal liberty and control of their own property. The debates on slavery attended by women especially sharpened their awareness, since many of the basic human rights issues carried implied analogies to women's deprivation and its basis in their material possession by white men.[36]

Most American women in the relatively leisured middle classes rejected the feminist implications in the moral-guardian theory which would extend their traditional domain to social controversy. While these women shared with the feminists an uneasiness with the ideals of gentility and idleness, they responded to a new functionalism of woman's domestic role. The growth of "domestic science" for the home, the spread of teachers' schools for women, and the rationalization of new modes of child-rearing all provided reassertions in new forms of woman's distinct contribution to society. However, the attempt to shore up family life and wifeliness through further training inevitably undercut the very aim of domestication, for some women exposed to outside influences were bound to create, as did Jane Addams and other reformers, still newer patterns for women's social guardianship.

In a popular tract written in 1885, Mrs. A. J. Graves expressed a warning against the danger inherent in over-refinement. Luxurious habits were sapping the strength of the female character, drawing women out of their true sphere. "Home is our palladium," she explained, "our post of honor and of duty, and here we must begin the work of reform." Thus practicality became the counterpart of moral greatness. But in order for women to accept this responsibility, other sources of activity had to be provided within the home. The new standards focused on women as supervisors of a renewed domestic life, responsible for quality of consumption and expanded child-care. Similarly, new standards of cleanliness arose in the nineteenth century, complemented by mechanical developments which made housework less burdensome but not less time-consuming for the devoted housewife. Catharine Beecher, Emma Willard, and others publicized new forms of domestic science, stressing the demands of the newer business and scientific methods on woman's responsibilities. The influential *Godey's Lady's Book* meanwhile mixed colorful fashions with detailed advice on domesticity. And various writers warned women against the "foreign influences" represented by the emerging servant class of Irish rather than native-born women, resolving upon the necessity of able women to manage without such help.[37]

In the early years of the nineteenth century, literature addressed to women had come increasingly to focus on their motherhood, encouraging them to raise good, Christian citizens. This literature glorified the contributions mothers made to society by careful attention to the environment and potential of each child, thereby providing a careerlike responsibility to the job. Theology slowly discovered children and presented a religious experience for young people different from that of their parents: descriptions of their experience and the expectations set for them became less strict, and the Calvinist stress upon their original sin was replaced by notions of childhood innocence. The psychology of John Locke and the pedagogues following him was transferred into popular writings about children, popularizing the impressionability of the human at birth, the need to implant the best hopes for each child and to discover the individual potential for each. These ideas were sharpened and their consequences for women deepened by the growing dichotomy established between men and women. Between passion and sensibility, mind and heart, the abstract and absent father and the leisured and confined mother, the gaps grew enormously. Women came to be viewed as peculiarly suited by nature and training to care for infants and their needs in the home. Culture was considered a feminine province in the world at large, but within each family respect for culture and communication of values was directly manifested by the relations between mother and child. The biological function of motherhood became elevated into a sophisticated and future-oriented definition of woman's social impact. The growing set of ideas with a wide range of detail about home, food, health, clothing, toys and religious training was disseminated almost universally in sermons, women's magazines, books, and newspapers.[38]

Meanwhile, special schools had been established, such as Mount Holyoke in 1837, for the purposes of domestic science and care and teaching of children. The very existence of these schools helped to legitimize women's education, and led to the establishment of the first true women's colleges, such as Vassar in 1867. Women who graduated from the colleges or the transformed special schools became the first professionals and were among the leading feminists of the late nineteenth century. Thus, the concern for rationalizing women's domestic role had at last been transformed, in part at least, to its opposite. Woman's moral guardianship was reinterpreted by such reformers as Florence Kelley and Vida Scudder to be responsibility for influencing the organic evolution of society.[39]

## IV

By mid-century, women's roles in the modern class structure of America were becoming clear. The needs of the increasingly complex society called into existence a new middle class of doctors, lawyers, and other professionals.

In the main, women attained this status vicariously through marriage; but in part, women too shared in the increase of opportunities for direct upward mobility through a variety of experiences and institutions, including women's colleges. Concurrently, a proletarianization process began on a wide scale for formerly rural populations, urban dwellers, and new immigrants. Here too women were for the most part wives, but in increasing numbers were industrial workers for at least a portion of their lives.

At the beginning of industrial capitalism in America, women constituted a basic industrial work force. As early as 1775, women had been employed during the first widespread use of spinning jennies. Government officials and entrepreneurs alike assumed that women were the best candidates for service in this promising sector, in part because work in the developing textile industry involved no encroachment upon traditional male dominated trades or crafts. Women were similarly encouraged to enter early factories because their presence as a surplus labor force allowed men and boys to labor in agricultural production or in the exploration of the West. The first women workers were typically recruited from the town poor-rolls, and for several decades thereafter orphans, widows, and unmarried women formed the ranks of the unskilled industrial laborers.[40]

New England textile mills provided the first opportunity for large numbers of women to work outside their immediate families in nondomestic labor. By the 1820s and 1830s, thousands of young women were attracted by the lure of the factory as an alternative to patriarchal farm life, and traveled to the company towns of Massachusetts and Rhode Island searching employment. On the other hand, due to migration of young men to the West, eastern women between the ages of fifteen and thirty greatly outnumbered their male counterparts and were forced to provide their own livings as single working women. Thus the choice for factory labor was for many more apparent than real, especially when they were faced with the alternative of servitude in a brother's family. Moreover, the prevailing secondary value attached to woman's work restricted women from receiving an education or training to enable them to compete in skilled or professional occupations. Nevertheless, their preference for self-sufficiency obscured this discrepancy, and women competed with one another to gain entry into these new occupations.[41]

The early mills commonly operated under the Waltham system, a form of paternalism which provided the women with boarding houses and a strict code of moral conduct. Despite the lack of individual freedom, the mill environment offered a chance to live in a community of women, to accumulate a small savings from earnings, and to set a pattern for independent living. Although the hours were long, the work was not usually hard, involving comparatively much free time and allowing the employee a chance for conversation and companionship. The first factories had not yet systematized the work process, and therefore production—although often experimental, sporadic, and irregular—had not yet been integrated into a rational routine of labor. Consequently the discipline of the wage earner was far from complete. The early strikes were usually spontaneous outbursts against announcements (or even rumors) of changed policies: wage cuts, speedups, or lengthening of hours. Most important, this semi-agricultural factory population could respond to intolerable changes in working conditions and periods of unemployment by returning to family farms.[42]

These first mills attracted attention for their superficially idyllic conditions. European visitors, familiar with the grim characteristics of British textile industries, marveled over the quaint towns operated by the mill owners and over the gentility and beauty of the young operatives. They were equally fascinated with the *Lowell Offering,* a journal devoted to the poetry written by the mill girls. However, these European promoters often missed the subtle fact that the *Offering* was published and funded by employers to advertise their enterprise rather than to popularize the cultural achievements of their employees. Conditions in the mills were tolerable, and wages were high enough to enable these early industrial workers to set aside a small savings. After four or five years of service, most women permanently left the industry: some moved West where women (and especially teachers) were in demand; some secured an education to set themselves on a brighter path; and others retreated to a life of alleged marital bliss.

By the 1830s, industrialism was developing rapidly, introducing new social and mechanical changes that would fundamentally alter the work situation. Technological improvements in the machinery allowed greater efficiency and promoted speedup of the work process. The new ethos of discipline destroyed the aura of gentility of earlier days, making the mill girl's position less appealing for a rising middle class of women. The depressions of the 1830s as well as western competition destroyed a large number of New England family farms, forcing many daughters into a permanent factory population. Similarly, the Irish immigration beginning in the mid-1830s introduced a new class of women into the mills. Thus, while factory conditions deteriorated (more looms to tend, speeding up, more noise, dust, longer hours) the women who entered the textile industries represented a transformed working population and took these jobs for their lifework. Labor in the mill became a permanent experience and was no longer the first step toward a broader range of opportunities.

By mid-century, the growing work force of women had developed an internal hierarchy. While the unskilled, industrial workers showed life-styles and attitudes characteristic of the proletariat, women in growing professions such as teaching and nursing set themselves apart from their sisters. Moreover, the division between women who worked and those who remained at home was accentuated by the culturally defined "proper sphere" of women. Thus, while a working woman of colonial America had been considered on her own merits, by 1850-60 her counterpart was no longer perceived as an individual attempting to earn a living; rather, she was likely to be judged as a woman who had stepped out of her place and who thereby invited negative evaluation from her society.[43]

Middle-class women who had gained their new leisure in part from the sweat of their working-class sisters customarily returned the favor with deprecation. Although the realization of True Womanhood was possible only as an aspiration for most women, its acceptance by influential and educated groups in society furthered the degradation of lower-class women beyond their physical exploitation. The middle- or upper-class woman who was privileged to work in the privacy of her own home was spared from the spectacle of her indelicacy, while the laboring woman was easily identifiable through appearance, dress, rough manner, and attitude toward life.

Working-class women were inevitably marked by their participation in activities considered masculine. They shared with men a life in the world of business, a material existence which seemed inherently lacking in virtue and purity. In a Victorian culture, class stratification was culturally broadened to divide women into The Good and The Bad. Because the American ideal of femininity was so widely held, even minor deviations from the image, such as dress, carriage, speech, and manners, placed lower-class women outside the pale of respectability. For their part, working women had only one advantage: they alone retained a right to sexual fulfillment. Without birth control and general sexual freedom, this right constituted a negative differentiation. Lower-class white and black women became recognized as prime objects of sexual exploitation, thus preserving the most precious virtue of the Fair Lady. Most lower-class women who entered prostitution did so because the way of life appealed to them, particularly as an alternative to the tedious and restrictive patterns of factory work. Meanwhile, middle-class reformers organized into social-purity associations designed to "save" women from a life of degradation. Reformers were usually careful to attribute the rise of the Social Evil to the new industrial and urban order rather than to the individual wickedness of the prostitutes, but in general ascetic sexual standards were considered the appropriate alternative. Interest in prostitutes was usually limited to charity orphanages and female reform schools designed to educate lower-class children into the ethics of self-control and repressive sexuality. For the individual prostitute, "rehabilitation" was thought unlikely, for Victorian morality was based upon a standard which considered the woman who had lost her virginity as "ruined."[44]

With their own particular needs and desires, working women discerned only slight significance in the demands of organized middle-class women. The ballot, legal rights, and other social reform issues seemed irrelevant or secondary compared to the more pressing problems of daily life. As they explained to social workers later, they wished the "secret" of preventing conception, and when told it was abstinence, scoffed at such a solution as unreal. They envied the leisure of women who complained of boredom. And they viewed the women's educational movement from afar, as designed for those of a privileged class.

Working women shared with their men the opportunities for earning money and participating in wage labor. Consequently, their first expression of feminist consciousness was determined by their status as workers. By and large, they tended to join men in the ranks of organized labor, and they experienced their own sense of strength and power in trade unions. During the late 1830s, factory women became involved in the first genuine trade union protests against the fundamental technological changes in the industrialization process. The formation of a Factory Girls Association, which soon attracted a membership of 2,500, marked an organizational stage which transcended the spontaneous forms of earlier protests and strikes against employers. By the late 1840s, the Lowell Female Reform Association was strong enough to buy out the *Voice of Industry,* a paper which had long benefited from the participation of women. The *Voice* projected a profound critique of True Womanhood, urging its female readers to attend the meetings of the New England Workingmen's Association "without false delicacy." Thus, in 1848, while their middle-class sisters met at Seneca Falls to discuss property rights and suffrage discrimination, advanced factory operatives, such as Sarah Bagley and Huldah Stone, directed their attention to topics of wages and hours. They realized their wages were three to four times lower than those of men working in comparable jobs, due to the inferiority ascribed to their position as workers. As working women, they pronounced a total rejection of the ideal woman that prevented their full participation and remuneration in industry. They rejected notions of feminine frailty, of weakness, of social purity and moral superiority, and passivity.[45]

## V

The accelerating industrialization and urbanization in the closing decades of the nineteenth century offer difficulties of interpretation which women's history has only begun to overcome. The fragmentation of social relations between classes and between men and women again transformed the nature and shape of women's roles. American women passed to new and more specialized relationships with each other through the situation of factory labor and the growth of political and social organizations. Gentility became a widespread ideal, but even where it was realizable in middle-class and upper-class homes, it was undermined by an activist redefinition of moral guardianship. On the other hand, working-class women, a marginal force in the early decades of the century, were by its end coming to discover their class interests and their own special problems.

In the twentieth century, these changes in women's conditions were to develop fully.[46] Structural shifts in the economy and two world wars brought ever-increasing numbers of women into the labor force. Work for women, including married middle-class women, became respectable and desirable. At the same time, the breakdown of the old pre-industrial family unit raised women to the new pedestal of society's primary agents of domestic consumption. Through all this, the ideological pattern of assumptions and stereotypes concerning the nature of woman and the role she was to play proved remarkably adaptable. Overall, women possessed little active capacity for expressing their common difficulties and collective power and generally attempted individual solutions to problems of identity, sexuality, work and self-fulfillment. Only the generalized social fragmentation of the 1960s posed again a *political* intervention, lost since the days of the woman suffrage movement and operating only indirectly through the intervening decades. Women, by all indications, began moving toward a new, collective self-consciousness.

"Woman's awareness of herself," Simone de Beauvoir has noted, "is not exclusively defined by her sexuality; it reflects a situation that depends on the economic organization." In the course of three and a half centuries, that awareness was reflected through the prisms of a colonial community, a transitional Victorian industrializing society, and a commodity-rich but labor-alienated modern capitalist order. There has been no single definition of woman, but rather a succession of definitions in which self-conscious feminism has been provoked, transformed or suppressed, and provoked again. There are signs that self-consciousness has gained new heights and promises to reach still further. For this effort to succeed, women must comprehend the interior and exterior worlds of the growth, both the heightened perceptions of self and the heightened contradictions of a society whose most basic problems remain unresolved.

NOTES

1. Cited in Eugenie A. Leonard, *The Dear-Bought Heritage* (Philadelphia: University of Pennsylvania Press, 1965), 33.

2. Cited in Thomas Woody, *A History of Women's Education in the United States* (New York: Science Press, 1929), I, 135.

3. An excellent study exists of an exception to this statement at the Moravian Brethren's settlement in Bethlehem, Pa. Gillian Lindt Gollin, *Moravians in Two Worlds: A Study of Changing Communities* (New York: Columbia University Press, 1967), describes the colonial community's development in comparison with its German counterpart. In a separate article, Gollin wrote a good study of the attempt to replace family structures in the community: "Family Surrogates in Colonial America: The Moravian Experiment," *Journal of Marriage and the Family* XXXI (1969), 650–58.

4. Until recent years, historians concerned with long-range developments in colonial America were little concerned with social history, and those who dealt with the smaller world of women and children were oblivious to broader questions about society. The most efficient way to begin gathering information about the period is through an extensive bibliography, *The American Woman in Colonial and Revolutionary Times, 1565–1800* (Philadelphia: University of Pennsylvania Press, 1962), compiled by Eugenie A. Leonard, Sophie H. Drinker, and Miriam Y. Holden. Bernard Bailyn, *Education in the Forming of American Society: Needs and Opportunities for Study* (New York: Vintage, 1960), provides some suggestions and bibliography for studying the impact of social change on family structures. Lawrence A. Cremin, *American Education: The Colonial Experience* (New York: Harper and Row, 1970), lists studies on colonial households which are useful in analyzing forces affecting family growth in the New World. Unfortunately, all of these studies are remarkably unimaginative when it comes to piecing together the changes for women; important family changes apparently occur only between fathers and sons.

5. Edmund S. Morgan, *The Puritan Family: Religion and Domestic Relations in Seventeenth Century New England*, rev. ed. (New York: Harper and Row, 1966), deals primarily with the *idea of*, rather than the *practice of*, New England families, but it is valuable for understanding the ideological and religious roles of families in Puritan communities. Insights about family practices can be gained from John Demos, *A Little Commonwealth: Family Life in Plymouth Colony* (New York: Oxford University Press, 1970).

6. Julia C. Spruill, *Women's Life and Work in the Southern Colonies* (New York:

Norton, 1972) is the most thorough documentation of the world of women for any geographical area and a gold mine of information. Chapter one of her book describes the "womanless" years and efforts to import wives. Walter Hart Blumenthal, *Brides from Bridewell: Female Felons Sent to Colonial America* (Rutland, Vt.: C. E. Tuttle Co., 1962), supplements Spruill's account with more detail about procuring the wives.

7. The major study of the colonial sex ratio is Herbert Moller, "Sex Composition and Correlated Culture Patterns of Colonial America," *William and Mary Quarterly*, 3d ser., II (1945), 113–53. His statistics are helpful but the suggestions he offers about cultural effects are so riddled with bad psychology and elementary sexist assumptions that they are useless. Changes in marriage age during the seventeenth century can be found in John Demos, "Notes on Life in Plymouth Colony," *William and Mary Quarterly*, 3d ser., XXII (1965), 264–86, and in Philip J. Greven, Jr., *Four Generations: Population, Land and Family in Colonial Andover, Massachusetts* (Ithaca, N.Y.: Cornell University Press, 1970).

8. Alice Morse Earle, *Home Life in Colonial Days* (New York: Macmillan Co., 1898) still offers a detailed treatment of household production (particularly its tools and processes) in the period. See also Spruill, *Women's Life and Work*, and Leonard, Drinker, and Holden, *The American Woman*. Although not on the colonial period, Jerena East Giffen's " 'Add a Pinch and a Lump': Missouri Women in the 1820's," *Missouri Historical Review* LXV (1971), 478–504, provides detail about production and women's work in another pre-industrial setting.

9. Morgan, *The Puritan Family*, discusses the child-trading phenomenon in New England extensively, although his conclusions about parental fear of intimacy need revision since the appearance of Philippe Ariès, *Centuries of Childhood: A Social History of Family Life*, trans. Robert Baldick (New York: Knopf, 1962). David Rothman, "A Note on the Study of the Colonial Family," *William and Mary Quarterly*, 3d ser., XXIII (1966), 627–34, reviews Bailyn and Morgan in light of Ariès. See also Elizabeth B. Schlesinger, "Cotton Mather and His Children," *William and Mary Quarterly*, 3d ser., X (1953), 181–89.

10. Anne Grant, *Memoirs of an American Lady, With Sketches of Manners and Scenery in America* (New York, 1846), and E. W. and C. M. Andrews, eds., *Journal of a Lady of Quality, Being the Narrative of a Journey from Scotland to the West Indies, North Carolina and Portugal in the Years 1774 to 1776* (New Haven: Yale University Press, 1923). Most of Grant's frequent digressions on the glories of home and mother do not ring true to the pre-Revolutionary time and seem to reflect the early nineteenth-century period in which she wrote. Laws about education for bastards and orphans are discussed in Marcus W. Jernegan, *Laboring and Dependent Classes in Colonial America, 1607–1783* (Chicago: University of Chicago Press, 1931).

11. Henry D. Biddle, ed., *Extracts from the Journal of Elizabeth Drinker, from 1759–1807* (Philadelphia: Lippincott, 1889), shows one woman releasing this role to schools. Anne L. Kuhn, *The Mother's Role in Childhood Education: New England Concepts, 1830–1860* (New Haven: Yale University Press, 1947) shows the results and Woody, *A History of Women's Education*, vol. I, describes the training girls received to raise children.

12. Spruill, *Woman's Life and Work*; Morgan, *The Puritan Family*; and Edmund S. Morgan, *Virginians at Home: Family Life in the Seventeenth Century* (Williamsburg, Va.: Colonial Williamsburg, 1952), are useful here. Puritan attitudes toward sex and evidence of freer practice in the late eighteenth century are described in Charles F. Adams, "Some Phases of Sexual Morality and Church Discipline in New England," Massachusetts Historical Society *Proceedings*, ser. 2, VI (1891), 477–516; in Edmund S. Morgan, "Puritans and Sex," *New England Quarterly*, XV (1942), 591–607; and in John Demos, "Families in Colonial Bristol, Rhode Island: An Exercise in Historical Demog-

raphy," *William and Mary Quarterly*, 3d. ser., XXV (1968), 40–57. The liveliest personal account of sex in the southern colonies is William Byrd, *The Great American Gentleman* . . . (New York: Putnam, 1963), a diary from Virginia.

13. Ironically, the solidarity of pre-industrial American society is illustrated by the Salem witch trials. Nearly everyone in town was involved in the trials. Most accused witches were women, but there were also men; most were white, but there was also a West Indian slave. Witchcraft was a problem for every resident of the village, and its extirpation a collective responsibility. Within that framework, young and old, men and women, poor and well-to-do mobilized.

14. The "outstanding" women of this period have received their share of biographies, most of them terrible, but some providing at least outlines of the possible differences for women of the time. Hutchinson needs to be saved from the outrages of her latest biographer, Emery Battis, *Saints and Sectaries: Anne Hutchinson and the Antinomian Controversy in the Massachusetts Bay Colony* (Chapel Hill: University of North Carolina Press, 1962). Elizabeth Wade White, *Anne Bradstreet: The Tenth Muse* (New York: Oxford University Press, 1971), is a sensitive account of America's first poet. Mary Agnes Best, *Rebel Saints* (New York: Harcourt, Brace, 1925), is a collection of biographies of heroic Quakers, including those women who martyred themselves in Massachusetts. Sarah Harrison was the unsung heroine who refused to swear obedience; see Morgan, *Virginians at Home*, 47.

15. Most writers on colonial children are agreed on this point. Alice Morse Earle, *Child-Life in Colonial Days* (New York: Macmillan Co., 1889); Sandford Fleming, *Children and Puritanism: The Place of Children in the Life and Thought of the New England Churches, 1620–1847* (New Haven: Yale University Press, 1933); and Monica M. Keifer, *American Children through Their Books, 1700–1835* (Philadelphia: University of Pennsylvania Press, 1948). None of these examine practice, but make their judgments on the basis of artifacts.

16. Elisabeth Anthony Dexter, *Colonial Women of Affairs: Women in Business and the Professions in America before 1776* rev. ed. (Boston: Houghton Mifflin, 1931). Dexter's examples, without her concluding discussion about reasons for the decline of this phenomenon, have been picked up by most colonial historians. Her work was one of the first to deal with the transition into the nineteenth century.

17. This discussion is based on Alice Clark's excellent study, *Working Life of Women in the Seventeenth Century* (New York: A. M. Kelley, 1968). Unfortunately her insights and methods have been ignored by American historians.

18. Cited in Leonard, *The Dear-Bought Heritage*, 222.

19. From an advertisement in the *Pennsylvania Gazette*, cited in Woody, *History of Women's Education*, I, 227–28. The triumph of this move is discussed by Gerda Lerner, "The Lady and the Mill Girl," *Midcontinent American Studies Journal*, X (1969), 5–15. Although a number of histories of midwifery in Europe exist, virtually every one is a history of men's contributions to the field. A good but brief account of midwives' resisting of control by doctors in England appears in Thomas Rogers Forbes, *The Midwife and the Witch* (New Haven: Yale University Press, 1969).

20. Sophie H. Drinker, "Women Attorneys of Colonial Times," *Maryland Historical Magazine* LVI (1961), 335–51.

21. Ethel Armes, ed., *Nancy Shippen: Her Journal Book . . . with Letters to Her and about Her* (Philadelphia: Lippincott, 1935). This fascinating story includes her education, marriage, divorce, and Philadelphia social life. For a lengthy commentary by a young girl on the images and choices of women in the same period, see Elizabeth Southgate Bowne, *A Girl's Life Eighty Years Ago* (New York, 1887). Discussions about femininity are especially frequent in newspapers in the 1780s; most of these are available on microfilm. Bertha Monica Stearns, "Early Philadelphia Magazines for Ladies," *Penn-*

*sylvania Magazine of History and Biography* LXIV (1940), 479–91; Mary S. Benson, *Women in Eighteenth-Century America: A Study of Opinion and Social Usage* (New York: Columbia University Press, 1935).

22. Woody, *History of Women's Education,* is the most complete collection of information on women's education. Histories of education are undergoing great changes through redefinition of learning to include what occurs outside of schools and analysis of changes in the relations between family members and between social classes which induce people to formalize learning in schools. Unfortunately very little of this re-thinking has been directed toward women; Cremin's *American Education,* for example, ignores the problem.

23. Benjamin Rush, *Thoughts upon Female Education, Accommodated to the Present State of Society, Manners, and Government in the United States,* in *Essays on Education in the Early Republic,* ed. Frederick Rudolph (Cambridge, Mass.: Harvard University Press, 1965).

24. The extent of feminism during and after the Revolution is a puzzle, in need of clearer categories of analysis and more detailed examination. Many individual women expressed discontent with the image. For one girl's comments on Wollstonecraft, see Bowne, *A Girl's Life,* 58–62. The novelist Charles Brockden Brown wrote two feminist dialogues in *Alcuin* (New York: Grossman, 1971). New Jersey "forgot" to include the word "man" in its new constitution, so that for a short time women could vote. This sort of information is catalogued in a few articles but is confused in vague intellectual history and hazy definitions of feminism.

25. Herbert Brown, *The Sentimental Novel in America, 1789–1860* (Durham, N.C.: Duke University Press, 1940). Hannah Foster, *The Coquette* (Boston: privately printed, 1797). *Memoir of Miss Hannah Adams, Written by Herself* (Boston, 1832) provides an account of a woman making a career of writing. Rush and Hannah Foster and others expressed distaste for female novel-reading but seemed not to have made a dent in its popularity. For a young woman's reaction to *Pamela,* see Sam S. Baskett, "Eliza Lucas Pinckney: Portrait of an Eighteenth Century American," *South Carolina Historical Magazine* LXXII (1971), 207–19.

26. Karl Marx, *Capital* (Modern Library edition), I, 89–90. For an historical overview of pre-industrial conditions and the rise of manufacturing in relation to women, see Edith Abbott, *Women in Industry: A Study in American Economic History* (New York: Appleton, 1910, 1969 Arno reprint), chaps. 1–3.

27. William R. Taylor, *Cavalier and Yankee* (New York: Anchor Books, 1963), 96–99, 118–19; David M. Kennedy, *Birth Control in America* (New Haven: Yale University Press, 1970), 40; William Bridges, "Family Patterns and Social Values in America, 1825–1875," *American Quarterly* XVII (Spring 1965), 3–11; C. Richard King, ed., *Victorian Lady on the Texas Frontier: The Journal of Ann Raney Coleman* (Norman: University of Oklahoma Press, 1971).

28. For examples of colonial definitions see Wallace Notestein, "The English Woman, 1580–1650," in J. H. Plumb, *Studies in Social History, A Tribute to G. M. Trevelyan* (London: Longmans, Green, 1955), 69–107, which describes some of the English seventeenth-century elements of this image; Anne Firor Scott, in *The Southern Lady: From Pedestal to Politics, 1830–1920* (Chicago: University of Chicago Press, 1970), traces the continuation of this ideal of southern womanhood in the antebellum period. For counterparts of women's lives in the frontier, see William Sprague, *Women and the West* (Boston: Christopher, 1940), and Dee Brown, *The Gentle Tamers: Women of the Old Wild West* (New York: Putnam, 1958). Both books contain interesting contrasts with the genteel image of northeastern urban women. See also Janet James, "Changing Ideas about Women in the United States, 1776–1825," Ph.D. dissertation, Radcliffe College, 1954.

29. Barbara Welter, "The Cult of True Womanhood, 1820–1860," *American Quarterly* XVIII (Summer 1966), fully delineates this stereotype. Fuller treatment is accorded by Glenda Riley, "Changing Image of the American Woman in the Early Nineteenth Century," Ph.D. dissertation, Ohio State University, 1967. An interesting, although unfairly critical, analysis of femininity appears in a rarely used source, Fred Vigman's *Beauty's Triumph* (Boston: Christopher, 1966). For one of the earliest descriptions of American Victorian women, see an early work by Mary Roberts Coolidge, *Why Women Are So* (New York: Holt, 1912), which traces the notion of femininity from its origins in the pre-Victorian setting. The single, best collection of documents on women's lives in the nineteenth century is Nancy F. Cott, ed., *Root of Bitterness* (New York: Dutton, 1972). Ronald Hogeland, "The Female Appendage: Feminine Life Styles in America, 1820–1860," *Civil War History* XVII (June 1971), sets up a system of categories for analysis.

30. Many of these restrictions closely resembled and imitated British Victorian culture. Two useful, although sexist, sources are Gordon R. Taylor, *Sex In History* (London: Thames and Hudson, 1953), and Walter E. Houghton, *The Victorian Frame of Mind* (New Haven, Conn.: Yale University Press, 1957).

31. One of the most interesting compilations and analyses of fashions can be found in Bernard Rudolfsky's *The Unfashionable Human Body* (Garden City, N.Y.: Doubleday, 1971); see also Robert Riegel, "Women's Clothes and Women's Rights," *American Quarterly* XV (Autumn 1963), 390–401, for a survey of feminists' responses to and description of Victorian fashion. Thorstein Veblen, *Theory of the Leisure Class* (New York: Macmillan Co., 1899), provides a pointed and still pertinent political interpretation. For an excellent critique of Victorian furnishings, see Siegfried Giedion, *Mechanization Takes Command*, 2d ed. (New York: Oxford University Press, 1948). Harriet Martineau, in *Society in America*, abridged ed. (Garden City, N.Y.: Anchor, 1962), and B. Welter, in "The Cult of True Womanhood, 1820–1860," refer to the interaction of British and American women.

32. Stephen Nissenbaum, "Careful Love: Sylvester Graham and the Emergence of Victorian Sexual Theory in America, 1830–1840," Ph.D. dissertation, University of Wisconsin, 1968, has fully developed the intellectual rationales of repressive sexuality. Similarly, Sidney Ditzion's *Marriage, Morals, and Sex in America* (New York: Bookman Associates, 1953), contains much useful information on male attitudes and theories of sexuality. See also Ben Barker-Benfield, "The Spermatic Economy: A Nineteenth Century View of Sexuality," *Feminist Studies* I, no. 1 (Summer 1972), 45–74. Ironically, one of the most sexist treatments, Erik Dingwall's *The American Woman, An Historical Study* (New York: Rinehart, 1956), describes at length women's denial of their own sexuality; unfortunately, he assigns to women the blame for all the ramifications of the total repressive ethic in America.

33. For a fine but dated scholarly treatment, see Norman Himes, *A Medical History of Contraception* (Baltimore: Williams and Wilkins, 1936); Kennedy's *Birth Control in America* contains a most useful second chapter, "The Nineteenth Century Heritage; The Family, Feminism, and Sex," 36–76.

34. William O'Neill, *Everyone Was Brave: The Rise and Fall of Feminism in America* (Chicago: Quadrangle, 1969), 4–14.

35. William R. Taylor and Christopher Lasch, "Two Kindred Spirits: Sorority and Family in New England, 1839–1846," *New England Quarterly* XXXVI (March 1963). See also Keith Melder, "Beginnings of the Woman's Rights Movement in the United States, 1800–1840," Ph.D. dissertation, Yale University, 1965, and Melder's "Ladies Bountiful: Organized Women's Benevolence in Early Nineteenth Century America," *New York History* XLVIII (1967), 231–55. There is a growing literature on this theme: Carroll Smith-Rosenberg, "Beauty, the Beast and the Militant Women: A Case Study in

Sex Roles and Social Stress in Jacksonian America," *American Quarterly* XXIII (October 1971), 562–84; Glenda Riley, "The Subtle Subversion: Change in the Traditionalist Image of the American Woman," *The Historian* XXXII (February 1970), 210–27; Barbara Welter, "Anti-Intellectualism and the American Woman, 1800–1860," *Mid-America* 48 (October 1966), 258–70; Ann Wood, "Mrs. Sigourney and the Sensibility of Inner Space," *New England Quarterly* XLV (June 1972), 163–81; Ann Wood, "The 'Scribbling Women' and Fanny Fern: Why Women Wrote," *American Quarterly* XXIII (Spring 1971), 2–24.

36. For specialized studies on women and abolitionism, see Samuel Sillen, *Women against Slavery* (New York: Masses and Mainstream, 1955); Aileen Kraditor, *Means and Ends in American Abolitionism* (New York: Pantheon, 1969); Helen M. Lewis, *The Woman Movement and the Negro Movement—Parallel Struggles for Rights* (Charlottesville: University of Virginia Press, 1949); Alma Lutz, *Crusade for Freedom: Women in the Anti-Slavery Struggle* (Boston: Beacon Press, 1968); Jane Pease, "Role of Women in the Anti-Slavery Movement," *Canadian Historical Association Historical Papers* (1967), 67–123; James McPherson, "Abolitionists, Woman Suffrage, and the Negro, 1865–1869," *Mid-America* XLVII (January 1965), 40–47.

37. Mrs. A. J. Graves, *Woman in America* (New York: Harper's Family Library, 1843), 254; Catharine Beecher's best work is *The American Woman's Home: Or Principles of Domestic Science* (Boston: J. B. Ford, 1869); also *Woman's Profession As Mother and Educator* (Philadelphia: George Maclean, 1872) is useful. Helen Papashivily, *All the Happy Endings* (New York: Harper, 1956) traces the glorification of the common woman in the popular domestic novels of the nineteenth century. Other contemporaty works on domesticity include *The Young Lady's Own Book* (Philadelphia: J. Locken, 1841); Lydia Maria Child, *The American Frugal Housewife* (Boston: Carter, Hendee, 1832); Marie McIntosh, *Woman in America: Her Works and Her Rewards* (New York: Appleton, 1850); Mrs. L. Abele, *The Young Ladies' Choice; or Gems by the Way-Side. An Offering of Purity and Truth* (Boston: Higgins, Bradley and Dayton, 1858). See also Elizabeth Bacon, "The Growth of Household Conveniences in the United States, 1865–1900," Ph.D. dissertation, Radcliffe College, 1942.

38. Changes in theology and church practice are described in Fleming's *Children and Puritanism*. The most complete intellectual history of the motherhood literature is Anne L. Kuhn, *The Mother's Role in Childhood Education: New England Concepts, 1830–1860* (New Haven, Conn.: Yale University Press, 1947). Neither book pays attention to the possible chasm between ideas and practice but the sense of development of the ideas is quite good. The elements of the new care are discussed by Kiefer in *American Children through Their Books*, and in a short but provocative article by Barbara Garlitz, "The Immortality Ode: Its Cultural Progeny," *Studies In English Literature* VI (1966), 639–49, in which the influence of Wordsworth and the haloed child is the center of discussion. See Garlitz, "The Cult of Childhood in Nineteenth Century England and America," Ph.D. dissertation, Radcliffe College, 1959, for a fuller examination. Charles Strickland, "A Transcendentalist Father: The Child-Rearing Practices of Bronson Alcott," *Perspectives In American History* III (1969), 5–73, tells an interesting tale of a male theoretician setting rules for his wife. Although his ideas were not particularly successful, more telling is the mother's failure to transcend herself and to meet the standards of idealized warmth and understanding toward her difficult daughters. She simply could not avoid hitting her children or making speedy punishments under the pressures she lived with.

39. Woody, *History of Women's Education*, vol. I; Eleanor Thompson, *Education for Ladies, 1830–1860* (New York: King's Crown Press, 1947); Helen Campbell, *Household Economics* (New York: Putnam, 1898); Albert H. Leake, *Vocational Education of Girls and Women* (New York: Macmillan Co., 1918).

40. David Montgomery, "The Working Classes of the Pre-Industrial American City, 1780–1830," *Labor History* IX (Winter 1968). For information on women who were wards of the state, indentured servants, or simply trained as laborers, see Abbott, *Women in Industry;* Jernagen, *Laboring and Dependent Classes in Colonial America;* Richard B. Morris, *Government and Labor in Early America* (New York, 1946); and A. E. Smith, *Colonists in Bondage: White Servitude and Convict Labor in America* (Chapel Hill: University of North Carolina Press, 1947). Only Abbott deals particularly with women but the other sources provide invaluable information about landless residents of the colonies and provide the legal history defining their lives.

41. Helen L. Sumner, *History of Women in Industry in the U.S.,* vol. IX, Report of the Condition of Woman and Child Wage-Earners in the U.S., U.S. Senate Document 645, 61st Cong. 2d Sess. (Washington, D.C., 1911), is an invaluable source; see also Alice Hyneman Rhine, "Woman in Industry," in *Woman's Work in America,* ed. Annie Meyer (New York: Holt, 1891). Edith Abbott assessed Martineau's findings on the extent of occupations open to women: "Harriet Martineau and the Employment of Women in 1836," *Journal of Political Economy,* XIV (December 1906). For an unusual cataloging of the variety of jobs supposedly open to women at midcentury, see Virginia Penny, *The Employments of Women: A Cyclopedia of Woman's Work* (Boston: Walker, Wise, 1863).

42. Norman Ware, *The Industrial Worker, 1840–1860* (Boston: Houghton Mifflin, 1924), chaps. 5–9, has much background information on industrialism and its effects on the wage-earner, with special reference to the New England mill girls; see also Hannah Josephson, *The Golden Thread, New England Mill Girls and Magnates* (New York: Duell, Sloan, Pearce, 1949); Caroline Ware, *Early New England Cotton Manufacture* (New York: Russell and Russell, 1931, 1966). Lucy Larcom, an early operative, mentions her mill experience in her memoirs, *A New England Girlhood* (Boston: Houghton Mifflin, 1889), chaps. 7–11. She also composed an epic-length poem about life in the mill town, *An Idyl of Work* (Boston: Osgood, 1875). Historians have recently been making new investigations into conditions of life and work in the mills, which may throw into question the interpretations and descriptions offered in this article, especially those suggesting a period of relative freedom of choice during the first years of factory life.

43. Elisabeth Dexter, *Career Women of America, 1776–1840* (Francestown, N.J.: M. Jones, 1950), 218–25, discusses the restrictions placed on working women after the Revolution. The best analysis of class stratification in this period is Lerner's "The Lady and the Mill Girl: Changes in the Status of Women in the Age of Jackson." For a contemporary account, see Helen Campbell, *Prisoners of Poverty: Women Wage Workers, Their Trades and Their Lives* (Boston: Little, Brown, 1887).

44. William Sanger, *A History of Prostitution* (New York: Harper, 1869), one of the earliest attempts at an investigation and analysis of local conditions. Some interesting contemporary accounts offer insights into the prevalence and forms of nineteenth-century prostitution: G. Ellington, *The Women of New York, Or, The Underworld of the Great City* (New York: Arno, 1972, from 1869 ed.); J. D. McCabe, *Secrets of the Great City* (Philadelphia: Jones Bros., 1868) and *New York by Sunlight and Gaslight* (Philadelphia: H. N. Hinckley, 1882). For attitudes toward prostitution, see David Jay Pivar, "The New Abolitionism: The Quest for Social Purity, 1876–1900," Ph.D. dissertation, University of Pennsylvania, 1965, published as *Purity Crusade: Sexual Morality and Social Control, 1868–1900* (Westport, Conn.: Greenwood, 1973). Robert Riegel, "Changing American Attitudes toward Prostitution, 1800–1920," *Journal of the History of Ideas* XXIX (1969), 436–52; Egal Feldman, "Prostitution, the Alien Woman, and the Progressive Imagination, 1910–1915," *American Quarterly* XIX (1967), 192–206. For an interesting account of the two most famous madams of the period, see Charles Washburn's *Come into My Parlor: A Biography of the Aristocratic Everleigh Sisters of*

*Chicago* (New York: Arno, 1974, from 1936 ed.); see also *Nell Kimball, Her Life As an American Madame* (New York: Berkley Publishing Co., 1971); Theodore Rosebury, *Microbes and Morals: The Strange Story of Venereal Disease* (New York: Viking, 1971); D. R. M. Bennett, *Anthony Comstock: His Career of Cruelty and Crime* (New York: De Capo, 1971); Charles Winick and Paul M. Kinsie, *The Lively Commerce: Prostitution in the United States* (Chicago: Quadrangle, 1971), chap. 1.

45. Ware, *The Industrial Worker, 1840–1860;* John B. Andrews and W. D. P. Bliss, *History of Women in Trade Unions,* Senate Doc. no. 645, X, 61st Cong., 2d Sess. (Washington, D.C., 1911); Alice Henry, *Women and the Labor Movement* (New York: Doran, 1923).

46. See Ann Gordon, Mari Jo Buhle, and Nancy Schrom, "Women in American Society," *Radical America* 5, no. 4 (July–August 1971), and Nancy Schrom, "Women in the Twentieth Century," in *Past Imperfect: Alternative Essays in American History,* ed. Blanche Cook, Alice Harris, and Ronald Radosh (New York: Knopf, 1973). For a full historical treatment of economic and political conditions, see William Chafe, *The American Woman: Her Changing Social, Economic, and Political Roles, 1920–1970* (New York: Oxford University Press, 1972).

# Beyond *Kinder, Küche, Kirche:*
# Weimar Women in Politics and Work

## *Renate Bridenthal and Claudia Koonz*

It is a commonplace that the National Socialist assumption of power in Germany in 1933 was to a large extent made possible by a clever manipulation of irrational fears provoked by the economic, social, and political tensions of the time. More than once since the Frankfurt School's famous study on authority and the family it has been suggested that the authoritarianism of the German family contributed to the susceptibility of the population to the siren call of the leadership principle and that threats to the traditional structure of society, especially the family, made people fearful and desperate enough to see a savior in Hitler.[1] Certainly his call for women to return to hearth and home found a responsive audience. The *Kinder, Küche, Kirche* issue in Nazi propaganda implied that women were deserting their homes, their children, and their morality, challenging men's authority by asserting their independence, and by flooding the labor market to such an extent that honest *Familienväter* found themselves without "work or bread," to use the compassionate terms of the otherwise dispassionate 1933 census.[2] Carl Gustav Jung, in his pamphlet *Die Frau in Europa*, was only one of the more distinguished spokesmen for the widely held view that women's emancipation was responsible for endangering not only the institution of marriage but also the whole spiritual balance between the masculine and feminine principles.[3]

The traditional view of liberal historians proceeds on many of the same assumptions, though it appears to welcome the "progress" women made during the years of the Weimar Republic. David Schoenbaum, in *Hitler's Social Revolution,* draws the common picture when he writes of "the economic liberation of thousands of women sales clerks . . . an ever increasing contingent of women doctors, lawyers, judges and social workers . . . thousands of women in shops, offices, and professions in competition with men. . . . The campaign against the democratic republic was a repudiation of the equality of women."[4]

If liberation had been proceeding apace, it is not difficult to understand

Portions of this essay, in a different form, were published by Renate Bridenthal in *Central European History* 6, no. 2 (June 1973); reprinted by permission.

why men would react against it. But how do we account for the fact that large numbers of women voted for Hitler and the conservative parties in spite of the fact that it was the Socialist government of 1918 which gave them the vote and equal civil rights? Prevailing opinion holds that with these legal changes and with equalized employment and educational opportunities, the status of women improved dramatically. If this were so, why did the *Kinder, Küche, Kirche* issue in Nazi propaganda not deflect their votes? An American journalist was incredulous after the 1931 elections: "Why does she [the German woman] vote for a group that intends to take the ballot from her? Why does she support anti-feminism? How are we to account for the fact that in nine cities where the sexes voted separately last autumn, more women than men voted for the Nazis?"[5]

German women did not merely lose the fight for equality; they joined the opposition. How do we account for this enigma? Was there something dubious about these new options? We will show that the conservatism of Weimar women must be seen in the context of the fraudulence of their supposed emancipation. Despite the rhetoric about women's emancipation, patriarchal ideology continued to dominate all institutions of German economic and political life.

### I

German women received the right to vote as part of that spate of reforms commonly termed the "November Revolution" of 1918. They voted for the first time in the National Assembly elections two months later. When the Weimar constitution was drafted, women were assured that "women and men have basically the same rights and duties," and promised that all discrimination against women in the civil service would end.[6] Prior to November 1918, only the Socialists had advocated women's suffrage as an official party demand. But once the reform became law, all political parties hastily inserted planks on the "woman question" into their platforms, issued numerous pamphlets to attract the new voters, and included women in lists of candidates for office. No politician publicly opposed women's suffrage. Even the leader of a women's organization opposed to women's rights quickly dropped her crusade and ran for election to the National Assembly.[7] All obvious hostility to women in politics disappeared as women were officially welcomed into public life.

Judging from the first elections, women responded enthusiastically to their newly granted right. Nearly 80 percent of all eligible women voters cast their ballots in 1919—a slightly higher percentage than that of the eligible male voters.[8] Nearly 10 percent of the National Assembly delegates were women and between 5 and 10 percent of the state legislators elected shortly thereafter were women.[9] Most contemporaneous observers believed this immediate acceptance of women into political life augured well for the future of women's rights.

Such an auspicious beginning would lead, they predicted, to legal reforms, widespread social legislation, wage equalization, improved protection for women workers, and increased educational opportunities for women and girls. As one Social Democrat put it: "We have voted, we have sent women to all levels of local and state government, and we have helped to write the Constitution. . . . We have created the necessary foundation upon which we can build that equality which alone will make us free."[10] Non-Socialist women were also optimistic. "A new Golden Age dawns! The outlines of a new German realm become clear. And we will help build it!" exclaimed a journalist in a popular middle-class women's magazine.[11]

The right to vote was not regarded as an end, but as the means by which women could work toward complete equality. After 1918 women could continue their fight for emancipation within the political structure instead of outside it. Rights, therefore, became linked with new responsibilities;[12] demands transformed into duties.[13] Socialists had always welcomed women into their ranks and vigorously opposed any autonomous women's organization. Now liberals and conservatives also incorporated women into their party organizations and the women agreed it was time for women to cease being "equal righters" (*Frauenrechtlerinnen*) and to become party members.[14] This did not mean that these women intended to end their struggle for equal rights, but it did indicate that they were convinced this struggle could best be waged from within the party structure.

This optimism proved to be unfounded. Despite the frequent praise of the emancipated German woman, the progress of women's rights was disappointing. Judicial decisions upheld women's legal inequality in family law and property rights. Wages, job security, and working conditions continued to be more favorable for men than for women. Even sweeping legislation to protect mothers and improve health care for children failed to pass in the Reichstag. The "woman question" continued to be one of the most controversial topics of the 1920s, but the economic and legal status of women did not improve. As one psychologist commented in 1932, "The fact that there is a woman here and there has not altered the status quo in the slightest."[15]

Perhaps most disillusioning to proponents of emancipation was the fact that women's participation in the political process did not increase after 1919. Quite to the contrary, in each election fewer eligible women bothered to vote at all. With every election fewer women appeared among the Reichstag delegates.[16] Although most of the leaders from the women's movement joined the Democratic party and Socialists had long advocated women's rights, German women in general did not heed their call and voted instead for those parties which had for so long opposed women's rights. This trend was established in the earliest elections of Weimar and did not change thereafter. For example, the women's vote affected the 1928 Reichstag in the following ways: it increased the delegates of the Catholic Center by twelve, those of the Nationalists by nine, and those of the Right liberals by two; it decreased the delegates of the Democrat, Socialist, Economic, and Nazi parties by one to four, and of the Communists by eight. (See Table I.)[17]

The explanation for women's persistent loyalty to conservative parties can be found in the reactions of politicians to their new women constituents. Before examining the responses of various parties, several generalizations

Table 1. Impact of the women's vote on 1928 Reichstag elections

| Party | Total delegates elected | Estimated delegations based on male vote only | Loss or gain due to female vote |
|---|---|---|---|
| Catholic Center | 62 | 50 | + 12 |
| National Fatherland | 73 | 64 | + 9 |
| People's | 45 | 43 | + 2 |
| Democratic | 25 | 26 | − 1 |
| Social Democratic | 153 | 157 | − 4 |
| Economic | 23 | 24 | − 1 |
| Communist | 54 | 62 | − 8 |
| National Socialist | 12 | 16 | − 4 |

about all parties may be considered. Both male and female politicians hoped that women would one day participate equally in politics. But women politicians would not be the same as men. Women could bring into political life special feminine concerns and ideals. They were more able than men to stand above party squabbles and strive for distant objectives. Both men and women agreed that further reforms were necessary to realize women's equality in public life. However, no one imagined that motherhood would cease to be the major concern of all normal women. Special legislation should protect women factory workers who were forced to work for wages; "exception women" in the professions were not to be hindered by sex discrimination; expanded social legislation would encourage more women to devote themselves exclusively to homemaking. Women, idealists predicted, would retain their separate identity, but be treated equally.

## The Socialist Parties

According to Marxist theory, the basis for women's special oppression in society is capitalism. While reforms within that system might ameliorate some conditions, no satisfactory emancipation of women can occur until the ultimate triumph of Socialism. Similarly, the inferior place of women within the family was attributed, not to vague entities like the male ego, but to the system of private property. It followed that for women to achieve true emancipation, they must join the ranks of socialism and fight for the overthrow of capitalism. Bourgeois women who organized in separate groups to win women's rights were called "female parasites" by Socialists.[18] Any woman Socialist who devoted too much attention to the potentially divisive "woman question" was regarded with suspicion. The woman Socialist's job was to educate other women and convince them that a Socialist state was worth fighting for. This meant fighting "shoulder to shoulder" with the men to achieve broad Socialist victory.

In 1918 and 1919 the Communists ignored the woman question altogether. Revolution, they believed, would soon solve all the problems of capitalism. Issuing broadsides, planning lectures or otherwise recruiting women supporters seemed unrelated to achieving the immediate overthrow of bourgeois society. Of the twelve million leaflets and three million pamphlets distributed by the KPD during the year following the "November Revolution" none mentioned the "woman question."[19] As it became clear that the anticipated overthrow would not occur, however, the party entered electoral politics and simultaneously began to devote some attention to attracting women voters. "Agitation among women" appeared on an earlier agenda, but this issue was removed from the discussion until the third party congress in February 1920.[20] Comrade Marz, who introduced the subject, assured her audience that it was understood that party agitation among women would not rest "on any sort of exclusively women's interests," but would aim at encouraging "proletarian women to join their male class comrades in the fight for communist goals."[21] This type of disclaimer did not, it should be noted, accompany the debates about agitation among other special groups, such as soldiers, youths, and peasants. But, despite women's promises to subordinate their concerns, the woman question was especially divisive throughout the Weimar years.

Unlike the Communists, both wings of the Socialist party realized they had to attract women voters from the very beginning of the Weimar Republic. From the earliest postwar days women's issues appeared in party literature and women candidates were placed on Socialist ballots. The Social Democrats, Independent Socialists and Communists each urged women to eschew the other Socialist parties. However, despite this rivalry there was very little difference among the three parties where the woman question was concerned. All Socialists demanded guarantees of the woman's right to work; protective legislation and improved factory inspection; increased maternity and health care benefits; the granting of full legal status to out-of-wedlock children; the establishment of day care facilities; better social welfare protection for families with insufficient incomes; and, finally, cooperation between Socialist men and women.[22] Equal pay for equal work did not appear as a demand. Except for some Communist pamphlets, Socialist propaganda did not mention demands for the overthrow of the family. Quite to the contrary, left-wing parties consistently attacked the right for allowing capitalism to destroy the family. Specific party statements on the woman question were dictated by expediency. This meant emphasizing issues which would attract the maximum number of women supporters without alienating Socialist men voters.

Socialists and Communists set out to recruit more women members in similar ways. Organizations for women workers, proletarian girls' clubs, educational courses in homemaking and political theory, consumer cooperatives, lectures or reading evenings and weekend outings comprised the major activities for members and supporters. Although the female vote never exceeded the male vote for any Socialist party, the ratio of women members to men members improved in the Social Democratic party after several years of organizing. In 1924 women comprised 15.8 percent of the Socialist party; by 1928 this percentage had risen to 21.1 percent, and in 1930 it was 23 percent.[23] It was mainly in the urban areas where women comprised an increasing proportion of party members—in rural areas the ratio of men to women was as high as fifty to one.[24]

As women increased their constituencies, they received a decreasing share of party offices, party budgets, and influence. Invariably these requests were circumvented or denied. With each election, fewer Socialist and Communist women were sent to the Reichstag; fewer party offices were held by women.[25]

On several occasions (usually in the semiprivacy of party meetings or in the pages of *Die Genossin,* the newsletter for leading party women) SPD women did protest their poor representation. When they did, Socialist men (and sometimes women, too)[26] usually responded with accusations that women had not yet been successful in marshaling women workers to the cause of socialism. Often they even blamed the failure of so many Socialist reforms on the granting of women's suffrage. It was the conservative women's vote, they asserted, which prevented the Socialist parties from obtaining a majority in the Reichstag.[27] Sometimes the women countered this charge.

> You accuse us of not correctly utilizing the ballot. . . . The big brother scolds us, the little sister. If, in the 38 years during which we have worked [for Socialism], we had encountered a little more practical socialism within the family, then women might have a little more love and understanding for socialism. . . . The guilt belongs with big brother. Before you did not think it worthwhile to bother enlightening the inferior woman. Now we all must suffer.[28]

Neither Socialists nor Communists integrated their positions on women's oppression into the general framework of party ideology. No party pamphlet or newspaper addressed to the general reader discussed women's oppression. Even an exhortation to Communist men telling them to send their women to party meetings appeared in the women's pages of the party paper.[29] Of between twenty-five and thirty-six books listed as suggested reading for Communists in the 1920s, none mentioned women (although four were written by Luxemburg and three by Zetkin).[30] Similarly, an annual Socialist publication, *Our Program in Word and Picture,* never mentioned women—except in one picture which urged, "Women, organize yourselves!"[31] Socialist journals, pamphlets, and newspapers were addressed to men. Contrary to Socialist appeals about marching shoulder to shoulder, the women's organizations were regarded merely as useful auxiliaries.

Socialists and Communists understood that the "woman question" could become an extremely divisive issue. Occasionally someone would comment on the fact that "between men and women erupts an abrasive fight over bread and work,"[32] but these discussions were dropped at once. Socialist theory dictated that antifeminism stemmed from male workers' insufficient understanding of capitalism—their true enemy. Hostility toward women indicated some form of dissatisfaction (however crude) with the capitalist system. Rather than directly attacking this false consciousness, Socialists sought to redirect it against the capitalist system. The parallel with Socialists' views on anti-Semitism is striking in this respect.[33] The Marxist parties did not want to eliminate antifeminism; they wanted to use it. Their rhetoric was designed primarily to attract women voters, which was not necessarily the same as emancipating women.

## Liberal and Conservative Parties

The non-Socialist parties, of course, campaigned vigorously to attract the "woman vote." Their appeals stressed protection for women workers and mothers, improved educational opportunities for women, and increased social services to aid families with many children. To a greater extent than the Socialists, bourgeois politicians stressed the importance of legal reforms to implement the equality of women in the family and in professions.[34] Liberal and conservative women promised to infuse German public life with a new idealism, and male politicians welcomed this promise with enthusiasm. What the nation needed, according to this analysis, was not a socialist or economic revolution, but rather a spiritual revolution. At best what they wanted could be termed a "reformation" and, at worst, "counter revolution." In any case, women of the center and right believed they had a very special role to play in the reconstruction of Germany. Both men and women would have to change their traditional attitudes to encourage women to contribute to public life. But this new outlook did not mean that women were to abandon their feminine nature or concerns. Quite to the contrary, they were encouraged to assert their femininity and play a leading role in pressing for domestic reforms. After four years of wartime propaganda which urged women to maintain morale on the home front and which built up women's self-esteem, this message was already a familiar one in 1918–19. The non-Socialist parties simply redirected this basic appeal away from the defense of the fatherland and toward the victory of their own parties. As with the left-wing parties, the center and right wing stressed one message to woman voters: "we need you." But these parties added, "without you Germany will collapse and fall into the chaos of Socialism."

One nationalist poster addressed its appeal to the rural women: "TO THE DEAR, GERMAN COUNTRY GIRLS! You wonderful, energetic, brave German country girls with the healthy red cheeks and the fresh, pious hearts—we are counting on every one of you!"[35] Another conservative woman, Clara Viebig, called on women to fight socialism: "we do not want civil war—whether we live in villas or huts!"[36] Democratic party leader Gertrud Bäumer reminded her readers, "The Revolution called us into political life; but now we are also called on to oppose the Revolution."[37] Right-wing liberal Clara Mende urged bourgeois women to plunge themselves into politics in order to defeat the "women's troops" of the socialist parties.[38]

The non-Socialist parties had a distinct advantage in recruiting women. They could capitalize on women's self-image as housewives and mothers. Socialists had to re-form women's view of themselves from "wife" to "worker" before their propaganda could be fully effective. Bourgeois propaganda emphasized the importance of women within traditional roles and accorded to the *Kinder, Küche, Kirche* ethos a higher status than formerly.

This attitude toward women and their traditional role has become known as the "pedestal" mystique. In Weimar Germany, the application of this mystique had an unusually deleterious effect. Even before Ludendorff's testimony about the "Stab in the Back" legend, women had begun to blame themselves for the low morale on the home front. The brave young men marched gallantly off to the front with the song "Deutsche Frauen, Deutsche Treue" on their lips,[39] while the women at home could not even prevent disorder and lawlessness.[40]

If Germans had been defeated on the home front, were not women largely to blame? Democrat Marianne Weber was horrified that just before the surrender, "Minor shoplifting went unpunished; no one had any respect for rationing. Cunning, selfishness, vile profiteering, dishonor, shameless hoarding and swindling permeated all circles."[41] She uttered not a word about the responsibility for the outbreak of the war or about the conditions created by the blockade; instead, she heaped recriminations upon herself and other women at home for not preventing this "spiritual decay"! This was to be a persistent motif throughout the Republic. Women, disappointed with the new government, would wonder wherein they had failed or what remained for them to do in order to achieve that putative utopia, "The New Germany." While it may inflate the ego to be praised for "spiritual" superiority, the theory is a pernicious one. However flattering, it is futile to accept responsibility for a phenomenon over which one has no control. Germany's malaise in the twenties was not created by women; nor would it be overcome by their efforts—spiritual or otherwise.

The obstacles to creating a spiritual revolution or reformation may have been formidable, but women of the center and right were undaunted because the tasks assigned to them were already so familiar. Mrs. Friedrich Naumann (whose husband founded the German Democratic party) listed the priorities for women in the "New Germany": (1) Avoid de-population; (2) maintain national unity; (3) make the people's state (*Volksstaat*) a pleasant place for all; (4) improve public school education; (5) maintain Germanic traditions and high health standards; (6) feel oneself to be a German citizen.[42]

The Catholic Center party belatedly welcomed new women voters and expressed the hope that women's new status would aid the national effort to attack decadence. In fact, the party platform linked demands for protection of the woman and family with a call "forcefully to oppose any degenerate art and all avant-garde literature . . . [we must] allow women free opportunity to cooperate . . . utilizing the full capabilities of the feminine nature."[43] Although the Catholic Center party sent only a few women delegates to the Reichstag during the Weimar Republic, it remained the most successful in attracting women's votes.[44] The right-wing liberal German People's party also insisted that women's political activity was the natural consequence of their newly elevated status as wives and mothers. Katarina von Kardorff railed against the "irrational and emotional" Weimar constitution which had been written by men. She called on German women to attack male values and protect democracy. "Women by nature reject dictatorship and injustice more than men do."[45] Nationalist politicians explicitly recognized that housework must be accorded new status if women were to remain satisfied with their traditional role. "The irreplaceable value created by the work of housewife and mother must be socially and economically recognized."[46]

Thus the parties of the center and right agreed that while women's self-image would not undergo a basic change after women's suffrage was granted, the *image* of women had to be refurbished. *Kinder, Küche, Kirche* were expanded to include education, home economics, and social work. Simultaneously, the need for such services was emphasized by politicians of all parties. Since the Reichstag consistently rejected increased spending for social welfare projects and deferred basic legal changes that would affect women's lives, this posture was hypocritical.

Moreover, there was a basic contradiction in the rhetoric of the liberal and conservative parties. On the one hand they claimed that women's suffrage marked an important landmark in the progress of women's emancipation; on the other, they claimed that it would not initiate drastic changes in the social structure or family. One of the most dramatic examples of this hypocrisy may be found in a Democratic party pamphlet of 1919 which suggested themes for local campaign posters. After some general appeals for "peace, solidarity, and unity" came a second set of appeals to the "family father." Recalcitrant men who still opposed women's suffrage were told, "You do not need to fear the loss of your position in your home: remain just who you were and who you will be! But bring your daughter and your wife along with you to vote. As odd as it may seem, you *should* discuss politics with them. . . . You must become their political educator!" The next set of suggestions was directed at women voters, who were reminded that "your vote is your own business. No one—either in your family or where you work—ought to tell you how to vote."[47]

Within each of the center and right-wing parties, women did press for more far-reaching changes. As in the Socialist parties, women requested more party funds for their activities and greater recognition of women's issues from the party as a whole. "You rely too strongly on the loyalty of the woman," warned one Democratic woman in 1927. "We need publicity, literature and funds for educational activities just like all other groups."[48] Catholic women wished that their party would devote more attention to moral, educational, and religious issues.[49] Katarina von Kardorff warned in 1930 that she might form a "Mother's League" if the People's party did not accord more importance to women's demands.[50] Anna Mayer, lawyer and member of the liberal People's party, complained that many legal reforms were essential if women were to become equal citizens.[51] Nationalist women assured their male colleagues that "we do not want to be a party within a party," but added, "women do need their own special forum to discuss the issues which concern them."[52]

Despite the requests for greater attention to women's issues, the percentages of women in Reichstag delegations from liberal and conservative parties did not increase during the Weimar Republic. The Democrats' 1920 delegation included 9 percent women in 1920 and declined to 7 percent in 1930; Catholic Center representation dropped from 6.3 percent in 1919 to

4.6 percent in 1924 and rose to 5.9 percent in 1930; The People's party delegation included 4.5 percent women in 1919 and 3.5 percent in 1930; the Nationalist representation included 7 percent women in 1919, 2.6 percent in 1928, and 7.3 percent in 1930.[53] While these percentages were not as high as similar statistics for liberal and socialist parties, representation of women at state and local levels was far lower—typically under 1 percent.[54] Moreover, German women displayed little concern about the relative absence of women on the ballots and persisted in their preference for the parties of the right. These parties emphasized the primacy of the family and encouraged women to participate in politics in order to preserve and enhance their status within their traditional role.

## II

The ethos of *Kinder, Küche, Kirche* was further reinforced by developments in German economic life. Modernization, usually held to be a progressive, liberating force for women, appears on closer scrutiny to have been a retrogressive, constricting force.

### Labor Force Participation

To begin with, the much-vaunted increase of women in the German labor force was itself partly a statistical delusion. The first postwar census of 1925 showed 35 percent of all women to be working, an increase of 5 percent over 1907. Less remarked upon was the increase in the proportion of men working: 6.6 percent to include 68 percent of the total male population. Thus, while there was a somewhat larger relative increase in the proportion of women working, within the framework of a generally expanding work force, the change was not spectacular. Before the war, women made up 34 percent of the working population; after the war, 36 percent.[55] Hardly a great leap forward. Three million more women entered the work force, but so did four million more men. Women's presence was felt more because it had never really been accepted in the first place and because inflation and depression made jobs scarce and competitive.

Some of the upsurge in women's work was due to the imbalance in population caused by the war and was considered to be temporary. In 1925 there were 32.2 million women to 30.2 million men, or 1,072 women to 1,000 men, a differential which, it was hoped, would be reduced by the time of the next census in 1933.[56] The participation of women in the work force was not seen to be on an upward trajectory, but was expected to decline as women got busy replacing the "lost" population.[57] The falling birth rate was anxiously watched as were the suspiciously high figures for miscarriages reported by sickness insurance agencies.[58] Women were not supposed to be working or independent; they were supposed to be producing babies.

A second statistical misinterpretation is due to the fact that the census of 1925 gave women more latitude in defining their status. They could now register as gainfully occupied full time if they considered their main subsistence to derive from participation in the business of the head of household. This immediately accounted for one-third of the reported female working population, or 4.1 million women, only half of whom had reported themselves in this category before the war.[59] Part of the reason was definitional and part was real: with the impoverishment of the small establishment, hired help was let go and wives took over more of the work. As "helping dependents," however, they can hardly be considered liberated. For one thing, they were working harder than ever, and for another, they had no control over the property mutually acquired with their husbands.

Most of the remaining 7.4 million gainfully occupied women were wage earners, whom the Revolution of 1918 had promised equal pay for equal work and for whom special legislation was enacted regarding night work, midday breaks, and maternity leave.

A good way of looking at all of these eleven and a half million economically productive women is by economic sectors, not only because the census material is organized that way, but because such a division is useful for an analysis of change. Agriculture, industry, distribution, and services are not only contemporaneous activities. The development of each in relation to the others indicates change along an historical continuum. Keeping in mind that the period of the Weimar Republic was itself a moving point along a longer line of national industrialization, we can look at the place of women in each sector and analyze their changing role in at least this one case of rapid modernization.

### Agriculture

Nearly half of all the working women in the Weimar Republic were in agriculture, most of them peasant wives, that is, "helping dependents," upon whom the war, the blockade, and postwar reconstruction had placed a very heavy burden. Industrialization in the late nineteenth century had drawn men out of the country, leaving women to do more and more of the farm work, a trend intensified by male absence during World War I, so that in 1925 there were actually more women than men working in agriculture.[60] In the second period of the republic, however, when the rationalization of industry and some aspects of agriculture intensified, women were drawn into the former and pushed out of the latter. By 1933, men again dominated in agriculture and even the total female population in the countryside fell disproportionately, leading to complaints of *Frauenmangel* (lack of women) while the rest of the nation worried about its *Frauenüberschuss* (surplus of women).[61]

What this means is that when the family farm became more labor-intensive relative to other sectors of the economy, women assumed an increasing share of the work. Peasant wives suffered the most, since the eight-hour day and regulated wages now made hired help unprofitable and put a greater burden on the family, creating conditions which probably did not endear the republic to peasant women. Many maids were let go. However appealing city lights may have been to the young women who left the country, it should be remembered that it was mainly economic pressure that forced their departure.[62] Meanwhile, the peasant woman toiled in field and garden, did the dairying and poultrying which brought her an independent income for household expenses, and carried out her normal household duties. A cross section of the Württemberg peasant economy showed the wife working an average of 12 percent more hours a year than her husband and 40 percent more than the hired help, while it was reckoned that she consumed only 80 percent of the food needed by an adult male.[63] Even before the war, the peasant wife had begun to murmur: she chafed against the "raw despotism" of her husband who, she complained, seemed to care more for his cattle and fields than for his wife, treated her like a dog or a baby-producing machine, and rarely appreciated her until she was dead.[64]

As modern techniques began to penetrate agricultural life in the second half of the Weimar period, they tended to displace the woman rather than give her a new and more prestigious role. Thus, when dairying and poultrying became big businesses with state subsidies, they became male-dominated. Women were forced to turn for every household need to their husbands, whose income before had been reserved for farm maintenance and taxes. This new situation caused family friction and, on the part of women, an increasing sense of dependence and frustration. Their daughters had no incentive to stay and become like their mothers. Many, like their lesser cousins, the maids, left for the city.[65]

Furthermore, women literally lost ground as heads of farms. In 1907 they made up 14 percent of the independent heads of farm households; in 1925, this had slipped to 12 percent; by 1933, it was down to 10 percent.[66] Moreover, most of their farms were tiny: women owned about half the miniplots under one hectare and a diminishing proportion of larger farms. With inflation and depression, the smallest ones were absorbed by the middle-sized ones, reducing the number of female owners.[67]

Nor did women come to occupy an important place in the new agricultural ventures. They held only one-sixth of the management positions in 1925 and only one-twelfth, in 1933.[68] Prewar optimists about women's future in agriculture gave way after the war to more cautious prognosticators. A women's vocational guide for agricultural professions stressed the teaching of home economics and suggested gardening as a career, provided that candidates not set their sights much higher than gardener's aide. It acknowledged the fact that males were preferred in large-scale poultrying or dairying; smaller enterprises were more likely to welcome women, of whom they also expected domestic services. It concluded by reminding women that, in general, management positions were closed to them since men resented female supervisors.[69]

### Industry

If half the agricultural working population was female, only one-third, and later only one-fourth, of the industrial working population was female, another indication of the reduced role women played in the modernizing sectors. Urban nonworking wives of industrial laborers became dependent on their husbands for the income needed to purchase essential items they might once have produced, such as food and clothing. They lost their economic indispensability, a condition whose psychological effects are only now being explored in depth. On the other hand, the wife of a worker whose income did not provide the basic necessities had to work for wages in order to buy them. If she had small children, she usually did piece work at home, which often meant crowding an already overcrowded city apartment and working for the most exploitative rates of all. If she worked in a factory, her life became divided, introducing the familiar split from which many women still suffer, with all its attendant guilt for not being at home all day.

In addition, much of the legislation designed to protect women was a sham. The eight-hour day did not account for work taken home at night by underpaid women workers. Midday breaks were curtailed because women preferred to leave earlier in the evening in order to prepare dinner for their families—and were grateful for the right to do so. Maternity-leave policy was consistently violated by women who could not afford six unpaid weeks. The result was job instability, since women had to report pregancy to their employer. There was also a suspiciously high rate of miscarriages, as reported by firms and insurance agencies.[70]

The war brought women of all the belligerent countries into industry, but Germany sustained the largest proportional increase and generally maintained, though did not enlarge, this increase during the postwar years.[71] In March 1917, women first outnumbered men at work and their number grew until the end of the war.[72] Defense-related needs brought them into industries that had never employed them before: for example, Krupp, which hired no women in 1913, reported 28,302 of them by 1918; and roughly three-fifths of the metal industries in Rhineland Westphalia introduced women for the first time during the war. Other fields, such as chemicals, opened wider, and even some closed crafts, such as the printing trades and locksmiths, admitted women for the first time. In light industry women predominated up to 75 percent in many plants during the war and in those of heavy industry they often reached 25 percent.[73] Social work expanded to meet the needs of fatherless families and the bourgeois women of the organized feminist movement rushed to help with food distribution, job information, housing, and child care.[74] Behind the lines, women did the traditional sewing, cooking, and nursing for the army, but they also freed men for the front by getting into the heaviest work, such as construction of munitions dumps, road building, dynamiting, setting up barbed wire, and so on. A communications division uniformed in blue almost became an official news corps of the army, but the war ended before its formation. Insufficient statistics prevent any clear picture of the entire extent of female participation in the war effort, but it seems clear that while some sex barriers to work were dropped, most of the new jobs were unskilled and did not promise much in the way of professional advancement for women.[75]

Backlash was evident as early as the winter of 1917 when the war ministry, preparing demobilization, established guidelines for women to relinquish their jobs to returning veterans. Demobilization set the tone for later arguments used especially during the Depression that women competed with men for work. With the worsening economic situation of the early 1920s, tension between the sexes over jobs increased. Women were either sent home (which might mean back to the country), or released into the economic custody of their returning husbands or fathers or brothers, or placed in domestic service, or retrained in some traditionally feminine line like sewing.[76] Those who kept their jobs suffered a revived discrimination in wages. The socialist-backed demand for equal pay for equal work, written into some contracts immediately after the revolution, was gradually retracted beginning in 1920, when male-dominated unions adjusted to capitalist realities. Wage differentials between men and women settled around 30 percent to 40 percent. This was an improvement over prewar levels which had been 50 percent to 60 percent, but disappointed the proponents of women's equality, who now had to settle for merely a reduced inferiority.[77]

Although the unions bitterly fought home industry, the old standby for women who had to work, it proved ineradicable.[78] The most exploitative of all wage labor, since it drew on the vulnerable group of mothers, invalids, and pensioners, and since it placed the costs of overhead such as rent and utilities on the worker, home industry was nevertheless a *sine qua non* of many a household. The government's and the unions' attempts to suppress this source of income encountered bitterness and suspicion on the part of many women who had already been deprived of their factory jobs.[79]

What ultimately made female employment seem threatening to men was the extensive rationalization of industry after 1925. Generally this meant standardization of parts, and serial or flow production, that is, improved movement of the product along assembly lines. Intensive mechanization was more rare, since the amount of available capital was limited. The breakdown of work into small, simple, mechanical, repetitive tasks made the hiring of cheap, unskilled labor possible, and women were the most available source. They did not, however, actually displace men in most cases. What happened was that industries which already employed many women expanded. Most affected were those industries which had rationalized even earlier and whose products now came into greater demand, such as the electro-technical, chemical, paper, and duplicating industries, and metalware manufacturing. These had employed women on a fairly large scale for some time, ostensibly for their patience, precision, and dexterity—arguments rarely advanced on behalf of female surgeons—but in fact for their low wages as unskilled and docile labor.[80]

After 1925, consumer industries grew in Germany. The chemical industry developed soaps, perfumes, and cosmetics, enlarging the branches which employed women. Those of men, largely in factory maintenance and transport, remained about the same. Similarly, the amount of electrical products made mainly by women, such as bulbs, telegraph and telephone equipment, wires, and radios, grew faster than the items produced mainly by men in the heavy-current industry, such as turbines and transformers.[81] The clothing and food industries, which traditionally employed many women, expanded, as did the proportion of women in them—again because the kind of work they did was related to production, which increased; men, however, worked in the more unchanging areas of plant and delivery.[82] Only in optics and precision tools and in the manufacture of metal wares did the development of standardized parts actually displace men, but to a very small degree.[83]

As noted earlier, the proportion of men in the labor force also increased. Of the one and a half million new jobs added in the period from 1925 to 1933, 77 percent were taken by men.[84] Their jobs came from gains in construction and in the development of heavy industries, such as iron and steel and auto manufacture, as well as in the machine industry. Thus, the picture of women streaming into assembly-line jobs while men were pounding the pavement looking for work gave a superficially persuasive but fundamentally misleading impression. The actual proportion of women in the labor force did not so much rise as shift. In some cases, rationalization even worked against women. For example, textiles, traditionally the most female-dominated field, began to languish in the face of competition from new synthetic fibers such as rayon, in which men predominated.[85] Contrary to the commonly held view, loudly voiced during the Depression, women were not displacing men. Rather, they were themselves displaced, moving out of agriculture and home industry into factories where they were more visible as a work force and more likely to provoke resentment. "Women's work" became a scapegoat.

Meanwhile, the federal employment-counseling offices adjusted to the increased availability of unskilled jobs for women by steering girls away from learning a skill, since fewer apprenticeships were available to them than to boys. A government representative resorted to prejudice to help the counselors cope with the situation:

> We will have to revise our one-sided emphasis on artisan and trades skills for girls in favor of semi-skilled work. . . . Many a girl with mediocre or weak intelligence will prefer a semi-skilled trade, in which she will find greater satisfaction than in a skilled trade whose requirements are too difficult. . . . The skilled trades can use only lively and intelligent people . . . less-talented girls will be happier with simple assembly work.[86]

No reference was made to simple-minded boys.

Rationalization was pernicious in other ways too. The speedup on the assembly line, a new form of industrial brutality, resulted in many cases of physical and nervous exhaustion.[87] The accident rate was higher for women than for men. Most of the factory inspection reports attributed this to women's greater carelessness, nervousness, and distractibility. One of them did note that in a metalware factory women worked at the lighter presses, which operated faster than the heavy ones worked by men, who could take time to be careful.[88] The same inspector did not, however, remember that fatigue also affected the women's performance, since most of them had two jobs, the other being housework and child-care. More than half the female industrial workers were married and even unmarried women living alone or with their families were seldom relieved of domestic chores then as now.[89]

Rationalization in industry also encouraged bigness, and this trend cost

•

women ownership or management positions, even more than men, just as it did in agriculture. In the clothing industry, for example, where the number of women nearly equaled that of men, the number of independent women, excluding those in home industry, dropped by one-third from 1925 to 1933, while that of men fell only one-eighth.[90] In the food and beverages industry, in which women were also heavily represented, the number of independent women fell 14 percent, while that of men dropped by only .5 percent.[91] The larger the establishment, the less likely was a woman to hold a high position in management. This tendency, which had begun before the war, was accelerated by the mergers under the Weimar Republic. A test sample of industries in Baden, Hamburg, and Wurttemberg in 1925 showed that the percentage of female managers in industry had just about halved since the last census of 1907, twice as steep a drop as the overall average.[92]

## Trade

In trade, the proportion of female shop owners declined from 1907 to 1925, though it picked up again to prewar levels by 1933.[93] However, the proportion of women heads of inns and taverns fell from 30 percent in 1907 to 25 percent in 1933, while that of men rose again after an initial drop, probably indicating the increase in large hotels under predominantly male ownership and management.[94]

Turning to white-collar work, we find it to have been the fastest growing area of female employment, though it had the lowest absolute number of women. Structural changes in the public and private sectors, such as the mushrooming of bureaucracies in government, in the political parties and unions, in offices, and the development of the distributive sector, created thousands of clerical and sales jobs. This, too, was related to modernization, as the use of adding machines and typewriters derogated many aspects of office work to the level of simple mechanical tasks to be performed by low-paid semiskilled female labor. Male white-collar jobs, being higher level, grew more slowly.[95]

Meanwhile, hordes of saleswomen streamed into the small shops and department stores, where an integral part of their job was to sell a product by seduction, symbolically, that is, through the use of feminine wiles.[96] Indeed, not until that phase of modernization concerned with distribution and services fully developed did appearance and sexual role-playing come to be so important a part of women's work. One of the more pathetic medical cases to come to the attention of one of the few women doctors in Germany was that of a twelve-year-old girl whose face had been disfigured by tuberculosis and who, unaware that she was about to die, worried that the disfigurement would bar her from an office or sales job when she grew up—a problem surely not an obstacle for peasant women or industrial workers.[97]

Not only good looks, but youth also became an essential part of the new working woman's equipment. Most clerks and salesgirls became obsolete by thirty, a condition which again did not hold true of their sisters in industry or agriculture.[98] Newspapers advertised for twenty-five-year-olds.[99] Businesses phased out older women rather than promote them through the hierarchy. In 1925, less than 1 percent of the female white-collar workers held management positions, compared with 6 percent of the males. To put it another way, men held 95 percent of the top posts, though they constituted only three-fourths of the white-collar force. Women, who made up one-fourth of the total contingent, held only 5 percent of the top posts.[100]  Many a girl who had had some enthusiasm for a career lost it once she realized that she had no future.

Social pressure to marry, in addition to lack of opportunity at work, led most young women to regard their jobs as temporary, a fact which made them hard to organize into unions. Filled with Cinderella fantasies encouraged by the media, they dreamed of marrying the boss rather than uniting against his exploitation of their labor and sex. Though they often worked extra long hours for barely subsistence wages and had dependents such as aged parents or younger siblings, they scrimped to buy the fashionable clothes and cosmetics their proletarian sisters turned out on the assembly line.[101]  Once married (though rarely to the boss), they did not return to work, since they usually allied themselves with someone from the same white-collar group—a male better paid than themselves. Here again, we see women leaving the economy as it modernizes.

## Services and Professions

Agriculture occupied nearly half the female labor force, industry a third to a fourth, and the service and distributive sectors an eighth, the remainder being the women in the free professions. In the fields of health, education, and the arts, women who had access to higher learning did make some significant advances. A majority taught, and women comprised one-third of the teachers; they made up more than half in the health profession, though mostly as nurses; and they provided four-fifths of social welfare workers. [102] The number of women doctors multiplied by thirteen after the war and nearly doubled again before the Nazi take-over; the number of female dentists and dental technicians had nearly as dramatic a rise, and the number of lawyers quintupled from 1925 to 1933. Certainly an impressive set of gains, one would think, even if they did involve only 6 percent of the total female working population.[103]

Yet looked at in another way, women's progress in the professions was somewhat less spectacular. For example, while 30 percent of the teachers were women, this did not represent a rise in proportion over prewar levels. Only 7 percent headed schools and in fact they were losing ground compared to before the war. Men slowly took over the formerly private high schools and lyceums for girls, which had been founded and seen through their early financial crises by women.[104]  Even before the war, there had been a widespread fear of the feminization of public education.[105]  After the revolution, as the states took over more of the educational burden, male influence in the schools increased. Prussian legislation stipulated that in girls' schools, one-third of the faculties be men and one-third of the science work be done by them. A court decision of 1922 put women teachers on a salary schedule below that of men because "men teachers were contributing to the material restoration of Germany by training workmen, whereas the women were only making housewives."[106] In short, coeducation and state control increased the number of schools and the number of female and male teachers, but derogated the position of women in education relative to the prewar period.

The health profession underwent an interesting metamorphosis as the number of midwives declined by over 6,000 while the number of female doctors rose only 4,200 in the period from 1907 to 1933. Only 5 percent of all the doctors were women.[107] Of these, only half had an independent practice, compared with three-fourths of the male doctors, the rest being employed in clinics or hospitals or public health institutions. The majority of women in the health profession went into nursing. Here modernization, in the form of professionalization, seemed to be proletarianizing most women, though it allowed a few to achieve elite status.

Women made up less than .5 percent of lawyers in 1925 and this figure rose to 1.5 percent in 1933, for a grand total of 251 women lawyers—hardly an invasion of the field. Of these, two-thirds had their own practices, compared with 95 percent of the male lawyers, and most of them dealt with family law or protective factory legislation for women.[108]

In short, advances in the professions were indeed made over the prewar period, but one can hardly speak of the liberation of thousands of women in competition with men. Above and beyond social conditioning and the difficulties of combining a family life with employment, sex prejudice effectively blocked many a career.

### III

From the foregoing, it is possible to draw some clear conclusions regarding the position of women in the politics and economy of Weimar Germany.

No political party (with the possible exception of the Communists) undertook the task of reeducating women to accept full citizen status. Women voters were regarded much as American politicians might view the "ethnic vote." Their ballots were sought, but too large a participation in party leadership was not encouraged. Every party in the early years of the Weimar Republic made a great effort to include at least a few women in its upper echelons and regularly placed women's names on its lists of candidates. In the most conspicuous positions, women comprised between 5 and 10 percent of elected or party offices; but at local levels the percentage of women fell away to between 1 and 2 percent.[109] This contrasts sharply with Duverger's description of women's participation in government. According to his paradigm, women tend to be better represented in less important positions. As jobs increase in pay, responsibility and status, the percentages of women decline.[110]

Thus, the Weimar example seems to provide us with a dramatic case of "tokenism." The effect of this situation was not to provide role models and thereby encourage more women to enter local political activities. Instead, as long-time leaders of the women's rights movement observed women in many conspicuous places, they relaxed their efforts at further changes and turned their attention to national issues unrelated to the recruitment of additional women into public life. Meanwhile, opponents of women's participation in politics became alarmed at what they perceived to be an inundation of women into politics, and their intransigence against further reforms increased.

Another effect of this "tokenism" was to place in relatively important positions women who were not vigorous crusaders for women's rights. "Token" women are rarely militant feminists. Thus, when women party leaders requested more funds, autonomy, or status for their women's activities, they usually met resistance. And, more often than not, they accepted a rejection without strong protest. Socialist women were easily intimidated by accusations that they had not yet been sufficiently effective in recruiting more women party members; bourgeois women too often were mollified by promises that a subcommittee would investigate their demands. Similarly, when bills concerning legal rights of women failed to pass in a legislature, women delegates acquiesced and did not renew pressures for change. Not wishing to disrupt party or legislative harmony, women proved to be docile participants in the political process when it came to feminist issues.

All parties, it is clear, wanted to attract women's votes, but were less than enthusiastic about women's rights. Discussions of the "woman question" did not appear in the pamphlets or newspapers addressed to the general (male) readership of any party. Although bourgeois parties emphasized women's role in a putative spiritual revolution and the Socialist parties told women to view themselves as workers for the overthrow of capitalism, no party successfully integrated its rhetoric supporting women's rights into its theory or practice. Resentment toward women workers persisted and was even reinforced by the Socialists' hesitancy to fight for equal pay for equal work. In the liberal and conservative parties as well, women's participation in the economy was encouraged only insofar as women did not overstep the bounds of their traditional interests. No political party endorsed measures which would upset the traditional supremacy of German men—in the economy, the family, or the government. Male politicians supported emancipation only as long as the status quo was not threatened. Women politicians sensed this limitation on the good will of their fellow party members. Consequently they were careful to reaffirm their desire not to disrupt the time-honored division of labor between men and women. In short, no politician in Weimar Germany challenged the ideal of separate but equal.

On the economic front as well, war and postwar developments did not provide an unambiguous improvement for women. Thus, the traditional picture of women's economic liberation must be seriously modified. Modernization of techniques and concentration of ownership reshuffled jobs so that women as a group increasingly were pressed into unskilled work with lessened responsibility or out of the economy altogether. They lost status and sometimes relative independence and probably a corresponding sense of competence and self-esteem. Recriminated against for abandoning their families, suffering consequently from a sense of failure at home as well as at work, their socially induced feelings of inferiority were reinforced by low pay and lack of advancement.

In politics, however, the failure of major reforms and the reluctance of the parties to integrate women into their organizations cannot be attributed solely to male misogyny or female passivity. The right to vote and constitutional promises of equality between the sexes had come as part of the "revolution from above." In fact, the suffrage victory had come in 1918— when the women's movement was less active than it had been before war work claimed the full attention of its participants.[111] The right to vote had been given to women in the hope that women voters would help to insure the defeat of Bolshevism and to provide a progressive, liberal image of Germany at the Paris Peace Conference. When the crisis of 1918—19 subsided, so did loyalty to *all* of the Weimar reforms which had been dictated by opportunism, not idealism. In this respect, the fate of women's emancipation shared the fate of the Weimar Republic itself. Hitler stated his opposition to women in politics more boldly than other politicians. But there can be no question that the prevailing attitudes in Weimar Germany presaged the practices of the Third Reich.

Despite much rhetoric about the rights of women, Germans did not envision a change in the traditional role of women. Women had as little reason as men to seek a basic transformation of their role. When women did enter the traditionally masculine occupations, they were neither paid nor treated equally. And no political solution to this problem appeared to be forthcoming. Without an appealing alternative, women persisted in their loyalty to the familiar *Kinder, Küche, Kirche* ethos and saw emancipation more often as a threat than as a blessing.

Thus, it should not surprise us that the women of the Weimar Republic failed to embrace their putative emancipation and even rejected it politically. Conservative politicians understood the appeal of tradition in times of uncertainty. They, unlike liberal and left-wing parties, could make political propaganda out of this anxiety. The home was to the German woman what the workshop or small business or farm was to the German man. It meant status, independence, respectability, and security. It was, in short, territory to be defended. Women's apprehensions about losing their traditional niche in society were akin to men's fears of "proletarianization." The Depression exacerbated the resultant tensions. Hitler told women that politics was a dirty business and not suited for them; that women should be honored in their homes, not exploited in the factory; that they should sew brown shirts and inspire their menfolk. Obviously, he struck a responsive chord: German women had come a long way—in the wrong direction.

## NOTES

1. *Studien über Autorität und Familie: Forschungsberichte aus dem Institut für Sozialforschung*, intro. by Max Horkheimer; Schriften des Instituts für Sozialforschung, no. 5 (Paris: F. Alcan, 1936).

2. Germany, Statistisches Amt., *Statistik des deutschen Reichs* 453, pt. II, 6—7. Hereafter referred to as Stat.d.d.R.

3. Carl Gustav Jung, *Die Frau in Europa*, 3d ed. (Zurich: Rascher, 1948). It is interesting that this essay was reprinted in the post-World War II period.

4. David Schoenbaum, *Hitler's Social Revolution* (Garden City, N.Y.: Doubleday, 1966), 178.

5. Miriam Beard, "The Tune Hitlerism Beats for Germany" (June 7, 1931), in John Weiss, ed., *Nazis and Fascists in Europe, 1918–1945* (Chicago: Quadrangle, 1969), 96. Karl Dietrich Bracher is among the recent historians who have puzzled over this apparent paradox. Bracher, *The German Dictatorship* (New York: Praeger, 1970), 86–87, 338–39.

6. Siegfried Berger, *Einführung in die Deutsche Reichsverfassung von 11. August 1919* (Berlin, 1927), 49. For an excellent summary of women's legal status in the Weimar Republic, see Emma Oekinghaus, *Die gesellschaftliche und rechtliche Stellung der Frau* (Jena: Fischer, 1925).

7. Related by Clara Mende, *Die deutsche Volkspartei zur Frauenfrage* (Berlin: Staatspolitischer, 1919), 5.

8. Gabrielle Bremme notes that this relatively low percentage of male voters resulted in part from bureaucratic problems in registering recently demobilized soldiers. Bremme, *Die politische Rolle der Frau in Deutschland* (Göttingen: Vandenhoeck und Ruprecht, 1956), 31. Maurice Duverger observed that this percentage of women voting in their first election was larger than that of women in other countries just after suffrage reform. Duverger, *The Political Role of Women* (Paris: UNESCO, 1955), 56–60.

9. Gertrud Bäumer, *Die Frau im Deutschen Staat* (Berlin: Junker und Dünnhaupt, 1932), 43ff.; Alois Kloeckner, *Die Zentrumsfraktion* (Berlin: Prussian Center Party, 1919), 10; Oekinghaus, *Die gesellschaftliche und rechtliche Stellung der Frau*, 125.

10. Clara Böhm-Schuch, "Die Politik und die Frauen," *Frauenstimmen aus der Nationalversammlung: Beiträge der sozialdemokratischen Volksvertreterinnen zu den Zeitfragen* (Berlin: SPD, 1920), 16–17.

11. Käthe Schrey, "Advent 1918," *Deutsche Frauenzeitung, Illustrierte Familie Wochenschrift mit Modenzeitung* XXXII, 9, 1, November 30, 1918.

12. Clara Viebig, *Mütter und Frauen!* (n.d.), 1. This was a pamphlet published by the DVP in 1919 or 1920.

13. This was a fairly common theme in bourgeois publications. See for example *Die Frau*, 1918–19.

14. Marie Stritt, "Von der Frauenstimmrechtlerin zur Parteipolitiker," *Die Staatsbürgerin, Monatsschrift des deutschen Reichsverbandes für Frauenstimmrecht*, VII:10/11, 30, January and February 1919. See also G. Bäumer, *Lebensweg durch eine Zeitenwende* (Tübingen: R. Wunderlich, 1933), 430.

15. Alice Rühle-Gerstiel, *Das Frauenproblem der Gegenwart: eine psychologische Bilanz* (Leipzig: S. Hirzel, 1932), 387.

16. Fewer women voted as compared both with the percentage of eligible women voting in 1919 and with the percentages of eligible men who voted in each election. Bremme notes, however, that women tend to vote more sporadically than men. For example in the "crisis" situations of 1919, 1930–33, and 1945 the percentages of women voting increased dramatically.

17. Bäumer, *Die Frau im Deutschen Staat*, 45. Hans Beyer investigates in greater detail the impact of women's suffrage on each of the Weimar parties. Beyer, *Die Frau in der politische Entscheidung* (Stuttgart: F. Enke, 1932), 34–41. For a complete breakdown by sex and region of Weimar elections, see Duverger, *The Political Role of Women*, 52ff.

18. G. G. L. Alexander, *Kämpfende Frauen: historischematerialische Studien* (Berlin: Neuer Deutscher Verlag, 1921), 32. For a concise, eloquent statement of the Socialist position, see Clara Zetkin, "Frauenreichskonferenz," of 1920. KPD, *Bericht* (Berlin, 1920), 285ff.

19. KPD, *Bericht über den 2. Parteitag der Kommunistischen Partei (Spartakus) vom 20. bis 24. Oktober 1919* (Berlin, 1919), 29. Pamphlets and leaflets were, however, directed at soldiers, workers in special industries and peasants.

20. KPD, *Bericht über den 3. Parteitag der KPD (Spartakus) am 25. und 26. Februar 1920* (Berlin: KPD, 1920), 57. No other item was dropped from the agenda.

21. *Ibid.*, 58–59.

22. Besides the official party platforms of each party, see Oda Olberg, "Polemisches über Frauenfrage und Sozialismus," in Wally Zepler, ed., *Sozialismus und Frauenfrage* (Berlin: P. Cassirer, 1919), 38ff.; Luise Zietz, *USPD Protokoll über die Verhandlung des Parteitages in Leipzig vom 8. bis 12. Januar 1922 sowie über die zweite Reichsfrauenkonferenz, 1922* (Leipzig: A.G., n.d.), 184ff.; *Protokoll der Reichs-frauen-Konferenz der USP 29. und 30. November 1919* (Berlin: Freiheit, 1919), 461ff.; KPD, *Bericht, 3. Parteitag;* A. Blos, *Frauenfrage,* 165ff.; KPD, *Frauen Wacht auf!* (Berlin [1924?] ), 8.

23. Werner Thönnessen, *Die Frauenemanzipation in Politik und Literatur der Deutschen Sozialdemokratie, 1863–1933* (Gelnhausen, 1958), 120ff. Also noteworthy is the fact that the differential between male and female support for the SPD narrowed. In 1920, 25.4 percent of all males voted SPD as compared with 19.9 percent of the females. The statistics for 1930 are less complete, but in the districts which separated male and female votes, the differential had dropped to just under 3 percent. These observations are based on tables in Duverger, *The Political Role of Women,* 54.

24. Blos, *Frauenfrage,* 165, 180, 193.

25. The one exception to this rule was the Communist delegation of 1930—which included thirteen (17.1 percent) women. This compared very favorably with earlier representations of about 5 or 6 percent. Social Democratic representation declined from 13.3 percent in 1919 to 11.1 percent in 1930. Bremme, *Die politische Rolle der Frau in Deutschland,* 124.

26. For example, see Luise Zietz's tirade against conservative Socialist women, *USPD Protokoll über die Verhandlungen des Parteitages in Leipzig,* 187ff.

27. Even *Die Gleichheit* repeated this charge without criticism. "Without women's vote, progress would have already made greater strides." *Die Gleichheit,* no. 14/15 (1922) 1. See also *Vorwärts,* August 22, 1931.

28. *Protokoll über die Verhandlungen des Parteitages der SPD, abgehalten zu Gorlitz, 1921,* 189. Thönnessen discusses this issue in *Die Frauenemanzipation,* 101ff.

29. *Tribüne der proletarischen Frau* in *Die Rote Fahne,* no. 4, November 10, 1920, p. 1. This particular admonition urges men to send their women to party meetings and tells them not to worry that the housework won't be completed. The women's improved morale will help them do their household chores in much less time.

30. These lists appeared in advertisements in party pamphlets and in printed editions of party protocols throughout the 1920s.

31. Among twenty portraits of party leaders, none was of a woman. *Unser Program in Wort und Bild* (Berlin, 1931), 17.

32. Matilda Wurm, "Die Frauenarbeit," report read at the USPD Convention, *Protokoll; Leipzig 8–12. Januar, 1922* (Leipzig, n.d.), 511.

33. For a discussion of Socialism and anti-Semitism, see Peter Pulzer, *The Rise of Political Anti-Semitism* (New York: Wiley, 1964), 259–71; for a slightly different perspective, see Hannah Arendt, *Anti-Semitism* (New York, 1968), 42ff.

34. The one exception to this was the Catholic Center party's reluctance to sponsor any reforms which would have undercut complete male supremacy within the family.

35. Leaflet no. 6, Evangelische Frauenverein, Federal German Archive, Coblenz; Bestand nr. 34. Hereafter referred to as BA Koblenz.

36. Viebig, *Mütter und Frauen!,* 2.

37. Bäumer, *Lebensweg,* 360. *"Wir sind gerufen durch die Revolution. Aber wir sind auch gerufen gegen die Revolution."*

38. Mende, *Die deutsche Volkspartei zur Frauenfrage,* 3.

39. A. von Zann-Harnack, *Schriften,* 18–19.

40. Helene Lange, *Kampfzeiten II,* entry for November 1918, p. 227. For wartime propaganda on this theme, see Ursula von Gersdorff, *Frauen im Kriegsdienst* (Stuttgart: Deutsche Verlags-Anstalt, 1969), 107–78 *passim.*

41. M. Weber, "Die besonderen Kulturaufgabe der Frau" (1918), *Frauenfragen und Frauengedanken: Gesammelte Aufsätze* (Tübingen, 1919), 252.

42. Frau Fr. Naumann, *Was soll die Frau in der Politik?* (Berlin, 1918), 2. This combination of liberal politics and traditional views on women's role should come as no surprise to American readers who may have read Dr. Benjamin Spock on the subject: "Biologically and temperamentally I believe women were made to be concerned first and foremost with child care, husband care and home care." *Redbook,* March, 1969.

43. "Aufruf und Leitsätze des Reichausschusses" (Frankfurt, December 30, 1918), quoted in Wilhelm Mommsen and Günther Franz, *Die Deutschen Parteiprogramme 1918–1930* (Leipzig and Berlin: B.G. Teubner, 1931), 11–13.

44. Hans Beyer notes that while men had been dropping out of the Center party since before the war, women's votes more than compensated for this loss and maintained the Center as a leading party throughout the 1920s. Beyer, *Die Frau in der politische Entscheidung,* 34ff. In 1919, 6.3 percent of Center delegates were women; in 1930, the percentage dropped to 5.9. Bremme, *Der politische Rolle der Frau in Deutschland,* 124.

45. Kardorff Nachlass, "Wir brauchen eine Mutterliga!" item 12, Folio 40. Kardorff called women the "tragic sex" because they had been misled by male values, and closed her speech with the appeal "Mothers of all the World, Unite!"

46. DNVP, "Grundsätze," quoted in Mommsen and Franz, *Die Deutschen Parteiprogramme,* 60–71; see also p. 90 For a liberal statement of this view, see Dr. Jur. Anna-lise Schellwitz-Ueltzen, *Die Frau im neuen Deutschland* (Berlin: Staatspolitischer, 1920), 7ff.

47. *Frauen-Flugschriften der Deutschen demokratischen Partei,* pamphlet (Berlin: Demokratischer, 1918).

48. Frl. Wittstock, organization meeting at Bad Eilsen, September 17 and 18, 1927, BA Koblenz, R 45 III/29 (27–9), item. 31.

49. For a discussion of the Catholic women's movement, see Hilde Lion, *Zur Soziologie der Frauenbewegung (Die sozialistische und die Katholische Frauenbewegung)* (Berlin, 1932), 78ff.

50. Kardorff Nachlass, "Wir brauchen eine Mutterliga!"

51. Anna Mayer, *Die Rechtsstellung der Ehefrau und der ehelichen Mutter* (Berlin: Staatspolitischer, 1921). This is pamphlet no. 9 in the series, *Flugschriften der Deutschen Volkspartei.*

52. Frauenabteilung der Reichsgeschaftsstelle, *Winke fur Frauenausschüsse* (Berlin, n.d.), 2. BA Koblenz, Zsg 1 - 42/46 (26).

53. Bremme, *Der politische Rolle der Frau in Deutschland,* 124.

54. Rühle-Gerstiel, *Das Frauenproblem der Gegenwart,* 287ff.

55. *Stat.d.d.R.,* 402: 423 and 408: 9.

|  | Female | | Male | |
|---|---|---|---|---|
|  | *Total population* | *Gainfully occupied* | *Total population* | *Gainfully occupied* |
| 1907 | 27,884,309 | 8,501,005 | 27,106,774 | 16,655,012 |
| 1925 | 32,213,796 | 11,478,012 | 30,196,823 | 20,531,288 |

56. *Stat.d.d.R.*, 408: 8. Germany, Statistisches Amt, *Wirtschaft und Statistik*, 5 (1925), 12. Hereafter referred to as *W & S*. The differential came down to 1059/1000 in 1933. *W & S* 14 (1934), 159.

57. *Stat.d.d.R.*, 408: 318–19, projected that in 1933, 34 percent of the female population would be working. Forced displacement of women after the Nazi takeover made this figure accurate. *W & S* 5 (1925), Sonderheft 2, p. 5, looking worriedly at the hugh population of Russia, counted the German losses as between twelve and thirteen million: two million soldiers, three-quarter million civilians, three million unborn children, seven million in lost territories, and calculated that the normal population of Germany should be seventy-five million rather than sixty-two-and-a-half million. Even so, it was the largest population in Europe, with Great Britain following with forty-four million and France and Italy with thirty-nine million each.

58. *W & S* 5 (1929), "Beiträge zum deutschen Bevolkerungsproblem," 29.

59. *Stat.d.d.R.*, 408: 7.

60. *Stat.d.d.R.*, 221: 205, 132*; 402: 232; 453 (Pt. II), 36.

*Agricultural working population*

|  | Female | Male |
|---|---|---|
| 1895 | 2,730,216 | 5,315,225 |
| 1907 | 4,558,718 | 5,023,084 |
| 1925 | 4,969,279 | 4,793,147 |
| 1933 | 4,649,279 | 4,694,006 |

This shows male participation in absolute numbers steadily decreasing, women's increasing until 1933, when they, in turn, began their "flight from the country."

61. In the countryside, the ratio of females to males in 1933 was 1,002 to 1,000 and only 862 to 1,000 among the twenty-year-olds, indicating a high rate of emigration for young girls. The national average was 1,059 to 1,000 and in the big cities it was greater, with Berlin leading at 1,160 to 1,000. *W & S* 14 (1934), 160; 15 (1935), 197.

62. From 1925 to 1933, the total number of agricultural workers decreased by 12 percent, female workers alone by 22 percent. *W & S* 14 (1934), 632. The Chamber of Agriculture in Pomerania ascertained that from January 1, 1928, to June 30, 1929, about 20 percent of the *Mägde* from Eastern Pomerania emigrated. Max Sering, *Die deutsche Landwirtschaft unter volks- und weltwirtschaftlichen Gesichtspunkten* (Berlin: Reichsministerium für Ernährung und Landwirtschaft, 1932), 149.

63. The average number of hours a year worked by the peasant woman in Württemberg was 3,933, by the peasant man 3,554, by the hired help, 2,800. Adolf Münzinger, *Der Arbeitsertrag der bäuerlichen Familienwirtschaft; eine bäuerliche Betriebserhebung in Württemberg* (Berlin, 1929), II, 811–12, 835.

64. *Ibid.*, 809–10; Rosa Kempf, *Arbeits- und Lebensverhältnisse der Frauen in der Landwirtschaft Bayerns* (Jena: G. Fischer, 1918), 132.

65. *Ibid.*, 36, 133.

66. *Stat.d.d.R.*, 212: 606–7; 410: 70–71; 461: 52–53.

*Leading positions in agriculture*
*(owners, lessors, directors)*

|  | Female | Male |
|---|---|---|
| 1907 | 403,400 | 2,526,093 |
| 1925 | 428,244 | 3,158,318 |
| 1933 | 313,878 | 2,710,682 |

Note that while male ownership also dropped in the second period of the Republic, it remained above prewar levels, while that of women fell below.

67. *Stat.d.d.R.*, 410: 70–71; *W & S* 14 (1934), 444.
68. *Stat.d.d.R.*, 402: 232; 453 (Pt. II), 36.

*Managerial positions*
*in agriculture*

|  | Female | Male |
|---|---|---|
| 1925 | 1,577 | 8,248 |
| 1933 | 228[a] | 2,583[b] |

[a]Plus 52 unemployed: 14 percent
[b]Plus 180 unemployed: 6.5 percent

The *Stat.d.d.R.*, 211: 207, commented on the drop in the number of female heads of agricultural institutions from 1895 to 1907, relating it directly to the development of dairy co-ops; Kempf, *Arbeits- und Lebensverhältnisse der Frauen*, 129, noted that the commercial development of agriculture tended to exclude women and jeopardized the peasant wife's relative independence.

69. Emma Stropp, *Die landwirtschaftlichen Frauenberufe; ein Wegweiser für die Berufswahl* (Gotha: Verlag Die Landfrau, 1919). Lily Hauff, *Entwickelung der Frauenberufe in den letzten drei Jahrzehnten* (Berlin: Puttkammer und Mühlbrecht, 1911), 24–25, had expected educated women to make great headway in all these fields. Women's place in gardening underwent some dramatic changes from 1907 to 1933. From 1907 to 1925, the number of female gardeners dropped sharply, then picked up by 1933, though only to half the prewar level. The number of men in the profession climbed steadily. *Stat.d.d.R.*, 211 (Anhang), 53; 402: 410; 470: 35.

*Gardeners*

|  | Female | Male |
|---|---|---|
| 1907 | 26,833 | 121,404 |
| 1925 | 7,814 | 126,456 |
| 1933 | 13,701 | 164,949 |

70. These are recurrent themes in the reports of the factory inspectors. Germany, Arbeitsministerium, *Jahresberichte der Gewerbeaufsichtsbeamten und Bergbehorden*, 1919–34. Hereafter referred to as *GAB*. In 1928, one factory in Berlin reported 148 live births to 724 "miscarriages," and in 1926 a factory inspector remarked that if the unsafe conditions of some factories were known, women would queue up to work in them, given their tendency to try to abort. *GAB* (1926), I: 105; (1928), I: 113. In Prussia, the ratio of live births to miscarriages completely reversed itself from 1916 to 1922: from 8 live births to 5 miscarriages it became 5 live births to 8 miscarriages. *GAB* for Prussia (1922), 62.

As late as 1932, the criminal code still prohibited contraceptive devices; and abortion, permitted only for medical reasons, carried a penalty of six months to five years imprisonment for the patient and up to ten years for the doctor. Nevertheless, illegal abortions for those who could afford them were performed. The files of one doctor operating in a small town of 25,000 indicated that in one year he had performed 426 abortions, mostly on married women. Dr. Else Kienle, *Frauen: aus dem Tagebuch einer Ärztin* (Berlin, 1932), 25.

71. Antonina Vallentin, "The Employment of Women since the War," *International Labor Review* 25 (January-June 1932), 484; Helene Kaiser, *Der Einfluss industrieller*

*Frauenarbeit auf die Gestaltung der industriellen Reservearmee in der deutschen Volks-wirtschaft der Gegenwart* (Leipzig: Teicher, 1933), 22.

72. Harry Oppenborn, *Die Tätigkeit der Frau in der deutschen Kriegswirtschaft* (Hamburg: Hans Christians Druckerei und Verlag, 1928), 19.

73. *Ibid.*, 16–43; Ursula von Gersdorff, *Frauen im Kriegsdienst* (Stuttgart: Deutsche Verlagsanstalt, 1969), 25.

74. Oppenborn, *Die Tätigkeit der Frau*, 44–52.

75. Von Gersdorff, *Frauen im Kriegsdienst*, 37.

76. *GAB* (1919), I: 113.

77. Jürgen Kuczynski, *Die Geschichte der Lage der Arbeiter unter dem Kapitalismus* 18 (Berlin: Akademie Verlag, 1963), 223. In chap. 3, the author analyzes the wage differentials between men and women during the Weimar period and concludes that it tended to narrow during bad times, the inflationary twenties and the Depression, when men's real wages fell closer to subsistence level and thus to women's wages, while in good times, such as the period of relative stabilization, the differential tended to widen again as men's wages recovered.

78. *Ibid.*, 230; *GAB* (1919), I: 123.

79. *GAB* (Prussia, 1921), I: 113.

80. Kaiser, *Der Einfluss industrieller Frauenarbeit*, 49; *W & S*, 6 (1926), 792.

81. Robert Brady, *The Rationalization Movement in German Industry* (Berkeley: University of California Press, 1933), 171–72, 240.

82. *Ibid.*, 309.

83. Kaiser, *Der Einfluss industrieller Frauenarbeit*, 100–105.

84. Brady, *The Rationalization Movement in German Industry*, 309.

85. Employment in the textile industry:

|  | Female | Male |
|---|---|---|
| 1925 | 672,842 | 533,889 |
| 1933 | 586,077 (incl. unemployed) | 532,638 (incl. unemployed) |
|  | 465,512 (employed) | 391,169 (employed) |

Note that while women's participation in the diminishing textile labor force dropped much more sharply than that of men, 13 percent compared to 0.2 percent, their rate of unemployment was considerably lower, so that actual employment of women dropped only 16 percent while that of men dropped 27 percent. This kind of phenomenon gave rise to the impression that women were displacing men on the job market, when actually the structural change underlying the crisis was going in the opposite direction. *Stat.d.d.R.*, 402: 236; 453 (Pt. II), 40.

86. Germany, Arbeitsministerium, "Die öffentliche Berufsberatung in Deutschland nach der Berufsberatungsstatistik von 1926/1927," *Reichsarbeitsblatt* II (1928), no. 15, 253–57. There was one job available for every two male applicants who came for counseling and one for every three female applicants. Forty-three percent of the males were placed, 35 percent of the females.

87. Kuczynski, *Die Geschichte der Lage der Arbeiter unter dem Kapitalismus*, 238.

88. *GAB* (Prussia, 1922), 68.

89. Margarete Blum, *Neuzeitliche Arbeitsteilung zwischen Mann und Frau in Handel und Industrie* (Köln: Welzel, 1932), 41.

90. Independents in the clothing industry:

|  | Female | Male |
|---|---|---|
| 1925 | 298,867 | 316,714 |
| 1933 | 196,717 | 279,470 |

*W & S*, 7 (1927), 576 and 14 (1934), Sonderblatt no. 24, p. 8.

91. Independents in the food and beverages industry:

|  | *Female* | *Male* |
|---|---|---|
| 1925 | 21,677 | 228,579 |
| 1933 | 18,481 | 227,327 |

*W & S,* 7 (1927), 575 and 14 (1934), Sonderblatt no. 24, p. 8.

92. Percentage of employees in managerial positions:

|  | *Wurttemberg* | | *Baden* | | *Hamburg* | |
|---|---|---|---|---|---|---|
|  | *Women[a]* | *Total[b]* | *Women* | *Total* | *Women* | *Total* |
| 1925 | 18 | 20.8 | 15.4 | 17.2 | 27.5 | 18.3 |
| 1933 | 10.4 | 15 | 7.3 | 13.5 | 12 | 15.2 |

[a]Women in managerial positions as a percentage of all managers
[b]Managers as a percentage of all employees

*W & S,* 6 (1926), 915. The census of 1907 already noted the inverse relationship of numbers of workers and heads of managers of firms on a sexual basis. *Stat.d.d.R.,* 211: 207 remarked on the general tendency for the number of female clerks to increase more rapidly than that of male clerks while the number of female owners and managers fell more rapidly than that of males. The census of 1925 showed this to be a continuing trend. *Stat.d.d.R.,* 408: 133–34:

*Independents in industry and crafts*

|  | *1907* | *1925* | *% change* |
|---|---|---|---|
| Female | 307,295 | 241,489 | −21.4 |
| Male | 1,223,976 | 1,269,379 | 3.7 |

Meanwhile, the employment of women in home industry rose, while that of men fell.

*Home industry*

|  | *1907* | *1925* | *% change* |
|---|---|---|---|
| Female | 127,883 | 189,299 | 48 |
| Male | 109,274 | 84,946 | −22.3 |

In trade and commerce, the number of female independents increased, but considerably less than the number or proportion of male independents.

*Independents in trade and commerce*

|  | *1907* | *1925* | *% change* |
|---|---|---|---|
| Female | 224,879 | 265,863 | 18.2 |
| Male | 702,924 | 932,339 | 32.6 |

93. *Stat.d.d.R.,* 211: 205; 408: 124; 453 (Pt. II), 46.

*Independents in trade*

|  | *Female* | *Male* | *% Female* |
|---|---|---|---|
| 1907 | 169,670 | 497,568 | 25 |
| 1925 | 200,112 | 736,074 | 21 |
| 1933 | 250,943 | 737,369 | 25.5 |

94. *Ibid.*

Heads of inns and taverns

|  | Female | Male | % Female |
|---|---|---|---|
| 1907 | 69,503 | 169,173 | 30 |
| 1925 | 63,297 | 131,564 | 32 |
| 1933 | 44,849 | 136,346 | 25 |

95. *Stat.d.d.R.*, 453 (Pt. II), 7.

White-collar employees (to nearest thousand)

|  | Female | Male | % Female | % Total female work force |
|---|---|---|---|---|
| 1907 | 493,000 | 2,818,000 | 14.9 | 5.8 |
| 1925 | 1,446,000 | 3,996,000 | 26.6 | 12.6 |
| 1933 | 1,695,000 | 3,818,000 | 30.7 | 14.8 |

Note that men were affected more by the Depression, again leading to the impression that they were being displaced by women, when in fact men's and women's white-collar work was very different.

96. Blum, *Neuzeitliche Arbeitsteilung*, 17; Stephanie Herz, *Zur Typologie der kaufmännischen Angestellten* (Berlin: Druckerei des Studentenwerks e.V. 1931), 26.

97. Kienle, *Frauen*, 50.

98. Half the female clerks were under age twenty-five, compared with one-fourth of the males. Staffi M. Tarrasch, *Die weiblichen Angestellten: Das Problem ihrer Organisation* (Heidelberg, 1931), 15–16.

99. Herz, *Zur Typologie der kaufmännischen Angestellten*, 25.

100. *Stat.d.d.R.*, 408: 139.

101. Herz, *Zur Typologie der kaufmännischen Angestellten*, 17. Frieda Glass, "Einkommen und Lebensbedingungen berufstätiger Frauen; nach einer Erhebung der Arbeitsgemeinschaft deutscher Frauenberufsverbände," *Jahrbuch der Frauenarbeit* 7 (Berlin: Verband der weiblichen Handels- und Büroangestellten, 1931), 24–45.

102. *Stat.d.d.R.*, 408: 87, 93–94.

103. *Stat.d.d.R.*, 453 (Pt. II), 48–50; *W & S*, 7 (1927), 576–77.

104. *Stat.d.d.R.*, 408: 298; *W & S*, 15 (1935), Sonderbeilage no. 14, p. 18; Hauff, *Entwickelung der Frauenberufe*, 44.

Teachers

|  | Female | Male | % Female |
|---|---|---|---|
| 1907 | 89,110 | 188,043 | 32 |
| 1925 | 97,675 | 211,066 | 32 |
| 1933 | 94,140 | 212,469 | 30 |

105. Kempf, *Arbeits- und Lebensverhältnisse der Frauen*, 137.

106. Hugh Wiley Puckett, *Germany's Women Go Forward* (New York: Columbia University Press, 1930), 199.

107. *Stat.d.d.R.*, 211: 269–76; 408: 308–9; *W & S*, 15 (1935), Sonderblatt no. 14, p. 19.

Medical profession

|  | Doctors | | Midwives | Nurses |
|---|---|---|---|---|
|  | Female | Male |  |  |
| 1907 | 195 | 29,763 | 28,393 | 71,624 |
| 1925 | 2,572 | 45,332 | 23,452 | 117,128 |
| 1933 | 4,395 | 47,132 | 21,911 | 131,794 |

108. *Stat.d.d.R.*, 408: 299; *W & S*, 15 (1935), Sonderbeilage no. 14, p. 19.

109. Blos, *Frauenfrage*, 133–36; Alois Kloeckner, *Die Zentrumsfraktion in der Preussischen Landesversammlung* (Berlin, 1919), 10; Elisabeth Suersen, *Die Frau im Deutschen Reichs- und Landesstaatsdienst* (Mannheim, 1920); Bäumer, *Die Frau im Deutschen Staat*, 43ff.

110. Duverger, *The Political Role of Women*, 123. For further discussion on this, see Rühle-Gersteil, *Das Frauenproblem der Gegenwart*, 142, 251–65.

111. For an interesting array of opinions on why women were enfranchised, see DNVP, "Aufruf des Vorstandes, 27. December, 1918," in Mommsen and Franz, *Die Deutschen Parteiprogramme*, 19; Blos, *Frauenfrage*, 97–99; Ruth Kohler-Irrgang, *Die Sendung der Frau in der Deutsche Geschichte* (Leipzig, 1942), 277; Konrad Meyer, *Wahlrecht und Wahlpflicht der Frau* (Magdeburg, 1918), 2–9.

# Women, Work, and the Social Order

## Alice Kessler-Harris

In colonial New England, women routinely kept taverns, worked as compositors, operated printing presses, and ran their husbands' business affairs. Not infrequently, they also ran mills, served apprenticeships, and worked in saw mills. Yet in 1825, a young farm girl who wished to earn extra money by working in a textile mill had to board in a house where she was governed by stringent rules. Each girl had to sit at table during meals at a place assigned her according to the length of time she had worked in the factory. Doors were closed at 10 p.m. and boarders expected to retire then. Anyone "habitually absent from public worship on the Sabbath" was subject to discharge.[1] Not long thereafter, women were told by Sara Jane Clarke that the "true feminine genius is ever timid, doubtful, and clingingly dependent; a perpetual childhood."[2]

"Acceptable employments," pointed out one prominent ladies' magazine, were to be pursued only before marriage and in case of dire need.[3] But in World War I women successfully replaced male trolley drivers who had joined the army. Shortly after the men returned, they went out on strike to protest the fact that the women had not immediately been fired. During World War II, women "ran lathes, cut dies, read blueprints, and serviced airplanes. They maintained roadbeds, greased locomotives . . . worked as stevedores, blacksmiths, . . . and drill press operators."[4] After the war, a best-selling book proposed government programs to bolster the family, encourage women to bear children and revive the lost arts of canning, preserving, and interior decorating. In contrast, the contemporary women's liberation movement insists on equal opportunity, an end to the sex-stereotyping of jobs, and changes in family structure which would free all women who want to work outside the home.

How can we explain these dramatic changes in the kinds of work done by women? How can we understand accompanying shifts in attitudes toward working women? What are the relationships of these two to the work that men do? This essay will explore the interaction between ideas about women and their labor force participation. It will consider women's work in the

An earlier form of this essay was delivered at the Conference on Labor Market Segmentation, March 17, 1973, at Harvard University, Cambridge, Mass. A longer version of this essay appears in *Labor Market Segmentation*, ed. David Gordon et al. (Lexington, Mass.: Lexington Books, D. C. Heath, 1975).

context of changing economic needs, and explore the relationship between work outside the home and changing family functions. For each economic stage in America's past, it will attempt to understand both the ways in which women have participated in the labor force, and the ways in which working women of different classes and ethnic groups perceive their experiences.

The relationships among these factors are complex. While ideas about women's proper roles have historically confined women to work within the home and community, to exclude them from paid labor altogether would have deprived the industrializing process of workers badly needed in an American labor market characterized by chronic scarcity until the closing decades of the nineteenth century. For all women to work would threaten the integrity of home and family on which social order was believed to rest. Clearly some women had to be socialized into staying at home while others were encouraged to work. The varying needs of the economy as well as the changing functions of families have increasingly led women into the labor force. The resulting tension between family and work roles has been resolved historically in a variety of ways and with different consequences for women of various classes and ethnic groups. At the same time, women as a group have always worked in the lowest paid, least prestigious sectors of the work force. This essay will attempt to comprehend both the unity and the diversity of women's work experiences by exploring the interaction between the changing labor-force requirements of employers and the family's relationship to society.

The family had been a keystone of social order in Puritan New England. The Massachusetts Bay Colony self-consciously encouraged families to be "little cells of righteousness where the mother and father disciplined not only their children, but also their servants and any boarders they might take in."[5] Unmarried men and women were required to place themselves in the home of a family in order to be guided by them. Family members were encouraged to supervise each other to guard the morals of the community as a whole. John Demos sums up his study of the Plymouth colony by noting that the family functioned as a business, a school, a training institution, a church, and often as a welfare institution. "Family and community . . .," he concludes, "formed part of the same moral equation. The one supported the other and they became in a sense indistinguishable."[6]

While the functions of the family changed toward the end of the eighteenth century, certain assumptions remained. A pre-industrial society assumed that, except among the aristocracy, all family members would work as a matter of course. So widely accepted was this practice that colonial widows almost routinely took over businesses left by their deceased husbands, and in at least one instance the Plymouth Colony General Court revoked the license of an innkeeper whose wife had recently died. The court judged that without her services, the husband was not capable of keeping a public house.[7] But work for women was inseparable from the home and family. When Alexander Hamilton argued that putting women and children to work in incipient manufacturing enterprises would save them from the curse of idleness, his idea was scorned.

As the agrarian eighteenth-century society moved into the early industrialization of the nineteenth century, a growing mythology confirmed women's attachment to their homes. On a functional level, this is readily explained. Industrialization and concurrent urbanization increased the number of men who worked in impersonal factories beyond the immediate surroundings of home and community. With men removed from contact with children during the lengthy and exhausting day, women had to fill the breach. Simultaneously, laissez-faire economic policies which emphasized individualism, success, and competition, replaced the old Puritan ethic which emphasized morality, hard work and community. Men who worked hard and strove for success required wives who could competently supervise the household and exercise supportive roles as well. Ideas about what women should do conformed to these new societal requirements. In what Bernard Wishy calls a reappraisal of family life that took place after 1830, motherhood rose to new heights, and children became the focus of womanly activity. Mothers were asked to give up wealth, frivolity, and fashion in order to prepare themselves for a great calling. "The mother was the obvious source of everything that would save or damn the child; the historical and spiritual destiny of America lay in her hands."[8]

Simultaneously, the woman became a lady. Meek and submissive, modest and silent, women were expected to submerge their wills into those of husbands and fathers. Piety, purity, and submissiveness became the ideal. The art of homemaking now reached mystical proportions, with some educators arguing that women must be trained to that end. Homemaking became a profession. There could be no higher calling.[9] Girls of all classes went to school to learn to read, write, and do simple math; but those whose parents aspired to the middle class were treated differently from their brothers. Since they inhabited "a realm different from that of men, their education must also be different."[10] For the affluent, a little music, literature, and embroidery added to the three R's were enough. "Home, duty to the family, and religion" were the only concerns fit for women.

For a woman to neglect her duty meant social chaos. As one popular nineteenth-century schoolbook argued, "when a woman quits her own department ... she departs from that sphere which is assigned to her in the order of society, because she neglects her duty and leaves her own department vacant...."[11] Consistent with this feeling, one state after another, beginning in New York in 1778, and ending with New Jersey in 1844, deprived women of the suffrage rights they had possessed in the early years after the revolution. When the suffragists asked for their lost political rights in 1848, they were met with ridicule and antagonism. As Aileen Kraditor has argued, "it was not that social order required the subordination of women, rather ... it required a family structure that involved the subordination of women."[12] Until 1850, the decennial census recorded all data by families. In 1850, the name of each person was enumerated, but only the occupations of males over 15 were recorded. Finally, in 1860, occupations of females were included.[13]

Women became factory workers at a time when the family was understood as the basic social unit, essential to social order. Millowners, like most other

Americans, had a large stake in preserving social order, and removing women from their homes did not prove appealing to an affluent and largely agrarian population with a coherent conception of woman's role. But the need for labor was undeniable. In the early years after the revolution, New England millowners hired whole families, many of whom worked only during slack seasons on the farm. Independent farmers were reluctant to adapt to the discipline of the factory, and proved to be an unsatisfactory labor supply.[14]

The unmarried daughters of New England farmers seemed to be the only alternative. Could one reconcile the moral imperative of the home with the use of these young women in factories? It was the genius of Francis Cabot Lowell to conceive of a way of doing so. He appealed to the young single daughters of farm families in a way that played into both their sense of family responsibility and into the ethic of hard work. For the mill which finally opened in Lowell, Massachusetts, in 1821, he proposed carefully supervised boarding houses for girls who would spend a few years before marriage at the mills, and he offered salaries which were to be saved for their trousseaux, or used to help pay off mortgages, or send a brother through college. At the same time, parents were assured that their daughters would be given both hard work and discipline, experiences that would make them into better wives and mothers. The mills attracted a reliable labor force, easily disciplined in industrial routines, and far less expensive than male breadwinners. In return, they promised a training ground in morality.

The millowners' needs conspired with their conviction that they were providing a service for the nation. Millowners repeatedly stated "that one of their prime purposes in launching the textile industry was to give employment to respectable women to save them from poverty and idleness."[15] They argued that they were in fact preserving republican virtues of hard work, and raising the moral and intellectual tone of the country.[16] The mill girls themselves, at least in the early years, seemed to believe the rationale. In a manner reminiscent of the early Puritans, they "supervised" one another, ostracizing those whose morals were in question.[17] They were said to read poetry and to study together. The factory became a reputed cultural oasis.

For a variety of technological and economic reasons, employers could not long maintain high wages and good working conditions. Within twenty years after the mill's opening, the Lowell women complained of excessively long hours, wage cuts, and extra work. These complaints were echoed in textile mills throughout New England. Workers who had country homes to return to refused to work under deteriorating conditions. When Lowell operatives organized themselves into the Female Labor Reform Association in 1845, the millowners deserted their moral stance. Taking advantage of increasing Irish immigration, they rapidly eliminated the old work force. As late as 1845, only 7 percent of the employees in the eight Lowell mills were Irish. By 1852, the old New England mill girl had gone. The pages of the *Lowell Offering*, a worker-run but factory-supported paper, reveal the degree to which employers had chosen to place a cheap labor supply above their previous moral convictions. Some operators still continued to believe in 1849 that corporation owners would raise wages so as "to attract once more the sort of girl who had made the industry what it was."[18] Skeptics felt that the mills had lost the respect of the community because standards of morality and the old spirit of mutual surveillance had declined. Caroline Ware, historian of the textile industry, assesses the position of the employers: "Necessity had forced them to gain and hold the respect of the community in order to attract the requisite workers, and they were only too eager to be relieved of that necessity by the advent of a class of labor which had no standing in the community and no prejudice against mill-work."[19]

The rapid replacement of New England women by lower paid and more tractable Irish male and female workers, illustrates the double uses of the moral code in channeling the labor force as the nineteenth century progressed. By the mid 1850s, "respectable" women would not work in factories or as servants. The only sanctioned occupations for women were teaching and, when genteel poverty struck, dressmaking. The labor force needs of employers encouraged class divisions which were reflected in the prevailing myths about women. None of the extensive and elaborate network aimed at preventing the middle-class woman from leaving her sphere applied to immigrants, working class, or black women. These women constituted the growing number who, from 1850 on, took jobs in expanding industries.[20] While financial need drove them into the labor force, their practical exclusion from the moral code which defined a woman's role had a number of tangible benefits for employers.

In the first place, the existence of the moral code and the middle-class feminine ideal of domesticity provided employers with a labor force of women who, for the most part, were convinced that their real calling lay in marriage and child-rearing and had only a transient interest in their jobs. The drive toward respectability provided working women with a set of aspirations (equivalent to upward mobility for men) which mitigated class consciousness and complaints about present exploitation. For those who were married and working, the desire to stay home provided a goad to prod unfortunate husbands into working harder and earning more.

Second, insisting that women belonged at home permitted employers to exploit working women by treating them as though their earnings were merely supplemental. Any examination of women's wages, which were always substantially below those of men and seldom sufficient even for a single woman to support herself, reveals that this was the common practice of employers. Thus, John Commons estimated that while in 1914 a living wage for a single person was defined as eight dollars per week, 75 percent of all female wage earners received less than that, and 50 percent received less than six dollars per week. A 20 percent unemployment rate further reduced these wages.[21] The assumption that women belonged at home occasionally led employers to ask that the help received by women living at home be taken into account in calculating "living wages."[22] The same assumption led employers to refuse to train women to perform skilled jobs and to deny their aspirations for upward mobility.[23]

A third effect of the domestic code was to keep women out of unions. Since many felt their work life to be temporary, women had little incentive to join one another in a struggle for better conditions. Employers clearly felt this to be a tangible benefit, for in the few instances in the nineteenth century where women created successful unions, they were quickly crushed. Because unions would negate the advantages of low wages and docility they could not be tolerated.[24]

Fourth, employers gained an inestimable advantage from the dual work force in their relationships with male workers. Working men argued that women workers held wages down. Repeatedly in the 1830s they insisted that wages paid to them would be higher if women were excluded from the work force. In 1836, a National Trades Union Committee urged that female labor be excluded from factories. After explaining that the natural responsibility and moral sensibility of women best suited them to domesticity, the report argued that female labor produced "ruinous competition, . . . to male labor" whose end finally would be that "the workman is discharged or reduced to a corresponding rate of wages with the female operative."[25] The report continued:

> One thing . . . must be apparent to every reflecting female, that all her exertions are scarce sufficient to keep her alive; that the price of her labor each year is reduced; and that she in a measure stands in the way of the male when attempting to raise his prices or equalize his labor, and that her efforts to sustain herself and family, are actually the same as tying a stone around the neck of her natural protector, Man, and destroying him with the weight she has brought to his assistance. This is the true and natural consequence of female labor when carried beyond the family.[26]

The president of the Philadelphia Trades Association advised women to withdraw altogether from the work force: " . . . the less you do, the more there will be for the men to do and the better they will be paid for doing it, and ultimately you will be what you ought to be, free from the performance of that kind of labor which was designed for man alone to perform."[27]

Male fears of displacement and of wage reductions seemed justified. While men and women normally did not compete for the same jobs, employers often substituted one for the other, over a period of time. The work force in New England textile factories, which was 90 percent female in 1828, was only 69 percent female in 1848.[28] In Massachusetts, 61 percent of the teachers were male in 1840; by 1865, 86 percent were female.[29]

Finally, the "cult of true womanhood" glorified a family structure and stability that encouraged, even coerced the male head to work harder, in order to support his family and provide for his wife. For one's wife to be working meant that the husband had failed. The need to preserve the wife's position on a pedestal pushed men into an endless search for upward mobility and financial success. Sacrificing for one's family became a pattern still prevalent among working-class Americans. The idea that women should be able to stay at home, the better to mother their children, justified hard work, long hours, economic exploitation, and a host of other evils for male workers.

The moral injunction that confined women to their homes served many purposes. It maintained social order by providing stable families. It kept most married women out of the labor force, confining them to supportive roles in relation to the male work force. It divided women from each other along class lines, and helped to ensure that those women who did work would stay in the labor force only briefly, remaining primarily committed to their families and satisfied with low-paying jobs. The special position of women as the least-paid and least-skilled members of the work force induced hostility from unskilled male labor. Afraid that women might take their jobs, some workingmen might have hesitated to demand justice from intransigent employers.

For most of the nineteenth century, the tension between the need for labor and the need for social order was contained by the domestic code. Toward the end of the century, a number of factors operated to break down the code so that it could no longer contain the underlying contradiction. The industrial strife that enveloped America in the late nineteenth century led many contemporary observers to fear that social order was giving way. Under these conditions several factors seem to have had special significance for women.

Increasing immigration had provided a plentiful labor supply of precisely the kinds of men and women who fell outside the moral code.[30] But as employers took advantage of the labor supply to lower wages and to coerce hard work out of this group of people, strikes spread and public attention was drawn to their grievances. Newspaper exposes and government investigations noted the injurious effects on all workers, but especially on women, of harsh working conditions and of wages insufficient to keep body and soul together. Some investigators pointed to spreading prostitution as one consequence of low industrial wages.[31] Others argued that stunted and warped mothers endangered the health of the unborn, and objected to "latchkey" children. Pressure for legislation to "protect" these women began to build up.

Simultaneously, it became apparent both to the investigators and to male workers that women were finding it increasingly necessary to work. Sickness, accident, and death rates among industrial workers reached all-time highs between 1903 and 1907. Unemployment fluctuated cyclically. Despite rises in real wages after 1897, wages remained too low to meet normal family needs. Whether consequentially or not, the proportion of married women in the nonagricultural work force almost doubled between 1890 and 1920.[32] Workingmen now voiced new fears that women would undermine the male labor force. While a few made sporadic attempts to organize women into trade unions, most supported legislation that would effectively limit women's participation in the labor force by raising their wages, limiting the hours they could work, and prescribing the kinds of jobs in which they could be employed.

A further breakdown in the moral code and an explanation for women's increasing participation in the work force lay in the character of the immigrant population. Ambitious and anxious to fulfill the American Dream, women from pre-industrial origins whose traditions incorporated both strong family loyalty and strong work orientations saw little need to play confined roles. Though the kinds of jobs they would take often depended on their ethnic origins, they were both willing and eager to work at least before marriage and often before having children.[33] To convince them of their errors, movements to "Americanize" the immigrant, of which the social settlement was a prime example, appeared in the 1890s. Those movements continued through the 1920s, and were often directed at teaching the immigrant woman the arts of homemaking, bathing and caring for children, sewing, and cooking. All seemed designed to convince immigrant women that in America women stayed at home.

But probably the most telling failure of the moral code to contain the contradictions between the need for social order and the need for labor lies in its rejection by some middle-class women. While social values dictated leisure and an absence of work for women, these things themselves bred a challenge to social order. The number of women by the end of the nineteenth century exceeded the number of men. What were spinsters to do? For wealthy married women, affluence, servants, and a decline in the birth rate all added up to boredom. Excess energies spent themselves in ways which often had significance for working women. Some women, seeking the suffrage, allied themselves with working women, thus momentarily breaking down class barriers that had consistently divided them. Their involvement in the trade-union movement not only contributed markedly to the success of women attempting to organize themselves, but revealed the common disabilities of the two groups. Other women became reformers, investigating and exposing conditions of child labor and the abuse of women, and as a consequence, publicizing the conditions on which their own leisure rested.

Still a third group crossed class lines more dramatically, attracted by new jobs opening in offices. Between 1890 and 1920, the percentage of women employed as clerks, saleswomen, stenographers, typists, bookkeepers, cashiers, and accountants increased from 5.3 percent of the nonagricultural female work force to 25.6 percent.[34] During the same period, among the women who worked, the proportion who were born in America of native parents also increased rapidly (35.3 percent to 43.8 percent); the percentage of native-born women of foreign parents increased slightly (20.9 percent to 24.9 percent); the percentage of foreign-born women dropped slightly (19.8 percent to 18.8 percent), and that of Negro women dropped markedly (23.4 percent to 17.6 percent).[35] Increases were accompanied by enormous shifts to the clerical sectors of the work force.[36] The needs of employers for people who were both relatively well educated and willing to work for relatively low pay seem to have encouraged the creation of a new market. In part this was met by rising educational levels among immigrant daughters who had traditionally worked. But in part it was met by native white women entering the labor market for the first time.

Changing needs of employers, on the one hand (which encouraged the influx of native Americans into the labor force) and an overabundant labor supply of unskilled and semiskilled workers on the other (providing leisure for the middle-class and encouraging exploitation of immigrants) seem together to have cracked the moral code which had served so many useful functions in the nineteenth century. The compromises which emerged from this period of uncertainty indicate new attempts to preserve social order in some sectors, while providing new freedom to work in others. They are best seen in the context of broader value changes then affecting the whole society. In the early 1900s America moved from laissez-faire economic policies to government regulation in a corporate state. The change reflected growing public willingness to accept corporate efficiency and rationality as the basis for industrial society. Large-scale industry encouraged both the homogenization of the labor force (by devaluing and removing control from skilled labor) and the artificial creation of distinctions among workers (by emphasizing expertise, credentials, and ethnic and sexual characteristics).[37] The division of the labor force in this way, effectively limiting occupational mobility for many groups, was sanctioned by legislation which legitimized these new hierarchies. State licensing requirements for medicine and social work as well as for many technical training schools illustrate this trend. So does protective labor legislation for women.

"Protective" legislation served the twofold function of segmenting the labor force and of returning some women to their homes by regulating the kinds of jobs they could hold. From about 1900 into the middle 1920s women found themselves subject to an increasing barrage of legislation limiting their working hours, establishing minimum wages, and defining the sanitary conditions under which they could work. Whatever its real value in eliminating the most gruesome abuses against a large working population, legislation effectively served to channel women into selected areas of the labor force.

Many women even then declared that protective legislation discriminated against working women. Supporters quite specifically argued that these laws were in the best interests of the state. Oregon, for example, preceded its minimum wage law with a preamble: "The welfare of the State of Oregon requires that women and minors should be protected from conditions of labor which have a pernicious effect on their health and morals, and inadequate wages . . . have such a pernicious effect."[38] John Commons interpreted the principle as follows: "In proportion as certain classes of laborers . . . are recognized by the courts as suffering an injury, and in proportion as the injured persons are deemed to be of importance to the public as well as unable to protect themselves, then legislation requiring the employer to remove the injury and prohibiting the laborer from even voluntarily consenting to the injury . . . begins to be sustained as 'reasonable.' "[39] Men did not benefit from minimum wage laws in this period, and courts repeatedly struck down legislative restrictions on hours which applied to men. Clearly the state's vital interest in women placed them in a special category. Protective legislation affected deeply the unskilled poor working woman, while it had minimal effect on the new office clerk. Workingmen favored minimum wage legislation for women because it effectively reduced a downward pull on their wages.[40] As one authority phrased it, "The wage bargaining power of men is weakened by the competition of women and children, hence a law restricting the hours of women and children may also be looked upon as a law to protect men in their bargaining power."[41]

In other ways too, legislation recognized the needs of employers. A

Federal Vocational Education Act passed in 1917 which provided for both men and women was widely supported by educators, manufacturers, trades unionists, businessmen, social workers, and philanthropists. Schools and professional agencies opened their doors to women who were encouraged to become teachers and social workers. Corporations and the state took over some social-insurance functions formerly provided by the family. Women got the vote. The 1920s witnessed an elaborate reappraisal of the free-spirited, now middle-class, office girl *cum* flapper. But married women and poor women were encouraged not to work unless absolutely necessary, and employers, discouraged by minimum wage rules and short hours, often looked elsewhere for labor. That compromise satisfied both employers with an abundance of immigrant labor and workingmen. It maintained the tenuous compromise between social order vested in the home and passed down by women, and the need for labor, by arguing that women's place was in the home, most of the time. Between 1900 and 1940, the percentage of women participating in the work force rose only very slowly.[42] When it increased dramatically under the impetus of war in the 1940s, it was accompanied by elaborate justifications.

Since World War II, changing economic needs have simultaneously opened new jobs and altered the nature of families and of women's functions within them. Job structures have shifted dramatically from primarily blue-collar and manual labor before World War II to white-collar and service work in the postwar period. Teaching, social work, the human services, health, publishing, advertising: these expanding sectors have long been considered the preserves of women. While the spread of mass education and the demand for office workers of various kinds have encouraged women to enter the labor force, the concomitant need that these workers not seek advancement or high compensation has nevertheless encouraged the belief that their work experience is and ought to be secondary to their home roles.[43] Popular magazines, advertising, prevalent truths about child-rearing, and the glorification of femininity have conspired to support this belief. Together they add up to what Betty Friedan has called the "feminine mystique": the belief that a woman's satisfaction rests in competently and creatively running the household. For the most part the myth has served its purpose. Until the present, women have not agitated for more responsible jobs, higher wages, or release from their family roles. Even professional women who are married had until recently routinely accepted channeling that kept them out of the top reaches of their professions.

But the feminine mystique seems no longer able to contain the contradictions that have emerged from the ongoing tension between the need for labor on the one hand and the belief that social order is vested in the family on the other. Large numbers of women, as opposed to the relatively few turn-of-the-century pioneers for women's rights, seem dissatisfied with their family roles.[44] Increased affluence and improved household technology as well as expanding consumer services have reduced the need for women to work at home. Longer life spans for men and women and declining birth rates have reduced the proportion of a lifetime spent in child-rearing. Changes in life styles raise questions about how to socialize children, and what values to instill in them.

As the family changes, more and more women begin to work.[45] Working women as a group are becoming older, better educated, less likely to take time off for babies, and more likely to be married and to have children. Available job opportunities raise questions about proper roles for women. The expansion of jobs in precisely those sectors in which women have been working leads to demands for upward mobility. Women with seniority rights and prior experience become discontented when they are consistently overlooked for top jobs.

Changes in the family as well as changes in perceptions of jobs seem to have produced the women's liberation movement. Its demands for more jobs and equal opportunities may help to satisfy the needs of the expanding service sector of the labor market for secretaries, clerks, and assistants of various kinds. There is some evidence that jobs for women are opening faster than they can be filled by the available pool of single or childless women.[46] Short of a dramatic re-channeling of men toward secretarial and low-level office jobs (which would involve major adjustments in social values), large-scale bureaucracies will have to make allowances for women with children if they wish to fill jobs. In some ways, these women may be ideal candidates for the secondary labor force. Their education and values have groomed them for office jobs, yet their primary commitments to children forestall claims to advancement. There is little evidence that the number of women holding prestige jobs has increased, or that women's wages have risen in comparison with those of men. Moreover, government responses to working women seem to preserve class lines. Recent federal legislation encourages women who can afford the cost of child care or household help to work, while current executive action deprives those who are poor of federally financed day-care centers.

The enormous number of women now working prompts questions about whether their commitments to jobs will undermine the basis of the family, and whether the family is any longer crucial to maintaining social order. Rising divorce rates, the recent Supreme Court decision on abortion, and public affirmations of homosexuality all testify to increasing conflict about the traditional role of the family. Attempts to alter sex-role stereotypes and to create communal shopping, child-care, and housework facilities; questions about mass-consumption psychology and the rejection of material goods; demands for individual fulfillment and authenticity—all emerge from the changing function of the family and challenge its relationship to prevalent ideology. Because the leaders of the current movement question the ideology that upholds the family, women's liberation may have the potential for long-term change.

Changes in women's participation in the work force must be understood partly as a function of the ideology of the family, and therefore of the roles that women, like men, are convinced they must play. That ideology emerges both from the objective needs of families and from a complex of societal goals which derive from a changing political economy. Women are used in the work force in ways which encompass the ideological justifications of a whole society and its immediate labor force needs. These together provide part of the complex reality that translates back into class divisions among working and nonworking women, and into specific policies as they affect women workers.

## NOTES

1. Edith Abbott, *Women in Industry* (New York: Appleton, 1910), 374–76.

2. Barbara Welter, "The Cult of True Womanhood, 1820–1860," *American Quarterly* XVIII (Summer 1964), 160.

3. Glenda Gates Riley, "The Subtle Subversion: Changes in the Traditionalist Image of the American Woman," *The Historian* XXXII (February 1970), 220.

4. William Chafe, *The American Woman: Her Changing Social Economic and Political Roles, 1920–1970* (New York: Oxford University Press, 1972).

5. Edmund Morgan, *The Puritan Dilemma* (Boston: Little, Brown, 1958), 71; see also John Demos, *A Little Commonwealth: Family Life in Plymouth Colony* (New York: Oxford University Press, 1970), 78.

6. Demos, *A Little Commonwealth*, 186.

7. *Ibid.*, 89.

8. Bernard Wishy, *The Child and the Republic: The Dawn of Modern American Child Nurture* (Philadelphia: University of Pennsylvania Press, 1972), 28.

9. Ruth Miller Elson, *Guardians of Tradition: American Schoolbooks of the Nineteenth Century* (Lincoln: University of Nebraska Press, 1964), 309; Siegfried Giedion, *Mechanization Takes Command: A Contribution to Anonymous History* (New York: Norton, 1969 [1948]), 514; for discussions of the nineteenth-century woman, see also Welter, "The Cult of True Womanhood," and Riley, "The Subtle Subversion."

10. Elson, *Guardians of Tradition*, 309; Gerda Lerner, "Women's Rights and American Feminism," *American Scholar* (Spring 1971), 238.

11. Quoted in Elson, *Guardians of Tradition*, 309.

12. Aileen Kraditor, *Up from the Pedestal* (New York: Quadrangle, 1968), 13. Kraditor continued: "The home was the bulwark against social disorder, and woman was the creator of the home . . . she occupied a desperately necessary place as symbol and center of the one institution that prevented society from flying apart."

13. Joseph A. Hill, *Women in Gainful Occupations, 1870–1920*, Census Monographs IX (U.S. Government Printing Office, 1929), 3.

14. Caroline T. Ware, *The Early New England Cotton Manufactures: A Study in Industrial Beginnings* (Boston: Houghton Mifflin, 1931), 198. Hannah Josephson, *The Golden Threads: New England's Mill Girls and Magnates* (New York: Duell, Sloan and Pearce, 1949), 22; Oscar Handlin, *Boston's Immigrants: 1790–1880* (New York: Atheneum, 1971 [1941]), 74–76; Reinhard Bendix, *Work and Authority in Industry: Ideologies of Management* (New York: Wiley, 1956), 39.

15. Josephson, *The Golden Threads*, 63, 23; see also John Kasson, "Civilizing the Machine: Technology, Aesthetics, and Society in Nineteenth Century American Thought," Ph.D. dissertation, Yale University, 1971; and see also Holland Thompson, *From the Cotton Field to the Cotton Mill: A Study of the Industrial Transition in North Carolina* (Freeport, N.Y.: Books for Libraries Press, 1971 [1906]), 52, for a similar example of paternal employment in the South. About one-half of the employees in the New England textile mills were recruited this way.

16. Kasson, "Civilizing the Machine," 41.

17. *Ibid.*, 53–55.

18. Ware, *Early New England Cotton Manufactures,* 231.

19. *Ibid.,* 234.

20. Handlin, *Boston's Immigrants,* 82.

21. John R. Commons et al., eds., *A Documentary History of American Industrial Society,* vol. VI, *The Labor Movement* (Cleveland, Ohio: Arthur H. Clark Co., 1910), 195; Emilie Josephine Hutchinson, *Women's Wages: A Study of the Wages of Industrial Women and Measures Suggested to Increase Them* (New York: AMS Press, 1968), 24, 25. Handlin, *Boston's Immigrants,* 81, notes that women earned an average of $1.50 to 3.00 per week, while men earned from $4.50 to $5.50.

22. Commons, *A Documentary History,* 210.

23. The constant employment of women at low-skilled jobs bears this out.

24. Hutchinson, *Women's Wages,* 159–60. See Alice Kessler-Harris, "Where Are the Organized Women Workers?" *Feminist Studies* III (Fall, 1975), 92–110, for an elaboration on this point.

25. Commons, *A Documentary History,* 282.

26. *Ibid.,* 284.

27. Hutchinson, *Women's Wages,* 159, quoted from *The Report on the Conditions of Women and Child Wage Earners,* X, 48.

28. Elizabeth F. Baker, *Technology and Women's Work* (New York: Columbia University Press, 1964), 17.

29. Michael Katz, *The Irony of Early School Reform* (Cambridge, Mass: Harvard University Press, 1968), 12; and Hutchinson, *Women's Wages,* 34, 158.

30. The increasing percentage of women workers was especially significant. In nonagricultural occupations, the percentage of women workers increased from 12.8 of all women over fifteen to 21.3 in 1920. There was only a slight increase from 1920 to 1930. Hill, *Women in Gainful Occupations,* 19. In 1920, 20 percent of native-born women of native parents were working; 47.8 percent of those women who were foreign born or born of foreign parents were working; and 43 percent of Negro women were working. *Ibid.,* 11. Between 1890 and 1930, the proportion of women over fifteen who were employed increased by one-third. Donald Lescohier, "Working Conditions," in John Commons, *History of Labor in the United States: 1896–1932* (New York: Macmillan, 1935), III, 37.

31. See *Report on Conditions of Women and Child Wage Earners,* V, 70; XV, 93.

32. The percentage of married women among those who worked increased from 12.1 in 1890 to 19.8 in 1910. The percentage of married women who worked increased from 3.3 in 1890 to 6.8 in 1910. Lescohier, "Working Conditions," 37; and Hill, *Women in Gainful Occupations,* 76, 77.

33. Caroline Manning, *The Immigrant Woman and Her Job* (New York: Arno Press, 1970 [1930]), *passim.*

34. Hill, *Women in Gainful Occupations,* 39–41. The percentage of women employed in factories increased from 17.6 in 1870 to 23.8 in 1920.

35. *Ibid.,* 85, 94, 102, 110.

36. *Ibid.,* 90, 96. See also Margery Davies, "The Feminization of the Clerical Labor Force," paper given at the Conference on Labor Market Segmentation, Harvard University, Cambridge, Mass., March 17, 1973.

37. See David M. Gordon, Richard Edwards, and Michael Reich, "Labor Market Segmentation in American Capitalism," paper given at the Conference on Labor Market Segmentation, Harvard University, March 16, 1973, which outlines the historical development of the segmentation process. Kathy Stone, "The Origins of Job Structures in the Steel Industry," in a paper given at the same conference and subsequently published in *Radical America* VII (November-December 1973), traces motivation for segmentation in one industry.

38. Hutchinson, *Women's Wages*, 81.

39. John R. Commons and John B. Andrews, *Principles of Labor Legislation*, rev. ed. (New York: Harper, 1927), 30.

40. Hutchinson, *Women's Wages*, 161.

41. Commons and Andrews, *Principles of Labor Legislation*, 69.

42. See the extended discussion of this question in Valerie Kincaide Oppenheimer, *The Female Labor Force in the United States: Demographic and Economic Factors Governing Its Growth and Changing Composition*, Population Monograph Series, no. 5, (Berkeley: University of California Press, 1970), 1–5.

43. Michael J. Piore's "The Dual Labor Market: Theory and Implications," in *Problems in Political Economy: An Urban Perspective*, ed. David Gordon (Lexington, Mass.: D. C. Heath, 1971), 90–94, is a concise statement of the way these divisions in the labor force work.

44. See for example Susan Jacoby, "What do I do for the next 20 Years?" *New York Times Magazine*, June 17, 1973, 10.

45. Cf. Alice Harris and Bertram Silverman, "Notes on Women in Advanced Capitalism," *Social Policy*, June-July 1973, for elaboration.

46. Valerie Kincaide Oppenheimer, "Demographic Influences on Female Employment and the Status of Women," *American Journal of Sociology* LXXVIII (January 1973).

# PART IV

# Toward a Future Human Past

The concluding four essays in this volume, like those in Part I, contain contributions to a critical historiography of the field of women's history. In these essays, however, the emphasis falls on efforts to advance the perspective with proposals for new approaches to study and research.

Gerda Lerner's essay, "New Approaches to the Study of Women in American History," was the first serious effort in recent years to assess the current state of work in the field and define some urgent needs. Though briefly stated, her remarks in this paper suggest in essence a number of directions later developed more fully by others. Thus Lerner notes the need to differentiate "women" into more specifically defined groups and "to distinguish among their economic status, family status, and political-legal status," as well as their class position; the need to consider the gap between myth and reality with respect to the alleged "place" and actual position of women in any given time or location; the need to devise new scales of measurement appropriate to evaluating women's achievements; the need to examine whether women have wielded previously unrecognized forms of power; and the need to analyze the patterns and significance of changes in women's role over time. Lerner's second article, "Placing Women in History: A 1975 Perspective," provides a more recent assessment. These two articles span a five-year interval and mark the shifting definition of conceptual problems in women's history as well as changes in the state of the field.

Hilda Smith, in "Feminism and the Methodology of Women's History," takes us in a different direction. While Lerner is inclined to reject "the feminist frame of reference" as too limiting and hampered by bias, Smith argues strongly for a feminist approach to women's history. Without denying the significant differences which distinguish women from each other, Smith argues that the main basis for the separate study of women's history is that women have indeed had a unique past. Smith defines feminism as "a view of women as a distinct sociological group for which there are established patterns of behavior, special legal and legislative restrictions, and customarily defined roles," and suggests a number of corollaries expanding this definition. However much the position of women may have varied over time, culture, class or other conditions, the distinguishing feature of their history as a group is that which relates to "the determination of one's existence in regard to one's sex." Seen in this light, feminism applied to history involves not a narrow focus on feminist movements, nor an uncritical hagiography of women's achievements, nor an unrelieved account of women's oppression. Rather: "For feminists, the idea that women are a sociological group whose behavior is both overtly and covertly regulated is the starting point from which extended analyses of society are conducted." Smith proceeds then to suggest a number of ways in which a feminist approach will influence the methodology and interpretation of history, from the search for source materials to the analysis of theories of childhood.

The selection by Juliet Mitchell reprinted here from *Woman's Estate* (first published as part of the well-known essay, "Women: The Longest Revolution"), was originally set in a critical analysis of socialist writings on the position of women, which space limitations preclude us from reproducing here. In a spirit akin to Smith, Mitchell finds past socialist theory inadequate in its failure to deal with the specific conditions of women's oppression; like Lerner, she rejects the idea of "woman" as an undifferentiated whole. In the selection included here, Mitchell proposes that women's position be analyzed as a complex unity composed of a number of different elements appearing in varying combinations. The key elements, she argues, are: production, reproduction, sexuality, and socialization of children. The actual condition of women in any particular time and place will be the product of these four structures. Specific conditions within these structures may vary at different rates, so that amelioration on one scale may be offset by reinforcement on another ("as increased socialization has made up for decreased reproduction"). Whether for purposes of analysis or as a basis for action, all four structures must be taken into account.

In the concluding essay, Sheila Johansson carries further the attempt to understand women's historical experience as a complex set of conditions, specific to women and yet varying greatly over time. Like Smith, Johansson is conscious of the importance of customarily defined roles and legal statuses, and she places considerable emphasis upon the influence of ideology, attitudes, and values; as Mitchell does, she includes sexuality, reproduction, socialization, and production (economic roles and status) among the key conditions to be analyzed in assessing the situation of women. But on the whole, Johansson is probably closest to Lerner in the spirit of her approach, and her analysis takes up almost all of the themes touched on earlier by Lerner. Johansson develops these themes in far greater detail—the diversity of "women," the complexity and variability of their roles and statuses as measured by multiple scales and criteria, the need to recognize changing patterns over time. Beyond this, Johansson is especially concerned with exploring the modes by which women have exercised power, influence, or creativity, and affected the direction of social change. As do Gordon, Buhle, and Dye in "The Problem of Women's History" in Part I of this volume, Johansson concludes: ". . . the nature of long-term social change will never be understood unless the study of women becomes a part of any attempt to unravel the mysteries of the past and the dim outlines of the future."

# New Approaches to the Study
# of Women in American History

*Gerda Lerner*

The striking fact about the historiography of women is the general neglect of the subject by historians. As long as historians held to the traditional view that only the transmission and exercise of power were worthy of their interest, women were of necessity ignored. There was little room in political, diplomatic, and military history for American women, who were, longer than any other single group in the population, outside the power structure. At best their relationship to power was implicit and peripheral and could easily be passed over as insignificant. With the rise of social history and increasing concern with groups out of power, women received some attention, but interest was focused mainly on their position in the family and on their social status.[1] The number of women featured in textbooks of American history remains astonishingly small to this day, as does the number of biographies and monographs on women by professional historians.

The literature concerning the role of women in American history is topically narrow, predominantly descriptive, and generally devoid of interpretation. Except for the feminist viewpoint, there seems to be no underlying conceptual framework.

Feminist writers, not trained historians, were the first to undertake a systematic approach to the problem of women's role in American life and history. This took the forms of feminist tracts, theoretical approaches, and compilations of woman's "contributions."[2] The early compilers attacked the subject with a missionary zeal designed, above all, to right wrong. Their tendency was to praise anything women had done as a "contribution" and to include any women who had gained the slightest public attention in their numerous lists.[3] Still, much positive work was done in simply recounting the history of the woman's rights movement and some of its forerunners and in discussing some of the women whose pioneering struggles opened opportunities to others. Feminist writers were hampered by a twofold bias. First, they shared the middle-class, nativist, moralistic approach of the Progressives and tended to censure out of existence anyone who did not fit into this pattern. Thus we find that women like Frances Wright and Ernestine Rose received

This essay is reprinted from the *Journal of Social History* IV, no. 4 (Fall 1969), 333–56, by permission of the editor; © 1971 by Peter N. Stearns.

little attention because they were considered too radical. "Premature feminists" such as the Grimké sisters, Maria Weston Chapman, and Lydia Maria Child are barely mentioned. The second bias of the feminists lies in their belief that the history of women is important only as representing the history of an oppressed group and its struggle against its oppressors.

This latter concept underlies the somewhat heroic, collectively authored *History of Woman Suffrage*. This work, probably because it represents an easily available though disorganized collection of primary sources, has had a pervasive influence on later historians. Following the lead and interpretation of the feminists, professional historians have been preoccupied with the woman's rights movement in its legal and political aspects. Modern historians, too, think that what is important to know about women is how they got the ballot.[4]

The only serious challenge to this conceptual framework was offered by Mary Beard in the form of a vigorous though often fuzzy polemic against the feminists.[5] What is important about women, said Mary Beard, is not that they were an oppressed group—she denied that they ever were—but that they have made a continuous and impressive contribution to society throughout all of history. It is a contribution, however, which does not fit into the value system generally accepted by historians when they make decisions as to who is or is not important to history. Mary Beard undertook in several of her books to trace the positive achievements of women, their social role, and their contributions to community life. Her concepts are most successfully reflected in *The Rise of American Civilization,* which she wrote with her husband Charles Beard. In it the position of women is treated throughout in an integrated way with great attention to the economic contributions made by women.[6] But the Beards' approach to the subject of women had little influence on the historical profession. Perhaps this was due to the fact that in the 1930s and 1940s both the general public and historians became somewhat disenchanted with the woman's rights movement.

The winning of suffrage had made only a slight change in the actual status of women, and other factors—technological and economic changes, access to higher education, changing sexual mores—now loomed a great deal larger. The impact of Freudianism and psychology had made reformers in general somewhat suspect. Feminism was not infrequently treated with the same humorous condescension as that other successful failure: temperance.

Women have received serious attention from economic historians. There is a good deal of excellent literature dealing with the problem of women workers. Women as contributors to the economy from colonial times on, the laws affecting them, their wages and working conditions, and their struggle for protective legislation have been fully described.[7] Although female labor leaders have not generally been given much attention, their activities are on record. Excellent collections of material pertaining to women at Radcliffe and Smith College are available but remain insufficiently explored.

Modern historians of the reform movements have done much to restore a sane balance to female achievement in reform; yet one still finds excluded from notice certain women who would have been included as a matter of course had they been men. Sophie Loeb, Grace Dodge, and Mary Anderson could be cited as examples.[8]

The historical literature on the family in America is quite scanty, but there seems to be a revival of interest in the subject. Several interesting monographs have begun to deal with the family role of women in its various aspects. This approach is promising and will, one hopes, be pursued by other historians.[9]

A new conceptual framework for dealing with the subject of women in American history is needed. The feminist frame of reference has become archaic and fairly useless. The twentieth-century revolution in technology, morality, education, and employment patterns has brought enormous changes in the status and role of American women; these changes demand a historical perspective and understanding. The emergence of a recent "new feminism" is a social phenomenon requiring interpretation. Most important, women themselves are as entitled as minority group members are to having "their" history fully recorded.

Yet the subject is complex. It is difficult to conceptualize women as a group, since they are dispersed throughout the population. Except for special-interest organizations, they do not combine. The subject is full of paradoxes which elude precise definitions and defy synthesis.

Women at various times and places were a majority of the population, yet their status was that of an oppressed minority, deprived of the rights men enjoyed. Women have for centuries been excluded from positions of power, both political and economic, yet as members of families, as daughters and wives, they often were closer to actual power than many a man. If women were among the most exploited of workers, they were also among the exploiters. If some women were dissatisfied with their limited opportunities, most women were adjusted to their position in society and resisted efforts at changing it. Women generally played a conservative role as individuals and in their communities, the role of conserving tradition, law, order, and the status quo. Yet women in their organizations were frequently allied with the most radical and even revolutionary causes and entered alliances with the very groups threatening the status quo.

If women themselves acted paradoxically, so did society in formulating its values for women. The rationale for women's peculiar position in society has always been that their function as mothers is essential to the survival of the group and that the home is the essential nucleus of society as we know it. Yet the millions of housewives and homemakers have throughout our history been deprived of the one tangible reward our society ranks highest: an income of their own. Neither custom, law, nor changes of technology, education, or politics have touched this sacred tradition. The unpaid housewife-and-mother has affected attitudes toward the women who perform homemaking services for strangers. Traditionally women in the service trades have been the lowest paid among all workers. Nor has this pattern been restricted to the unskilled groups. When women have entered an occupation in large numbers, this occupation has come to be regarded as low status and has been rewarded by low pay. Examples for this are readily found in the teaching and nursing fields. Even intellectual work has been treated with the same double standard. Creative fields in which women excel—poetry, the short story—have been those carrying the lowest rewards in money and esteem. Only in the performing arts has individual female talent had the same opportunity as male talent. Yet a cursory glance at the composition of any major symphony orchestra even today will reveal that in this field, too, opportunities for women have been restricted.

In dealing with the subject of women, studies frequently use other distinctive groups in our society as models for comparison. Women's position has variously been likened to that of the slaves, oppressed ethnic or racial minorities, or economically deprived groups. But these comparisons quickly prove inadequate. The slave comparison obviously was a rhetorical device rather than a factual statement even at the time when Harriet Martineau first made it.[10] While the law denied women equal citizenship and for certain purposes classed them with "Indians and imbeciles," it never denied them physical freedom nor did it regard them as "chattel personnel." In fact, even within the slavery system, women were oppressed differently from men. The "minority group model" is also unsatisfactory. All members of a minority group which suffers discrimination share, with a very few exceptions, in the low-status position of the entire group. But women may be the wives of cabinet members, the daughters of congressmen, the sisters of business leaders, and yet, seen simply as persons, they may be disfranchised and suffer from economic and educational discrimination. On the other hand, a lower-class woman may advance to a position of economic or social power simply by marriage, a route which is generally not open to members of racial minority groups. In one particular respect the minority group comparison is illuminating: like Negroes, women suffer from "high visibility"; they remain more readily identifiable for their group characteristics than for their personal attainments.[11]

Modern psychology, which has offered various conflicting theories about the role and place of women, has further complicated the task of the historian. A social historian who wishes to study a particular ethnic or religious minority can study its location and economy, its culture, leadership, adjustment to American society, and contributions. The question of psychology would only arise in dealing with personal biographies. But the historian of women is at once faced with the necessity of making psychological judgments. Is it not a basic fact that the psychology as well as the physiology of women is different from that of men? Therefore they must of necessity have different expectations, needs, demands, and roles. If so, is the difference in "rights" not simply natural, a reflection of reality? The problems become more vexing when dealing with individual women. The biographer feels obliged first of all to concern himself with his subject's sexual role. Was she married? A mother? If she was not, this indicates that whatever she achieved was the result of sexual frustration. If she was married, one is under an obligation to explain that she did not neglect her children or perhaps that she did. And always there is the crucial question: "What was her relationship to her father?" This is not intended to disparage the efforts of those biographers who wish to enlist the aid of modern psychology for their work. But it should be pointed out that a great deal of excellent history about men has been written without the author's feeling compelled to discuss his subject's sex life or relationship to his mother in explaining his historical significance. In dealing with women, biographers are impeded by the necessity of dealing first with sex, then with the person. This is an approach which must be examined in each case for its applicability: where it is useful, it should be retained; where it is not, it should be discarded without apology.

In order to broaden the study of women in American history, it is not really necessary to suggest new sources. Primary research material is readily available, not only in the several manuscript collections devoted to the subject, but in the usual primary sources for social historians: local historical records, letters, diaries, the organizational records of women's clubs, religious and charitable organizations, labor unions in fields employing women workers. There are numerous magazines especially written for women which provide good source material. Archives of Congress and of state governments contain petitions and statements made at hearings which can yield valuable information about the activities and interests of women. Many of these readily available sources remain neglected.

A fresh approach to known material and to available sources could provide valuable new insights. The following suggestions might make a useful beginning.

First, the subject "Women" is too vast and diffuse to serve as a valid point of departure. Women are members of families, citizens of different regions, economic producers, just as men are, but their emphasis on these various roles is different. The economic role of men predominates in their lives, but women shift readily from one role to another at different periods in their lives. It is in this that their function is different from men and it is this which must form the basis for any conceptual framework. In modern society the only statement about women in general which can be made with validity concerns their political status. Therefore the subject should be subsumed under several categories and any inquiry, description, and generalization should be limited to a narrower field. It is useful to deal with the *status* of women at any given time—to distinguish among their economic status, family status, and political-legal status. There must also be a consideration of class position, as has been usefully proven in recent studies of the feminist movement.[12]

Second, we should look at different aspects of women's role in American history. We must certainly be concerned with the woman's rights movement, but only as part of the total story. Historians must painstakingly restore the actual record of women's contributions at any given period in history. It is interesting that the history of women before the advent of the feminist movement has been more fully recorded and in a more balanced way than it has afterward, so that the story of colonial women can be quite fully traced through secondary literature.[13] But when we deal with the period after 1800, it often proves difficult to establish even descriptive facts. During the early national period, women organized elaborate welfare and relief systems which they staffed and administered. This story should be part of the history of the period; it is not now. Women were the teachers in most of the nation's public schools during the nineteenth century; this is worth recording and exploring. Women made a significant contribution to the growth and development of frontier communities. These are but a few of the many areas in which more research and uncovering of factual information are needed.

Third, we might well discard the "oppressed group model" when discussing women's role in the political life of the nation. Instead, we might start with the fact that one generalization about women which holds up is that they were, longer than any other group in the nation, deprived of political and economic power. Did this mean they actually wielded no power or did they wield power in different forms? My research has led me to believe that they wielded considerable power and in the middle of the nineteenth century even political power. They found a way to make their power felt through organizations, through pressure tactics, through petitioning, and through various other means; these later became models for other mass movements for reform.

Fourth, another important fact is that women are a group who for a considerable period of history were deprived of equal access to education. While they were not illiterate, their education was limited, usually to below the high school level. This was true of the majority of women until the end of the nineteenth century. It might be very useful to investigate what impact this had on female behavior and more specifically, women's performance as a group in terms of outstanding achievement. To put it another way, how many generations of educated women are necessary to produce a significant number of outstanding women academicians? How many generations of college-trained women are necessary before women in sizable numbers make contributions in the sciences? When do women begin to move from the small-scale, home-centered creative forms, the fiction, poetry, and article-writing, to the larger-scale work within the framework of cultural institutions? Is the proverbial dearth of female philosophers really a result of some innate distinctiveness of female mental function or rather the product of centuries of environmental and institutional deprivation? This type of inquiry lends itself to a comparative cross-cultural approach. A comparison between the educational deprivation of women and that suffered by certain minority groups might lead us to a demonstrable correlation between educational deprivation and a gap of several generations before adequate and competitive performance is possible. This could explain a great deal about some of our problems with minority groups, public schooling, and academic achievement.

Fifth, it would be most worthwhile to distinguish the ideas society held at any given moment in regard to woman's proper "place" from what was actually woman's status at that time. The two do not necessarily overlap. On the contrary, there seems to be a considerable gap between the popular myth and reality. Social historians might legitimately be concerned with the significance of this gap, how to account for it, and whether it fits any distinguishable pattern. It would also be important to understand the function of ideas about women in the general ordering of society. Was the fact that colonial women were idealized as thrifty housewives and able helpmeets a cause or effect of the labor shortage in the colonies? Are the idealized suburban housewife, the fashion-conscious teenager, the sex-symbol model, causes or effects of our consumer-oriented society? And what effect does the societally held concept of woman's role have on the development of female talent, on woman's contribution to the society?

Finally, we come back to the initial problem of how to judge the contribution of women. Are women noteworthy when their achievement falls exactly in a category of achievement set up for men? Obviously not, for this is how they have been kept out of the history books up to now. Are women noteworthy then, as the feminists tended to think, if they do anything at all? Not likely. The fact remains that women are different from men and that their role in society and history is different from that of men. Different, but equal in importance. Obviously their achievements must also be measured on a different scale. To define and devise such a scale is difficult until the gaps in our historical knowledge about the actual contributions of women have been filled. This work remains to be done.

But we already know enough about the subject to conclude that the role women played at different times in our history has been changing. The patterns and significance of these changes, the continuities and discontinuities, the expectations and strivings of the pioneers, and the realities of the social scene—all these await study and new interpretations. One would hope at once for a wider framework and a narrower focus—a discarding of old categories and a painstaking search of known sources for unknown meanings. It is an endeavor that should enlist the best talents of the profession and, hopefully and at long last, not primarily female talent.

### NOTES

1. Cf. Arthur Schlesinger, Sr., *New Viewpoints in American History* (New York, 1922), chap. 6. For a contemporary historian's viewpoint, see David M. Potter, "American Women and the American Character," in *American History and Social Sciences*, ed. Edward N. Saveth (New York, 1964), 427–28.

2. The most important feminist tracts before the launching of the woman's rights movement are: Charles Brockden Brown, *Alcuin: A Dialogue* (Boston,1798); Sarah M. Grimké, *Letters on the Equality of the Sexes and the Condition of Woman* (Boston, 1838); and Margaret Fuller, *Woman in the Nineteenth Century* (Boston, 1844). The publications of the feminist movement are too numerous to list here; a representative collection is incorporated in Elizabeth C. Stanton, Susan B. Anthony, and Matilda J. Gage, *History of Woman Suffrage*, 6 vols. (New York, 1881–1922).

3. Typical of the "compilers" are: Lydia M. Child, *History of the Condition of Women*, 2 vols. (New York, 1835); Sarah J. Hale, *Woman's Record* ... (New York, 1853); Phebe A. Hanaford, *Daughters of America, or Women of the Century* (Augusta, Me., n.d.); and Frances E. Willard and Mary A. Livermore, *American Women* (New York, 1897).

4. Cf. Eleanor Flexner, *Century of Struggle: The Woman's Rights Movement in the United States* (Cambridge, Mass., 1959); Aileen S. Kraditor, *The Ideas of the Woman Suffrage Movement* (New York, 1965).

5. Mary R. Beard, *Woman As Force in History* (New York, 1946).

6. Mary R. Beard, *America through Women's Eyes* (New York, 1934), *On Under-*

*standing Women* (New York, 1931), and *Women's Work in Municipalities* (New York, 1915); Charles R. and Mary R. Beard, *The Rise of American Civilization* (New York, 1927).

7. For the economic life of colonial women see: Elisabeth A. Dexter, *Colonial Women of Affairs: Women in Business and Professions in America before 1776* (Boston, 1931), and *Career Women of America: 1776–1840* (Francestown, N.H., 1950); Richard B. Morris, *Government and Labor in Early America* (New York, 1946); and Julia C. Spruill, *Women's Life and Work in the Southern Colonies* (Chapel Hill, N.C., 1938). For women's economic role in nineteenth- and twentieth-century America, see: Edith Abbott, *Women in Industry* (New York, 1918); J. B. Andrews and W. D. P. Bliss, *Report on Condition of Woman and Child Wage-Earners in the United States*, 19 vols. (Doc. No. 645, 61st Congress, 2d Session; Washington, 1910); and Elizabeth Baker, *Technology and Women's Work* (New York, 1964).

8. For women in reform movements, see: Robert Bremner, *American Philanthropy* (Chicago, 1960); Clarke E. Chambers, *Seedtime of Reform: American Social Service and Social Action, 1918–1933* (Ann Arbor, 1963); Christopher Lasch, *The New Radicalism in America: 1889–1963* (New York, 1965); and Daniel Levine, *Varieties of Reform Thought* (Madison, Wis., 1964).

9. For a history of the family, see Arthur W. Calhoun, *A Social History of the American Family*, 3 vols. (Cleveland, 1918); Sidney Ditzion, *Marriage, Morals, and Sex in America* (New York, 1953); Paul H. Jacobson, *American Marriage and Divorce* (New York, 1959); and William O'Neill, *Divorce in the Progressive Era* (New Haven, 1967).

10. Harriet Martineau, *Society in America* (New York, 1837), I, 158.

11. Helen Hacker, "Women As a Minority Group," *Social Forces* XXX (1951–52), 60–69.

12. See Kraditor, *Ideas of the Woman Suffrage Movement*, and Lasch, *The New Radicalism*.

13. A full bibliography of colonial women is to be found in Eugenie A. Leonard, Sophie H. Drinker, and Miriam Y. Holden, *The American Woman in Colonial and Revolutionary Times: 1565–1800* (Philadelphia, 1962).

# Placing Women in History:
## A 1975 Perspective

### Gerda Lerner

In the brief span of five years in which American historians have begun to develop women's history as an independent field, they have sought to find a conceptual framework and a methodology appropriate to the task.

The first level at which scholars trained in traditional history approach women's history is by writing accounts of "women worthies" or "compensatory history."[1] Who are the women missing from history? Who are the women of achievement and what did they achieve? The resulting history of "notable women" does not tell us much about those activities in which most women engaged, nor does it tell us about the significance to society as a whole of women's activities. The history of notable women is the history of exceptional, even deviant women, and does not describe the experience and history of the mass of women. Also, women of different classes have different historical experiences. To comprehend the full complexity of society at a given stage of its development, it is essential to take account of such differences.

Women have a different experience as to consciousness, depending on whether their activity is male-defined or woman-oriented. They are indoctrinated in a male-defined value system and conduct their lives accordingly. Thus, colonial and early nineteenth-century female reformers directed their activities into channels which were merely an extension of their domestic concerns and traditional roles. They taught school, cared for the poor, the sick, the aged. As their consciousness developed, they turned their attention toward the needs of women. Becoming woman-oriented, they began to "uplift" prostitutes, organize women for abolition or temperance, and seek the upgrading of female education, though only in order to equip women better for their traditional roles. Only at a later stage, growing out of the recognition of the

This is a revised version of an article which appeared in *Feminist Studies* 3, no. 1–2 (1975), 5–15. The article was based on papers given by the author at a panel at the Second Berkshire Conference on the History of Women, October 25–27, 1974, at Radcliffe College, Cambridge, Mass., and at a Sarah Lawrence College Workshop-Symposium, March 15, 1975. The author has greatly benefited from discussion with co-panelists Renate Bridenthal and Joan Kelly-Gadol, and from the comments and critiques of audience participants at both conferences.

separate interests of women as a group, and of their subordinate place in society, did their consciousness become woman-defined. Feminist thought starts at this level and encompasses the active assertion of the rights and grievances of women. These various stages of female consciousness need to be considered in historical analysis.

The next level of conceptualizing women's history has been "contribution history": describing women's contribution to, their status in and their oppression by male-defined society. Under this category we find quite a variety of questions being asked: What have women contributed to abolition, to reform, to the Progressive movement, to the labor movement, to the New Deal? The movement in question stands in the foreground of inquiry; women made a "contribution" to it; the contribution is judged first of all with respect to its effect on the movement and second by standards appropriate to men. The ways in which women were aided and affected by the work of these "great women," the ways in which they themselves grew into feminist awareness, are ignored. Jane Addams's enormous contribution in creating a support network for women and new structures for living are subordinated to her role as a Progressive, or to an interpretation which regards her as merely representative of a group of frustrated college-trained women with no place to go. In other words, a deviant from male-defined norms. Margaret Sanger is seen merely as the founder of the birth-control movement, not as a woman raising a revolutionary challenge to the centuries-old practice by which the bodies and lives of women are dominated and ruled by male-made laws. In the labor movement, women are described as "also there" or as problems. Their essential role on behalf of themselves and of other women is seldom considered a central theme in writing their history. Women are the outgroup, Simone de Beauvoir's "other."

Another set of questions concerns oppression and its opposite, the struggle for woman's rights. Who oppressed women and how were they oppressed? How did they respond to such oppression?

Such questions have yielded detailed and very valuable accounts of economic or social oppression, and of the various organizational, political ways in which women as a group have fought such oppression. Judging from the results, it is clear that asking of history the question "Why and how were women victimized?" has its usefulness. We learn what society or individuals or classes of people have done to women, and we learn how women themselves have reacted to conditions imposed upon them. But the limitation of this approach is that it makes it appear either that women were largely passive or that, at the most, they reacted to male pressures or the restraints of patriarchal society. Such inquiry fails to elicit the positive and essential way in which women have functioned in history. The ongoing and continuing contribution of women to the development of human culture cannot be found by treating them only as victims of oppression, as Mary Beard was the first to point out.[2] I have in my own work learned that it is far more useful to deal with the question of victimization as one aspect of women's history, but never to regard it as the *central* aspect of women's history. Essentially, treating women as victims of oppression once again places them in a male-defined conceptual framework: oppressed, victimized by standards and values established by men. The true history of women is the history of their ongoing functioning in that male-defined world, *on their own terms.* The question of oppression does not elicit that story, and is therefore a tool of limited usefulness to the historian.

A major focus of women's history has been on women's rights struggles, especially the winning of suffrage, on organizational and institutional history of the women's movements, and on its leaders. This, again, is an important aspect of women's history, but it cannot and should not be its central concern.

Recent literature has dealt with marriage and divorce, with educational opportunities, and with the economic struggles of working women. Much of recent work has been concerned with the image of women and "woman's sphere," with the educational ideals of society, the values to which women are indoctrinated, and with gender role acculturation as seen in historical perspective. A separate field of study has examined ideals, values, and prescriptions concerning sexuality, especially female sexuality. Ronald Walters and Ben Barker-Benfield have tended to confirm traditional stereotypes concerning Victorian sexuality, the double standard, and the subordinate position of women. Much of this material is based on the study of such readily available sources as sermons, educational tracts, women's magazines, and medical textbooks. The pitfall in such interpretation, as Carl Degler has pointed out, is the tendency to confuse prescriptive literature with actual behavior. In fact, what we are learning from most of these monographs is not what women did, felt or experienced, but what men in the past thought women should do. Charles Rosenberg, Carroll Smith-Rosenberg, and Carl Degler have shown how to approach the same material and interpret it from the new perspective of women's history.[3] They have sharply distinguished between prescription and behavior, between myth and reality.

Other attempts to deduce women's status from popular literature and ideology demonstrate similar difficulties. Barbara Welter, in an early and highly influential article, found the emergence of "the cult of true womanhood" in sermons and periodicals of the Jacksonian era. Many historians, feminists among them, have deduced from this, that Victorian ideals of woman's place pervaded the society and were representative of its realities. More detailed analysis reveals, that this mass media concern with woman's domesticity was, in fact, a response to the opposite trend in society.[4] Lower-class women were entering the factories, middle-class women were discontented with their accustomed roles, and the family, as an institution, was experiencing turmoil and crisis. Idealization is very frequently a defensive ideology and an expression of tension within the society. To use ideology as a measure of the shifting status of women, it must be set against a careful analysis of social structure, economic conditions, institutional changes and popular values. With this caution, society's attitudes toward women and toward gender role indoctrination can be usefully analyzed as manifestations of a shifting value system and of tensions within patriarchal society.

"Contribution" history is an important stage in the creation of a true history of women. The monographic work which such inquiries produce is essential to the development of more complex and sophisticated questions, but it mostly describes what men in the past told women to do and what men in the past thought women should be. This is just another way of saying that historians of women's history have so far used a traditional conceptual framework. Essentially, they have applied questions from traditional history to women, and tried to fit women's past into the empty spaces of historical scholarship. While the value and utility of such work is unquestioned, the limitation of such work is that it deals with women in male-defined society and tries to fit them into the categories and value systems which consider *man* the measure of significance. Perhaps it will be useful to refer to this level of work as "transitional women's history," seeing it as an inevitable step in the development of new criteria and concepts.

Another methodological question which arises frequently concerns the connection between women's history and other recently emerging fields. It is obvious that there has already been rich cross-fertilization between the new social history and women's history, but it has not been nor should it be a case of subsuming women's history under the larger and already respectable field of social history.

Women are part of the anonymous in history, but unlike them, they are also and always have been part of the ruling elite. They are oppressed, but not quite like either racial or ethnic groups, though some of them are. They are subordinate and exploited, but not quite like lower classes, though some of them are. We have not yet really solved the problems of definition, but it can be suggested that the key to understanding women's history is in accepting— painful though that may be—that it is the history of the *majority* of humankind. Women are essentially different from all the above categories, because they are the majority now and always have been at least half of humanity, and because their subjection to patriarchal institutions antedates all other oppression and has outlasted all economic and social changes in recorded history.

Historians working in family history ask a great many questions pertaining to women, but family history is not in itself women's history. It is no longer sufficient to view women mainly as members of families. Family history has by and large neglected unmarried and widowed women. In its applications to specific monographic studies, such as the work of Philip Greven, family history has been used to describe the relationships of fathers and sons and the property arrangements between them.[5] The relationships of fathers to daughters and mothers to their children have been ignored. The complex family-support patterns, for example those whereby the work and wages of daughters are used to support the education of brothers and to maintain aged parents while that of sons is not so used, have been ignored.

Another way in which family history has been interpreted within the context of patriarchal assumptions is by using a vaguely defined "domestic power" of women, power within the family, as a measure of the societal status of women. Daniel Scott Smith has discovered in the nineteenth century the rise of something called "domestic feminism," expressed in a lowered birth rate from which he deduces an increasing control of women over their reproductive lives.[6] One might, from similar figures, as easily deduce a rise of desire on the part of men to curb their offspring due to the demands of a developing industrial system for a more highly educated labor force, hence for fewer children per family.

Demographic data can indeed tell us something about female as well as male status in society, but only in the context of an economic and sociological analysis. Further, the status of women within the family is something quite different and distinct from their status in general society. I learned in studying the history of black women and the black family that relatively high status for women within the family does not signify "matriarchy" or "power for women," since black women are not only members of families, but persons functioning in a larger society. The status of persons is determined not in one area of their functioning, such as within the family, but in several. The decisive historical fact about women is that the *areas* of their functioning, not only their status *within* those areas, have been determined by men. The effect on the consciousness of women has been pervasive. It is one of the decisive aspects of their history and any analysis which does not take this complexity into consideration must be inadequate.

Then there is the impact of demographic techniques, the study of large aggregates of anonymous people by computer technology based on census data, public documents, property records. Demographic techniques have led to insights which are very useful for women's history. They have yielded revealing data on fertility fluctuations, on changes in illegitimacy patterns and sex ratios, and aggregate studies of life cycles. The latter work has been done very successfully by Joseph Kett, Robert Wells, Peter Laslett, and Kenneth Keniston.[7] In the United States the field has been largely dominated by male historians, mostly through self-imposed sex role stereotyping by women historians, who have shared a prejudice against the computer and statistics. However, a group of younger women scholars, trained in demographic techniques, have begun to research and publish material concerning working-class women. Alice Kessler-Harris, Virginia McLaughlin, Judith Walkowitz, Susan Kleinberg, and Tamara Hareven are among those who have elicited woman-oriented interpretations from aggregate data.[8] They have demonstrated that social history can be enriched by combining cliometrics with sophisticated humanistic and feminist interpretations. They have added gender as a factor for analysis to such familiar concepts as class, race and ethnicity.

The compensatory questions raised by women's history specialists are proving interesting and valuable in a variety of fields, but a limitation of this approach is that it tends to separate the work and activities of women from those of men, even where they were essentially connected. As yet, synthesis is lacking. For example, the rich history of the abolition movement has been told as though women played a marginal, auxiliary, and at times mainly disruptive role in it. Yet female anti-slavery societies outnumbered male societies; women abolitionists largely financed the movement with their fund-raising activities and did much of the work of propaganda writing in and distribution of abolitionist newspapers and magazines. The enormous political significance of petition campaigns organized by women remains unrecorded.

Most important, no historical work has as yet taken the organizational work of female abolitionists seriously as an integral part of the anti-slavery movement.

Slowly, as the field has matured, historians of women's history have become dissatisfied with old questions and old methods, and have come up with new ways of approaching historical material. They have, for example, begun to ask about the actual *experience* of women in the past. This is obviously different from a description of the condition of women written from the perspective of male sources, and leads one to the use of women's letters, diaries, autobiographies, and oral history sources. This shift from male-oriented to female-oriented consciousness is most important and leads to challenging new interpretations.

Historians of women's history have studied female sexuality and its regulation from the female point of view, making imaginative use of medical textbooks, diaries, and case histories of hospital patients. Questions concerning women's experience have led to studies of birth control, as it affects women and as an issue expressing cultural and symbolic values; of the physical conditions to which women are prone, such as menarche, pregnancy and women's ailments; of customs, attitudes, and fashions affecting women's health and women's life experience. Historians are now exploring the impact of female bonding, of female friendship and homosexual relations, and the experience of women in groups, such as women in utopian communities, in women's clubs and settlement houses. There has been an interest in the possibility that women's centuries-long preoccupation with birth and with the care of the sick and dying has led to some specific female rituals.[9]

Women's history has already presented a challenge to some basic assumptions historians make. While most historians are aware of the fact that their findings are not value-free and they are trained to check their biases by a variety of methods, they are as yet quite unaware of their own sexist bias and, more important, of the sexist bias which pervades the value system, the culture, and the very language within which they work.

Women's history presents a challenge to the periodization of traditional history. The periods in which basic changes occur in society and which historians have commonly regarded as turning points for all historical development, are not necessarily the same for men as for women. This is not surprising when we consider that the traditional time frame in history has been derived from political history. Women have been the one group in history longest excluded from political power as they have, by and large, been excluded from military decision-making. Thus the irrelevance of periodization based on military and political developments to their historical experience should have been predictable.

Renate Bridenthal's and Joan Kelly-Gadol's papers confirm that the history of women demands different periodization than does political history.[10] Neither the Renaissance, it appears, nor the period during which women's suffrage was won, were periods in which women experienced an advance in their status. Recent work on women by American historians, such as Linda Kerber's on the American Revolution and my own work, confirms this conclusion. For example, neither during or after the American Revolution nor in the age of Jackson did women share the historical experience of men. On the contrary, they experienced in both periods status loss and a restriction of options as to occupations and role choices, and certainly in Jacksonian America, there were restrictions imposed upon their sexuality, at least in prescriptive behavior. If one applies to both of these cases the kind of sophisticated and detailed analysis Joan Kelly-Gadol attempts—that is, differentiations between women of different classes and comparisons between the status of men of a given class and women of that class—one finds the picture further complicated. Status loss in one area—social production—may be offset by status gain in another—access to education.

What kind of periodization might be substituted for the periodization of traditional history, in order for it to be applicable to women? The answer depends largely on the conceptual framework in which the historian works. Many historians, in their search for a unifying framework of women's history, have tended to use the Marxist or neo-Marxist model supplied by Juliet Mitchell[11] and recently elaborated by Sheila Rowbotham.[12] The important fact, says Mitchell, which distinguishes the past of women from that of men is precisely that until very recently sexuality and reproduction were inevitably linked for women, while they were not so linked for men. Similarly, child-bearing and child-rearing were inevitably linked for women and still are so linked. Women's freedom depends on breaking those links. Using Mitchell's categories we can and should ask of each historical period: what happened to the link between sexuality and reproduction? What happened to the link between child-bearing and child-rearing? Important changes in the status of women occur when it becomes possible through the availability of birth control information and technology to sever sexuality from inevitable motherhood. However, it may be the case that it is not the distribution of birth control information and products, so much as the level of medical and health care, which are the determinants of change. That is, when infant mortality decreases, so that raising every child to adulthood becomes the normal expectation of parents, family size declines.

The above case illustrates the difficulty that has vexed scholars of women's history in trying to locate a periodization more appropriate to women. Working in different fields and specialities, many historians have observed that the transition from agricultural to industrializing society and then again the transition to fully developed industrial society entails important changes affecting women and the family. Changes in relations of production affect women's status as family members and as workers. Later, shifts in the mode of production affect the kinds of occupations women can enter and their status within them. Major shifts in health care and technological development, related to industrialization, also affect the lives of women. It is not too difficult to discern such patterns and to conclude that there must be a causal relationship between changes in the mode of production and the status of women. Here, the Marxist model seems to offer an immediately satisfying solution, especially if, following Mitchell, "sexuality" as a factor is added to such factors as class. But in the case of women, just as in the case of racial castes, ideology and prescription internalized by both women and men seem to be as much a causative factor as are material changes in production relations. Does the entry of lower-class women into industrial production really bring them closer to "liberation"? In the absence of institutional changes such as the right to abortion and safe contraception, altered child rearing arrangements, and varied options for sexual expression, changes in economic relations may become oppressive. Unless such changes are accompanied by changes in consciousness, which in turn result in institutional changes, they do not favorably affect the lives of women.

Is smaller family size the result of "domestic freedom" of choice exercised by women, the freedom of choice exercised by men, the ideologically buttressed coercion of institutions in the service of an economic class? Is it liberating for women, for men, or for corporations? This raises another difficult question: what about the relationship of upper-class to lower-class women? To what extent is the relative advance in the status of upper-class women predicated on the status loss of lower-class women? Examples of this are: the liberation of the middle-class American housewife in the mid-nineteenth century through the availability of cheap black or immigrant domestic workers; the liberation of the twentieth century housewife from incessant drudgery in the home through agricultural stoop-labor and the food-processing industry, both employing low-paid female workers.

Is periodization then dependent as much on class as on gender? This question is just one of several which challenge the universalist assumptions of all previous historical categories. I cannot provide an answer, but I think the questions themselves point us in the right direction.

It appears to me that all conceptual models of history hitherto developed have only limited usefulness for women's history, since all are based on the silent assumptions of a patriarchal ordering of values. The structural-functionalist framework leaves out class and sex factors, the traditional Marxist framework leaves out sex and race factors as *essentials,* admitting them only as marginal factors. Mitchell's neo-Marxist model includes these, but slights ideas, values, and psychological factors. Still, her four-structures model and the refinements of it proposed by Bridenthal are an excellent addition to the conceptual working tools of the historian of women's history. They should be tried out, discussed, refined. But they are not, in my opinion, the whole answer.

Joan Kelly-Gadol[13] offers the useful suggestion that attitudes toward sexuality should be studied in each historical period. She considers the constraints upon women's sexuality imposed by society a useful measure of women's true status. This approach would necessitate comparisons between prescribed behavior for women and men as well as indications of their actual sexual behavior at any given time. This challenging method can be used with great effectiveness for certain periods of history and especially for upper- and middle-class women. I doubt that it can be usefully employed as a general criterion, because of the difficulty of finding substantiating evidence, especially as it pertains to lower classes.

I raised the question of a conceptual framework for dealing with women's history in 1969, reasoning from the assumption that women were a sub-group, a particular and problematic group, different from any other sub-group in history.[14] Neither caste, class, nor race quite fit the model for describing us. I have now come to the conclusion that the idea that women are some kind of a sub-group is wrong. It will not do—there are just too many of us. No single framework, no single-factor, four-factor, or eight-factor explanation can serve to contain all that the history of women is. Picture, if you can, an attempt to organize the history of men by using four factors. It will not work; neither will it work for women.

Women are and always have been at least half of humanity and most of the time have been the majority of humanity. Their culturally determined and psychologically internalized marginality seems to be what makes their histori-cal experience essentially different from that of men. But men have defined their experience as history and have left women out. At this time, as during earlier periods of feminist activity, women are urged to fit into the empty spaces, assuming their traditional marginal, "sub-group" status. But the truth is that history, as written and perceived up to now, is the history of a minority, who may well turn out to be the "sub-group." In order to write a new history worthy of the name, we will have to recognize that no single methodology and conceptual framework can fit the complexities of the historical experience of all women.

The first stage of "transitional history" may be to add some new cate-gories to the general categories by which historians organize their material: sexuality, reproduction, the link between child-bearing and child-rearing; role indoctrination; sexual values and myths; female consciousness. Further, all of these need to be analysed taking factors of race, class, ethnicity, and possibly religion into consideration. What we have here is not a single framework for dealing with women in history, but new questions to all of universal history.

The next stage may be to explore the possibility that what we call women's history may actually be the study of a separate women's culture. Such a culture would include not only the separate occupations, status, experiences and rituals of women but also their separate consciousness, which internalizes patriarchal assumptions. In some cases, it would include the tensions created in that culture between the prescribed patriarchal assump-tions and women's efforts to attain autonomy and emancipation.

A following stage may develop a synthesis: a history of the dialectic, the tensions between the two cultures, male and female. Such a synthesis could be based on close comparative study of given periods in which the historical experience of men is compared to that of women, their tensions and inter-actions being as much the subject of study as their differences. Only after a series of such detailed studies can we hope to find the parameters by which to define the new universal history. My guess is that no one conceptual frame-work will fit so complex a subject.

Methods are tools for analysis—some of us will stick with one tool, some of us will reach for different tools as we need them. For women, the problem really is that we must acquire not only the confidence needed for using tools, but for making new ones to fit our needs. We should do so relying on our learned skills and on our rational skepticism of handed-down doctrine. The recognition that we had been denied our history came to many of us as a staggering flash of insight, which altered our consciousness irretrievably. We have come a long way since then. The next step is to face the reality, once and for all and with all its complex consequences, that women are the majority of humankind and have been essential to the making of history. Thus, all history as we now know it, is merely pre-history. Only a new history firmly based on this recognition and equally concerned with men, women, the establishment and the passing of patriarchy, can lay claim to being a truly universal history.

## NOTES

1. For the term "women worthies," I am indebted to Natalie Zemon Davis, University of California at Berkeley.

2. Mary Beard, *Woman As Force in History* (New York: Collier, 1972). See also the discussion of this question in Gerda Lerner, "New Approaches to the Study of Women in American History," in this volume.

3. Ronald G. Walters, ed., *Primers for Prudery* (Englewood Cliffs, N.J.: Prentice-Hall, 1974); Ben Barker-Benfield, "The Spermatic Economy: A Nineteenth Century View of Sexuality," *Feminist Studies* I, no. 1 (Summer 1972), 59ff.; Carl Degler, "What Ought to Be and What Was: Women's Sexuality in the Nineteenth Century," *American Historical Review* 79, no. 5 (December 1974), 1467–90. For a different approach, see also: Carroll Smith-Rosenberg and Charles Rosenberg, "The Female Animal: Medical and Biological Views of Women in Nineteenth Century America," *Journal of American History* 60, no. 2 (September 1973), 332–56; Carroll Smith-Rosenberg, "The Hysterical Woman: Some Reflections on Sex Roles and Role Conflict in 19th Century America," *Social Research* (Winter 1972), 652–78; and Charles Rosenberg, "Sexuality, Class and Role," *American Quarterly* 25, no. 2 (May 1973), 131–53.

4. Barbara Welter, "The Cult of True Womanhood 1820–1860," *American Quarterly* 18, no. 2 (Summer 1966), 151–57; Gerda Lerner, "The Lady and the Mill Girl: Changes in the Status of Women in the Age of Jackson," *Midcontinent American Studies Journal* 10, no. 1 (Spring 1969), 5–15.

5. Philip J. Greven, Jr., *Four Generations: Population, Land and Family in Colonial Andover, Massachusetts* (Ithaca, N.Y.: Cornell University Press, 1970). For a good sampling of recent work in family history, see Michael Gordon, ed., *The American Family in Social-Historical Perspective* (New York: St. Martin's Press, 1973).

6. Daniel Scott Smith, "Family Limitation, Sexual Control and Domestic Feminism in Victorian America," *Feminist Studies* 1, no. 3–4 (Winter–Spring 1973), 40–57.

7. See *Journal of Interdisciplinary History* 2, no. 2 (Autumn 1971) for articles by Joseph Kett, Robert Wells, Peter Laslett, and Kenneth Keniston.

8. Virginia Yans McLaughlin, "Patterns of Work and Family Organization: Buffalo's Italians," *Journal of Interdisciplinary History* 2, no. 2 (Autumn 1971), 219–314; Tamara Hareven, "The History of the Family As an Interdisciplinary Field," in *ibid.*, 399–414; Susan Kleinberg, University of California at San Diego, "Women's Work: The Lives of Working Class Women in Pittsburgh, 1870–1900" (unpublished paper) and Alice Kessler-Harris, Sarah Lawrence College, "Problems of Clan and Culture in Organizing Women Workers, 1900–1920," Second Berkshire Conference on the History of Women, October 25–27, 1974, at Radcliffe College, Cambridge, Mass.

9. For a good overview of this work see the unpublished papers of the Second

Berkshire Conference on the History of Women. See also Carroll Smith-Rosenberg, "Puberty to Menopause: The Cycle of Femininity in Nineteenth Century America," *Feminist Studies* 1, no. 3–4 (Winter–Spring 1973), 58–72.

10. Renate Bridenthal, "Effects of Women's History on Traditional Historiography, with Specific Reference to Twentieth-Century Europe," and Joan Kelly-Gadol, "Women in the Renaissance and Renaissance Historiography," papers read at the Second Berkshire Conference on the History of Women; revised versions of these papers appear in *Feminist Studies* 3 (1975), no. 3–4.

11. Juliet Mitchell, *Woman's Estate* (New York: Pantheon Books, 1972); see the excerpt from that work, "Four Structures in a Complex Unity," reprinted in this volume.

12. Sheila Rowbotham, *Woman's Consciousness, Man's World* (Baltimore, Md.: Penguin Books, 1973), and *Women, Resistance and Revolution* (New York: Pantheon, 1972).

13. Kelly-Gadol, "Women in the Renaissance and Renaissance Historiography."

14. See Lerner, "New Approaches to the Study of Women in American History," in this volume.

# Feminism and the Methodology of Women's History

## Hilda Smith

### I

There are many questions which come to mind when contemplating the study of women in the past. Did women, as a group, have a history separate from the history of society in general? Can one use the same criteria for defining the historical significance of individual women that are applied to men? What relationship does women's history hold to the field of social history? Does one need a particular perspective or conceptual or ideological framework when studying women or is it possible to employ the perspective of social or radical historians? These questions lead one to the most basic issue—why study women at all, or why study them outside the context of normal historical selection? If a woman fills a crucial role in the progression of "historical events," then she cannot be ignored. However, most women have not done so, and one certainly does not need a separate field of women's history to deal with those few queens and great ladies of the past.

If this be so, why study women's history? First, there is the general argument presented primarily by social historians that history should not be equated with an understanding of elites, that its content should not be of political, diplomatic, or intellectual achievements alone; that for the majority of people the line separating them from others is not the significant fact in their lives. And, that perhaps all the mass of documents rushed to and fro in diplomatic pouches may tell us little about the past. These arguments have become somewhat commonplace, and, to a large extent, are accepted by a large body of historians writing today. However, the acceptance of women's history as a legitimate field of study is not so evident. For this reason, these arguments need to be applied more specifically to a study of women's past.

History is a selective view of the past whose scope is limited more by the realities of the present than through a clear understanding of the past. As historians perceive shifts in the present power structure they consciously or unconsciously alter their view of who was important in the past. When entrepreneurs became powerful during the latter part of the nineteenth century, historians came to interpret the actions of seventeenth-century gentry and merchants more in terms of the development of an entrepreneurial spirit. Likewise, members of the socialist and labor movements fostered an increased interest in workers living in past ages; and, in our country an interest in black history has been intricately connected with the impetus of the civil rights movement. Anyone who has worked in the area of women's history is aware of the innumerable titles on women's subjects written between 1880 and 1920 and the dearth of such material following that period. Feminist agitation and interest in the history of women spurred such investigation; and only recently, with the newest feminist movement, has that interest returned. When a group of people come to think of themselves as significant beings or are pushing for such recognition from society, and further, when historians recognize or experience such pressure, then an interest in that group's past is enhanced. In this way historical research has expanded to include increasing numbers of people who have obtained or pressed for power—in the present, not in the past. And this is a necessary process in reconstructing the past. History, at its best, should be a recounting of how members of a particular society lived and not merely a designation of who was "important" in that society. Women's history, along with other studies of the powerless groups of the past, is based on that assumption.

But this is not sufficient to justify a study of women. Why not place them into other social categories—put working-class women into social and labor history; let black women be studied as part of black history; in other words, why not fit women into the appropriate group and remove the necessity of having a separate field for women's history? But that will not do, because— and here is the central justification for studying the history of women— women have had a unique past. Women, as a group, have held a particular position in society regardless of the other restrictions of their lives.

Sexual division has been one of the most basic distinctions within society encouraging one group to view its interests differently from another. Just as class and race and religion and locality help formulate a man or woman's view of himself or herself, so sex has been used to create a separate identity for men and women. And by studying the history of men in the past, one by no means knows what the realities of women's lives were during a given era. It is necessary, therefore, to view the development of women's history from the feminist perspective of women as a distinct sociological group which has experienced both overt and covert controls through legal, political, and social restrictions.

## II

One difficulty which arises when applying a feminist perspective to the study of women's history is the lack of exactitude in works which discuss feminism. Most authors assume their readers know what is meant by femi- nism and therefore fail to define it. Because they limit their definitions (when given) and their discussion to a nineteenth-century political phenomenon centered around the issue of women's rights, their works suffer from a limited applicability both in a chronological and ideological sense. This difficulty is a result of the failure to view feminist thinking at its origin. Rather, authors discuss only the end products of a feminist train of thought, i.e., specific goals, and they ignore the process which led the feminist to designate those aims as significant for women. It is neither fruitful nor valid to devise a definition from the goals of one particular feminist movement or organization, for one must look for the unifying element in all periods and varieties of feminist thought. The logical beginning to such a search is to pose the question: how are the ways feminists view women different from the ways nonfeminists view them? One must first look at feminism as an ideology about the determination of one's existence in regard to one's sex. Then it is possible to proceed to a study of the varying feminist goals of particular periods and societies.

I would like, therefore, to define feminism as a view of women as a distinct sociological group for which there are established patterns of behavior, special legal and legislative restrictions, and customarily defined roles. This definition includes the obvious corollary that women's roles and behavior are based on neither rational criteria nor physiological dictates. It assumes a process of indoctrination from earliest childhood, both by overt and covert means, which determines the differing life styles of men and women. And, finally, it views the role of women as more restricted and less personally fulfilling than that of men.

The above, however, is only the broadest generalization which can be made about feminist thinking throughout history. Within this general definition there are standard categories through which feminists view the status of women. These categories aid feminists in specifying the intellectual and social systems which are the bases for controlling women's lives. These categories are normally constructed around the institutions and/or attitudes of a given society. For example, if a feminist views a particular society with the aim of discovering the position of its women, she will examine its government, religion, education, and family structure, and the relationship between women and each of these. She will look, as well, at the art and literature of the period to determine the number of antifeminist writings and the general presentation of women. Feminist thinking, organized within these specific categories, poses, again and again, these two questions: what did men think of women at a particular period, and were women allowed to develop freely their individual talents and were they eventually permitted to hold positions of power and responsibility?

In order to clarify the above definition I would like to discuss more explicitly the conclusions drawn from viewing women as a sociological group. To begin, one does not see women always as individuals with problems distinct from the other members of their sex. If a woman faces a particular problem, it is the feminist's first inclination to place this problem into the context of women's defined sexual role. She (and feminists are overwhelmingly female) will more quickly than a nonfeminist pose the question "why" about any difficulty which befalls an individual woman.

To help understand what this means, I think it may be useful to speak of what is not, per se, a feminist viewpoint. Complaints about the position of women or displeasure expressed about the life of a particular woman do not, by themselves, constitute feminism. Nor do negative comments on men or on a particular man. Neither do complaints about the lives of women seen in the context of the normal, individualistic sexual relationships between men and women. Unless the writer asks the question "why" about the actions she considers detrimental to women, she is no feminist. And further, if she does ask "why," and her answer does not include an understanding of women as a sociological group (as opposed to merely a sex or biological entity), then again she is no feminist. Feminism is a system of thought devised to explain the relationships between men and women, and people can plug into that system at various points (depending on whether their interest is women's education, the role of the wife, etc.). To do so, however, an individual must develop a feminist explanation of social phenomena in addition to formulating complaints about the position of either men or women.

Thinking of women as a group with interests distinct from men encourages feminists to place women's rights in the context of the historical progression of movements for political and social emancipation. Women are simply another group whose rights have been restricted systematically by the powerful within a particular society. As early as the seventeenth century, feminists were comparing the role of the wife with that of the slave. Not only is there a belief in the close relationship between women and other deprived peoples, but feminists employ similar explanations for women's lack of accomplishments. It is lack of opportunity and not lack of skill which prevents women's advancement. The woman has no more choice to live the life of the man than do the poor to lead the life of the wealthy. Feminism is, therefore, a logical step in that progression of thought, perhaps most accurately termed "liberalism," which views the development of individual potential as a good and any limits on such development as regrettable. Further, it is clear that one must first view women as a social and political entity before they can be thought of as one more group denied fulfillment.

Finally, I would like to elaborate on feminists' views of women's defined role as being constrictive and as being thus limited for the benefit of men. In arriving at the view that women are either discriminated against or oppressed there are two essential prior assumptions—first, that women in some way are treated as a group, and second, that others possess sufficient power to inflict their will upon women. For feminists, the idea that women are a sociological group whose behavior is both overtly and covertly regulated is the starting point from which extended analyses of society are conducted. As stated earlier, if a feminist learns of the restrictions placed upon an individual woman her immediate response is to place this instance within her understanding of the general pattern of women's existence. And it is this chain of thought, above all else, which stamps an individual as a feminist.

Perhaps a modern example will help to clarify. In contrasting the position of blacks and women in the United States the nonfeminist would find little similarity. If questioned he would agree that women are as absent from powerful positions as blacks, or earn less than blacks (providing he were familiar with employment statistics), and that the types of skills which they perform are equally restricted. But, although he will admit the obvious truths of such statements of fact, he will not conclude that women's behavior is restricted in ways comparable to that of the black population. He will not do so because he views women as individuals who have choices to make and who make those choices which limit their role outside of the home and beyond occupations normally followed by women. The crucial ingredient in feminism, therefore, is not an exaggerated view of women's inferior state, but the understanding that the choices made by any woman must be placed first within the context of her sex; just as to understand the choices made by a contemporary black one can never forget the limitations placed on his or her decision by race.

### III

Accepting this working definition, I would like to apply the feminist perspective to studying women's history. At the most basic level, that of source material, certain problems arise about the discovery of sources and their proper interpretation. First, one discovers that if the historian searches for material on women in the same way as she has searched for material on men, she is likely to find little. If women had a separate existence, then the search for their materials must work from an awareness of that separation. Historical materials are preserved when it is in someone's interest to preserve them. For women, it has seldom been in the interest of the institutions of society to preserve their papers—the two exceptions are family memorabilia and feminist collections.

In the family documents, material on women is often hidden or lost because family papers are seldom indexed under women's names. On the other hand, as a result of the efforts of women's organizations and particularly feminist groups to preserve their work, we have a disproportionate amount of work in women's history focusing on the history of feminism. Second, because of the lack of interest in women's papers, one does not have the same quantity of materials when working on women who are of comparable importance or equal station, or historical significance with men. For instance, when searching the single-letters catalogs of the Bodleian Library at Oxford, one is struck by the massive materials of obscure seventeenth-century scholars whose voluminous correspondence the Bodleian had chosen to preserve, while one can locate only a handful of letters by women. Church libraries contain materials of comparably obscure ministers, but it is rare to find any institution which has a similar interest in the activities of women.

To find materials for women's history, one must search among the numerous and unorganized collections of family papers. Further, one has to be aware of social custom which has made it improper for women to write publicly, or when so doing, to sign their works. For this reason, guides such as Haklett's *Dictionary of Anonymous Works* are essential to bring women out of their hiding. As a general guide, then, to researching women's past, one must start from the assumption that only a general search among bibliographic materials for a certain era will lead to any except the most renowned of public women. The historian seldom has any but a handful of women's names, if that, with which to begin the search and he or she will quickly find additional names shrouded in anonymity. It is therefore often necessary to peruse indexes of works printed from such and such a time in a particular city or area, and simply pull out those works written by or about women. Such a search is terribly time consuming, but essential. Of course materials are more readily available for periods following 1800, and especially in American history. In the absence of more of this type of research, work in this area has concentrated too heavily on the leadership and the development of the feminist and suffragist movements, though less so in recent years.

One must begin, then, from the assumption that women lived different lives from men, and we must ask in what areas are those differences most pronounced. For the early modern period, biological, spiritual, and intellectual distinctions separated men from women. One may turn to an analysis of gynecological tracts, or debates about woman's preaching, or the rationales for excluding her from higher education, as logical sources for research.

## IV

As suggested earlier in this book in "Ideology and Gynecology in Seventeenth-Century England," the distinctions drawn between men and women on biological and intellectual grounds were closely interrelated. The first sentence of *The Womans Doctour* established quite clearly the interlocking nature of general sex roles and the supposed role of women's physiology in supporting these roles:

> Women are made to stay at home, and to look after Household employments, and because such business is accomplished with much ease, without any vehement stirrings of the body, therefore hath provident Nature assigned them their monthly courses, that by the benefit of these evacuations, the feculent corrupt bloud might be purified, which otherwise, as being the purest part of the bloud, would turne to ranke poyson; like the seed ejaculated out of its proper vessells.[1]

This intricate linking of the physician's perception of women's everyday lives with their health is typical of the same sort of linking in all types of works directed especially toward a discussion of women. Such values must be studied not in an isolated manner, but rather in their relationship to a broader analysis of the operation of sex division on our judgments of proper human behavior. Unquestionably, women are defined more readily by their sexuality than men are, but as I hope to show later, society's conception of masculinity, or more explicitly manhood, has helped to shape the actions of men in a way comparable to the force of femininity on the lives of individual women. Women consistently, and men occasionally, work against their own interests to conform to their view of proper femininity or masculinity. One of the goals of women's history should be an understanding of the forcefulness of such demands for conformity, and their actual operation in the lives of women.

It is not a simple task to understand the distinction between men's and women's existence. We know so little about women's past and we have never studied men from the perspective of a general sexual identity as a motivation for their behavior. Although most historians agree on the importance of sexual attitudes in defining women's proper role, there is little agreement on the extent of their importance in contrast to the more overt restrictions of women's economic, social, and political roles.

The nebulous and informal nature of attitudinal control presents a serious difficulty in analyzing critically the role attitudes play in shaping social relationships. There is no direct connection between the statement of a particular attitude and its influence on human behavior, but one's view of how one should behave influences and modifies the more explicit limitations of life. For instance, whether a woman decides to nurse a child is not totally determined by whether she has an alternative which allows her not to do so; but her choice is influenced by what she holds to be the "natural" thing to do, her conception of motherhood, or her acceptance of the medical arguments for nursing.

Attitudes are especially crucial to a study of women's history, for they have been particularly effective in curtailing women's lives. Not merely have women had an existence distinct from men; they have lived differently from other groups as well. The greatest force for social control has been exclusion. Keep the poor away from the sources of wealth, the blacks away from whites, and you effectively prevent their grasping power within a particular society. It has never been possible to exclude women in the same ways as it has been to exclude other out-groups, because of women's vital importance in the fulfillment of men's needs for pleasure and procreation. This has meant that women have always been close to the centers of power but prevented from exercising this power themselves. For this reason, it has been necessary to bombard them with a massive literature of religious, social, and biological content explaining why they should remain in a role secondary to men. If one is to postulate, as I believe most of us do, that people seldom place unnecessary restrictions on themselves for the mere purpose of limiting what they can do in life, then we must take seriously the effect of sexual propaganda on women's social position.

Although there are many areas to which attention must be directed, I think we should first concentrate on the wide-sweeping nature of sexist attitudes. Much work has been done on the content of these attitudes at various periods, but very little on the breadth of their scope and the manner and effectiveness of their implementation. In reviewing, even in a cursory fashion, the literature of the Western world, one comes away with some impression of the nature of sexual stereotyping. It is virtually impossible when surveying this literature to find women portrayed as characters who have experienced intellectual or philosophical crises of conscience comparable to that of Faust or who have wrestled with the moral and religious dilemma of a Job. Often women do not develop as characters in literature, and when they do, it is in terms of personal interaction, usually male-female sexual relationships. I think we have come to believe that there is something ludicrous about a woman viewing herself against the background of the universe, agonizing over the meaning of her existence, or sparring with God or the devil for her soul. Even with Joan of Arc, it was her voices who told her what her destiny must be.

Attitudes, then, should be studied not for their content alone, but for an evaluation of their forcefulness and extensiveness as well. In reaching such an understanding of sexual norms, I would like to suggest that they are a continuous stream—a diverse, but interrelated set of beliefs about the nature of men and women that seldom become explicit, but are constantly at work in day-to-day experience. They are, above all, unspoken and ill-defined justifications for daily interactions which can be used, if necessary, to defend an individual's action. Seldom are they carefully thought out; when a man tells his wife, for instance, that women are meant to do housework, he has not carefully analyzed proper social customs as a basis for his statement. Rather, he is mouthing a truism which is actually an inchoate reference to a vague, but powerful compilation of views about men and women. The significance of his statement lies not in its content, but rather in its symbolic relationship to general sexual attitudes. For this reason such attitudes are understood more clearly when not studied in a particularly literal sense, but rather viewed as part of a loosely joined system of beliefs which exists substantially unchanged over several centuries. It is essentially ahistorical, although the purpose for which it is used may have great significance for the position of women at any given period.

## V

In trying to reach an understanding of the structure and forcefulness of sexual attitudes, I wish to focus on the massive quantity of such literature and the involvement of the most prominent thinkers in its production. When searching bibliographies for writings about women, one is struck first by the lack of neutral material. No one seems able to write about women without making judgments as to their proper nature or station in life. Most of this material is negative (for example, seeing some failure or moral flaw in the female character which must be controlled or overcome). A small portion are defenses against the general attacks. Even when one comes across material that would appear neutral—gynecological tracts, or sermons on being a proper Christian—they prove to be misogynist. "Misogynist" is used here not merely to denote scurrilous attacks, but for those writings which are based on a view of feminine incompetence and moral laxity, and which follow this judgment with arguments to restrict women's activities. At the most basic, and perhaps simpleminded level, it is those writers who don't like women and believe they can't be trusted, and who therefore, believe society will prosper only if women's role in it is severely limited. The rationalizations for such restriction depend on the focus of the particular work. While the reason seventeenth-century Presbyterian sermons argued that women should have no active role in the church and should be submissive at home was to prevent them from leading their husbands to Separatist congregations, gynecologists wanted them to do little outside of the home because of their physiologically imposed weaknesses, both mental and physical. The arguments could vary, but the conclusions were consistently the same. One's first reaction to the discovery of such views is, "so what," sexual equality is something only recently suggested (and far from generally accepted now), why would one expect to find it in the seventeenth century? However, this immediate reaction is itself a significant expression of the total acceptance of sexual bias, that makes us say "so what" to a continually false and negative view of women.

One is reminded of the impressions which came to Virginia Woolf following a study of such writings. Her description, although specifically relevent to the antifeminist literature of her era, accurately sums up one's reaction to the authors of such works; first, in their educated veneer, and second, in their genuine dislike of women.

But while I pondered I had unconsciously, in my listlessness, in my desperation, been drawing a picture where I should, like my neighbor, have been writing a conclusion. I had been drawing a face, a figure. It was the face and the figure of Professor von X engaged in writing his monumental work entitled *The Mental, Moral and Physical Inferiority of the Female Sex.* He was not in my picture a man attractive to women. He was heavily built; he had a great jowl; to balance that he had very small eyes; he was very red in the face. His expression suggested that he was labouring under some emotion that made him jab his pen on the paper as if he were killing some noxious insect as he wrote, but even when he had killed it that did not satisfy him; he must go on killing it; and even so, some cause for anger and irritation remained. . . . How explain the anger of the professors? Why were they angry? For when it came to analyzing the impression left by these books there was always an element of heat. This heat took many forms; it showed itself in satire, in sentiment, in curiosity, in reprobation. But there was another element which was often present and could not immediately be identified. Anger, I called it. But it was anger that had gone underground and mixed itself with all kinds of other emotions. To judge from its odd effects, it was anger disguised and complex, not simple and open.[2]

When Woolf asks how we explain the anger of the professors, she poses a very real difficulty in getting beneath the surface of such writing to discover the motivation of the author. One has only rare clues or hints as to why men write misogynist works. One Puritan minister who was particularly vehement on the question of wifely obedience admits later in his work that his young wife had deserted him. Joint domicile, he contends, is a directive from God. But seldom are we fortunate enough to have such references, and most works are highly repetitive and devoid of any serious analysis of social relationships. Yet their intellectual poverty and endless repetition does not subtract from their continual and widespread distribution. The endless theme of woman's incompetence and sensuality, her lack of practical and intellectual accomplishments, and her general weakness in mind and body confronts one at every turn. The magnitude of such writings is suggested in Ruth Kelso's chapter "Women in the Scheme of Things" in her work entitled *Doctrine for the Lady of the Renaissance.*[3] Even in a collection such as the Thomason

Tracts of seventeenth-century Puritan writings, the vast majority of the works indexed under "women" are either misogynist or semipornographic, or both.

In moving from the study of attitudinal content to an understanding of how attitudes operate on human behavior, we must search for a key to measuring the force of particular views during a given era. One such key may be the subtle and indistinct, but real relationship of respectability to the acceptance of attitudes. The level of respectability of a particular view can be determined by observing which members of society hold such views and how public they are willing to make their commitment to them. There is significance, therefore, to the numbers of great minds who have written misogynist literature. When men have written attacks against women they have known their support would be legion, and that their views were grounded solidly in the theological and social commentaries of their age. In pinpointing one common reference in these works, it is interesting to note the continual comments on Eve's indiscretion in the Garden, and the subsequent use of Eve as a symbol of women's shortcomings. One such use is presented in Juan Luis Vives's *The Instruction of a Christian Woman* written in 1523:

> Therefore, because a woman is a frail thing, and of weak discretion, and that may lightly be deceived, which thing our first mother Eve sheweth, whom the Devil caught with a light argument, Therefore a woman should not teach, lest when she hath taken a false opinion and belief of any thing, she spread it unto the hearers, by the authority of mastership and lightly bring others into the same errors, for the learners commonly do after the teacher with good will.[4]

The Bible, of course, was an endless source for antiwoman thoughts. If one wanted variety from the typical Pauline admonitions about silence in the church and obedience at home, one could always rely on the third chapter of Genesis as solid support of women's proper limitations. Eve, after admitting that "the serpent beguiled me," was told, "I will greatly multiply thy sorrow and thy conception; in sorrow thou shalt bring forth children; and thy desire shall be to thy husband, and he shall rule over thee." And Adam was punished "because thou hast harkened unto the voice of thy wife."[5] Here, then, was a succinct outline for the proper relationship between the sexes that could be and was used again and again to justify female subordinance. Aristotle's works were the second most popular source to buttress arguments contending feminine weakness. His analysis of women's incomplete reasoning power justified her exclusion from higher education, and from any vocation requiring such skill.

The church fathers, scholastics, ancient and contemporary medical writers, and patriarchal political theorists such as Bodin and Filmer offered endless intellectual justification for general sexual biases. Thus the more vulgar misogynist literature of the time was not wholly a deviant form of expression, but rather reflected a solid base of support in the more respectable literature of the period.

Next, in moving from the intellectual bases for mysogynist respectability there is the connection between respectability and the means of altering attitudes. One comes to change one's views on a particular group not so much because former beliefs have been rationally demolished, but rather because one believes (for a number of reasons) that it is no longer proper to hold a particular view, at least not publicly. Those who wish to overturn such attitudes can make an individual ashamed to profess them publicly if they can connect their espousal with unsavory elements within the society. Make a man feel he loses status because of his beliefs, and he will at least be cautious about holding them openly. Other than through the use of disreputable images, attitudes are changed through a general alteration in a society's thought patterns so that a previously accepted view now becomes "old-fashioned" or "superstitious." Such an alteration came on the question of witchcraft near the end of the seventeenth century. Although the early decades of that century had seen widespread persecution of witches, by the end of that century, no educated person accepted witchcraft as a serious possibility.

## VI

I would now like to look at seventeenth-century British feminism both as a phenomenon of the kind of radical change in thinking (exemplified by the demise of witchcraft), and as an overt attempt to change sexual attitudes by shaming those who held such views. Although seventeenth-century feminists were few in number, and their impact was localized and subsequently hidden, their feminism is highly articulate and forms a coherent set of writings. The earliest appeared during the early 1660s and the largest group were published during the two decades before and after the year 1700. These feminists viewed women as a group who were oppressed by men for their benefit; and they linked this oppression to an intricate system of external controls and customary pressures. The Duchess of Newcastle, writing in 1662, sets the uncompromising tone of most of their works:

> ... wish I were so Fortunate, as to persuade you to make a frequentation, association, and combination amongst our sex, that we may unite in Prudent consels, to make ourselves as Free, Happy, and Famous as Men, whereas now we live and Dye, as if we were produced from Beast rather than from Men; for men are Happy, and we women are miserable, they possess all the ease, rest, pleasure, wealth, Power, and Fame whereas women are Restless with Labour, Easeless with pain, Melancholy for want of power, and Dye in Oblivion for want of Fame; nevertheless, men are so unconscionable and cruel against us, as they endeavour to Barr us all Sorts or kinds of Liberty, as not to suffer us Freely to associate amongst our own sex, but, would fain Bury us in their houses or Beds, as in a Grave; the truth is, we live like Bats or owls, Labour like Beasts, and Dye like worms.[6]

For the most part, the feminists were from the lesser gentry, or sisters of the local curate; occasionally they were governesses and teachers in schools for girls. They resented women's lack of education and the triviality of their lives, and attacked those men and institutions which excluded them. Their basis of attack came from an abiding faith in reason and the precepts of the scientific revolution. Custom and the reliance on authority were their two great enemies. Their reaction to women's customary role is put well by Sarah Egerton in her poem, "The Liberty," written in the first decade of the eighteenth century.

> Shall I be one, of those obsequious Fools,
> That square there lives, by customs scanty Rules,
> Condemn'd for ever, to the puny curse,
> of Precepts taught, at Boarding-school, or nurse,
> That all the business of my life must be,
> Foolish, dull Trifling, Formality.
> Confin'd to a strict Magick Complaisance,
> And round a Circle, of nice visits Dance,
> Nor for my life beyond the Chalk advance.[7]

The feminists' acceptance of women as a sociological group whose existence was systematically restricted caused them not merely to think differently about women, but to write about them differently as well. During the sixteenth century there had been a debate on the advisability of educating women, but the conflict was fought around individual examples of women's brilliance or stupidity, and worth or worthlessness. Those opposing such education looked back to examples of trifling or immoral women, and to particular authorities bolstering such views, while those favoring female education noted brilliant women of the past, and pointed to those scholars who allowed women's education. For the seventeenth-century feminist, however, individual examples were inconclusive. She spoke not of individual women, but of the general conditions determining all women's lives.

Such views of women broke radically with the past, and feminists wrote to convince others of the logic and humanity of such views. They did not take sexual attitudes at face value, but looked beneath their veneer to why certain men and groups held such views. Seldom did they attack individual views, but rather those who held the views and the general system of women's subordination from which they arose. Mary Astell, author of *A Serious Proposal to the Ladies,* subtly undermines men's good behavior as based on the chivalric code: ". . . nor is there a Man of Honour amongst the whole Tribe that would not venture his Life, and his Salvation too in their [women's] Defence, if any but himself attempts to injure them."[8] Not merely did they turn men's actions against them, they turned general political beliefs against the men as well: "For whatever may be said against Passive-Obedience in an other case, I suppose there's no man but likes it very well in this; how much sever[e] Arbitrary Power may be dislik'd on a Throne, not Milton himself wou'd cry up Liberty to poor Female Slaves, or plead for the Lawfulness of Resisting a Private Tyranny."[9]

The feminists kept their harshest words for those groups whom they believed legitimized sex prejudice. Physicians were viewed as special enemies. Lady Anne Winchilsea describes them:

No more Vapours, your belov'd Disease,
Your Ignorance's Skreen, your *what-you please*
With which you cheat poor Females of their Lives,
Whilst men dispute not, so it rid their wives.[10]

Although the feminists had few good words for scholars, they satirized them rather than directly criticizing them. The anonymous author of *A Defence of the Female Sex* sees men as "great hunters of ancient Manuscripts, [who] have in great Veneration anything, that has scap'd the teeth of Time and Rats," and then castigates them as follows: "These Superstitious, bigotted Idolaters of time past, are children in their understanding all their lives; for they hang so incessantly upon the leading strings of Authority. . . ."[11] Seventeenth-century feminists, then, did not attack misogynist writings or sexual attitudes in a piecemeal fashion, but struck generally at women's subordinate role and at those groups which benefited from such subordination. They continually compared their lives with men's and found their lives wanting.

## VII

It is the need for such comparison that is often overlooked in women's history. Women's past cannot be studied in a vacuum. Women were a part of the society in which they lived and absorbed its values. It is our duty to learn how their peculiar experience affected this absorption, not to isolate them from their historical setting. In attempting to argue the significance of comparing male and female life-styles and value systems for the study of women's history, I want to present an interrelated analysis of the limitations of Renaissance views toward women's education and a critique of Phillipe Ariès's *Centuries of Childhood*.

Ariès, because he ignores the importance of sexual distinction as a factor in human behavior, fails to discover any significance in his equation of boyhood with childhood. This is not to say that he ignores the failings of girls' education, or that he does not see a clear difference between their education and that of boys in the sixteenth and seventeenth centuries; however, he devotes only a few paragraphs in his lengthy work to girls and fails to appreciate the significance of his own observation that only boys were beginning to experience childhood with the advent of the early modern period:

It is interesting to note that the attempt to distinguish children was generally confined to the boys: the little girls were distinguished only by the false sleeves, abandoned in the eighteenth century, as if childhood separated girls from adult life less than it did boys. The evidence provided by dress bears out the other indications furnished by the history of manners: boys were the first specialized children. They began going to school in large numbers as far back as the late sixteenth century and the early seventeenth century. The education of girls started in a small way only in the time of Fénelon and Mme de Maintenón and developed slowly and tardily. Without a proper educational system, the girls were confused with the women at an early age just as the boys had formerly been confused with the men, and nobody thought of giving visible form, by means of dress, to a distinction which was beginning to exist in reality for the boys but which still remained futile for the girls.[12]

Ariès, then, does contend quite clearly that there was a vast difference between the existence of boys and girls during this period; yet, he does not connect such a contrast to the broader context of sexual distinction in general. For this reason, his work deals with the less important of the two aspects of the changing conception of manhood, and its concomitant, an increased significance and uniqueness for the years of boyhood. The men of the sixteenth and seventeenth centuries were becoming independent creatures, both economically and intellectually. They differ quite significantly from their medieval predecessors. If the medieval knight were the ideal for his age, then the Renaissance gentleman replaced him as the model for the sixteenth century. The medieval knight and Renaissance gentlemen were two very different types of people. The medieval knight possessed many qualities which were later ascribed to women. First, he was both economically and socially dependent. He lived not to serve himself, but to serve others. One of his first duties was to conform to a code of social behavior, the chivalric code. Further, he was a child all of his life in that he played at games in the form of tournaments and stylized warfare. He was poorly educated and was unskilled and uninterested in the ways of economic success. It is difficult to imagine a transition from childhood to knighthood, as Ariès outlines for the sixteenth and seventeenth centuries. But with the growth of national bureaucracies and the intricacies of Renaissance courts, the gentleman was required to be a skilled adult. He was expected to be well educated and independent.

What Ariès fails to grasp, then, is that the phenomenon he is witnessing comes more from a changing conception of manhood than from a developing view of childhood. This is the only way one can understand the omission of women from this process. Men are becoming adults in the modern sense of that term, while women are kept children and there is no need to distinguish a childhood for their younger years. It is not so much that "boys were confused with men" in the medieval period, but that the ideal of the adult male had not taken its form as yet. That ideal is intricately connected with all of those changes Ariès notes in his work—educational advancement, economic independence, and a general emphasis on individual accomplishment. In practical terms this development led to an exclusion of women from the humanist brand of learning because of their limited vocation. Their domestic service did not require the training of the diplomat, or bureaucrat, or merchant. Richard Mulcaster, an English educator writing in 1581, notes the proper distinction between male and female education: "Our training is without restriction either as regards subject-matter or method, because our employment is so general; their functions are limited, and so must their education be also. . . ."[13] The lot of the gentleman was changing, while that of his wife was not.

Those scholars who look merely at what Renaissance figures have to say about women and find it more encouraging than medieval views, assume that the Renaissance opened new educational opportunities for women. However, women were actually better off during the medieval period when the general ignorance of both men and women was greater, and the lack of a good education was not considered such a serious flaw. One must therefore, look at what is happening to both sexes during a particular period to gauge women's progress, for if men take a giant stride, and women only a tiny step, woman may easily be worse off than she was before her slight advancement.

VIII

In conclusion, and working from the question of women's progress, I think we must reevaluate women's role in the general "progress of mankind." Her special existence has often excluded her from such progress, and, on the contrary, this advance has worked to her detriment. Women have fared better in nonstructured, nonintellectual, localized institutions and have been excluded from institutions which set rigid standards and operate on the basis of an established hierarchy. Women gain most from periods of social dysfunction such as war or rebellion in which the normal connections of power are severed. Although this is true of all out-groups, it is particularly true of women who are so close to the centers of power and the obvious choices to take over responsibilities vacated by absent males. Two major developments of modern society have harmed women—professionalization and industrialization. The professionalization of medicine in England in the seventeenth century was closely tied to the effort to force women out of their traditional roles in the field. In this country in the nineteenth century, the growth of medical schools led to the exclusion of women from medicine. Whenever a group organized around professional standards, a seemingly necessary concomitant was the exclusion of women. Alice Clark in *Working Life of Women in the Seventeenth Century* and David Montgomery in his article on the working classes of pre-industrial America both argue that there existed a collusion between poor-law overseers or charitable organizations and employers to keep wages at pauper level for women.[14] The United States Navy was allowed to pay only twelve and a half cents a shirt, or the same prices women could obtain in the almshouses. The industrial revolution removed the role of the independent wife in the family economy and turned women into either economically dependent beings, or the poorest of the industrial workers.

Nor was the general improvement in the position of the middle class reflected directly in the lives of women. For instance, we speak of middle-class men and women as if they lived comparable lives which would designate them as being "middle class," when in reality the middle-class wife lives an existence quite different from that of her husband, in terms of leisure, power, status, and quality of work. "Class," like so many of our general social terms, is based upon a view of society which is centered on men. Although occupation is considered the single most important determinant of class in this country, a woman's class is not determined by her occupation, but rather by her husband's. Her occupation becomes relevant only if she is a single, self-supporting adult and has no man to define her class for her.

As a possible alternative to viewing women's class outside of the context of their husbands' occupations, I would contend that number of children is as determining a factor in a woman's class as her husband's income. If "middle class" in some way denotes leisure and the opportunity to pursue interests other than those dictated by day-to-day existence, then a woman whose husband's income qualifies her for middle-class status, but who has seven children, may lead a more encumbered existence than one whose husband is poorer, but who has only one or two children. What we must do, then, when attempting a study of women, is not to assume that they live lives comparable to men, but to pose questions and develop hypotheses which take into account the specially restricted life women have been encouraged to follow.

In short, when approaching the study of women's history, we must from the outset apply what we know about women's position to our historical investigation. We cannot uncover the realities of women's past if we look at them as adjuncts to or minor participants in the male power structure. Further, we must realize that we are working with a group whose lives have been hidden and distorted by the society in which they lived and by future chroniclers of that society. It makes little difference whether such errors were consciously or unconsciously wrought. Historical language must come under scrutiny through applying to it a feminist understanding of women's lives. "Progress," "civilization," even "class" may appear in a light very different from that of their general historical usage, when viewed from the perspective of women's history.

## NOTES

1. Nicholas Fontanus, *The Woman Doctour: or, an exact and distinct Explanation of all such Diseases as are peculiar to that Sex with Choise and Experimental Remedies against the same* (London, 1652), 1.

2. Virginia Woolf, *A Room of One's Own* (New York: Harcourt, 1957), 31–32.

3. Ruth Kelso, *Doctrine for the Lady of the Renaissance* (Urbana: University of Illinois Press, 1956).

4. Foster Watson, *Vives and the Renaissance Education of Women* (London, 1909), 56.

5. Gen. 3:13, 16–17.

6. Margaret Lucas, Duchess of Newcastle, "Female Orations," *Orations of Divers Sorts* (London, 1662), 225–26.

7. Sarah Fyge Egerton, "The Liberty," *Poems on Several Occasions* (London, n.d.), 20.

8. Mary Astell, *Reflections upon Marriage* (London, 1700), 24.

9. *Ibid.*, 30–31.

10. Anne Winchilsea, "For the Better," *Miscellany Poems on Several Occasions* (London, 1713), 138.

11. *An Essay in the Defence of the Female Sex* (London, 1696), 29.

12. Philippe Ariès, *Centuries of Childhood: A Social History of Family Life,* trans. Robert Baldick (New York: Knopf, 1962), 58

13. James Oliphant, ed., *The Educational Writings of Richard Mulcaster* (London, 1903), 51.

14. Alice Clark, *Working Life of Women in the Seventeenth Century* (London, 1919), 66–73; David Montgomery, "The Working Classes of the Pre-Industrial American City, 1780–1830," *Labor History* 9 (1968), 18–21.

# Four Structures in a Complex Unity

*Juliet Mitchell*

Past socialist theory has failed to differentiate woman's condition into its separate structures, which together form a complex—not a simple—unity. To do this will mean rejecting the idea that woman's condition can be deduced derivatively from the economy (Engels), or equated symbolically with society (early Marx). Rather, it must be seen as a *specific* structure, which is a unity of different elements. The variations of woman's condition throughout history will be the result of different combinations of these elements—we will thus have not a linear narrative of economic development (de Beauvoir) for the elements will be combined in different ways at different times. In a complex totality each independent sector has its own autonomous reality though each is ultimately, but only ultimately, determined by the economic factor. This complex totality means that no contradiction in society is ever simple. As each sector can move at a different pace, the synthesis of the different time-scales in the total structure means that sometimes contradictions cancel each other out, and sometimes they reinforce one another. Because the unity of woman's condition at any time is in this way the product of several structures, moving at different paces, it is always "overdetermined."[1]

The key structures of woman's situation can be listed as follows: production, reproduction, sexuality, and the socialization of children. The concrete combination of these produce the "complex unity" of her position; but each separate structure may have reached a different "moment" at any given historical time. Each then must be examined separately in order to see what the present unity is, and how it might be changed. The notes that follow do not pretend to give a historical account of each sector. They are concerned only with some general reflections on the different roles of women and some of their interconnections.

## 1. Production

The biological differentiation of the sexes into male and female and the division of labor that is based on this have *seemed,* throughout history, an

Reprinted by permission of the author and publishers from *Woman's Estate,* © 1971 Pantheon Books, a division of Random House, Inc., and from the Penguin Books, Ltd., edition, pp. 100–122, © 1966, 1970, 1971 by Juliet Mitchell. This selection first appeared as part of an essay entitled "Women: The Longest Revolution," in *New Left Review,* no. 40 (1966).

interlocked necessity. Anatomically smaller and weaker, woman appears to be rendered by her physiology and psychobiological metabolism a less useful member of a work force. It is always stressed how, particularly in the early stages of social development, man's physical superiority gave him the means of conquest over nature which was denied to women. Once woman was accorded the menial tasks involved in maintenance while man undertook conquest and creation, she became an aspect of the things preserved: private property and children. Marx, Engels, Bebel, de Beauvoir—the major socialist writers on the subject—link the confirmation and continuation of woman's oppression after the establishment of her physical inferiority for hard manual work with the advent of private property. But woman's physical weakness has never prevented her from performing work as such (quite apart from bringing up children)—only specific types of work, in specific societies. In primitive, ancient, oriental, medieval and capitalist societies, the *volume* of work performed by women has always been considerable (it has usually been much more than this). It is only its form that is in question. Domestic labor, even today, is enormous if quantified in terms of productive labor.[2] It has been calculated in Sweden that 2,340,000,000 hours a year are spent by women in housework compared with 1,290,000,000 hours in industry. The Chase Manhattan Bank estimated a woman's overall working week averaged 99.6 hours. In any case women's physique alone has never permanently or even predominantly relegated them to menial domestic chores. In many peasant societies, women have worked in the fields as much as, or more than, men.

*Physical Weakness and Coercion*

The assumption behind most socialist analyses is that the crucial factor starting the whole development of feminine subordination was women's lesser capacity for demanding physical work. But, in fact, this is a major over-simplification. Even in these terms, historically it has been woman's lesser capacity for violence as well as for work, that has determined her subordination. In most societies woman has not only been less able than man to perform arduous kinds of work, she has also been less able to fight. Man not only has the strength to assert himself against nature, but also against his fellows. *Social coercion* has interplayed with the straightforward division of labor, based on biological capacity, to a much greater extent than is generally admitted. Women have been *forced* to do "women's work." Of course this force may not be actualized as direct aggression. In primitive societies women's lesser physical suitability for the hunt is assumed to be evident. In agricultural societies where women's inferiority is socially instituted, women are given the arduous task of tilling and cultivation. For this, coercion is necessary. In developed civilizations, and more complex societies, women's physical deficiencies again become relevant. Women are thought to be of no use either for war or in the construction of cities. But with early industrialization, coercion once more becomes important. As Marx wrote: " . . . insofar as machinery dispenses with muscular power, it becomes a means of employing labourers of slight muscular strength, and those whose bodily development is incomplete, but whose limbs are all the more supple. The labour of women and children was, therefore, the first thing sought for by capitalists who used machinery."[3]

René Dumont points out that in many zones of tropical Africa today men are often idle, while women are forced to work all day: "The African woman experiences a three-fold servitude: through forced marriage; through her dowry and polygamy, which increases the leisure time of men and simultaneously their social prestige; and finally through the very unequal division of labour."[4] This exploitation has no "natural" source whatever. Women may perform their "heavy" duties in contemporary African peasant societies, not for fear of physical reprisal by their men, but because these duties are "customary" and built into the role structures of the society. A further point is that coercion implies a different relationship from coercer to coerced than does exploitation. It is political rather than economic. In describing coercion, Marx said that the master treated the slave or serf as the "inorganic and natural condition of its own reproduction." That is to say, labor itself becomes like other natural things—cattle or soil: "The original conditions of production appear as natural prerequisites, *natural conditions of the existence of the producer,* just as his living body, however reproduced and developed by him, is not originally established by himself, but appears as his *prerequisite."*[5] This is preeminently woman's condition. For far from woman's *physical* weakness removing her from productive work, her *social* weakness has in these cases evidently made her the major slave of it.

This truth, elementary though it may seem, has nevertheless been constantly ignored by socialist writers on the subject, with the result that there is an unfounded optimism in their predictions of the future. For, if it is just the biological incapacity for the hardest physical work which has determined the subordination of women, then the prospect of an advanced machine technology, abolishing the need for strenuous physical exertion, would seem to promise the liberation of women. For a moment industrialization itself thus seems to herald women's liberation. Engels, for instance, wrote: "The first premise for the emancipation of women is the reintroduction of the entire female sex into public industry. . . . And this has become possible only as a result of modern large-scale industry, which not only permits of the participation of women in production in large numbers, but actually calls for it and, moreover strives to convert private domestic work also into a public industry."[6]

What Marx said of early industrialism is no less, but also *no more* true of an automated society: ". . . it is obvious that the fact of the collective working group being composed of individuals of both sexes and all ages, must necessarily, *under suitable conditions,* become a source of human development; although in its spontaneously developed, brutal, capitalist form, where the labourer exists for the process of production, and not the process of production for the labourer, that fact is a pestiferous source of corruption and slavery."[7]

Industrial labor and automated technology both promise the preconditions for women's liberation alongside man's—but no more than the preconditions. It is only too obvious that the advent of industrialization has not so far freed women in this sense, either in the West or in the East. De Beauvoir hoped that automation would make a decisive, qualitative difference by abolishing altogether the physical differential between the sexes. But any reliance on this in itself accords an independent role to technique which history does not justify. Under capitalism, automation could possibly lead to an ever-growing structural unemployment which would expel women (along with immigrants)—the latest and least integrated recruits to the labor force and ideologically the most expendable for a bourgeois society—from production after only a brief interlude in it. Technology is mediated by the total structure, and it is this which will determine woman's future in work relations. It is the relationship between the social forces and technology that Firestone's "ecological" revolution ultimately ignores.

Physical deficiency is not now, any more than in the past, a sufficient explanation of woman's relegation to inferior status. Coercion has been ameliorated to an ideology shared by both sexes. Commenting on the results of her questionnaire of working women, Viola Klein notes: "There is no trace of feminine egalitarianism—militant or otherwise—in any of the women's answers to the questionnaire; nor is it even implicitly assumed that women have a 'Right to Work.' "[8] Denied, or refusing, a role in *production,* woman does not even create the preconditions of her liberation. But even her presence in the work force does not erode her oppression in the family.

## 2. Reproduction

Women's absence from the critical sector of production historically, of course, has been caused not just by their assumed physical weakness in a context of coercion—but also by their role in reproduction. Maternity necessitates withdrawals from work, but this is not a decisive phenomenon. It is rather women's role in reproduction which has become, in capitalist society at least, the spiritual "complement" of men's role in production. Bearing children, bringing them up, and maintaining the home—these form the core of woman's natural vocation, in this ideology. This belief has attained great force because of the seeming universality of the family as a human institution. There is little doubt that Marxist analyses have underplayed the fundamental problems posed here. The complete failure to give any operative content to the slogan of "abolition" of the family is striking evidence of this (as well as of the vacuity of the notion).

The biological function of maternity is a universal, atemporal fact, and as such has seemed to escape the categories of Marxist historical analysis. However, from it is made to follow the so-called stability and omnipresence of the family, if in very different forms.[9] Once this is accepted, women's social subordination—however emphasized as an honorable, but different role (cf. the "equal-but-separate" ideologies of Southern racists)—can be seen to follow inevitably as an *insurmountable* bio-historical fact. The causal chain then goes: maternity, family, absence from production and public life, sexual inequality.

The linchpin in this line of argument is the idea of the family. The notion that "family" and "society" are virtually coextensive or that an advanced society not founded on the nuclear family is now inconceivable, despite revolutionary posturings to the contrary, is still widespread. It can only be seriously discussed by asking just what the family is—or rather what women's role in the family is. Once this is done, the problem appears in quite a new light. For it is obvious that woman's role in the family—primitive, feudal, or bourgeois—partakes of three quite different structures: reproduction, sexuality, and the socialization of children. These are historically, not intrinsically, related to each other in the present modern family. We can easily see that they needn't be. For instance, biological parentage is not necessarily identical with social parentage (adoption). Thus it is essential to discuss not the family as an unanalysed entity, but the separate *structures* which today compose it but which tomorrow may be decomposed into a new pattern.

As I have said, reproduction is seen as an apparently constant atemporal phenomenon—part of biology rather than history. In fact this is an illusion. What is true is that the "mode of reproduction" does not vary with the "mode of production"; it can remain effectively the same through a number of different modes of production. For it has been defined till now by its uncontrollable, natural character, and to this extent has been an unmodified biological fact. As long as reproduction remained a natural phenomenon, of course, women were effectively doomed to social exploitation. In any sense, they were not "masters" of a large part of their lives. They had no choice as to whether or how often they gave birth to children (apart from precarious methods of contraception or repeated dangerous abortions); their existence was essentially subject to biological processes outside their control.

## Contraception

Contraception, which was finally invented as a rational technique only in the nineteenth century, was thus an innovation of world-historic importance. It is only just now beginning to show what immense consequences it could have, in the form of the Pill. For what it means is that at last the mode of reproduction potentially could be transformed. Once child-bearing becomes totally voluntary (how much so is it in the West, even today?) its significance is fundamentally different. It need no longer be the sole or ultimate vocation of woman; it becomes one option among others.

History is the development of human beings' transformation of nature, and thereby of themselves—of human nature—in different modes of production. Today there are the technical possibilities for the transformation and "humanization" of the most natural part of human culture. This is what a change in the mode of reproduction could mean.

We are far from this state of affairs yet. In Italy the sale of contraceptives remains illegal. In many countries it is difficult to get reliable means. The oral contraceptive is still the privilege of a moneyed minority in a few Western countries. Even here the progress has been realized in a typically conservative and exploitative form. It is made only for women, who are thus guinea pigs in a venture which involves both sexes.

The fact of overwhelming importance is that easily available contraception threatens to dissociate sexual from reproductive experience—which all contemporary ideology tries to make inseparable, as the *raison d'être* of the family.

### Reproduction and Production

At present, reproduction in our society is often a kind of sad mimicry of production. Work in a capitalist society is an alienation of labor in the making of a social product which is confiscated by capital. But it can still sometimes be a real act of creation, purposive and responsible, even in the conditions of the worst exploitation. Maternity is often a caricature of this. The biological product—the child—is treated as if it were a solid product. Parenthood becomes a kind of substitute for work, an activity in which the child is seen as an object created by the mother, in the same way as a commodity is created by a worker. Naturally, the child does not literally escape, but the mother's alienation can be much worse than that of the worker whose product is appropriated by the boss. The child as an autonomous person inevitably threatens the activity which claims to create it continually merely as a *possession* of the parent. Possessions are felt as extensions of the self. The child as a possession is supremely this. Anything the child does is therefore a threat to the mother herself, who has renounced her autonomy through this misconception of her reproductive role. There are few more precarious ventures on which to base a life.

Furthermore, even if the woman has emotional control over her child, legally and economically both she and it are subject to the father. The social cult of maternity is matched by the real socioeconomic powerlessness of the mother. The psychological and practical benefits men receive from this are obvious. The converse of woman's quest for creation in the child is man's retreat from his work into the family: "When we come home, we lay aside our mask and drop our tools, and are no longer lawyers, sailors, soldiers, statesmen, clergymen, but only men. We fall again into our most human relations, which, after all, are the whole of what belongs to us as we are ourselves."[10]

Unlike her nonproductive status, her capacity for maternity *is* a definition of woman. But it is only a physiological definition. Yet so long as maternity is allowed to remain a substitute for action and creativity, and the home an area of relaxation for men, woman will remain confined to the species, to her universal and natural condition.

### 3. Sexuality

Sexuality has traditionally been the most tabooed dimension of women's situation. The meaning of sexual freedom and its connection with women's freedom is a subject which few socialist writers have cared to broach. "Socialist morality" in the Soviet Union for a long time debarred serious discussion of the subject within the world communist movement. Marx himself—in this respect somewhat less liberal than Engels—early in his life expressed traditional views on the matter: " . . . the sanctification of the sexual instinct through exclusivity, the checking of instinct by laws, the moral beauty which makes nature's commandment ideal in the form of an emotional bond—[this is] the spiritual essence of marriage."[11] Yet it is obvious that throughout history women have been appropriated as sexual objects, as much as progenitors or producers. Indeed, the sexual relationship can be assimilated to the statute of possession much more easily and completely than the productive or reproductive relationship. Contemporary British sexual vocabulary bears eloquent witness to this—it is a comprehensive lexicon of reification—"bird," "fruit," "chick," etc. Later Marx was well aware of this: *"Marriage . . . is incontestably a form of exclusive private property."*[12] But neither he nor his successors ever tried seriously to envisage the implications of this for socialism, or even for a structural analysis of women's conditions. Communism, Marx stressed in the same passage, would not mean mere "communalization" of women as common property. Beyond this, he never ventured.

Some historical considerations are in order here. For if socialists have said nothing, the gap has been filled by liberal ideologues. In his book, *Eros Denied*, Wayland Young argues that Western civilization has been uniquely repressive sexually, and, in a plea for greater sexual freedom today, compares it at some length with oriental and ancient societies.[13] It is striking, however, that his book makes no reference whatever to women's status in these different societies, or to the different forms of marriage-contract prevalent in them. This makes the whole argument a purely formal exercise—an obverse of socialist discussions of women's position which ignore the problem of sexual freedom and its meanings. For while it is true that certain oriental or ancient (and indeed primitive) cultures were much less puritanical than Western societies, it is absurd to regard this as a kind of "transposable value" which can be abstracted from its social structure. In effect, in many of these societies sexual openness was accompanied by a form of polygamous exploitation which made it, in practice, an expression simply of masculine domination. Since art was the province of man, too, this freedom finds a natural and often powerful expression in art—which is often quoted as if it were evidence of the total quality of human relationships in the society. Nothing could be more misleading. What is necessary, rather than this naïve, hortatory core of historical example, is some account of the co-variation between the degrees of sexual liberty and openness, and the position and dignity of women in different societies.

### Sexuality and the Position of Women: Some Historical Examples

Some points are immediately obvious. The actual history is much more dialectical than any liberal account presents it. Unlimited juridical polygamy—whatever the sexualization of the culture which accompanies it—is clearly a total derogation of woman's autonomy, and constitutes an extreme form of oppression. Ancient China is a perfect illustration of this, a sensual culture and a society in which the father as head of the household wielded an extraordinary despotism. The Chinese paterfamilias was "a liturgical [semi-official] policeman of his kin group."[14] In the West, however, the advent of monogamy was in no sense an *absolute* improvement. It certainly did not create a one-to-one equality—far from it. Engels commented accurately: "Monogamy does not by any means make its appearance in history as the reconciliation of man and woman, still less as the highest form of such a reconciliation. On the contrary, it appears as the subjugation of one sex by the other, as the proclamation of a conflict between the sexes entirely unknown hitherto in prehistoric times."[15]

But in the Christian Era, monogamy took on a very specific form in the West. It was allied with an unprecedented regime of general sexual repression. In its Pauline version, this had a markedly antifeminine bias, inherited from Judaism. With time this became diluted—feudal society, despite its subsequent reputation for asceticism, practiced formal monogamy with considerable actual acceptance of polygamous behavior, at least within the ruling class. But here again the extent of sexual freedom was only an index of masculine domination. In England, the truly major change occurred in the sixteenth century with the rise of militant puritanism and the increase of market relations in the economy. Lawrence Stone observes: "In practice, if not in theory, the early sixteenth century nobility was a polygamous society, and some contrived to live with a succession of women despite the official prohibition on divorce. . . . But impressed by Calvinist criticisms of the double standard, in the late sixteenth century public opinion began to object to the open maintenance of a mistress."[16]

Capitalism and the attendant demands of the newly emergent bourgeoisie accorded woman a new status as wife and mother. Her legal rights improved; there was vigorous controversy over her social position: wife-beating was condemned. "In a woman the bourgeois man is looking for a counterpart, not an equal."[17] At the social periphery woman did occasionally achieve an equality which was more than her feminine function in a market society. In the extreme nonconformist sects women often had completely equal rights: the Quaker leader George Fox argued that the Redemption restored Prelapsarian equality and Quaker women thereby gained a real autonomy. But once most of the sects were institutionalized, the need for family discipline was reemphasized and woman's obedience with it. As one historian, Keith Thomas, says, the Puritans "had done something to raise women's status, but not really very much."[18] The patriarchal system was retained and maintained by the new economic mode of production—capitalism. The transition to complete effective monogamy accompanied the transition to modern bourgeois society as we know it today. Like the capitalist market system itself, it represented a historic advance, at great historic cost. The formal, juridical equality of capitalist society and capitalist rationality now applied as much to the marital as to the labor contract. In both cases, nominal parity masks real exploitation and inequality. But in both cases the formal equality is itself a certain progress, which can help to make possible a further advance.

### Sexuality and the Position of Women: Today

The situation today is defined by a new contradiction. Once formal conjugal equality (monogamy) is established, sexual freedom as such—which under polygamous conditions was usually a form of exploitation—becomes, conversely, a possible force for liberation. It then means, simply, the freedom of both sexes to transcend the limits of present sexual institutions.

Historically, then, there has been a dialectical movement in which sexual expression was "sacrificed" in an epoch of more-or-less puritan repression, which nevertheless produced a greater parity of sexual roles and in turn created the precondition for a genuine sexual liberation, in the dual sense of equality *and* freedom—whose unity defines socialism.

## Love and Marriage

This movement can be verified within the history of the "sentiments." The cult of *love* emerges only in the twelfth century in opposition to legal marital forms and with a heightened valuation of women (courtly love). It thereafter gradually became diffused, and assimilated to marriage as such, producing that absurdity—a free choice for life. What is striking here is that monogamy as an institution in the West anticipated the idea of love by many centuries. The two have subsequently been officially harmonized, but the tension between them has never been abolished. There is a formal contradiction between the voluntary contractual character of "marriage" and the spontaneous uncontrollable character of "love"—the passion that is celebrated precisely for its involuntary force. The notion that it occurs only once in every life and can therefore be integrated into a voluntary contract, becomes decreasingly plausible in the light of everyday experience—once sexual repression as a psycho-ideological system becomes at all relaxed.

Obviously, the main breach in the traditional value-pattern has, so far, been the increase in premarital sexual experience. This is now virtually legitimized in contemporary society. But its implications are explosive for the ideological conception of marriage that dominates this society: that it is an exclusive and permanent bond. An essay in an anthology called *The Family and the Sexual Revolution* reveals this very clearly: "As far as extra-marital relations are concerned, the anti-sexualists are still fighting a strong, if losing, battle. The very heart of the Judaeo-Christian sex ethic is that men and women shall remain virginal until marriage and that they shall be completely faithful after marriage. In regard to premarital chastity, this ethic seems clearly on the way out, and in many segments of the populace is more and more becoming a dead letter."[19]

The current wave of sexual liberalization, in the present context, *could* become conducive to the greater general freedom of women. Equally, it could presage new forms of oppression. The puritan-bourgeois creation of "counterpart" (not equal) produced the *precondition* for emancipation, but it gave statutory legal equality to the sexes at the cost of greatly intensified repression. Subsequently—like private property itself—it has become a brake on the further development of a free sexuality. Capitalist market relations have historically been a precondition of socialism; bourgeois marital relations (contrary to the denunciation of the *Communist Manifesto*) may equally be a precondition of women's liberation.

## 4. Socialization of Children

Woman's biological "destiny" as mother becomes a cultural vocation in her role as socializer of children. In bringing up children, woman achieves her main social definition. Her suitability for socialization springs from her physiological condition: her ability to produce milk and her occasional relative inability to undertake strenuous work loads. It should be said at the outset that suitability is not inevitability. Several anthropologists make this clear. Lévi-Strauss writes: "In every human group, women give birth to children and take care of them, and men rather have as their specialty hunting and warlike activities. Even there, though, we have ambiguous cases: of course, men never give birth to babies, but in many societies . . . they are made to act as if they did."[20] Evans-Pritchard's description of the Nuer tribe depicts just such a situation. Margaret Mead comments on the element of wish-fulfillment in the assumption of a natural correlation of femininity and nurturance: "We have assumed that because it is convenient for a mother to wish to care for her child, this is a trait with which women have been more generously endowed by a careful teleological process of evolution. We have assumed that because men have hunted, an activity requiring enterprise, bravery and initiative, they have been endowed with these useful attitudes as part of their sex-temperament."[21]

However, the cultural allocation of roles in bringing up children—and the limits of its variability—is not the essential problem for consideration. What is much more important is to analyze the nature of the socialization process itself and its requirements.

The sociologist Talcott Parsons, in his detailed analysis, claims that it is essential for the child to have two "parents," one who plays an "expressive" role, and one who plays an "instrumental" role.[22] The nuclear family revolves around the two axes of generational hierarchy (parents and children), and the two parental roles (mother-expressive and father-instrumental). The role division derives from the mother's ability and the father's inability to breast-feed. In all groups, Parsons and his colleagues assert, even in those primitive tribes where the father appears to nurture the child (such as those discussed by Evans-Pritchard and Mead), the male plays the instrumental role *in relation* to the wife-mother. At one stage the mother plays an instrumental and expressive role vis-à-vis her infant; this is in the very first years when she is the source of approval and disapproval as well as of love and care. However, after this, the father, or male substitute (in matrilineal societies the mother's brother) takes over. In a modern industrial society two types of role are clearly important: the adult role in the family of procreation, and the adult occupational role in outside work. The function of the family as such reflects the function of the women within it; it is primarily expressive. The person playing the integrated-adaptive-expressive role cannot be off all the time on instrumental-occupational errands—hence there is a built-in inhibition of the woman's work outside the home. Parsons's analysis makes clear the exact role of the maternal socializer in contemporary American society.[23] It fails to go on to state that other aspects and modes of socialization are conceivable.

What is valuable in Parsons's work is simply his insistence on the central importance of socialization as a process which is constitutive of any society (no Marxist has provided a comparable analysis). His general conclusion is that:

> It seems to be without serious qualification the opinion of competent personality psychologists that, though personalities differ greatly in their degrees of rigidity, certain broad fundamental patterns of "character" are laid down in childhood (so far as they are not genetically inherited) and are not radically changed by adult experience. The exact degree to which this is the case or the exact age levels at which plasticity becomes greatly diminished, are not at issue here. The important thing is the fact of childhood character formation and its relative stability after that.[24]

## Infancy

This seems indisputable: one of the great revolutions of modern psychology has been the discovery of the decisive specific weight of infancy in the course of an individual life—a psychic time disproportionately greater than the chronological time. Freud began the revolution with his work on infantile sexuality; Melanie Klein radicalized it with her work on the first year of the infant's life. The result is that today we know far more than ever before how delicate and precarious a process the passage from birth to childhood is for everyone. It would seem that the fate of the adult personality can be largely decided in the initial months of life. The preconditions for the later stability and integration demand an extraordinary degree of care and intelligence on the part of the adult who is socializing the child, as well as a persistence through time of the same person.

These undoubted advances in the scientific understanding of childhood have been widely used as an argument to reassert women's quintessential maternal function, at a time when the traditional family has seemed increasingly eroded. The psychoanalyst John Bowlby, studying evacuee children in World War II, declared: "essential for mental health is that the infant and young child should experience a warm, intimate, and continuous relationship with his mother,"[25] setting a trend which has become cumulative since. The emphasis of familial ideology has shifted from a cult of the biological ordeal of maternity (the pain which makes the child precious, etc.) to a celebration of mother-care as a social act. This can reach ludicrous extremes:

> For the mother, breast-feeding becomes a complement to the act of creation. It gives her a heightened sense of fulfillment and allows her to participate in a relationship as close to perfection as any that a woman can hope to achieve. . . . The simple fact of giving birth, however, does not of itself fulfill this need and longing. . . . Motherliness is a way of life. It enables a woman to express her total self with the tender feelings, the protective attitudes, the encompassing love of the motherly woman.[26]

The tautologies, the mystifications, the sheer absurdities point to the gap between reality and ideology.

*Family Patterns*

This ideology corresponds in dislocated form to a real change in the pattern of the family. As the family has become smaller, each child has become more important; the actual *act* of reproduction occupies less and less time, and the socializing and nurturance process increases commensurately in significance. Contemporary society is obsessed by the physical, moral, and sexual problems of childhood and adolescence. Ultimate responsibility for these is placed on the mother. Thus the mother's reproductive role has retreated as her socializing role has increased. In the 1890s in England a mother spent fifteen years in a state of pregnancy and lactation: in the 1960s she spent an average of four years. Compulsory schooling from the age of five, of course, reduces the maternal function very greatly after the initial vulnerable years.

The present situation is then one in which the qualitative importance of socialization during the early years of the child's life has acquired a much greater significance than in the past—while the quantitative amount of a mother's life spent either in gestation or child-rearing has greatly diminished. It follows that socialization cannot simply be elevated to the woman's new maternal vocation. Used as a mystique, it becomes an instrument of oppression. Moreover, there is no inherent reason why the biological and social mother should coincide. The process of socialization is, in itself, invariable—but the person of the socializer can vary. Observers of collective methods of child-rearing in the kibbutzim in Israel note that the child who is reared by a trained nurse (though normally maternally breast-fed) does not suffer the backwash of typical parental anxieties and thus may positively gain by the system. This possibility should not be made a fetish in its turn (Jean Baby, speaking of the post-four-year-old child, goes so far as to say that "complete separation appears indispensable to guarantee the liberty of the child as well as the mother."[27] ) But what it does reveal is the viability of plural forms of socialization—neither necessarily tied to the nuclear family, nor to the biological parent, or rather to *one* of the biological parents—the mother.

## Conclusion

The lesson of these reflections is that the liberation of women can only be achieved if *all four* structures in which they are integrated are transformed—production, reproduction, sexuality, and socialization. A modification of any of them can be offset by a reinforcement of another (as increased socialization has made up for decreased reproduction). This means that a mere permutation of the form of exploitation is achieved. The history of the last sixty years provides ample evidence of this. In the early twentieth century, militant feminism in England and the U.S.A. surpassed the labor movement in its violence. The vote—a political right—was eventually won. Nonetheless, though a simple completion of the formal legal equality of bourgeois society, it left the socioeconomic situation of women virtually unchanged. The wider legacy of the suffrage was practically nil: the suffragettes, by and large, proved unable to move beyond their own initial demands, and many of their leading figures later became extreme reactionaries. The Russian Revolution produced a quite different experience. In the Soviet Union in the 1920s, advanced social legislation aimed at liberating women above all in the field of sexuality; divorce was made free and automatic for either partner, thus effectively liquidating marriage; illegitimacy was abolished, abortion was free, etc. The social and demographic effects of these laws in a backward, semi-literate society bent on rapid industrialization (needing, therefore, a high birthrate) were— predictably—catastrophic.[28] Stalinism soon produced a restoration of traditional iron norms. Inheritance was reinstated, divorce made inaccessible, abortion illegal, etc.

> The State cannot exist without the family. Marriage is a positive value for the Socialist Soviet State only if the partners see in it a lifelong union. So-called free love is a bourgeois invention and has nothing in common with the principles of conduct of a Soviet citizen. Moreover, marriage receives its full value for the State only if there is progeny, and the consorts experience the highest happiness of parenthood.[29]

Women still retained the right and obligation to work, but because these gains had not been integrated into the earlier attempts to free sexuality and abolish the family, no general liberation has occurred.

In China, today there is still another experience. At this stage of the revolution the emphasis is being placed on liberating women in *production.* This has produced an impressive social promotion of women. But it seems to have been accompanied by some repression of sexuality and a rigorous puritanism (rampant in civic life). This corresponds not only to the need to mobilize women massively in economic life, but to a deep cultural reaction against the brutality, corruption, and prostitution prevalent in Imperial and Kuomintang China (a phenomenon unlike anything in Czarist Russia). Because the exploitation of women was so great in the *ancien régime* women's participation at village level in the Chinese Revolution was uniquely high. As for reproduction, the Russian cult of maternity in the 1930s and 1940s has not been repeated for demographic reasons: indeed, China may be one of the first countries in the world to provide free state-authorized contraception on a universal scale to the population. Again, one must remember the effect of the low level of industrialization and the fear produced by imperialist encirclement. It is too early to estimate the Chinese achievement as regards the liberation of women.

Possibly it is only in the highly developed societies of the West that an authentic liberation of women can be envisaged today. But for this to occur, there must be a transformation of *all* the structures into which they are integrated, and all the contradictions must coalesce, to explode—a *unité de rupture.* A revolutionary movement must base its analysis on the uneven development of each structure, and attack the weakest link in the combination. This may then become the point of departure for a general transformation.

NOTES

1. See Louis Althusser, "Contradiction and Overdetermination," in *For Marx* (London: Allen Lane, 1970). To describe a movement of this complexity, as I have mentioned above, Althusser uses the Freudian term "overdetermination." The phrase *"unité de rupture"* (mentioned below) refers to the moment when the contradictions so reinforce one another as to coalesce into the conditions for a revolutionary change.

2. Apologists who assume that housework, though time-consuming, is light and relatively enjoyable, are refusing to acknowledge the dull and degrading routine it entails. Lenin commented crisply: "You all know that even when women have full rights, they still remain factually downtrodden because all housework is left to them. In most cases housework is the most unproductive, the most barbarous and the most arduous work a woman can do. It is exceptionally petty and does not include anything that would in any way promote the development of the woman." Lenin, *Collected Works* (London: Lawrence and Wishart, 1961), XXX, 43.

3. Karl Marx, *Capital* (London: Lawrence and Wishart, 1963), I, 394.

4. René Dumont, *L'Afrique noire est mal partie* (1962), 210.

5. Karl Marx, *Precapitalist Economic Formations,* ed. E. J. Hobsbawm (London: Lawrence and Wishart, 1964), 87.

6. Friedrich Engels, *Origin of the Family, Private Property, and the State* from *Selected Works* (London: Lawrence and Wishart, 1958), II, 233, 311.

7. Marx, *Capital,* I, 394.

8. Viola Klein, "Working Wives," *Institute of Personnel Management Occasional Papers,* no. 15 (1960), 13.

9. Philippe Ariès in *Centuries of Childhood: A Social History of Family Life,* trans. Robert Baldick (New York: Knopf, 1962), shows that though the family may in some form always have existed it was often submerged under more forceful structures. In fact, according to Ariés, it has acquired its present significance only with the advent of industrialization.

10. J. A. Froude, *Nemesis of Faith* (1849), 103.

11. Karl Marx, "Chapitre de Mariage," *Oeuvres Complètes,* ed. Molitor, *Oeuvres Philosophiques,* I, 25.

12. Karl Marx, *Private Property and Communism,* in *Early Writings,* ed. T. B. Bottomore (London: Watts and Co., 1963), 153.

13. Wayland Young, *Eros Denied: Sex in Western Society* (New York: Grove, 1964).

14. Karl Wittfogel, *Oriental Despotism: A Comparative Study of Total Power* (New Haven, Conn.: Yale University Press, 1957), 116.

15. Engels, *Origin of the Family . . . ,* II, 224.

16. Lawrence Stone, *The Crisis of the Aristocracy, 1558–1641* (New York: Oxford University Press, 1965), 663–64.

17. Simone de Beauvoir, *The Long March* (Cleveland, Ohio: World, 1958), 141.

18. Keith Thomas, "Women and the Civil War Sects," *Past and Present,* no. 13 (April 1958), 43.

19. Albert Ellis, "The Folklore of Sex," in *The Family and the Sexual Revolution,* ed. E. M. Schur (Bloomington: Indiana University Press, 1964), 35.

20. Claude Lévi-Strauss, "The Family," in *Man, Culture and Society,* ed. H. L. Shapiro (New York: Oxford University Press, 1956), 274.

21. Margaret Mead, "Sex and Temperament," in Schur, ed., *The Family and the Sexual Revolution,* 207–8.

22. Talcott Parsons and Robert F. Bales, *Family, Socialization and Interaction Process* (Chicago: Free Press, 1955), 47. "The area of instrumental function concerns relations of the system to its situation outside the system . . . and 'instrumentally'

establishing the desired relations to *external* goal-objects. The expressive area concerns the 'internal' affairs of the system, the maintenance of integrative relations between the members, and regulation of the patterns and tension levels of its component units."

23. One of Parson's main theoretical innovations is his contention that what the child strives to internalize will vary with the content of the reciprocal role relationships in which he or she is a participant. R. D. Laing in *Family and Individual Structure* (1966), contends that a child may internalize an entire systen—i.e., "the family."

24. Talcott Parsons, *The Social System,* (Glencoe, Ill.: Free Press, 1952), 227. There is no doubt that the Women's Liberation Movement, with its practical and theoretical stress on the importance of child-care, has accorded the subject the seriousness it needs. See, for instance, "Women's Liberation: Notes on Child-Care," produced by the Women's Center, 36 W. 22d st., New York.

25. John Bowlby, cit. by Bruno Bettelheim, "Does Communal Education Work? The Case of the Kibbutz," in Schur, ed. *The Family and the Sexual Revolution,* 295. These evacuee war children were probably suffering from more than mother-loss, e.g. bombings and air-raids.

26. Betty Ann Countrywoman in *Redbook,* June 1960, cit. by Betty Friedan, *The Feminine Mystique* (Baltimore, Md.: Penguin, 1965), 51.

27. Jean Baby, *Un Monde Meilleur* (Maspero, 1964), 99.

28. For a fuller account of this, see Chap. IVa of Kate Millett's *Sexual Politics* (New York: Doubleday, 1970).

29. From the official journal of the Commissariat of Justice, *Sotsialisticheskaya Zakonnost,* 1939, no. 2, cit. by N. Timasheff, "The Attempt to Abolish the Family in Russia," in *Modern Introduction to the Family,* ed. N. W. Bell and E. F. Vogel (Chicago: Free Press, 1960), 59.

# "Herstory" As History:
# A New Field or Another Fad?

*Sheila Ryan Johansson*

## 1. The Study of Women As a Contemporary Historical Specialty

Clio, the muse of history, is now a liberated woman. No longer does she accept the traditional norms which defined certain themes as her proper pursuit. One now finds those she inspires investigating all manner of peculiar topics—mobs, magic, madness, famines, families, and funny papers are only a few of the new topics intriguing historians. In the meantime, new techniques as diverse as quantification and psychoanalysis are being used by some historians. Traditional scholars have frequently expressed doubts that much good could come of all this innovation, and as women's history makes its appearance and claims recognition as a legitimate new field of research, they must wonder still more about the future of their discipline. Surely the study of women must be the ultimate harbinger of scholarly chaos. What could have less to do with the "serious" study of social change? Scholars suffering from this lingering "Victorianism" might well feel that women are too eternal or unworldly to have much to do with politics and economics. Others might wonder whether topicality isn't the sole reason for the increasing attention paid to the history of women.

It must be admitted that past interest in women's history has had a faddish character. Stored in the dark recesses of large university libraries are hundreds of books about women in the remote and recent past, produced when the status of women had become a temporarily fashionable topic. Thus this "new field" has a literature dating back at least to the seventeenth century.[1]

Until very recently, however, the vast majority of books on the history of women have centered around the theme of "Woman's" intrinsic goodness or badness. Of the hundreds of books which address themselves wholly or partly to the history of women only a few are free from this orientation, an orientation which is fatal to balanced, scholarly treatment. Some books argued that women, as embodiments of the eternal feminine, had always provided the necessary support and inspiration for the more visible achievements of men throughout history. More commonly, other books tried to

An abbreviated version of this essay was read at the annual meeting of the American Historical Association, December 1973, in San Francisco.

show that behind every war, persecution, or disaster was a woman's passion for power, sex, or revenge. The belief in Woman's goodness reached its height in the middle of the nineteenth century, just as organized feminism began to challenge the patriarchal structure of power in America and England. But by the turn of the century, the backlash against feminism revived the view that women, particularly famous women, were basically troublemakers. Thus Emil Reich, author of a multivolume study called *Woman through the Ages,* felt comfortable telling his readers that if the primary function of history was to teach, then ". . . of what use today are the female makers of history, except to show posterity the exaggerated errors into which their excessive egotism runs?"[2]

Recently, women have come to dominate the writing of women's history. But if contemporary feminists have rejected the interpretative absurdities of the saga of Woman-the-Good or Woman-the-Bad, they have for the most part only replaced these two venerables with Woman-the-Passive-Victim. Whatever the limitations of the first two perspectives, they gave some importance to women in history. The present emphasis upon the utter, total, and complete victimization of women in the past leads only to the conclusion that for one half of humanity, time has meant nothing more than survival, or a cowlike submission to inscrutable natural processes and outrageous social customs.

It is Simone de Beauvoir who is most responsible for reestablishing in recent years the intellectual validity of the "victim" interpretation. Herself brilliant and famous, she publicly apologized in *The Second Sex* (1949) for her sex, and defensively explained why it had meant so little to history. "Woman," according to de Beauvoir, was a weak creature basically dependent upon man for survival because of the disabilities connected with reproduction. As such, "Woman" was perceived by "Man" as a different and rather contemptible being, one easily manipulated to serve his own ends.

Openly and by implication de Beauvoir argued that masterful Man pioneered and monopolized all forms of creative endeavor and cultural achievements. Man was objective, imaginative, heroic; man was both ruler and rebel. Woman appeared to have no virtues which were admirable in themselves. Her traits and skills, such as they were, came out of oppression and weakness. If women were at last free to become fully human it was only because birth control and paid employment had emancipated them. With this emancipation they could become more and more like men, and hence finally capable of participating in history.[3]

It is not surprising that de Beauvoir's book was generally well received by men. After all, her defense of injured Woman is shot through with an extravagant and quite unrealistic vision of historic Man. Yet if pressed, even the most chauvinistic male historian might admit that history, if it has been dominated by Man, has also been filled with more heat than light, more injustice, selfishness and violence than enlightened detachment, and certainly more conservatism than progressive creativity. Furthermore, by her own evidence Man, when contemplating Woman, was for the most part a pretty conventional fellow, anything but heroic and objective, quite derivative and often stale in his handling of the woman question.

The West's current cultural malaise and the ecological crisis have led some
to reassess the relative merits of "masculinity" and "femininity" (as presently
defined). Many forces are combining to create a climate more favorable to the
appreciation of women and things feminine. These trends form the background for the renewed attention being paid to the historical work of Mary
Beard.[4]

Beard was a historian who had long fought against intellectual trends
which tended to devaluate the positive contributions of women to history. In
*On Understanding Women* (1931) and *Woman As Force in History* (1946) she
argued that only the conventions of contemporary historical methods made
women seem potentially victimized and unimportant. In the spirit of John
Stuart Mill, she insisted upon the manifold civilizing influence of women in
history—the collective pressure females had exerted for "civilization" and
against barbarism. Even so, she did not have a well-structured theory about
women's civilizing mission, only a lot of examples here and there of women
who had done something positive for their culture. Unfortunately, Beard
ignored most of the historical evidence relating to the victimization of women
and produced, instead, an interpretation which is just as one-sided as de
Beauvoir's.

It is not surprising that de Beauvoir, and not Beard, has been able to
convince many contemporary feminists of the merits of her case.[5] De
Beauvoir, displaying an impressive erudition, used material from many fields
to structure a fairly consistent general theory about women, while Mary
Beard stuck faithfully to history, rarely attaining in her own field the
brilliance de Beauvoir displayed in so many.

Nevertheless, the general ideas of Mary Beard may yet have their day.
Historians with an interest in the history of the family, sexual behavior,
population history, and collective psychology can scarcely neglect women.
They need information about what women have been doing in, to, and for
their cultures, as much or more than they need material on the victimization
of women. But if the study of women as either agents or victims expects to
establish itself as both a legitimate and useful perspective on the past, certain
basic methodological changes must be made. The most obvious one involves
abandoning "Woman" altogether.

*Women vs. "Woman"*

"Woman" was the main character in the historical sagas of both Beard and
de Beauvoir. To the latter "Woman" had an unquestionable status as a useful
philosophic category, while to Mary Beard it radiated an old-fashioned
dignity. But "Woman" as a collective noun is as full of traps as it is
convenient; as a unit of analysis for a historical narrative it is awkward and
dangerous.

Over time men have changed their minds again and again about who and
what "Woman" is. Depending on the author, place, and period, Woman has
been declared innately mysterious or simple, altruistic or selfish, bold or
timid, cruel or loving, spiritual or materialistic, mindless or too clever, sensual
or sexless, more moral, less moral, more aesthetic, less aesthetic, more

sensitive, less sensitive, more frivolous, more serious and so forth. Triumphs over simple logic have been achieved when an individual man has been able to maintain contradictory things about Woman at one and the same time or from page to page. Outside of the difficulty in treating such a changeable creature as the heroine of a historical narrative, timeless abstractions by their very nature do not have histories, they simply persist without change. Although by a careful selection of quotes from here and there over time, one can create the illusion that everywhere Woman has been the same (and hence has no history), it is just as easy to assemble a set of remarks by the great and near-great that show the opposite.

Most often it has been those hostile to women who have written of "Woman" and her true unchanging essence. Descriptions and analyses of the eternal feminine have usually been put forth by those anxious to justify the continuance of various forms of social and legal restrictions which confine women to one or two highly circumscribed social roles, and which condemn rebellious women to the category of genetic sports, nature's mistakes, or exceptions that prove the rule. Thus categorized, the complaints of rebels are dismissed as unfortunate outcries about which nothing can be done. Although some writers sympathetic to women have written of "Woman," the remarks of Millicent Fawcett, a nineteenth-century British feminist, still apply: "We talk about 'women' and 'women's suffrage,'" she said: "we do not talk about Woman with a capital W. That we leave to our enemies."[6]

Although Mary Beard and Simone de Beauvoir are not enemies of women, in talking about "Woman" they fell into the obvious traps inherent in the use of such an abstract term. De Beauvoir, defining Woman as perpetually passive and unimportant, cannot help classifying all the standard "great" women, for example, Joan of Arc and Elizabeth I of England, as exceptions who some-how managed to appropriate the properties of masculinity. Mary Beard, noting that *some* women have been cruel and violent (and thus exceptions to the rule of Woman's pacific and civilized benevolence) also defines such women out of their sex. But when enough exceptions are judiciously ad-mitted to generalizations about "Woman," any "rule" can be proved.

In future attempts to write about women in history "Woman" should be abandoned, and left to second-rate poets. Historians must deal with women, and most important, with well-defined groups of women.

### Social Roles and Classes

The most historically central distinctions between kinds of women are those which involve both social class and social roles. Working historians do not find it possible to ignore the gulf between men who are kings and men who are commoners, and still produce meaningful generalizations about social change. However, it is still common practice to suspend common sense when thinking about the female sex, even though queens, burgesses, artisan women, and peasant women were divided by differences in outlook and life-styles which were as profound as those which divided men.

It is perhaps easier to understand the necessity of making distinctions between groups of women, when we consider the importance of "social roles" to the study of women's history. In daily life women exist and relate to other human beings through specific social roles—female infant, female child, daughter, sister, maiden, wife (first, second, third, etc.), mother, grandmother, widow, divorcee, mistress, whore, nun—rarely does a woman interact with others simply and only as a woman. What women can do in each social role differs widely in all cultures and all times. In one and the same culture an "agressive" maiden might inspire horror, while an "authoritative" grandmother or mother-in-law might be considered natural and worthy of respect. In most Western cultures each social role seems to have a history of its own which deserves separate, detailed treatment, since what is declared natural and appropriate to each changes over time.

In writing about women and the law throughout history, it becomes very apparent that women as women scarcely exist. Law codes distribute rights, responsibilites and property to females according to their age, marital status, blood relationships, and so forth. The legal status of any particular woman in any stage or state of life is further complicated by class distinctions, and sometimes by race and religion. There are few if any laws about women per se, and each legally recognized category which distinguishes among women also has a history of its own.

As Mary Beard argued, the slavelike legal status of Victorian married women under the common law has received disproportionate historical attention. Indeed one sometimes gets the impression that all women, irrespective of their marital status, were equally vulnerable to the common law. But for any cohort of women born in Europe after the fifteenth century, 10 to 20 percent remained permanently single; at any one time, moreover, one-fourth to one-half of all women under thirty were apt to be unmarried.[7] How these women made use of their property rights is relatively unexplored.

Obviously political roles were also affected by considerations of class and social role. Until various "democratic" revolutions officially decided that women should be widely excluded from the formal political realm, there were many areas in Europe where upper-class women as widows habitually took part in local power struggles. There were certain areas in Europe, even in the nineteenth century, where propertied women (if they were not married) voted in local elections.[8]

Sometimes historians are careful about making the necessary descriptive distinctions among groups of women. But the more careful a scholar is to note the profusion of differences among women in various roles, ranks, and culture epochs, the less willing she (or he) seems to be to account analytically for these differences. Recent detailed treatments of English and French women in history are almost purely descriptive, providing a profusion of detail and (in the French case) pictures, in very large and ambitious volumes.[9] But the descriptive work is marked by an absence of coherent and sustained attempts to explain the differences observed and the changes over time. An abundance of details without a theoretical context simply reinforces the impression that information about women hasn't much connection with the mainstream concerns of historians.

A fruitful fusion of the empirical and analytic approaches will probably not come about until scholars have been convinced that studying women of the past can offer something more than a wealth of interesting but trivial details. Toward this end, the following sections of this paper examine selected aspects of women's history with a view to suggesting some relationships between the lives and social roles of women, and the pace and direction of social change. I have already discussed the need for making certain distinctions of class and social role among women. In section 2, I apply these observations to the history of the "victimization" of women, through a more complex analysis of the "status" of women. In section 3, I consider the implications of treating men as agents in women's history, and in section 4, I return to the more fundamental theme: the necessity for continuing Mary Beard's work on the role of *women as agents* in history.

## 2. Victimization and the Status of Women

If women ever participated in history as something more than passive and rather ineffectual victims, much of the form and content of that participation must have been influenced by sexual discrimination. If we ought to pay more attention to Mary Beard's Woman-As-Force, we cannot forget de Beauvoir's Woman-As-Victim. For although the oppression of women has been treated at great length, there is still much to be learned about the historical sources, causes, nature and extent of discrimination based on sex.

### The Complex Problem of Status

The conceptual, descriptive, and analytic weaknesses which plague women's history are very noticeable in the treatment of women's "oppression." This and other central terms are rarely defined; some of the basic assumptions which lie behind the selection and presentation of evidence are highly questionable, and many of the explanatory generalizations are vague, poorly supported, or internally contradictory. Sweeping theories perch on a rickety empirical base, and sometimes the facts used to support various statements are not facts at all. Since both the methodology and the basic data of women's history are underdeveloped it is not surprising that there is a plethora of "whys" and "hows" of the status of women. As yet there are almost none which involve a thorough discussion of what the status of women means. "Status" is used as if it were a perfectly self-evident concept, and most explanations of the changing status of women seem to assume that one social variable can be both the cause and effect of the overall position of women in a society.

Thus, "Woman's" role in either economics, or religion, or education, or the family, or reproduction, or sexual life, or her image in philosophy and literature, or her legal rights, or her physical weakness, or her temperament is singled out as the one thing worthy of attention. Such assumptions are often accompanied by vague beliefs that all women have the same status at any one time and that this status can be meaningfully characterized as "high" or "low," although the comparative basis of such a judgment remains obscure.

In the literature on the status of women in modern societies or even some anthropological treatments of women, it is recognized that the status of women is a composite of many details about the rights, duties, privileges, disabilities, options, and restrictions that the women of a specific group experience as they move through an inevitable progression of age-groups and social roles. Such an approach involves a recognition that there is no such animal as *Woman* and that oversimplifications of complex situations in her name are neither useful nor scholarly.[10]

## The Status Pattern

To break away from misleading simplicities about status we must first outline as many as possible of its major components. It seems that dozens of bits of information would be needed in order to describe the "status" of women as they are distributed among various national, temporal, socioeconomic or ethnic and religious divisions. When all the information deemed relevant is assembled we might call it a *status pattern,* a pattern which goes beyond descriptions of women (i.e., adult females) and extends into material about girls and even female babies.

A relatively complete "status pattern" would provide the basis for the sort of structured and comparable observations about women which better theorizing (about the extent of status differences between groups of women and men, or understanding the nature of status permutations over time) would require. The following is simply the skeleton of a *status pattern.* It is one of several possible complex guides to assembling and organizing material pertinent to understanding the phrase "status of women" in a comprehensive sense.

*Infancy and childhood:* (1) infanticide practices, (2) attitude toward newborn babies, (3) sex-differential feeding, fondling and scolding, (4) cultural habits affecting diet, exercise, and play patterns (as they differ between boys and girls), (5) opportunities to identify with and imitate adult role models, (6) formal beliefs about being a female as presented to young children (early self-image and self-esteem).

*Youth:* (1) amount and quality of instruction (mental stimulation and challenge) preparatory to adult role, (2) opportunities to explore individual proclivities—elasticity in role choice, (3) opportunities to move freely in one's environment, (4) customs governing the expression of sexual urges before marriage, (5) nature of exposure to formal cultural teaching about women and women's roles, (6) nature, content, and formal rites of passage marking maturity.

*Work:* (1) amount and extensiveness of vocational training or higher education, (2) range of work choices offered and their importance to the culture as well as their formal status, (3) sex-differential wages, (4) the possibility of economic independence from husband or family, (5) freedom to migrate in search of work, (6) access to social institutions which relate to success or pleasure in one's work, (7) economic status in old age or retirement, as compared with equivalent male groups.

*Marriage:* (1) customs governing the choice of marriage as a state, (2) customs governing choice of spouse and the number of spouses, (3) customs governing the relative age of marriage, (4) customs governing the social, economic, and sexual rights, and duties of wives as compared with husbands, (5) effect of aging on wife's status, (6) expression of sexual urges outside marriage—rights and restrictions, (7) conditions under which a marriage can be terminated by divorce or annulment, (8) customs governing remarriage.

*Motherhood:* (1) nature and extent of the average maternity regimen, birth intervals, medical care, infant and maternal mortality, (2) extent to which women control reproduction, (3) economic and cultural duties of mothers, (4) legal rights of mothers, (5) position of unwed mothers, (6) status of barren women, (7) right of mothers over children when marriage is terminated.

*Widowed, divorced, and unmarried women:* (1) legal, social, economic and sexual rights of permanently unmarried women and single women of marriageable age, (2) connotations attached to singleness, (3) right to choose not to marry, (4) rights and duties of widows, (5) rights, duties, and image of divorced women, (6) rights of lesbians and other "deviants" to pursue a chosen life-style.

*Legal rights:* Outside of those aspects of legal status already mentioned one has to consider (1) comparative rights of daughters and sons under age, (2) age of majority, (3) extent to which women in various ages and social roles can inherit, manage, purchase, sell, and bequeath property, or earn and control wages, (4) the legal capacity of women at various ages and in various social roles to testify, sue, be sued, sign contracts, witness, take oaths, sit on juries, be tried and imprisoned as criminals, etc., (5) extent to which women can act as guardians or wards for their own and other's children, (6) extent to which women can take training in law, practice law, teach law, and act as a judge.

*Political and military factors:* (1) right to give advice, vote or make decisions in family councils or local (community) organizations, e.g., village councils, (2) right to participate, express opinions, vote or organize for political purposes at higher levels of government, (3) right to hold positions of formal power in local and national political elites, (4) sex-linked customs governing training in and access to the means of legal uses of force, since this involves training in the ability to defend oneself, or participation in official military organizations.

*Religion:* (1) symbolic roles of females and the feminine in the images and beliefs of standard creeds, (2) role and participation of lay women in religious ceremonies or household cults, (3) role of women in the "clergy" or structure of religious leadership, (4) role of women in the nonofficial religious power structure, i.e., prophets, sibyls, or witches, (5) nature of ceremonies or taboos which apply to women, (6) freedom to choose religion, irrespective of family's or spouse's wish.

*Cultural and intellectual variables:* (1) comparative formal education of men and women, (2) comparative customs governing artistic/intellectual self-expression, i.e., rules of whatever nature which encourage, permit, or train talent in art, music, literature, philosophy, and science, (3) access to patronage systems, (4) opportunities to act as patrons (personal or institutional), (5) right to receive training as singer, actress, dancer, speaker, etc., (6) right to perform in public, (7) right to be evaluated irrespective of sex, (8) popular, literary, philosophical, and scientific "image" of women.

*Miscellaneous social variables:* (1) dress customs of women and whether they promote or damage women's health, freedom, etc., (2) standard diets of women in various classes and ages, (3) opportunities for healthy exercise, (4) customs governing movements and travels outside the home proper, (5) general medical care available, and (6) death rates.

*Subjective perceptions of status:* (1) ways in which women experiencing life in a given group themselves evaluated their own status (part of understanding status is understanding how various women said it *felt* to be a woman in a society), (2) opportunities women had to learn about or participate in alternative status patterns (useful to know for evaluating first-person reports), (3) extent of resignation, fatalism, or self-abnegation promoted generally in the society (thus influencing the degree of enthusiasm or contentment with various features of status).

### Comparing and Evaluating Status

One might wonder, even granting the necessity of gathering all this material, whether it is possible to obtain it all, and, if so, what it would mean. For most groups of women in modern history it is possible. Much of the necessary information exists already, scattered in various books, monographs, or unpublished primary sources; it needs only to be drawn together. Studying the complete status of women becomes more and more difficult as one goes further back in time, but the difficulties are repaid with new perspectives on the nature of women's status.

It becomes evident very quickly that a wealth of information makes informal evaluative assessments ("high" vs. "low") rather meaningless, or even impossible. As paradoxes and internal contradictions appear, new ways to compare and assess the overall import of a status pattern are called for. Consider, for example, legal status alone. There are no cultures that deprive *all* groups of women of every form of legal rights or privileges; what one finds instead is a melange of benefits and disabilities that varies markedly from group to group (depending upon age, role, and class) and, taken as a whole, from culture to culture. Several problems immediately arise: how does one make sense of an inconsistent pattern, and then compare it to other patchwork assemblies of legal rules? More important, how does legal status affect or relate to the other aspects of status?

In sixteenth-century Europe married English women had less protection from economic exploitation or general mistreatment by husbands than any women in Western Europe. Yet travelers from the continent were fairly agreed upon the fact that as wives, English women had the most spirited and independent temperaments and the most freedom from their husbands' supervision. Propertied Spanish married women had the best legal position in Europe at the time, yet after the sixteenth-century counter-reformation their legal privileges could not protect them from increasingly severe social and educational disabilities. As one becomes acquainted with the necessary profusion of details, each of which has some importance to the status of women, one is forced more and more into the making of complex and highly qualified evaluations that are very far from "high" and "low," "better" or "worse." We are forced to ask "high" with respect to what? "Favorable" when compared to what alternatives? Rarely, if ever, has the standard of comparison implied by these terms been made explicit.

There are many constructive approaches to evaluating and comparing status patterns. One way involves comparing each element in the status pattern of a specific group of women with those possessed by a comparable group of men or women of another age, class, religion, or other subclassification. The numbers of differences among patterns could be used as a crude approximation of inequality. The net number of "unfavorable" differences might even be used as a first approach to understanding how and in what degree the women of this group were more or differently "oppressed" than their male counterparts. As things presently stand, "women's oppression," for all its importance as a central concept in talking about the victimization of women, has more emotive than cognitive content. This is unfortunate because the very vagueness of the term hinders the development of concrete speculations about and planning for social change.

Another very different approach to comparing and evaluating status patterns involves the construction of a timeless and supercultural model of an ideal human status pattern. Once defined, the ideal could be compared with any number of actual status patterns as they applied to groups of women and men. The relative distance between the ideal and the various real status patterns could then be used as a basis for comparison.

Either approach necessarily involves the making of many value judgments; and, the world being what it is, various scholars can be expected to disagree about whether or not certain provisions regarding divorce, marriage, abortion, birth control, economic opportunities, political participation, and religious roles are liberating or oppressive, good or bad, favorable or unfavorable. In discussing the status of women there is no way of escaping value judgments and the different perspectives these necessarily introduce. But if they are made overtly, so that the reader is aware of what is happening, the reasons for differing evaluation will become clear. As it is now, value judgments are made covertly and sometimes unconsciously, so that the disputes of various researchers about whether or not "Woman's" status was high or low, although seeming to be empirical in character, are not about the "facts" of status, but about the different values each researcher brought to the assessment of various status elements.

Nowhere is this clearer than in the nineteenth-century European and American debates about the status of women. It was a common belief in nineteenth-century Europe that the status of women (no distinctions being made by class but middle-class women the reference point) was the general indicator of social progress. Socialists like Fourier and Marx accepted this idea; conservatives like Spencer completely agreed. But socialists thought the status of women was "low" in this, the heyday of darkest capitalism, while conservatives said it was "high" in this time of advanced material progress and freedom. Socialists took as proof of their case that women (upper- and middle-class women) did not work; while conservative or liberals took this same observation as proof that women's status was high. In terms of a socialist value framework, work meant dignity and independence; but from the point of view of a traditional and still popular aristocratic perspective, idle people, if they lived in luxury, quite obviously had "high" status. Those people who had to work for a living were to be pitied, not envied. Since "primitive" women could be observed doing heavy work, they were therefore considered by conservatives to be oppressed. But to socialists the hard labor of primitive women meant that they *necessarily* had a certain importance and power that civilized women lacked altogether.

Although there is no settling who is correct in some absolute objective sense, there are good arguments for and against both sides. On the whole, however, the debate is too simple to cast much light on the overall status of women. In terms of European history, doing work has not necessarily meant that one would possess other "favorable" rights and responsibilities. One has only to look at the overall status pattern of peasants, serfs, or slaves to see that. Conversely, women who are idle and completely dependent upon men for food, clothing, and shelter, as Victorian middle-class women were, may not be powerless altogether. Indeed, they may *feel* they are much better off than women who must share the workload with their husbands.

Finally, the detailed knowledge about status that a whole pattern of rights, responsibilities, duties, privileges, options, and commands will give us provides in itself the basis for any serious historical work about why the status of women changes, as it certainly does, over time. There have been spectacular status revolutions and slow status evolutions, wherein bit by bit most of the elements in a status pattern changed over time till the whole pattern was noticeably different. But to explain the occurrence of either pattern one first must know when and where the changes took place. This is especially necessary if the absurdities of some of the current explanations for why women's status has changed are to be avoided in the future.

As it is, Christianity, Protestantism, capitalism, chivalry, and romanticism are blamed for initiating all manner of unfavorable status elements that either existed previously or are not unique to European cultures. Explanations which place the cause after the effect, or which mistake a widespread feature of "civilized" cultures for something uniquely European have little value either for historians or interested feminists. Yet it is the quest for better explanations that will rightly be at the center of future research in women's history. How one or more aspects of the status of women have changed over time, why they have changed, or why they have remained relatively immune to change—all these questions bring us to the next subject, the treatment of men in women's history.

### 3. Men in Women's History

If modern historians have been able to pretend that women have not been part of history, historians of women would probably not be able to or wish to return the insult to the same degree. Men have had too much to do with the status of women to be ignored. But the ideas outlined in the previous sections might at least return women to the center stage of "herstory." Much of what is regarded as feminist historical analysis is simply the study of men—what men have written about women in poems, plays, essays, novels, and "scientific" studies. This situation is understandable, in that male attitudes are among the most visible aspects of past sexism; but it is counterproductive in that it perpetuates the tendency to regard women as passive and femininity as culturally unimportant. The love-hate relationship that many feminists have had with men and masculinity is never more apparent than in the angry fixation with male-produced literature that leads some to an intellectual assault on ideas which they nevertheless portray as of ultimate importance.

What de Beauvoir or Millett reveal about the implications of some male writing about women is often brilliant and incisive. But their general de-emphasis of women prevents any detailed investigation into the material effects of literary misogyny on the daily life of either ordinary or exceptional women. Literary trends are presented both as something which affect and reflect general beliefs about the nature and role of women in society; but we are rarely treated to any detailed elaboration about the relation of literature to, for example, legal or economic status, or even the daily drudgery of ordinary women.

Finally, in a parody of the male tendency to regard all women as alike, the individuality as well as the social background of men writing about women is ignored or treated with extreme and misleading brevity.[11] In Kate Millett's *Sexual Politics,* which some regard as one of the most influential works of the feminist revival, "Man" is presented as a callous patriarch—a creature basically contemptuous of the humanity of the women he finds it so easy to oppress. Confident and egoistic to an extreme degree, "he" stalks through life relentlessly pursuing his own self-interest. This picture of arrogant strength must flatter and please many of the would-be "Marlboro men" of modern life. But it must strike many more as absurd, since it bears so little relation to their own reactions toward and experiences with women. One can disregard all the male complaints about the women who have deceived, misled, abused, frightened, or dominated them only if one is determined also to write off or ignore the spirit, intelligence, strength, and resilience that many women have displayed through time. In spite of all the discrimination that has hampered women in history, females have a certain amount of built-in power over males, as mothers, wives, lovers, and sisters. Many men, certainly, have been willing to acknowledge this.

At least two male authors have written honestly of the fear and terror that so many men experience at the very depths of their encounters with women. Wolfgang Lederer's *The Fear of Women* (1968) and H. P. Hays's *The Dangerous Sex* (1964) present men not as confident patriarchs, but as perpetually insecure sons and lovers forever fighting the deep-rooted power of a mother or the withering capacity of adult women to reject and ridicule, and thus destroy, men. In this light many of the masculine moves to oppress women appear as defensive responses to the real and perceived powers of women, rather than as a confidently undertaken manipulation of a weak and despised "other."

When Kate Millett analyzes the ideas of John Ruskin, the Victorian art and social critic, she presents him as a calculating fellow who was rationally, if cynically, reacting to feminist assaults on male privileges. In particular his doctrine of "separate spheres" (in which "the home" was defined as the queenly domain of Woman, while "the world" remained the kingly domain of Man) was presented as a rational attempt to stifle the increasing intellectual respectability of sexual egalitarianism. From the standpoint of his personal dealings with women (which Millett does not discuss), Ruskin appears more like a frightened and defensive man than a confident patriarch. As a boy he had been thoroughly dominated by his imposing Victorian mother. Although he managed to marry against her will, he could never bring himself to consummate his marriage. His wife was forced to make his impotence public when she sought an annulment in order to marry another man. Ruskin was never able afterward to relate to females over twelve years of age. His terror of adult women, more than patriarchal cynicism, may have been behind his desire to see adult women confined to "the Home." That would leave him free to seek refuge in a reassuringly all-male "World."

More to the point, perhaps, is whether or not Ruskin's essays had any effect on the minds of his readers. Certainly there is no evidence that he succeeded in stopping the progress of reformist feminism in England, or did anything more than preach to the converted.

The lives of many of the great woman-haters of history were filled with similar sex-linked torments. If as males their societies gave them every theoretical advantage in dealing with women in their lives, as individuals they could not manage to convert abstract advantages into concrete benefits in dealing with individual women. Thus, the defeats and humiliations suffered in daily life were transformed into harsh and unflattering assessments of "Woman." Words were used as weapons in individual sex-wars which men found themselves losing. To present all misogynists as straightforwardly contemptuous of women, ignoring the background of fear and possible humiliation which inspired their remarks, is unfair. It reminds us again of our present inability to believe that women are or ever could have been something more than mere victims.

If psychological perspectives on male attitudes toward women are presently underdeveloped, sociological approaches are all but nonexistent. Even feminists who believe that class analysis is essential to historical understanding frequently treat the abstract category "Man" as if it were indivisible. This is understandable, since specialists rarely agree on the best way to subdivide men into groups, socioeconomic or otherwise. One scholar's "lower-middle" is another's "upper-lower." But even by using the standard (and admittedly crude) upper-middle-lower model of class structure some initial contrasts in male attitudes by class can be outlined. (These contrasts do not cover all cases, irrespective of place and time, nor are they intended to; they are simply a first and tentative approximation of variations by class.)

It is in the traditional sort of ruling class that we might, at first, expect to find males who most approximate to the patriarchal type as now outlined by feminists. For the most part, European countries have been ruled by males who came from titled and landed families. Close to the centers of visible power, they often behaved with the aggressive, confident, casually cruel, dominant, and callous demeanor that some feminists attribute to men in general. Hence it is in the upper reaches of society that we might expect to find the greatest contempt for women and the cruelest constraints upon their freedom.

Actually, it is in the literature of castle and court (whether written by or simply for an audience of ruling-class families) that one finds pervasive sexism least developed. The oppositeness of the sexes is not stressed; sometimes it is invisible. Men and women come in a comparable range of human types; women are often depicted as beings capable of aggressive, intelligent and often cruel behavior. This is most pronounced in the mythological and saga literature of early feudal Europe, whether Celtic, Scandinavian, German, or Slavic. Sometimes, women appear as warriors who can defeat men in forms of physical combat. In the original Nibelungenlied (not in Wagner's operatic version) Brünhilde has a series of would-be suitors put to death because they cannot defeat her in stone-heaving. Apparently, her strength and cruelty only enhance her desirability as a beautiful and wealthy mate in the eyes of Gunther.[12] In the Icelandic *Laxdaela Saga* females appear almost universally as strong, unsentimental, no-nonsense types who are not averse to shedding blood or stirring up violence. This is perhaps even more revealing since the saga itself is much more historical than mythical. The women in it are not goddesses or witches who use magic.[13]

Although there were institutions and customs which were unfavorable to women in upper-class life, the women of ruling-class families generally had unusual privileges and opportunities as well. For every period which fastened real or symbolic chastity belts on upper-class women, there was another which granted them something like unofficial sexual license. In general, ruling-class men could not afford to have wives and mothers who were much different, temperamentally and intellectually, from themselves. Husbands too often went off to war; if they died in battle or from natural causes without a mature male heir, wives were expected to substitute for them. Substituting for absent husbands meant that feudal women managed estates, held court, and even organized and led military actions. Husbands depended on the class and family loyalty of their wives to a great degree; they simply could not afford the luxury of helpless, weak, or stupid women.[14] Furthermore, since male rulers had ample opportunities to dominate and abuse men less powerful than themselves, they might have felt comparatively less threatened by strong women.

Moving down the social scale to the amorphous and problematic group of men called "middle class" (a group for which there are numerous and conflicting definitions) we find an ideal quite different from the one described above.[15] Nothing is more abhorrent to the recognizable middle-ranking male than that women either could or should be substitutes for males, temporarily or otherwise. Economically it was usually infeasible and psychologically it was threatening to an extreme degree. The middle-class male's psyche was heavily affected by the daily reality of competition and the perpetual awareness that real security in life is impossible. This, combined with a preference for using family resources with maximum effectiveness, shaped a distinctive perspective on the role and nature of "Woman," one which involved the maximization of her difference from "Man."

The life-styles of middle-class men, for example, often included a long period of intensive and expensive training in some occupation (something regarded as "wasted" on women). Very often getting started in life required further investments of family capital. Men in such a position usually married in their late twenties or mid-thirties. The female children of middle-ranking families had an upbringing and a life-style as different from that of their typical male counterparts as could be possible. As girls they were sheltered and usually uneducated. As daughters they cost their families money, principally through the marital dowry. Before the sixteenth century, middle-class girls often married in their early teens and quickly began an intensive and constraining maternity regimen. The death or absence of their husbands usually left them totally unprepared to take over the men's occupations, since they had little or no experience in "the world" or any extensive professional training. (This was less true in the lower middle classes.)

Not surprisingly, the ideals of feminine behavior usually preferred by middling males include docility, dependence, and timidity, and not a rough-and-ready generalized competence. What middling males usually wanted were obedient cooperative daughters, and helpful, reassuring, soothing wives who offered little in the way of competition or criticism. The numerous middle-class women who revolted against prevailing temperamental ideals and social constraints usually did so through sexual or consumer indulgence, or, often, just plain nagging and sloth. Such women could be clearly and safely defined as sinful, disloyal or, increasingly from the sixteenth century, "unladylike." In contrast, middle-class women who asked for the same education or professional opportunities as their menfolk were branded "unnatural" or "masculine." To middle-class males, their work above all was in some sense the heart and soul of their masculine identity. Temperamental and occupational similarity between women and men threatened the economic, psychological, and social security of middle-class male-dominated families.

It is thus unfortunate that most of the written historical artifacts that discuss the nature of "Woman" or the differences between the sexes have been produced by insecure, competitive, "middle-ranging" men who come from urban cultures. Thus, Athenians, Florentines, and Victorians, although widely separated in time and space, tended to single out the same sort of supposedly innate differences between men and women. But the physical, temperamental and mental contrasts which they observed to exist between themselves and their own women (who naturally were taken as *the* model of normal women) were based on similar social patterns, in particular, the marked contrasts between the upbringing and opportunities afforded to young males and females.

Occasionally middle-class males have spoken in defense of the basic equality of men and women, but for the most part middle-class women have had to be their own and their sex's defender. There is a definite correlation between the rise of a feminist or proto-feminist literature in Europe after the fifteenth century, and the slow breakdown of rules and conventions which barred middle-class women from formal education.

Even today, male writing on women is produced primarily by those men who can be recognized as middle class in the sense used here. Many still argue that women are so different from men, that their lives and opportunities must be radically different as well. Thus, even in fairly "modern" times middle-class women had to contend with the argument that higher education for "the fair sex" would lead either to their insanity or sterility. As recently as the mid-twentieth century, "experts" were worried about the harmful effects that education and employment for women would have on their children. Actually, in both periods the experts were most worried about what effects such changes in opportunities for women would have on the men who for ages have regarded their mothers, sisters, and wives as pillows, comforters, and larger-than-life reflecting mirrors, not competitors in the race for life's most desired prizes.

Lower-class men (those who come from families where the main wage earner was relatively uneducated and was employed in a nonprestigious position) have had different uses for their womenfolk. Traditionally, lower-class life has demanded much of its women. Female peasants often worked longer and harder than men. Artisan women were often expected to learn their husband's skills as well as fulfill their heavy domestic responsibilities. Physical weakness or a cultivated psychological delicacy was not something that was desired or fostered among traditional working-class women. But despite the hard work and sacrifice that characterize the lot of so many lower-class women, the few lower-class men who have written about "Woman" have quite often been intensely chauvinistic.

The strength that working-class women contribute to family life does not necessarily translate itself into formal social-sexual equality. Instead, peasant or working-class life is commonly shot through with *symbolic* manifestations of male superiority. Women must walk behind their husbands, or speak deferentially. The best chairs must be saved for the men, and so forth; hard-working peasant women must cook meals, serve the best to their menfolk, and then make do with the leftovers for themselves and the children.[16]

The courtship games of chivalry and courtesy that enliven the love rituals of the sentimental middle classes (and which pretend to reverse the roles of superior and inferior between men and women) are not to the taste of the poor. Instead, men who experience daily humiliation and frustration because of their economic and social disadvantages find their most important form of solace in looking down on and abusing women. This psychological cushion against oppression makes class exploitation more bearable; perhaps, as some feminists argue, it makes it more durable.[17]

While it can be argued that underneath the visible forms of sexual inequality, a real day-to-day partnership in work and struggle makes the lower-class husband and wife more "equal" than spouses in higher social ranks, it should be noted again that masculinity in the lower classes confers real and tangible advantages. Among these are a higher-protein diet (men get more meat), a chance for greater leisure, and a much better opportunity to be educated. And woe to the lower-class woman who rebels! Her impertinence is met with a sock in the jaw, and a kick in the ribs; not, as in the more genteel classes, with an essay full of biblical quotations, or a book on true, ladylike womanhood.

This complex situation is often faithfully reproduced in realistic novels of lower-class life. Women sometimes appear as the true foundations of strength who hold family life together, while men more often give way and drink themselves and their family to ruin. Nevertheless, when peasant or working-class authors and essayists discuss "Woman" they often rabidly insist that men are superior regardless, and darkly hint that without this illusion men would simply fall apart.

If this simple model ignores an impressive array of variations and exceptions, it nevertheless goes beyond the undifferentiated treatments of sexism which are common today. Male attitudes toward women are diverse in the extreme, and ways must be developed which can help us to understand the variations encountered. We need to take the widest, rather than the narrowest, possible perspectives in studying male attitudes as part of women's history.

## 4. Beyond Victimization: Women As Social Agents

The recorded attitudes of men toward women (or "Woman") ought not to be the central focus of women's history. The most interesting and significant aspect of the history of women as a field is its potential for showing us that females, handicapped or not, did things as individuals and groups that affected the structure, functioning and historical unfolding of their societies. Historians have been able to ignore this fact, which is after all rather obvious, only because they habitually focus on the thoughts and actions of the most easily observed elites. Since women have been only a tiny minority of those who have run countries, armies, banks, or factories, and are almost entirely unrecognized in histories of "great" thinkers and spectacular rebels, it is natural that most establishment historians believe that history will remain "a stag affair" (as J. H. Hexter puts it).[18]

But it is the nearly exclusive focus on the behavior of traditional elites that many newer historians are challenging. Those who research the lives and attitudes of peasants, workers, children, mobs, families or any aspect of popular culture or population history have implicitly or explicitly begun to believe that understanding the past requires much more than understanding elites. Marxism inspires some of these scholars of "the people" (although traditional Marxism is quite compatible with the view that ordinary people don't count, except when the proper stage of history has arrived). Other "anti-elitists" are simply repulsed by the disproportionate attention given to such small minorities of all those who have ever lived. But the quasi-moral repulsion which elite-centered research prompts is not enough to justify turning away from such research to seek radically new perspectives on the past.

Much more fundamental is the emergence of an interpretive perspective which declares that decentralized, collective forms of decision-making and behavior are ultimately the main source of fundamental forms of social change. Berenice A. Carroll has offered such a perspective in her discussion of the "powers of the 'powerless' " in relation to war and peace. Carroll argues that the allegedly "powerless," i.e., those lacking the power of dominance or control over others, nevertheless exercise important forms of social power which, though difficult to mobilize in conscious, organized ways, are probably those forms of power on which all major, long-term social change depends.[19]

Carroll's discussion of the normally overlooked "powers of the 'powerless' " is applicable to women's history. In the following discussion, her analytic categories have been adapted and extended for use in women's history. The categories introduced here are only rudimentarily developed; they are suggestive rather than definitive, and should be read in that spirit. Their major purpose is to present conceptual avenues through which some escape from the stultifying obsession with women as victims is possible. Although women may not have been a force in the machinations of elected assemblies or boards of trade, female beings have had other ways of contributing to social change.

*Women and Sexuality*

Now that it is once more becoming permissible to discuss the "facts of life," and even to acknowledge that sexuality is an important force in both personal and collective history, women will necessarily receive greater attention.[20] However, some historians still manage to minimize the treatment of women when doing research on sexual history—so deep, it seems, is the feeling that if a subject is important it must be exclusively associated with men.[21]

In pre-nineteenth-century history, particularly court history, ignoring women was not considered either necessary or desirable. Historians felt free, indeed obliged, to discuss the role that sexual politics played in domestic and foreign policy. During the late nineteenth century such frankness became forbidden, and only recently have modern historians regained the "right" (should they have the inclination) to discuss the role of women in any aspect of changing sexual morals or sexual behavior. Non-historians have already done some interesting work on the importance of sexual history to cultural history, and of women to sexual history.[22] Certainly it would seem that society's attempts to inculcate and enforce certain forms of highly unnatural sexual behavior (or the lack of it) has centered and depended on the cooperation of women more than men.

In a few recent articles which have tried to examine the impact of collective sexual anxieties on history, new perspectives on old problems have emerged. Theodore Roszak, for example, has written about the relationship between the rise of nineteenth-century feminism and the outbreak of World War I. He presents some suggestive evidence linking the strident and self-justifying militarism among prewar intellectuals to the successes and continued advance of the feminist movement.[23]

In general, the history of sexuality (in addition to being one perspective on change through which women could again be integrated into the study of history) could be used to show us how the changing relationships between the sexes has always had widespread cultural ramifications.

## Reproduction

Frequently in feminist theory the role of women in reproducing the species is considered a liability. But through most of history the survival of the species has been dependent upon the willingness of women to bear (on the average) six to eight children so that two or three might survive to adulthood. Until the decline of mortality rates in the nineteenth century, the rebellion of even a minority of women from this taxing maternity regimen could threaten a group with slow or rapid extinction. Governing elites, for example, have always needed and desired a large supply of tax-payers, laborers, true believers, or soldiers, so that almost all governments have passed laws which forbid birth control or abortion. These laws, more-over, are usually explicitly designed to prevent women from taking control of their own physiological processes (since many forms of reproduction control are designed to be used by women, or depend on women for their effectiveness).

But throughout history, whenever small groups of women gained a rela-tively high degree of autonomy over their persons and behavior, many of them chose to restrict their fertility in order to become free for other activities. The relative emancipation of upper-class Roman women during the last years of the Republic (lasting through most of the Empire) was apparently accompanied by a significant resort to birth control and abortion. Emperors and senators condemned the behavior of women, and offered still more legal and economic concessions to women who would bear at least three children. But the bribes and concessions had little or no effect. Within several genera-tions, the old Roman families who had put together the empire were nearly extinct. Rome itself became generally ruled by non-Romans.[24]

In the later Middle Ages midwives were frequently persecuted as witches because of the close connection between their activities and the transmission of birth control and abortion techniques. The two Dominican authors of the classic witch-hunting manual, *Malleus Mallificarum,* accused midwives of conspiring with wives to cheat husbands of their rightful progeny.[25]

On the other hand, in the early nineteenth century the local authorities in many German states felt threatened because women were producing too many, rather than too few, babies. By law they limited marriage to couples with sufficient funds. Poor women could not, or did not want to cooperate, and illegitimacy became so prevalent (in some areas as many as 25 percent of all babies born were bastards) that it constituted a social problem in itself.[26]

In the future women's history can explore the impact that women have had through reproduction patterns on both the existence and welfare of local and national populations.

## Socialization

As children are born and survive the hazards of infancy, they must be socialized. One can argue that men dictate the patterns of socialization, but this is far from being anything like a "fact" or an indisputable observation. What we can see is that women directly participate in and shape the earliest and most crucial form of education children ever receive.

The quality of individual care given to each child is something that social institutions or value systems can do little directly to control or supervise: and, collectively, nothing is more important to the transmission of values and behavior patterns than the ways women develop or use to inculcate early habits and beliefs in young minds. The unity of culture, mass psychology, and national temperament are thought by some to be an outgrowth of early childhood socialization patterns.[27] This has long been recognized in Jewish history, for this otherwise patrilineal and patriarchal culture has institutionalized a form of spiritual matrilineality: you can't be Jewish without a Jewish mother.

Historians of early Christianity have usually recognized that in the long run it was the attraction that Christianity had to urban family women which gave it an edge over its other competitors. Russian communists made conscious efforts in the early revolutionary days to attach women to the revolution, recognizing that the rooting of revolutionary values and their transmission to the future would be difficult without the cooperation of child-rearing women. How women cooperate with or initiate new ways of raising children will be a part of women's history in the future.

### Social Roles: Acceptance and Rebellion

Societies can function smoothly only when ordinary people work, pay taxes, buy goods, obey the law, marry, and have children in the accepted way. When rebellion against any of these various roles becomes widespread the authorities quite rightly fear that the basis of their own power is being threatened. Women as individuals and groups have often been involved in spectacular role revolts, which tend to get overlooked by historians (and hence lost to collective consciousness) or interpreted in some other way.

Of course on the individual level, it has long been acknowledged that small numbers of women have revolted against the wife-mother role altogether; while others have tried to redefine or support moves for the redefinition of these roles. Still others have tried to create new roles for women. But widespread role-revolts (which do not necessarily go under that name) do not always involve formal leaders or organizations. More often they are diffuse and disorganized changes of mind and behavior that are similar in form to changing fashions.

In fact the history of fashion itself can tell us much about the nature of feminine role internalization in various classes or eras. Until the nineteenth century, women were more or less in direct control of fashions. Changes in hair style and dress were often the most visible part of widespread role discontent or the collective desire for role redefinition. For example, there was a fascinating little sex war in early seventeenth-century London which saw some women writing essays in defense of their sex, while many others simply changed their clothes. Women wore men's hats, mock swords at their sides, and other forms of male apparel. King James was alarmed by all the other evidence of feminine aggressiveness and he instructed bishops to see that these "new" women were denounced from the pulpit, and measures taken to stop them.[28]

Even today, changes in the ordinary woman's perception and acceptance of her role can still be gauged through dress customs. Although women do not control the fashion industry, as consumers they still have the power to make or break fashion trends. In recent years, the "midi-length" skirt, definitely a call to go back rather than forward, was rejected by independent women who in the mass prefer pants, long, short or otherwise.

Role revolts have existed all through women's history. The popularity of perpetual virginity in the Christian world of the fourth, fifth, and sixth centuries had the character of a role revolt for many women. Before virginity became institutionalized (through monasteries) a Christian woman could escape early arranged marriage and the difficulties and restrictions of domestic life by dedicating herself to Christ. The status of perpetual virginity gave a woman both respect and relative mobility, in addition to a life-style built around spiritual self-fulfillment, something not otherwise available to many women. Several patristic essays in defense of virginity were inspired by requests from groups of women who felt they needed more theological backing for their way of life, especially in view of the reluctance Christian parents sometimes felt at seeing their daughters take up rather unconventional lives, escaping their parents' powers.[29]

Modern history has been filled with widespread role revolts by women who have rejected the economic, sexual, and intellectual limitations placed on them by male-dominated societies. But even medieval society, through various heretical movements, saw women behaving in similar ways.[30] Later, the Protestant Reformation itself was partly successful because it appealed to rather ordinary married women who saw in its rejection of virginity and redefinition of marriage a way to improve the status of their roles as wives.

The history of the wife role and the mother role has been ignored until now because it has generally been believed no significant changes have taken place in it. Like everything else, wifehood-motherhood has varied; and until we know more about the nature and significance of these variations the history of the family as a social institution will remain incomplete. A 1970 study of seventeenth-century family life in France acknowledged the problems presented by gaps in our knowledge about the real social roles of women in the family, as opposed to what was unreflectingly said about them.[31]

At present, the ordinary middle-class housewife who is relatively highly educated but who functions in the home as an unpaid domestic servant, as well as a children's nurse, is almost unprecedented when compared to the middle-class women of past societies. Similarly, the woman who imagines or hopes that she and her husband can be "friends" has a unique attitude when compared with wives of the past.

On the whole, little has been done with the changing nature of the relations between the sexes through history. Natalie Davis has remarked that ". . . there were important and little understood changes going on in the relations between men and women in the fifteenth and sixteenth centuries."[32] Actually, the same could be said for almost any century, and in the future the study of such a nebulous topic could well anchor itself in the study of changes in the major social roles of women.

## Economic Roles and Community Participation

If women have generally been barred from decision-making positions as merchants, industrialists, or government officials (by a now-withering combination of social, educational, and legal discrimination) the same has not been true of economic life in general. We have a fairly good idea of the diversity and nature of feminine contributions to the economy because several historians have specifically treated this topic.[33] From hard-working peasant women to clever and resourceful artisans or small merchants (market women) ordinary women have carried the civilization of the world on their backs, as much if not more than ordinary men.[34] Even women who were principally housewives were an important and necessary part of the production of food and the manufacture of life's necessities until fairly recently.

Although we have a good deal of general information about the types of women's work in the past, the all-important details, and particularly the basic quantitative data, have not been gathered. The duties of peasant women often change over time but we know very little about why. A detailed history of women's work in the urban centers of Europe would be very useful. From the sixteenth century on, when the age of marriage for women rose to the mid-twenties, the opportunities to work and the kinds of work available to single women became crucial to their survival in a new way. As the labor force sometimes expanded and sometimes contracted, women, more than men, seem to have functioned as a reserve army of labor. Certainly European poverty and charity was something directed more toward women and children than men. On the other hand, working women in Europe often saved their own dowries, which made it possible for some poor couples to purchase or have more material possessions at the time of their wedding than would otherwise have been possible. This possibly helped contribute to the higher standard of living in Europe which was widespread by the eighteenth century.

Sometimes the active participation of lower-class women in economic life gave them other social and economic privileges. In some areas they were allowed to participate in village affairs.[35] In others they were not. Very little, as yet, can be said about the overall importance of female participation in the peasant or artisan economies of modern Europe, and the impact of women's work on other aspects of their status.

## The Migration, Distribution, and Age-Specific Mortality of Women

It would be very helpful historically in assessing to what extent ordinary women were mere victims or active agents in controlling their daily lives, if we had more quantitative information about the geographical movements of women. By voluntarily migrating, particularly as unmarried adults, women have shown a sense of adventure or desperation similar to that of male migrants. Males dominate long-range migration, but women seem often to outnumber men as rural-urban migrants (at least in modern European history). Very little is known about why women migrate and cluster in certain places. The habitual migration of single female factory workers in the English industrial revolution was one reason it was so difficult to organize them into unions. Since single women were the majority of the female work force in English factories, this migration—not, as is sometimes asserted, the natural disinclination of women for organization—foredoomed attempts to organize women in industry.

Why women permanently outnumber men in some localities, and vice versa in others, is not well understood, nor are the socioeconomic effects of such imbalances in the sex ratio. Finally, while everybody dies, the age-specific patterns of dying often differ between the sexes. For example, until the nineteenth century, women may have had a lower overall life expectancy than men, as women still do in India.[36] One of the central indexes of modernization is an increasing gap between the life expectancy of the two sexes, with women tending to live longer and longer than men. In pre-industrial Europe, not only childbirth hazards, but famines may have contributed disproportionately to female mortality. Apparently, women, more than men, went without food during times of dearth so that their children could have what was available, or husbands sometimes refused to share what was available. Both aspects have different implications for women's history, one pointing to the heroism and the other to the victimization of women.

### Life-styles and Cultural/Moral Influence

One often finds women vaguely credited for raising or lowering the quality of cultural and moral life. Although this belief attributes a certain importance to women, detailed explanations about how women do either are rarely found. Certainly women have usually had a certain amount of consumer power which carries with it the power to approve of or veto new trends in foods, clothes, books, movies, and the quality of popular culture in general. Women are influential in determining life-styles at "higher" levels of society as well. At the family level, women, particularly in socially and economically lower strata, often determine what face the family will show to the world. Even if the man is the principal breadwinner, a woman's managerial skills often make the difference between putting on a respectable front and slipping slowly into greater penury. This too is part of the study of living standards.

In earlier times, it was at the level of popular culture that ordinary women had their only means of self-expression. Through music,[37] decorative art, and story telling, women actually originated or perpetuated forms of popular culture which sometimes made their influence felt in higher circles. The evolution of language, particularly dialects, might be heavily influenced by women as providers of the first models of speech that children encounter, as implied by the phrase "mother tongue."

In the eras that immediately preceded the dawn of civilization, the cultural influence of women may have been pervasive.[38] According to many reputable experts on prehistory (a field in which much speculation necessarily abounds) there is a fair amount of evidence that unknown women first pioneered and spread the domestication of plants. Their development of primitive agriculture (the first great breakthrough in human control over nature) was followed by the invention of pottery, something which is also credited to women, as is weaving, a technical skill of some complexity. In general, the great and small influences of women upon culture remain to be systematically explored.

## Values, Beliefs, and Attitudes

Women in general often influence the content of the value systems they transmit as mothers. If male value-authorities influence the general beliefs of women, women have ways of making their own preferences felt, and of influencing the value and attitude preferences of men. The seeming attractions that women have for certain kinds of men can make that male type seem desirable to men themselves. The reputed appeal that twentieth-century dictators have had to large numbers of "ordinary" women may have added a certain luster to the otherwise ridiculous posturing of these men. Only a few authors have tried to analyze the reasons that so many women were, or were not, reputed to be supporters of right-wing rather than left-wing parties in the Europe of the 1920s and 30s.[39]

Since women have long been regarded by men as some kind of supreme audience, the praise, mockery, or rejection of women can have important if subtle effects on the male psyche. In nineteenth-century France, the heirs of the revolutionary Jacobins were fond of blaming formally powerless women for the failure of revolutionary institutions and values to take permanent hold on the French nation. They said that the inherent conservatism of women caused them to continue to value and support the remnants of church and monarchy. What they would not admit is that the revolution itself and those who continued to go forward in its name had been less favorable to the interests of women than the old regime. The heirs of the Jacobins neglected women's education (something important to middle-class women) and charity and welfare measures (something important to working-class women). Leftists long maintained the antifeminist tendencies of the Napoleonic code and repeatedly refused to support the political aspirations of activist women. Under such circumstances it would have been a miracle to find revolutionary traditions popular among many women.

If some women have cooperated in blocking value transformations, other groups of women have promoted new values and attitudes. Modern nationalism in Italy was first promoted in early nineteenth-century salons, by aristocratic women who refused to recognize Napoleon as a liberator. Later Italian nationalists were indebted to their women for support and encouragement of every kind.[40] The greatest period of Italian history, the Renaissance, was filled with the influence of women as patrons and even creators. One Italian Renaissance historian has recently argued that since in upper-class households women were the major influence on their sons' upbringing, it was they who encouraged their charges to value manners and beauty over war or trade.[41] This thesis, which gives to women an important influence in fostering a value shift, has been rejected by many merely because it affords them this significance. But the proliferation of religious organizations for boys in

Florence in the 1400s is thought by another Renaissance historian to have been partly a response to the dominating influence of women over boys.[42]

Along similar lines, psychohistorian Robert Lifton recognized the importance of maternal support in the lives of Japanese radical students. Backing from their mothers was the only source of praise and validation they received in an otherwise conservative and authoritarian society; in this way the mothers of radicals provided a "psychic mandate" for change.[43]

Women have done more than simply influence change. Hundreds of women through history have overcome material obstacles and social prejudice to present their sometimes original and sometimes borrowed ideas. The belief persists that feminist ideas were first fostered by men; but this is simply another illusion created by the tendency of the majority of writers to ignore what women have done in behalf of their own sex. From Christine de Pisan in the late fourteenth century to now, there has been a continuous tradition of women who wrote in a feminist but by no means uniform vein. It has been the thoughts of these women which kept alive ideas about improving the status of women up to the great nineteenth-century flowering of feminist thought.

### Organizations: Revolt and Support

If large numbers of men and women begin to reject their traditional roles and values, unofficially developing new life-styles and attitudes, their efforts will often culminate in formal organizations of one kind or another, or in organized protests, up to and including violent rebellion. On the other hand, popular support for a government or a ruler just as easily leads to organized efforts to support and favor the existing order.

Nineteenth-century feminists in their various subclassifications are the best examples of the ability of women to sustain an organized but peaceful protest against laws which were unfair and institutions or professions which excluded women.[44] The counterparts of the organized feminists were the more conservative charitable women who in nineteenth-century England were among the first individuals and groups to deal with the social casualties of economic transformation and urbanization. Their charitable efforts could not solve the problem of poverty but their pioneering efforts later influenced the form and content of welfare legislation.

Working-class women had different forms of organized protest. In seventeenth- and eighteenth-century Europe they formed the bulk of the crowds rioting over the price of bread. Women, through bread riots, had their own forms of dealing out a rough justice to grain speculators and bakers who tried to cheat the poor.[45] In the great revolutions of modern Europe, mobs of women have often played key roles, from the women's march to Versailles (which brought the king back under the control of the revolutionary assembly)[46] to the strike activities of women workers of the 1905 and 1917 revolutions in Russia. Earlier in Russia, forms of organized anarchist terrorism were almost dominated by women. The successful plot to kill the czar in 1881 was led and engineered by a woman terrorist, Sophia Perovskaya, and there were several dozen assorted officials who were either shot at, wounded, or killed by terrorist women.[47] Through wide-ranging activities, organized women have had an impact on modern history.

## Women in Elite Groups

The statement that women have not been prime ministers, presidents, or elected representatives is often taken to imply that females have had little effect on the machinations of elites.[48] Even if it were true, one might well consider the implications of such exclusion. For our purposes, however, it is just as relevant to consider the ways women *have* made their presence felt in elite groups. The exclusion of women from formal and visible participation in politics is really only operative in traditional "democratic" or republican forms of government. Previous to twentieth-century suffrage reforms, democracies or republics always defined themselves as inherently male, by granting suffrage and other political rights exclusively to men. But for most of world history, politics has been aristocratic in character, and women of the aristocracy could wield political power. A self-perpetuating group of ruling families (often dominated themselves by one family) claimed that power was naturally a *family* affair, an aspect of kinship.

Women were very important to the political and social machinations of such ruling families. As queens, regents, influential consorts, mothers, or sisters, women had a great deal of formal power on their own and/or as influences over those males who made the formal decisions traditional historians regard as so important. This influence is currently discounted by historians who read back into history the largely male-only infighting of contemporary elected representatives. Colorful aristocrats with their penchant for sexual politics are thus recreated as dry-as-dust parliamentarians. The long-credited stories about the great mistresses who influenced kings and ministers are dismissed as anecdotal, and it is simply assumed (not proved) by academic historians that women could not possibly have had anything to do with decision making, since this is "obviously" a male prerogative.[49]

Aside from this bias, and apart from individual influence, women were an important part of the family alliances which characterized aristocratic politics. Whether as symbolic links which, through a marriage, bound countries in an alliance, or as real diplomatic links between allied families, women were an intrinsic part of politics for *most* of history. In classically feudal Europe, before the extensive bureaucratization of government, the personality of a woman could make and break an alliance and determine peace or war.[50] In medieval Europe in general the wife of a ruling baron was expected to substitute for him in his absence or at his death (if there were no mature heirs.) This included leading armies. In the time of Joan of Arc, as well as both before and after her, many women led armies and directed extensive military operations as a normal part of feudal life.

If some women were once part of aristocratic political elites other women have been active in cultural elites. In medieval times, women as outstanding abbesses were in the intellectual forefront of their eras, as poets, artists, and thinkers.[51] Since the Renaissance there has been a continuous history of secular women artists. Some of their work was so good it has been passed off as the masterpieces of famous male artists, thus fetching much higher prices.[52] As patrons and creators of other supportive cultural forms, women have influenced "high" culture. The most outstanding innovation was perhaps the perfection of the salon by the aristocratic women of seventeenth-century France. The salon gave a semi-organized focus to French genius, but the salonières not only acted as patrons and inspirations to innovative males, but some wrote and created influential masterpieces on their own.

Generally it has been in literature that female genius has made a mark on high culture. This is not so much due to an innate literary bent in females, but because comparatively large numbers of women since the sixteenth century have been exposed to the basic skills (reading and writing); and because the talented among them have not experienced many difficulties in getting hold of pens and paper. With or without a vote of confidence from the familial and cultural powers that be, writing can be done and manuscripts sent off without fear of public ridicule and exposure, thanks to a nom de plume. Thus, many women have written fiction, and from the thousands that tried, instances of genius emerged.

Women in modern Europe music have not had as happy a history.[53] For a while in the Renaissance courts of Italy and later in France women were encouraged to write music and conduct orchestras (usually all-woman orchestras) as well as sing and play instruments. A few women composers and conductors were widely praised. But, increasingly from the eighteenth century, opportunities in music for women were restricted to singing. We know of women who continued to try to write music, but the doors of conservatories were barred to them. In general, any woman who wanted to do more than sing found it difficult or impossible to get the intensive training, helpful patronage, and official encouragement that, for example, gives aspiring young conductors access to an orchestra. Yet these things are usually part of the background of any successful composer. Since the basic population of practicing women musicians remained very tiny (except in the vocal arts) the probability that a genius might emerge from their ranks was very low.

*Great Women*

As it stands now the only exceptions to the belief that women have been nothing but victims in history are the "great" women. Compared to other kinds of women's history, biographies of exceptional women form a relatively well developed and accessible literature. There is even one statistical study of their characteristics.[54] But generally, great women are presented as so special that the study of their lives and accomplishments has nothing to do with the history of more ordinary women.

It is possible to take another perspective on their greatness, and to see them as the tip of an iceberg—the most visible representatives or extreme instances of certain trends in the history of women.

Elizabeth I of England was a great woman and a great ruler. But she was not just a lucky accident. Like other aristocratic Renaissance women she was unusually well educated by a group of thinkers who believed in the intellectual capacity of women. When she took the throne, Elizabeth was one of the most educated persons—not merely women—in England. The confidence and skills her education gave her undoubtedly contributed to her performance as a monarch. The many other outstanding Renaissance women were also affected similarly. It would be interesting to see how many great women could be reinterpreted as exceptionally striking instances of a type of woman becoming more common in a given era.[55]

## Conclusion

As many feminists have noted, history remains very much *his* story. It is not surprising that most women feel that their sex does not have an interesting or significant past. However, like minority groups, women cannot afford to lack a consciousness of a collective identity, one which necessarily involves a shared awareness of the past. Without this, a social group suffers from a kind of collective amnesia, which makes it vulnerable to the impositions of dubious stereotypes, as well as limiting prejudices about what is right and proper for it to do or not do. Being aware of what those who are like oneself have been doing all this time, or what they have been like in other places and times, is often a healthy antidote to stale but venerable clichés. Even if one believes that a sense of the past has no practical applications, it remains a uniquely human form of consciousness. Women, like men, need to know what the flow of time has meant to them.

For both sexes, history has been more like a tragedy than a melodrama. Until the recent spread of industrialization, most cultures have been characterized by high death rates, pervasive poverty, extreme insecurity, ignorance, and fatalism. In the general scramble for something more than the worst that life had to offer, small groups of men, with their women, have oppressed other groups of men and women. But to understand this, or any other aspect of our tragic but fascinating human past, we must begin to understand more fully than we do the ways in which women really function in society, and the ways in which the relationships between men and women affect and are affected by other aspects of social and economic change. I think it is not too much to say that the nature of long-term social change will never be understood unless the study of women becomes a part of any attempt to unravel the mysteries of the past and perceive the dim outlines of the future.

## NOTES

1. Thomas Heywood, *Nine Books of Various History Concerning Women* (London, 1624). Reissued in 1657 as *The General History of Women*. Earlier in the fifteenth and sixteenth centuries many general essays on women used historical material to make various points about the limitations and capabilities of "the sex."

2. Emil Reich, *Woman through the Ages* (London, 1908), II, 243.

3. For further comment on de Beauvoir's approach, see Berenice A. Carroll, "Mary Beard's *Woman As Force in History:* A Critique," in this volume.

4. See *ibid.* and Gerda Lerner, "New Approaches to the Study of Women in American History," in this volume.

5. Two recent American feminists whose books have been widely read are Kate

Millett, *Sexual Politics* (New York, 1970) and Shulamith Firestone, *The Dialectic of Sex* (New York, 1970); both reflect positions closer to that of Simone de Beauvoir than to that of Mary Beard.

6. Fawcett is quoted in Theodore Stanton, *The Woman Question in Europe* (London, 1884), 6.

7. See J. Hajnal, "European Marriage Patterns in Perspective," in D. V. Glass and D. E. C. Eversley, *Population in History* (Chicago, 1965), 101–47.

8. In Austria, Russia, and elsewhere, single women of age who owned enough property had the right to cast ballots in local political matters through a proxy. Previous to the 1832 reforms in England, a small body of women in a similar position also had this restricted local franchise.

9. See Doris Mary Stenton, *The English Woman in History* (London, 1957), and *Histoire Mondial de la Femme*, ed. Pierre Grimal, 4 vols. (Paris, 1965); Gerda Lerner's *The Woman in American History* (Reading, Mass., 1971), is similar. Stenton's and Lerner's books are good descriptive treatments, which means they make careful, detailed, descriptive comparisons of socioeconomic classes of women. The links of this material with general currents of social change are weak, although more so in Stenton than Lerner. Ironically, both create the impression that what they say is all that can be said.

10. There are several recent examples of the complex approach to delineating the status of women: one on modern Russian women is Donald R. Brown, ed., *The Role and Status of Women in the Soviet Union* (New York, 1968); another is Iris Andreski, *Old Wives' Tales: Life-Stories from Ibibioland,* (New York, 1970). In addition to presenting first-person autobiographies, the latter is an attempt to present the complex interpretation of their own status held by the women of one African tribe.

11. Katherine M. Rogers, *The Troublesome Helpmate: A History of Misogyny in Literature* (Seattle, 1966), is a partial exception.

12. *Nibelungenlied*, trans. D. G. Mowatt (New York, 1962), 1–50.

13. *Laxdaela Saga*, trans. Magnus Magnusson and Hermann Palsson (Baltimore, 1964).

14. In the nineteenth century, male aristocrats, who had longer life spans and hardly ever went away to extended wars, began to cultivate a taste for a more dependent and less resilient type of femininity.

15. Here "middle class" refers to males who come from families who have something in the way of position and wealth, or the pretense of being something more than poor and obscure in their communities. Generally, middling types are found in urban communities, but sometimes middle-class patterns are found in rural or village settings.

16. For a detailed treatment of the nature and effects of symbolic and real manifestations of male social superiority in peasant life, see Robert E. Kennedy, Jr., "The Social Status of the Sexes and their Relative Mortality in Ireland," *Readings in Population,* ed. William Peterson (New York, 1972), 121–35.

17. See Kathy McAffee and Myrna Wood, "Bread and Roses," in *The American Left,* ed. Loren Baritz (New York, 1971), 480–81.

18. See Carroll, "Mary Beard's *Woman As Force in History.*"

19. Berenice A. Carroll, "Peace Research: The Cult of Power," *Journal of Conflict Resolution* (December, 1972), 585–616. Carroll suggests a preliminary "inventory" of nine forms of power exercised by the "powerless," including: (1) disintegrative, (2) inertial, (3) innovative or norm-creating, (4) legitimizing or socializing, (5) expressive, (6) explosive, (7) resisting, (8) collective or cooperative, (9) migratory or population power. While the categories developed in Section 4 of this paper were partially suggested by this inventory, they are substantially different in character from Carroll's definitions.

20. See for example Edward Shorter, "Sexual Change and Illegitimacy: The Euro-

pean Experience," in *Modern European Social History,* ed. Robert Bezucha (Lexington, 1972), 230–69.

21. For example, see Peter T. Cominos, "Late-Victorian Sexual Respectability and the Social System," *International Review of Social History* XIII (1963). Cominos almost ignores the role of women in the ethos of respectability among Victorians.

22. G. Rattray Taylor's *Sex in History* (London, 1954) is a good example. More detailed is the same author's *The Angel Makers.*

23. Theodore Roszak, "The Hard and the Soft: The Force of Feminism in Modern Times," in *Masculine/Feminine: Readings . . .*, ed. Betty and Theodore Roszak (New York, 1969), 87–104.

24. J. P. V. D. Boldson, *Roman Women* (New York, 1963).

25. *Malleus Mallificarum,* trans. Montague Summers (London, 1968).

26. Shorter, "Sexual Change and Illegitimacy," 231–69.

27. The best-known treatment of this is Erik Erikson's *Childhood and Society* (New York, 1963). Another recent study of the side effects of motherhood is found in Peter Loewenberg's "The Psychohistorical Origins of the Nazi Cohort," *American Historical Review* 77 (December 1971), 1480–85.

28. Carroll Camden, *The Elizabethan Woman* (Houston, Tex., 1952).

29. *The Select Letters of St. Jerome,* trans. F. A. Wright (London, 1933).

30. Frederick Heer, *The Medieval World* (London, 1962).

31. David Hunt, *Parents and Children in History* (New York, 1970), 71–73. The title of this otherwise interesting book is somewhat misleading. It is principally about fathers and sons. The material about mothers is minimal, and there are almost no contrasts made between boys and girls as children.

32. Natalie Davis, "The Reasons of Misrule," *Past and Present* (February 1971), 66.

33. Some examples: Ivy Pinchbeck, *Women Workers and the Industrial Revolution, 1750–1850* (New York, 1930); Margaret Hewitt, *Wives and Mothers in Victorian Industry* (London, 1958); F. W. Tickner, *Women in English Economic History* (London, 1923). These deal with principally English data. There is a large literature in French as well.

34. A. V. Chayanov, *The Theory of Peasant Economy* (Homewood, Ill., 1966). See p. 180 for some quantitative material relevant to sex-differences in Russian peasant labor. Beyond this one attempt to measure and compare the relative labor of men and women in peasant economies, the impression is general that women work harder than men. In other words, the men seize what leisure they can and make it a male prerogative.

35. Jerome Blum, "The Internal Structure and Policy of the European Village Community from the Fifteenth to the Nineteenth Century," *Journal of Modern History* (December 1971), 564–66.

36. One book that has quite a few relevant statistics for these and other matters concerning modern women is Evelyne Sullerot's *Woman, Society and Social Change,* trans. M. S. Archer (New York, 1971), p. 47.

37. Sophie Drinker, *Music and Women* (New York, 1948).

38. For a modern, detailed, and scholarly review of women in prehistory see the chapters by Louis-René Nougier, *Préhistoire et Antiquité,* vol. 1 of *Histoire de la Femme,* ed. Pierre Grimal, 4 vols. (Paris, 1965).

39. One attempt to make sense of this is Clifford Kirkpatrick's *Nazi Germany: Its Women and Family Life* (Indianapolis, 1938). See also, however, Renate Bridenthal and Claudia Koonz, "Beyond *Kinder, Küche, Kirche,*" in this volume.

40. Priscilla Robertson, *Revolutions of 1848* (Princeton, 1952), 312–13.

41. D. Herlihy, "Vieillir au Quattrocento," *Annales* (November–December 1969).

42. See Richard Trexler, "Ritual in Florence: Adolescence and Salvation in the Renaissance," in *The Pursuit of Holiness in Late Medieval and Renaissance Religion,* ed. C. Trinkaus with H. A. Oberman (Leiden, 1974), 200–264.

43. Robert Jay Lifton, *History and Human Survival* (New York, 1961), 275.

44. See William L. O'Neill, *Everyone Was Brave: The Rise and Fall of Feminism in America* (Chicago, 1969).

45. E. P. Thompson, "The Moral Economy of the English Crowd in the Eighteenth Century," *Past and Present* (February 1971), 114–18.

46. Olwen Hufton, "Women in Revolution," *Past and Present* (February 1971), 91–107.

47. Nina Selivanova, *Russia's Women* (New York, 1923), 170–203.

48. The term "elites" covers a wide range of groups. Elites can be social as well as political in nature. Frederic Cople Jaher has made some interesting observations about the roles and powers of women in the various social elites of Eastern American cities in the nineteenth century. In New York, the leading ladies of the four hundred families who dominated "society" rarely used their powers to benefit the appearance of their city or the welfare of its people. Furthermore, by refusing to patronize or socialize with writers and artists, they have contributed to the migration of nineteenth-century American talent to Europe. Socially influential women in Boston, in contrast, often became patrons of the arts and even of reformer-intellectuals. See Jaher, "Style and Status: High Society in Late-Nineteenth-Century New York," in *The Rich, the Well Born, and the Powerful,* ed. Frederic Cople Jaher (Urbana, 1974).

49. An example of unexamined dismissal of the influence of mistresses over monarchs is Pierre Goubert's treatment of Madame de Maintenon's influence on Louis XIV. Her power is persistently questioned or dismissed in a very offhand manner. *Louis XIV and Twenty Million Frenchmen* (New York, 1966).

50. Joel T. Rosenthal, "Marriage and the Blood Feud in 'Heroic' Europe," *British Journal of Sociology* (June 1966), 133–42.

51. Lina Eckenstein, *Women under Monasticism* (Cambridge, 1963).

52. See Linda Nochlin, "Why Have There Been No Great Women Artists?" in *Art News* (January 1971), 22, and the editorial in that issue (p. 49) for a comment on some female geniuses.

53. Drinker, *Music and Women, passim.*

54. Cora Castle, *A Statistical Study of Eminent Women* in *Archives of Psychology,* no. 7 (August 1913). Nevertheless, there is still much that can be done with the biographical side of women's history. Some great women still do not have multiple or relatively modern treatments of their lives.

55. The historical examples used in the preceding sections were mostly European in origin, solely because of the teaching and research background of the author. Many similar examples could be found for American and non-European civilizations as well.

# Contributors

KAY BOALS teaches in the Department of Politics at Princeton University and is currently working on a book on the politics of male-female relations. Her previous publications in international law, Middle East politics, and male-female relations all reflect a continuing concern with the politics of personal and political transformation.

RENATE BRIDENTHAL teaches history at Brooklyn College of the City University of New York, where she is currently Director of the Women's Studies Program. She and Claudia Koonz are editing a book entitled *Becoming Visible: Women in European History,* to be published by Houghton Mifflin, which coordinates the efforts of twenty historians to describe and analyze women's experience in Europe from pre-literate times to the present.

MARI JO BUHLE teaches courses in American women's and labor history at Brown University. She has taught also in the Women's Studies Program at Sarah Lawrence College. Her dissertation, for the University of Wisconsin, was on "American Socialism and Feminism, 1820-1920," and she is co-editor of a new edition of the *History of Woman Suffrage,* forthcoming from the University of Illinois Press.

BERENICE A. CARROLL has taught history and political science at the University of Illinois, Urbana, the University of Texas at Austin, and the University of Maryland at College Park, where she has also served as Director of Women's Studies. She is author of *Design for Total War: Arms and Economics in the Third Reich* (Mouton, 1968) and editor of *Peace and Change: A Journal of Peace Research.* She has been active in various professional and civic groups, particularly in the peace movement and the women's movement.

KATHLEEN CASEY received her Ph.D. in history from the University of California at Berkeley in 1974, after a twenty-year absence from academic life. She has taught at Berkeley, at the University of Wyoming, and at the State University of New York at Binghamton, and has recently joined the faculty of Sarah Lawrence College.

NANCY SCHROM DYE is a member of the faculty of the University of Kentucky, where she teaches courses on American women's and social history.

ANN D. GORDON has taught social studies education at Northwestern University and is currently Associate Editor of the Jane Addams Papers Project at Jane Addams Hull-House, University of Illinois, Chicago Circle. She holds a Ph.D. in American colonial history from the University of Wisconsin.

LINDA GORDON teaches history at the University of Massachusetts at Boston. She is the author of *Woman's Body, Woman's Rights: A Social History of Birth Control in America,* to be published by Random House/Vintage, and is co-editor of a documentary history of U.S. working-class women, to be published by Random House.

AMY HACKETT is completing a dissertation on the German women's movement, at Columbia University. She has taught history there and at Washington University. She is on the editorial board of *Feminist Studies.*

PERSIS HUNT teaches French history at the University of North Carolina, Chapel Hill. Her article on women in the Paris Commune, entitled "Feminism and Anti-clericalism under the Commune," appeared in *Massachusetts Review* (Summer, 1971).

ROBIN MILLER JACOBY is a member of the History Department at the University of Michigan, where she teaches women's history and women's studies courses. She is the author of "The Women's Trade Union League and American Feminism," *Feminist Studies,* vol. 3, no. 1, and is completing a book on the British and American women's trade union leagues.

SHEILA JOHANSSON has taught women's history and European social history at the University of California at Berkeley and at the University of Illinois, Urbana. Her Ph.D. dissertation, for the University of California at Berkeley, was on changing mortality and fertility patterns in nineteenth-century England.

ALICE KESSLER-HARRIS is currently directly the Women's Studies Program at Sarah Lawrence College; she is on leave from Hofstra University, where she is Associate Professor of History. Her previous publications include *Past Imperfect: Alternative Essays in American History* (co-editor), and several essays on women in the labor force. She is currently writing a book on the social history of wage-earning women in America, to be published by Oxford University Press.

CLAUDIA KOONZ teaches history at The College of the Holy Cross, Worcester, Massachusetts, and is editing with Renate Bridenthal a book entitled *Becoming Visible: Women in European History.*

JOYCE A. LADNER teaches sociology at Hunter College, City University of New York. She is author of *Tomorrow's Tomorrow: The Black Woman* (Doubleday, 1971) and of numerous articles published in anthologies and journals. She has also taught at Southern Illinois University and at Howard University, and has been Senior Research Fellow at the Institute of the Black World in Atlanta. She was the first recipient of the Black Woman's Community Development Foundation Fellowship, to study the African woman's involvement in nation-building in Tanzania.

ANN J. LANE teaches history at John Jay College, City University of New York. She is author of *The Brownsville Affair: National Outrage and Black Reaction* (Kennikat, 1971) and editor of *The Debate over "Slavery": Stanley Elkins and His Critics* (University of Illinois Press, 1971). She was a founder of the Socialist Scholars Conference, and has served on the executive board of the Columbia University seminar on Women and Society. She is currently working on a study of Mary Ritter Beard.

ASUNCIÓN LAVRIN holds a Ph.D. in history from Harvard University. Most of her research has focused on women in religious and secular life in colonial Mexico and Spanish America. She has taught in several institutions and at present is associated with Georgetown and Howard universities.

GERDA LERNER teaches history at Sarah Lawrence College, where she has also served as Director of Women's Studies. She is author of a number of books, of which the most recent is *Black Women in White America: A Documentary History* (Pantheon, 1971). She is currently completing a documentary social history of American women to be published by Bobbs-Merrill.

JULIET MITCHELL has lectured in English literature at Leeds and at Reading universities, England. She is author of *Woman's Estate* (1971) and *Psychoanalysis and Feminism* (1974), and has served as an editor of *New Left Review.* She has also written and lectured extensively on women and women's liberation in England, Scandinavia, Canada, and the United States.

ANN M. PESCATELLO has been working for several years in Iberian imperial history. She has taught history and served as chairperson of Latin American Studies at Washington University, and as Director of Latin American Studies and Dean of the Center for International Affairs at Florida International University. She is currently Director of the Council on Intercultural and Comparative Studies. She is the author of *Female and Male in Latin America: Essays* (University of Pittsburgh Press, 1973); *The African in Latin America* (Random House, 1975); and *Power and Pawn: Females in Iberian Families, Cultures, and Societies* (Greenwood, 1976).

ELIZABETH PLECK teaches American social and urban history at the University of Michigan. She has written an article entitled "Two-Parent Households: Black Family Structure in Late-Nineteenth Century Boston," *Journal of Social History* (Fall, 1972).

SARAH B. POMEROY is a member of the Classics Department at Hunter College of the City University of New York. She is author of *Goddesses, Whores, Wives, and Slaves: Women in Classical Antiquity* (Schocken, 1975).

ROCHELLE GOLDBERG RUTHCHILD is a member of the Core Faculty for Feminist Studies at the Goddard/Cambridge Graduate Program in Social Change. She is working on several articles about the Russian women's movement, and is active at the Cambridge Women's Center.

DOLORES BARRACANO SCHMIDT is Assistant Vice-Chancellor for Affirmative Action and Special Assistant to the Chancellor, State University of

New York. She has taught English at several institutions of higher education, and published articles on sexism in textbooks and other topics. She is co-editor of *The Deputy Reader: Studies in Moral Responsibility* (Scott, Foresman, 1965). She has served as president of the women's caucus of the Modern Language Association.

EARL SCHMIDT teaches history at California State College, California, Pennsylvania.

MARCIA SCOTT teaches history at Massachusetts College of Pharmacy, where she has served as acting chairperson of the Department of the Social Sciences.

ADELE SIMMONS is Dean of Student Affairs at Princeton University, where she is encouraging undergraduates of both sexes to become more aware of the opportunities and implications of the women's movement. She is co-author, with Ann Freedman, Margaret Dunkle, and Francine Blau, of *Exploitation from 9 to 5: Report of the Twentieth Century Fund Task Force on Women and Employment.* She is currently completing a manuscript on decolonization in the island of Mauritius.

HILDA SMITH teaches women's history at the University of Maryland, College Park, and has chaired the Advisory Committee on Women's Studies there. She received her Ph.D. from the University of Chicago and is currently working on a book entitled "Reason's Disciples: Seventeenth-Century English Feminism."